Praise for Islamic Philosophy *from Its Origin to the Present*

"Nasr explores varied approaches to the Muslim philosophic concepts of hikmah and falsafah throughout history, but at all times stresses the inexorable connection in Islamic thought between the philosophic sciences and the Muslim faith, emphasizing that Islamic philosophy 'functions in the world of prophecy.'"

— *Middle East Journal*

"Combining history with metaphysical exposition and mature contemplation on the unique character of a philosophy which can flourish 'in the land of prophecy', it is not so much a coherent overview as a series of contemplations, crammed with information and ideas, drawing on a lifetime of scholarship and experience ... This is a rich and rewarding book, full of information and always concerned to address contemporary issues."

— *Temenos Academy Review*

"Nasr once again tackles a complex subject ... [he] demonstrates that philosophical rationalism remains largely foreign to the Muslim ethos, even though such rationalism (which led to secularism in the West) was rarely a complete stranger to the Muslim world (despite attempts by Sunni Ash`arites, among others, to suppress it) ... Nasr goes far beyond a discussion of 'Arab' philosophy, affirming that Islam is a multicultural, polyglot mosaic united in its allegiance to the one God who reveals himself through prophecy."

— *CHOICE*

ISLAMIC PHILOSOPHY FROM ITS ORIGIN TO THE PRESENT

SUNY series in Islam
Seyyed Hossein Nasr, editor

ISLAMIC PHILOSOPHY FROM ITS ORIGIN TO THE PRESENT

Philosophy in the Land of Prophecy

Seyyed Hossein Nasr

State University of New York Press

Published by
State University of New York Press

For information, contact State University of New York Press, Albany, NY
www.sunypress.edu

Production by Marilyn P. Semerad
Marketing by Fran Keneston

Library of Congress Cataloging-in-Publication Data

Nasr, Seyyed Hossein.
Islamic philosophy from its origin to the present : philosophy in the land of prophecy / Seyyed Hossein Nasr.
p. cm. — (SUNY series in Islam)
Includes bibliographical references and index.
ISBN 0-7914-6799-6 (hardcover : alk. paper) — ISBN 0-7914-6800-3 (pbk. : alk. paper)
1. Philosophy, Islamic. I. Title. II. Series.

B741.N384 2006
181'.07—dc22 2005023943

ISBN-13: 978-0-7914-6799-2 (hardcover : alk. paper)
ISBN-13: 978-0-7914-6800-5 (pbk. : alk. paper)

10 9 8 7 6 5 4 3 2 1

بسم الله الرحمن الرحيم

The Quranic revelation is the light which enables one to see. It is like the sun which casts light lavishly. Philosophical intelligence is the eye that sees this light and without this light one cannot see anything. If one closes one's eyes, that is, if one pretends to pass by philosophical intelligence, this light itself will not be seen because there will not be any eyes to see it.

—Mullā Ṣadrā

Contents

Preface ix

Transliteration x

Introduction: Philosophy and Prophecy 1

PART 1. ISLAMIC PHILOSOPHY AND ITS STUDY

1. The Study of Islamic Philosophy in the West in Recent Times: An Overview 13
2. The Meaning and Role of Philosophy in Islam 31
3. *Al-Ḥikmat al-Ilāhiyyah* and *Kalām* 49

PART 2. PHILOSOPHICAL ISSUES

4. The Question of Existence and Quiddity and Ontology in Islamic Philosophy 63
5. Post-Avicennan Islamic Philosophy and the Study of Being 85
6. Epistemological Questions: Relations among Intellect, Reason, and Intuition within Diverse Islamic Intellectual Perspectives 93

PART 3. ISLAMIC PHILOSOPHY IN HISTORY

7. A Framework for the Study of the History of Islamic Philosophy 107
8. Dimensions of the Islamic Intellectual Tradition: *Kalām*, Philosophy, and Spirituality 119
9. The Poet-Scientist ʻUmar Khayyām as Philosopher 165
10. Philosophy in Azarbaijan and the School of Shiraz 185
11. The School of Isfahan Revisited 209

12. Mullā Ṣadrā and the Full Flowering of Prophetic Philosophy 223

13. From the School of Isfahan to the School of Tehran 235

PART 4. THE CURRENT SITUATION

14. Reflections on Islam and Modern Thought 259

15. Philosophy in the Land of Prophecy Yesterday and Today 273

Notes 281

Index 343

Preface

This book is the result of nearly fifty years of study and meditation upon philosophy and philosophical issues as seen in light of the realities revealed through prophecy both objective and inward in the form of illumination. In a world in which philosophy has become so divorced from revealed realities and secular thought has sought to marginalize and even annihilate knowledge imbued with the sacred, it is necessary to return, whenever possible, to the theme of the relation between philosophy and prophecy through different perspectives and angles of vision. Years ago we dealt with the heart of the question of the relation between knowledge and the reality of the sacred in *Knowledge ad the Sacred* and have returned to this subject from other angles of vision in later works such as *The Need for a Sacred Science.*

In the present work we turn our gaze specifically upon philosophy and especially Islamic philosophy. We deal with over a millennium of Islamic philosophy, its doctrines, history, and approaches, from the angle of vision of the relation between that long philosophical tradition and the realities of prophecy that have always dominated the horizon of the Islamic cosmos and the intellectual climate and space of the Islamic people. Some of the chapters of this book were written as essays over the years. They have all been thoroughly revised and integrated into the framework of this book. Many other chapters are new and were written specifically as integral parts of the present work in order to complete the picture that we have sought to depict in the pages that follow.

We wish to thank the Radius Foundation, which provided financial help to make the preparation of this text possible. We are also especially grateful to Katherine O'Brien, who prepared and readied the text for the press. Having had to endure reading hundreds of pages of handwritten material and numerous alterations required patience, know-how, and energy to carry out a Herculean task. Without her help it would not have been possible to present the text for publication.

Transliteration

Arabic Letter	Transliteration
ء	ʾ
ب	b
ت	t
ث	th
ج	j
ح	ḥ
خ	kh
د	d
ذ	dh
ر	r
ز	z
س	s
ش	sh
ص	ṣ
ض	ḍ
ط	ṭ
ظ	ẓ
ع	ʿ
غ	gh
ف	f
ق	q
ك	k
ل	l
م	m
ن	n
و	w
ه	h
ة	t
ي	y

Short Vowels

ـَ	a
ـُ	u
ـِ	i

Long Vowels

ـَا	ā
ـُو	ū
ـِي	ī

Diphthongs

ـَوْ	aw
ـَيْ	ay
ـِيّ	iyy
ـُوّ	uww

Persian Letters

پ	p
چ	ch
ژ	zh
گ	g

Introduction
Philosophy and Prophecy

In the current cultural climate in the West as well as other parts of the globe affected by modernism and postmodernism, philosophy and prophecy are seen as two very different and, in the eyes of many, antithetical approaches to the understanding of the nature of reality. Such was not, however, the case in the various traditional civilizations preceding the advent of the modern world. Nor is it the case even today to the extent that the traditional worldview has survived. Needless to say, by "prophecy" we do not mean foretelling of the future, but bringing a message from higher or deeper orders of reality to a particular human collectivity. Now the modes of this function have differed from religion to religion, but the reality of "prophecy" is evident in worlds as diverse as the ancient Egyptian, the classical Greek, and the Hindu, not to speak of the Abrahamic monotheisms in which the role of prophecy is so central. If we do not limit our understanding of prophecy to the Abrahamic view of it, we can see the presence of prophecy in very diverse religious climes in nearly all of which it is not only of a legal, ethical, and spiritual significance but also of a sapiental one concerned with knowledge. We see this reality in the world of the *rishis* in India and the shamans of diverse Shamanic religions as well as in the *iatromantis* of the Greek religion and the immortals of Taoism, in the illumination of the Buddha and later in the Zen Buddhist masters who have experienced illumination or *satori*, as well as the prophets of the Iranian religions such as Zoroaster and of course in the Abrahamic prophets. Consequently in all of these worlds, whenever and wherever philosophy in its universal sense has flourished, it has been related to prophecy in numerous ways.

Even if we limit the definition of philosophy to the intellectual activity in ancient Greece known by that name, an activity that the modern Western understanding of history considers to be the origin of philosophical speculation as such, the rapport between philosophy and prophecy can be seen to be a very close one at the very moment of the genesis of Greek philosophy. We also come to realize that the two drifted apart only later and were not separated from each other at the beginning of the Greek philosophical tradition. Let us just consider the three most important figures at the origin of Greek philosophical speculation. Pythagoras, who is said to have coined the term *philosophy*, was certainly not an ordinary philosopher like Descartes or Kant. He was said to have had extraordinary prophetic powers and was himself like a prophet who founded a new religious community.[1] The Muslims in fact called him a monotheist (*muwaḥḥid*) and some referred to him as a prophet.

The person often called the "father" of Western logic and philosophy was Parmenides, who is usually presented as a rationalist who happened to have written a poem of mediocre quality. But as the recent brilliant studies of Peter Kingsley have clearly demonstrated, far from being a rationalist in the modern sense, he was deeply immersed in the world of prophecy in its Greek religious sense and was a seer and visionary.[2] In his poem, which contains his philosophical message, Parmenides is led to the other world by the Daughters of the Sun who came from the Mansion of Light situated at the farthest degree of existence.[3] The answer to the question as to how this journey took place is "incubation," a spiritual practice well known in Greek religion, one in which a person would rest completely still until his or her soul would be taken to higher levels of reality, and the mysteries of existence would be revealed.

Thus Parmenides undertakes the inner journey until he meets the goddess who teaches him everything of importance, that is, teaches him what is considered to be the origin of Greek philosophical speculation. It is remarkable that when the goddess confronts Parmenides, she addresses him as *kouros*, that is, young man. This fact is remarkable and fascinating because in the Islamic tradition the very term for spiritual chivalry (*futuwwah* in Arabic and *jawānmardī* in Persian) is associated with the word for youth (*fatā/jawān*), and this spiritual chivalry is said to have existed before Islam and to have been given new life in Islam where its source is associated with 'Alī,[4] who received it from the Prophet of Islam and where it was integrated into Sufism. Furthermore, 'Alī has been associated by traditional Islamic sources with the founding of Islamic metaphysics.[5]

Another Greek figure who was given the title *kouros* was Epimenides of Crete who also journeyed to the other world where he met Justice and who brought back laws into this world. Like Parmenides, he also wrote poetry. Now Epimenides was known as a healer-prophet or *iatromantis* to whom everything had been revealed through incubation while he lay motionless in a cave for years.[6]

Parmenides was associated with this tradition. The *iatromantis* journeyed into other worlds like shamans and not only described their journeys but also used language in such a way as to make this journey possible for others. They used incantations and repetitions in their poems that we also see in Parmenides. They also introduced stories and legends of the East even as far as Tibet and India, which is of great interest because the community of Parmenides in southern Italy itself hailed originally from the East in Anatolia where the god Apollo was held in special esteem as the divine model of the *iatromantis* whom he inspired as his prophets to compose hypnotic poetry containing knowledge of reality.

Excavations in recent decades in Velia in southern Italy, which was the home of Parmenides, have revealed inscriptions that connect him directly to Apollo and the *iatromantis*. As Kingsley writes, "We are being shown Parmenides as a son of the god Apollo, allied to mysterious Iatromantis figures who were experts in the use of incantory poetry and at making journeys into other worlds."[7] If we remember that, esoterically speaking, "Apollo is not the god of light but the Light of God,"[8] it becomes clear how deeply philosophy as expounded by its Greek father Parmenides was related at the moment of its genesis to prophecy even conceived in Abrahamic terms provided one does not overlook the inner meaning of prophecy to which we shall turn soon. A whole tradition of healer priests was created in the service of Apollo Oulios (Apollo the Healer), and it is said that Parmenides was its founder. It is interesting to note that although these aspects of Parmenides were later forgotten in the West, they were remembered in Islamic philosophy where Muslim historians of philosophy associate not only Islamic but also Greek philosophy closely with prophecy.[9] One must recall here the famous Arabic dictum *yanba' al-ḥikmah min mishkāt al-nubuwwah*, that is, "philosophy issues from the niche of prophecy."

It is also of interest to note that the teacher of Parmenides is said to have been obscure and poor and that what he taught above all else to his student was stillness or *hesychia*. This was so important that later figures such as Plato, who sought to understand Parmenides, used the term *hesychia* more than any other word to describe the latter's understanding of reality. "For Parmenides it's through stillness that we come to stillness. Through stillness we come to understand stillness. Through the practice of stillness we come to experience a reality that exists beyond this world of the senses."[10] Again it is of remarkable interest to remember the usage of '*hesychia*' associated with the founder of Greek logic and philosophy in Hesychasm, which embodies the esoteric teachings of the Orthodox Church, teachings whose goal is the attainment of sanctity and gnosis.

In the poem of Parmenides he is told explicitly by the goddess to take what she has taught him back to the world and to be her messenger. Kingsley makes clear what the term *messenger* means in this context. "There is one particular name that well describes the kind of messenger Parmenides finds himself becoming: prophet. The real meaning of the word 'prophet' has nothing to do with being able to look into the future. In origin it just meant someone whose job is to speak on behalf of a great power, of someone or something else."[11] This "prophetic function" of Parmenides included not only being a philosopher, poet, and healer but also, like Epimenides, a bringer of law.

The relation between Parmenides and prophecy was not, however, primarily social, legal, and exoteric but inward, initiatic, and esoteric. His poem, if correctly understood, is itself initiation into another world, and "all the signs that only a fool would choose to miss, are that this is a text for initiates."[12] In this he joins both Pythagoras and Empedocles whose philosophy was also addressed only to those capable of receiving its message and was properly speaking wed to the esoteric rather than exoteric dimension of the Greek religion, requiring initiation for its full understanding. It is remarkable how again in this question Islamic philosophy resembles so much the vision of philosophy of these pre-Socratic figures such as Pythagoras, Parmenides, and Empedocles, all of whom were deeply revered by Islamic philosophers, especially of the *ishrāqī* (Illuminationist) school.

Coming to the mysterious figure of Empedocles, again we see a philosopher who was also a poet as well as a healer and who was considered by many to be also a prophet. "As well as being a sorcerer, and a poet, he was also a prophet and healer: one of those healer-prophets I have already talked about."[13] Empedocles also wrote on cosmology and the sciences of nature such as physics, but even in these domains these works were not written only to provide facts but "to save souls,"[14] very much like the cosmology of a number of Islamic philosophers, including Suhrawardī and even Ibn Sīnā in his *Visionary Recitals*.[15] What is essential is to realize most of all that Empedocles saw himself as a prophet and his poem as an esoteric work.

It is of interest to mention that all three of these figures who came at the origin of the Greek philosophical tradition were also poets. This is a characteristic of much of philosophy that flourished over the ages under the sun of prophecy. One need only recall the ancient Hindu sages who were poets and also fathers of Hindu philosophical thought in its traditional sense or the many Chinese sages who expressed themselves in poetry. In the world of Abrahamic monotheism this is to be seen among a number of Jewish and Christian philosophers but is again to be found especially among Islamic philosophers from Ibn Sīnā , Nāṣir-i Khusraw, Khayyām, and Suhrawardī to Afḍal al-Dīn Kāshānī, Mīr Dāmād, and Mullā Ṣadrā to Ḥājjī Mullā Hādī Sabziwārī, who lived in the thirteenth/nineteenth century.[16]

In a world such as the one in which we live today where philosophy is reduced to rationalism or more and more irrationalism and in which not only esoterism but religion itself is either denied or marginalized, the interpretation given above of the founders of Western philosophy will be rejected in many circles, and the nexus between philosophy and prophecy in general and philosophy, poetry and esoterism in particular will be dismissed or considered as being of little consequence. But strangely enough for the Western reader the relation among philosophy, prophecy, and esoterism, affirmed by a number of contemporary Western scholars, are found to be central to the Islamic philosophical tradition with which most of this book will be concerned. We have included the discussion of these Greek figures here in order to demonstrate that the relation between philosophy and prophecy, although severed to an ever greater degree in the West from the end of the Middle Ages onward, is of great significance not only for the understanding of Islamic philosophy but also for a deeper comprehension of the origins of Western philosophy itself, origins that Western philosophy shares with Islamic philosophy but that have come to be understood in radically different ways by these two currents of thought as Western philosophy has come to distance itself to an ever greater degree from both the perennial philosophy and Christian theology.

There are of course different modes and degrees of prophecy, a fact that one realizes if one studies various religious traditions and even if one limits oneself to a single tradition as we see in Judaism and Islam where the prophetic role of Jonah or Daniel is not the same as that of Moses or the Prophet of Islam. And yet there are common elements in various understandings of prophecy as far as the challenges posed to philosophy are concerned. First of all prophecy implies levels of reality whether these are envisaged as an objective or a subjective hierarchy. If there were to be only a single level of reality associated objectively with the corporeal world and subjectively with our ordinary consciousness considered as the only legitimate and accepted form of consciousness, then prophecy as the function of bringing a message from another world or another level of consciousness would be meaningless because there would not be another world or level of consciousness, and any claims to their existence would be rejected and considered as subjective hallucinations. Such is in fact the case with modern scientism and the prevalent desacralized worldview, both of which exclude in their perspectives the transcendent Reality and even higher levels of existence vis-à-vis this world as well as the Immanent Self and levels of consciousness deeper than the ordinary. But in all the worlds in which the reality of prophecy has been operative in one mode or another, acceptance of higher levels of reality and/or deeper levels of consciousness has been taken for granted as the correct manner of understanding the nature of the total reality in which human beings live.[17] Formulated in this way, this assertion includes Abrahamic monotheisms along with the Indian religions, Taoism and Confucianism as well as the ancient Mediterranean and Iranian religions, and Shamanism along with Buddhism, which emphasizes levels of consciousness rather than degrees of objective existence.

In all these worlds, prophecy, which is a central reality, creates consequences with which philosophy has to deal. Prophecy provides laws and moral teachings for society that ethical, political, and legal philosophy have to consider. Moreover, prophecy claims to provide knowledge of the nature of reality, including knowledge of the Origin or Source of all things, of the creation of the cosmos and its structure or cosmogony and cosmology, of the nature of the human soul, which would include both what should properly be called "pneumatology" and traditional psychology and of the end of things, or eschatology. The fruit of prophecy is knowledge of all the major aspects of reality experienced or speculated about by human beings, including the nature of time and space, form and substance, causality, destiny, and numerous other issues with which philosophy in general is also concerned.

Furthermore, certain forms of prophecy have had to do with inner knowledge, with the esoteric and the mystical, with visions of other levels of reality not meant for the public at large. We have already seen the relation of the origin of Greek philosophy to the esoteric dimension of the Greek religion, and we can find many other examples in other traditions including Buddhism and especially Islam where philosophy became related more and more in later centuries to the inner dimension of the Quranic revelation. The relation between philosophy and esoterism, which is a dimension of prophecy as defined here in its universal sense, also has a long history in the West lasting until the German Romantic movement.

From the seventeenth century onward Western philosophy felt forced to philosophize about the picture of the world painted by modern sciences and became more and more a handmaid of modern science especially with Kant and culminating with much of twentieth century Anglo-Saxon philosophy, which is little more than logic tied to the scientific worldview. In an analogous way, in various traditional worlds in which the reality of prophecy and revelation was central, whether the embodiment of this prophecy has been a book or some other form of the message brought from heaven or the messenger himself as in the case of the Hindu *avatārs,* the Buddha, or Christ, philosophy has had no choice but to take this central reality into consideration. Philosophy has to philosophize about something, and in the traditional worlds in question that something has always included the realities revealed through prophecy, which have ranged in form from the illuminations of the *rishis* of Hinduism and the Buddha, to God speaking to Moses on Mt. Sinai or the archangel Gabriel revealing the Quran to the Prophet of Islam.

In the traditional worlds in question, philosophy has not been simply theology as some have contended unless one limits philosophy to its modern positivistic definition in which case there is in reality no non-Western philosophy or for that matter medieval Western philosophy to speak of. But if we accept the definition of philosophy given by the person who is said to have first used the term—that is, Pythagoras—and see it as love of *sophia,* or if we accept its definition according to Plato as "the practice of death" according to which philosophy includes both intellectual activity and spiritual practice, then certainly there are many schools of philosophy in various traditional worlds, some existing until now only in oral form as among the Australian aborigines and Native Americans,[18] while others having produced volumes of philosophical writings over the centuries.

Even if one were to decide to deal only with written philosophical works, one could compose volumes on the subject of philosophy in the land of prophecy dealing with the Taoist and Confucian Chinese philosophical traditions, with those of Tibetan and Mahāyāna Buddhism including the schools of Japan, all of which possess their own special characteristics, and of course with the very rich philosophical traditions of Hindu India. One could also turn to the Abrahamic world and write on Jewish, Christian, and Islamic philosophical schools from the perspective of philosophical activity in worlds dominated by prophecy. Nor would such a treatment be completely parallel for the three sister Abrahamic traditions—despite notable similarities—because while the Jewish and Islamic conceptions of prophecy and the sacred book are close together, that of Christianity, in which the founder of the religion is seen as the incarnation of the

Divinity, is different in many ways from both the Jewish and the Islamic views of the matter. This difference is especially important philosophically as we see in the philosophical treatments of the incarnation in Christian philosophy and "prophetic philosophy" in its Islamic context.[19]

In this work we shall limit our discussion of philosophy in the land of prophecy primarily to Islamic philosophy. This limitation is due mostly to the nature of our own studies in philosophy over the past five decades, which have been concerned mostly with Islamic philosophy. But we have also studied other traditions enough to be able to assert that a similar work could be written for the Greek, Jewish, Christian, or for that matter Neo-Confucian and Hindu philosophical traditions with both the similarities and differences that are to be found between these traditions. In a sense the similarities would be much more fundamental than the differences for they concern the basic metaphysical truths common between them, truths for which we use the term *philosophia perennis*. But there are also differences of expression of the perennial philosophy depending on the intellectual climate in which the perennial philosophy is expressed in the same way that there is an inner unity among religions along with diversity on the formal level.[20]

In any case our attempt in this work is to present Islamic philosophy in its teachings as well as history as a philosophy that functions in a world dominated by prophecy and, this being the world of Islam, by a sacred book. We have concentrated especially on the later periods of Islamic philosophy especially in Persia, which, after the Mongol invasion in the seventh/thirteenth century, became the main arena for the continuation of the life of Islamic philosophy and where philosophy drew even closer to the inner realities made available through prophecy. There is also the important reason that this later period is still not well known in the West despite the research carried out during the second half of the twentieth century by a number of scholars in European languages. In fact the last part of the book presents many figures and ideas not known in the West at all. This emphasis on later Islamic philosophy is also of interest from the point of view of comparative studies for it shows how two philosophical traditions, the Islamic and the Christian, parted ways and followed such different destinies from the eighth/fourteenth and ninth/fifteenth centuries onward. In the West philosophy became more and more distanced from theology after the eighth/fourteenth century, and gradually the main schools of philosophy, in the West ceased to be Christian philosophy, and in fact philosophy in many of its schools turned against religion in general and Christianity in particular, pitting philosophy as the main rival to religion. In contrast, in the Islamic world philosophy continued to function within a universe dominated by the reality of prophecy, and this situation has persisted to a large extent to this day despite the appearance of secular philosophies here and there in various Islamic countries.

Strangely enough, while a number of secularized Muslim scholars of Islamic philosophy who write about it but do not belong to the Islamic philosophical tradition tend these days to criticize the very notion of "prophetic philosophy" and want to separate philosophy from prophecy à la the modern West, a notable number of American philosophers, have now joined the society of Christian philosophers, while interest in Jewish philosophy as a living philosophy is also on the rise in the West. In such a context the continued living presence of the Islamic philosophical tradition, which has always functioned in a world dominated by prophecy, can also be of interest as living philosophy to Western philosophers in quest of the resuscitation of Jewish or Christian philosophy. Furthermore, this study can perhaps also be of some help to certain Muslims who are philosophically inclined but who have become severed from their own philosophical tradition without having forsaken the reality of prophecy.

PART 1

Islamic Philosophy and Its Study

CHAPTER 1

The Study of Islamic Philosophy in the West in Recent Times: An Overview

The study of Islamic philosophy has had a long history not only in the Islamic world itself but also in the West. The tradition of the study of this philosophy in the West is nearly one thousand years old and can be divided into three phases, namely, the medieval period of translation, analysis, and study of Arabic texts; the second wave of translation and study in the Renaissance following the medieval effort, and finally a new attempt to study Islamic philosophy, which began in earnest in the nineteenth century and which continues to this day. There is a certain continuity in this long history and connection between these three phases, but there are also discontinuities. It is, however, essentially with the last period that we shall concern ourselves in this appraisal. Moreover, by 'philosophy' we understand *al-falsafah* or *al-ḥikmat al-ilāhiyyah* of the traditional Islamic sources as defined in the chapters that are to follow[1] and not the general meaning of 'philosophy' as used in modern European languages, which would extend to many other traditional Islamic disciplines such as the Quranic commentary (*tafsīr* and *taʾwīl*), principles of religion (*uṣūl al-dīn*), the principles of jurisprudence (*uṣūl al-fiqh*), Sufism, the natural sciences, and the sciences, of language.

In the common parlance of European languages, 'philosophy' evokes the idea of something having to do with general principles, governing reasoning laws, conceptual definitions, the origin, and end of things, and still to some extent wisdom, and one speaks not only of pure philosophy but also of the philosophy of art, religion, or science. In the classical Islamic languages, however, *al-falsafah* refers to a specific set of disciplines and to a number of distinct schools such as the *mashshāʾī* (Peripatetic) and *ishrāqī* (Illuminationist), not to just any school of thought that contains "philosophical" ideas. Moreover, in later Islamic history in the eastern lands of Islam the term *al-ḥikmat al-ilāhiyyah* became common and practically synonymous with *al-falsafah,* whereas in the western lands of Islam the older term *al-falsafah* continued to be used to denote the activity of the "philosophers." In both cases, however, these terms have always been used as names for specific types of intellectual activity that Muslims came to identify with philosophy or what one could also translate in the second case, "theosophy," whereas other disciplines cultivated within Islamic civilization and possessing notable philosophical dimensions in the Western sense of 'philosophy' have not been categorized in the classical period of Islamic history as either *al-falsafah* or *al-ḥikmat al-ilāhiyyah.* It must be added, however, that although we have limited ourselves here to the discussion of *falsafah* in its traditional sense, it is necessary to remember its relation to various fields such as Sufism, theology (*kalām*), law, the natural and mathematical sciences, and the sciences of language. But we shall not deal here with these disciplines in themselves or with the philosophy they contain in the general Western sense of the term.

Just as in the context of Islamic civilization, philosophy, though a very distinct discipline, has been closely related to the sciences on the one hand and Sufism and *kalām* on the other, it has also had ramifications in fields dealing with the practical aspects of human life, especially political science and jurisprudence. The classical division of the "intellectual sciences" and also philosophy by many early Islamic philosophers (and following for the most part Aristotle) into the theoretical and the practical, the first comprised of metaphysics, physics, mathematics, and logic and the second of ethics, politics, and economics (in its traditional sense), reveals its relation to various fields and sciences including in some classifications even the religious sciences such as theology, Quranic commentary, and the principles of jurisprudence. Not only do these fields possess a "philosophy" of their own as philosophy is currently understood—the work of Harry A. Wolfson on the philosophy of the *kalām* being an outstanding proof[2]—but also *falsafah* as a separate discipline has been inextricably related to many aspects of their development. It is this second aspect that belongs to any integral treatment of the study of Islamic philosophy and that in fact calls for an interdisciplinary approach that should bear much fruit in the future.

Several schools can be distinguished in the history of the study of Islamic philosophy in the West since the nineteenth century. Here we shall mention first of all these schools up to the 1960s when important changes began to take place due to diverse factors and then turn in the second part of this discussion to the last decades of the twentieth century. The various Western approaches to the study of Islamic philosophy include first of all the Christian scholastic tradition cultivated mostly by Catholic scholars, who in a sense continued the medieval study of Islamic philosophy within the matrix of Thomism or Neo-Thomism, especially up to Vatican II when the study of Thomism itself became somewhat diluted in many Catholic circles. Some of these scholars such as Etienne Gilson and Maurice De Wulf relied mostly on Latin translations of Islamic texts and were interested only in the role played by Islamic philosophy in Latin scholasticism, and others were well acquainted with the Arabic material and the structure of Islamic thought in general, such as Louis Massignon, A. M. Goichon, and Louis Gardet.[3] There was, moreover, a special school of Catholic scholars in Spain in whom a sense of "Spanish identity" and reliance upon Catholic theology were combined. This school also produced a number of scholars of repute, such as Miguel Asín Palacios, Miguel Cruz Hernández, and Gonzales Palencia, who made major contributions to the study of Islamic philosophy and related fields but were confined in their creative thought and research mostly to Spain and the Maghreb. The historians of Islamic scientific thought, Millás-Vallicrosa and Juan Vernet, were also in a sense related to this group in their Spanish orientation, although not closely identified with Catholic thought.

Another school that parallels the Catholic in its long history and that issued from the same type of scholastic background is that of Jewish scholarship, which had its roots directly or indirectly in rabbinical training and medieval Jewish scholasticism, with which elements from the Western humanist schools had sometimes become mixed. This school produced outstanding scholars in the nineteenth century, such as Moritz Steinschneider and Salomo Munk, and continued to produce some of the most outstanding scholars of Islamic philosophy and of Islamic thought in general during the early part of the twentieth century, such as Ignaz Goldziher, A. J. Wensinck, Saul Horovitz, Harry Wolfson, Erwin I. J. Rosenthal, Georges Vajda, Simon van der Bergh, Shlomo Pines, Paul Kraus, and Richard Walzer. The political turmoils following the partition of Palestine, however, changed the attitude of many, but not all, scholars of this type of background toward both Islamic philosophy and traditional Jewish thought itself, making many of them less sympathetic interpreters of traditional forms of Islamic thought.

Altogether the approaches of the scholars in the two groups already mentioned have important similarities in that most of them drew in different degrees from traditional Christian and Jewish philosophy and theology, which themselves possessed certain basic common features with Islamic thought and of course with each other. Quite different from both groups was another group of scholars who appeared on the scene in the late nineteenth century. Their background was modern European philosophy and not Christian or Jewish scholasticism, and they tried to understand the contents of Islamic philosophy in terms of different schools of thought prevalent in the West at the time they were writing. From Ernst Renan, followed by Léon Gauthier, who sought to make Ibn Rushd the father of rationalism, to Henry Corbin, who made use of the insights of phenomenology and more esoteric currents of Western thought to penetrate into the inner meaning of Islamic philosophy, there appeared a number of scholars who approached Islamic philosophy as thinkers and scholars immersed in the various schools of Western philosophy current in their day and also in modern methods of scholarship rather than as scholars of texts or men with medieval scholastic training in philosophy. In the case of Corbin, which is unique, there was, however, in addition to his immersion in German philosophy especially that of Martin Heidegger, profound knowledge of medieval Christian thought which he studied under Gilson. In the category of scholars such as Renan, who were influenced by the secularist philosophies of their day, which served as background for their study of Islamic philosophy, one cannot fail to mention also the large number of Marxist thinkers and scholars during the twentieth century in both the Soviet Union and the West who produced numerous works on Islamic philosophy within the framework of Marxist philosophy.

In contrast to these groups, there also developed from the nineteenth century onward a large school of orientalists with primarily philological rather than theological or philosophical training who studied Islamic philosophy textually and philologically without deep understanding of the philosophical and theological dimensions of their study. This group was responsible for the careful edition of many important texts but produced few meaningful interpretations. From the mid-1950s training in the social sciences supplemented that of philology and history, and a certain number of works appeared on Islamic philosophy from the point of view of current theories of the social sciences in the West. Most such works were related mostly to political philosophy rather than pure philosophy, although in Islamic thought the two cannot be completely separated from each other.

With the extension in the West after the Second World War of the awareness of the existence of several intellectual traditions in the world other than the Western, a school of scholarship based on the comparative method came into being. With the relative success that this approach had had in the fields of Far Eastern and Indian metaphysics and philosophy, a group of scholars began to turn to the study of Islamic philosophy in a comparative context usually in relation to the West but also occasionally to other Oriental intellectual traditions. The works of Toshihiko Izutsu and Noriko Ushida (both Asians but writing in English), and Henry Corbin, Gardet, and others mark a beginning in this potentially fecund field of study.[4]

Finally, there came into being, again only during the second half of the twentieth century, a school that began to study Islamic philosophy as a living school of thought rather than as a matter of solely historical interest. The inner need of Western man for a new "existential" knowledge of the Oriental traditions turned a number of seekers to search within the Islamic philosophical tradition for answers to questions posed by the modern world on the intellectual level. Already earlier in the twentieth century Bernard Carra de Vaux, Max Horten, and a few other figures had been concerned to some degree with the philosophical content of Islamic philosophy. Now this concern began to increase, and such men as Corbin; Gardet; Gilbert Durand in the West; and S. H. Nasr, Toshihiko Izutsu, Mehdi Mohaghegh, and Naquib al-Attas in the East began a new type of scholarship in Islamic philosophy, which, without sacrificing in any way the scholarly aspect of such studies, turned them directly into the service of the philosophical and metaphysical quest of those contemporary men and women who were aware of the profound intellectual crisis of Western civilization and were seeking authentic philosophical knowledge elsewhere.

This development, if pursued more extensively and in depth, could help to overcome the excessive historicism of earlier works by treating Islamic metaphysical and philosophical ideas as something of innate philosophical value rather than being of only archaeological interest. Until now so much of the research in Islamic philosophy has been devoted to tracing historical influences that few have bothered to ask what a particular philosophical idea must have meant as philosophical idea to those who held it and contemplated it, whatever might have been its apparent historical origin. Somehow the significance of the saying that truth has no history has rarely been realized in the modern West in the case of Oriental philosophy in general and Islamic philosophy in particular with the result that, besides exceptions, some of which have been already cited, few European thinkers of importance in modern times have been attracted to Islamic philosophy as philosophy. Nor have other non-Western philosophical traditions fared much better. The combination of philosopher and orientalist that one finds in a scholar such as Corbin has only rarely appeared on the scene of the Western study of Islamic philosophy, because this philosophy has been presented too often as nothing more than Greek philosophy in Arabic dress, without anything of innate philosophical value in it that could not be found in the Greek sources themselves. Only an extension of the activity of the group that considers Islamic philosophy as a living intellectual tradition worthy of study on its own basis can remedy the shortsightedness that has prevented to a large extent a true appreciation of this subject in the West.

In addition to all the groups cited so far, who were mostly part of or connected in one way or another to the Western intellectual scene, the twentieth century, especially in its middle decades, produced also numerous Muslim scholars and a few non-Muslims from the Arab world such as George Anawati and Majid Fakhry who made many contributions to Islamic philosophy. This group includes scholars trained in modern methods of research, and writing often in both Islamic and Western languages, such as Muṣṭafā ʻAbd al-Rāziq, Ibrāhīm Madkour, ʻAlāʾ al-Dīn Affifi, Fuʾād El-Ahwany, Muḥammad Abū Rīdah, ʻAbd al-Raḥmān Badawī (who was particularly productive in both French and Arabic), and somewhat later Muhsin Mahdi, Fazlur Rahman, S. H. Nasr, Muhammad Arkoun, Mian Muhammad Sharif, and many others, some of whom also participated in the activities of the other groups mentioned above. There were also those who continued the traditional method of cultivating and studying Islamic philosophy. This latter group was to be found especially in Persia and included, as far as figures whose works appeared also in the West, Sayyid Muḥammad Ḥusayn Ṭabāṭabāʾī, Sayyid Jalāl al-Dīn Āshtiyānī, Murtaḍā Muṭahharī, Mīrzā Mahdī Ḥāʾirī, Mehdi Mohaghegh, and a number of others whose writings are only now becoming known in Europe and America.[5] But a great deal more effort must be made to make the works of Muslim scholars on Islamic philosophy known to the West and to facilitate genuine cooperation between Eastern scholars and those in the West whose field of interest is Islamic philosophy.

During the last few decades of the twentieth century a number of events took place that caused a new chapter to be written in the history and methods of study of Islamic philosophy in the West. As a result of Vatican II Thomism became less emphasized in many Catholic circles with the result that the earlier approach of Catholic scholars rooted in Thomism and also interested in Islamic philosophy became less common, although still a number of important scholars with such a background continue to make significant contributions to the field of Islamic philosophy as we see for example in the case of David Burrell.[6] Likewise, the old rabbinical training that some Jewish scholars of Islamic philosophy of the earlier period had undergone became rarer, although Jewish scholars with knowledge of Hebrew and the Jewish philosophical tradition such as Lenn Goodman and Oliver Leaman have continued to make important contributions especially to earlier Islamic philosophy.

Also during these decades, the philosophical scene on the European continent and in the Anglo-Saxon world began to part ways more sharply than before with existentialism and phenomenology becoming dominant on the Continent and analytical philosophy in Britain, Canada, and the United States, with deconstructionism appearing also on the scene late in the twentieth century but with different interpretations of it as far as philosophy is concerned in the two worlds. Moreover, a new generation of Western scholars of Islamic philosophy appeared who, if not strictly speaking philosophers, were nevertheless influenced by those diverse currents of thought, the influence upon them depending on their background and educational training. Also during this period as a result of the earlier efforts of Corbin, Izutsu, Nasr and others later Islamic philosophy became a subject of interest for a whole new generation of students in the West.

Furthermore, during these decades the number of Muslim scholars of Islamic philosophy who wrote in a European language increased dramatically. Some of these figures such as Muhsin Mahdi, Fazlur Rahman, Jawād Falaṭūrī, Ḥā᾿irī Yazdī, and Nasr have taught in Western universities and trained numerous students, both Muslim and non-Muslim. Others such as Naquib al-Attas returned to the Islamic world but wrote mostly in English. Moreover, a number of Western students went to the Islamic world for a period to study philosophy and related subjects, and some such as Herman Landolt, James Morris, William Chittick, and John Cooper became well-known authorities on Islamic thought in general and Islamic philosophy in particular. In fact a great deal of activity in Islamic philosophy in the West by these and a number of older Muslim scholars, as well as by a later generation such as Hossein Ziai and Mehdi Aminrazavi is having an impact within the Islamic world itself. Today many students from the Arab world, Turkey, Iran, Pakistan, Indonesia, Malaysia, and other Muslim lands are coming to the West to study with such scholars, the case of McGill

University being particularly notable in this process. As a result, activity in Islamic philosophy in the West has become closely related to the life of Islamic philosophy in the Islamic world itself.

The last decades of the twentieth century were also witness to the gradual penetration into and interaction with Western philosophy of the living Islamic philosophical tradition. This is evident most of all in France as a result of the influence of Corbin as can be seen in the works of such younger French philosophers as Christian Jambet. But there has also now come into being a gradual interaction between Islamic philosophy and analytical philosophy[7] and semiotics as we see in the works of Ian Netton and Oliver Leaman. All of these currents led at the end of the twentieth century to the establishment of a whole center in Britain devoted to not only the dissemination of Islamic philosophy, especially in its later forms, but also to its interaction with Western philosophy, particularly the analytical school. This center publishes the journal *Transcendent Philosophy*, under the direction of a young Islamic philosopher Gholam Ali Safavi, among whose writers are to be found many of the younger scholars, both Muslim and Western, interested in Islamic philosophy as philosophy and also in serious comparative studies.

The field of the study of Islamic philosophy in the West has become as a result a much more extensive one than it was in the early decades of the twentieth century. It is enough to consult the voluminous bibliography of Hans Daiber, already cited, to see the very large number of works appearing every year in European languages on this subject, works written by both Western and Muslim scholars, and to realize how scholarly activity in the field has expanded in nearly every major European country as well as in the United States and Canada. And yet the chasm between the scholarly study of Islamic philosophy as intellectual history and from a Western point of view and as living philosophy remains as does the understanding of the Islamic philosophical tradition as viewed by those within that tradition and as seen by most Western scholars who still for the most part seek to apply categories drawn from ever-changing philosophical fashions of the West to a philosophical tradition cultivated in the land of prophecy and concerned with truths that stand above and beyond the transient fashions of the day.

This chasm can in fact be seen between all forms of traditional philosophy, which are so many expressions of the *philosophia perennis*,[8] and various currents of modern philosophy. The traditional exponents of the *philosophia perennis* in the twentieth century, especially René Guénon, Ananda K. Coomaraswamy, and Frithjof Schuon[9] were all adamant in pointing out the profound distinctions between traditional and modern philosophies.[10] Their criticisms of modern thought and exposition of traditional metaphysics and cosmology, which lie at the heart of the *philosophia perennis*, have led many of the scholars of the younger generation to the serious study of Islamic philosophy, but the works of traditional authors have not been able to eradicate completely the mental distortions and incorrect presumptions about the nature of the intellect and knowledge that still prevent many Western scholars of Islamic philosophy to grasp its real nature and its significance as a philosophy that remains aware of the realities of prophecy.

Despite conceptual perspectives held by many Western scholars that are not acceptable by those who belong to the Islamic intellectual tradition and who live within its framework, Western scholars of Islamic philosophy have made some notable contributions to this field of study. For over a century they have cataloged many libraries in East and West and have discovered thereby numerous manuscripts of Islamic philosophy of the greatest importance. Today nearly all the major libraries in the West are fairly well cataloged, there being only a few exceptions such as parts of the Vatican Library. In any case one does not expect it to be likely that any major discoveries in the field of Islamic philosophical manuscripts will be made in these libraries, although the possibility of course always exists. The situation is not, however, the same in the Islamic world itself where almost every year new manuscripts of significance come to light even in Iran and Turkey whose holdings are better cataloged than most other Islamic countries. There is most likely much to be discovered in the way of philosophical manuscripts when libraries of India, Pakistan, Syria, Yemen, Mali and many other lands not to speak of private collections all over the Islamic world are better cataloged.[11] Western scholars have already done much in developing scholarly methods for the cataloging of manuscripts, methods that have been used not only by themselves but also to an ever greater degree by Muslim specialists in manuscripts such as Fuʾād Sezgin and Muḥammad Tāqī Dānishpazhūh. Although it is often overlooked by students of philosophy, this type of scholarly activity is of the utmost importance for making the basic texts of Islamic philosophy available to the scholarly community for study.

A closely related domain is the correction and preparation of critical editions of manuscripts. In the traditional Islamic world the major texts of Islamic philosophy that were usually taught to students, such as the *Shifā'* (Healing) of Ibn Sīnā or *Sharḥ al-hidāyah* (Commentary upon the Guidance) of Mullā Sadrā and Athīr al-Dīn Abharī, were corrected by the teachers as they went along, and the existing oral tradition was always involved as the written text was taught. With the coming of printing into the Islamic world, some texts were lithographed and later even printed in modern form by scholars trained traditionally in Islamic philosophy but in many other cases faulty texts began to appear in printed form and still do so.

From the late nineteenth century onward, a number of Western scholars began to edit Arabic and Persian philosophical texts critically as such major series as the Bibliothèque Iranienne of the Institut Franco-Iranien directed by Henry Corbin bears witness.[12] Long collaboration with Western scholars of manuscripts taught several generations of Muslim scholars how to edit texts critically, something that became ever more necessary as the oral tradition became less available. Today the editing of Islamic philosophical texts often appears as a thankless task, and fewer and fewer Western scholars are willing to devote much time to it. This task is now being accomplished mostly by Arab, Persian, Turkish, and other Muslim scholars, but it cannot be forgotten that in this area of providing critical editions of texts the work of Western scholars has been of great importance. Yet, alas, even today there is not one major Islamic philosopher all of whose works have been edited critically on the basis of all the known manuscripts. Needless to say, this is a shortcoming that has to be overcome soon. Meanwhile, the critical and dependable printed editions of works of Islamic philosophy that do exist owe much, either directly or indirectly, to Western scholars of this field.

The knowledge of Islamic philosophy in the West would not of course be possible outside the small circles of scholars of Islamic languages without translations of basic texts into European languages. This task has been carried out by a number of Western scholars for over a century, and they have been joined in this task during the past half century by a number of Muslim scholars with mastery of one or more European languages. Yet there is a remarkable dearth of trustworthy translations available to the Western reader when one compares the case of Islamic philosophical texts with that of Hindu or Buddhist texts. As far as translation into English is concerned, the number is limited and still does not include the totality of such basic Islamic philosophical texts as the *Shifā'* and *al-Ishārāt wa'l-tanbīhāt* (The Book of Directives and Remarks) of Ibn Sīnā, the *Sharḥ al-ishārāt* of Naṣīr al-Dīn al-Ṭusī, and *al-Asfār al-arba'ah* (The Four Journeys) of Mullā Ṣadrā. Still there are notable translations by Western scholars of which the *Tahāfut al-tahāfut* (The Incoherence of the Incoherence) by van den Bergh is in many ways exemplary. Other noteworthy translations into English include the *Metaphysics* of al-Kindī by Alfred Ivry; several texts of Ismā'īlī philosophy by Vladimir Ivanow and Paul Walker; several works of al-Fārābī by Richard Walzer and Fritz W. Zimmerman; *The Spiritual Physick* and *The Philosophical Life* of al-Rāzī by Arthur J. Arberry; the *Al-Amad 'alaʾl-abad* (On the Soul and Its Fate) of Abuʾl-Ḥasan al-'Āmirī by Everett K. Rowson; *The Life of Ibn Sīnā* by William E. Gohlmann and selections of Ibn Sīnā's philosophical theology by Arthur J. Arberry; a long epistle of the Ikhwān al-Ṣafāʾ by Lenn Goodman; *Ḥayy ibn Yaqẓān* (Living Son of the Awake) of Ibn Ṭufayl also translated by Lenn Goodman; *The Mystical Treatises* of Suhrawardī by Wheeler Thackston; *Averroes' Commentary on Plato's "Republic"* by Erwin Rosenthal; Ibn Rushd's *Metaphysics* by Charles Genequand; and a number of his logical works and commentaries on Aristotle by S. Kurland, Harry Blumberg, Herbert Davidson, and Charles Butterworth who has also translated his *Faṣl al-maqāl* (The Decisive Treatise); a selective translation of the works of Afḍal al-Dīn Kashānī by William Chittick; the *Muqaddimah* (Prolegomena) of Ibn Khaldūn by Franz Rosenthal; *al-Ḥikmat al-'arshiyyah* (Wisdom of the Throne) of Mullā Ṣadrā by James Morris; *Iksīr al-'ārifīn* (The Elixir of the Gnostics) also of Mullā Ṣadrā by Chittick; and *Ḥujjat Allāh al-bālighah* (The Conclusive Argument from God) of Shāh Walī Allāh of Delhi by Marcia Hermansen. There are of course many other worthy translations, and this list does not mean to be in any way complete but only illustrative.[13] Furthermore, there are also many important translations in other European languages especially in French,[14] German, Spanish, Italian, and Russian. There are also translations of numerous works of philosophical theology and doctrinal Sufism, which bear directly on Islamic philosophy, but which we have not cited here.

As already mentioned, this effort to make works of Islamic philosophy available in English has been joined by a number of Islamic scholars as well as a number of Christian Arabs during the past few decades. As far as the English language is concerned, one can mention Muhsin Mahdi, a major authority as editor, commentator, and translator of al-Fārābī, George Hourani, Michael Marmura, Majid Fakhry, Selim Kamal, M. S. Khan, Fawzī al-Najjār, Shams Inati, Hossein Ziai (sometimes in collaboration with John Walbridge), and Parviz Morewedge, just to cite some of the better known names. And again there are a number of scholars of Islamic background who have made important translations into French and German.[15]

As a result of all these efforts, some primary sources of Islamic philosophy are now available in European languages but not to the extent that one could understand Islamic philosophy in depth without the knowledge of Arabic and in the case of many philosophers, Persian, and for Ottoman philosophical thought also Turkish. Much remains to be done in this domain, but this effort is hampered by many factors, including the lack of critical editions of many important primary texts, a shortage of philosophical dictionaries,[16] and most of all a lack of the necessary scholars to carry out the difficult task of making competent translations. This latter factor is further aggravated by the fact that in many Western universities translation of a philosophical text, which is often a daunting task, is not even considered in the scholarly works of a young scholar when he or she is being considered for academic promotion.

What is needed for Islamic philosophy is something like the Loeb Library for Greek and Latin texts where the text in the original appears on one side of the page and the English translation on the opposite page. Fortunately during the last few years Brigham Young University has embarked upon such a series in which already a few important titles have appeared.[17] Some other publishers in America are also beginning to produce works of this kind.[18] In any case in order to have the main corpus of Islamic philosophy available to be studied in the West by those interested in philosophy, much more careful translation has to be carried out. Furthermore, the vocabulary chosen for the translation of technical philosophical terms must reflect the character of Islamic philosophy engaged with the realities manifested in the land of prophecy rather than the rationalistic or skeptical bent of mind of many of those who embark upon the arduous task of translation. Otherwise the Italian adage *traduttore traditore*, that is, a translator is a betrayer, becomes the reality as we in fact see in a number of translations in many fields of Islamic studies, including philosophy.

The history of philosophy in the modern sense began in the West in the nineteenth century following certain philosophical developments, especially in Germany. Much earlier, classical Muslim scholars had written works that dealt with the lives and writings of Islamic thinkers, including philosophers. These works included not only the *al-Milal waʾl-niḥal* literature, meaning literally religious creeds and schools of philosophy or thought, by such figures as al-Bāghdādī, Ibn Ḥazm, and al-Shahrastānī, but also well-known treatises dealing with philosophers, scientists, and theologians and bearing other titles such as the works of Ibn al-Nadīm, Ibn Abī Uṣaybiʿah, Ibn al-Qifṭī, Ibn Khallakān, and Ḥājjī Khalīfah. There are also classical works devoted more specifically to philosophers, including pre-Islamic ones, works such as those of Muḥammad Shams al-Dīn Shahrazūrī,[19] Quṭb al-Dīn Ashkiwarī, and Muḥammad Tunakābunī. These treatises usually reflect knowledge of not only earlier Islamic works including anthologies of sayings of Greek and Muslim philosophers by such figures as Ibn Fātik and Abū Sulaymān al-Sijistānī, but also directly or indirectly of Greek works such as those of Theophrastus, Diogenes Laertius, and Galen dealing with Greek philosophers.

It is of great interest in the context of the present book to note that in most of these traditional histories of Islamic philosophy, the idea that philosophy was related at the beginning to prophecy has been confirmed and emphasized, and it has been asserted that *ḥikmah* began with the prophet Idrīs identified with Hermes.[20] But the works on Islamic philosophy that began to be written in the West from the nineteenth century onward were based on very different premises and methods. They were for the most part rooted in positivistic historicism and disregarded the traditional Islamic understanding of the history of philosophy nearly completely. From the middle of the nineteenth century European scholars began to write histories of Islamic philosophy, usually called "Arabic" philosophy following the medieval usage of this term.[21] Starting with the pioneering works of Augustus Schmölders and Salomo Munk, a number of well-known works on the history of Islamic philosophy appeared in various European languages by such figures as Bernard Carra de Vaux, Miguel Cruz Hernández, De Lacy O'Leary, Gustave Dugat, Léon Gauthier, and Goffredo Quadri.[22] The most influential among these works in the Islamic world itself was Tjitze De Boer's *Geschichte der Philosophie im Islam*,[23] which in its English version remained a standard text in Pakistani and many Indian universities until the 1970s and in some places until more recently.

These works, often of a scholarly nature, nevertheless looked upon Islamic philosophy from the point of view of the modern European perspective on its own philosophical heritage. All of them disregarded more or less later Islamic philosophy from the thirteenth century onward as if it had never existed. Most of them saw what they knew of Islamic philosophy even of the earlier period, that is, the main figures of *mashshāʾī* or Islamic Peripatetic philosophy, as being of little more value than a bridge between late medieval European philosophy and the Greek past. They disregarded for the most part the relation between Islamic philosophy and the Quranic revelation and ignored the view of Islamic philosophy itself about its origins and its relation to prophecy.

During the first six or seven decades of the twentieth century, many Muslims who had become aware of Western approaches to the history of philosophy also wrote histories of Islamic philosophy but based mostly on the current Western models. Some dealt more with the issue of the relation of Islamic philosophy to *kalām* and the Quranic revelation itself than their Western counterparts. Those writing in Arabic also provided much information on the original Arabic philosophical texts not found in the Western histories of Islamic philosophy. During the period in question most of the Muslim authors in this field were Arabs such as Muṣṭafā 'Abd al-Rāziq, 'Uthmān Amīn, Ibrāhīm Madhkūr, Ḥusām al-Ālūsī, 'Alī Sāmī al-Najjār, and the very prolific 'Abd al-Raḥmān Badawī, who wrote in both French and Arabic. Among this group 'Abd al-Ḥalīm Maḥmūd was exceptional in his grasp of the relation of *falsafah* to the inner teachings of Islam. Some of the notable scholars writing on the history of Islamic philosophy were also Christian rather than Muslim Arabs. This latter category included among others Georges Anawati, Ḥannā al-Fākhūrī, and Khalīl al-Jurr. The works in Arabic on the history of Islamic philosophy often contain many insights and analyses not found in the works of European scholars, but the model of most of these works remained to a large extent the histories written by Western scholars. This is especially true in their conception of Islamic philosophy as terminating with Ibn Rushd, to which Ibn Khaldūn came to be added as a kind of postscript. These works in fact disregarded, like their Western counterparts, the whole later tradition of Islamic philosophy, to which much of the present book is devoted, and therefore did not emphasize at all the living nature of the Islamic philosophical tradition.

During this period histories of Islamic philosophy were also written by Turkish, Indo-Pakistani, and to a lesser extent Persian scholars. One needs only to recall Zia Ülken from Turkey and Saeed Shaikh from Pakistan, whose works became fairly popular. Although these works did not suffer from any attachment to Arab nationalistic ideology, their treatments nevertheless ignored much of later Islamic philosophy and were to a large extent based on European models. The only figure of this period who sought to deal with later Islamic philosophy, although in a truncated version, was Muḥammad Iqbāl in his *The Development of Metaphysics in Persia,* which contains important insights, although it is also very incomplete and contains certain basic errors. It is interesting to note that in Persia, where Islamic philosophy was more active as a living tradition than anywhere else, less attention was paid to the history of Islamic philosophy as cultivated in the West than in the Arab world, the reason being precisely *because* the tradition that always emphasized that truth stands ultimately above time and that philosophy cannot be reduced to its history was still so strong. It has been only during the past three decades that Persian scholars such as 'Alī Aṣghar Ḥalabī and Ghulām Ḥusayn Ibrāhīm Dīnānī have written extensive works on the history of Islamic philosophy and where translations of works on this subject from European languages and Arabic have also attracted a number of figures who belong to the authentic Islamic intellectual tradition to the modern treatment of the history of Islamic philosophy.

A major turning point occurred in the writing of the history of Islamic philosophy in the 1960s. First of all Henry Corbin, who was the first Western scholar to have discovered the whole continent of later Islamic philosophy and who opposed strongly the historicism that issued from nineteenth-century European philosophy, asked myself and Osman Yahya, a Syrian expert on doctrinal and philosophical Sufism, to collaborate with him to write a history of Islamic philosophy for the popular encyclopedic collection *Pléiades*. The result of this cooperation was the *Histoire de la philosophie islamique,*[24] which was soon translated into many European and Islamic languages and became very popular. Although this work was only the first volume of our project and ended with the life of Ibn Rushd, it treated Islamic philosophy and its history in a completely different way from other works in European languages and took fully into consideration the rapport between philosophical speculation and revelation in Islam. Neither Yahya nor I had time to complete this project; so Corbin completed it in a somewhat more summary fashion, and it is this completed version that has been translated into English as *The History of Islamic Philosophy.*[25]

Two years before the appearance of our *Histoire de la philosophie islamique*, I delivered a set of three lectures at Harvard University, in which, while dealing with Ibn Sīnā, Suhrawardī, and Ibn 'Arabī, I sought to combine the Islamic view that philosophical truth has ultimately no history and that in Islamic history what was important was intellectual perspectives and not individuals with careful historical scholarship making use of both Western and Islamic sources. My lectures were in reality a response from within the Islamic philosophical tradition to the historiography of Islamic philosophy developed in the West. The book resulting from these lectures was entitled *Three Muslim Sages.*[26] Translated into Arabic, Persian, Turkish, Urdu, Bengali, and many other languages, it remains to this day a text studied in many Islamic as well as Western universities and represents an interaction between the living Islamic intellectual tradition and Western scholarship on the subject of the history of Islamic philosophy.

Meanwhile, the government of Pakistan had created a center under the direction of Mian Muḥammad Sharīf to compile a major history of Islamic philosophy in which scholars from East and West would collaborate. The original plan for the book followed mostly the

Western histories of Islamic philosophy with chapters added on culture, the arts, and more recent developments in the Islamic world. Around 1960, I began to cooperate with M. M. Sharīf on this project and convinced him to add chapters on later Islamic philosophy, which he accepted with the proviso that I would write them, which I did. Nevertheless, the work, which became standard reference for several decades[27] and was translated into a number of languages, is a rather composite work and does not as yet represent a satisfactory integration between the traditional Islamic understanding of Islamic philosophy and Western historiography of the subject.

Since those defining years of the 1960s, a number of histories have appeared by Western scholars with greater awareness of the integral Islamic philosophical tradition. Such works include *Historia del pensamiento en el mundo islámico* of Miguel Cruz Hernández[28] and Ian Netton's *Allāh Transcendent.*[29] But the most popular work in English written by a single author during this period on the subject has been Majid Fakhry's *History of Islamic Philosophy,*[30] which in its original version followed the earlier European and Arabic works that limited Islamic philosophy to only certain schools and the earlier period of Islamic thought. But subsequent editions have continued to embrace to an ever greater degree the later Islamic philosophical tradition, although the section on recent schools of Islamic philosophy in Persia and India is still rather scanty.

Finally, in the 1990s Routledge requested that Oliver Leaman and I edit a major two-volume work on the history of Islamic philosophy, which would also include a section on Jewish philosophy as part of their general series on the history of philosophy. The plan of this work was based on both a historical and a morphological treatment of the subject and taking full account of the relation of Islamic philosophy to the Islamic revelation, as well as the whole of the Islamic intellectual tradition. Again we invited scholars from both the West and the Islamic world, and, as in nearly all works in which a large number of scholars of different backgrounds participate, the result was that there are differences and sometimes discordant views expressed. But this work, entitled *History of Islamic Philosophy,* which first appeared in 1996, is now perhaps the most extensive work available on the subject, a work in which Western and Islamic scholarship are combined with the aim of creating a bridge between the two.

There are very few fields in which Western scholarship has been as influential upon philosophical activity in the Islamic world as that of the history of Islamic philosophy. Works written on this subject in the West continue to influence Muslims themselves and their view of their own intellectual tradition. At stake for Muslims is the meaning of philosophy and its relation to prophecy. A full history of Islamic philosophy, which would include all periods of Islamic history and all the different schools of thought with an Islamic philosophical dimension and full awareness of the nexus between philosophy and prophecy, must await more monographic studies of figures and periods not yet fully known. But during the past few decades at least a framework for the study of the history of Islamic philosophy has been created that is deeply rooted in the nature of Islam and its intellectual tradition. Western scholarship on this subject originally opposed the Islamic view almost completely and for the most part looked upon philosophy as a secularized mental activity. However, later at least some voices in the West began to look at the subject differently often more in accordance with the Islamic view of things. In any case the Western challenge to the Muslims' self-understanding of their own intellectual tradition has been very significant in the Muslim response of the past few decades, a response that is bound to grow in both depth and breadth in the future.

Western scholars have also of course carried out many analyses of various figures and texts of Islamic thought often in total disagreement with the Muslims' own understanding of the figure or subject at hand. A blatant example of this is the study by Renan, the French rationalistic and agnostic philosopher, of Ibn Rushd, a study that has had far-reaching influence. Nor have such studies, which claim to know an Ibn Sīnā or a Suhrawardī better than those who belong to the living Islamic philosophical tradition including oral teachings that go back to these masters, ceased to appear in the West. But in this domain also such analyses are rarely followed blindly by Western educated Muslims as they were in days of old. Usually they are catalysts for philosophical deliberation, especially among younger Muslim philosophers and scholars of philosophy who are well versed in a European language. In any case Western scholarship on Islamic philosophy continues to have an influence upon the Islamic world itself in the domain of philosophical analysis as in the other fields mentioned above. Moreover, this interaction, which is in reality a form of comparative philosophy, cannot but bear positive fruit if on the Islamic side the authentic and traditional Islamic view of philosophy is not abandoned and forgotten as was the case with an earlier generation of Western-educated Muslims.

In the chapters that follow we shall be discussing both philosophical questions and the ideas of particular Islamic philosophers and schools of philosophy seen from the point of view of the Islamic philosophical tradition itself. Yet our language and mode of presentation will incorporate Western scholarship and address the Western as well as the Muslim audience. We hope to remain faithful to philosophy cultivated in the land of prophecy while presenting features of this philosophy in such a manner that they can speak even to those beyond the borders of this "land," even to those who think that they do not need to heed the voice of prophecy or do not even hear it, but who are nevertheless drawn to the teachings of the *ḥikmah* or wisdom contained in the Islamic philosophical tradition.

CHAPTER 2

The Meaning and Role of Philosophy in Islam

As already mentioned in the preceding chapter, 'philosophy' is used in so many different ways in Western languages today that in discussing the meaning and role of philosophy in Islam we must turn before anything else to the exact meaning corresponding to this term in Arabic, that is, *falsafah* and *ḥikmah,* and also to the structure of Islam in its essence and historical deployment in relation to philosophy. Islam is hierarchic when considered in its total reality and also in the way it has manifested itself in history.[1] The Islamic revelation possesses within itself several dimensions and has been revealed to humanity on the basic levels of *al-islām, al-īmān,* and *al-iḥsān* (submission, faith, and virtue) and from another perspective as *al-Sharī'ah, al-Ṭarīqah* and *al-Ḥaqīqah* (the Law, the Path and the Truth).[2] When we speak of the role of philosophy in Islam we must first of all ask with which aspect and dimension of Islam we are dealing. In any case we must avoid the mistake made only too often by many orientalists during the past century of identifying Islam with only the *Sharī'ah* or *kalām* and then studying the relationship of "philosophy" or metaphysics with that particular dimension of Islam. Rather, in order to understand the real role of "philosophy" in Islam we must consider Islam in all its amplitude and depth, including especially the dimension of *al-Ḥaqīqah,* where precisely one will find the point of intersection between "traditional philosophy" and metaphysics and that aspect of the Islamic perspective into which *sapientia* in all its forms has been integrated throughout Islamic history.[3] Likewise, the whole of Islamic civilization must be considered in its width and breadth, not only a single part of *dār al-islām,* for it is one of the characteristics of Islamic civilization that the totality of its life and the richness of its arts and sciences can only be gauged by studying all of its parts. Only in unison do these parts reveal the unity of the whole that is reflected in all the genuine manifestations of Islam. One cannot understand the role of "philosophy" or any other intellectual discipline in Islam by selecting only one dimension of Islam or one particular geographical area, no matter how important that dimension or that area may be in itself.

As for "philosophy," the sense in which we intend to use it in this discussion must be defined with precision, for here we are dealing with a question of some complexity. First of all it must be remembered that terms dealing with the intellectual sciences have a precise meaning in the sciences of traditional civilizations such as the Islamic. We can use "philosophy" as the translation of the Arabic *al-falsafah* and inquire into the meaning of the latter term in Islam and its civilization. Or we can seek to discover how 'philosophy' as used today in English must be understood within the context of Islamic civilization. Or again we can seek to find all those Islamic sciences and intellectual disciplines which possess a "philosophical" aspect in the sense of dealing with the general worldview of man and his position in the universe. For our own part, we must begin by making the basic affirmation that if by philosophy we mean secularized philosophy as currently understood in the West, that is, the attempt of people to reach the ultimate knowledge of things only through the use of their own rational and sensuous faculties and cut off completely from both the effusion of grace and knowledge made available through prophecy and revelation as well as the light of the Divine Intellect, then such an activity is peripheral in the Islamic intellectual universe. It is a fruit of a humanism that did not manifest itself in Islam except for very few instances of a completely secondary nature. It is what some Persian philosophers and sages have called "mental acrobatics" or literally "weaving" (*bāftan*), in contrast to philosophy as the gaining of certainty, or literally the discovery of truth (*yāftan*). But if by philosophy we mean a traditional philosophy based on certainty rather than doubt, where the mind of a human being is continuously illuminated by the light of the Divine Intellect and revelation and protected from error by the grace provided by a traditional world in which he or she breathes, then we certainly do have an Islamic philosophy that possesses illimitable horizons and is one of the richest intellectual traditions in the world, a philosophy that is of necessity concerned with religious realities and prophecy as well as logic, the natural sciences, and so on, and has been often wedded to illumination (*ishrāq*) and gnosis (*'irfān*).[4] If we view philosophy in this light, then the title of "philosopher" cannot be refused to those in Islam who are called the *"falāsifah"* as well as those known as *ḥukamāʾ* and *'urafāʾ*.[5]

Moreover, if one takes the whole of the Islamic world into account, including the Persian, the Ottoman, and the Indian parts of it, one certainly cannot call Islamic philosophy a transient phenomenon that had a short-lived existence in a civilization whose intellectual structure did not permit its survival. One can no longer speak of

Christian and Jewish philosophy and then refuse to accept the reality of Islamic philosophy.[6] One can with some logic assert, as has been done by Fernand van Steenberghen[7] and certain others, that philosophy, as understood by the scholastics was not called specifically "Christian" by them but was conceived of as philosophy as such, but that did not make it any less Christian. In the same way in classical Islamic texts one reads usually of the term *al-falsafah* (philosophy), but not *al-falsafat al-islāmiyyah* (Islamic philosophy), which is of a more current usage, just as most classical Islamic authors have usually referred to *al-dīn* (*the* religion), when writing about Islam rather than using the term *al-islām*. The homogeneity and unity of traditional civilization was such that for its members their world was *the* world. Western civilization certainly produced Christian art during the Middle Ages, but this art was usually called "art" as such. Islam produced some of the greatest architectural marvels in the world, which were, however, very rarely referred to as "Islamic architecture" by their own creators. They simply called them "architecture." This characteristic is a profound aspect of the medieval world and of traditional civilizations in general, which must be taken into full consideration in the present discussion. But if we stand "outside" of these worlds and study them in comparison with the secular modern world or with other sacred civilizations, then in the same way that we can call Chartres "Christian architecture" and St. Thomas a "Christian philosopher" we can refer to the Alhambra as "Islamic architecture" and Ibn Sīnā and Suhrawardī as "Islamic philosophers."

In all honesty and taking into consideration the long tradition and the still living character of Islamic philosophy we cannot refuse to recognize the reality of this distinct type of traditional philosophy as being just as closely allied to the structure of Islam, and just as closely related to a particular dimension of it, as other traditional philosophies such as the Hindu or Neo-Confucian are related to the tradition in whose bosoms they have been cultivated. For the Islamic philosophers, especially those of the later period, traditional philosophy has always been a way in which the truths of revelation have been seen and discussed through intellectual and rational discourse and the philosophical significance of the message of prophecy and of reality itself as it reveals itself in the land of prophecy brought out. The truth reached by traditional philosophy is for the *ḥukamā*ʾ, an aspect of the Truth itself, of *al-Ḥaqq*, which is a Divine Name and therefore the source of all revealed truth.[8] For the Islamic *ḥukamā*ʾ, as for Philo, philosophy was originally a form of revealed Truth, closely allied to revelation. For Muslims it was connected with the name of the prophet

Idrīs, who was identified by them with Hermes, and who was entitled "The Father of Philosophers" (Abū'l-ḥukamā'). The identification of the chain of philosophy with an antediluvian prophet reveals a profound aspect of the concept of philosophy in Islam—far more profound than that any historical criticism could claim to negate.[9] It was a way of confirming the legitimacy of *ḥikmah* in the Islamic intellectual world and showing its relation to prophecy, a way that we also observe among certain Jewish and Christian philosophers who saw in Moses, Solomon, and other prophets the origins of their philosophical tradition.

Having established the existence of Islamic philosophy as a distinct type of traditional philosophy, we must now probe into its meaning and definition. We must first of all make a distinction between philosophy in the general sense as *Weltanschauung* and philosophy as a distinct intellectual discipline in the technical sense. If we think of philosophy in the general sense of *Weltanschauung*, then outside of *falsafah* and *al-ḥikmah*, with which philosophy has been identified by most schools, we must search within several other traditional Islamic disciplines for "philosophy," as mentioned in the last chapter. Among these disciplines the intellectual form of Sufism which is also called al-*al-'irfān* or *al-ma'rifah*, that is, gnosis understood as unitive and illuminative knowledge, is particularly significant. This fact is especially true of the later period of Islamic history when in most of the Arab world *falsafah* as a distinct school disappeared, and the intellectual needs corresponding to it found their fulfillment in *kalām* and doctrinal Sufism.[10]

As for philosophy in the technical sense, it embraces not only Peripatetic philosophy in its early phase, known in the West thanks to medieval translations and modern research following the earlier tradition, but also later Peripatetic philosophy after Ibn Rushd and beginning with Khwājah Naṣīr al-Dīn al-Ṭūsī, the school of Illumination (*ishrāq*) founded by Suhrawardī , metaphysical and gnostic forms of Sufism identified closely with the school of Ibn 'Arabī, and the "transcendent theosophy" (*al-ḥikmat al-muta'āliyah*) of Mullā Ṣadrā, not to speak of philosophies with specific religious forms such as Ismā'īlī philosophy, which possesses its own long and rich history.[11] We shall turn to this integral history in later chapters of this work.

Because of the vastness of the subject we shall confine ourselves in this chapter to the role and meaning of *falsafah* or *ḥikmah*, or philosophy in its technical sense, in Islam, always keeping in mind, however, the richness of Sufism, *kalām*, and some of the Islamic cosmological sciences in the domain of ideas that concern the Islamic and more generally universal views of man's position in the universe and vis-à-vis God. The most profound metaphysics in Islam is in fact to be found in the writings of the Sufi masters, especially those who have chosen to deal with the doctrinal aspects of the spiritual way, or with that *scientia sacra* called "gnosis" (*al-'irfān*) or (*al-ma'rifah*). A more general treatment of the meaning of philosophy in Islam would have to include Sufism, *kalām, uṣūl,* and some of the other Islamic sciences as well, but as already mentioned, these lie outside the boundaries of the present discussion, which concerns only *falsafah* or *ḥikmah* as these terms have been understood by the traditional Islamic authorities themselves.

To understand the meaning of Islamic philosophy it is best to examine the use of the terms *falsafah* and *ḥikmah* in various traditional sources and the definitions provided for them by the Islamic philosophers themselves.[12] The term *'ḥikmah'* appears in twenty places in the Quran, of which perhaps the most often cited, when referring to philosophy, is, "He giveth wisdom [*ḥikmah*] unto whom He willeth, and he unto whom wisdom is given, he truly hath received abundant good" (Quran, 2, 269, Pickthall translation).[13] It also appears in the *Ḥadīth* literature in such sayings as "The acquisition of *ḥikmah* is incumbent upon thee: verily the good resides in *ḥikmah*,"[14] and "Speak not of *ḥikmah* to fools."[15]

Different Muslim authorities have debated as to what *'ḥikmah'* means in such verses and sayings, and many theologians such as Fakhr al-Dīn al-Rāzī have identified it with *kalām* rather than *falsafah*. However, throughout Islamic history many have identified it with the intellectual sciences (*al-'ulūm al-'aqliyyah*) in general and traditional philosophy in particular. In fact during later centuries traditional philosophy came to be known, especially in Persia, as *al-ḥikmat al-ilāhiyyah*, or literally *theosophia* in its original sense. Even early in Islamic history certain authorities used *'ḥikmah'* in the sense of the intellectual sciences and philosophy, as for example Jāḥiẓ, who in *al-Bayān wa'l-tabyīn* (Declaration and Explations) refers to it in connection with Sahl ibn Hārūn,[16] and Ibn Nadīm, who calls Khālid ibn Yazīd, known for his interest in the "pre-Islamic" or *awā'il* sciences, the "*ḥakīm* of Āl al-Marwān."[17]

The definitions given by the Islamic philosophers themselves are more revealing than those of literary figures in elucidating the meaning of philosophy for Islam. In his well-known definition of *falsafah*, the first of the great Muslim Peripatetics, al-Kindī, writes: "Philosophy is the knowledge of the reality of things within man's possibility, because the philosopher's end in his theoretical knowledge is to gain truth and in his practical knowledge to behave in accordance with truth."[18] His successor al-Fārābī accepted this definition in principle, making in addition a distinction between "philosophy rooted in certainty" (*falsafah yaqīniyyah*), which is based on demonstration (*burhān*),[19] and "philosophy deriving from opinion" (*falsafah maẓnūnah*), based upon dialectics and sophistry.[20] He also gives the well-known definition of philosophy as "the knowledge of existents *qua* existents" and also states that "there is nothing among existents in the world with which philosophy is not concerned."[21]

The master of Peripatetics, Ibn Sīnā, adds another element to the definition of *ḥikmah* and relates it more closely to realization and perfection of the being of man when he writes: "*Ḥikmah* is the perfecting of the human soul through the conceptualization of things and the judgment of theoretical and practical truths to the measure of human capability."[22] This close accordance between knowledge and its practice, so important for later Islamic philosophy, is repeated in the definition of the Ikhwān al-Ṣafā᾿ when they say: "The beginning of philosophy is the love of the sciences; its middle is knowledge of the reality of things to the extent to which man is capable; and its end is speech and action in conformity with this knowledge."[23]

With Suhrawardī and the *ishrāqī* school, the close rapport between philosophy and religion or more precisely between philosophy as an aspect of the inner dimension of revealed truth and the ascetic and spiritual practices related to religious discipline, which in Islam are connected with Sufism and also Shi'ite gnosis, becomes fully established. Not only was Suhrawardī himself a Sufi and a *ḥakīm* at the same time, but also he conceived of a true *faylasūf* or *ḥakīm* as one who possesses both theoretical knowledge and spiritual vision.[24] He calls such a person "*muta᾿allih*," literally, one who has become "God like," and speaks in his *Partaw-nāmah* (The Book of Radiance) of *ḥikmah* as "The act of the soul's becoming imprinted by the spiritual truths and the intelligibles."[25] After him philosophy and spiritual realization became for the most part wedded except among those who followed only the Peripatetic school, and *al-ḥikmat al-ilāhiyyah* became, especially in Persia and other eastern lands of Islam, the bridge between the formal religious sciences and the verities of pure gnosis.

The Safavid *ḥakīms*, who brought many trends of Islamic philosophy to their full fruition and flowering, continued to relate philosophy closely to the esoteric dimension of religion, as had many earlier philosophers including Ismā῾īlī thinkers, and considered the traditional philosopher as the person who possesses not only theoretical knowledge but also a direct vision of the truth so that he speaks to mankind as a sage fulfilling a certain aspect of the prophetic function after the close of the cycle of prophecy. In the Twelve-Imam Shi'ite world many an authority such as Mullā Ṣadrā has identified the term *scholars* (*'ulamā'*) in the famous prophetic saying, "The scholars of my community are like the prophets of the Children of Israel,"[26] with the *ḥukamā'*, who in the later period were mostly also Sufis and gnostics. *Ḥikmah*, therefore, continued its close relation with Islamic esoterism and became identified in the context of Shi'ism with the "cycle of initiation" (*dā'irat al-walāyah/wilāyah*) following the cycle of prophecy (*dā'irat al-nubuwwah*). Mīr Firdiriskī, for example, considers the *ḥukamā'* as standing in the class immediately below the prophets and writes: "The utmost extremity reached by the *falāsifah* is the point of departure for prophecy."[27]

With Ṣadr al-Dīn Shīrāzī (Mullā Ṣadrā), who achieved such a vast synthesis of the various schools of Islamic philosophy and intellectuality, the definition of '*ḥikmah*' also reaches a fullness and synthetic quality that embraces much that came before him. In one of his famous definitions, which echoes in part the words of Plato, he writes: "*Falsafah* is the perfecting of the human soul to the extent of human possibility through knowledge of the essential realities of things as they are in themselves and through judgment concerning their existence established upon demonstration and not derived from opinion or through imitation. Or if thou liketh thou canst say, it is to give intelligible order to the world to the extent of human possibility in order to gain 'resemblance' to the Creator, Transcendent is He."[28] Similarly in another definition he considers *ḥikmah* as the means whereby "man becomes an intelligible world resembling the objective world and similar to the order of universal existence."[29] Referring to the first principles discussed in *ḥikmah* Mullā Ṣadrā says: "It is this *ḥikmah* that the Blessed Prophet had in mind in his prayer to his Lord when he said: 'O Lord! Show us things as they really are.' "[30] Moreover, he gives a spiritual exegesis of the Quranic verse 'Surely We created man of the best stature, then We reduced him to the lowest of the low, save those who believe and do good works' (Quran, 95, 4–6) in this way: "Of the best stature" refers to the spiritual world and the angelic part of the soul, 'the lowest of the low' to the material world and the animal part of the soul, 'those who believe' to theoretical *ḥikmah* and those who 'do good works' to practical *ḥikmah*."[31] Seen in this light *ḥikmah*, in its two aspects of knowledge and action, becomes the means whereby man is saved from his wretched state of the lowest of the low and enabled to regain the angelic and paradisal state in which he was originally created. *Ḥikmah* is, in his view, completely wedded to religion and the spiritual life and is far removed from purely mental activity connected with the rationalistic conception of philosophy that has become prevalent in the West since the post-Renaissance period.

Having surveyed the meaning of philosophy through the eyes of some of its major expositors and supporters, a few words must now be said about the different forms of "opposition" to it, before turning to its role and function in Islam. It must, however, be remembered that "opposition" in the context of a traditional civilization is very different from the opposition of contending modern philosophical schools that have no principles in common. In Islam there has often been a tension between the various components and dimensions of the tradition but a tension that has been almost always creative and has never destroyed the unity of Islam and its civilization.[32] With this reserve in mind it can be said that opposition to *falsafah* in Islam came mainly from three groups, but for different reasons: the purely religious scholars dealing with *fiqh* and *uṣūl*, the theologians (*mutakallimūn*), especially of the Ash'arite school, and certain of the Sufis.

Some of the scholars of the religious sciences criticized *falsafah* simply because it stood outside of the domain of the *Sharī'ah* with which they were solely concerned. Some, like Ibn Taymiyyah in Sunnism and Mullā Bāqir Majlisī in Shi'ism, wrote specifically against the *falāsifah* and in the case of the former against logic, although he himself made use of logical discourse. Their opposition to *falsafah* is related to their mission to preserve the purely transmitted sciences on the exoteric level. Thus they refused to be concerned with either the intellectual sciences or the esoteric dimension of Islam, which alone could integrate these sciences, and chief among them philosophy, into the Islamic perspective.

As for the theologians, the opposition of the Ash'arites to *falsafah* was of course much greater than that of the Mu'tazilite school of *kalām*, while in the Shi'ite world, Ismā'īlī *kalām* was always close to Ismā'īlī philosophy, and Twelve-Imam Shi'ite *kalām* became closely wedded to *falsafah* with the *Tajrīd* (Catharsis) of Naṣīr al-Dīn al-Ṭūsī. In fact as we shall see in the next chapter, in Shi'ism later *falsafah* or *al-ḥikmat al-ilāhiyyah* itself claimed to fulfill the true role of theology and in reality contains much that in Western terms would be considered as theology.[33] The well-known attack of al-Ghazzālī against *falsafah* was not simply a negative act of demolishing *falsafah*. First of all, it attacked only Peripatetic philosophy and moreover the rationalistic tendencies within it. Second, the criticism was of such a nature that it changed the direction of the flow of Islamic intellectual life rather than put an end to it.[34] The background that made possible the spread of the sapiential teachings of Suhrawardī and Ibn 'Arabī owes much to al-Ghazzālī, while the later revival of Peripatetic philosophy by al-Ṭūsī is related closely to the criticism of Ibn Sīnā by another Ash'arite critic of *falsafah*, Fakhr al-Dīn al-Rāzī.[35] The criticism of *falsafah* by the *mutakallimūn*, therefore, was for the most part a creative interplay between *falsafah* and *kalām*, which left an indelible mark upon both of them. *Kalām* forced *falsafah*, even the Peripatetic school, to deal with certain specifically religious issues, while *falsafah* influenced ever more the formulation and argumentation of *kalām* itself, even Sunni *kalām*, starting with Imām al-Ḥaramayn al-Juwaynī, continuing with al-Ghazzālī, and al-Rāzī, and in a sense culminating with 'Aḍud al-Dīn al-Ījī in his *Kitāb al-mawāqif* (The Book of Stations), which is concerned with philosophical *kalām*. This trend is also to be seen in the works of Jalāl al-Dīn Dawānī. In Shi'ism also it is difficult to distinguish some of the later commentaries upon the *Tajrīd* from works on *falsafah*. The "opposition" of *kalām* to *falsafah*, therefore, far from destroying *falsafah*, influenced its later course and in much of the Sunni world absorbed it into itself after the seventh/thirteenth century, with the result that, as already mentioned, such a figure as Ibn Khaldūn was to call this later *kalām* a form of philosophy.

As for the criticism of *falsafah* made by certain Sufis, it too must be seen in light of the nature of Islamic esoterism as well as certain local and temporal conditions. Sufi metaphysics could not become bound to the "lesser truth" of Aristotelianism against whose inherent limitations it reacted and whose limits it criticized. But the criticism against the substance of *falsafah* came, not from the whole of Sufism, but from a particular tendency within it. In general one can distinguish two tendencies within Sufi spirituality, one that takes the human intellect to be a ladder to the luminous world of the Spirit and the other that emphasizes more the discontinuity between human reason and the Divine Intellect and seeks to reach the world of the Spirit by breaking completely the power of ratiocination within the mind. The final result, which is reaching God, is the same in both cases, but the role played by reason is somewhat different in the two instances. The first tendency can be seen in some of the members of the school of Ibn 'Arabī such as 'Abd al-Karīm al-Jīlī, Ṣadr al-Dīn al-Qunyawī,[36] and the like, and the second in some of the famous Persian Sufi poets such as Sanā'ī and Mawlānā Jalāl al-Dīn Rūmī[37] and in the Arab world in certain early Sufi poets. Moreover, later in Islamic history there were important figures who were both Sufis and philosophers such as Suhrawardī, Dā'ūd al-Qayṣarī, and Shah Walī Allāh of Delhi.[38] In the case of those following the first tendency many sapiential doctrines belonging to ancient schools of philosophy such as Hermeticism, Neopythagoreanism and Neoplatonism were integrated into Islamic esoterism through the light of Islamic gnosis as we see in the writings of Ibn 'Arabī. It is interesting to note, however, that while Ibn 'Arabī was called "the Plato of his day," he was critical of the rationalistic philosophers who had preceded him.

In the second case there is a greater criticism of ratiocination (*istidlāl*) for spiritual reasons, and throughout Islamic history followers of this type of Sufism have criticized *falsafah,* particularly of the Peripatetic kind, severely, in order to open before people the luminous skies of illumination and gnosis while they have emphasized the centrality of love which in the Sufi context is not, however, in any way opposed to *ma'rifah* or gnosis as we see so clearly in the *Mathnawī* of Rūmī. In fact the *Mathnawī* has been called quite rightly "an ocean of gnosis."[39] Without Sufism and other aspects of Islamic esoterism contained in Shi'ism the rise of a Suhrawardī or a Mullā Ṣadrā would be inconceivable. In fact both tendencies within Sufism have played a critical role in the later history of *falsafah,* one more positive, and the other in a sense more negative, while both aspects of Sufism have remained the guardians and in many cases expositors of traditional *falsafah* or *ḥikmah* in its profoundest and most essential sense or what in Western parlance is called the *"philosophia perennis." Falsafah* for its part benefited immensely from this interaction with Sufism and gradually became itself the outer courtyard leading those qualified to enter the inner garden of gnosis and beatitude.

The criticism of Sufism against *falsafah* and the rebuttals of the *ḥukamā'* are well illustrated in the following assertion of Rūmī and the responses it brought forth. In his *Mathnawī,* he says:

> The leg of the syllogisers is a wooden one,
> A wooden leg is very infirm.[40]

This verse was answered by Mīr Dāmād in his own well-known poem in these terms:

> O thou who hast said that reasoning is like a wooden leg
> —Otherwise Fakhr al-Dīn Rāzī would have no peer—
> Thou hast not distinguished between intellect and fantasy,
> Do not reproach demonstration, O thou who hast not
> understood correctly.[41]

Later in the twelfth/eighteenth century the famous Sufi master of Shiraz, Mawlānā Sayyid Quṭb al-Dīn Muḥammad Shīrāzī, rose to defend Rūmī from the attack of Mīr Dāmād in yet another poem, some of whose lines are as follows:

O thou who reproacheth Mawlawī [Rūmī],
O thou who art deprived of an understanding [of the *Mathnawī*],
The *Mathnawī* is the ocean of the light of the soul,
Its poetry is replete with pearl and coral.
If thou hadst an understanding of the *Mathnawī*,
Thou wouldst never raise thy tongue in its reproach.
Although the weaknesses of the faculty of reason,
Have been accounted by Mawlawī in the *Mathnawī*
He did not intend by reason (*'aql*) the Universal Intellect (*'aql-i kull*),
For the latter is the guide upon all paths.
Rather, he meant the philosophical and particular reason,
For this is without the light of the face of Joseph.[42]
Since the particular intellect [reason] is mingled with fantasy,
Therefore it is considered blameworthy by the saints.[43]

The criticism made by certain Sufis of *falsafah* and their influence upon its development was like the transformation brought about by the alchemist through the presence of the philosopher's stone. The very substance of *falsafah* was changed during later Islamic history from a rational and systematic system of thought with an Islamic form and concerned as well with certain specifically Islamic issues to a wisdom related to esoterism and closely wedded to illumination and gnosis while retaining its distinct character as philosophy and making use of rational thought. Likewise, Islamic philosophy was saved by Islamic esoteric teachings and gnosis from the deadlock it had reached with the type of excessive Aristotelianism of an Ibn Rushd and was enabled to channel itself into a new direction, a direction that bestowed upon it renewed vigor and made it a major aspect of Islamic intellectual life in the eastern lands of Islam during the eight centuries following the death of the Andalusian master of Aristotelianism with whom the earlier chapter of Islamic philosophy had drawn to a close.

In discussing the role and function of *falsafah* in Islam and Islamic civilization we must note the change that took place to some degree after the period leading to Ibn Sīnā in the East and Ibn Rushd in the West. During the early period, which is also the formative period of the Islamic intellectual sciences, *falsafah* performed a central role in the process of the absorption and synthesis of the pre-Islamic sciences and the formulation of the Islamic sciences. The science of logic, the problem of the classification of the sciences, the methodology of the sciences, and their interaction with the rest of Islamic culture were all deeply concerned with and of concern to *falsafah* and its particular elaboration in Islam. Moreover, during this early period most of the great scientists were also philosophers so that we can speak during the early centuries, and even later, of a single type of Muslim savant who was both philosopher and scientist and whom we have already called "philosopher-scientist."[44] The development of Islamic science in the early period is related to that of Peripatetic philosophy as well as the philosophical trends of an anti-Peripatetic nature. Not only al-Fārābī and Ibn Sīnā, but also Muḥammad ibn Zakariyyā᾽ al-Rāzī and al-Bīrūnī were all prominent figures of Islamic science. In fact the anti-Peripatetic view, which is nevertheless *falsafah,* is particularly significant in the development of many new ideas in the sciences.[45] In any case during early Islamic history the cultivation and the development of the sciences would have been inconceivable without *falsafah.* The meaning of '*ḥakīm*,' which denotes at once a physician, scientist, and philosopher, is the best proof of this close connection.[46]

Not only did *falsafah* play a central role in the development of the intellectual sciences, of which it was like the head compared to the rest of the body, but also it was the major discipline in which tools and instruments of analysis, logic, and rational inquiry were developed for the transmitted sciences and other aspects of Islamic culture. The tools of logic developed mostly by the *falāsifah* and in conformity with the particular genius of Islam, in which logic plays a positive role from a soteriological point of view and prepares the mind for illumination and contemplation, were applied to fields ranging far and wide, from grammar and rhetoric to even the classification and categorization of *Ḥadīth,* from organizing economic activity in the bazaar to developing the geometry and arithmetic required to construct the great monuments of Islamic architecture. To be sure the function of the *falsafah* with which we are concerned here does not involve only the rationalizing tendencies of the Graeco-Alexandrian doctrines adopted by the Muslim Peripatetics or specific Aristotelian teachings. It concerns more generally the development of a climate of rational thought and of the instrument of logic and logical reasoning, which, once developed, were adopted by the various Islamic arts and sciences for their own ends and in accordance with the nature of Islam and its teachings.

Also during this early period when Islam made its first contacts with the arts and sciences of other civilizations, *falsafah* played an important role in enabling the Muslims to integrate the pre-Islamic sciences into their own perspective. Its role on the formal level complements that of Islamic esoterism, whose insistence on the universality of revelation on the supra-formal level made possible a positive encounter with other religions and traditions.[47] For the *falāsifah,* as al-Kindī asserted so clearly from the beginning, the truth was one; therefore, they were certain that the truth, wherever and whenever it might be discovered, would conform to the inner teachings of Islam, simply because the instrument of knowledge for both *falsafah* or *ḥikmah* and religion was the same, namely, the Universal Intellect or Logos, which plays such an important role in the theory of knowledge of the Islamic philosophers. Such facts as the identification of Hermes with Idrīs and the Sabaeans with the followers of Hermes, the belief that the early philosophers of Greece learned their *sophia* from Solomon and other prophets, and, looking eastward, the open interest shown by the *falāsifah* in the wisdom of India and ancient Persia both of which had a strong religious color all attest to the rapport between *falsafah* and prophecy and religion.

One must always remember the important role of *falsafah* in early Islam in providing the appropriate intellectual background for the encounter of Muslims with the arts, sciences, and philosophies of other civilizations. This role was in fact crucial during the early period of Islamic history when Muslims were translating the heritage of the great civilizations that had preceded them into their own world of thought and were laying the foundations for the rise of the Islamic sciences. This role was particularly important then, but it did not cease to be significant even later. The translation of the Chinese sciences during the Īl-Khānid period was supported by men whose background was that of *ḥikmah,* such men as Rashīd al-Dīn Faḍl Allāh, who was both vizier and philosopher-scientist.[48] Moreover, during the Moghul period in India the movement of translation of Sanskrit works into Persian incited by Akbar and reaching its culmination with Dārā Shukūh, a movement whose great religious and cultural significance is not as yet generally recognized outside the Indo-Pakistani subcontinent, is again closely connected with the later tradition of *falsafah* and *ḥikmah* as it spread from Persia, starting mostly with the reign of Skandar Lodi, to the Indian subcontinent. Finally, it must be reasserted that during the earlier phase of Islamic history one of the important and enduring roles of *falsafah* was its struggle with *kalām* and the particularly "philosophical" structure it finally bestowed upon that science. The difference between the treatises of *kalām* of al-Ash'arī himself or his student Abū Bakr al-Bāqillānī and Fakhr al-Dīn al-Rāzī, 'Adūḍ al-Dīn al-Ījī and Sayyid Sharīf al-Jurjānī is due solely to the long struggle of *kalām* with *falsafah.* Through *kalām,* therefore, *falsafah,* as an Islamic discipline, left its indelible mark upon the later intellectual life of Sunnism, where, at least in the Sunni parts of the Arab world in contrast to the Shi'ite world, *falsafah* as a distinct discipline had begun to wane after the eighth/eleventh century.

Something must also be said about the position of *falsafah* in Islamic universities during this early period. The official position accorded to *falsafah* in the curriculum of the Islamic universities varied greatly from land to land and period to period, depending upon theological and political factors of a complex nature, which we cannot analyze here.[49] In Jundishapur and the Bayt al-ḥikmah in Baghdad, *falsafah* was respected and taught, as it was also in the Azhar, after its establishment by the Fāṭimids. But its teaching in official *madrasahs* came to be banned with the rise of Ash'arite power among the Abbasids and Seljuqs, to the extent that in his will and testament for the trust (*waqf*) of the Niẓāmiyyah school system, Khwājah Niẓām al-Mulk ordered specifically that the teaching of *falsafah* be banned from the university system founded by him. This ban in fact continued in most of the Sunni part of the Arab world afterward except for logic, which was always taught there. But later in Islamic history the teaching of *falsafah* was made once again a part of the curriculum by Khwājah Naṣīr al-Dīn al-Ṭūsī at Maraghah and Rashīd al-Dīn Faḍl Allāh in the Rab'-i Rashīdī in Tabriz, as well as in certain Ottoman *madrasahs*, and despite a checkered career, it has continued as a part of the *madrasah* curricula in Persia and many schools of the Indo-Pakistani subcontinent and Iraq to this day. As noted elsewhere in this book, in India especially as a result of the influence of the scholars of Farangi Mahall in Lucknow Islamic philosophy continued in the curriculum of *madrasahs* until the fourteenth/twentieth century. In any case, however, the extent of the role of *falsafah* must not be judged solely by whether it was taught in universities or not, making a comparison with the situation in the West. In Islam, because of the very informal structure of traditional education, much of the instruction in *falsafah* as well as in the esoteric sciences has always been carried out in private circles outside the *madrasahs* and continues so to this day.

When we come to later Islamic history, or what we might call the "post-Ibn Rushdian phase" of Islamic philosophy, the role and function of *falsafah* became somewhat different from what it had been until then. The Islamic sciences, both the intellectual and transmitted, had by now become already elaborated and were following their own course of development. Peripatetic philosophy, moreover, had reached an impasse, as seen in the far-reaching attacks of al-Ghazzālī and the much less influential rebuttal of Ibn Rushd. New intellectual forces had appeared upon the scene, of which the most important were those identified with the names of Suhrawardī and Ibn 'Arabī. Politically also the symbolic unity of the Islamic world was soon brought to an end by the destruction of the Abbasid caliphate by the Mongols and the emerging of a new pattern, which finally led to the establishment in the central regions of the Islamic world of the three major Muslim empires of the Ottomans, Safavids, and Moghuls. In this new situation *falsafah* was to have a different function and role in the western and the eastern lands of Islam.

In the western lands of Islam, after Ibn Rushd *falsafah* ceased to exist as an independent and rigorously defined discipline, with a few exceptions in the Arab world such as Ibn Sab'īn and Ibn Khaldūn. Among the Turks and the Sunni Arabs of Syria and Iraq a certain amount of philosophic activity did continue, associated mostly with the school of Suhrawardī and the metaphysical doctrines of Ibn 'Arabī, but unfortunately this tradition has not been investigated thoroughly until now.[50] In the western lands of Islam the life of the main substance of *falsafah*, however, both in its logical aspects and cosmological and metaphysical doctrines, continued to pulsate within *kalām* and also within Sufism of the gnostic and metaphysical type, associated with Ibn 'Arabī and his commentators such as Ṣadr al-Dīn al-Qunyawī, Mu'ayyīd al-Dīn al-Jandī, Dā'ūd al-Qayṣarī, Shams al-Dīn al-Fanārī, 'Abd al-Wahhāb al-Sha'rānī, Bālī Afandī, and 'Abd al-Ghanyī al-Nabulusī. The continuation of the intellectual life of the Muslims of the western regions, a life that manifested itself in *falsafah* as well as *kalām* and *taṣawwuf* in the early centuries, is to be found during the later period primarily in *kalām* and Sufism. One would, therefore, have to say that although until the revival of Islamic philosophy in Egypt by Jamāl al-Dīn al-Asadābādī (known as al-Afghānī) in the thirteenth/nineteenth century *falsafah* or *ḥikmah* as a separate and distinct discipline was only pursued sparsely and was not cultivated avidly in the western lands of Islam, it nevertheless continued to possess a certain mode of life within the matrix of *kalām* and Sufism.

In the eastern lands of Islam and particularly in Persia the role of *falsafah* was quite different as we shall see in the last chapters of this book. Thanks to Suhrawardī and Ibn 'Arabī new schools of *ḥikmah* grew while the teachings of Ibn Sīnā were revived by al-Ṭūsī. As a result, a rich intellectual life came into being, which reached its apogee in many ways in the Safavid period with Mīr Dāmād and Mullā Ṣadrā[51] and which also played a major role among the Muslims of the Indian subcontinent. Besides its function in aiding to sustain the intellectual sciences, which continued to be cultivated in Persia and India—and also to a certain extent among the Ottomans—up to the thirteenth/nineteenth century, and besides its role in the various aspects of the religious life of the community, *falsafah* or *ḥikmah*, which by now had come much closer to the heart of the Islamic message and had left the limitative confines of Peripatetic philosophy, became the bridge for many to Sufism and Sufi metaphysics. In the same way that in the Arab world one observes in many circles to this day a certain wedding between Ash'arite *kalām* and Sufism, in Persia and to a certain extent in the Ottoman world and in the Indian subcontinent there came into being a notable wedding between *ḥikmah* and *'irfān*, and many masters appeared who were both *ḥakīms* and *'ārifs* (gnostics). On the one hand, *ḥikmah* became profoundly imbued with the gnostic teachings of Ibn 'Arabī and his school and was able to present in such cases as Mullā Ṣadrā a more systematic and logical interpretation of Sufi metaphysics than found in many of the Sufi texts themselves. On the other hand, it became in turn the major point of access to the teachings of Sufism for many of intellectual inclination with a rational bent of mind who were engaged in the cultivation of the official religious sciences. As a result of the transformation it received and the role it fulfilled, *falsafah* or *ḥikmah* continued its own life and remains to this day in Persia and certain adjacent lands as a living intellectual tradition independent of *kalām* and *'irfān*.

In conclusion and in summary it can be said that *falsafah* in Islam satisfied a certain need for causality that exists everywhere among certain human types, provided the necessary logical and rational tools for the cultivation and development of many of the arts and sciences, enabled Muslims to encounter and assimilate the learning of many other cultures, in its reactions with *kalām* left a deep effect upon the latter's future course, and finally became wed to illumination and gnosis, thus creating a bridge between the rigor of logic and the ecstasy of spiritual union, while influencing in some cases the expression of gnostic teachings themselves.

What we have said about traditional Islamic philosophy holds true to a large extent today wherever Islamic philosophy remains a living intellectual tradition. This philosophy remains of the greatest pertinence to the contemporary world because of the harmony it has achieved between logic and spiritual vision and also because of the profound metaphysical and cosmological doctrines it contains within the pages of its long and extended historical unfolding.[52] Furthermore, because of the present encounter of Islam with an alien philosophy and science—this time from the West—Islamic philosophy must be called upon once again to play the role it fulfilled in early Islamic history, namely, to provide the necessary intellectual instruments and the requisite intellectual background with the aid of which Muslims can face various alien philosophies and sciences from a position of discernment and intellectual rigor. Otherwise the encounter with the West can only result in calamity for the future of Islamic intellectual life and threaten even more than what happened in the colonial period the continuation of the life of *falsafah* itself. Only in remaining true to its own genius, to its own roots, and to the role it has always played in Islamic history in a land dominated by the reality of prophecy can *falsafah* (and *ḥikmah*) fulfill this vital function of providing the Muslims themselves with the necessary intellectual background to confront the modern and now postmodern West and to remind the world at large about the long-forgotten but urgently needed truths that Islamic philosophy has been able to preserve within its treasury of wisdom over the centuries and that it is able to present in a contemporary language to the world today.

CHAPTER 3

Al-Ḥikmat al-Ilāhiyyah and *Kalām*

In trying to understand the role of philosophy within the context of the Islamic tradition in its totality, one of the most interesting subjects to investigate is the relation between later Islamic philosophy in its metaphysical aspects or what came to be known as *al-ḥikmat al-ilāhiyyah* and *kalām* which is usually translated as Islamic theology in Western languages. When we speak of *al-ḥikmat al-ilāhiyyah* we do not mean simply the *ilāhiyyāt* of the works of Muslim Peripatetics such as Ibn Sīnā and Ibn Rushd, nor the *ḥikmah* to which some of the theologians such as Fakhr al-Dīn Rāzī refer as being synonymous with *kalām*. Rather, we mean that blend of rational philosophy, illumination, gnosis, and the tenets of revelation that formed into a synthesis after Suhrawardī and to a large extent, thanks to him, that reached its peak with Ṣadr al-Dīn Shīrāzī and his students.[1] In this chapter we wish to examine the relation between the followers of the school of *al-ḥikmat al-ilāhiyyah*, or *ḥikmat-i ilāhī* (especially that part concerned with "the general principles" (*al-umūr al-'āmmah*) and *kalām*. Although not all the *ḥukamā*ʾ of this school have the same view concerning *kalām*, there is enough unity of view among them to warrant such a study, in the same way that one can speak of the relation between *mashshā*ʾ*ī* philosophy and *kalām* even though not all of the Muslim Peripatetic philosophers have held the same views concerning *kalām*.

In the history of the struggle and reciprocal influence between *falsafah* and *kalām* in Islam, we can, for the sake of the present discussion, distinguish five periods:

1. The earliest period, from the beginning to the end of the third/ninth century, when the Mu'tazilite school was dominant in *kalām*, and *falsafah* was passing through its period of genesis and early development with such figures as Īrānshahrī and al-Kindī and his students. This period was one of distinct but parallel developments and of close association between *falsafah* and *kalām* in an atmosphere of more or less relative mutual respect, at least in the case of al-Kindī himself, although from the side of *kalām* certain

of its branches such as the school of Basra opposed *falsafah* strongly even during this early period.

2. The period from the end of the third/ninth to the fifth/eleventh century, from the rise of Ash'arite theology and its elaboration to the beginning of the gradual incorporation of certain philosophical arguments into *kalām* by Imām al-Ḥaramayn al-Juwaynī and his student al-Ghazzālī. This was a period of intense opposition and often enmity between *falsafah* and *kalām*, a period whose phases have been so ably studied along with those of the first period by many Western scholars, from Munk, Steinschneider, Horovitz, and Horten to Anawati, Gardet, and especially Wolfson, whose studies in the domain of the relation between *falsafah* and *kalām* during the early period of Islamic history mark one of the highlights of Occidental scholarship on Islamic thought.[2] Names of more recent scholars such as Joseph von Ess, David Burrell, and Wilfred Madelung can be added to this list.

3. The period from al-Juwaynī and al-Ghazzālī to Fakhr al-Dīn al-Rāzī and including Abū᾿l-Fatḥ al-Shahrastānī, that is, from about the fifth/eleventh century to the seventh/thirteenth century. During this period strong opposition between *falsafah* and *kalām* continued as can be seen in the well-known critiques of Ibn Sīnā by al-Ghazzālī and al-Rāzī, but at the same time each school became influenced in many ways by the other. *Falsafah*, going back to Ibn Sīnā, who lived at the beginning of this period, began to discuss more than before such problems as the meaning of prophecy and the Divine Word, the question of human and Divine Will connected with the issue of predestination and free will, the Divine Attributes, and so on, issues that had always been central to *kalām*. Meanwhile, *kalām* became even more "philosophical," employing both ideas and arguments drawn from *falsafah*. In fact such a famous Ash'arite theologian as Fakhr al-Dīn al-Rāzī had extensive knowledge of philosophy. That is why Ibn Khaldūn, who appeared shortly after this period, wrote that there appeared men whom it was difficult to classify exclusively in the category of *faylasūf* or *mutakallim* and who could be legitimately considered as belonging to either or both groups. Still, during the period in question the attacks of Ash'arite *kalām*, although itself "philosophized," continued against *falsafah* to the extent that they eclipsed Peripatetic philosophy in the eastern lands of Islam as we shall see more fully in later chapters.

4. From the seventh/thirteenth century to the tenth/sixteenth century a more peaceful relationship existed between *falsafah*, which now included the newly established school of Illumination or *ishrāq*, and *kalām*. In the Sunni world many figures appeared who were masters of both *falsafah* and Ash'arite *kalām* (of the later school) such as Sayyid Sharīf Jurjānī, Jalāl al-Dīn Dawānī, and even Dāʾūd al-Qayṣarī. In the Twelve-Imam Shi'ite world systematic *kalām* was established by Naṣīr al-Dīn al-Ṭūsī who was himself one of the greatest of Islamic philosophers. His student 'Allāmah al-Ḥillī, who is considered one of the most outstanding authorities in Shi'ite *kalām*, was also a master philosopher. One can see during this period in both the Sunni and Shi'ite worlds a much less contentious relationship between *falsafah* and *kalām* and the appearance of many more figures such as those to whom Ibn Khaldūn had alluded, that is, men who were at once *faylasūf* and *mutakallim*. Meanwhile, after the rise of Suhrawardī and development of his school, *al-ḥikmat al-muta'āliyah* began to develop rapidly in the School of Isfahan with which we shall discuss in chapter 11 of this work.

5. From the tenth/sixteenth century to modern times when in the Shi'ite world, following the full development of *al-ḥikmat al-muta'āliyah* by Mullā Ṣadrā, philosophy seen as *al-ḥikmat al-ilāhiyyah* began to eclipse *kalām* to the extent that Shi'ite *kalām* soon ceased to occupy the important position it had held earlier and became marginalized. As for the Sunni world, especially in India, the teachings of the masters of philosophy understood as *ḥikmat al-ilāhiyyah* flourished. There, however, in contrast to Persia, this *ḥikmah* tradition did not completely supplant and eclipse Ash'arite *kalām*, but the two were often integrated together, along with Sufism, into a grand synthesis as we see in the writings of Shāh Walī Allāh of Delhi and Mawlānā 'Alī Ashraf Thanwī.

During the last two periods in question the opposition of the followers of *al-ḥikmat al-ilāhiyyah* to *kalām*, and especially to the *kalām* of the Ash'arite school, did not disappear and even grew, as far as Shi'ite philosophers were concerned. The opposition to Ash'arism did not, however, come only from philosophers or Shi'ite theologians. As far as Ash'arite theology is concerned, it is too often taken in the West as representing Islamic theology as such; although more recent scholarship has shown that even in Sunni circles it has never represented all religious thought or "theology" in its Christian sense and has always been opposed by a segment of the Sunni religious community.[3] The Quran and the Sunnah, on the one hand, and the pure metaphysics and gnosis derived from the esoteric teachings of Islam and contained in Sufism, on the other hand, were there to show some of the innate shortcomings of the whole Ash'arite approach.[4] This matter must be taken into full consideration when one discusses the opposition of the followers of *al-ḥikmat al-ilāhiyyah* to *kalām* in general and Ash'arite *kalām* in particular.

The followers of *al-ḥikmat al-ilāhiyyah* considered the methods of *kalām* as being illegitimate, but the problems with which it dealt as being of vital importance. While they held the same reverence for the Quran and *Sunnah* as the followers of *kalām* and also drew from these sources for their doctrines, they refused to accept the methods of *kalām* as sufficient or even legitimate in solving the more profound questions of religion and their metaphysical implications. In fact it can be said that the *ḥukamāʾ-i ilāhī* (that is, philosophers who belonged to the school of *al-ḥikmat al-ilāhiyyah*), as they came to be called in Persian, believed themselves to be exactly that class of religious scholars who possessed the necessary intellectual means to explain the intellectual content of religion and answer the questions posed for religion by the discursive mind, or in other words to accomplish those very goals which the *mutakallimūn* attempted to accomplish but failed to do so in a satisfactory manner in the eyes of the *ḥukamāʾ*.

The change from opposition to *kalām* to replacing its very role and function, at least in the cultural orbit of Persia where *ḥikmat-i ilāhī* flourished for the most part, can be seen already in the intermediary figures between Suhrawardī and Mullā Ṣadrā, to whom we shall turn later in this book. Suhrawardī himself makes singularly little reference to *kalām*, while at the same time he discusses the most essential problems of *kalām* such as Divine Attributes, the nature of the human soul, and God's knowledge of the world, in light of his own *ishrāqī* doctrines.[5] Naṣīr al-Dīn al-Ṭūsī, who followed him by a century, was both *ḥakīm* and *mutakallim* and in fact the founder of Shi'ite systematic theology thanks mostly to his *Tajrīd* (Catharsis).[6] His student Quṭb al-Dīn al-Shīrāzī, the commentator of Suhrawardī and at the same time a Peripatetic philosopher, showed less interest in *kalām* than his master while being aware of its arguments. But another of Naṣīr al-Dīn's students, 'Allāmah al-Ḥillī, was again both a foremost theologian and a *ḥakīm*.

The tendency toward a synthesis between *ḥikmat-i ilāhī* and *kalām* especially in its Shi'ite form but also including Ash'arite *kalām* became even more accentuated in the eighth/fourteenth and ninth/fifteenth centuries. While specifically Shi'ite theologians such as Ibn Abī Jumhūr Aḥṣā'ī and Sayyid Ḥaydar Āmulī were well versed in the doctrines of *ḥikmat-i ilāhī*, some of the best known *ḥakīms* of the age, such as Jalāl al-Dīn Dawānī, Ṣadr al-Dīn and Ghiyāth al-Dīn Manṣūr Dashtakī, and Mīr Sayyid Sharīf Jurjānī were as much at home with *kalām* as *ḥikmah* and also *'irfān*. It is hardly possible to say whether Dawānī was a *ḥakīm-i ilāhī* or a *mutakallim* in the same way that later in India numerous figures appeared who were both *mutakallim* and *faylasūf or ḥakīm*. It is important to note, however, that while Ṭūsī was well versed in both schools but expressed the viewpoint of each in separate works and did not combine their arguments in a single book or a single doctrinal synthesis, Dawānī and many other later figures combined arguments and methods of both schools in their exposition of the nature of things and attempted a synthesis between them. This is a hallmark of much of the thought of the eighth/fourteenth and ninth/fifteenth centuries.

With Mullā Ṣadrā the new relation between *kalām* and *al-ḥikmat al-ilāhiyyah*, which had been developing since the seventh/thirteenth century, reaches a new peak and the summit of its development.[7] Mullā Ṣadrā knew well the important Mu'tazilite and Ash'arite theologians, especially al-Ghazzālī and Fakhr al-Dīn al-Rāzī, and also the most important Shi'ite theologians before himself. In fact among the later Islamic philosophers probably none was as well acquainted with both Sunni and Shi'ite *kalām* as he. *Kalām* represents, along with Peripatetic philosophy, *ishrāqī* theosophy and *'irfān*, one of the basic elements from which he created his vast synthesis. He turns to the arguments of *kalām* again and again especially in the *Asfār*, and he confirms and praises some of the arguments of the *mutakallimūn* in certain places[8] while rejecting them violently in others.[9]

What is, however, most interesting in Mullā Ṣadrā's views about *kalām* is not his acceptance of some of their beliefs and arguments nor the fact that nearly every single problem discussed by *kalām* is also considered by him in his "transcendent theosophy" (*al-ḥikmat al-muta'āliyah*); rather, it is his views concerning the very nature of *kalām* and the shortcomings of the knowledge acquired through its methods. According to him, the *mutakallimūn* in general have not purified their inner being sufficiently so as to enable the intellect within them to perceive directly the Divine Realities without the dimming and obscuring influence of the carnal soul. In the *Si aṣl* (Three Principles) he says in bitter words that reflect the hardship he suffered at the hands of some of the superficial *'ulamā'* and *mutakallimūn* who opposed his teachings, "Some of those who pretend to be scholars and are full of evil and corruption and some of the *mutakallimūn* who have no logic or reason . . . have made opposition to the Sufis their slogan."[10] He continues,

> O dear scholar and o conceited *mutakallim*! Until when and for how long will you mark the face of intimacy with the mole of fear and cast the earth of darkness upon the eye of faithfulness through distress and be busy with admonition and oppression of the people of purity and faithfulness? Until when and for how long will you wear the dress of deception and hypocrisy and the robe of trickery and imposture, and drink the cup of conceit from the hands of the fiend that appears as an angel, and use your effort in destroying the truth and spreading falsehood, in vilifying the man of knowledge and praising the ignorant?[11]

In his *Kasr aṣnām al-jāhiliyyah* (Breaking the Idols of the Age of Ignorance), Mullā Ṣadrā makes clearer the reason why *kalām* cannot reach the heart of religious truth. He writes,

> The differences that occur among scholars of *kalām* and jurisprudence (*fiqh*) in the important questions and the general principles of religious injunctions, and not in secondary details where differences can exist, originate in the failure of their effort to seek the truth of things and in the fact that they do not penetrate into all of the aspects of the truth. The way to reach certainty (*yaqīn*) in the inquiry into religious truths and the inner meaning of the teachings of the Prophet is not through discussions of *kalām* and disputations. Rather, it is through the acquiring of inner and intuitive knowledge, the abandoning of what one's nature is accustomed to, the rejection of worldly and base things and the disregarding of the opinions of creatures, the praise of men and the attention of rulers. In summary, it is through the realization of real asceticism before the world, its children, its wealth and its glory.
>
> Worldly glory is a greater temptation than wealth. And worldly glory deriving from a social status based upon [pretended] knowledge and righteousness is a worse corruption in the hearts [of men] than the worldly glory derived from authority over their bodies and based upon might and power. For from the former originate most disputa-

> tions and discussions of *kalām* and the rivalries and controversies of *fiqh*, whose origin is the desire for fame and social prestige throughout the land, the love to rule and to control the servants of God, the great hope in [acquiring] what is desirable physically, the wish to continue to subsist on this earth and to cling to it, satisfaction with the life of this world and being removed from the good pleasure of God, the Exalted, on the Day of Resurrection.[12]

With this stern judgment, which concerns not the result but the very roots of the thoughts and words of the *mutakallimūn*, Mullā Ṣadrā attacks the basis of *kalām* at the same time that he integrates so much of its heritage into his own intellectual synthesis.

The writings of one of Mullā Ṣadrā's foremost students, 'Abd al-Razzāq Lāhījī,[13] are particularly significant for an understanding of the relation between *al-ḥikmat al-ilāhiyyah* and *kalām* in later centuries. Although he had studied the *al-Asfār al-arba'ah* (The Four Journeys), *al-Shawāhid al-rubūbiyyah* (Divine Witnesses), and *al-Mabdaʾ waʾl-ma'ād* (The Origin and the End) of Mullā Ṣadrā with the master himself and was also well versed in *ishrāqī* philosophy, as a result of the radically changed conditions at the end of the Safavid period to which we shall turn later in this book, he distanced himself from his teacher's *al-ḥikmat al-muta'āliyah* and wrote his most famous works on *kalām* and publicly at least showed himself to be closer to the Peripatetics than to Mullā Ṣadrā in questions pertaining to philosophy. Among his works on *kalām* the most famous are *Gawhar-i murād* (The Sought Jewel) and *Shāwariq al-ilhām* (Orients of Divine Inspiration), the latter being a commentary upon Ṭūsī's *al-Tajrīd*. These works, the first written in Persian and the second in Arabic, have become among the most authoritative works on Shi'ite *kalām*.

Although a defender of Shi'ite *kalām*, Lāhījī did not extend his approval to all schools of *kalām*. The famous theologian Taftāzānī, like Ibn Khaldūn, distinguished between the *kalām* of the *mutaqaddimīn* or "ancients" and the *mutaʾakhkhirīn*, "those who came later," but identified the first with the Mu'tazilites and the second with the Ash'arites. Lāhījī used the same distinction but with a different meaning. For him the *kalām* of the *mutaqaddimīn* is identified with Sunni *kalām* in general and that of the *mutaʾakhkhirīn* with Shi'ite *kalām*. He criticizes the first type of *kalām* because of its opposition to *ḥikmah* and defends the second, which he finds in harmony with the *ḥikmah* tradition. He considers the method of the first to be merely dialectic (*jadal*) and the second, like philosophy, demonstration (*burhān*).[14]

It is important to note that while Lāhījī was a notable authority on *kalām*, he was also deeply rooted in both Sufism and *al-ḥikmat al-ilāhiyyah,* although he hid to some extent his attachment to his master's teachings. Lāhījī wrote a number of works on logic and philosophy and even a commentary upon the *Sharḥ al-ishārāt* (Commentary upon the Directives and Remarks [of Ibn Sīnā]) by Ṭūsī. Some of his philosophical and gnostic views are also to be found in his poetry, which is of high quality.[15] Lāhījī was also deeply interested in the relation between *kalām* and Sufism, a domain in which he held a position not far removed from that of al-Ghazzālī. In light of all these qualifications it is, therefore, of particular significance to read what he writes about the relation between *al-ḥikmat al-ilāhiyyah* and *kalām* in his *Gawhar-i murād.*

He writes,

> Know that the types of differences existing among the *'ulamā'* in matters pertaining to the divine sciences (*ma'ārif-i ilāhī*) are limited to the differences between the schools of *ḥikmat* and *kalām.* . . .
>
> The difference between *kalām* and *ḥikmat* lies in the following facts: It must first of all be known that the intellect (*'aql*) possesses complete independence in the acquiring of the divine sciences and other intellectual matters, and in these matters it does not depend upon the *Sharī'ah.* Once this is realized it can be concluded that the way of the *ḥukamā'* is acquiring true science and proving the definite principles that govern over the essences of things in a way that is in accordance with the nature of reality. And this way is based upon reasoning and purely intellectual demonstration leading to self-evident premises that no intellect can refuse or resist to accept and in which the agreement or disagreement of any particular circumstances of peoples or religious communities does not have any effect. The knowledge acquired in this way is called in the terminology of learned men "the science of *ḥikmat.*" Of necessity this science is in conformity with authentic revealed laws, for the truth of the *Sharī'ah* is ascertainable in its reality through intellectual demonstration, but this agreement does not enter into the proof of the problems of *ḥikmat,* which do not depend upon the *Sharī'ah* for their proof. . . .

As for the term *kalām,* it has two meanings: the *kalām* of the ancients and the new *kalām.* The *kalām* of the ancients is an art which enables man to defend the statutes of the *Sharī'ah* through demonstration composed of well-known premises that are established with certainty among the followers of religion whether they lead to self-evident premises or not. This art has nothing in common with *ḥikmat,* either in subject matter, in reasoning or in its usefulness. The subject of *ḥikmat* is the real nature of things not circumstances. Its reasoning is composed of truths that are established with certainty resulting from self-evident premises, whether these are uncontested and well-known or not. Its usefulness is in the acquiring of knowledge and the perfection of the theoretical faculty of the mind and not in the preservation of statutes. Thus it is clear that this art [*kalām*] cannot be one of the means of acquiring knowledge (*ma'rifat*).

The ancients among the Muslims needed this art for two reasons: one was to protect the doctrines of the *Sharī'ah* from the people of opposition [to it] among followers of other denominations and religions. This need concerned the general public among Muslims. The other was to prove the particular aims of each school and sect of Islam and to protect the condition of each school from the attacks of the other Islamic schools. Naturally the relationship [created by the type of defense given] to each school is different.

What we have said concerns the origin of *kalām* among Muslims. But gradually the borders of *kalām* were extended. People were no longer satisfied with guarding the situation but began to document and explain the arguments for the principles and foundations of religion, basing their arguments upon well-known and evident premises. They left the straight path of the most perfect among the Companions (*ṣaḥābah*) and their followers (*tābi'īn*), which consisted of contemplation and meditation as well as reference to the scholars (*'ulamā'*) among the Companions and leaders (*imāms*) among their followers. They considered their own way as the way to acquire knowledge and even considered it as the only possible way. . . .

This then is the new *kalām*, which is the counterpart of *ḥikmat*. It shares the same subject and aim with *ḥikmat* but differs from it in the primary arguments and reasoning. It has been said concerning the definition of the new *kalām* that it is a knowledge of the state of creatures according to the mode of the injunctions of the *Sharī'ah*. By adding this last condition the definition of *ḥikmat* has been avoided, for agreement with the injunctions of the *Sharī'ah* means basing one's arguments upon premises that are well-known and evident among the followers of the *Sharī'ah*. And this is not acceptable in the definition of *ḥikmat*, for it is not necessary for premises that are well-known and [appear as] evident to be among truths that are known with certainty. Therefore, if by chance the premises are truths possessing certainty they [the followers of *ḥikmat*] use them as such, and if not, they do not consider premises based upon opinion as valid in intellectual matters (*masā᾿il-i 'ilmiyyah*).

A group of the ignorant, who have appeared in the guise of learned men, have been in error concerning this condition (*qayd*) [about the definition of *kalām* and its difference from *ḥikmat*] or have on purpose made simple souls fall into the error of thinking that in the concept of *ḥikmat* opposition to the injunctions of the *Sharī'ah* is considered valid. For this reason the condemnation of *ḥikmat* and its followers has become prevalent among Muslims. Whereas, from what we have said it has become clear that the acquiring of knowledge (*ma'rifat*) in a way that is not dependent upon simple imitation (*taqlīd*) is limited to the way of demonstration (*burhān*) and the basing of arguments upon premises that are certain, whether this knowledge be called *ḥikmat* or *kalām*.

It is not right to condemn *ḥikmat* because some of the *ḥakīms* have committed errors in certain problems. Rather, that group is condemnable that extends its prejudice concerning particular well-known personalities to *ḥikmat* itself, considering their [the *ḥakīms'*] imitation as necessary and believing every single word they have uttered to be the truth. He who is satisfied with mere imitation, why should he not imitate the prophets and *imāms*?—which act would of course bring him salvation, especially if he is not among those possessing capability [for intellectual penetration] and is

> not able to conceive of real perfection.[16] It is certain that simply to imitate philosophers and to consider perfection to reside solely in transmitting their words and guidance to reside solely in following them is pure error and the very essence of wretchedness. Rather, the sure way of acquiring the divine sciences (*ma'ārif*) is pure demonstration and the simple acquiring of certainty. Therefore, it is neither necessary to be a *mutakallim* nor a philosopher. Rather, one must be a believer (*mu'min*) who has faith in Divine Unity (*muwaḥḥid*) and one must have confidence in correct action, begging assistance in one's action from the true *Sharī'ah*. And if a person is not capable of achieving true perfection, he must never cease to imitate the truly perfect men.[17]

Shi'ite *kalām* soon became eclipsed completely in Persia with the revival of *ḥikmah*, especially of the school of Mullā Ṣadrā at the end of the twelfth/eighteenth and beginning of the thirteenth/nineteenth centuries. Two of the sons of Lāhījī, Mīrzā Ibrāhīm and Mīrzā Ḥasan, were also authorities in both *kalām* and *ḥikmah*. Hasan is the more important of the two. He studied in Qom where he died in 1121/1709.[18] He wrote on both *kalām* and philosophy, which he defended against its opponents. His works include *Zawāhir al-ḥikam* (The Flowers of Philosophical Sciences) which has a strong Avicennan color; *Āʾīna-yi ḥikmat* (The Mirror of Philosophy) which is also of a philosophical nature; and glosses upon the *Shawāriq* of his father on *kalām*. It is said that he first began to write on *ḥikmah* and the relation between *ḥikmah* and Sufism and only after being condemned by some of the exoteric religious authorities turned to writing on *kalām* and ethics. It is also interesting to note that although he was the grandson of Mullā Ṣadrā, he does not refer to the *ḥikmat al-muta'āliyah* at all.

The life of Ḥasan Lāhījī coincides with the end of the Safavid period and opposition to both *ḥikmah* and *'irfān* in Shi'ite religious circles in Persia and Iraq. But strangely enough it also coincides with the swan song of Shi'ite *kalām* as the *al-ḥikmat al-ilāhiyyah* tradition becomes revived and soon replaces *kalām* almost completely. Henceforth, great religious scholars appear such as Mullā Mahdī Narāqī who are both jurisprudents and philosophers, but no authority on Shi'ite *kalām* appears with the prominence of an al-Ḥillī or Lāhījī. Only in the past two decades has a new school of *kalām* called "*kalām-i jadīd*" been established in Qom and other centers of Shi'ite learning to confront the challenges of modernism and postmodernism. But even in this domain of providing religious and theological responses to the philosophical and cultural tidal waves coming from the West, the *ḥikmah* tradition plays the most important role, as we see in the case of a pivotal figure of the fourteenth/twentieth century, 'Allāmah Sayyid Muḥammad Ḥusayn Ṭabāṭabā'ī.

As for the Sunni world, the *al-hikmat al-ilāhiyyah* tradition did not take root in the Arab world except in Shi'ite circles in Iraq, so the question of its relation to *kalām* in that world does not arise until Jamāl al-Dīn Asadābādī, known as al-Afghānī, revived the study of *falsafah* in Cairo in the late thirteenth/nineteenth century. Even then most Arab scholars of Islamic philosophy, contented themselves with early Islamic philosophy, and little interest was shown in the later *ḥikmah* tradition until quite recently. In the Turkish part of the Ottoman Empire, Islamic philosophy mostly of the schools of Ibn Sīnā and Suhrawardī continued to be cultivated until modern times, and as already stated many figures appeared who sought to create a harmony between *ḥikmah/falsafah* and *kalām*.

As far as the Sunni world is concerned, the most interesting relationship between al-*ḥikmat al-ilāhiyyah* and *kalām* is to be found in India where the later *ḥikmah* tradition spread widely in Sunni as well as Shi'ite circles. It is quite interesting to note that many of the major Sunni intellectual figures of India, chief among them Shāh Walī Allāh, were both *ḥakīm* and *mutakallim* and sought to harmonize *ḥikmah* and Ash'arite *kalām* as we see in Shāh Walī Allāh's *Ḥujjat Allah al-bālighah* (The Conclusive Argument from God).[19] We can also see the same rapport between the two in the writings of the early fourteenth/twentieth-century figure Mawlānā 'Alī Thanwī, who was both *faylasūf/ḥakīm* and *mutakallim* in addition to being, like Shāh Walī Allāh, a Sufi.

The destiny of the relation between *al-ḥikmat al-ilāhiyyah* and *kalām* was therefore to be different in Persia and India. In the Shi'ite climate of Persia, *al-ḥikmat al-ilāhiyyah,* which to be sure had incorporated certain elements of *kalām* into its structure, ultimately devoured and more or less replaced *kalām*. In Sunni India in contrast, Sunni *kalām*, which in its later form had become more philosophical, continued to survive in a more distinct manner in the grand syntheses of Shāh Walī Allāh and others than one finds in the case of Shi'ite *kalām* among later *ḥakīms*, some of whom we shall discuss in chapter 13 of this book. In any case, all those diverse modes of relationship between philosophy and theology in the Islamic contexts represent so many different possibilities of philosophical activity in a land in which the sun of prophecy shines upon a world in which a human collectivity has lived, has thought, and has carried out philosophical speculation.

PART 2

Philosophical Issues

CHAPTER 4

The Question of Existence and Quiddity and Ontology in Islamic Philosophy

THE SIGNIFICANCE OF THE SUBJECT

There is no issue more central to Islamic philosophy and especially metaphysics than *wujūd* (at once Being and existence) in itself and in its relation to *māhiyyah* (quiddity or essence). For eleven centuries Islamic philosophers and even certain Sufis and theologians (*mutakallimūn*) have been concerned with this subject and have developed on the basis of their study of *wujūd* worldviews that have dominated Islamic thought and have also had a deep influence upon Christian and Jewish philosophy. Islamic philosophy is most of all a philosophy concerned with *wujūd* and hence with its distinction from *māhiyyah*. To understand the meaning of these basic concepts, their distinction, and relationship is, therefore, to grasp the very basis of Islamic philosophical thought.[1]

It is true that Islamic metaphysics places the Absolute above all limitations, even beyond the ontological Principle as usually understood. It knows that the Divine Essence (*al-Dhāt al-ilāhiyyah*) stands above even Being, that it is Non-Being or Beyond-Being[2] in that it stands beyond all limitation and even beyond the qualification of being beyond all limitation. Nevertheless, the language of this metaphysical doctrine revolves around *wujūd* in most schools of Islamic thought. Hence, the discussion concerning the distinction between *wujūd* and *māhiyyah* and their relation remains central to Islamic metaphysical thought even while most Muslim gnostics and metaphysicians have remained fully aware of the supra-ontological nature of the Supreme Reality and have not limited metaphysics to ontology.

Only too often the concern of Islamic philosophers with *wujūd* and *māhiyyah* has been traced back solely to Greek philosophy and especially to Aristotle. There is of course no doubt concerning the debt of al-Fārābī, who was the first Muslim philosopher to discuss fully the distinction between *wujūd* and *māhiyyah* to the Stagirite. The manner, however, in which he and especially Ibn Sīnā, who has been called the "philosopher of being" *par excellence*,[3] approached the subject and the centrality that the study of *wujūd* gained in Islamic thought have very much to do with the Islamic revelation itself. The Quran states explicitly, "But His command, when He intendeth a thing, is only that he saith unto it: Be! and it is (*kun fa-yakūn*)" (36: 82); it also speaks over and over of the creation and destruction of the world. This world as experienced by the *homo islamicus* is, therefore, not synonymous with *wujūd*. It is not "an ontological block without fissure in which essence, existence and unity are but one."[4]

Moreover, the origin of the "chain of being" is not simply the first link in the chain but is transcendent vis-à-vis the chain. The levels of existence (*marātib al-wujūd*) to which Aristotle and Theophrastus and before them Plato refer are, therefore, from the Islamic point of view, discontinuous with respect to their Source, which is above and beyond them. The Quranic teachings about Allah as Creator of the world played a most crucial role in the development of Islamic philosophy, as far as the study of *wujūd* is concerned. On the one hand, it made central the importance of the ontological hiatus between Being and existents and, on the other hand, bestowed another significance on the distinction between *wujūd* and *māhiyyah* by providing a meaning to the act of existentiation or the bestowal of *wujūd* upon *māhiyyah* other than what one finds in Aristotelian philosophy as it developed among the Greeks.

A Historical Survey of the Study of *Wujūd* and *Māhiyyah* in Islamic Thought

Already in his *Fuṣūṣ al-ḥikmah*,[5] al-Fārābī distinguishes clearly *huwiyyah*, which in the terminology of early Islamic philosophy means that by which something is actualized, hence *wujūd*, from *māhiyyah*. Ibn Sīnā, deeply influenced by al-Fārābī, makes this distinction the cornerstone of his ontology and treats it amply in many of his works, especially the metaphysics of the *Shifāʾ* (Healing) and the *Najāh* (Salvation) as well as in his final major philosophical opus, *al-Ishārāt waʾl-tanbīhāt* (Directives and Remarks).[6] Fakhr al-Dīn al-Rāzī, although a theologian, continued his concern for this issue while his contemporary Shihāb al-Dīn Suhrawardī, the founder of the school of Illumination or *ishrāq*, constructed a whole metaphysics of essence that would be inconceivable without the basis established by Avicennan ontology.[7] A century later in the seventh/thirteenth century, both Naṣīr al-Dīn al-Ṭūsī and his student 'Allāmah al-Ḥillī dealt extensively with the question of *wujūd* and *māhiyyah* even in their theological writings[8] as did most of the major philosophical figures between Ṭūsī and the Safavid period, such as Quṭb al-Dīn Shirāzī, Ghiyāth al-Dīn Manṣur Dashtakī, Ibn Turkah, and Jalāl al-Dīn Dawānī.[9]

Finally, with the Safavid renaissance of Islamic philosophy in Persia and the founding of what has now come to be known as the "School of Isfahan,"[10] Islamic metaphysics, based on the question of *wujūd*, reaches its peak with Mīr Dāmād and especially Ṣadr al-Dīn Shirāzī (Mullā Ṣadrā) who in his *al-Asfār al-arba'ah* has provided the most extensive discussion of *wujūd* to be found in the annals of Islamic philosophy.[11] This sage founded a new school of *ḥikmah* called the "transcendent theosophy" (*al-ḥikmat al-muta'āliyah),* which became the most dominant, although not the only, philosophical school in Persia, especially as far as the issue of *wujūd* and *māhiyyah* and their relation are concerned.

From the generation of Mullā Ṣadrā's students, such as 'Abd al-Razzāq Lāhījī and Fayḍ Kāshānī, to the Qajar revival of this school by Mullā 'Alī Nūrī, Ḥājjī Mullā Hādī Sabziwārī and Mullā 'Alī Mudarris Ṭihrānī,[12] numerous works on *wujūd* and *māhiyyah* continued to appear in Persia, while there was no less of an interest in this subject in India where the foremost thinkers, such as Shāh Walī Allāh of Delhi, dealt extensively with the subject.[13] In fact, the centrality of *wujūd* and *māhiyyah* in Islamic philosophy persists to this day wherever authentic Islamic philosophy has survived, as in Persia where several major works have centered on the issue over the past few decades.[14]

The Meaning of *Wujūd* and *Māhiyyah*

Traditional teachers of Islamic philosophy begin the teaching of *ḥikmat-i ilāhī* (literally *"theo-sophia"*) as it is called in Persian,[15] by instilling in the mind of the student a way of thinking based upon the distinction between *wujūd* and *māhiyyah.* They appeal to the immediate perception of things and assert that man in seeking to understand the nature of the reality he perceives can ask two questions about it: (1) Is it (*hal huwa*)? and (2) What is it (*mā huwa*)? The answer to the first question relates to *wujūd* or its opposite (*'adam* or nonexistence), and the answer to the second question concerns *māhiyyah* (from the word *mā huwa* or *ma hiya,* which is its feminine form).

Usually in Islamic philosophy terms are carefully defined, but in the case of *wujūd* it is impossible to define it in the usual meaning of definition as used in logic that consists of genus and specific difference.

Moreover, every unknown is defined by that which is known, but there is nothing more universally known than *wujūd* and therefore nothing else in terms of which *wujūd* can be defined. In traditional circles it is said that everyone, even a small baby, knows intuitively the difference between *wujūd* and its opposite, as can be seen by the fact that when a baby is crying, to speak to it about milk is of no avail, but as soon as "real" milk, that is, milk possessing *wujūd* is given to it, it stops crying.

Rather than define *wujūd*, therefore, Islamic philosophers allude to its meaning through such assertions as "*wujūd* is that by virtue of which it is possible to give knowledge about something" or "*wujūd* is that which is the source of all effects."[16] As for *māhiyyah*, it is possible to define it clearly and precisely as that which provides an answer to the question What is it? There is, however, a further development of this concept in later Islamic philosophy that distinguishes between *'māhiyyah'* in its particular sense (*biʾl-maʿnaʾl-akhaṣṣ*), which is the response to the question What is it?, and *'māhiyyah'* in its general sense (*biʾl-maʿnaʾl-aʿamm*), which means that by which a thing is what it is. It is said that *'māhiyyah'* in this second sense is derived from the Arabic phrase *mā bihi huwa huwa* (that by which something is what it is). This second meaning refers to the reality (*ḥaqīqah*) of a thing and is not opposed to *wujūd*, as is the first meaning of *'māhiyyah.'*[17]

As far as the etymological derivation of the term *wujūd* is concerned, it is an Arabic term related to the root *wjd*, which possesses the basic meaning "to find" or "come to know" about something. It is etymologically related to the term *wijdān*, which means "consciousness," "awareness," or "knowledge," as well as to *wajd*, which means "ecstasy" or "bliss."[18] The Islamic philosophers who were Persian or used that language also employed the Persian term *hastī*, which comes from Old Persian and is related to the Indo-European terms denoting being, such as *ist* in German and *is* in English.

'Wujūd' as used in traditional Islamic philosophy cannot be rendered in English simply as existence. Rather, it denotes at once Being, being, Existence, and existence, each of which has a specific meaning in the context of Islamic metaphysics. The term *Being* refers to the Absolute or Necessary Being (*wājib al-wujūd*); *being* is a universal concept encompassing all levels of reality, both that of creatures and that of the Necessary Being Itself. *Existence* (capitalized) refers to the first emanation or effusion from the Pure or absolute Being, or what is called *"al-fayḍ al-aqdas,"* the Sacred Effusion in later Islamic philosophy; while *existence* refers to the reality of all things other than the Necessary Being.

Technically speaking, God is, but He cannot be said to exist, for one must remember that the English word *'existence'* is derived from the Latin *ex-sistere*, which implies a pulling away or drawing away from the substance or ground of reality. The very rich vocabulary of Islamic philosophy differentiates all these usages by using *'wujūd'* with various modifiers and connotations based upon the context, whereas the single English term 'existence' cannot render justice to all the nuances of meaning contained in the Arabic term. Thus throughout this chapter we use the Arabic *'wujūd'* rather than a particular English translation of it. There are also terms derived from *'wujūd'* that are of great philosophical importance, especially the term *mawjūd* or "existent," which Islamic philosophy, especially of the later period, clearly distinguished from *wujūd* as the "act of existence." Muslim metaphysicians knew full well the difference between the terms *ens* and *actus essendi* or *Sein* and *Dasein*, and therefore followed a path that led to conclusions very different from those in the West, which finally led to modern Western *Existenz Philosophie* and existentialism.[19]

The Distinction between *Wujūd* and *Māhiyyah*

The starting point of Islamic ontology is not the world of existents in which the existence of something, that something as existent, and the unity of that thing are the same as is the case with Aristotelian metaphysics. For Aristotle the world could not not exist. It is an ontological block that cannot conceivably be broken; thus the distinction between *wujūd* and *māhiyyah* is not of any great consequence. For Islamic thought, on the contrary, the world is not synonymous with *wujūd*. There is an ontological poverty (*faqr*) of the world in the sense that *wujūd* is given by God who alone is the abiding Reality, all "other" existents coming into being and passing away. The conceptual distinction between *wujūd* and *māhiyyah*, therefore, gains great significance and, far from being inconsequential, becomes in fact the key for understanding the nature of reality. The difference between the Avicennan and Aristotelian understanding of *wujūd* and *ón*, respectively, has in fact very much to do with the message of prophecy in the world in which Ibn Sīnā philosophized.

According to traditional Islamic philosophy, the intellect (*al-'aql*) is able to distinguish clearly between the *wujūd* and *māhiyyah* of anything, not as they are externally where there is but one existent object, but in the "container of the mind." When one asks oneself the question "What is it?" with respect to a particular object, the answer given is totally distinct from concern for its existence or nonexistence. The "mind" has the power to conceive of the quiddity of something, let us say man, purely and completely as *māhiyyah* and totally distinct from any form of *wujūd*. *Māhiyyah* thus considered in itself and in so far as it is itself (*min haythu hiya hiya*) is called in Islamic philosophy, and following the terminology of Ibn Sīnā, "natural universal" (*al-kullī al-ṭabī'ī*). *Māhiyyah* also appears in the mind, possessing "mental existence," and in the external world *in concreto*, possessing external existence; but in itself it can be considered completely shorn of any concern with *wujūd*,[20] such as when the "mind" conceives of the *māhiyyah* of man which includes the definition of man without any consideration as to whether man exists or not.

Moreover, *māhiyyah* excludes *wujūd* as one of its constituent elements. Or to use traditional terminology, *wujūd* is not a *maqawwim* of *māhiyyah* in the sense that animal, which is contained in the definition of man as rational animal, is a constituent or *muqawwim* of the *māhiyyah* of man. There is nothing in a *māhiyyah* that would relate it to *wujūd* or necessitate the existence of that *māhiyyah*. The two concepts are totally distinct as are their causes. The causes of a *māhiyyah* are the elements that constitute its definition, namely, the genus and specific difference, while the causes of the *wujūd* of a particular existent are its efficient and final causes, as well as its substratum.[21] For a *māhiyyah* to exist, therefore, *wujūd* must be "added to it," that is, become wedded to it from "outside" itself.

In the history of Islamic thought, not to speak of modern studies of Islamic philosophy, there has often been a misunderstanding about this distinction and about the relation between *wujūd* and *māhiyyah*. It is essential, therefore, to emphasize that Ibn Sīnā and those who followed him did not begin with two "realities," one *māhiyyah* and the other *wujūd*, which became wedded in concrete, external objects, even if certain philosophers have referred to existents as "combined pairs" (*zawj tarkībī*). Rather, they began with the single, concrete external object, the *ens* or *mawjūd*, which they analyzed conceptually in terms of *māhiyyah* and *wujūd* and which they studied separately in their philosophical treatises.[22] These concepts, however, were to provide a key for the understanding of not only the relation between the "suchness" and "is-ness" of existents, but also the ontological origin of things and their interrelatedness, as we see especially in the "transcendent theosophy" of Ṣadr al-Dīn Shirāzī.

THE QUESTION OF THE "ACCIDENTALITY" OF *WUJŪD*

One of the problems that concerned philosophers who followed in the wake of Ibn Sīnā was whether *wujūd* is an accident (*'araḍ*) that occurs to *māhiyyah* or not. Fakhr al-Dīn al-Rāzī and certain other later Muslim thinkers took Ibn Sīnā to task for calling *wujūd* an "accident," while in the Latin West on the basis of an erroneous interpretation by Ibn Rushd of the Avicennan thesis as stated in the *Shifā'*[23] and elsewhere, such philosophers as the Latin Averroist Siger of Brabant and even St. Thomas himself understood Ibn Sīnā to mean that *wujūd* is an accident that occurs to *māhiyyah*. If one understands accident in the ordinary sense of, let us say, a color being an accident, and the wood that bears that color is the substance upon which the accident alights from the outside (or *en in alio*, as the Scholastics would say), then insurmountable problems arise. In the case of the wood, which is the place or locus where the accident occurs, the substance exists whether the accident occurs to it or not. The wood remains wood and possesses a concrete reality whether it is to be painted red or green. The wood has a subsistence, and only at a later stage does the accident of color occur in it.

In the case of *wujūd*, the question would arise as to what state the *māhiyyah* would be in "before" the occurrence of the accident of *wujūd*. If it is already an existent, then *wujūd* must have occurred to it before, and the argument could be carried back ad infinitum. If *māhiyyah* were nonexistent, then it could not possess any reality like that of wood that would later be painted red or green.

This type of interpretation of Ibn Sīnā, which would understand "accident" in the case of *wujūd* to mean the same as the ordinary sense of the word *accident*, is due partly to the fact that Ibn Sīnā did not fully clarify the use of the term *'araḍ* or accident as used in relation to *wujūd* in the *Shifā'*. In his *Ta'līqāt* (Glosses), however, which although not known in the Latin West, had a profound influence upon post-Avicennan philosophy in the Eastern lands of Islam and especially in Persia, Ibn Sīnā makes clear that by '*ʿaraḍ*' as used in relation to '*wujūd*' and '*māhiyyah*' he does not mean accident in relation to substance as usually understood, and he asserts clearly that *wujūd* is an *'araḍ* only in a very special sense. Ibn Sīnā writes,

> The 'existence' of all 'accidents' in themselves is their 'existence for their substrata,' except only one 'accident,' which is 'existence.' This difference is due to the fact that all other

'accidents,' in order to become existent, need each a substratum (which is already existent by itself), while 'existence' does not require any 'existence' in order to become existent. Thus it is not proper to say that its 'existence' (i.e. the 'existence' of this particular 'accident' called 'existence') in a substratum is its very 'existence,' meaning thereby that 'existence' has 'existence' (other than itself) in the same way as (an 'accident' like) whiteness has 'existence.' (That which can properly be said about the 'accident'—'existence') is, on the contrary, that its 'existence in a substratum' is the very 'existence' of that substratum. As for every 'accident' other than 'existence,' its 'existence in a substratum' is the 'existence' of that 'accident.'[24]

What is essential to note is that this whole analysis is conceptual and not based upon the external world where no *māhiyyah* is ever to be found without *wujūd*. In contrast both to Latin interpreters of Ibn Sīnā and to such Muslim thinkers as Fakhr al-Dīn al-Rāzī and Ibn Rushd, who misunderstood Ibn Sīnā on this point, Naṣīr al-Dīn al-Tūsī was fully aware of Ibn Sīnā's intentions when he wrote,

> Quiddity can never be independent of 'existence' except in the intellect. This, however, should not be taken as meaning that 'quiddity' in the intellect is separated from 'existence,' because 'being in the intellect' is itself a kind of 'existence,' namely, 'mental existence' [*wujūd dhihnī*], just as 'being in the external world' is 'external existence' [*wujūd khārijī*]. The above statement that *māhiyyah* is separated from *wujūd* in the intellect (*al-'aql*) must be understood in the sense that the intellect is of such a nature that it can observe 'quiddity' alone without considering its 'existence.' Not considering something is not the same as considering it to be non-existent.[25]

To understand the accidentality of *wujūd* as understood in the later tradition of Islamic philosophy that followed Ibn Sīnā's teachings, it must be remembered that in the "container of the mind," or as the intellect analyzes the nature of reality in itself and *not* in the external world, *māhiyyah* can be considered purely as itself to which then *wujūd* is "added" or "occurs" from the outside. In the outside world, however, it is in reality the *māhiyyāt* that are "added to" or "occur in" *wujūd*, at least according to the school of the principiality of *wujūd* (*aṣālat al-wujūd*), to which we shall soon turn. *Māhiyyāt* (plural of *māhiyyah*) must be understood not as extrinsic limitations or determinations of *wujūd* but as intrinsic ones that are nothing in themselves and have a reality only in relation to *wujūd,* which alone possesses reality.

Necessity, Contingency, Impossibility

One of the fundamental distinctions in the Islamic philosophy of being is that between necessity (*wujūb*), contingency or possibility (*imkān*), and impossibility (*imtinā'*). This distinction, which, again, was formulated in its perfected form for the first time by Ibn Sīnā and stated in many of his works,[26] is traditionally called "the three directions" (*al-jahāt al-thalāthah*) and is basic to the understanding of Islamic metaphysics. It possesses, in fact, at once a philosophical and a theological significance to the extent that the term *wājib al-wujūd,* the Necessary Being, which is a philosophical term for God, has been used throughout the centuries extensively by Islamic theologians, Sufis, and even jurists and ordinary preachers.

If one were to consider a *māhiyyah* in itself in the "container of the mind," one of three conditions would hold true:

1. It could exist or not exist. In either case there would be no logical contradiction.
2. It must exist because if it were not to exist, there would follow a logical contradiction.
3. It cannot exist because if it were to exist, there would follow a logical contradiction.

The first category is called "*mumkin,*" the second "*wājib,*" and the third "*mumtani*ᶜ." Nearly all *māhiyyāt* are *mumkin*, such as the *māhiyyah* of man, horse, or star. Once one considers the *māhiyyah* of man in itself in the mind, there is no logical contradiction, whether it possesses *wujūd* or not. Everything in the created order in fact participates in the condition of contingency so that the universe, or all that is other than God (*ma siwa*ʾ*Llāh*), is often called the "world of contingencies" (*'ālam al-mumkināt*).[27]

It is also possible for the mind (or strictly speaking *al-'aql*) to conceive of certain *māhiyyāt,* the supposition of whose existence would involve a logical contradiction. In traditional Islamic thought the example usually given is *sharīk al-Bāri*ʾ, that is, a partner taken unto God.

Such an example might not be so obvious to the modern mind, but numerous other examples could be given, such as a quantity that would be quantitatively greater than the sum of its parts, for the supposition of that which is impossible in reality is not itself impossible.

Finally, the mind can conceive of a *māhiyyah* that must possess *wujūd* of necessity, that *māhiyyah* being one that is itself *wujūd*. That Reality whose *māhiyyah* is *wujūd* cannot not be; it is called the "Necessary Being" or *wājib al-wujūd*. Furthermore, numerous arguments have been provided to prove that there can be but one *wājib al-wujūd* in harmony with the Quranic doctrine of the Oneness of God. The quality of necessity in the ultimate sense belongs to God alone, as does that of freedom. One of the great masters of traditional Islamic philosophy of the beginning of the twentieth century, Mīrzā Mahdī Āshtiyānī who was devoted to the school of the "transcendent unity of being," in fact asserted that after a lifetime of study he had finally discovered that *wujūb* or necessity is none other than *wujūd* itself.

This analysis in the "container of the mind" might seem to be contradicted by the external world in which objects already possess *wujūd*. Can one say in their case that they are still contingent? This question becomes particularly pertinent when one remembers that according to most schools of Islamic philosophy what exists must exist and cannot not exist. Naṣīr al-Dīn al-Ṭūsī summarizes this doctrine in his famous poem:

> That which exists is as it should be,
> That which should not exist will not do so.[28]

The answer to this problem resides in the distinction between an object in its essence and as it exists in the external world. In itself, as a *māhiyyah*, every object save God is contingent, a *mumkin al-wujūd*. But now that it has gained *wujūd*, for it to exist necessarily requires the agency of a reality other than itself. Existents are, therefore, *wājib biʾl-ghayr*, necessary through an agent other than themselves. They are necessary as existents by the very fact that they possess *wujūd* but are contingent in their essence in contrast to the Necessary Being, which is necessary in Its own Essence and not through an agent outside Itself.

The distinction between necessity and contingency makes possible a vision of the universe in perfect accord with the Islamic perspective where to God alone belongs the power of creation and existentiation (*ījād*). It is He who said "Be!" and it was. Everything in the universe is "poor" in the sense of not possessing any *wujūd* of its own. It is the Necessary Being alone which bestows *wujūd* upon the *māhiyyāt* and brings them from the darkness of nonexistence into the light of *wujūd*, covering them with the robe of necessity, while in themselves they remain forever in the nakedness of contingency.

The Concept and Reality of 'Wujūd'

Islamic philosophy followed a different course from postmedieval Western philosophy in nearly every domain despite their common roots and the considerable influence of Islamic philosophy upon Latin Scholasticism. In the subject of ontology most of the differences belong to later centuries when Islamic and Western thought had parted ways. One of these important differences concerns the distinction between the concept (*mafhūm*) and reality (*ḥaqīqah*) of '*wujūd*,' which is discussed in later Islamic metaphysics in a manner very different from that found in later Western thought.

There are some schools of Islamic philosophy, similar to certain Western schools of philosophy, that consider *wujūd* to be merely an abstraction not corresponding to any external reality that consists solely of existents. The most important school of Islamic philosophy, however, that flowered during the later centuries under the influence of Ṣadr al-Dīn Shīrāzī distinguishes clearly between the concept of *wujūd* and the Reality to which it corresponds. The concept 'being' is the most universal and known of all concepts, while the Reality of *wujūd* is the most inaccessible of all realities, although it is the most manifest. In fact, it is the only Reality for those who possess the knowledge that results from illumination and "unveiling."[29]

All further discussions of *wujūd* and *māhiyyah* must be understood in light of the distinction between the concept of *wujūd*, which exists in the "mind," and the Reality of *wujūd*, which exists externally and can be known and experienced provided man is willing to conform himself to what Being demands of him. Here, philosophy and gnosis meet, and the supreme experience made possible through spiritual practice becomes the ever-present reality that underlies the conceptualizations of the philosophers.

It is also in light of this experience of *wujūd* that Islamic metaphysics has remained always aware of the distinction between *ens* and *actu essendi* and has seen things not merely as objects that exist but as acts of *wujūd*, as *esto*. If Islamic philosophy did not move, as did Western philosophy, towards an ever-greater concern with a world of solidified objects, or what certain French philosophers have called "*la chosification du monde*," it was because the experience of the Reality of Being as an ever-present element prevented the speculative mind of the majority of Islamic philosophers either from mistaking the act of *wujūd* for the existent that appears to possess *wujūd* on its own while being cut off from the absolute Being, or from failing to distinguish between the concept of *wujūd* and its blinding Reality.[30]

The Unity, Gradation, and Principiality of *Wujūd*

The Transcendent Unity of Being (waḥdat al-wujūd)

The crowning achievement of Islamic philosophy in the domain of metaphysics and especially in ontology is to be found in the later period in Persia in the school that, as already mentioned, has now come to be known as the School of Isfahan,[31] whose founder was Mīr Dāmād and whose leading light was Ṣadr al-Dīn Shīrāzī. It is in the numerous writings of this veritable sage that the rigorous logical discussion of al-Fārābī and Ibn Sīnā, the critiques of al-Ghazzālī and Fakhr al-Dīn al-Rāzī, the illuminative doctrines of Shihāb al-Dīn Suhrawardī, and the supreme experiential knowledge of the Sufis as formulated by such masters of gnosis as Ibn 'Arabī and Ṣadr al-Dīn al-Qunyawī became united in a vast synthesis whose unifying thread was the inner teachings of the Quran as well as the *Ḥadīth* and the sayings of the Shi'ite Imams.[32] All of the discussions about *wujūd* and *māhiyyah* that were going on for some seven centuries before the advent of the School of Isfahan in the tenth/sixteenth century (and that have been summarized above) are to be found in the grand synthesis of Ṣadr al-Dīn whose metaphysical doctrine is based upon the unity (*waḥdah*), gradation (*tashkīk*), and principiality (*aṣālah*) of *wujūd*.

As far as the "transcendent unity of Being" or *waḥdat al-wujūd* is concerned, it must be said at the outset that this doctrine is not the result of ratiocination but of intellection and inner experience. If correctly understood, it stands at the heart of the basic message of Islam, which is that of unity (*al-tawḥīd*) and which is found expressed in the purest form in the testimony of Islam, *Lā ilāha illa'Llāh*, there is no divinity but Allah. This formula is the synthesis of all metaphysics and contains despite its brevity the whole doctrine of the Unity of the Divine Principle and the manifestation of multiplicity, which cannot but issue from that Unity before whose blinding Reality it is nothing. The Sufis and also Shi'ite esoterists and gnostics have asked, "What does divinity (*ilāh*) mean except reality or *wujūd*?" By purifying themselves through spiritual practice, they have come to realize the full import of the testimony and have realized that Reality or *wujūd* belongs ultimately to God alone, that not only is He One, but also that He is the only ultimate Reality and the source of everything that appears to possess *wujūd*. All *wujūd* belongs to God while He is transcendent vis-à-vis all existents. The Quran itself confirms this esoteric doctrine in many ways, such as when it asserts that God is "the First and the Last, the Outward and the Inward" (53: 3) or when it says, "Whithersoever ye turneth, there is the Face of God.' "[33]

The experience of the "oneness of Being" or the "transcendent unity of Being" is not meant for everyone. Rather, it is the crowning achievement of human existence, the supreme fruit and also goal of gnosis or divine knowledge attainable only through arduous spiritual practice and self-discipline to which must, of course, be added the grace of God and His affirmation (*taʾyīd*).[34] Yet the possibility of this experience has always been present throughout the history of Islam as in other integral traditions. Its realization could not but have the deepest effect upon philosophy, which must of necessity be related to and concerned with the fruits of human experience. But how different are these fruits in a civilization such as that of the modern West where experience is limited to what is derived from the external senses and based upon existents considered as mere objects or things, and in traditional Islamic civilization dominated by the reality of prophecy where the supreme experience has been not of existents but of Pure Being, which can be reached through the inner faculty of the heart and whose act causes the existentiation of all quiddities.

Yet, because the doctrine of *waḥdat al-wujūd* is by nature an esoteric one reserved for the spiritual and intellectual elite (*al-khawāṣṣ*), it has met opposition from within the ranks of exoteric *'ulamāʾ* throughout the history of Islam while encountering bewildering misunderstandings on the part of many Western orientalists during the modern period. Some among the former have accused the followers of *waḥdat al-wujūd* of incarnationalism, lack of faith, infidelity (*kufr*), and the like. As for the latter, they have used their favorite pejorative categories such as pantheism, monism, and the like, used in a Western philosophical context and with all the theological anathema that is attached to such terms in Christian theology, to denigrate the doctrine and experience of *waḥdat al-wujūd*.

The early Sufis and gnostics spoke of *waḥdat al-wujūd* only through allusions or in daring theophanic locutions (*shaṭḥ*).[35] Only from the sixth/twefth and seventh/thirteenth centuries with such figures as Abū Ḥāmid Muḥammad al-Ghazzālī, Ibn Sab'īn and especially followers of the school of Ibn 'Arabī did this doctrine become formulated more explicitly, soon to become the dominant metaphysical doctrine in Sufism. Of course it was not accepted by all Sufis. Some simply remained silent on the subject and thought that the doctrine of *waḥdat al-wujūd*, which is the fruit of "presential knowledge" (*al-'ilm al-ḥuḍūrī*), of divine unveiling (*kashf*), and of illumination (*ishrāq*), should not be expounded explicitly beyond a certain degree. Such an attitude is to be seen in some of the greatest masters of gnosis, such as Shaykh Abū'l-Ḥasan al-Shādhilī, the founder of the Shādhiliyyah Sufi Order, which remains to this day one of the most important of Sufi orders from Morocco to the Yemen. Others, while being attached to a Sufi order, openly opposed the doctrine, one of the most famous examples being Taqī al-Dīn ibn Taymiyyah who was a Qādirī Sufi yet strongly opposed Ibn 'Arabī's formulations.

There were also those who opposed the doctrine of *waḥdat al-wujūd* by substituting the pole of subject for the object, formulating the doctrine that is known as *waḥdat al-shuhūd* or "unity of consciousness." This school, founded by 'Alā' al-Dawlah Simnānī in the eighth/fourteenth century, was to attract many followers in India including Shaykh Aḥmad Sirhindī, who in the tenth/sixteenth century provided one of the most widely accepted formulations of *waḥdat al-shuhūd* in the Indian subcontinent. In fact, much of the intellectual history of Muslim India revolves around the debate between the doctrines of *waḥdat al-wujūd* and *waḥdat al-shuhūd* with repercussions not only in the domain of religion but also in the social and political life of the Islamic community.[36]

In the central lands of the Islamic world itself, the doctrine of *waḥdat al-wujūd* received extensive treatment in the hands of the later commentators of Ibn 'Arabī and of his immediate student Ṣadr al-Dīn Qunyawī, such figures as Mu'ayyid al-Dīn al-Jandī,[37] 'Afīf al-Dīn al-Tilimsānī, Dā'ūd al-Qayṣarī, 'Abd al-Raḥmān Jāmī, and others.[38] This doctrine also began to attract the attention of philosophers and even theologians, especially Shi'ite figures such as Sayyid Ḥaydar Āmulī[39] and Ibn Turkah Iṣfahānī.[40] In fact, as Islamic philosophy became ever more closely wedded to gnosis and the experiential knowledge associated with it,[41] philosophical expositions of the meaning of *waḥdat al-wujūd* became more prevalent, until with Ṣadr al-Dīn Shirāzī, the doctrine of *waḥdat al-wujūd* became the keystone of his whole metaphysics.

There are, to be sure, several different interpretations of *waḥdat al-wujūd*. For many of the gnostics of the school of Ibn 'Arabī only God may be said to possess *wujūd*. Nothing else even possesses *wujūd* so that the question of how the *wujūd* of a particular existent is related to absolute Being does not even arise. For Mullā Ṣadrā and his followers, however, the most common understanding of *waḥdat al-wujūd* is that absolute Being bestows the effusion of *wujūd* upon all *māhiyyāt* in such a manner that all beings are like the rays of the sun of Being and issue from It. Nothing possesses any *wujūd* of its own. A vast and elaborate philosophical structure is created by Mullā Ṣadrā to demonstrate *waḥdat al-wujūd*. But the aim of the sage is really to guide the mind and prepare it for a knowledge that ultimately could be grasped only intuitively. The role of philosophy is in a sense to prepare the mind for intellection and the reception of this illumination, to enable the mind to gain a knowledge which in itself is not the result of ratiocination (*baḥth*) but of the "tasting" (*dhawq*) of the truth.

Gradation (tashkīk)

As for gradation or *tashkīk*, it is closely related to the Ṣadrian interpretation of *waḥdat al-wujūd* and must be understood in its light although the doctrine itself had a long history before Mullā Ṣadrā. The idea of gradation of existence or the "chain of being" is already to be found in Greek thought, especially in Aristotle and his Alexandrian commentators, and has played a major role in the history of Western thought.[42] Western medieval and Renaissance philosophers and scientists envisaged a universe in which there was a hierarchy stretching from the *materia prima* through the mineral, vegetable, and animal kingdoms, man and the angelic realms, and leading finally to God. Each creature in the hierarchy was defined by its mode of being, the more perfect standing higher in the hierarchy.

This scheme, attributed in the West to Aristotle, was not in fact completed in its details until the time of Ibn Sīnā who in his *Shifā*ʾ dealt for the first time with the whole hierarchy, encompassing all the three kingdoms together, in a single work. The *De Mineralibus* attributed for centuries to Aristotle, a work that complemented the works of Aristotle and Theophrastus on animals and plants, respectively, was actually a translation of Ibn Sīnā's chapter on minerals from the *Shifā*ʾ. The idea of the hierarchy or chain of being (*marātib al-wujūd*) was in fact central to his thought and to Islamic philosophy in general, the doctrine of the hierarchy of beings having its roots in the teachings of the Quran and *Ḥadīth*.[43]

In the *al-ḥikmat al-muta'āliyah* or the "transcendent theosophy" of Ṣadr al-Dīn Shīrāzī and later Islamic philosophy in general, this universally held doctrine of gradation gained a new meaning in light of the doctrine of the transcendent unity (*waḥdah*) and principiality (*aṣālah*) of *wujūd*. According to this school, not only is there a gradation of existents that stand in a vast hierarchy stretching from the "floor" (*farsh*) to the Divine Throne (*'arsh*), to use a traditional metaphor, but the *wujūd* of each existent *māhiyyah* is nothing but a grade of the single reality of *wujūd* whose source is God, the absolute Being (al-*wujūd al-muṭlaq*). The absolute Being is like the sun and all existents like points on the rays of the sun. These points are all light and are distinguished from other lights not by a specific difference (*faṣl*) as one would have in Aristotelian logic, but by nothing other than light itself. What distinguishes the *wujūd* of various existents is nothing but *wujūd* in different degrees of strength and weakness.[44] The universe is nothing but degrees of strength and weakness of *wujūd* stretching from the intense degree of *wujūd* of the archangelic realities to the dim *wujūd* of the lowly dust from which Adam was made. Gradation is characteristic of *wujūd,* while *māhiyyah* cannot accept gradation. To understand the meaning of gradation as it pertains to *wujūd* is to gain the key to the comprehension of that reality that is at once one and many, that is in Itself Oneness and at the same time the source of the multiplicity that issues from and returns to that Unity.

Principiality of Wujūd *(*aṣālat al-wujūd*)*

From the time of Mīr Dāmād and Mullā Ṣadrā, that is, the eleventh/seventeenth century, Islamic philosophers have been deeply concerned with the question of the principiality of *wujūd* or *māhiyyah* and in fact have carried this debate backward to embrace the whole of the history of Islamic philosophy. The basic question asked by later Islamic philosophies is the following: granted that there is a basic distinction between the concepts of *wujūd* and *māhiyyah,* which of these concepts is real in the sense of corresponding to what is real in the concrete object that exists in the external world? The answer to this question is not as simple as it might at first appear, for not only is there the question of *wujūd* and *māhiyyah,* but also of the existent or *mawjūd* and the central problem of the relation between the *wujūd* of various existents.

The whole of Islamic philosophy has been divided by later thinkers into two schools on the basis of this distinction, and numerous treatises have been written by the champions of *aṣālat al-wujūd* against *aṣālat al-māhiyyah* and vice versa. The great champions of *aṣālat al-māhiyyah* are usually considered to be Suhrawardī and Mīr Dāmād, who hold that the *māhiyyāt* are real, and *wujūd* is merely posited mentally (*i'tibārī*); Mullā Ṣadrā and Ibn Sīnā, along with his followers such as Naṣīr al-Dīn al-Ṭūsī, have been considered to be followers of *aṣālat al-wujūd*. Because Ibn Sīnā did not accept the unity and gradation of *wujūd* in the Ṣadrian sense, however, his *aṣālat al-wujūd* is in a sense similar to *aṣālat al-māhiyyah.* Mullā Ṣadrā himself wrote that at the beginning of his life as a philosopher he was also a follower of the school of *aṣālat al-māhiyyah* and that only after receiving special divine guidance and inspiration did he come to see the truth of the position of *aṣālat al-wujūd.*[45] Thus it might be said that there are two grand versions of Islamic metaphysics, one "essentialistic" or based on *aṣālat al-māhiyyah* and identified mostly with the name of Suhrawardī, and the other "existentialistic" or based on *aṣālat al-wujūd* and associated with the name of Mullā Ṣadrā.[46] Needless to say, both owe a very great deal to the basic works of al-Fārābī and especially Ibn Sīnā.

Suhrawardī, while interpreting Ibn Sīnā's thesis that *wujūd* is an accident (*'āriḍ*), considers it to be merely posited in the mind (*i'tibārī*) without corresponding to any reality in the external world; hence his defense of the correspondence of the concept of *'māhiyyah'* to the reality of an object. Mullā Ṣadrā, on the contrary, after his conversion to the truth of the doctrine of *aṣālat al-wujūd*, raised this principle to the very center of his metaphysical teachings, bringing about a profound transformation in Islamic philosophy, which H. Corbin has called a "revolution in Islamic thought." In the *Asfār* he takes the followers of *aṣālat al-māhiyyah* to task and provides numerous arguments to prove his position, some of the most important being based on the unity of the external object and the impossibility of gradation in the *māhiyyāt.* Some of the arguments were later summarized by Sabziwārī in rhyming couplets in his *Sharḥ-i manẓūmah* and have become common knowledge among students of traditional Islamic philosophy in Persia.[47] The basis of acceptance of *aṣālat al-wujūd* by Mullā Ṣadrā, Sabziwārī, and other masters of this school resides, however, not in rational arguments but in the experience of the Reality of *wujūd* in which the intellect itself functions on a level other than that of ordinary life, even if it be the life of a philosopher of great rational powers and analytical acumen.

The acceptance of the unity, gradation, and principiality of *wujūd* together constitutes a veritable transformation of earlier schools of Islamic thought and marks the summit of the discourse on ontology in Islamic philosophy. Associated with the name of Mullā Ṣadrā, this perspective in which *wujūd* is seen as the single reality possessing grades and modes from which the *māhiyyāt* are abstracted has also come to be identified with the Khusrawānī or Pahlawī sages and philosophers (*khusrawāniyyūn* and *fahlawiyyūn* in Arabic). These terms refer to the ancient sages of Persia and are derived from the writings of Suhrawardī, who saw in their teachings the perfect combination of rational and intuitive knowledge which he identified with the theosophers (sing. *ḥakīm muta᾽allih*).[48] It might appear paradoxical that, although Suhrawardī is identified with the school of *aṣālat al-māhiyyah,* the followers should be called the Pahlawī sages, using the terminology of the master of the school of Illumination. This paradox disappears, however, if one remembers that although Suhrawardī considered *wujūd* to be merely "mentally posited" (*i'tibārī*), he bestowed all the attributes of *wujūd* upon light (*al-nūr*), while Mullā Ṣadrā and other later philosophers of his school who accepted the unity, gradation, and principiality of *wujūd* often identified *wujūd* with light and in fact used the term *kathrah nūrāniyyah* (luminous multiplicity) when they referred to the multiplicity resulting from the gradation of *wujūd.*

The Structure of Reality

The analysis of the previous pages on ontology in Islamic philosophy can be summarized as follows: External reality appears as one ontological block as it presents itself to man through his immediate experience but can be conceptually analyzed into *wujūd* and *māhiyyah.* As far as *wujūd* is concerned, one can distinguish between the concept of *wujūd* and its reality.[49] Furthermore, the concept or notion of *wujūd* is either of absolute *wujūd* or of a particular mode of existence called "portion" (*ḥissah*) of *wujūd* in Islamic philosophy. As for the reality of *wujūd,* it refers either to the all-embracing and general Reality of *wujūd* (*fard 'āmm*) or to particular "units" of the reality of *wujūd* (*fard khāṣṣ*).

The structure of reality is envisaged differently by different schools of Islamic thought depending on how they conceive of these four stages or meanings of *wujūd.* The Ash'arite theologians simply refuse to accept these distinctions, whether they be conceptual or belonging to the external world. The school of Mullā Ṣadrā, at the other end of the spectrum of Islamic thought, makes clear distinctions among all four meanings of *wujūd.* Certain philosophers accept only the concept of *wujūd* and deny its reality, while certain Peripatetics accept the reality of *wujūd* but identify the multiplicity in the external world not with the multiplicity of existents but with that of *wujūd* itself so that they identify *wujūd* not with a single reality with grades but with realities (*ḥaqā᾽iq*). Then there are those thinkers identified with the "tasting of theosophy" (*dhawq al-ta᾽alluh*), especially Jalāl al-Dīn Dawānī, who believe that there is only one reality in the external world to which *wujūd* refers, and that reality is God. There are no other realities to which *wujūd* refers. Finally, there are several schools of Sufism with their own doctrines concerning the relation between the concept and reality of *wujūd*. The most metaphysical of these views sees *wujūd* as the absolute, single Reality beside which there is no other reality; yet there are other realities that, although nothing in themselves, appear to exist because they are theophanies of the single Reality, which alone Is as the absolutely unconditioned *wujūd*.

Later Islamic philosophy, following upon the wake of the teachings of Ibn Sīnā, displays a remarkable richness of metaphysical, philosophical, and theological teachings concerning the structure of reality, the rapport between unity and multiplicity, and the relation between *wujūd* and *māhiyyah*. All of these schools have sought to demonstrate the unity of the Divine Principle and the relation of the world of multiplicity to that Principle.[50] Among these schools, which include not only the Ash'arites and the Peripatetics but also Ismā'īlī philosophers and theologians, *ishrāqī* theosophers, and the various schools of Sufism, the "transcendent theosophy" associated with Mullā Ṣadrā represents a particularly significant synthesis of vast proportions. Therein one finds the echo of centuries of debate and analysis concerning *wujūd* and *māhiyyah* and the fruit of nearly a millennium of both the thought and spiritual experience of Muslim philosophers and gnostics.

In this school there is but one Reality, that of *wujūd*. There are not existing objects related to other existing objects. The very existence of objects is their relation to that one *wujūd* that partakes of modes and gradation as do rays of light, modes, and gradation from which the mind abstracts the *māhiyyāt*. There is in the universe nothing but the Reality of *wujūd*.

It might of course be asked how in such a perspective one can avoid identifying the world with God and what happens to the central thesis of the transcendence of God emphasized so much by Islam. The answer is provided by the distinction that the "Pahlawī sages" make between the "negatively conditioned" (*bi-sharṭ-i lā*), "non-conditioned" (*la bi-sharṭ*), and "conditioned by something" (*bi-sharṭ-i shay*ʾ) stages of *wujūd*. These aspects were originally applied by Naṣīr al-Dīn al-Ṭūsī to *māhiyyah*, which can be considered as negatively conditioned, that is, in a complete purity in itself, or as nonconditioned, as indeterminate in the sense that it can or cannot be associated with something, or as conditioned by something, that is, associated with some other concept.[51]

These distinctions have been applied by the "Pahlawī philosophers" to *wujūd*. Considered as such, negatively conditioned *wujūd* is the Absolute, Pure, and Transcendent Being of God. Nonconditioned *wujūd* is both the most universal concept and reality of being according to Sufi metaphysics and the expansive mode of *wujūd* that is indeterminate and yet can determine itself into various forms according to the philosophers. It is identified by some with the act of existentiation and the "Breath of the Compassionate" (*nafas al-raḥmān*) of the Sufis and is sometimes called the "expansive *wujūd*" (*al-wujūd al-munbasiṭ*). Finally, as conditioned by something, *wujūd* refers to the actual stages and levels of *wujūd* in particular existents. Moreover, these three levels of *wujūd* are hierarchical. Negatively conditioned *wujūd* is the Source and Origin of the Universe, the Reality that is transcendent and yet from which everything issues. Nonconditioned *wujūd,* if understood as "expansive *wujūd* and not as the most universal of concepts and realities stands below that supreme S ource and is itself the immediate source for the *wujūd* of the existentiated order. Finally, *wujūd* conditioned by something comprises the whole chain of being from the angels to the pebbles along the seashore.

The Sufi metaphysicians have gone a step beyond the "Pahlawī sages" and criticized them for identifying negatively conditioned *wujūd* with God since negatively conditioned still implies a limitation and a condition. The absolute Being cannot be conditioned or limited in any way even by the condition of being negatively conditioned. They identify, therefore, not negatively conditioned but nonconditioned *wujūd* with God. Herein lies a major distinction between the metaphysics of the Sufis (and in a modified manner of the Ismā'īlī thinkers) and of the later philosophers. Nevertheless, the basic structure of reality envisaged by them is the same in that both see beyond the multiplicity of the world a unity that transcends yet determines that multiplicity and in fact *is* that multiplicity in a *coincidentia oppositorum* that can be grasped only by that intellectual intuition that provides the immediate knowledge granted only to those whom the traditional Islamic sources, following the terminology of the Quran, call "people of vision" (*ahl al-baṣīrah*), those who in the words of the Quran are "deeply versed in knowledge."

The Experience of *Wujūd*

Man lives in the world of multiplicity; his immediate experience is of objects and forms, of existents. Yet he yearns for unity, for the Reality that stands beyond and behind this veil of the manifold. One might say that the *māhiyyah* in the sense of nature of man is such that he yearns for the experience of *wujūd*. It is in the nature of man, and in this realm of terrestrial existence of man alone, to seek to transcend himself and to go beyond what he "is" in order to become what he really is. Man's mode of existence, his acts, his way of living his life, his inner discipline, his attainment of knowledge, and his living according to the dictates of Being affect his own mode of being. Man can perfect himself in such a manner that the act of *wujūd* in him is intensified until he ceases to exist as a separate ego and experiences the Supreme Being, becoming completely drowned in the ocean of the Reality of *wujūd*.

Man's spiritual progress from the experience of existents to that of the absolute Reality of *wujūd* can be compared to seeing objects around a room whose walls are covered with mirrors. Soon the observer looking at the walls realizes that the walls are mirrors, and he sees nothing but the mirrors. Finally he sees the objects, yet no longer as independent objects but as reflections in the mirror. In the ascent toward the experience of *wujūd*, man first realizes that the objects do not have a *wujūd* or reality of their own. Then he experiences *wujūd* in its absoluteness and realizes that he and everything else in the universe are literally "no-thing" and have no reality of their own. Finally, he realizes that all things are "plunged in God," that the "transcendent unity of Being" means that *wujūd* is one yet manifests a world of multiplicity that does not violate its sacred unity.

The vast metaphysical synthesis of Islamic sages and philosophers has for its aim the opening of the mind to the awareness of that reality that can, however, be experienced only by the whole of man's being and not by the mind alone. Yet the doctrines in their diverse forms serve to prepare the mind for that intellection that is supra-rational and to enable the mind to become integrated into the whole of man's being whose center is the heart. Only the person who is whole can experience that wholeness that belongs to the One, to *wujūd* in its absoluteness.

These Islamic doctrines have also created a philosophical universe of discourse in which the inner dimension of revelation and of existing things has never been forgotten, where the act of *wujūd* has been an ever-present reality, preventing the reduction of the world to objects and things divorced from their inner dimension and reality as has happened with postmedieval philosophy in the West leading to dire consequences for the human condition. The message of Islamic philosophy, as it concerns the study of *wujūd* and *māhiyyah*, is therefore of great significance for the contemporary world, which is suffocating in an environment of material things and objects that have overwhelmed the human spirit. This philosophy is also of great significance for a world that lives intensely on the mental plane at the expense of other dimensions of human existence, for although this philosophy speaks to the mind, it draws the mind once again toward the heart. The heart is the center of the human being, the locus of inner illumination and seat of the intellect, through which man is able to know experientially that Reality of *wujūd* that determines what and who we are, from where we issue, and to whose embrace we finally return. It is only in experiencing *wujūd,* thanks to the means provided by revelation, not this or that *wujūd* but *wujūd* in its pure inviolability, in its absoluteness and infinity, that man becomes fully man and fulfills the purpose for which he was drawn from the bosom of *wujūd* to embark upon this short terrestrial journey, only to return finally to that One and Unique *wujūd* from which in reality nothing ever departs.

CHAPTER 5

Post-Avicennan Islamic Philosophy and the Study of Being

The role of ontology and the major ontological distinctions made by Ibn Sīnā and others such as that between *wujūd* and *māhiyyah* are so central to the whole structure of Islamic philosophy for the past millennium that it is necessary to turn to this issue again in this chapter. It is also especially important to point to the way that the philosophical traditions of Islam and the West gradually parted ways on this central issue of ontology despite the great influence that early Islamic philosophers such as Ibn Sīnā exercised by the Christian philosophy of the European Middle Ages.

The history of the quest of post-Avicennan Islamic philosophers for the understanding of being differs in fact markedly from that of Western philosophers following St. Thomas and other masters of Scholasticism. While gradually in the West the possibility of the experience of Being nearly disappeared with the eclipse of sapiental mysticism and the vision of Being gave way to the discussion of the concept of 'being' and finally to the disintegration of this very concept in certain schools, in the Islamic world philosophy drew ever closer to the ocean of Being Itself until finally it became the complement of gnosis and its extension in the direction of systematic exposition and analysis. If in the final chapters of the history of Western philosophy, at least in several of its major schools, philosophy became wed to external experience and experiment with the forces and substances of the material world, resulting in various forms of empiricism, in the Islamic world as well philosophy drew ever closer to experience. But in this case the experience in question was of a spiritual and inward character, including ultimately the experience of Pure Being, the tasting of the Reality that is the origin of the sapiential wisdom or *ḥikmah* that developed after the sixth/twelfth century, a wisdom that for this reason is called "*ḥikmah dhawqiyyah*" (intuitive or literally "tasted" philosophy), *dhawq* having the same meaning in Arabic as the root of sapiential (*sapere*) in Latin.

The early Islamic philosophers such as al-Fārābī and Ibn Sīnā,[1] who are known as masters of discursive philosophy (*ḥikmah baḥthiyyah*) rather than of sapiential wisdom, nevertheless established the conceptual framework within which later discussions of being occurred, although new meaning was often given to the terms and concepts that they had established. Al-Fārābī in his *Kitāb al-ḥurūf* (The Book of Letters)[2] and as already mentioned in the last chapter, Ibn Sīnā in numerous works, especially the *Shifāʾ Najāh*, and *Dānishnāma-yi ʿalāʾī* (The ʿAlāʾī Book of Science)[3] already established the major distinctions between existence (*wujūd*) and quiddity (*māhiyyah*), on the one hand, and necessity (*wujūb*), contingency (*imkān*), and impossibility (*imtināʿ*), on the other, as well as many of the other basic concepts that colored the study of being in both the later Islamic world and the Occident.

The period immediately following in the wake of Ibn Sīnā's magisterial exposition of Peripatetic philosophy—namely, the fifth/eleventh and sixth/twelfth centuries—was the era of the dominance of Ash'arite *kalām* in the eastern lands of Islam and therefore of an eclipse of interest in those lands in the study of that discipline that with Francisco Suarez followed by Christian Wolff came to be called "ontology" in the West. *Kalām* was based mostly on a voluntarism[4] that concentrated exclusively upon the Will of God and disregarded His Being and Nature, of which the Will is but one Quality. Hence, the champions of *kalām*, in contrast to Latin theologians, were not particularly interested in the study of being per se, even if they often used the terminology of the Peripatetics as far as the distinction between *wājib al-wujūd* and *mumkināt* was concerned.

The founder of the school of Illumination, Shaykh al-ishrāq Shihāb al-Dīn Suhrawardī, revived the interest in ontology but approached the entire problem of existence from a new angle of vision.[5] He considered existence to be only an accident added to the quiddities, which possess reality. As already mentioned in the last chapter, he, thereby created an "essentialistic" metaphysics that attracted many followers over the centuries. Yet he made of light the very substance of reality and attributed to light what all the other philosophers had considered as belonging to *wujūd*. To study the question of being in Suhrawardī and his school, it would not be sufficient to seek pages on which the word *wujūd* appears. It would be necessary to study his doctrine of light in its totality.

Almost contemporary with Suhrawardī, another major intellectual figure and the foremost expositor of Sufi metaphysics, Muḥyī al-Dīn ibn ʿArabī, expounded the most profound doctrine possible of Being and its manifestations in a manner that is, properly speaking, gnostic and metaphysical rather than simply discursive and conceptual. Ibn ʿArabī spoke of the Divine Essence (*al-Dhāt*), Names and

Qualities, theophany (*tajallī*), and the like, and although he also used the language of the Islamic philosophers who dealt with *wujūd*, he interpreted it in a different manner.[6] He expounded a metaphysics that transcends ontology as usually understood, a metaphysics that begins with the Principle, standing above Being, of which Being is the first determination (*ta'ayyun*). Yet his doctrine of necessity included the most penetrating exposition of the meaning of *wujūd* as both Being and existence, even if he viewed this question from quite another angle than did the philosophers. It is in fact of interest to note that he paid special attention to existence when dealing with the theme of Divine Mercy.[7] In any case, Ibn 'Arabī had the profoundest effect upon both later Sufism and later Islamic philosophy, especially as far as the study of *wujūd* was concerned. It was he who first discussed the reality of the doctrine of the "transcendent unity of being" (*waḥdat al-wujūd*), if not its name which probably goes back to Ibn Sab'īn and the students of Ibn 'Arabī. This doctrine crowns nearly all later studies of *wujūd* and represents in a certain sense the summit of Islamic metaphysical doctrines as we saw in the previous chapter. This doctrine was fully developed by later students and commentators belonging to the school of Ibn Arabī.[8]

The revival of Peripatetic philosophy by Naṣīr al-Dīn Ṭūsī in the seventh/thirteenth century brought the teaching of Ibn Sīnā back to life, but this time Ibn Sīnā was often interpreted in light of the doctrines of Suhrawardī and Ibn 'Arabī and not solely in the more rationalistic vein in which he came to be known in the West. Moreover, such later masters of gnosis as Ṣadr al-Dīn al-Qunyawī, 'Abd al-Razzāq Kāshānī, and Sayyid Ḥaydar Āmulī gave a more systematic exposition of the study of being than is to be found in Ibn 'Arabī. Such texts as the *Naqd al-nuqūd fī ma'rifat al-wujūd* of Āmulī had a profound effect upon later Islamic philosophy itself, especially in Persia.[9]

The School of Isfahan, founded by Mīr Dāmād in Safavid Persia, marks a sudden rise of interest in the study of *wujūd*. In fact, during this period a new chapter was added to the exposition of traditional philosophy under the name of "general matters" (*al-umūr al-'āmmah*), with which most later texts of philosophy start and that deals more than anything else with *wujūd*. It was also during this period, as already mentioned, that the distinction between the principiality of existence (*aṣālat al-wujūd*) and the principiality of quiddity (*aṣālat al-māhiyyah*) was discussed for the first time and the entire history of philosophy viewed accordingly.[10]

It is usually thought that the Safavid period was dominated by the teachings of Mullā Ṣadrā, but such is far from the case. This period was marked by a rather varied philosophical life, and at least three distinct trends are discernible: that of Mīr Dāmād and his students, who followed Ibn Sīnā with a Suhrawardian color; that of Mullā Rajab 'Alī Tabrīzī, whose views are somewhat similar to Proclus' interpretation of the teaching of Plato and who considered the Divine Principle to be above both Being and non-Being and totally discontinuous with the chain of existence; and finally Mullā Ṣadrā and his followers, such as Mullā Muḥsin Fayḍ Kāshānī, who transformed the "essentialistic" metaphysics of Suhrawardī into an "existentialistic" one.[11] In his *Asfār, al-Shawāhid al-rubūbiyyah,* and *al-Mashā'ir,*[12] Mullā Ṣadrā has given the most extensive and systematic exposition of the "philosophy of being" to be found anywhere in Islam, combining the vision of the gnostics and the logical acumen of the Peripatetics. His metaphysics, based on the three principles of the unity, gradation, and principiality of being marks the opening of a new chapter in the development of Islamic philosophy and more particularly ontology.[13]

The doctrines of Mullā Ṣadrā concerning being were so profound and all-embracing that they found their echo among most of the leading Persian philosophers of the centuries that followed and were also influential among many thinkers of Muslim India. As far as Persia is concerned, such thirteenth/nineteenth century figures as Mullā 'Alī Nūrī, Ḥājjī Mullā Hādī Sabziwārī, and Mullā 'Alī Mudarris added important commentaries to Mullā Ṣadrā's works on the subject of ontology. Moreover, during the twentieth century such traditional masters as Mīrzā Mahdī Āshtiyānī and Sayyid Muḥammad Kāẓim 'Aṣṣār continued this particular tradition of philosophy in which the study of being is carried out through a highly developed dialectic but is ultimately based upon the experience of Being and its epiphanies, this experience having been made possible through the aid of Being Itself in the form of that objective theophany of the Universal Intellect, which is prophecy and the bringing of a revelation that creates a traditional universe.

It is hardly possible to do justice in a short space to the depth and richness of this later Islamic philosophical school insofar as the study of being is concerned. Men of great intelligence and perspicacity have spent lifetimes in the study and contemplation of these doctrines. But it is possible to summarize at least some of the salient features of the mainstream of this school, which culminated with Mullā Ṣadrā and his disciples.

Perhaps the most striking feature of the discussion of being in this school is that it is concerned with the act of Being and not with the existent, with *esse*, the *actus essendi*, rather than with *ens*. Western Scholasticism was gradually led to the study, not of being itself, but of that which exists and, therefore, of things. The gradual forgetting of the reality of Being in favor of the concept of being and then the disintegration of even this concept in the mainstream of Western philosophy was directly connected to the dissociation of *ens* from the act and reality of Being itself. If it took several centuries before certain philosophers of existence in the modern West realized the importance of distinguishing between *das Sein* and *das Seiende*, the later Islamic philosophers had already based ontology on the act of Being centuries earlier when within the confines of Islamic philosophy the experience of the reality of Being became the source for the intellectual discussion of its concept.[14]

The doctrine of the unity, gradation, and principiality of being, which is the foundation of the transcendent theosophy (*al-ḥikmat al-muta'āliyah*) of Mullā Ṣadrā, sees the whole of reality as nothing but the stages and grades of existence, and the quiddity of each object that has been brought into existence as nothing but the abstraction by the mind of a particular determination of existence.[15] The essences of things are not realities to which existence is added, but abstractions made by the mind of a particular state of being that is called "existent" merely because the untrained mind perceives only the external and apparent aspect of things. Outwardly, existents seem to be quiddities that have gained existence. But true awareness created through the disciplining of the intellect and through spiritual vision allows the perceiver to see everything for what it really is: namely, the very act of existence, each of whose instances appears as a quiddity to which existence is added; whereas in reality it is only a particular act of existence from the limitations of which the quiddity is abstracted. The ordinary man is usually aware of the container, whereas the sage sees the content that is at once being (*wujūd*), presence (*ḥuḍūr*), and witness (*shuhūd*).

The later Islamic philosophers often insist on the identity of *wujūd*, *ḥuḍūr*, and *shuhūd* because their vision has penetrated into the depth of Reality, which *is* at once being and knowledge, awareness and presence. In fact, the degree of awareness of being is itself dependent upon the degree of awareness of the knower, the degree and mode according to which he *is*. The more man *is*, the more he is able to perceive being. The universe itself is a series of presences (*ḥadrah*, pl. *ḥaḍarāt*) that man is able to comprehend and penetrate, to the extent that he himself is *present*.

Islamic metaphysics envisages Reality as the Principle (*al-mabdaʾ*) that is also the giver of existence (*al-mubdiʿ*) and that stands above even Being. It is the Non-Being that comprehends Pure Being. The first determination of this Principial Reality is Being, which itself is the source of creation. The first effusion of Pure Being is at once the Intellect and Universal Existence, what the Sufis call the "Breath of the Compassionate" (*nafas al-Raḥmān*) and that is ultimately the very substance of the created order. Particular modes of existence are themselves the rays of Universal Existence (often called *"al-wujūd al-munbasiṭ* or *al-fayḍ al-muqaddas"*). Inasmuch as *wujūd* is also *ḥuḍūr*, these grades have also been enumerated by the gnostics such as Ibn 'Arabī as the "Five Divine Presences" (*al-ḥaḍarāt al-ilāhiyyat al-khams*) extending from the Divine Essence through the various stages of existence to the world of spatio-temporal existence.[16] Yet, despite the multiplicity of the levels of existence, there is but one Being, and all the presences are ultimately the Presence of the One who alone is.

The philosophy of being of the later Islamic philosophers has a direct bearing for man and his entelechy. Modern existentialism limits itself to the existence of individual man, and for many of the philosophers of this school this existence comes to an end with the death of the individual. However, in the Islamic perspective, existence is not an accidental and a faltering flame to be extinguished by the wind of death. Death is the gate to a more intense degree of existence, whether this be natural death or initiatic death accomplished through spiritual practice. Annihilation (*fanāʾ*), which is the goal of the spiritual life, ends, not in extinction in the ordinary sense of the word, but in subsistence in the Divine and, therefore, in the most intense mode of being possible. Through spiritual death man becomes never less than what he was but more.[17]

The study of being in later Islamic philosophy is related profoundly to the practical import of its teachings for human life, for it is inseparable from the practice of an inner discipline, which is the sole guarantee of a true understanding of the meaning of existence. Ordinary man is too deeply immersed in things, in existents, to become aware of the great mystery of existence itself. It is easy to perform this or that act, but it is very difficult simply to exist. It is much easier to play with concepts than to still the mind and to create an awareness to enable man to perceive the mystery of existence itself, to realize that "all things are plunged in God."

The study of existence in later Islamic philosophy is therefore only outwardly concerned with the analysis of the concepts of 'existence,' 'quiddity,' 'necessity,' 'contingency,' and the like. Beneath this rigorous logical analysis there stands the invisible presence of the profound spiritual experience of pure existence and ultimately of Being Itself. Therein lies the great message of this school for the modern world, which suffers profoundly from the divorce between conceptual knowledge and the mode and manner of one's being. Man is not only what he thinks, and his being does not necessarily follow his thinking; rather man's thought is the function of what he is. The *cogito ergo sum* of Descartes, which turned ontology in the West away from the study of Being to the analysis of its mental reflection, would be corrected by the sages of this sapiential tradition as *sum ergo est Esse*, to quote a formulation of Frithjof Schuon.[18] I am; therefore God is; Pure Being is. Being is inferred from human existence itself, provided one turns toward the Center of oneself to experience Being, rather than fleeing from the Center into the bosom of congealed forms, whether they be external objects and acts or concepts running through an agitated mind, and also provided that the human mind turn to the call of prophecy that issuing from Being and the Intellect can enable us to repose again in the Infinite Source of all that is.

The more one *is*, the more one is able to understand being. And the best way to study Being is to live in conformity with Its demands. The central message of the later tradition of Islamic philosophy and theosophy seems to be that the study of being might begin with the concept of being, but it must end with its reality. Man might study the concept of being without ever transcending the confines of his own limitations and the prison of his own accidental nature. This would be, not *ḥikmah*, but mental acrobatics. In contrast, the veritable study of the reality of being, which is the goal of *ḥikmah*, brings with it freedom and deliverance from all confinement, for it opens the limited existence of man to the revivifying rays of a Reality that is at once being, consciousness, and joy or bliss, *wujūd*, *wujdān*, and *wajd*. The correct study of being leads to that state of wonder that is the origin of all wisdom, as well as to participation in that joy or bliss the attainment of which is the goal of all knowledge and the end of human life itself, and that is woven into the very texture of the substance of human nature.

CHAPTER 6

Epistemological Questions: Relations among Intellect, Reason, and Intuition within Diverse Islamic Intellectual Perspectives

The question of how one knows is of course central to every philosophical tradition, and Islamic philosophy is no exception. Although centered on the study of Being and its manifestations, Islamic philosophy has also dealt extensively with the issue of epistemology and the means available to human beings to acquire authentic knowledge. Here again the presence of prophecy has loomed large on the horizon as the supreme source of knowledge, influencing the views of different schools of Islamic philosophy on this matter. Islamic philosophers have consequently had to deal with the relation between what is humanly accessible in the domain of knowledge and what has been revealed through prophecy. They have also had to deal with the matter of how human beings are able to gain access to revealed knowledge and come to know God and His messages as well as messengers. Moreover, functioning in the world of prophecy in its Abrahamic form, they have had to explain how God knows the world, a question alien to most of classical Greek philosophy especially as far as divine knowledge of particulars of the world of multiplicity and individual human actions are concerned.

It is not our aim to deal here with the vast subject of various schools of Islamic epistemology and how each school has dealt with the relation between faith and reason,[1] intellect/reason and intuition, human knowledge and prophecy, and so on. Rather, our goal is to deal with the understanding of the exact meaning of intellect and intuition in the major intellectual perspectives in Islam and show how the discourse of various schools on the epistemology was affected in one way or another by the sapiental dimension of prophecy and means of knowing made available by the prophetic agency. Within the Islamic world, a millennium of discussion on the relations among demonstration (*burhān*) related to the faculty of intellect/reason, gnosis (*'irfān*) related to the faculty of the heart/intellect associated with inner intuition and illumination, and *qur'ān* or revelation related to the prophetic function reached its peak in the synthesis of Mullā Ṣadrā to whom we shall turn later in this book. But before reaching that synthesis, it is necessary to clear the ground of possible misunderstandings of the basic terms employed in Islamic thought and to explain what various perspectives within the Islamic intellectual tradition have meant by intellect, reason, intuition, and related concepts that over the centuries came to possess a very different meaning in schools of later Western philosophy from what we find in the Islamic tradition.

We live in a world in which the intellect has become synonymous with reason and intuition with a "biological" sixth sense concerned with foretelling future events and usually rejected as a legitimate means of gaining knowledge by those devoted to the use of reason. It has therefore become difficult to understand what intellect, reason, and intuition, these key faculties upon which knowledge is based, can mean in the context of Islamic thought. To understand the meaning of these terms in the traditional Islamic universe where the light of the One dominates all multiplicity, and multiplicity is always seen in the light of Unity, and where the reality of prophecy is taken for granted, it is necessary to examine the actual classical terminology employed in Islamic languages, particularly Arabic and Persian, to denote the concepts of "intellect,' 'reason,' and 'intuition.'

In modern Western languages the fundamental distinction between intellect (*intellectus*) and reason (*ratio*) that one finds in medieval Christian philosophy is usually forgotten, and the term *intellect* is used for all practical purposes[2] as the equivalent of reason. In Arabic and other Islamic languages a single term, *al-'aql*, is used to denote both reason and intellect, but the distinction between the two as well as their interrelation and the dependence of reason upon the intellect is always kept in mind. *'Al-'aql'* in Arabic is related to the root *'ql*, which means basically to bind. It is that faculty that binds man to the Truth, to God, to his Origin. By virtue of being endowed with *al-'aql*, man becomes man and shares in the attribute of knowledge, *al-'ilm*, which ultimately belongs to God alone. The possession *al-'aql* is of such a positive nature that the Quran refers over and over to the central role of *al-'aql* and of intellection (*ta'aqqul* or *tafaqquh*) in man's religious life and even in his salvation.[3] But *'al-'aql'* is also used as reason, intelligence, keenness of perception, foresight, common sense and many other concepts of a related order usually using *' 'aql'* with a modifier such as *al-'aql al-juz'ī* (partial *'aql*), which is often used for reason. As far as reason is concerned, which is the reflection of the intellect upon the plane of the human mind, other terms such as *istidlāl* are also used. In any case, each school of Islamic thought has elaborated in great detail those aspects of the meaning of intellect that pertain to its perspective and inner structure.

As far as the word intuition is concerned, such terms as *ḥads* and *firāsah* have been often used. These terms imply a "participation" in a knowledge that is not simply rational but also not irrational or opposed to the intellectual as the term is understood in its traditional sense. Another set of terms also prevalent in texts of philosophy, theology, and Sufism are *dhawq, ishrāq, mukāshafah, baṣīrah, naẓar,* and *badīhah.* These terms are all related to the direct vision and participation in the knowledge of the truth in contrast to indirect and conceptual knowledge upon which all ratiocination is based. This contrast is emphasized also in the basic distinction made in later schools of Islamic philosophy between the term *al-'ilm al-ḥuḍūrī* or "presential knowledge" as opposed to *al-'ilm al-ḥuṣūlī,* or "representative knowledge."[4] These terms refer to the difference between intuitive knowledge based on immediate experience and presence on the one hand and ratiocination as indirect knowledge based on mental concepts on the other. In no way, however, do all these terms, as used in traditional Islamic languages, stand opposed to *'al-'aql'*; rather, they serve in the profoundest sense as its elaborations on various levels. The Islamic intellectual tradition has usually not seen a dichotomy between intellect and intuition but has created a hierarchy of knowledge and methods of attaining knowledge according to which degrees of both intellection and intuition become harmonized in an order encompassing all the means available to man to know, from sensual knowledge and reason to intellection and inner vision or the "knowledge of the heart." If there have appeared from time to time thinkers who confined knowledge to what can be attained by reason (*istidlāl*) alone and who have denied both revelation and intuition as sources of knowledge, they have for that very reason remained peripheral within the integral Islamic intellectual tradition.

To understand fully the relationships among intellect, reason, and intuition in Islam, it is necessary to turn to those Islamic intellectual perspectives that have brought to actualization various intellectual, spiritual and formal possibilities inherent in the Islamic revelation. They include, as far as the present discussion is concerned, the purely religious sciences such as Quranic and *Sharī'ite* studies, theology, various schools of philosophy, and finally Sufism.

In the religious sciences the function of the intellect is seen only in light of its ability to elucidate the verities of revelation. It is revelation that is the basic means for the attainment of the truth, and it is also revelation that illuminates the intellect and enables it to function properly. This wedding between revelation and the intellect makes it in fact possible for the mind to "participate" in the truth by means of that "act" or "leap" that is usually called "faith" and that is inseparable from that intuition that makes forms of knowledge of the truth beyond the merely rational possible.

There also developed within the religious sciences a special method of juridical (*fiqhī*) thinking that was based on what has been called technically "juridical reasoning." This use of 'reason' is not very different from its use in traditional Catholic jurisprudence, although there are some differences, but in both cases reason was made subservient to the data of revelation and subsequent tradition. As far as Islamic jurisprudence is concerned, this use of reason in *fiqh,* although using both terms '*'aql*' and *'istidlāl,'* was never confused with the meaning of *'aql* as *intellectus*. Even when a major philosopher such as Ibn Rushd wrote on both philosophy and jurisprudence, he kept the meaning of the technical terms used in each discipline quite distinct as was habitual in the traditional Islamic sciences.

Within the category of religious sciences, it is important to point to another discipline other than jurisprudence, and that is the science of Quranic commentary. Some of the more esoteric commentators of the Quran have emphasized the complementary nature of revelation and intellection, which in fact has been called "particular or partial revelation" (*al-waḥy al-juzʾī*), while objective revelation, which causes a new religion to become established, is called "universal revelation" (*al-waḥy al-kullī*). According to such commentators as Mullā Ṣadrā, only through the objective and universal revelation do the virtualities of the intellect become actualized. It is only by submitting itself to objective revelation that this subjective revelation in man, which is the intellect, becomes fully itself, capable not only of analysis but also of synthesis and unification. In its unifying function the intellect is salutary and is able to save the soul from all bondage of multiplicity and separateness. The instrument of revelation, the Archangel Gabriel, is also the Holy Spirit, and associated with the Universal Intellect which illuminates the human intellect and enables the human being to exercise the faculty of intuition, which is identified with illumination and inner vision. In the light of revelation, the intellect functions not merely as reason, which is its mental reflection, but also as the instrument of vision and intuition, which when wed to faith, enables man to penetrate into the inner meaning of religion and more particularly God's Word as contained in the Quran. Man must exercise his intelligence in order to understand God's revelation, but in order to understand God's revelation, the intellect must be already illuminated by the light of faith[5] and touched by the grace issuing from revelation.

As far as Islamic theology or *kalām* is concerned, it is engaged more in the understanding of the Will of God than reaching the universal dimensions of the intellect. This is especially true of the dominant school of Sunni theology founded by Abū'l-Ḥasan al-Ash'arī. The Ash'arite school is based on a voluntarism that reduces the function of the intellect to the purely human level and remains nearly oblivious to the aspect of the Divinity as objective Truth and Knowledge.[6] For this school, truth is what God has willed, and the intellect has no function outside the external tenets of the religion. Although the extreme form of voluntarism found in the earlier school of Ash'arism was somewhat modified by the later school (*al-muta'akhkhirūn*) of such men as al-Ghazzālī and Fakhr al-Dīn al-Rāzī as already mentioned, Ash'arism has remained throughout its history as a school of theology in which the intellect is identified practically with reason but of course made subservient to the Will of God and not considered in its function of returning man through inner illumination to the Divine and penetrating into the heart of *tawḥīd*.[7]

In other schools of *kalām*, whether it be Mu'tazilism and Māturidism in the Sunni world or Twelve-Imam Shi'ite theology, a greater role is given to reason in its interpretation of the understanding of God's Will as manifested in His revelation without, however, leading to the type of position known as rationalism in the modern Occident. Nor do these schools of theology envisage any more than Ash'arism, the role of the universal function of the intellect, which includes what is known as intuition, as a means of attaining ultimate knowledge. The function of *kalām* has remained throughout Islamic history to find rational means to protect the citadel of faith (*al-īmān*). It has not been to enable the intellect to penetrate into the inner courtyard of faith and become the ladder that leads to the very heart of the truth of religion. In fact it is not so much in theology but rather in philosophy, *ḥikmah,* and gnosis that we must seek an explanation of the full meaning of the intellect and intuition and a complete methodology of knowledge in Islam.

In Islamic philosophy we can distinguish at least three schools that have dealt extensively with the methodology of knowledge and the full amplitude of the meaning of the intellect in its relation to intuition: Peripatetic (*mashshā'ī*) philosophy, Illuminationist (*ishrāqī*) philosophy, and the "transcendent theosophy" of Ṣadr al-Dīn Shīrāzī.[8] Although the *mashshā'ī* school in Islam drew most of its teachings from Aristotelian and Neoplatonic sources, it is not a rationalistic school as this term is usually understood in Western philosophy. The *mashshāʾī* school is based on a view of the intellect that is properly speaking metaphysical and not only philosophical and distinguishes clearly between the reflection of the intellect upon the human mind, which is reason, and the intellect in itself, which transcends the realm of the individual and which is a substance (*jawhar*) of luminous nature with several levels of reality.[9]

A complete treatment of the intellect and "a theory of knowledge" are to be found in the writings of the master of Muslim Peripatetics, Ibn Sīnā. Basing himself on the treatises on the intellect (*al-Risālah fiʾl-ʿaql*) by al-Kindī and al-Fārābī,[10] Ibn Sīnā gave an extensive analysis of the meaning of the intellect in several of his works especially *The Book of Healing* (*al-Shifāʾ*), *The Book of Salvation* (*al-Najāh*), *Springs of Wisdom* (*ʿUyūn al-ḥikmah*), and his last masterpiece *The Book of Directives and Remarks* (*Kitāb al-ishārāt waʾl-tanbīhāt*). Basing himself upon the Alexandrian commentators of Aristotle, such as Themistius and Alexander Aphrodisias, and with full awareness of the Quranic doctrine of revelation, Ibn Sīnā distinguishes between the Active Intellect (*al-ʿaql al-faʿʿāl*), which is universal and independent of the individual, and the intellectual function within man. Each human being possesses intelligence in virtuality. This is called "material" or "potential" intelligence (*biʾl-quwwah*). As the human being grows in knowledge the first intelligible forms are placed in the soul from above, and man attains to the level of the habitual intelligence (*biʾl-malakah*). Further on, as the intellect becomes fully actualized in the mind, man reaches the level of actual intellect (*biʾl-fiʿl*) and finally as this process is completed, the acquired intelligence (*mustafād*). Finally above these stages and states stands the Active Intellect (*al-ʿaql al-faʿʿāl*), which is Divine, and which illuminates the mind through the act of knowledge.[11] According to Ibn Sīnā, every act of cognition involves the illumination of the mind by the Active Intellect, which bestows upon the mind the form whose knowledge *is* the knowledge of the subject in question. Although Ibn Sīnā denies the Platonic ideas, he stands certainly closer to the realists of the medieval West than to the nominalists. It is not accidental that the followers of St. Augustine were to rally around the teachings of Ibn Sīnā once his works were translated into Latin and that a school was developed that owed its origin to both St. Augustine and Ibn Sīnā.[12] In any case Ibn Sīnā does not in any way confuse reason with intellect, nor does he deny completely the role of intuition as when he speaks of *ḥads* or intuition, which in some ways resembles Aristotle's *agkhinoia* or quick wit, although it is not identical with it.

The *mashshāʾī* doctrine concerning the intellect and intuition can be summarized by saying that there are degrees of intellect that are attained as man advances in knowledge with the aid of the Active Intellect. As the intellect grows in strength and universality, it begins to acquire functions and powers that are identified with intuition rather than intellect in its analytical function connected with the act of ratiocination. The means of acquiring metaphysical knowledge is, according to Ibn Sīnā, intellectual intuition by which *ta'aqqul* should perhaps be translated rather than mere ratiocination. But by intuition here we mean not a sensual or biological power that leaps in the dark but a power that illuminates and removes the boundaries of reason and the limitations of individualistic existence.

In traditional Islamic sources the *mashshāʾī* school is usually called *"ḥikmah baḥthiyyah"* ("rational philosophy" or more precisely "argumentative philosophy") in contrast to the *ishrāqī* school, which is called *"ḥikmah dhawqiyyah"* ("intuitive or literally tasted philosophy") and where intuition is identified with the direct "tasting" of reality and illumination, which permits man to go beyond the confines of his reason left to its own devices. Although *mashshāʾī* philosophy is by no means merely rationalistic as shown above, it is in the *ishrāqī* or illuminative school of wisdom founded by Shaykh al-ishrāq Shihāb al-Dīn Suhrawardī that the intuitive aspect of the intellect is fully emphasized and a ladder described reaching from sensual to principial, metaphysical knowledge through the light of the intellect. Suhrawardī, like such Western metaphysicians as St. Augustine and St. Thomas, emphasizes the principle of adequation or *adaequatio* (*adaequatio rei et intellectus*) according to which to each plane of reality there corresponds an instrument of knowledge adequate to the task of knowing that particular level of reality. But what characterizes and distinguishes *ishrāqī* epistemology is that according to this school every form of knowledge is the result of an illumination of the mind by the lights of the purely spiritual or intelligible world. Even the act of physical vision is possible because the soul of the beholder is illuminated by a light that in the very act of seeing embraces the object of vision. In the same way, the knowledge of a logical concept is made possible by the illumination of the mind at the moment when the very form of the logical concept in question is present in the mind. As for higher forms of knowledge reaching into the empyrean of gnosis and metaphysics, they too are naturally the fruit of the light of the spiritual world shining upon the mind. In *ishrāqī* wisdom, therefore, there is no intellection without illumination (intellects being so many lights) and no true knowledge without the actual "tasting" (*dhawq*) of the object of that knowledge, that tasting that is none other than *sapientia* (whose Latin root *sapere* as already mentioned, means literally "to taste") or intuitive knowledge at its highest level of meaning.[13]

As for the third school associated with Mullā Sadrā, the views of both the Peripatetics and Illuminationists are incorporated by him along with the Sufi doctrine of the "knowledge of the heart," into a vast methodology of knowledge in which all the diverse faculties of knowing are to be found in a hierarchy leading from the sensual to the spiritual.[14] Each act of knowledge, according to Mullā Ṣadrā, involves the being of the knower, and the hierarchy of the faculties of knowledge correspond to the hierarchy of existence. Of particular interest is Mullā Ṣadrā 's insistence on the importance of the power of imagination (*takhayyul*) as an instrument of knowledge corresponding to the "world of imagination" (*'ālam al-khayāl*) or *mundus imaginalis,* which has an objective reality and stands between the physical and purely spiritual realms of existence.[15] Corresponding to this world, man possesses an instrument of knowledge that is neither sensual nor intellectual but that fills the domain in between. This power of creative imagination, which is only perfected in the Universal Man (*al-insān al-kāmil*), is able to create forms in the imaginal world and know these forms ontologically. According to Mullā Ṣadrā, the very existence of these forms is the knowledge of them in the same way that according to Suhrawardī God's knowledge of the world is the very reality of the world. In any case the harmony and balance between intellect and intuition are perfected by Mullā Ṣadrā through his recourse to this intermediate domain and the intermediate faculty of knowing this domain, the faculty that is none other than the power of "imagination" (*takhayyul*) residing in the soul and integrally related to the rational, intellectual, and intuitive faculties of the soul.

The fullest meaning of the intellect and its universal function is to be found in the *ma'rifah* or gnosis, which lies at the heart of the Islamic revelation and which is crystallized in the esoteric dimension of Islam identified for the most part with Sufism. There are verses of the Quran and *ḥadīths* of the Prophet that allude to the heart as the seat of intelligence and knowledge.[16] The heart is the instrument of true knowledge, as its affliction is the cause of ignorance and forgetfulness. That is why the message of the revelation addresses the heart more than the mind as the following verses of the Quran reveal:

> O men, now there has come to you
> an admonition from your Lord. and

> a healing for what is in the breasts (namely the heart)
> and a guidance, and a mercy to the believers.
>
> Sūrah (10:57)
> (Arberry translation)

In the same way, it is the knowledge gained by the heart that counts before the Divine. Again to quote the Quran:

> God will not take you to task for a slip
> in your oaths: but He will take you to task for what your hearts
> have earned: and God is All-forgiving, All-clement.
>
> Sūrah (2: 225)
> (Arberry translation)

Likewise, the knowledge of the heart at least at some level and especially for those whose path to God is the path of knowledge, is considered as essential for salvation. Many traditional masters have in fact written that those who refuse to identify themselves with the heart or center of their living forfeit the possibility of entering Paradise, which already resides at the center of the heart as the famous dictum of Christ "The Kingdom of God is with in you" testifies. The Quran asserts:

> We have created for Gehenna many jinn and men;
> They have hearts, but understand not with them.
> (*lahum qulūbun lā yafqahuna bihā*)
>
> Sūrah (8: 178)
> (Arberry translation)

In the *Ḥadīth* literature there are also numerous references to the knowledge of the heart, a knowledge that is principial and essential and identified with faith as the following *ḥadīth* quoted by Bukhārī demonstrates:

> Faith descended at the root of the hearts of men, then came down the Quran and (people) learned from the Quran and from the example (of the Prophet).[17]

Also, only the heart that grasps for knowledge is considered praiseworthy, for as the Prophet has said: "Blessed is he who makes his heart grasping."[18] It could in fact be said that in the language of the

Noble Quran and *Ḥadīth* the heart means essentially the seat of principial knowledge or the instrument for the attainment of that knowledge. It is upon this foundation that the Sufis have developed the doctrine of "the knowledge of the heart" that has occupied so many of the great masters of Sufism.

The Sufis speak of the "eye of the heart" (*'ayn al-qalb* in Arabic and *chishm-i dil* in Persian) as the "third eye" identified with the imminent intellect, which is able to gain a knowledge different from that gained by the physical eyes yet direct and immediate like physical vision.[19] As the famous Persian poet Hātif states:

> Open the 'eye of the heart' so that thou canst see the spirit,
> And gain vision of that which visible is not.

This knowledge that is identified with the heart is principial knowledge gained through an instrument that is identified with the heart or center of being of man rather than the mind, which knows only indirectly and which is a projection of the heart. The heart is not simply identified with sentiments that are contrasted in modern philosophy with reason. Man does not possess only the faculty of reason and the sentiments or emotions that are contrasted with it. Rather, he is capable of an intellectual knowledge that transcends the dualism and dichotomy between reason and emotions, or the mind and the heart as they are usually understood. It is the loss of gnosis or truly intellectual knowledge in an operative and realized manner in the modern world that has caused the eclipse of the traditional conception of the "knowledge of the heart," a knowledge that is at once intellectual and intuitive in the profoundest meaning of these terms and that can therefore be identified with intellectual intuition.

To understand fully the intellectual knowledge identified with the heart, it is necessary to return to the distinction between "presential" (*ḥuḍūrī*) and "attained" (*ḥuṣūlī*) knowledge. All rational knowledge related to the mind is made possible through concepts that are "attained" by the mind. Therefore, all mental knowledge is "attained" knowledge. Mentally and rationally man can only know 'fire' or 'water' through the concept of fire or water abstracted through the senses and made available by the various mental faculties for the analytical faculty of the mind identified with reason. But there is another type of knowledge, possible for all men, but in practice attained only by the few. It is a knowledge that is direct and immediate, a knowledge that is identified with the heart. The knowledge of the heart has the immediacy and directness of sensual knowledge but concerns the intelligible or spiritual world. When one gains knowledge of the perfume of a rose through direct experience of the olfactory faculty, he or she does not gain knowledge of the concept of the perfume of the rose but a direct knowledge of it. For most people this kind of knowledge is limited to the sensual world, but for the gnostic whose eye of his or her heart is opened through spiritual practice, there is the possibility of a knowledge that has the directness of sensual experience but concerns the supernal realities. From the point of view of this "presential" knowledge, this supreme form of knowing in which ultimately the subject and object of knowledge are the same, the most concrete of all realities is the Supreme Principle. Everything else is relatively speaking an abstraction. To know in an ultimate sense is to know God through a knowledge that is both intellection and intuition in the highest meaning of these terms. It is to know the fire by being burned and consumed in it; it is to know water by being immersed in the ocean of absolute Being.

In the Islamic perspective, therefore, one can speak of a hierarchy of knowledge ranging from the sensual, through the imaginary and the rational, to the intellectual, which is also intuitive and identified with the heart. But just as the rational faculty of knowledge is not opposed to the sensual, the intellectual and intuitive are not opposed to the rational. Rather, the mind is a reflection of the heart, the center of the microcosm. The Islamic doctrine of Unity (*al-tawḥīd*) has been able to embrace all modes of knowing into complementary and not contending stages of a hierarchy leading to that supreme form of knowledge, that gnosis of the purified heart that is ultimately none other than the unitive and unifying knowledge of the One and the most profound realization of the Unity (*al-tawḥīd*) that is the Alpha and Omega of the Islamic revelation.

PART 3

Islamic Philosophy in History

CHAPTER 7

A Framework for the Study of the History of Islamic Philosophy

In turning to the study of the history of Islamic philosophy, rather than its doctrines and ideas, and in wanting to remain faithful to the reality of the Islamic intellectual tradition where what has been said has always prevailed over who has said it, it is necessary to create a framework different from that of earlier histories of philosophy written by Europeans and their Muslim imitators. As indicated earlier such an attempt has been made since the 1960s in several different works, including those of Corbin and my own. In this chapter I wish to outline and summarize the framework developed by Corbin and myself and to point out some of its salient features. First of all, although in traditional Islamic circles Islamic philosophy has always been taught as truth transcending time rather than simply ever-changing ideas, a traditional Islamic conception of the history of philosophy has existed as we see in the works of Suhrawardī, Mullā Ṣadrā, and others. Second, the challenges of Western scholarship require that an authentic Islamic interpretation of the history of Islamic philosophy be presented in a contemporary language and yet remain faithful to the Islamic view of both philosophy and its origin and later historical development.

Early in the twentieth century a few figures such as Muṣṭafā 'Abd al-Rāziq in Egypt and Ḍiā᾿ al-Dīn Durrī in Iran sought to write histories of Islamic philosophy from the Islamic point of view, but their project remained incomplete. Furthermore, they wrote in Arabic and Persian, respectively, and exercised little influence in the West. In 1962, after I had written *Three Muslim Sages,* in which I tried to interpret the whole of the Islamic intellectual tradition both morphologically and historically, Corbin approached me to collaborate with him on the writing of *Histoire de la philosophie islamique,* which was to be part of the *Pléiades* collection and the first part of which first appeared in 1964. To accomplish this task we thought of a historical framework and periodization for the history of Islamic philosophy, one that would break completely with prevalent conceptualizations that limited Islamic philosophy temporally to the time of the death of Averroes, neglected schools of philosophy other than the *mashshāʾī* even in the earlier period, such as Ismāʿīlī philosophy, and paid little attention to philosophy outside of *falsafah,* such as the philosophical dimensions of Sufism, theology, the arts, and the sciences.

It became evident that the history of Islamic philosophy could not be limited geographically but had to take into account the whole width and breadth of the Islamic world and that after Ibn Rushd, its main home became Persia. Over the years I departed to some extent from the periodization and framework that Corbin and I had created together, and I applied my own modified framework to the *History of Islamic Philosophy,* which I edited with Oliver Leaman and in a more summary fashion in the next chapter. What follows is a brief outline of what the history of Islamic philosophy would look like if developed within the framework I developed over the years based on the early work done in collaboration with Corbin.[1]

From its genesis twelve hundred years ago to today, Islamic philosophy (*al-ḥikmah; al-falsafah*) has been one of the major intellectual traditions within the Islamic world, and it has influenced and been influenced by many other intellectual perspectives, including Scholastic theology (*kalām*) and doctrinal Sufism (*al-maʿrifah* or *al-taṣawwuf al-ʿilmī*) and theoretical gnosis (*ʿirfān-i naẓarī*). The life of Islamic philosophy did not terminate with Ibn Rushd nearly eight hundred years ago, as thought by Western scholarship for several centuries. Rather, its activities continued strongly during the later centuries, particularly in Persia and other eastern lands of Islam, and it was revived in Egypt during the last century.

The Origin of Islamic Philosophy

Islamic philosophy was born of philosophical speculation on the heritage of Greco-Alexandrian philosophy, which was made available in Arabic in the third/ninth century, by Muslims who were immersed in the teachings of the Quran and lived in a universe in which revelation was a central reality. As already mentioned, Muslims considered Greek philosophy itself to have been rooted in prophecy, and in contrast to how the West was to view Greek philosophy later, Muslims continued to identify the origin of the Greek philosophical tradition that they were now mastering with revelation. Islamic philosophers concentrated on philosophizing in a world dominated by the reality of prophecy and revelation and created a "prophetic philosophy," which in turn influenced deeply the philosophical life of the other two members of Abrahamic monotheism, namely, Judaism and Christianity. The Quran, as well as *Ḥadīth,* served as a central source of Islamic philosophical speculation and influenced the reflection of Muslim thinkers upon Greek texts.[2] In later Islamic philosophy the sayings of the Shi'ite Imams also played a major role, especially in the works of Ṣadr al-Dīn Shīrāzī (Mullā Ṣadrā). Far from being simply Greek philosophy in Arabic and Persian, Islamic philosophy integrated certain elements of Greek philosophy into the Islamic perspective, creating new philosophical schools. Although Islamic philosophy drew from the Greek sources, which Muslims considered to be the fruit of earlier revelations associated with such figures as the prophet Idrīs (Hermes), it belonged to an independent philosophical universe of discourse. A full study of the origins of Islamic philosophy must be able to deal with the Islamic as well as the Greek sources and their interactions.

The Early Peripatetics

The early centuries of Islamic philosophy were marked by the appearance of several schools of thought. The most prominent school, which is often identified with Islamic philosophy as such in Western sources, is the *mashshāʾī* (Peripatetic). This school is not simply Aristotelian, as the name might indicate, but marks a synthesis of Islamic tenets, Aristotelianism, and Neoplatonism. Its founder is Abū Ya'qūb al-Kindī (d. c. A.H. 260/873 C.E.), the "Philosopher of the Arabs." Some Islamic sources have spoken of the Persian philosopher Abūʾl-'Abbās Īrānshahrī as the first Muslim to have written on philosophy, but nothing survives of his works save a few fragments. In contrast, a number of al-Kindī's works have reached us, some only in Hebrew and Latin, for he was well known in the West. Al-Kindī, like most of the early Peripatetics, was at once a philosopher and a scientist. Although much of his voluminous corpus has been lost, enough has survived to reveal his mastery in both domains. Al-Kindī was the first Islamic thinker to grapple with the problem of the expression of Peripatetic thought in Arabic. He also confronted one of the central problems of philosophy in the monotheistic world, namely, harmonization of faith and reason. Among his philosophical works his treatises on the intellect, *Fīʾl-'aql* (On the Intellect), and metaphysics, *Fīʾl-falsafat al-ūlā* (On Metaphysics), were particularly influential in the Muslim world; *Fīʾl-'aql,* known as *De Intellectu* in Latin, also had a wide-spread influence in medieval Europe.

Most of al-Kindī's immediate students were more significant as scientists than as philosophers, and his real successor on the philosophical scene was not among them. Yet their philosophical views, especially those of Abū Ṭayyib al-Sarakhsī, deserve to be closely studied and integrated into general histories of the Peripatetic school. As for al-Kindī's real successor, this title must be given to Abū Naṣr al-Fārābī (d. 339/950), who hailed from Khurasan in Central Asia. Many consider al-Fārābī to be the real founder of Islamic Peripatetic philosophy, and it was he more than al-Kindī who formulated the Arabic philosophical language and wrote about the relation between the Arabic language and the expression of Aristotelian logic. He commented on Aristotle's *Organon* and is the father of formal logic in the Islamic world. He furthermore sought to synthesize the political philosophy of Plato and Islamic political thought in his masterpiece *Kitāb ārā᾽ ahl al-madīnat al-fāḍilah* (The Book of the Opinions of the Citizens of the Virtuous City), and is considered to be the founder of Islamic political philosophy. Al-Fārābī also wrote of the harmony between the views of Plato and Aristotle, as well as on these philosophers individually and on various metaphysical and epistemological questions. He is, moreover, the first Islamic philosopher to systematize the emanation scheme (*fayḍ*) of the ten intellects from the One, for which Peripatetic philosophy is known.

After al-Fārābī , Khurasan gradually became the major center of philosophical activity, but throughout the fourth/tenth century Baghdad continued as an important center, following the earlier activities of al-Kindī. In the second half of the tenth century, however, the philosophical scene in Baghdad turned mostly to the study of logic under the guidance of Abū Sulaymān al-Sijistānī, who was also known as al-Manṭiqī (the Logician). Meanwhile Abū᾽l Ḥasan al-'Āmirī from Khurasan was developing the Fārābian teachings further and adding a new chapter of his own to Islamic philosophy by attempting to incorporate certain pre-Islamic Iranian ideas into his political philosophy.

Early Peripatetic philosophy reached its peak soon after al-'Āmirī with another Persian philosopher, Abū 'Alī al-Ḥusayn ibn 'Abd Allāh ibn Sīnā (369–428/980–1037), usually known as Ibn Sīnā (Avicenna). Often considered the greatest Islamic philosopher, Ibn Sīnā created a vast synthesis of Peripatetic thought in his *Kitāb al-shifā᾽* (The Book of Healing), which dominated many dimensions of Islamic thought for centuries. His ontological distinction between *wujūb* (necessity) and *imkān* (contingency)[3] became central to Islamic thought and also deeply influenced Jewish and Christian philosophy and theology, as did his integration of the study of the three kingdoms within the scheme of the great chain of being, that is, the scheme that places all creatures in a chain or levels of being stretching from the dust to the highest angel.

Ibn Sīnā's major works, which also included *Kitāb al-najāh* (The Book of Salvation) and his last philosophical masterpiece, *Kitāb al-ishārāt wa᾽l-tanbīhāt* (The Book of Directives and Remarks), were widely read by defenders and opponents of Islamic philosophy alike. Moreover, Ibn Sīnā also wrote certain "visionary recitals" and philosophico-mystical treatises that contain what he called *"al-ḥikmah al-mashriqiyyah"* (Oriental philosophy), which is of great importance if one looks upon the later tradition of Islamic philosophy.

In writing of this period of Peripatetic philosophy, it is not, however, sufficient to go from al-Fārābī to Ibn Sīnā and even include a few words on al-'Āmirī and al-Sijistānī. A great deal more needs to be said of the philosophical dimension of the circle of al-Sijistānī and figures such as al-Tawḥīdī,[4] as well as of other Peripatetic figures. This period is in fact witness to many philosophical figures who are rarely mentioned in general histories of Islamic philosophy, even those that emphasize the Peripatetics. This is also a period, which although known as far as the most famous figures are concerned, needs monographic studies for the lesser known figures, including Ibn Sīnā's important students such as Bahmanyār.

Ismā'īlī Philosophy

With an emphasis on *ta᾽wīl* (spiritual hemeneutics), the Ismā'īlī school of philosophy, associated with the Ismā'īlī branch of Shi'ism, saw philosophy as an esoteric knowledge associated with the inner meaning of religion.[5] It drew its ideas from Islamic esoterism and Neoplatonism, as well as both Hermeticism and Neopythagoreanism. The first work of this school, the *Umm al-kitāb* (The Archetypal Book), belongs to the second/eighth century, and it is supposed to be the record of conversations between the fifth Shi'ite Imam, Muḥammad al-Bāqir, and his students. On the basis of this early Shi'ite gnosis, Ismā'īlī philosophy developed during the next two centuries and reached its full flowering in the fourth/tenth and fifth/eleventh centuries with such figures as Abū Ya'qūb al-Sijistānī, Ḥamīd al-Dīn al-Kirmānī (often called the "Ismā'īlī Ibn Sīnā"), the author of *Rāḥat al 'aql* (Repose of the Intellect), and finally Nāṣir-i Khusraw (d. around 470/1077), perhaps the greatest of the Ismā'īlī philosophers. The Ismā'īlī philosophers played an important role in the rise of Persian as the second major philosophical language of Islam, and Nāṣir-i Khusraw, the author of the major work *Jāmiʿ al-ḥikmatayn* (The Sum of Two Wisdoms), wrote all of his major works in Persian. Ibn Sīnā, however, was the pioneer in the use of Persian as a philosophical language, having written *Dānish-nāma-yi ʿalāʾī* (The Book of Science Dedicated to ʿAlāʾ al-Dawlah), the first work of Peripatetic philosophy in Persian.

The *Raṣāʾil* (Treatises) of the Ikhwān al-Ṣafāʾ (Brethren of Purity) is a collection of fifty-one treatises closely associated with Ismāʿīlī circles. These treatises, which appeared in the fourth/tenth century in Basra, have a strong Neopythagorean color. They were widely read by later philosophers and even theologians such as al-Ghazzālī, who wrote against the Peripatetics and also Ismāʿīlism. Ismāʿīlī philosophy survived the fall of the Fāṭimids and continued into the seventh/thirteenth century when centers of Ismāʿīlī power in Persia were destroyed by the Mongols. Even then, the tradition continued in Yemen and India and even in Persia itself, but much remains to be done before the history of this important school becomes known in its fullness.

Independent Philosophers during the Early Centuries

Although Islamic philosophy is predominantly associated with schools that transcend the individual, the early centuries did produce a few independent philosophers who wielded some influence. The first among them is Muhammad ibn Zakariyyāʾ al-Rāzī (d. around 320/932), known in Latin as Rhazes, the greatest Muslim physician after Ibn Sīnā, who was also a philosopher known especially for his denial of the necessity of prophecy. He was strongly attacked by the Ismāʿīlīs for this view, as well as for positing "five eternal principles" consisting of the Demiurge, the Universal Soul, *materia prima*, Space, and Time. But Rāzī remains an important philosopher worthy of further study.[6] Another independent philosopher and one of Islam's greatest scientists, Abū Rayḥān al-Bīrūnī (d. 421/1030), held a philosophical view different from Rāzī's but admired al-Rāzī's scientific works greatly. Al-Bīrūnī's most important philosophical contribution was his criticism of Avicennian natural philosophy,[7] as well as his introduction of Hindu philosophy into the Islamic world. Finally, an important independent philosopher, Aḥmad ibn Muskūyah (Miskawayh; d. 421/1030), wrote the first major Islamic work on philosophical ethics, *Tahdhīb al-akhlāq* (Purification of Morals), as well as a book entitled *Jāwīdān khirad* (*philosophia perennis*).

THEOLOGIANS AGAINST PHILOSOPHERS

From the fifth/eleventh to the seventh/thirteenth century, the domination of western Asia by Seljuqs led to the eclipse of philosophy in the eastern lands of Islam. The caliphate, supported by the Seljuqs, preferred the teaching of *kalām* in the *madrasahs* (Islamic schools) to philosophy, although *kalām* itself, as discussed earlier, developed over time in a more philosophical form. During this period, the only notable philosopher in the eastern lands was the Persian poet and mathematician Omar Khayyam to whom we shall turn later in this book. The major theologians of this era, such as Abū Ḥāmid Muḥammad al-Ghazzālī (d. 505/1111), Abūʾl-Fatḥ al-Shahrastānī (d. 548/1153), and Fakhr al-Dīn al-Rāzī (d. 606/1210), wrote treatises against Peripatetic and, in the case of Ghazzālī and Rāzī also against Ismāʿīlī philosophy, thereby curtailing philosophical activity in the eastern lands of Islam.[8]

The most famous attack against the *falāsifah* came from the great Sufi theologian al-Ghazzālī, who, however, dealt with philosophical themes himself and even composed treatises on formal logic. In his autobiography, *āl-Munqidh min al-ḍalāl* (The Deliverance from Error), al-Ghazzālī criticized the Peripatetic philosophers severely. Then he summarized their views in his *Maqāṣid al-falāsifah* (The Purposes of the Philosophers), which caused the Latin Schoolmen to think of al-Ghazzālī himself as a Peripatetic. Finally, in his *Tahāfut al-falāsifah* (Incoherence of the Philosophers), he sought to demolish the views of the philosophers, accusing them of deviating from Islam in their denial of the createdness of the world, God's knowledge of particulars, and bodily resurrection. Al-Ghazzālī's attack had the effect of curtailing the power of rationalism in Islamic philosophy, but it did not bring rational philosophy to an end, as some have thought.

The influence of Fakhr al-Dīn al-Rāzī on the technical discussions of later Islamic philosophy was even greater than that of al-Ghazzālī. Al-Rāzī's most important attack against Peripatetic philosophy came in the form of his detailed criticism of Ibn Sīnā's *Kitāb al-ishārāt* in a work entitled *Sharḥ al-ishārāt* (Commentary upon the *Ishārāt*), to which Naṣīr al-Dīn al-Ṭūsī (d. 672/1274) was to write the celebrated response that resuscitated Avicennian philosophy. In the fourteenth century this central debate was carried further by Quṭb al-Dīn al-Rāzī in his *al-Muḥākamāt* (Trials), in which he sought to judge between the commentaries of Fakhr al-Dīn al-Rāzī and al-Ṭūsī. Although going back to Max Horten[9] there has been awareness of the Rāzī-Ṭūsī debate, most Western histories of Islamic philosophy and their Islamic imitations continue to emphasize the importance of the Ibn Sīnā, Ghazzālī, and Ibn Rushd debates rather than the Ibn Sīnā, Rāzī, and Ṭūsī one, whereas the second is more important for the later history of Islamic philosophy than the first.

Islamic Philosophy in Spain

While philosophy was in eclipse in the eastern lands of Islam, it flourished in Islamic Spain. Islamic philosophy in the western lands of Islam actually began with the Sufi philosopher Ibn Masarrah (d. 319/931), who profoundly influenced later thinkers. This link between Sufism and philosophy continued in Spain to the end except for the major figure of Ibn Rushd. Another early thinker, Ibn Ḥazm (d. 454/1064), jurist, theologian, philosopher, and author of one of the first Muslim works on comparative religion, also composed a famous treatise on Platonic love entitled *Ṭawq al-ḥamāmah* (The Ring of the Dove).

The first major philosopher in the Maghrib to follow the eastern *mashshāʾī* school was Ibn Bājjah (d. 533/1138), known both for his significant commentaries on Aristotelian physics and his philosophical masterpiece, *Tadbīr al-mutawaḥḥid* (Regimen of the Solitary), which maintains that the perfect state can come about only through the perfection of individuals who can unite their intellects with the Active Intellect. This work has a definite mystical bent as does the masterpiece of his successor, Ibn Ṭufayl (d. 580/1185), who like Ibn Bājjah was a political figure and scientist but is likewise known for one major opus, *Ḥayy ibn Yaqẓān* (Living Son of the Awake), which has also a mystical meaning and which bears the name of Ibn Sīnā's visionary recital but with a different structure. The work deals in a symbolic language with the harmony between the inner illumination received by the intellect and the knowledge revealed through revelation. Ibn Ṭufayl's philosophical novel was translated immediately into Hebrew but not into medieval Latin until the seventeenth century, when it became famous in Europe as *Philosophos Autodidactus* and exercised wide influence in both philosophical and literary circles.

The most famous Islamic philosopher of the Maghrib, Ibn Rushd (523–95/1126–98) known in Latin as Averroes, chief religious judge of Cordoba and a physician, wrote the most famous medieval commentaries on the Aristotelian corpus and was referred to in the West as "The Commentator." He set out to revive Peripatetic philosophy by responding to al-Ghazzālī's *Tahāfut* in his own *Tahāfut al-tahāfut* (Incoherence of the Incoherence). In contrast to his image in the West as a rationalist "free-thinker" and author of the double-truth theory, however, Ibn Rushd was a pious Muslim and in fact a religious functionary who set out to harmonize faith and reason, especially in his *Faṣl al-maqāl* (The Decisive Treatise). His influence in the West, however, was greater than in the Islamic world, where the later destiny of philosophy was more closely associated with the name of Ibn Sīnā, than with his.

After Ibn Rushd, Islamic philosophy began to wane in the Maghrib but did not disappear completely. 'Abd al-Ḥaqq ibn Sab'īn (d. 669/1270) wrote a number of important treatises based on the doctrine of *waḥdat al-wujūd* (the transcendent unity of being), and the Tunisian 'Abd al-Raḥmān ibn Khaldūn (d. 780/1379) developed a philosophy of history in his *al-Muqaddimah* (Prolegomena). The most important of these later figures from the Maghrib, however, was Muḥyī al-Dīn ibn 'Arabī (d. 638/1240), expositor of Sufi metaphysics. Although not a philosopher in the sense of *faylasūf,* he is one of the greatest expositors of mystical philosophy in any time and clime, and he exercised a profound influence on Sufism as well as later Islamic philosophy.

Although Islamic philosophy in the Maghrib seems to have come suddenly to an end, philosophical thought did not disappear completely but took refuge mostly in philosophical Sufism and philosophical theology as we see also in much of the rest of the Arab world. This later phase has hardly ever been treated in general histories of philosophy but needs to be studied.

Suhrawardī and the School of Illumination

A new school of philosophy, which could perhaps more properly be called "theosophy" in the original sense of this term, was established by Shihāb al-Dīn Suhrawardī (d. 587/1191), who considered discursive philosophy as developed by Ibn Sīnā to be only the first, necessary step in the attainment of true philosophy, which must also be based on intellectual intuition or *ishrāq* (illumination). Suhrawardī integrated Platonic philosophy, Neoplatonism, the wisdom of the ancient Persians, especially Mazdaean angelology, and Avicennian philosophy in the matrix of Islamic gnosis to create a widely influential new school of thought. His works, written in both Arabic and Persian, include many treatises written in a symbolic rather than discursive language, and they culminate in his masterpiece, *Ḥikmat al-ishrāq* (Theosophy of the Orient of Light). When he was executed in Aleppo, his followers went underground, but commentaries by Shams al-Dīn

Muḥammad Shahrazūrī a generation later, followed by the better-known commentary of Quṭb al-Dīn Shīrāzī (d. 710/ 1311), revived the teachings of *ishrāq*. Henceforth, the school exercised a deep influence not only in Persia but also in Ottoman Turkey and the Indian subcontinent, and it continues as a living school of thought to this day.

Rapprochement between Various Schools of Thought

The period from the thirteen to the sixteenth century marks the coming together of various schools of thought. The main arena of philosophical activity during this era was Persia, especially Shiraz; Iraq and eastern Anatolia, which were closely related culturally to Persia, were also important centers. This period is witness to the revival of Ibn Sīnā's philosophy by Naṣīr al-Dīn al-Ṭūsī (d. 672/1273), who also wrote the most famous work on philosophical ethics in Persian, *Akhlāq-i nāṣirī* (The Naṣīrean Ethics). Other notable figures of this rapprochement, such as Quṭb al-Dīn Shīrāzī, sought to integrate *mashshāʾī* and *ishrāqī* doctrines. These centuries also mark the spread of the doctrinal school of Sufism of Ibn 'Arabī, mostly through his foremost student, Ṣadr al-Dīn Qunyawī, and the latter's students and successors, such as Muʾayyid al-Dīn al-Jandī, 'Abd al-Razzāq al-Kāshānī, and Dāʾūd al-Qayṣarī. Likewise this period coincides with the spread of the school of *ishrāq* and philosophical *kalām* associated with such figures as Sayyid Sharīf Jurjānī.[10]

During this era several philosophers appeared who sought to synthesize these various schools. One such figure is Ibn Turkah Iṣfahānī (d. 830/1427), who was at once an *ishrāqī*, a *mashshāʾī*, and an *'ārif* of the school of Ibn 'Arabī. There was also a closer integration of philosophical activity and Twelver Shi'ite theology, as seen in the works of Naṣīr al-Dīn al-Ṭūsī, who, besides being a philosopher, was also the author of the major work of Shi'ite *kalām*. The background was thus set for the synthesis associated with the Safavid period.[11]

The School of Isfahan and Philosophy in India and Ottoman Turkey

In the tenth/sixteenth century, with the establishment of the Safavid dynasty in Persia, there began a new phase in Islamic philosophy associated with the School of Isfahan. Its founder, Mīr Dāmād (d. 1041/1631), taught in that city, although students came to him from all parts of Persia and many other lands. His most famous student,

Ṣadr al-Dīn Shīrāzī (Mullā Ṣadrā) (d. 1050/1640, is considered by many to be the greatest of all Islamic metaphysicians. In what he called the "transcendent theosophy" or *al-ḥikmah al-muta'āliyah,* he integrated the schools of *mashshā*ʾ, *ishrāq, 'irfān,* and *kalām* in a vast synthesis that has influenced most Islamic philosophy to this day. The message of his magnum opus, *al-Asfār al-arba'ah* (The Four Journeys), a veritable summa of Islamic philosophy, came to be known as *al-ḥikmat al-ilāhiyyah,* literally "divine wisdom" or "theosophy" which we have already discussed.

Mullā Ṣadrā's philosophy was taught in India and was revived in Qajar Persia by Mullā 'Alī Nūrī, Ḥājjī Mullā Hādī Sabziwārī, Āqā 'Alī Mudarris, and others and has continued as a powerful intellectual tradition into the present century.[12] Parallel philosophical schools with distinct features were also active in India and Ottoman Turkey during this period. But little is known of their history.

Islamic Philosophy in the Contemporary Islamic World

Islamic philosophy has continued as a living intellectual tradition and plays a significant role in the intellectual life of the Islamic world. Jamāl al-Dīn al-Afghānī, a student when in Persia of the school of Mullā Ṣadrā, revived the study of Islamic philosophy in Egypt, where some of the leading religious and intellectual figures, such as 'Abd al-Ḥalīm Maḥmūd, the late Shaykh al-Azhar, have been its devotees. In the Indo-Pakistani subcontinent, Muḥammad Iqbal was a student of Islamic philosophy, and even Mawlānā Mawdūdī, the founder of the Jamā'at-i Islāmī of Pakistan, translated some of Mullā Ṣadrā's *al-Asfār* into Urdu in his youth.

The main arena of Islamic philosophy in modern times has continued to be Persia despite the opposition of a sector of the Shi'ite *'ulamā*ʾ. Toward the end of the Qajar period a number of outstanding philosophers appeared, such as Mīrzā Mahdī Āshtīyānī and Mīrzā Ṭāhir Tunikābunī, who were active into the Pahlavi period, when such outstanding teachers as Sayyid Abūʾl-Ḥasan Qazwīnī, Sayyid Muḥammad Kaẓīm 'Aṣṣār, and 'Allāmah Ṭabāṭabāʾī came to dominate the scene. From the 1960s onward a veritable revival of Islamic philosophy occurred in the traditional schools as well as in circles of Western-educated Iranians, a revival that continues to this day. It must be remembered that Ayatollah Rūḥ Allāh Khumaynī (Khomeini) studied and taught *ḥikmat* for decades in Qom before entering the political arena and that the first head of the Council of the Islamic Revolution after the Iranian

Revolution of 1979, Murtaḍā Muṭahharī, was a noted philosopher. Likewise in Iraq Muhammad Bāqir al-Ṣadr, the well-known religious and political leader, belonged to the tradition of Islamic philosophy.

In most Islamic countries today there is renewed interest in various aspects of the Islamic intellectual tradition in which Islamic philosophy plays a central role. This philosophy is being studied and developed to an ever-greater degree to provide responses to the intellectual challenges from the West. It is also appealing to an ever increasing number of Western students, who are interested in it not only historically but as a living philosophy. In Islamic philosophy one can discover harmony between reason and revelation and the fruits of inner vision and ratiocination. Islamic philosophy is the repository of a knowledge that, on the basis of rational thought, leads ultimately to illumination and that is never divorced from the sacred.[13]

The Philosophy of Various Disciplines

A history of Islamic philosophy would not be complete without taking into account such disciplines as the philosophy of science, the philosophy of art, the philosophy of law, and so on. The outline mentioned above must not concern itself only with metaphysics, epistemology, psychology, and logic as is usually the case but take full account of the branches of philosophy mentioned previously.[14] An ideal history of Islamic philosophy would include all such studies within the treatment of each philosopher, period, or school. Also as a complement to such a treatment, there is need of full-fledged separate studies of the history of each of these branches such as the history of the Islamic philosophy of science or art.[15] But we are far from being able to achieve such a task now and must remain content for the moment with a thorough history of Islamic philosophy that from the Islamic view covers the main tenets of various philosophers and schools of thought. Therefore, we now turn to this issue seeking to provide first of all a fuller presentation of the various dimensions of the Islamic intellectual tradition and especially philosophy on the basis of the outline given above and then to more in-depth study of later philosophy mostly in Persia, which became the main arena for Islamic philosophical activity from the seventh/thirteenth century onward. Before dealing with this later period, however, we shall devote a chapter to the earlier and much better known period of Islamic philosophy and cosmology and to the unique figure of Khayyam, who is a solitary link between the earlier period, culminating with Ibn Sīnā and the revival of Islamic philosophy in the seventh/thirteenth century.

CHAPTER 8

Dimensions of the Islamic Intellectual Tradition: *Kalām*, Philosophy, and Spirituality

It is now time to turn more fully and in a more extensive manner to the development of Islamic philosophy historically and in relation to the other major dimensions of the Islamic intellectual tradition seen in its entirety. In a land whose horizons are illuminated by prophecy or what one can call a "traditional universe" one can observe at least three intellectual dimensions that may be called "theological," "philosophical," and "gnostic"—if this latter term is understood as referring to a knowledge that illuminates and liberates. Islam is no exception to this principle and has developed within its bosom all three types of intellectual activity, each possessing a millennial tradition with numerous illustrious representatives. The relative significance of each dimension is, however, not the same in Islam and Christianity, nor do these categories correspond exactly to schools into which their names are translated in a European language such as English as we have had occasion to discuss earlier in this book.

In the Islamic intellectual universe, there exists first of all *al-ma'rifah* or *al-'irfān* (gnosis). Then there is *falsafah,* which corresponds to philosophy in the older sense of the term, before it became limited to its positivistic definition. This school in turn became transformed for the most part in later centuries as we have seen into *al-ḥikmat al-ilāhiyyah* (literally, *"theosophia"*). Finally, there is *kalām,* usually translated as theology, whose propagators, the *mutakallimūn,* were referred to by Thomas Aquinas as the *"loquentes."* The significance of these intellectual dimensions is not the same in Islam as corresponding perspectives in the West. This is especially true of *kalām,* which does not at all occupy the same central role in Islamic thought as theology does in Christianity. Furthermore, the Islamic schools have interacted with each other in a totally different manner from what one observes in the Christian West. Gnosis has played a more central role in the Islamic tradition than it has in the West, and the destiny of philosophy has been very different in the two worlds despite their close affinity in the European Middle Ages. As for theology, it has continued to harbor over the centuries the profoundest religious and spiritual impulses of Christianity, whereas in Islam it has always been less central than in Christianity. As was mentioned earlier, much that is considered to be theology in the West is to be found in Islamic philosophy, especially during later centuries.

In Christianity not only has theology attempted to provide a rational defense for the faith, but it has also sought to provide access to the highest realms of the life of the spirit, as one finds in the mystical theology of Dionysius the Areopagite or, in the Protestant context, in the *Theologica Germanica* of Martin Luther. Such has never been the case in Islam, where *kalām*, literally "word," continued to be "the science that bears responsibility of solidly establishing religious beliefs by giving proofs and dispelling doubts."[1] The deepest spiritual and intellectual expressions of Islam are not to be found in works of *kalām*. Yet, this science is important for the understanding of certain aspects of Islamic thought and must be dealt with in this overall treatment of the Islamic intellectual tradition, especially since *kalām* has interacted in so many ways with philosophy, the main subject of this book.

Early *Kalām*

Traditionally, 'Alī ibn Abī Ṭālib, the cousin and son-in-law of the Prophet, is credited with having established the science of *kalām*, and his *Nahj al-balāghah* (Path of Eloquence) contains the first rational proofs among Muslims of the unity of God, following upon the wake of the Quran and the *Ḥadīth*. Already in the first Islamic century, the early community was confronted with such problems and questions as the relation between faith and works, who is saved, the nature of the Quran, and the legitimacy of political authority, all of which became crystallized later into the structure and concerns of *kalām*. Moreover, the debates held in Syria and Iraq between Muslims and followers of other religions—especially Christians, Mazdaeans, and Manichaeans, all of whom had developed philosophical and theological arguments for the defense of the tenets of their faith—caused the Muslims to seek to develop a rational edifice of their own for the protection and defense of Islam. This response to the theology of other religions is particularly true for the case of Christianity, whose theology directly challenged the young faith of Islam to construct its own theological edifice. Greco-Alexandrian philosophy, which early Christian thinkers had already encountered and with which Muslims were also becoming acquainted, was also an important factor in the formation of the early schools of *kalām*.

The rapid spread of Islam had brought diverse groups within the fold of the Islamic community and necessitated a clear definition of the creed to prevent various kinds of error. Because of the emphasis of Islam upon the Divine Law and its practice, these creeds are not as important as the *credo* in traditional Christianity, but they are nonetheless of significance for an understanding of the early theological concerns of the Islamic community. These creeds include the *Fiqh al-akbar* (The Great Knowledge) and the *Waṣiyyah* (Testament) either by or based upon the teachings of Imam Abū Ḥanīfah (d. 150/767), who was also the founder of one of the major Sunni schools of Law. These creeds emphasize above all else the unity of God and His power over human life. They usually also emphasize the importance of gaining knowledge of God to the extent possible. There were later theologians who insisted that every Muslim must know as many proofs for the existence of God as he is able to master.

THE MU'TAZILITES

The first systematic school of *kalām* grew out of the bosom of the circle of traditional scholars of the Quran and *Ḥadīth* in the second/eighth century and came to be known as the Mu'tazilite. Its founder, Wāṣil ibn 'Aṭāʾ (d. 131/748), is said to have been a student of the famous scholar of *Ḥadīth* and Sufism in Basra, Ḥasan al-Baṣrī, but he separated from his master and established his own circle in that city.

The Mu'tazilites, who were seen as the "freethinkers" and rationalists of Islam by early Western Islamicists, dominated the theological scene in Iraq for more than a century and developed an imposing theological edifice based on emphasis on the use of reason in matters pertaining to religion and the importance of human free will. The outstanding Mu'tazilites were either from Basra—for example, Abūʾl-Hudhayl al-'Allāf (d. 226/840), Abū Isḥāq al-Naẓẓām (d. 231/845), and the famous literary figure 'Amr ibn Baḥr al-Jāḥiẓ (d. 255/869)—or from Baghdad, among whose leaders were Bishr ibn al-Mu'tamir (d. 210/825) and Abū 'Alī al-Jubbāʾī (d. 303/915). After al-Maʾmūn, early in the third/ninth century, the fortunes of the Mu'tazilites began to wane, and soon they were replaced as the dominant school of *kalām* by the Ash'arites. They did not completely die out, however, but continued to survive for at least another two centuries in various parts of the heartland of the Islamic world, as can be seen in the vast Mu'tazilite encyclopedia of the Persian theologian Qāḍī 'Abd al-Jabbār, composed in the fifth/eleventh century. Their school survived even longer in the Yemen, where their teachings became adopted by the Zaydīs of that land.[2]

In the history of Islamic thought the Mu'tazilites came to be known for five principles or affirmations (*al-uṣūl al-khamsah*), which in fact summarize their basic teachings. These are unity (*al-tawḥīd*), justice (*al-'adl*), the promise and the threat (*al-wa'd wa'l-wa'īd*), in-between position in relation to a Muslim who commits a sin (*al-manzilah bayn al-manzilatayn*), and exhorting to perform the good and forbidding to commit evil (*al-amr bi'l-ma'rūf wa'l-nahy 'an al-munkar*).

The Mu'tazilites possessed a rational concept of the unity of God, and as a result they emphasized God's transcendence in such a manner as to reduce God almost to an abstract idea. In an atmosphere in which a great deal of debate was taking place concerning the meaning of God's Attributes and Qualities as mentioned in the Quran, they sought to avoid all possible anthropomorphism. As a result, they claimed that man cannot understand the real meaning of such Divine Attributes as Hearing or Seeing and that such Attributes have no reality of their own. Rather, they are identical with the Divine Essence. They also denied the possibility of knowledge of God's Nature. In denying any reality to Attributes, the Mu'tazilites also denied the eternity of the Quran as the Word of God. This view became their most famous and contested thesis because of its sociopolitical implications.

The Mu'tazilites also emphasized justice to the extent that they became known as the "people of unity and justice." Justice for them meant that God, being All-Wise, must have a purpose in the creation of the universe and that there is objective justice and good and evil in God's creation even if one puts aside the teachings of the Divine Law (*al-Sharī'ah*) concerning good and evil. Because God is just and good and cannot go against His Nature, He must always act for the best and is just. Furthermore, God does not will evil. Rather, evil is created by human beings, who have been given by God the freedom to act in either a good or an evil manner. They are therefore responsible for their actions and will be rewarded or punished by God accordingly.

The third principle, *al-wa'd wa'l-wa'īd*, which means literally "promise and threat," refers to the ultimate fate of various classes of people, namely, the believers (*mu'minūn*), those who are nominally Muslims but who have committed sin (*fāsiqūn*) and those who are unbelievers (*kuffār*). The Mu'tazilites had a severe view of sin and condemned both sinners and infidels to the punishment of hell. For the Mu'tazilites, faith (*īmān*) was not only the assertion of the unity of

God and consent to the truth of religion with the heart. It was also the avoidance of any grievous sins.

A major problem that confronted the early Islamic community was the question of who was saved and who was a Muslim. Was the sole condition faith, or was it necessary also to practice the tenets of the religion and avoid what was forbidden by the *Sharī'ah*? Amid this debate, the Mu'tazilites had to express their position clearly, which they did in the fourth of their five principles, one that follows directly from the principle of promise and threat. Their "in-between" position for sinners, *al-manzilah bayn al-manzilatayn*, asserts that the Muslim sinner (*fāsiq*) occupies a position between the believer and the unbeliever and is still a member of the Islamic community in this world although condemned to damnation in the world to come.

Finally, the Mu'tazilites emphasized the principle of *al-amr bi'l-ma'rūf wa'l-nahy 'an al-munkar*. This well-known Islamic principle, emphasized also by several other schools, asserts that man not only must exhort others to perform the good but also must forbid people from committing evil. It implies an active attitude toward the establishment of a just religious order and a morality that is not simply a matter of private conscience but involves Islamic society as a whole.

The Mu'tazilites were the first group of Muslim thinkers to apply rational arguments systematically to various questions of religion and also to natural philosophy. They, moreover, knew some of the tenets of Greek thought, which was being translated into Arabic at the time of the peak of their intellectual activity in Baghdad in the third/ninth century and had a share in the introduction of Hellenic and Hellenistic thought into the Islamic intellectual world. Most of the Mu'tazilites devoted themselves to purely theological and politico-theological questions, and all were concerned with ethics. They in fact developed a "rational ethics," for which they became well known in later Islamic history.[3] A few were also interested in physics or natural philosophy, chief among them al-Naẓẓām, who developed the theory of leap (*ṭafrah*) to explain the possibility of motion over a space that is infinitely divisible. He is known also for the theory of latency and manifestation (*kumūn wa burūz*), according to which God created everything at once in a state of latency and then gradually various forms from minerals to animals became actualized or manifested. Abū'l-Hudhayl al-'Allāf developed the theory of atomism, which later became central in Ash'arite theology. It is above all for the development of a rational theology that the Mu'tazilites are known in the history of Islamic thought. In this way, they influenced not only later Sunni theological thought but also Shi'ite thought and Islamic philosophy. Furthermore, they provided the theological atmosphere in which early Islamic philosophy was developed.

AL-ASH'ARĪ AND EARLY ASH'ARISM

During the third/ninth century, following Maʾmūn's policy of making Mu'tazilism compulsory and introducing a test of faith in these doctrines (*miḥnah*), a strong reaction set in against the "rationalist" *kalām* of the Mu'tazilites. The strict followers of the *Ḥadīth* and the jurisprudents (*fuqahāʾ*), especially the followers of Imam Aḥmad ibn Ḥanbal, opposed all rational proofs of the tenets of the faith. Muslims were asked to accept the doctrines of the faith without asking how (*bilā kayfa*), but this extreme reaction against the rationalist tendencies of the Mu'tazilite *kalām* could not last indefinitely. The emphasis of the Quran on the use of the intellect (*al-'aql*) necessitated the creation of a theology that would use rational arguments and be at the same time orthodox and acceptable to the Islamic community at large. It was to this task that Abūʾl-Ḥasan al-Ash'arī addressed himself, founding a new theological school that became the most widespread in the Sunni world. This school has come to be known in the West as that of orthodox theology, although the term *orthodox* in Islam has levels and nuances of meaning beyond the confines of Ash'arism.

Abūʾl-Ḥasan al-Ash'arī was born in Basra around 260/873 and died in Baghdad around 330/941. During his younger days, he was a student of the famous Basrean Mu'tazilite al-Jubbāʾī, but at the age of forty, possibly as the result of a dream of the Prophet, he turned against Mu'tazilite teachings and sought to return to the authentic teachings of the Quran. He went to the mosque of Basra and stated:

> He who knows me, knows who I am, and he who does not know me, let him know that I am Abūʾl-Ḥasan al-Ash'arī, that I used to maintain that the Quran is created, that eyes of men shall not see God, and that the creatures create their actions. Lo! I repent that I have been a Mu'tazilite. I renounce these opinions and I take the engagement to refute the Mu'tazilites and expose their infancy and turpitude.[4]

Following this public statement made at the age of forty, al-Ash'arī set out to develop a theology that used reason in the defense of the tenets of the faith and yet remained loyal to the dicta of revelation while making use of dialectic. He composed more than ninety works, many of which have survived. Among the most famous are *al-Ibānah 'an uṣūl al-diyānah* (Elucidation concerning the Principles of Religion), in which he sought to draw to his side the extreme "traditionalists," who were opposed to the use of dialectic in matters of religion; *Kitāb al-luma'* (The Book of Light), which contains the principles of Ash'arite *kalām*; and *Maqālāt al-islāmiyyīn* (Doctrines of the Muslims), a later work, which sets out to describe the views of various theological schools and sects.[5]

Al-Ash'arī sought to charter an intermediate course between two extremes: that of Mu'tazilite rationalists, who made revelation subservient to reason, and that of "externalists" of different persuasions, who rejected the role of reason completely and remained satisfied with the purely external meaning of the verses of the Quran and the teachings of the *Ḥadīth*. One of the great Ash'arite theologians of later centuries, al-Juwaynī, stated in fact that al- Ash'arī was not really a theologian (*mutakallim*) but a reconciler of the two extreme views prevalent in Islamic society at his time.

To combat the extreme views of the day, al-Ash'arī held, against the view of the Mu'tazilites, that the Divine Attributes were real but added that they were not like human attributes as claimed by the anthropomorphists. He believed that on the Day of Judgment man could see God, but without there being an incarnation (*ḥulūl*) of God in a human or nonhuman form. He believed that the Quran was uncreated and eternal, yet its ink and paper, individual letters and words were created. Again in contrast to the Mu'tazilites and their extreme opponents on this matter (the Murji'ites), al-Ash'arī believed that the Muslim who sins is in God's Hands and can be forgiven by God and go to paradise, or he can be punished in hell for a temporary period. Also against the view of Mu'tazilites, who believed that the Prophet could not intercede for Muslims before God, and the extreme Shi'ites, who believed that the Prophet and 'Alī could intercede for Muslims on their own, al-Ash'arī held that the Prophet could intercede on behalf of a sinner but with God's permission.

Altogether, al-Ash'arī sought to create a moderate position in nearly all the theological issues that were being debated at that time. He made reason subservient to revelation and negated the free will of man in favor of a voluntarism that deprives man of his creative free will and emphasizes the omnipotence of God in a way that according to many schools goes beyond even the text of the Quran. In the Sacred Book, on the one hand, God's omnipotence and omniscience are constantly emphasized, and, on the other, human beings are held responsible for their actions. In emphasizing the doctrine of voluntarism, al-Ash'arī in a sense reduced the Divine Nature to the Divine Will and conceived of God as an All-Powerful Will rather than the Supreme Reality, which is and also wills.[6]

Ash'arism is concerned not only with specifically religious issues but also with epistemology and the philosophy of nature. The most salient feature of Ash'arism in this domain is the justly famous atomism, which has also come to be known as occasionalism, a doctrine that was refuted explicitly by St. Thomas Aquinas.[7] Developed mostly by his student Abū Bakr al-Bāqillānī, who was the most important of the early Ash'arites after the founder of the school, this thoroughgoing atomism takes away from the created world and all things in it their specific nature. All things are composed of atoms (*juzʾ lā yatajazzā*, literally, the "part that cannot be further divided"), which are themselves without extension. Space is likewise composed of discontinuous points, and time of discontinuous moments. There is no horizontal causality. Fire does not burn because it is in its nature to do so but because God has willed it. Tomorrow He could will otherwise, and as a result fire would cease to burn. There is no such thing as the nature of fire. What in fact appears to us as cause and effect—for example, fire causing a piece of cotton to burn—is nothing but a habit of the mind (*'ādah*), because we have seen fire being brought near a piece of cotton and the cotton then burning in flames.[8] God is in reality the only cause; it is His Will that makes fire burn the cotton. Miracles are in fact nothing other than the breaking of this habit of mind (literally, "*khāriq al-'ādah*," which is one of the Arabic terms for miracles).

Ash'arism dissolves all horizontal causes into the vertical cause, which is God's Will. It thereby reduces the whole universe to a number of atoms moving in a discontinuous time and space in a world where nothing possesses any specific nature. No wonder then that Ash'arism was strongly opposed to Islamic philosophy, which sought to know the cause of things leading finally to the Ultimate Cause. Ash'arism did not contribute to the flowering of Islamic science, because most Islamic scientists were also philosophers, and very few were *mutakallim* or Ash'arite theologians. Moreover, as we have seen, Ash'arism remained an opponent of *falsafah* over the centuries.

Māturīdism and Ṭaḥāwism

Several other contemporaries of al-Ash'arī sought, like him, to formulate a theology that would be acceptable to the majority of Muslims, among them Abū Ja'far al-Ṭaḥāwī from Egypt (d. 321/933) and Abū Manṣūr al-Māturīdī (d. 337/944) from what is now known as Central Asia. The former was a great scholar of *Ḥadīth* and *fiqh* and developed a more "dogmatic" theology. The latter was given more to "speculative" theology; both were Ḥanafīs and sought to follow the theological as well as juridical views of Imam Abū Ḥanīfah. This is especially true of al-Ṭaḥāwī, whose theology is in reality another version of the theological thought of Imam Abū Ḥanīfah. Al-Māturīdī held a position in many ways close to that of al-Ash'arī but with more importance placed on reason than his contemporary would allow. For example, he considered it incumbent upon all human beings to seek to know God whether they followed the Divine Law or not, whereas al-Ash'arī believed that it was as a result of following the injunctions of the *Sharī'ah* that man was required to seek to know God. For a whole century, Ash'arism remained popular only among the Shāfiʿīs, while Māturīdism and to some extent Ṭaḥāwism held sway among the Ḥanāfīs. But finally Ash'arism triumphed over its rivals, mostly thanks to the work of the later Ash'arites, especially al-Ghazzālī, although not all the theological works of al-Ghazzālī can be considered as Ash'arite. It became widespread in Persia and other eastern lands of the Islamic world as well as in the Maghrib, where Ash'arite teachings became influential under the Almohads, whose founder, Ibn Tūmart, was a disciple of al-Ghazzālī.

Later Ash'arism

It was the later Ash'arites or the people whom Ibn Khaldūn called the "theologians of the *via nova*,"[9] who opened a new chapter in the history of *kalām* and made possible its spread throughout the Islamic world. These "later theologians" (*muta'akhirrūn*) include Imām al-Ḥaramayn al-Juwaynī (d. 478/1085), the author of the classical work of Ash'arism, *Kitāb al-irshād* (The Book of Guidance); his student Abū Ḥāmid Muḥammad al-Ghazzālī (d. 505/1111), the most celebrated of all Muslim theologians and an outstanding figure in the history of Sufism, who wrote numerous theological works, especially *al-Iqtiṣād fi'l-i'tiqād* (The Just Mean in Belief), which is of a more specifically Ash'arite nature than his other works; and Abū'l-Fatḥ al-Shahrastānī (d. 548/1153), the author of *Nihāyat al-iqdām* (The Extremity of Action or Summa Philosophiae), who as we have already mentioned also had Ismā'īlī tendencies. This later Ash'arism, which became more and more philosophical during later centuries, reached the peak of its development through Fakhr al-Dīn al-Rāzī (d. 606/1209), perhaps the most learned of all Ash'arite theologians,[10] with the *Sharḥ al-mawāqif* ("Commentary upon the Stations"), the commentary being by Mīr Sayyid Sharīf al-Jurjānī (d. 816/1413) and the text by 'Aḍūd al-Dīn al-Ījī (d. 756/1355). This work, which marks the peak of philosophical *kalām*, is taught to this day in such centers of Islamic learning as al-Azhar, along with the works of Sa'd al-Dīn al-Taftāzānī (d. 791/1389), who represented a competing school of *kalām* that was more opposed to Islamic philosophy while seeking itself to deal with the issues of philosophy.

There were other notable Ash'arite theologians of the later period, for example, Muḥammad al-Sanūsī (d. ca. 895/1490), whose short "creed," *al-Sanūsiyyah*, is popular to this day; Jalāl al-Dīn Dawānī (d. 907/1501), at once theologian and philosopher, who is said to have embraced Twelve-Imam Shi'ism toward the end of his life and whom we shall study more fully in chapter 11; and many other figures whose summaries and commentaries have been studied over the centuries. But the peak of this philosophical Ash'arite *kalām* was reached in the ninth/fifteenth century, and the later authors represent for the most part the continuation of the teachings of the earlier masters. The most important development in the later centuries was the wedding of Ash'arism and Sufism that is found among so many of the later Ash'arites, including al-Sanūsī and some of the Sufi theologians of India.

Kalām in the Modern World

Until the last century, many manuals of Ash'arite *kalām* continued to appear summarizing the earlier classics, for example, the manual *Jawharat al-tawḥīd* (The Substance of Unity) by the thirteenth/nineteenth century Egyptian scholar al-Bājūrī. But it was also at this time that a number of Sunni thinkers sought to inaugurate modernism in Islamic thought and some sought to resuscitate *kalām* as a way of reviving Islamic religious thought. Foremost among these modern scholars of *kalām* was Muḥammad 'Abduh (d. 1323/1905), who in his *Risālat al-tawḥīd* (The Treatise of Unity) delineated the "new theology," which paid greater attention to the use of reason and revived certain Mu'tazilite theses. His path was followed by several later Egyptian scholars, including the early fourteenth/twentieth-century figure Shaykh Muṣṭafā 'Abd al-Rāziq (d. 1366/1947), who, like 'Abduh, became a rector of al-Azhar University. Similar attempts to formulate a modern *kalām* were carried out in India by such well-known modernist thinkers as Sayyid Aḥmad Khān (d. 1316/1898) and Syed Ameer

Alī (d. 1347/1928). Even Muḥammad Iqbāl (d. 1337/1938), although more a philosopher than a *mutakallim*, could be included in this group if one considers his *Reconstruction of Religious Thought in Islam*. To what extent these and similar works reflect traditional Islamic intellectuality and spirituality is another matter. Whatever one's view might be of these tendencies, one can say with certitude that they reflect more the concern for an apologetic defense of Islam and the accommodation of modernity than the preservation of traditional Islamic intellectual life.

THE MESSAGE OF ASH'ARISM

When one ponders the message of Ash'arism and its philosophical and spiritual significance, one becomes aware of the central concern of this school to bring the reality of God into the everyday world by making intelligence subservient to the Will of God. It therefore corresponds to a possibility that was bound to manifest itself in a world dominated by the reality of prophecy as we also see in traditional Jewish and Christian thought. Ash'arism also envisages man as a being who is in obedience to God because his being is determined by God, not as a being who is free with a freedom that is of necessity granted to him by God by virtue of his being created in "His form" and as a creature who is the central reflection of God's Names and Qualities. In a similar manner Ash'arism takes away from the intellect its function of being able to know God and His revelation starting with the freedom and independence of the human agent.

> Omnipotentialism [of the Ash'arite school], which in practice denies the human mind all capacity to understand Divine motives, and which refers our intelligence to Revelation alone, has the function of suggesting that it is "God alone who knows," but it does this arbitrarily *ab extra* and forgets that, if it is indeed God who is always the thinker, then He is also the thinker in us and in pure intellection or inspiration. . . . But Ash'arism thinks only of one thing: to make the immensity of God concretely present in the world; and it is perfectly realistic in its presentiment that for the average man, the acceptance of higher truths passes through the will and not through the Intellect, and that consequently it is the will that must receive the shock; this shock, both crushing and sacramental, is provided precisely by all but blind omnipotentialism.[11]

Ash'arite voluntarism or omnipotentialism possesses a positive aspect, although against the reality of human intelligence and freedom and impervious to God's Nature, which is Pure Goodness, while accentuating His will. It emphasizes the presence of God in the day-to-day life of man and the assertion of His Will in the running of the world that surrounds man. To achieve this end fully, the Ash'arites posited the previously mentioned atomism or occasionalism, which reduces the reality of the phenomenal world to disconnected units and holds that the world is annihilated and recreated at every moment, thereby reasserting the dominance of God's Will over all things and at all moments. This atomistic doctrine, which stood opposed to the view of the Islamic metaphysicians, philosophers, and scientists, follows also a direction that is in a sense totally opposed to that of modern science, which since the Scientific Revolution has accepted atomism but only "horizontal" causes in the explanation of phenomena, denying all "vertical" causes. In contrast, Ash'arism denies all "horizontal" causes and helped to create an ambience in which a secular science such as that of the seventeenth century could not possibly have taken root.

> In summary, the purpose of this doctrine—or this atomism or occasionalism—is to remind us constantly that God is present and active in all things, and to suggest to us that this world here below would only be a discontinuous chaos were it not for the Divine Presence. Regarded in this way, Ash'arite atomism is a reminder of the Divine Presence, or an introduction of the transcendent—of the marvelous, one might say—into everyday life. Man must feel that faith is something other than ordinary logic and that it sees things in terms of God and not in terms of the world; and by this fact, the believer is himself not entirely of this world, his faith is not a "natural" thought, but a "supernatural" assent; what is divinely true seems absurd to unbelievers, who follow only an earth-bound process of thought. According to this perspective, the unbeliever thinks in a horizontal direction, whereas the believer thinks in a vertical and ascending direction, according to the "straight path"; and this divine transparency of earthly things—since the Divine Cause is everywhere and since it alone is really present—confers on faith a sort of concrete and sacramental mystery, in short, an element of the marvelous which makes of the believer a being marked by the super-natural.

> From the point of view of metaphysics, this is an unnecessary luxury, since the intellect has resources other than pious absurdity; but from the theological point of view it doubtless marks a victory. In a word, if unbelief in the form of atheistic scientism admits only physical causes and denies the transcendent causality which works in them, Ash'arism has replied in advance, and has done so radically, by denying physical causes; it is like a surgical operation or a preventive war. The Renaissance certainly could not have hatched in an Asharite climate.[12]

Ash'arite atomism also possesses a metaphysical significance beyond its immediate theological meaning. There is at once continuity and discontinuity between the Divine Principle and its manifestations. The Ash'arites emphasize this discontinuity, whereas the Islamic philosophers in general accentuate the continuity. This discontinuity is not only of cosmological significance. It also reflects, on the level of cosmic reality, the discontinuity between the Supreme Principle as Beyond-Being and Being as the immediate Principle of cosmic reality. Ash'arite atomism also echoes on the theological level a discontinuity or atomism that is to be seen in the Arabic language itself, in which one observes an intuitive leap from one idea to another or even from the subject to the predicate, whereas Indo-European languages possess a plasticity and continuous flow that is reflected also in the metaphysical expositions of people who think in such languages. A metaphysical treatise in Arabic by an Arab gnostic such as Ibn 'Arabī is like a series of discontinuous bolts of lightning striking a mountaintop, whereas—to use an example within the citadel of Islam—the Persian metaphysicians such as Mullā Ṣadrā present a more systematic and flowing exposition of metaphysics as if pouring honey from a jar.

It is remarkable that despite its "anti-intellectualism" Ash'arism not only became the prevalent *kalām* in the Sunni world, but also became combined in certain circumstances with Sufism, at whose heart lies the gnosis that is illuminative knowledge actualized with the help of revelation through the immanent intellect whose symbol is the heart. One need only think of al-Ghazzālī, who was more responsible than any other figure for the spread of Ash'arism beyond its early confines in the Arab East, although, as mentioned already, not all of his theological works are of an Ash'arite character. This great theologian was not only an eminent Sufi but also one who wrote many luminous pages concerning intellection through the heart and the cultivation of *al-ma'rifah* or Divine Knowledge. Many later Sufi figures, including several of the important authorities of North African, eastern Arabic, Turkish, and Indian Sufism, were to continue this wedding between Ash'arism and Sufism. Yet, many other Sufi masters and authorities of Islamic gnosis stood against Ash'arism and criticized its limitations severely, as did the Islamic philosophers, many of whom during later centuries did not believe that Ash'arism possessed the intellectual requirements necessary for dealing with the questions of God's Names and Qualities or other problems related to *theo-logia* in the original sense of this term. This is to be seen especially in Mullā Ṣadrā's attitude to *kalām* and has already been discussed in chapter 5.

Ash'arism, while not ceasing to oppose both the Islamic philosophers and certain types of Sufi metaphysics, nevertheless became itself more philosophical and turned to the basic philosophical and metaphysical issues dealt with by its adversaries. Its later treatises are concerned with such issues as being and nonbeing, necessity and contingency, the relation of the one to the many, substance and accidents—all of which were treated primarily by Islamic philosophers. Later Ash'arism also deals with the "science of God" (*ilāhiyyāt*), which is so amply treated in works of theoretical Sufism such as those of Ibn 'Arabī and Ṣadr al-Dīn al-Qunyawī, not to speak of the philosophers who used the term in their own way and identified it with metaphysics as expounded in their philosophical treatises. Ash'arism thus became one of several major schools of Islamic thought vying with the philosophers, on the one hand, and the theosophers and gnostics, who dealt with matters of more direct spiritual concern than the Ash'arites, on the other. In the final account Ash'arism provided a rational defense of the tenets of the faith and created a climate in which religious truths were real and the Will of God reigned supreme. For those who wanted to know God as well as obey His will, Ash'arism appeared either as an impediment as seen by most of the philosophers or, at best, the walls of the city of Divine Knowledge. It protected the city, but one had to pass beyond the wall in order to reach the treasures of the city itself, the city to which the Prophet referred when he said, "I am the city of knowledge and 'Alī is its gate."

Shi'ite *Kalām*

In addition to Sunni *kalām*, there developed in Islam other schools of *kalām* associated with the Ismā'īlīs and Twelve-Imam Shi'ites. As for the Zaydīs, the third school of Shi'ism, they adopted more or less

Mu'tazilite *kalām* as a result of which this form of *kalām* lasted in Yemen, the home of Zaydī Shi'ism, long after it had ceased to exist as a notable school of thought elsewhere in the Islamic world. Ismā'īlī thought, both philosophical and theological, developed early in the history of Islam, and the two remained close to each other. Some of the earlier Ismā'īlī thinkers, for example, Ḥamīd al-Dīn al-Kirmānī (d. ca. 408/1017) and Nāṣir-i Khusraw (d. between 465/1072 and 470/1077), were more philosophers than theologians. Others, including Abū Ḥatīm al-Rāzī (d. 322/933) and al-Mu'ayyid fi'l-Dīn al-Shīrāzī (d. 470/1077), were more theologians than philosophers. But both groups dealt with the major themes of Ismā'īlī thought, such as the meta-ontological status of the "unknowable" God or *Deus absconditus*, the inabililty of the intellect to know the Divine Essence, the illumination of the intellect by the Prophet and the Imams, the celestial archetype of Adam, the relation between the function of prophecy (*nubuwwah*) and initiatic power (*walāyah/wilayah*), and esoteric hermeneutics (*ta'wīl*).[13]

Twelve-Imam Shi'ite *kalām*, however, developed much later. The early concern of Twelve-Imam Shi'ite thinkers was mostly *Ḥadīth*, Quranic commentary, and jurisprudence, although earlier Shi'ite thinkers, including Shaykh al-Mufīd (d. 413/1022), must also be considered as theologians. It was, however, only in the seventh/thirteenth century that the first systematic treatise on Twelve-Imam Shi'ite *kalām* was written by none other than the celebrated mathematician and philosopher Nāṣir al-Dīn al-Ṭūsī (d. 672/1273). This is probably the only instance in history in which the major theological text of a religious community was composed by a scientist of the order of Nāṣir al-Dīn. The work of Ṭūsī entitled *Tajrīd al-i'tiqād* (Catharsis of Doctrines) became rapidly the standard theological text, and more than a hundred commentaries came to be written on it before this century. Perhaps the most notable commentary is the *Kashf al-murād* (The Unveiling of the Desired) by 'Allamāh Jamāl al-Dīn al-Ḥillī (d. 726/1326), who is the most notable Shi'ite *mutakallim* after Ṭūsī.

In studying this major opus, one can see clearly how Twelve-Imam Shi'ite *kalām* differs in its concerns from early Ash'arism. The work begins with a discussion of being and nonbeing and modes and grades of being. It develops an elaborate ontology that reminds one more of the ontology of Ibn Sīnā than the atomism of al-Ash'arī.[14] The work then proceeds to a discussion of quiddity or essence, which complements that of existence. Finally, the first section of the work turns to the relation between cause and effect and the discussion of causality in general. Again, in this basic issue, the work confirms the reality of horizontal causality in direct opposition to the Ash'arite view.

The second section (*maqṣad*) of the book turns to the discussion of substance and accidents. Once again in contrast to Ash'arism, the *Tajrīd* rejects all forms of atomism and asserts along with Ibn Sīnā that a body can be divided *ad infinitum* potentially but that such a division can never be actualized. Ṭūsī also confirms the reality of substances that are free of all potentiality and entanglement in matter and are immortal. These substances include both the intellect (*al-'aql*) and the human soul (*nafs*), which for Shi'ite *kalām* is an immortal substance and not a perishable configuration of atoms as in Ash'arism. Ash'arism does not accept a reality for the soul independent of the body but believes that the soul is recreated by God at the Day of Judgment along with the resurrection of the body.

It is only in the third *maqṣad* that Ṭūsī turns to theology properly speaking, in contrast to general metaphysics, with which he is occupied in the first two sections of the book. In the third, fourth, and fifth sections, he turns to God, prophecy, and imamology, respectively, dealing with general Islamic doctrines first and turning to the specifically Shi'ite doctrines concerning the Imam only in the fifth *maqṣad*. Finally, in the sixth and last section, he turns to questions of eschatology (*al-ma'ād*), explaining both the metaphysical and theological meaning of general Islamic eschatological doctrines and the theological meaning of specific Islamic images and symbols used in the explanation of complex posthumous realities. This manner of treating theological subjects became a model for many a later treatise, and many theologians and philosophers began to distinguish between *al-ilāhiyyat bi ma'na'l-'āmm* (metaphysics in its general sense, corresponding to the first two sections of Ṭūsī's work) and *al-ilāhiyyat bi ma'na'l-khāṣṣ* (theology dealing with the nature of God, prophecy, and other specifically religious issues).[15]

From the time of Ṭūsī to the Safavid period in the tenth/sixteenth century, a number of Shi'ite scholars of *kalām* appeared, some of whom, like Sayyid Ḥaydar Āmulī (d. after 787/1385), were also Sufis. Others, including Jalāl al-Dīn Dawānī, who was first a Sunni theologian and later turned to Shi'ism, and as we shall see later, were at once theologians and philosophers. During the Safavid period, Islamic philosophy associated with the School of Isfahan eclipsed *kalām*. But as we have already discussed, strangely enough, during the latter part of Safavid rule, the most famous students of the greatest of Safavid philosophers, Ṣadr al-Dīn Shīrāzī, Mullā Muḥsin Fayḍ Kāshānī (d. 1091/1680) and 'Abd al-Razzāq Lāhījī (d. 1071/1660)—were more scholars of *kalām* and other religious sciences than philosophers. This is especially true of Lāhījī who has already been mentioned. This tradition became mostly eclipsed in the Qajar period, and the main arena of Shi'ite thought became dominated more by philosophy or theosophy (*ḥikmah*), on the one hand, and the science of the principles of jurisprudence (*'ilm al-uṣūl*), on the other—not to speak of jurisprudence itself. To understand fully later Shi'ite *kalām*, it is necessary to turn not only to texts of *kalām* following the tradition of Ṭūsī, but also to those major works of theosophy (*al-ḥikmat al-ilāhiyyah*) that deal with all the traditional problems of *kalām* and claim to possess the intellectual means necessary to deal with these problems more than did the *mutakallimūn* themselves, while masters of this school refused to use the term *kalām* for their teachings.

Islamic Philosophy

It is in this religious and intellectual climate dominated to some extent by *kalām*, especially Ash'arism, and also impregnated by Sufism that Islamic philosophy flourished over the centuries. Both *kalām* and Sufism were of course directly related to the reality of revelation and prophecy. The first sought to preserve the citadel of faith and use rational arguments for the defense of the revelation. The second sought to reach the inner meaning of the revelation and attain that principial knowledge or *ma'rifah* that resides at the heart of Islam. The first challenged the unbridled use of *'aql* and sought to make it subservient to the revelation, and the second, especially in its more sapiental aspects, sought to illuminate the mind with the help of the light of God and the angelic and intelligible agents and to activate the heart/intellect as the organ for the attainment of supreme knowledge. Islamic philosophy followed its own history but in continuous reaction to and interaction with both *kalām* and Sufism in addition to certain aspects of the *Sharī'ah* and other religious sciences.

Over the centuries there appeared some Islamic philosophers opposed to *kalām* and some impervious to Sufism. There also appeared Islamic philosophers who were also scholars of *kalām*. Furthermore, there were many Islamic philosophers, especially of the later centuries, who were deeply imbued with the teachings of Sufism, especially its doctrinal and metaphysical formulations in the hands of Ibn 'Arabī and his students. These latter teachings in fact swept over the Islamic world as a whole from the seventh/thirteenth century onward, and it would not be an exaggeration to say that Ibn 'Arabī is the most influential intellectual figure in the Islamic world during the past seven centuries, if the whole of that world is considered. In any case *kalām* and spirituality in its intellectual mode are the other main dimensions of the Islamic intellectual tradition with which Islamic philosophy interacted in the most profound way possible. This philosophical tradition remained authentically philosophical while functioning in an intellectual universe dominated by the reality of prophecy, which made other intellectual dimensions such as *kalām* and doctrinal Sufism possible as well as also making possible the development of Islamic philosophy itself with all its distinct characteristics and attributes.

Early Peripatetic (*Mashshāʾī*) Philosophy

The best-known school of Islamic philosophy, the *mashshāʾī* or Peripatetic, which is a synthesis of the tenets of the Islamic revelation, Aristotelianism, and Neoplatonism of both the Athenian and Alexandrian schools, was founded in the third/ninth century in the rich intellectual climate of Baghdad by Abū Yaʿqūb al-Kindī (d. ca. 260/873).[16] The so-called philosopher of the Arabs was a prolific author who composed over two hundred treatises, in which he dealt with the sciences as well as philosophy, beginning a trend that characterizes the whole class of Muslim sages who were philosopher-scientists and not only philosophers.[17] His main concern was the discovery of the truth wherever it might be found. In a famous statement that has been repeated often over the centuries and characterizes all Islamic philosophy, he said: "We should not be ashamed to acknowledge truth and to assimilate it from whatever source it comes to us, even if it is brought to us by former generations and foreign peoples. For him who seeks the truth there is nothing of higher value than truth itself; it never cheapens or abases him who reaches for it, but ennobles and honours him."[18]

It was this universal conception of truth that has always characterized Islamic philosophy—a truth, however, that is not bound by the limits of reason. Rather, it is the illimitable Truth reached by the intellect that al-Kindī, like other Islamic philosophers, distinguished clearly from reason as the analytical faculty of the mind as discussed in chapter 6 of this work. This intellect is like an instrument of inner revelation for which the macrocosmic revelation provides an objective cadre.[19] The Islamic philosophers considered the call of the truth to be the highest call of philosophy, but this did not mean the subservience of revelation to reason, as some have contended. Rather, it meant to reach the truth at the heart of revelation through the use of the intellect, which, in its macrocosmic manifestation usually identified with the archangel of revelation, Gabriel, is the instrument of revelation itself. The treatise of al-Kindī on the intellect known as *De intellectu* in the Latin West points to the significance that the doctrine of the intellect was to have for later Islamic philosophers and even many Latin Scholastics.

Al-Kindī was also deeply interested in the relation between religion and philosophy or faith and reason. In his classification of the sciences, he sought to create harmony between divine and human knowledge[20] and wrote the first chapter in the long history of the relation between faith and reason that occupied nearly all Islamic philosophers for the next millennium. This was of course a necessary consequence of philosophy functioning in the land of prophecy, and we see similar concerns among Jewish and Christian philosophers. Al-Kindī also helped create the Arabic philosophical terminology that soon became a powerful vehicle for the expression of Islamic philosophy. Much of the translation of Greek philosophical works was made in Baghdad during his lifetime. He knew in fact some of the translators, and it is said that the summary of the *Enneads* of Plotinus, which came to be known to Muslims as the *Theology of Aristotle*, was translated for him by Ibn al-Nā'imah al-Ḥimsī. In any case, one of the major achievements of al-Kindī was the molding of the Arabic language as a vehicle for the expression of philosophy, as one sees in his celebrated treatise *Fiʾl-falsafat al-ūlā* (On Metaphysics). Although some of the terminology used by him was rejected by later philosophers writing in Arabic,[21] he remained a pioneer in the creation of Arabic philosophic vocabulary and the father of Islamic philosophy. He was the first devout Muslim who knew Greco-Alexandrian philosophy well and sought to create a philosophical system in which this philosophy was integrated into the Islamic worldview with its emphasis on the unity of God and the reality of revelation.

Al-Kindī's immediate students were mostly scientists, although some of them such as Aḥmad ibn Ṭayyib al-Sarakhsī are of philosophical interest, and his real successor as the next major figure in early *mashshāʾī* philosophy did not appear until a generation later in Khurasan. He was Abū Naṣr al-Fārābī (d. 339/ 950), who was born and raised in Farab in Central Asia in a family of Turkish background living within a Persian cultural milieu. He was already a famous philosopher when he came to Baghdad for a short period at midlife only to migrate once again westward to settle in Damascus, where he spent the rest of his life. At once a logician and musician, metaphysician and political thinker, al-Fārābī formulated *mashshāʾī*, a philosophy in the form it was to take in later Islamic history.

Al-Fārābī was attracted to the spiritual life from an early age and was a practicing Sufi. He was also one of the greatest theoreticians of music in Islam and a composer, some of whose compositions can still be heard in the repertory of Sufi music in India and Anatolia. Yet, he was an acute logician who commented on all the logical works of Aristotle. He also composed *Fi iḥṣāʾ al-'ulūm* (On the Enumeration of the Sciences), which classified and categorized the sciences and left a deep impact on later Islamic thought.[22] It was entitled *De Scientiis* in the West. Al-Fārābī in fact came to be known as the "Second Teacher" (*al-mu'allim al-thānī*) not because he taught philosophy or the sciences but because he was the first to enumerate and delineate clearly the sciences in the context of Islamic civilization, as Aristotle, the "First Teacher," had done for the Greek sciences.[23]

Al-Fārābī knew Aristotle well and in fact wrote commentaries not only on the Stagirite's logical writings but also on his cosmological and metaphysical works. Al-Fārābī's commentary on the *Metaphysics* exercised a great influence on Ibn Sīnā. But al-Fārābī was not interested so much in pure Aristotelianism as in synthesizing the teachings of Aristotle and Plato and the Neoplatonists within the universal perspective of Islam. This intellectual effort is seen most of all in his *Kitāb al-Jam' bayn raʾyay al-ḥakīmayn Aflāṭūn al-ilāhī wa Arisṭū* (The Book of Accord between the Ideas of the Divine Plato and Aristotle). This work did not prevent him, however, from writing separate treatises on the philosophy of Plato and Aristotle without seeking to synthesize their views.

Al-Fārābī was also the founder of Islamic political philosophy in which he sought to harmonize the idea of the philosopher-king of Plato with the idea of the prophet in monotheistic traditions. His definitive masterpiece, *Kitāb ārāʾ ahl al-madīnat al-faḍīlah* (The Book of the Opinions of the Citizens of the Virtuous City), influenced not only later political philosophical thinkers such as Ibn Rushd but the *mutakillimūn* as well. This major opus, which reflects so clearly the concerns of a philosophy functioning in a world dominated by the reality of prophecy, was supplemented by several works on practical philosophy and ethics, including *Kitāb taḥṣīl al-sa'ādah* (The Book of the Attainment of Happiness), which established al-Fārābī once and for all as a prime authority in this domain of philosophy in Islam.

From the spiritual point of view, the *Fuṣūṣ al-ḥikmah* (Bezels of Wisdom) of al-Fārābī, sometimes attributed to Ibn Sīnā, is of particular significance. Besides being rich in technical vocabulary,[24] this work represents the first important synthesis between speculative philosophy and gnosis in Islam. Many commentaries have been written on it, and it is taught to this day in Persia as a text of both philosophy and gnosis.[25] The work reflects the mind and soul of al-Fārābī, in whom critical philosophical analysis was combined with intellectual synthesis and in whose perspective both the musical and logical dimensions of reality were combined without any contradiction, both issuing from that *coincidentia oppositorum* that is realized in gnosis alone.

Al-Fārābī's most famous immediate student was Yaḥyā ibn 'Adī, a Christian theologian,[26] but his real successor in the field of Islamic philosophy was Abū 'Alī Sīnā (the Latin Avicenna), who lived two generations after him. Between these two giants of Islamic thought there stand a number of figures who are of some importance in the development of *mashshā'ī* philosophy. In Baghdad, the imposing figure was Yaḥyā ibn 'Adī's student Abū Sulaymān al-Sijistānī (d. 371/981), who was most of all a logician. As already mentioned his circle drew to itself philosophers as well as men of letters such as Abū Ḥayyān al-Tawḥīdī (d. 399/1009).[27] Meanwhile the locus of philosophical activity was shifting to an ever greater degree to Khurasan, where the most significant figure preceding Ibn Sīnā was Abū'l-Ḥasan al-'Āmirī (d. 381/992), known for his works on ethics as well as the philosophical defense of Islam, particularly in his *al-I'lām bi-manāqib al-islām* (Declaration of the Virtues of Islam), which is unique in *mashshā'ī* literature for its manner of defense of the Islamic religion.

Al-'Āmirī trained a number of scholars and philosophers, including Ibn Muskūyah (usually pronounced Miskawayh) (d. 421/1030),[28] known especially for his major work on philosophical ethics, the *Tadhhīb al-akhlāq* (Purification of Morals) and a doxography entitled *Jawīdān-khirad* in Persian or *al-Ḥikmat al-khālidah* in Arabic (Eternal Wisdom or *Philosophia Perennis*). This book marks a genre of philosophical writing in which sayings of sages of antiquity—not only Greek but also Indian and Persian—were assembled to point to the permanence and universality of the truth asserted in its final form in the Islamic revelation and developed by Islamic philosophers. This type of writing continued during later centuries with such figures as Ibn al-Fātik, who lived in Egypt in the fifth/eleventh century, Shams al-Dīn Shahrazūrī (d. ca. 680/1281), who was a commentator of Suhrawardī, and the Safavid philosopher Quṭb al-Dīn Ashkiwarī and pointed to the significance of the idea of the *philosophia perennis* among Islamic philosophers long before Steuco and Leibnitz wrote of it and made it famous in the West.[29]

Islamic Peripatetic or *mashshā'ī* philosophy reached its peak with Ibn Sīnā, who is perhaps the greatest and certainly the most influential Islamic philosopher and in a sense the father of specifically medieval philosophy to the extent that this philosophy is concerned basically with being. This incredible intellectual figure, who was at once a philosopher and the most famous physician of the period the West calls the "Middle Ages," was a Persian born in Bukhara in 370/980. He wandered most of his life in various Persian cities, especially Rayy, Isfahan, and Hamadan, and finally died from colic in the latter city in 428/1037 before reaching old age.[30] Despite a tumultuous life marked by externally unsettled conditions in Persia, Ibn Sīnā composed more than two hundred works, including the monumental *Kitāb al-shifāʾ*, which is an encyclopedia of Peripatetic philosophy and science. He also wrote *al-Qānūn fiʾl-ṭibb* (The Canon of Medicine), which is the most celebrated single work in the history of medicine. We have already cited some of his other works and need to recall here only a number of visionary recitals from his pen that concern his "Oriental Philosophy."

In his *mashshā'ī* works crowned by the *Shifāʾ*, Ibn Sīnā created that final synthesis of Aristotelian and Neoplatonic philosophy in the framework of Islam that became a permanent intellectual dimension in the Islamic world and survives as a living philosophical school to this day. Toward the end of his life, however, he criticized *mashshāʾī* philosophy, including his own as being the common philosophy meant for everyone, while pointing to the philosophy that he considered to be for the intellectual elite, which he called "Oriental Philosophy" (*al-ḥikmat al-mashriqiyyah*).[31] This philosophy is oriental because it is related to the world of light and not because of the geographic Orient. It is based on the illumination of the soul as well as ratiocination and sees the cosmos as a crypt through which the true philosopher must journey with the help of the guide, who is none other than the Divine Intellect. The language of this philosophy is eminently symbolic rather than discursive. It points to a path that was to be followed fully and to its ultimate end a century and a half after Ibn Sīnā by the founder of the school of Illumination (*al-ishrāq*), Shihāb al-Dīn Suhrawardī. Ibn Sīnā was therefore at once the elaborator of the most complete and enduring version of *mashshāʾī* philosophy and the guide to the threshold of that philosophy or theosophy of illumination, which marked the indissoluble union between philosophy and spirituality.

After Ibn Sīnā, *mashshāʾī* philosophy became temporarily eclipsed in the eastern lands of Islam as a result of the attacks of Ash'arism against it. Journeying to the western lands of Islam, it experienced a period of marked activity. Some of the students of Ibn Sīnā such as Bahmanyār ibn Marzbān (d. 458/1066), the author of *Kitāb al-taḥṣīl* (The Book of Attainment), continued the teachings of the master well into the fifth/eleventh century. Moreover, the few important philosophers of the sixth/twefth century, such as Abūʾl-Barakāt al-Baghdādī (d. ca. 560/1164), whose *Kitāb al-muʿtabar* (The Book of What Is Established by Personal Reflection) contains important ideas in the domain of physics as well as epistemology, and ʿUmar Khayyām (d. ca. 526/1132), at once poet, metaphysician, and mathematician, were deeply influenced by and indebted to Ibn Sīnā .[32]

Avicennan Ontology and Cosmology

The philosophy of Ibn Sīnā, which marks the peak of Islamic Peripatetic philosophy, is based on ontology, as mentioned in chapter 5, and Ibn Sīnā has been called the "philosopher of being" and the founder of what is characteristically medieval philosophy whether it be Jewish, Christian, or Islamic.[33] Here we wish to elucidate further his basic ontological ideas which were treated from another perspective in chapter 4. For Aristotle, existence is a "block without fissure," whereas for the Islamic philosophers, God is Pure Being and transcends the chain of being and the order of cosmic existence, while the existence of the world is contingent. To distinguish Pure Being from the existence of the world, Ibn Sīnā made the fundamental distinctions among necessity (*wujūb*), contingency (*imkān*), and impossibility (*imtināʿ*). The Necessary Being is that reality that must be and cannot not be, the reality whose nonexistence would imply logical contradiction. There is only one such reality, and that is the Necessary Being (*wājib al-wujūd*), which is the God revealed in monotheistic religions. Impossible being (*mumtaniʿ al-wujūd*) is that quiddity which cannot exist objectively, for that would imply contradiction. All beings apart from the Necessary Being are contingent beings (*mumkin al-wujūd*); considered as quiddities that could exist or not exist. This key distinction is one of the most fundamental in the whole history of philosophy. It influenced deeply all later Islamic philosophy and even theology. It also traveled to the West to become one of the key concepts of philosophy. This key distinction was itself related to the basic distinction between existence (*wujūd*) and quiddity (*māhiyyah*), discussed extensively in chapter 4.[34]

The contemplation by the Necessary Being of Itself generates the First Intellect; and the First Intellect's contemplation of the Necessary Being as well as of itself as contingent being and as necessitated by the Necessary Being (*al-wājib biʾl-ghayr*) leads to the generation of the Second Intellect, the Soul of the First Sphere, and the First Sphere. The process continues in this manner until the Tenth Intellect and the Ninth Sphere and its Soul are generated. This Ninth Sphere is the sphere of the Moon in accordance with the nine heavens of Ptolemaic astronomy as modified by Muslim astronomers. Below that level stand the spheres of the four elements governed by the Tenth Intellect, which is the "giver of forms" (*wāhib al-ṣuwar*) for all the existents in the sublunar region.[35] The sublunar region is also organized in a hierarchical order consisting of the three kingdoms crowned by man, who represents the point of return to the Origin. By means of knowledge, he can ascend through the levels of cosmic manifestation to gain union with the Active Intellect (*al-'aql al-fa''āl*). His mind ascends from the state of potentiality to actuality in which it becomes *intellectus in actu*.

The universe consists of a vast hierarchy beginning with the ten Intellects, which emanate from each other and ultimately from the Necessary Being. Below them stand the sublunar beings stretching from the *materia prima* to man, in whom the arc of ascent commences, terminating with the return to the purely intelligible world. The universe is generated through contemplation and returns to its origin through knowledge. The world is not created in time because time is a condition of the world, but it is not eternal in the sense that God is eternal. There is, rather, a basic distinction between the world and God, for God is the Necessary Being in need of nothing but Itself, and all existents are contingent in themselves, gain their existence from the Necessary Being, and remain in utter existential poverty in themselves. The Avicennan universe is one that preserves the transcendence of God through the radical distinction between necessity and contingency and at the same time emphasizes the emanation of the levels of cosmic existence from the Necessary Being as a result of the very nature of the Origin that generates the universe like the sun that radiates light by its very nature. Ibn Sīnā also accepts fully prophecy and seeks to explain it through his theory of the soul and the intellect.[36] Avicennan philosophy is a major expression of philosophy in the land of prophecy and has exercised wide influence over many other schools of philosophy in both East and West.

Some Independent Philosophers

Although Islamic philosophy developed for the most part in schools rather than being identified with individual philosophers as in the postmedieval West, there were some independent philosophers who cannot be classified as members of any of the major schools such as the Peripatetic, Ismā'īlī, or Illuminationist. Among these independent thinkers some such as Miskawayh, although possessing many independent features, were close to the *mashshāʾī* school. Others such as Abuʾl-Barakāt al-Baghdādī, although in many ways anti-Peripatetic, especially in the field of natural philosophy, sought to improve upon Ibn Sīnā's philosophy.[37] Yet others were completely independent. As mentioned in the last chapter of this group the most important are Muḥammad ibn Zakariyyāʾ al-Rāzī (the Latin Rhazes) and Abū Rayḥān al-Bīrūnī. Between these two colossal figures Rāzī is philosophically more important, while al-Bīrūnī is possibly the greatest scholar/scientist that Islamic civilization has produced. Before turning to Rāzī, however, a word must be said about two thinkers who are considered as epitomes of antiprophetic and antireligious thought in Islam and who antedated Rāzī. The first is Abū Isḥāq al-Warrāq, who lived in Baghdad in the beginning of the third/ninth century. Originally a Mu'tazilite theologian, he left the Mu'tazilite circle and was then accused of heresy, Manichaeanism, dualism, and even atheism. Since his works have been lost, we know him only through fragments of his writings quoted by others who were often his enemies. It is certain, however, that he had Shi'ite tendencies, and the accusations against him came from the Mu'tazilite camp, which he had abandoned. Certain later Shi'ite authorities such as the famous Safavid philosopher Mīr Dāmād even praised him. However, what is interesting is that because he was accused of the rejection of religion based on the Oneness of God, his many works, which some have considered to be as many as eighty, including a number of philosophical and theological works, were lost. This means that this kind of thought could not flourish in the climate where prophecy remained a central reality. We see the same situation in the case of the writings of Rāzī.

A second figure, Ibn al-Rāwandī, who lived in the second half of the third/ninth century and who was a student of al-Warrāq, has had the same reputation as his teacher as far as heretical antireligious ideas are concerned, although he harbored enmity against his teacher. Ibn al-Rāwandī was also originally a Mu'tazilite who left the school. It is said that as a result of becoming destitute and having to live in extreme poverty, he lost faith in God's justice and turned against religion. His *Kitāb al-zumurrud* (The Book of the Emerald), which rejected prophecy was later criticized strongly and refuted by the Ismā'īlī thinker al-Muʾayyad fiʾl-Dīn Shīrāzī. Throughout Islamic history his name has become, along with those of al-Warrāq and Rāzī, exemplary of thinkers and philosophers who lived in the land of prophecy but who did not heed its call and therefore cannot be properly called members of the Islamic philosophical tradition in its mainstream, although their ideas were debated by many later thinkers, this being especially true of Rāzī.

Let us now turn to Rāzī. It might seem strange to discuss Rāzī, a person who denied the necessity of prophecy, and who even wrote a work on the "tricks" of the prophets, in a book devoted to philosophy in the land of prophecy. But the study of the destiny of such an antiprophetic philosophy in a world dominated by prophecy is itself of much interest. Rāzī (d. 313/925 or 320/932) was born in Rayy and became celebrated as a physician, musician, and alchemist, as well as philosopher. He is in fact one of the greatest physicians of history who exercised immense influence upon both Islamic and Western medicine. As far as philosophy is concerned, however, he stood as a solitary figure criticized by many contemporary and later thinkers from the Ismā'īlī philosopher Abū Ḥātim al-Rāzī, who carried out polemics against him, to al-Bīrūnī, who admired him so much as a scientist that he prepared a catalog of his works while criticizing his religious and philosophical ideas.[38]

For reasons already mentioned in the case of al-Warrāq, most of al-Rāzī's philosophical writings have been lost. Some fragments have, however, survived in later works,[39] in addition to a few independent short treatises, chief among them *al-Sīrat al-falsafiyyah* (The Philosophical Way of Life) and *al-Ṭibb al-rūḥānī* (Spiritual Physick), which is related to both philosophy and medicine.

On the basis of these works one can draw a sketch of Rāzī's philosophical views, which were drawn not only from Greek but also possibly Persian and Indian sources, the latter perhaps through the influence of the enigmatic early philosopher Abū'l-'Abbās al-Īrānshahrī. In any case the type of atomism that he espoused as well as the "five preeternal principles" that constitute the foundation of his philosophy are very similar to the Nyāya-Vaiśeṣka school of Hindu philosophy.[40]

Al-Rāzī considered himself a completely independent thinker, although he showed much respect for Socrates and Plato but showed no use for prophecy and believed that God gives guidance to everyone.[41] He posited five "pre-eternal principles," God (or strictly speaking the Demiurge), Soul, matter, space, and time against the views of both Islamic theologians and philosophers. Also he believed in an atomism where atoms had dimensions but were physically indivisible in contrast to Mu'tazilite and Ash'arite theories of atomism. Also in contrast to Democritus, Rāzī was not a complete atomist because God and the Soul, which for him were preeternal principles, are not atoms. As for his ethics, although influenced by the *Timaeus* of Plato, upon which he wrote a commentary, Rāzī is closer to certain Epicurean theses in contrast to nearly all other Islamic philosophers.

Al- Rāzī was in fact an independent philosopher in two ways. He was independent of other schools of thought and also independent of the reality of prophecy. This latter position separated him from "prophetic philosophy" and the well known schools of Islamic philosophy that can be characterized as such. It even affected his study of alchemy in the deepest way. Alchemy is a symbolic science based on penetrating into the inner reality of both the soul and the cosmos. By rejecting prophecy, Rāzī also rejected *taʾwīl* or the hermeneutic interpretation of both the revealed and the cosmic book. The materials of alchemy thus became for him external substances, and he transformed alchemy into chemistry.[42] In any case, the figure of al-Rāzī is of much significance for the understanding of the intellectual climate dominated by the reality of prophecy and the types of thought that can blossom or wither away in such a climate. Al-Rāzī was venerated over the centuries as an outstanding physician and scientist, but as a philosopher, who was to a large extent an empiricist he had no followers, and his way of philosophical thinking could not generate a living current which could continue to bear fruit over the centuries.

Not all independent philosophers were, however, also independent of prophecy. A major case in point is Abū Rayḥān al-Bīrūnī. Perhaps the greatest Muslim scientist cum scholar that Islamic civilization has produced, as mentioned above, he admired Rāzī but opposed his "anti-prophetic" philosophy. Al-Bīrūnī did not write specifically philosophical treatises except for his exchange with Ibn Sīnā concerning natural philosophy[43] and sections of his unique work on Hinduism entitled *Taḥqīq mā liʾl-hind* (Investigations concerning India) which deal with philosophical issues and more especially the philosophy of religion. What is interesting in his case is that we find here an anti-Peripatetic philosophy that nevertheless displays a type of thought that was in accord with the reality of prophecy and demonstrates the diversity of philosophical views possible in the land of prophecy.[44]

Ismāʿīlī and Hermetico-Pythagorean Philosophy

During the early centuries of Islamic history, Islamic philosophy was not confined to the *mashshāʾī* school, which is the best known of the early schools and as already mentioned is usually considered to be synonymous with Islamic philosophy as such in most Western works on the history of Islamic philosophy and their imitations in Islamic languages. Even before al-Kindī, one can observe the beginning of

Ismā'īlī philosophy, that was to have a long and fecund history and that is of special interest in the relation between philosophy and prophecy. In this tradition, philosophy is identified with the inner truth of religion (*ḥaqīqah*) and possesses an esoteric character. As a result, Ismā'īlism became not only a congenial ground for the development of philosophy but also an impetus for the growth and cultivation of a distinct philosophical tradition, which, while dealing with basic Islamic themes such as unity (*al-tawḥīd*) and the reality of the Sacred Book, differed in many ways from Islamic Peripatetic philosophy.

The earliest text of this school dates back to the second/eighth century and is known as the *Umm al-kitāb* (The Archetypal Book). As mentioned in the last chapter it purports to be the record of a conversation held between Imam Muḥammad al-Bāqir (d. 115/733), the fifth Shi'ite Imam, and three of his disciples and reflects Shi'ite gnosis in its earliest forms of elaboration. The work emphasizes the esoteric science of letters (*al-jafr*) so prevalent in early Shi'ite circles and expounds a cosmology based on the number 5 and reminiscent of certain Manichaean cosmological schemes.

The systematic elaboration of Ismā'īlī philosophy came two centuries later with such figures as Abū Ya'qūb al-Sijistānī (d. sometime after 360/971), the author of the *Kashf al-maḥjūb* (Unveiling of the Veiled); Ḥamīd al-Dīn al-Kirmānī, whose *Rāḥat al-'aql* (Repose of the Intellect) is the most systematic work of this early school of Ismā'īlī philosophy; and the works of the greatest Ismā'īlī philosopher, Nāṣir-i Khusraw. This celebrated Persian poet and philosopher wrote all his major philosophical works in Persian rather than Arabic.[45] His most important opus is the *Jāmi' al-ḥikmatayn* (The Sum of Two Wisdoms), in which he compares and contrasts the philosophy derived from the Islamic revelation with Greek philosophy.[46]

Ismā'īlī philosophy continued to flourish in both Persia and Yemen even after the downfall of the Fatimids in Egypt. In Persia, Ḥasan al-Ṣabbāḥ declared the "Grand Resurrection" in the mountain fortress of Alamut in 557/1162 and established the new Ismā'īlī order in the formidable fortresses of northern Persia. Consequently, a new period of Ismā'īlī history began, during which Ismā'īlism and Sufism came closer together. In fact, certain Sufis such as the poets Sanā'ī and 'Aṭṭār as well as Qāsim-i Anwār (d. 837/1434) are claimed by the Ismā'īlīs as their own, as is the Ash'arite theologian al-Shahrastānī. The Ismā'īlīs even wrote commentaries on certain major Sufi works such as the *Gulshan-i rāz* ("Rose Garden of Divine Mysteries") of Shabistarī. Also during this period important Ismā'īlī philosophical tracts were composed in prose, mostly in Persian, such as the well-known *Taṣawwurāt* (Notions), attributed to Nāṣir al-Dīn al-Ṭūsī, and the tradition continued well into the tenth/sixteenth century.

In Yemen, a form of Ismā'īlism that was closer to the Fatimids continued, culminating in the works of the ninth/fifteenth missionary (*dā'ī*) of the Yemen, Sayyidunā Idrīs 'Imād al-Dīn (d. 872/1468). Interestingly enough, this branch of Ismā'īlism was finally to make its home in India along with the continuation of the Alamut tradition, which has become known since the last century as the Āghā-Khānid. The Yemeni authors followed by and large the theses presented in the earlier classical philosophical works of Ḥamīd al-Dīn Kirmānī and Nāṣir-i Khusraw, whereas the tradition of Alamut represented more the close link between imamology and mystical experience, between Ismā'īlī theosophy and Sufi metaphysics. There was also the much earlier Ismā'īlī tradition in Gujarat with its own more and more eclectic literature, which became enmeshed with the Ismā'īlī schools that became settled in India during later centuries.

While Ismā'īlī philosophy was developing, a number of works of Hermetic and Neo-Pythagorean inspiration appeared that have been claimed by some to be of Ismā'īlī inspiration and by others to belong more generally to Shi'ite circles—in fact to Islamic esoterism itself. The Hermetic corpus was translated into Arabic and was known to both alchemists and many philosophers.[47] Jābir ibn Ḥayyān, who lived in the second/eighth century and is the father of Islamic alchemy, wrote many philosophical works that are of Hermetic inspiration. This was to continue among later alchemists such as Abū᾿l-Qāsim al-'Irāqī, 'Izz al-Dīn al-Jaldakī, and Abū Maslamah al-Majrīṭī.[48] One must remember that both the *Turba Philosophorum* and the *Picatrix* were translated into Latin from Arabic and that there is, in addition to alchemical texts, a copious Islamic Hermetic literature of considerable philosophical importance. On the one hand, the visionary recitals of Ibn Sīnā reflect Hermetic prototypes, whereas the works of Suhrawardī are replete with references to Hermes and Hermeticism. On the other hand, one can see Hermetic themes in the works of many Sufis from Dhu᾿l-Nūn al-Miṣrī to Ibn 'Arabī. This Islamic Hermetic philosophy dealt on many levels with the reality of prophecy.

Neo-Pythagorean philosophy too found a place in the Islamic intellectual citadel early in the history of Islam. The concern with the symbolism of numbers in early Shi'ite and Sufi circles points to this fact, and in the fourth/tenth century there appeared a major work entitled *Rasā᾿il ikhwān al-ṣafā᾿* (Epistles of the Brethren of Purity), which contains an elaborate summary of philosophy, cosmology, and the natural sciences bound together by the unifying thread of Pythagorean mathematical symbolism.[49] Although this work is also claimed by many scholars to be of Ismā'īlī origin, it issued from a more general Shi'ite background and wielded an influence reaching nearly all sectors of Islamic intellectual life, including such a figure as al-Ghazzālī, who had read the work. Islamic spirituality has an inner link with what has been called "Abrahamic Pythagoreanism," as seen in the sacred art of Islam. This inner link has manifested itself in many forms in philosophical expositions throughout Islamic history and among numerous philosophers and is far from being confined to the Brethren of Purity. Furthermore, one can see its manifestation not only in the eastern lands of Islam but also in Andalusia in the works of Ibn al-Sīd of Badajoz (d. 521/1127), whose works, especially the *Kitāb al-ḥadā'iq* (The Book of Circles), are concerned with mathematical symbolism.

The metaphysics expounded by the classical Ismā'īlī philosophers such as al-Sijistānī, Ḥamīd al-Dīn al-Kirmānī, and Nāṣir-i Khusraw and followed for the most part by the later Yemeni school is based not on Being, as is the case with Ibn Sīnā and his followers, but on the Supreme Principle or Originator (*al-Mubdi'*) which is Supra-Being, beyond all categories and delimitations, including even Being and beyond the capacity of the human intellect to grasp. It lies even beyond the negation of being. Being is the first act of *al-Mubdi'*, the command stated in the Quran when God says, "But His command, when He intendeth a thing is only that he saith into it: Be! and it is" (36: 81). This *kun* or *esto* is the origin of the chain of being, of all realms of existence. It is the One (*al-Wāḥid*), and the Originator or *al-Mubdi'* is the maker of oneness (*al-muwaḥḥid*), which is also called the "Mystery of mysteries" (*ghayb al-ghuyūb*). The Supreme Principle has the function of "monadizing" and unifying all beings, and unity or *al-tawḥīd* "then takes on an aspect of monadology. At the same time that it disengages this Unifying Principle from all the ones which it unifies; it is by them and through them that it affirms It."[50]

The first being, which is called also the "First Originated" (*al-mubda' al-awwal*), is the Word of God (*Kalām Allāh*) and the First Intellect. From it emanate the beings in the hierarchy of existence according to the basic Ismā'īlī concept of 'limit' or 'degree' (*ḥadd*). Each being has a *ḥadd* by virtue of which it is delimited (*maḥdūd*) in a hierarchy of beings or "monads" unified by virtue of the unifying act of the Originator. This hierarchy stretches from the celestial pleroma created by the imperative *kun* and called the "World of Origination" (*'ālam al-ibdā'*) or the "World of Divine Command" (*'ālam al-amr*) to the world of creation (*'ālam al-khalq*). According to the earlier Ismā'īlī philosophers, followed by the Yemeni school, emanation of lower states of being (*inbi'āth*) commences with the First Intellect. The relation of all the lower levels of being reflects the rapport between the first limit (*al-ḥadd*) and the first delimited (*al-maḥdūd*), namely, the First Intellect and the Second Intellect, which proceeds from it and has its limit in it. This dual relationship is referred to by the Ismā'īlīs as "*sābiq*" (that which comes before) and "*tālī*" (that which follows) and is considered to correspond to the Pen (*al-qalam*) and the Guarded Tablet (*al-lawḥ al-maḥfūẓ*) of Quranic cosmology. This archetypal relationship is reflected in the lower states of being and has its counterpart on earth in the rapport between the prophet (*al-nabī*) and his inheritor (*al-waṣī*), who is the imam.

In the procession of the Intellects, the Third Intellect is the Celestial Adam (*al-Adam al-rūḥānī*), who is the archetype of humanity. The Celestial Adam, however, refused to see the *ḥadd* that defined his horizon as leading through hierarchy to the Originator and thereby sought to reach the Originator directly. He fell as a result into the worst metaphysical idolatry of setting himself up as the Absolute. He finally awakened from this stupor and realized his error, but as a result he was already passed by the procession of the Celestial Intellects and found himself as the Tenth Intellect. This drama in heaven is the origin of time. Celestial Adam must now redeem himself with the help of the Seven Intellects separating him from his original station and degree. These Intellects are called the "Seven Cherubim," and they indicate the distance of his fall. Time is in a sense "retarded eternity," and henceforth the number 7 becomes the archetypal number governing the unfolding of time.

The Ismā'īlīs have a cyclic view of history dominated by the number 7. There are seven cycles, each with its own prophet followed by his imam. Within Islam, it was after the sixth Shi'ite Imam, Ja'far al-Ṣādiq, that the Ismā'īlīs parted from the main branch of Shi'ism, considering Ismā'īl as their seventh imam. The number 7 has henceforth continued to be of major significance in their sacred history as well as in their cosmology. It must be recalled that Ismā'īlī philosophy is based on the principle of *ta*ʾ*wīl* or esoteric hermeneutic interpretation. Everything has an outward (*al-ẓāhir*) and an inward (*al-bāṭin*) aspect, and *ta*ʾ*wīl* is the process of going from the outward to the inward. In the domain of religion, the outward is represented by the prophet and the inward by the imam. The role of philosophy is precisely to make possible the discovery of the inward or the esoteric. Its language is therefore eminently symbolic, and its function, ultimately esoteric. In the context of Ismā'īlism, philosophy became synonymous with the truth (*al-ḥaqīqah*) lying at the heart of religion, which establishes rites and practices on the exoteric level with the ultimate aim of leading man to that knowledge that the Ismā'īlī philosophers and theosophers considered to have been expounded in their works for the intellectual elite among their community.[51] It is obvious how closely this philosophical tradition is related to prophecy understood in both its outward and inward aspects.

Islamic Philosophy in the Western Lands of Islam

Islamic philosophy had a shorter life in the western lands of Islam than in the eastern, but even in that faraway region of the Islamic world—and especially in Andalusia—there appeared many illustrious Islamic philosophers who left an indelible mark on Western philosophy while creating an important chapter in the history of Islamic philosophy itself. The founder of this chapter in the history of Islamic thought was Ibn Masarrah (d. 319/931), the mysterious founder of the school of Almeria, who was both mystic and philosopher and who led a group of disciples in the Cordovan Sierra until his death. He combined in his vision philosophy and Sufism and more generally Islamic esoterism, and this fusion became characteristic of Andalusian philosophy with the major exception of Ibn Rushd (Averroes). The works of Ibn Masarrah are for the most part lost, and only two, *Kitāb al-tabṣirah* (The Book of Penetrating Explanations) containing the key to his metaphysical teachings, and the *Kitāb al-ḥurūf* (The Book of Letters), dealing with "mystical algebra," are known to have circulated among his disciples. His influence was nevertheless immense, and his teachings have been reconstituted by Miguel Asín Palacios, thanks to many later references to him.[52]

At the heart of Ibn Masarrah's teachings stands a cosmology named after Empedocles and often referred to as pseudo-Empedoclean and insistant on the esoteric character of philosophy and even psychology.[53] His doctrines emphasized the absolute simplicity and ineffability of the absolute Being, the emanation of the levels of existence, the hierarchization of souls, and their emanation from the Universal Soul. The so-called pseudo-Empedoclean cosmology is especially interesting because of its vast influence on later Andalusian Sufism, from Ibn al-'Arīf and Ibn Barrajān to Ibn 'Arabī, as well as on later Islamic philosophers such as Mullā Ṣadrā and also Jewish philosophers such as Solomon ben Gabirol. As already mentioned, Empedocles was seen by Ibn Masarrah as the first of the great Greek philosophers, followed by Pythagoras, Socrates, Plato, and Aristotle. Empedocles was viewed by him as by certain other Islamic philosophers as a prophet-like figure who had received his teachings from Heaven. The cosmology attributed to him is based on the theory of hierarchic emanation of five substances: the *materia prima* (which is the first of intelligible realities and is not understood in the same way as the Aristotelian *materia prima*), the Intellect, the Soul, Nature, and *materia secunda*. The *materia prima* is "intelligible matter" existing in actuality and the first emanation of the Divine, while the Divine Principle Itself is above this schema, much like the Originator (*al-Mubdi'*) of the Ismā'īlīs. Ibn Masarrah also mentions the well-known Empedoclean theory of the two cosmic energies, namely, love and discord, which he, however, interprets in a different manner from modern scholars' interpretations of Empedocles and uses the term *qahr* (which means "dominion" or "victory" and has an astrological color) rather than discord. What was basic to Ibn Masarrah's teachings, however, was the idea of "intelligible matter," which stood opposed to the teachings of both the Aristotelians and the Neoplatonists and is seen elaborated later by Ibn 'Arabī, who speaks of "spiritual matter."

One of the major early intellectual figures of Islamic Spain was Abū Muḥammand 'Alī ibn Ḥazm (d. 454/1063). At once jurist, moralist, historian, theologian, and philosopher, he represents a remarkable intellectual presence in the Cordova of the fifth/eleventh century. He was a Ẓāhirite in jurisprudence and a theologian of note who remained sharply critical of the Ash'arites. His vast literary output, marked often by seething attacks on his opponents, touches on many branches of Islamic learning, including comparative religion and philosophy. His *Kitāb al-fiṣal fi'l-milal wa'l-ahwā' wa'l-niḥal* (The Book of Critical Detailed Examination of Religions, Sects, and Philosophical Schools) is considered by many to be one of the first works in the field of comparative religion, along with the *Taḥqīq mā li'l-hind* (India) of al-Bīrūnī. Ibn Ḥazm's *Ṭawq al-ḥimāmah* (The Ring of the Dove), translated many times into European languages, is the most famous Islamic treatise on Platonic love.[54] In this beautifully written work, Ibn Ḥazm follows upon the wake of earlier Muslim Platonists such as the Persian philosopher Muḥammad ibn Dā'ūd al-Iṣfahānī (d. 297/909) and echoes the teachings of Plato in the *Phaedrus*. The beauty of the soul attracts it to a beautiful object, and, as a result of the existence in the beautiful object of something corresponding to the nature of the soul, love is created. One finds in Ibn Ḥazm a full development of Platonic love, which marks him as a notable philosopher in addition to being a jurist and theologian and makes him a congenial companion of the *fedeli d'amore* among the Sufis despite certain differences of perspective.

The first major Muslim follower of eastern *mashshāʾī* philosophy in Spain was Abū Bakr ibn Bājjah, the famous Latin Avempace, who had a great influence on Ibn Rushd and Albert the Great as well as on many Jewish philosophers. Originally from northern Spain, he led a difficult life in a Spain torn by local wars; he settled in Fez in Morocco, where he became vizier and was finally imprisoned and died in 533/1138. Ibn Bājjah was an accomplished physician, astronomer, physicist, and natural historian, as well as philosopher, but his work remained incomplete, and much of it perished. He is, however, quoted extensively by later authorities, and one can surmise from these sources his importance in the anti-Ptolemaic astronomy and cosmology being developed in Spain in the sixth/twelfth century, as well as his crucial role in the history of the critique of the Aristotelian theory of projectile motion.

As far as the philosophical significance of his work is concerned, one must turn especially to his major opus *Tadbīr al-mutawaḥḥid* (Regimen of the Solitary), which is one of the most significant works of Islamic philosophy in the Maghrib.[55] In this work, the author speaks of the perfect state that is created not by external transformations, reforms, or revolutions but by the inner transformation of those individuals who have become inwardly united with the Active Intellect (*al-'aql al fa''āl*) and whose intellects are completely in act. These individuals are solitary figures, strangers, and exiles in a world that is comprised for the most part of human beings who cannot raise their gaze to the realm of the purely intelligible. Ibn Bājjah opposed explicitly the Ghazzālian type of mysticism and proposed a more intellectual and detached form of mystical contemplation. Yet in many ways he belongs to the same family as Sufi gnostics, and his *Tadbīr* is reminiscent of the *Occidental Exile* of Suhrawardī and the *gharīb* or stranger to the world emphasized in so many Sufi works. Unfortunately, this major opus was never completed, and we do not know how Ibn Bājjah envisaged the termination and completion of the actualization of the intellect in the solitary figure who becomes inwardly united with the Active Intellect, which is at the same time the Holy Spirit and therefore linked to revelation and the prophetic function.

If Ibn Bājjah was particularly drawn to the teachings of al-Fārābī, his successor upon the philosophical scene in Spain, Abū Bakr Muḥammad ibn Ṭufayl of Cadiz, was especially attracted to Ibn Sīnā. Ibn Ṭufayl was also a physician and scientist, as well as a philosopher, and, like Ibn Bājjah, he even became vizier in Morocco, where he died in 580/1185. He was also a friend of Ibn Rushd and asked the great commentator to undertake the study and the analysis of the works of

Aristotle. He was known as Abubacer in the Latin West, but his major opus, *Ḥayy ibn Yaqzān* (Living Son of the Awake), did not become known to the Scholastics. It was translated into Hebrew and later in the seventeenth century into Latin as *Philosophus autodidactus,* a work that had much influence on later European literature and is in fact considered by some to be the source of inspiration for the *Robinson Crusoe* story, as well as on certain forms of seventeenth-century mysticism concerned with the inner light. This major philosophical romance takes its title from the earlier work of Ibn Sīnā but seeks a path toward inner illumination in a manner similar to that of Suhrawardī, who was Ibn Ṭufayl's contemporary. It is of interest to note that at the beginning of his work Ibn Ṭufayl refers to the "Oriental Philosophy" that Ibn Sīnā was seeking in his later works and that Suhrawardī restored.

In Ibn Ṭufayl's "initiatic romance," the names in the Avicennan recital are retained, but their function changes. Ḥayy ibn Yaqẓān himself is the hero of the story rather than the Active Intellect. He appears in a mysterious manner through spontaneous generation from a matter that is made spiritually active by the Active Intellect. He is helped and brought up by a gazelle as a result of the sympathy (*sympatheia*) that relates all living beings together. As he grows up, he begins to attain knowledge first of the physical world, then of the heavens, the angels, the creative Demiurge, and finally of the Divine Principle and the universal theophany. Upon reaching the highest form of knowledge, he is joined by Absāl from a nearby island where he had been instructed in religion and theology. After mastering Ḥayy's language, Absāl discovers to his astonishment that all he had learned about religion is confirmed by Ḥayy in its purest form. Together they try to educate the people of the nearby island from which Absāl had come, but few understand what they say.

Far from being a treatise on naturalism denying revelation, as some have claimed,[56] *Ḥayy ibn Yaqẓān* is a work that seeks to unveil within man the significance of the intellect whose illumination of the mind is like an inner revelation that cannot but confirm the truths of the outer revelation and objective prophecy. Ḥayy is the solitary of Ibn Bājjah, whose inner experience to reach the truth through the intellect—a truth that is then confirmed to be in accord with the revealed religious truths learned by Absāl—points to one of the major messages that lies at the heart of Islamic philosophy. That message is the inner accord between philosophy and religion and the esoteric role of philosophy as the inner dimension of the truths expounded by revealed religion for a whole human collectivity. The eminently symbolic language of *Ḥayy ibn Yaqẓān* also indicates the esoteric character of veritable philosophy, whose meaning cannot be exhausted by the outer meaning of its language and mode of exposition.

It is in light of this background that one must examine the attempt of the most celebrated of the Islamic philosophers of Spain, Abū'l-Walīd ibn Rushd, to reconcile religion and philosophy. The philosopher who became a central intellectual figure in the Latin West under the name of Averroes was born in Cordova in 520/1126, where he was to become the chief judge (*qāḍī*) later in life. But the political situation of Andalusia changed, and Ibn Rushd fell from political favor. He spent the last part of his life in Marrakesh, where he died in 595/1198.

This greatest speculative philosopher of the Maghrib was to have two distinct destinies. In the West he became known as the commentator *par excellence* of Aristotle: hence the words of Dante, "*Averrois che'l gran comento feo*" (*Divine Comedy*, Inferno; iv, 144). It was through his eyes that for a long time the West saw Aristotle, and by mistake Averroes became known as the author of the double truth theory and the inspiration for a politicized Averroism. He even came to be known as the symbol of a rationalism opposed to religious faith, a view that continued into the modern period, as seen by the classical work of the nineteenth-century French rationalist Ernest Renan.[57] Averroes became a major figure in Western intellectual history, and in fact most of his works have survived not in the original Arabic but in Hebrew and Latin. As a result, there came into being a distinct school known as Latin Averroism.[58]

The Muslim Ibn Rushd was quite a different figure. Besides seeking to present the pure teachings of Aristotle, his main aim was to harmonize religion and philosophy. But his real thesis was not "double truth" but recourse to *ta'wīl*, which is so important for the understanding of the whole Islamic philosophical tradition. According to this principle as understood by Ibn Rushd, there are not two contradictory truths but a single truth that is presented in the form of religion and, through *ta'wīl*, results in philosophical knowledge. Religion is for everyone, whereas philosophy is only for those who possess the necessary intellectual faculties. Yet, the truth reached by one group is not contradictory to the truth discovered by the other. The principle of *ta'wīl* permits the harmony between religion and philosophy.[59] The whole thrust of the philosophy of Ibn Rushd, who was at once a pious Muslim and an authority in the *Sharī'ah* and a great philosopher, was to harmonize faith and reason. He represents yet another fruit of the tree of philosophy that has grown and thrived in the land of prophecy.

One of Ibn Rushd's most important works was his response to al-Ghazzālī's attack against the philosophers contained in the latter's *Tahāfut al-falāsifah*. Ibn Rushd took up the challenge of defending Islamic philosophy and sought to respond to al-Ghazzālī point by point in his *Tahāfut al-tahāfut* (Incoherence of the Incoherence), which is one of the major works of Islamic philosophy.[60] This work did not have the influence of al-Ghazzālī's attack, but it did not go without a further response by later Islamic thinkers. Ibn Rushd revived Aristotle, but he did not have the influence of the Peripatetic Ibn Sīnā, whom he criticized in many ways. Ibn Rushd was especially opposed to Ibn Sīnā's theory of emanation and emphasis on the soul of the spheres, as well as his doctrine of the intellect and the relation of the soul with the Active Intellect. The result of Ibn Rushd's critique was the banishment of the angels, of the *Animae caelestes*, from the cosmos. The influence of Averroes in the West could not but help in the secularization of the cosmos, preparing the ground for the rise of a totally secularized knowledge of the natural order.

Islamic philosophy itself, however, chose another path. It revived Avicennan philosophy rather than following Ibn Rushd and turned to the "Orient of Light" through the works of Suhrawardī and set out on a path whose first steps had been explored by Ibn Sīnā himself. With the death of Ibn Rushd something died—but not Islamic philosophy, as has been claimed by Western students of the Islamic philosophic tradition for seven centuries. Philosophy began a new phase of its life in Persia and other eastern lands of Islam, while its sun set in the Maghrib. But even in the western lands of Islam, there appeared at least two other major philosophical figures, 'Abd al-Ḥaqq ibn Sab'īn, who hailed from Murcia, spent the middle part of his life in North Africa and Egypt, and lived the last period of his life in Mecca, where he died around 669/1270, and Ibn Khaldūn who hailed from Tunisia. Ibn Sab'īn had definitely pro-Shi'ite tendencies and expounded openly the doctrine of "the transcendent unity of being," which caused him to fall into difficulty with exoteric religious authorities both in the Maghrib and in Egypt. Even in Mecca, where he was supported by the ruler, he was attacked from many quarters, and the circumstances of his death remain a mystery. Some have said that he was forced to commit suicide,[61] others that he committed suicide before the Ka'bah to experience the ecstasy of union, and still others that he was poisoned.

Ibn Sab'īn was at once a philosopher, a Sufi, and a follower of the Shawdhiyyah Order, which went back to the Andalusian Sufi from Seville Abū 'Abd Allāh al-Shawdhī and was characterized by its mixing of philosophy and Sufism, which we see already in Ibn Masarrah.

Ibn Sab'īn had an extensive knowledge of both traditions. He knew well the early classical Sufis of Baghdad and Khurasan such as al-Junayd, al-Ḥallāj, Bāyazīd, and al-Ghazzālī, as well as the earlier Andalusian masters such as Ibn Masarrah, Ibn Qasyī, and Ibn 'Arabī, who like him was born in Murcia, traveled to North Africa and Egypt, and lived for some time in Mecca. But Ibn Sab'īn is not a direct follower of the school of Ibn 'Arabī, some of whose later representatives he was to meet in Egypt.

Ibn Sab'īn also knew well both the eastern philosophers such as al-Fārābī and Ibn Sīnā and the Andalusian ones such as Ibn Bājjah, Ibn Ṭufayl, and Ibn Rushd. He even knew Suhrawardī, whom he, however, classified with the Peripatetics and criticized severely along with nearly all the earlier philosophers and many of the earlier Sufis. Ibn Sab'īn was a follower of the doctrine of "absolute Oneness," according to which there is only the Being of God and nothing else. He criticized the earlier Islamic thinkers for not having reached the level of this "absolute Oneness." He is in fact probably the first person to use the term *waḥdat al-wujūd*.

It is also of interest to note that Ibn Sab'īn had extensive knowledge of Judaism, Christianity, and even Hinduism and Zoroastrianism, as well as Greek philosophy, including Hermeticism. He was furthermore considered a master in the "hidden sciences,"[62] especially the science of the inner meaning of letters and words. His highly difficult writings often contain "kabbalistic" sentences whose meaning cannot be understood save through recourse to these sciences. These writings include also treatises on the hidden sciences, as well as works devoted to philosophy and practical Sufism.

Many of Ibn Sab'īn's works are lost, but a few survive and bear witness to the depth and fecundity of his thought. The most significant of his philosophical works is the *Budd al-'ārif* (The Object of Worship of the Gnostic), which starts with logic and terminates with metaphysics and must be considered the synthesis of his metaphysical teachings.[63] But his most influential work as far as the Western world is concerned is *Ajwibah yamāniyyah 'an as᾿ilat al-ṣiqilliyyah* (Yemeni Answers to Sicilian Questions), which consists of answers to four philosophical questions sent by Emperor Frederick II. The work was translated into Latin and became well known in Scholastic circles.

Ibn Sab'īn must be considered along with Suhrawardī and Ibn 'Arabī as a master of Islamic spirituality who combined the purification of the soul with the perfection of the intellectual faculties, who created a synthesis between spiritual life and speculative thought, between Sufism and philosophy, although in a different manner from his two illustrious predecessors. As the last great representative of the Maghribi-Andalusian school of Islamic philosophy, Ibn Sab'īn embodies that synthesis between the practical spiritual life and intellectual doctrine that one finds in Ibn Masarrah, who stands at the origin of this school.[64] The West may have seen in the Islamic philosophy of Spain a pure Aristotelian rationalism with which it was fascinated but which it feared. In light of the integral tradition of Islamic philosophy, however, it is this synthesis between practical Sufism and philosophy as metaphysics and gnosis that represents the central message of this school. The journey of Ibn Sab'īn to the East and his death in the holy city of Mecca, the heartland of Islam, are symbolic of the wedding of that knowledge that transforms and illuminates and the spiritual practice that opens the heart to the reception of such a knowledge. If with the journey of Ibn Sab'īn, the light of this type of philosophy became dimmed in Andalusia, it shone already brightly in the eastern lands of Islam thanks to the teachings of the master of the school of Illumination, Suhrawardī, whose commentators and students were Ibn Sab'īn's contemporaries.

The other major philosophical figure in the Maghrib after Ibn Sab'īn was the Tunisian Ibn Khaldūn. Born in Tunis in 732/1332 he spent his life in Algeria, Tunisia, and Egypt and died in Cairo in 808/1406. Although primarily a historian and diplomat and the author of the well-known historical work, *Kitāb al-'ibar* (The Book about Events which Constitute a Lesson), Ibn Khaldūn was also a major philosopher of history and in fact is considered by many to be the founder of this discipline in both East and West. His philosophy of human society and its history, which draws from both religious teachings and the study of history to which was added the rich experience of a full life, is to be found primarily in the introduction to the *Kitāb al-'ibar*, which is known as the *Muqaddimah* (Prolegomena).[65] A careful study of his work reveals how even this philosophy of history can be affected by the Islamic understanding of the rhythms of sacred history and the providence of God, or what Ibn Khaldūn calls "*mashiyyat Allāh*" (literally "what God has willed for the world"), which is an ever present reality in the transformations and upheavals of society.[66] Outside the domain of the philosophy of history, Ibn Khaldūn's philosophical ideas were of little consequence. He criticized as practically a jurisprudent and a theologian à la Ghazzālī the other Islamic philosophers and their political philosophy, for example the works of al-Fārābī.[66] Yet he was saddened by the decline of the intellectual sciences in the Maghrib. His interest in these sciences can be seen in the *Muqaddimah* itself, and he devised an important classification of the Islamic sciences.[67] In any case, he marks the swan song of classical Islamic philosophy in the

Maghrib and at the same time the beginning of the discipline of "the science of civilizations" and the philosophy of history as they were to develop later in the West from Vico to Hegel to Toynbee and the contemporary period.

SUHRAWARDĪ AND THE SCHOOL OF ILLUMINATION (*AL-ISHRĀQ*)

The complete harmonization of spirituality and philosophy in Islam was achieved in the school of Illumination (*al-ishrāq*) founded by Shaykh al-ishrāq Shihāb al-Dīn Suhrawardī. Born in the small village of Suhraward[68] in Western Persia in 549/1153, he studied in Zanjan and Isfahan, where he completed his formal education in the religious and philosophical sciences and entered into Sufism. He then set out for Anatolia and settled in Aleppo, where as a result of the opposition of certain jurists he met his death at a young age in 587/1191. Suhrawardī was a great Sufi mystic and philosopher and the restorer within the bosom of Islam of the perennial philosophy, which he called *"al-ḥikmat al-'atīqah,"* the *philosophia priscorium,* which as already mentioned was referred to by certain Renaissance philosophers, and whose origin he considered to be divine. He saw veritable philosophy—or one should rather say theosophy, if this word is understood in its original sense and as still used by Jakob Boehme—as resulting from the wedding between the training of the theoretical intellect through philosophy and the purification of the heart through Sufism. The means of attaining supreme knowledge he considered to be illumination, which at once transforms one's being and bestows knowledge.

During his short and tragic life, Suhrawardī wrote more than forty treatises, the doctrinal ones almost all in Arabic, and the symbolic or visionary recitals almost all in Persian. Both his Arabic and Persian works are among the literary masterpieces of Islamic philosophy. His doctrinal writings, which begin with an elaboration and gradual transformation of Avicennan Peripatetic philosophy, culminate in the *Ḥikmat al-ishrāq* (The Theosophy of the Orient of Light), which is one of the most important works in the tradition of Islamic philosophy.[69] His recitals include some of the most beautiful prose writings of the Persian language, including such masterpieces as *Fī ḥaqīqat al-'ishq* (On the Reality of Love) and *Āwāz-i par-i Jibraʾīl* (The Chant of the Wing of Gabriel).[70] Few Islamic philosophers were able to combine metaphysics of the highest order with a poetic prose of almost incomparable richness and literary quality.

Suhrawardī integrated Platonism and Mazdaean angelology in the matrix of Islamic gnosis. He believed that there existed in antiquity two traditions of wisdom (*al-ḥikmah*), both of divine origin and rooted in revelation. One of these traditions reached the pre-Socratics such as Pythagoras and then Plato, and other Greek philosophers and created the authentic Greek philosophical tradition, which terminated with Aristotle. The other was disseminated among the sages of ancient Persia whom he calls the "*khusrawāniyyūn*," (sages) who were followers of the Persian philosopher-king Kay Khusraw. Finally, these traditions became united in Suhrawardī. Like many Islamic philosophers, he identified Hermes with the prophet Idrīs, who was given the title Father of Philosophers (Wālid al-ḥukamāʾ or Abūʾl-ḥukamāʾ) and was considered to be the recipient of the celestial wisdom that was the origin of philosophy. It was finally in Islam, the last and primordial religion, that this primordial tradition became restored by Suhrawardī as the school of Illumination (*al-ishrāq*). This school is therefore profoundly related to the reality of prophecy.

The Master of Illumination insisted that there existed from the beginning an "eternal dough" (*al-khamīrat al-azaliyyah*), which is none other than eternal wisdom or *sophia perennis* within the being of men and women. It is hidden in the very substance of human beings ready to be "leavened" and actualized through intellectual training and inner purification.[71] It is this "eternal dough" which was actualized and transmitted by pre-Socratics to the Pythagoreans and Plato and then to the Sufis Dhuʾl-Nūn al-Miṣrī and Sahl al-Tustarī and through the Persian sages to Bāyazid al-Basṭāmī and Manṣūr al-Ḥallāj and that was restored in its full glory by Suhrawardī, who combined the inner knowledge of these masters with the intellectual discipline of such philosophers as al-Fārābī and Ibn Sīnā. Suhrawardī, however, never mentions historical chains connecting him to this long tradition of wisdom but insists that the real means of attainment of this knowledge is through God and His revealed Book. That is why he bases himself so much on the Quran and is the first major Muslim philosopher to quote the Quran extensively in his philosophical writings.

Suhrawardī created a vast philosophical synthesis, which draws from many sources and especially the nearly six centuries of Islamic thought before him. But this synthesis is unified by a metaphysics and an epistemology that are able to relate all the different strands of thought to each other in a unified pattern. What is most significant from the point of view of philosophy in its relation to spirituality is the insistence of *ishrāqī* philosophy on the organic nexus between intellectual activity and inner purification. Henceforth in the Islamic world, wherever philosophy survived, it was seen as lived wisdom. The philosopher or *ḥakīm* was expected to be not only a person possessing cerebral knowledge but a saintly person transformed by his knowledge. Philosophy as a mental activity divorced from spiritual realization and the inner life became marginalized as a legitimate intellectual category, and Islamic philosophy became henceforth what *sophia* has always been in Oriental traditions, namely, a wisdom lived and experienced as well as thought and reasoned.

Although as a result of his violent death Suhrawardī and his doctrines were not visible for a generation, the teachings of the school of Illumination reappeared in the middle part of the seventh/thirteenth century in the major commentary by Muḥammad al-Shahrazūrī (d. sometime after 687/1288) on the *Ḥikmat al-ishrāq*. This was followed by the second major commentary on this work by Quṭb al-Dīn al-Shīrāzī (d. 710/1311) to whom we shall turn in chapter 11. This work is the most enduring philosophical text of Quṭb al-Dīn for in his commentary on the *Ḥikmat al-ishrāq* he resuscitated the teachings of Suhrawardī and provided a key to a work that is read and studied in Persia, Turkey, and Muslim India to this day. After him a long line of *ishrāqī* philosophers appeared in both Persia and the Indian subcontinent, where the influence of Suhrawardī has been very extensive. Suhrawardī established a new and at the same time primordial intellectual dimension in Islam, which became a permanent aspect of the Islamic intellectual scene and survives to this day.[72]

What Is Ishrāqī Philosophy?

Ishrāqī philosophy—or theosophy, to be more precise—is based on the metaphysics of light. The origin and source of all things is the Light of lights (*nūr al-anwār*), which is infinite and absolute Light above and beyond all the rays that it emanates. All levels of reality, however, are also degrees and levels of light distinguished from each other by their degrees of intensity and weakness and by nothing other than light. There is, in fact, nothing in the whole universe but light. From the Light of lights there issues a vertical or longitudinal hierarchy of lights that comprises the levels of universal existence and a horizontal or latitudinal order that contains the archetypes (sg. *rabb al-naw'*) or Platonic ideas of all that appears here below as objects and things. These lights are none other than what in the language of religion are called "angels." Suhrawardī gives names of Mazdaean angels as well as Islamic ones to these lights and brings out the central role of the angels in cosmology as well as in epistemology and soteriology.[73]

The word *ishrāq* in Arabic itself means at once illumination and the first light of the early morning as it shines from the east (*sharq*). The Orient is not only the geographical East but the origin of light, of reality. *Ishrāqī* philosophy is both "Oriental" and "illuminative." It illuminates because it is Oriental and is Oriental because it is illuminative. It is the knowledge with the help of which man can orient himself in the universe and finally reach that Orient which is his original abode, while in the shadow and darkness of terrestrial existence man lives in the "occident" of the world of being no matter where he lives geographically. The spiritual or illuminated man who is aware of his "Oriental" origin, is therefore a stranger and an exile in this world, as described in one of Suhrawardī's most eloquent symbolic recitals *Qiṣṣat al-ghurbat al-gharbiyyah* (The Story of the Occidental Exile). It is through reminiscence of his original abode that man begins to have a nostalgia for his veritable home and with the help of illuminative knowledge that he is able to reach that abode. Illuminative knowledge, which is made possible by contact with the angelic orders, transforms man's being and saves him. The angel is the instrument of illumination and hence salvation. Man has descended from the world of the "signeurial lights" and it is by returning to this world and reunifying with his angelic "alter-ego" that man finds his wholeness once again.

Ishraqī philosophy depicts in an eminently symbolic language a vast universe based on the symbolism of light and the "Orient," a universe that breaks the boundaries of Aristotelian cosmology as well as the confines of *ratio* defined by the Aristotelians. Suhrawardī was able to create an essentialistic metaphysics of light and a cosmology of rarely paralleled grandeur and beauty which "orients" the veritable seeker through the cosmic crypt and guides him to the realm of pure light which is none other than the Orient of Being. In this journey, which is at once philosophical and spiritual, man is led by a knowledge that is itself light according to the saying of the Prophet who said *al-'ilmu nūrun* (knowledge is light). That is why this philosophy, according to Suhrawardī's last will and testament at the end of his *Ḥikmat al-ishrāq*, is not to be taught to everyone. It is for those whose minds have been trained by rigorous philosophical training and whose hearts have been purified through inner effort to subdue that interior dragon which is the carnal soul. For such people, the teachings of *ishrāq* reveal an inner knowledge which is none other than the eternal wisdom or *sophia perennis* that illuminates and transforms, obliterates, and resurrects until man reaches the pleroma of the world of lights and the original abode from which he began his cosmic wayfaring.

Between Suhrawardī and the School of Isfahan

The period stretching from the seventh/thirteenth to the tenth/sixteenth century is characterized by the ever greater rapprochement between various schools of Islamic philosophy as Persia becomes the main arena for activity in Islamic philosophy.[74] Early in this period, Ibn Sīnā's[74] philosophy was resurrected by Naṣīr al-Dīn al-Ṭūsī, who is one of the foremost Islamic *mashshāʾī* philosophers. As already mentioned, his commentary on the *Ishārāt waʾl-tanbīhāt* and his response to the criticisms of Fakhr al-Dīn al-Rāzī against Ibn Sīnā had a much greater influence on later Islamic philosophy than the *Tahāfut al-tahāfut* of Ibn Rushd. Ṭūsī was the leading light of a whole circle of philosophers, including not only the already mentioned Quṭb al-Dīn al-Shīrāzī but also Dabīrān-i Kātibī Qazwīnī (d. 675/1276) the author of the *Ḥikmat al-'ayn* (Wisdom from the Source). Another well-known Peripatetic philosopher of the same period who needs to be mentioned is Athīr al-Dīn Abharī (d. 663/1264), whose *Hidāyat al-ḥikmah* (Guide of Philosophy) became popular during later centuries, especially with the commentary of Mullā Ṣadrā.

Perhaps the most distinctive philosopher of this period who is said to have also been related to Naṣīr al-Dīn was Afḍal al-Dīn Kāshānī (d. ca. 610/1213) known also as Bābā Afḍal. An eminent Sufi whose tomb is a locus of pilgrimage to this day, Bābā Afḍal was a brilliant logician and metaphysician. He wrote a number of works in Persian, which rank along with the Persian treatises of Suhrawardī as among outstanding masterpieces of Persian philosophical prose. His works represent yet another wedding between Sufism and philosophy, and they are based on a self-knowledge or autology that leads from the knowledge of the self to the Self according to the prophetic *ḥadīth, man 'arafa nafsahu faqad 'arafa rabbahu* (he who knows himself know his Lord).

Parallel with the revival of Peripatetic philosophy by Ṭūsī and *ishrāqī* theosophy by his colleague at Maraghah, Quṭb al-Dīn Shīrāzī, theoretical Sufism of the school of Ibn 'Arabī spread rapidly in the East, while philosophical *kalām* was developing greatly. During the next three centuries important philosophers appeared who tried to synthesize these various schools of thought. Some, like Dawānī, were at once scholars of *kalām* and *ishrāqīs*. Others, such as the Dashtakī family of Shiraz, were followers of Ibn Sīnā and Suhrawardī. Still others, such as Ibn Turkah Iṣfahānī (d. ca. 835/ 1432), who is a major figure of this period, was an *ishrāqī* interpreter of Peripatetic philosophy and a gnostic of the school of Ibn'Arabī. These figures, to whom we shall turn later in this book, prepared the ground for the grand synthesis among the four schools of *ishrāq*, *mashshā*ʾ, *'irfān*, and *kalām*, which, however, was not achieved until the Safavid period with the establishment of what has become known as the School of Isfahan.

Islamic Philosophy after Suhrawardī

The later history of Islamic philosophy is much less known than that of the earlier period. The revival of Avicennan philosophy by Naṣīr al-Dīn al-Ṭūsī, the continuation of the school of Illumination, the spread of the philosophical Sufism of the school of Ibn 'Arabī, and the expansion of philosophical theology, both Sunni and Shi'ite, mark the centuries that were to follow. Moreover, gradually these perspectives became synthesized resulting finally in Mīr Dāmād, Mullā Ṣadrā, and the School of Isfahan in the tenth/sixteenth century and its aftermath.[75] The main arena for the development of Islamic philosophy during the past eight centuries has been primarily Persia with important developments in Ottoman Turkey and Muslim India. Therefore, rather than giving a brief description of the later phases of Islamic philosophy here, we shall devote the rest of the book to a fuller treatment of later Islamic philosophy primarily in Persia and with some references to the Ottoman world and Muslim India. However, to treat fully the latter subjects would require a separate work.

Before turning to this later period, which marks the full flowering of "prophetic philosophy in Islam," it is of some interest to turn to the most enigmatic and misconstrued of the Islamic philosophers, 'Umar Khayyām, whose message as ordinarily understood seems to negate the very nature of Islamic philosophy as being related to prophecy. We cannot turn to the later period coming down to our own days without reexamining the philosophical teachings of the most famous of all literary figures of Asia in the West, namely Khayyām, who more than being a poet was a philosopher and scientist and as we shall see, much more in line of the main tradition of Islamic philosophy than being a solitary deviant musing as a skeptic and a hedonist in a world dominated by the reality of revelation.

CHAPTER 9

The Poet-Scientist 'Umar Khayyām as Philosopher

It is now time to turn to the enigmatic figure of Khayyām, who, if understood only superficially, seems to represent a philosophical view in opposition to the realities of the land of prophecy. Yet, if his works, including those devoted specifically to philosophy, are studied in depth, he emerges as a figure much more in the line of Ibn Sīnā than Epicurus and the Skeptics of antiquity.

'Umar ibn Ibrāhīm Khayyām (also known as Khayyāmī) Nayshapūrī (439/1048–526/1131) known in the West simply as Omar Khayyam is the most famous poet of the East in the West,[1] and since the nineteenth century efforts by historians of science such as Amélie Sédillot and Franz Woepke followed by many twentieth century scholars, he has also become established as one of the major mathematicians and astronomers of the medieval period, the author of the most important treatise on algebra before modern times,[2] as well as a significant work on the criticism of the Euclidean parallel lines postulate.[3] His reputation is therefore well established as both poet and scientist. What is much less known about him, however, is his significance as a philosopher, and his few remaining philosophical works have not received anywhere the same attention in the Occident as have his scientific or poetic writings to the extent that he hardly figures in general histories of Islamic philosophy written in Europe.[4] It has usually become forgotten that in traditional Islamic sources he was known essentially as a philosopher-scientist. Zamakhsharī referred to him as "the philosopher of the world,"[5] and his son-in-law, Muḥammad Baghdādī, is said to have stated that Khayyām was busy teaching the metaphysics (*ilāhiyyāt*) of Ibn Sīnā's *al-Shifā'* when he died.[6] Many other sources have also testified that he taught for decades the philosophy of Ibn Sīnā in Nayshapur where Khayyām lived most of his life, breathed his last, and was buried and where his mausoleum remains today a famous site visited by many people every year.

It is in light of these diverse and sometimes contradictory evaluations of Khayyām and especially the eclipse of his significance as a philosopher within the Islamic philosophical tradition, which we have already discussed in previous chapters, that we wish to turn to a study of his philosophy on the basis of what has remained of his writings. Before embarking upon this task, however, it is necessary to confront his quatrains and the "philosophical" meaning that many have associated with it in the West and also in other areas of the world, including those parts of the Islamic world where people's knowledge of Khayyām has come primarily through Western sources. The quatrains in Fitzgerald's translation convey at least superficially a hedonistic, fatalistic, and this worldly philosophy combined with much skepticism about religious teachings if not God Himself. One might ask how could this Khayyām be the same man who wrote the extant philosophical works that are attributed to him with certainty or who was so respected as a scholar of religious stature that the Islamic judge of the province of Fars would send him a letter asking him philosophical and theological questions? Several responses are possible, each of which needs to be stated and then examined. One is that the philosopher-scientist Khayyām was not the same Khayyām who is the author of the quatrains bearing his name. A number of scholars in East and West have accepted this position, and many have sought to give as proof the fact that Niẓāmī 'Arūḍī Samarqandī in his *Chahār-maqālah* (Four Articles) mentions Khayyām in the third chapter of his work as an astronomer and not in the second chapter as a poet.[7] A second group has doubted the authenticity of most of the quatrains and has accepted that Khayyām may have written a few of these as a pastime without meaning to describe his complete philosophy of life therein. Another group asserts that the world-loving, skeptical, and fatalistic philosophy expressed in many of the quatrains expresses the thought of the "real" Khayyām, while the existing philosophical treatises are simply formalities that he produced because the conditions of the world in which he lived required his composing such works.

It is of interest to note that as modernism brought a wave of religious lukewarmness and even skepticism among a number of Iranians, it also made the Khayyām "packaged" in the West a cultural hero of those who had become philosophically skeptical and agnostic. For example, Taqī Irānī, who was the intellectual leader of the Iranian communists in the period before the Second World War, was much interested in Khayyām but because of his own "scientific materialism" turned to the study of Khayyām's mathematics rather than his poetry, which did not accord with communist teachings. Also Iran's most famous modern writer, Sadegh Hedayat, who was an agnostic and antireligious activist, did much to introduce the new skeptical view of

Khayyām among modernized Persians[8] to the extent that some by mistake think of him as the founder of Khayyām studies in Iran.[9] In fact no person in Persian literature has been used as often as Khayyām in modern times to depict whatever sense of rebellion against revelation, religious doubt, hedonistic tendency, or even feeling of suicide might have existed within the mind of certain figures who have then claimed to be the authentic interpreters of Khayyām in question.

In dealing with the philosophy of Khayyām and its interpretation we are therefore dealing not only with an intellectual question but also with one that for some is an existential matter and touches the very foundations of their secularized worldview for which they have sought historical legitimacy by identifying their personal and subjective states with the thought of Khayyām. Nevertheless, for the sake of intellectual honesty and the truth all these possibilities must be examined in light of Khayyām's written works even if there is a popularized Khayyām out there after whom night clubs are named all over the world, a figure whose image is difficult to erase from the minds of those, including a number of modernized Iranian writers, who are wooed by the Victorian Khayyām cult begun by Fitzgerald and its aftermath, which survives in a new form to this day.

As far as positing two Khayyāms is concerned, we believe that there is no cogent reason for doing so, especially if one accepts that only a few dozen of the quatrains are most likely authentic and the rest by other poets such as Ḥayyānī or Ḥayātī (as mentioned in some manuscripts of the *Rubā'iyyāt* in Persia and in Paris), which could have been easily mistaken (in the Arabic/Persian script) by later scribes for Khayyāmī. If we take this fact into consideration, there is no need to accept all of the poems in his name as being his or go to the other extreme to negate the authenticity of all the poems attributed to Khayyām. Furthermore, the poems found in the most ancient manuscripts do not contradict his philosophical writings in principle as we shall see later in this essay. In fact it was common among Persian Islamic philosophers to write a few quatrains on the side often in the spirit of some of the poems of Khayyām singing about the impermanence of the world and its transience and similar themes. One need only recall the names of Ibn Sīnā, Suhrawardī, Nāṣir al-Dīn Ṭūsī, and Mullā Ṣadrā, who wrote some poems along with their extensive prose works, not to speak of such philosophers as Nāṣir-i Khusraw, Afḍal al-Dīn Kāshānī, Mīr Dāmād, Mullā 'Abd al-Razzāq Lāhījī, and Sabziwārī, who in contrast to the earlier group were also accomplished poets and wrote poetry extensively. Moreover, this tradition has continued to our own day.[10] We therefore tend to agree with those who believe that some of the quatrains attributed by Khayyām were actually by him and must be considered as *a* source but not *the* source of his philosophical views.

As for those who rely solely on the quatrains, believing that Khayyām was hiding his skeptical and hedonistic views because of expediency, we find no logic in this argument except the psychological need of some modern skeptics to find historical precedence and therefore legitimacy for their innovations based on the premises of modernism. To accuse Khayyām of blatant hypocrisy while seeking to make of him a cultural hero for modern skeptics is itself the worst kind of hypocrisy hardly worthy of serious consideration.

In trying to understand the philosophy of Khayyām , therefore, we must turn to his own works in light of the intellectual and social conditions of his day and evaluations of Khayyām's works by such figures as Ẓahīr al-Dīn Bayhaqī, Niẓāmī 'Arūḍī Samarqandī, and Jār Allāh Zamakhsharī, as well as the Sufi poets and writers who came shortly after him such as 'Aṭṭār and Najm al-Dīn Rāzī. In this chapter it is not possible to investigate the secondary sources, but a word can be said about the intellectual conditions of Khayyām's time before turning to the three sources of his philosophy: namely, his scientific works, his philosophical texts, and his poetry.

The establishment of Seljuq rule over Persia, Anatolia, Iraq, and Syria led to a new political situation that, as already mentioned, also possessed consequences for the cultivation of philosophy. After over two centuries, the Seljuqs united Western Asia under the aegis of Sunni power, a power of which the Abbasid caliph remained the symbol, although in fact military and political power remained in the hands of the Seljuq sultans. To strengthen the central power of Sunni authority, the Seljuqs, like the Abbasid caliphs, supported Ash'arite *kalām* and by extension combated the propagation of *falsafah* to which Ash'arism was opposed. It is not accidental that from the middle of the fifth/eleventh century onward, *kalām* came to dominate the intellectual scene in Persia and other eastern lands of Islam, especially Khurasan, from which Khayyām hailed. One needs only to recall the name of such important figures of Ash'arite *kalām* as Imām al-Ḥaramayn Juwaynī and Abū Ḥāmid Muḥammad Ghazzālī, both from Khurasan, to confirm this fact. We now know that Ghazzālī was not only an Ash'arite *mutakallim*, but in his opposition to *falsafah* he certainly joined the Ash'arite ranks.

During this period the teaching of philosophy was marginalized in Persia and adjacent areas, to the extent that the Seljuq prime minister, Khwājah Niẓām al-Mulk, in his conditions for the endowment of the Niẓāmiyyah *madrasah* system, stipulates that philosophy should not be taught therein. This was the period of such works as the *Tahāfut al-falāsifah* of Ghazzālī, the *Muṣāri'ah* (Wrestling with the Philosopher) of Abū'l-Fatḥ Shahrastānī, and the *Sharḥ al-ishārāt* (Commentary upon the Book of Directives [and Remarks]) of Fakhr al-Dīn Rāzī, all works opposed to *falsafah*. It is usually said that between the middle of the fifth/eleventh century and the beginning of the seventh/thirteenth century, *falsafah* was eclipsed in the eastern lands of Islam and flourished only in the Maghrib, where Ibn Rushd was to write his response to Ghazzālī in his *Tahāfut al-tahāfut*. Furthermore, it is well known that in the East at the end of this period of Ash'arite domination, that is, in the seventh/thirteenth century, Khwājah Nāṣir al-Dīn al-Ṭūsī answered both Shahrastānī and Rāzī and resuscitated Ibn Sīnā's philosophy. In general one points to Suhrawardī as the only major philosopher in this period of the eclipse of philosophy in the East whose influence, however, really began in the decades that coincides with Ṭūsī's revival of Ibn Sīnā.

These statements are generally correct but should not be taken to mean that there was no philosophical activity in Persia and lands nearby during this period of domination of *kalām*. The most important proof of the continuation of the school of Ibn Sīnā in the fifth/eleventh and sixth/twelfth centuries is, in fact, 'Umar Khayyām himself. He lived in the middle of this period of eclipse of Avicennan philosophy, between Ibn Sīnā's students and Ṭūsī and must be considered an eminent philosophical figure during this period of suppression of philosophical thought in Persia and other eastern lands of Islam. His very existence is proof of the fact that philosophy had not disappeared totally from the scene in this area even during this period of eclipse. Nevertheless, the era during which he lived is also one of the reasons why in general histories of Islamic philosophy there is usually no mention of him as a philosopher belonging to the school of Ibn Sīnā. Had he lived earlier or later he probably would have been studied more extensively as a *mashshā'ī* philosopher like many others of the fourth/tenth or seventh/thirteenth century. But he was destined to remain a solitary figure between Ibn Sīnā's students Bahmanyār ibn Marzbān and Abū'l-'Abbās Lūkarī, on the one hand, and Naṣīr al-Dīn al-Ṭūsī and other philosophers of the seventh/thirteenth century, on the other. Yet, although a lonely figure who preferred solitude and did not like to accept students, he was highly revered as both philosopher and mathematician by scholars of his own generation, as well as those who came thereafter.

Although much attention has been paid during the past century both in the West and to some extent in the Islamic world itself to the history of mathematics in Islamic civilization, much less attention has been paid to the Islamic philosophy of mathematics with which many Islamic scientists such as Khayyām dealt. Needless to say, from the point of view of philosophy, the most important contribution of Khayyām's mathematical works is to the philosophy of mathematics. To illustrate this assertion, it is sufficient to draw attention to three basic mathematical ideas with which Khayyām deals and which possess a strong philosophical dimension. The first is mathematical order. From where does this order issue, and why does it correspond to the order dominant in the world of nature? Khayyām was fully aware of this basic question but answered it in one of his philosophical treatises on being to which we shall turn shortly rather than in a mathematical treatise. Khayyām's profound answer is that the Divine Origin of all existence not only emanates *wujūd* or being, by virtue of which all things gain reality, but It is also the source of order that is inseparable from the very act of existence. To speak of *wujūd* is also to speak of order, which the science of mathematics studies in turn as do certain other disciplines.

A second mathematico-philosphical question with which Khayyām was concerned is the significance of postulates in geometry and the necessity for the mathematician to rely upon philosophy in order to prove the postulates and principles of his own science, hence the importance of the relation of any particular science to prime philosophy. More specifically Khayyām was interested in the pertinence of the fact that the fifth postulate of Euclid, called the "parallel postulate," cannot be proven on the basis of existing axioms. Khayyām refused to enter motion into the attempt to prove this postulate as had Ibn al-Haytham because Khayyām associated motion with the world of matter and wanted to keep it away from the purely intelligible and immaterial world of geometry.[11] In providing his proofs, Khayyām had to have recourse to some non-Euclidean theorems.[12] Moreover, in his study of the fifth postulate Khayyām discussed concepts of space and geometric order, which are of much importance for the philosophy of mathematics. These are also dealt with in another manner in his *Algebra,* where the relation between algebraic equations and geometric figures plays a central role and where Khayyām in a sense geometrizes algebra.

A third important issue worth mentioning is the clear distinction made by Khayyām, on the basis of the work of earlier Islamic philosophers such as Ibn Sīnā, between natural body (*al-jism al-ṭabī'ī*) and mathematical body (*al-jism al-ta'līmī*). The first is defined as a body that is in the category of substance and that stands by itself, while the second, also called "volume" (*ḥajm*), is of the category of accident that does not subsist by itself in the external world. The first is the body with which the natural sciences deal, and the second is the concern of mathematics. Khayyām was very careful in respecting the boundaries of each discipline and criticized Ibn al-Haytham in his proof of the parallel postulate precisely because he had broken this rule and had brought a subject belonging to natural philosophy, that is, motion, which belongs to the natural body, into the domain of geometry, which deals with mathematical body.

In this distinction between *al-jism al-ṭabī'ī* and *al-jism al-ta'līmī* by Khayyām, Ṭūsī, and others there is a basic metaphysical principle involved that is of great significance even for the philosophy of quantum mechanics. Many people today think of atomic particles such as the electron and proton as if they were corporeal objects such as apples and pears except on a much smaller scale. In fact, however, the two classes of things belong to two different realms of existence and not to a single domain of reality. Wolfgang Smith in his brilliant work *The Quantum Enigma* calls the first, that is, electrons, and so on, physical and the second, that is, ordinary objects such as apples, corporeal. The first is potential and the second actual with the modification that needs to be made in such Aristotelian terms when dealing with modern physics.[13] The distinction made by Khayyām and others between the two types of body in question is in many ways related to the issue brought up by Wolfgang Smith and is of great significance for the philosophy of mathematics and the relation between mathematics and physics envisaged from a philosophical point of view.

In turning to Khayyām's properly speaking philosophical works, it is necessary to deal with each work separately since our concern in this chapter is after all with his philosophy.[14] Let us first turn to Khayyām's translation with brief commentary of Ibn Sīnā's *al-Khuṭbat al-gharrā'* (The Splendid Sermon) on the praise of God.[15] This beautifully composed treatise on Divine Unity is somewhat reminiscent of the poems of such figures as Abū Bakr Muḥammad ibn 'Alī Khusrawī.

Also after Khayyām, the famous poet laureate Fakhr al-Dīn As'ad Gurgānī in his *Wīs wa Rāmīn* (The Romance of Wīs and Rāmīn) composed lines similar to Ibn Sīnā's. The significance of this treatise is first of all in Khayyām's strong attestation to the reality of God and His Unity. In fact the content of the treatise, which he chose to translate and elucidate rather than criticize, meaning that he accepted and identified with its content rather than opposing it, stands diametrically opposed to the religious skepticism and agnosticism that some have read into Khayyām's philosophy, basing themselves solely on some of the poems attributed to him. Second, in light of the fact that Khayyām rarely praised or repeated predecessors, the very fact that he chose to translate a work of Ibn Sīnā proves the extent of his respect for Shaykh al-raʾīs and only confirms the assertion of all the traditional sources that in philosophy Khayyām was his follower. Some in fact have considered Khayyām to be a direct student of Ibn Sīnā, but this assertion cannot be taken as being literally true because of the birth and death dates of the two figures involved. Rather, it means that Khayyām was a student of the school of Ibn Sīnā, and his philosophical lineage in fact goes back through Lūkarī and Bahmanyār to Ibn Sīnā himself. This direct intellectual descent is of great importance in the case of Khayyām in situating him in the matrix of the general Islamic intellectual tradition. Moreover, such intellectual lineage is very pertinent for Islamic philosophical figures in general.

The Arabic treatise *al-Risālah fi'l-kawn waʾl-taklīf* (Treatise on the Realm of Existence and Human Responsibility) is one of Khayyām's substantial philosophical writings in which he mentions Ibn Sīnā explicitly as his master.[16] Much of the first part of this work in fact follows Ibn Sīnā closely; furthermore, some of its phrases are almost identical to those of Ibn Sīnā's *al-Ishārāt waʾl-tanbīhāt*. The treatise consists of answers provided by Khayyām to a number of questions sent to him by Abū Naṣr Nasawī, the judge (*qāḍī*) of the province of Fars, concerning the creation of the world and people's responsibility toward their Creator.[17] Khayyām, who in all of his works was to the point and disliked unnecessary verbiage, begins by stating that the subject of philosophy is essentially the response to three questions: whether something is, what it is, and why it is what it is. The answer to the first question leads in the discussion of being (*wujūd*), the second quiddity (*māhiyyah*), and the third causality (*'illiyyah*). Then he directs his attention to ontology following closely Ibn Sīnā in discussing the descending and ascending arcs of existence and the hierarchic chain of being.[18]

Khayyām then turns to the question of responsibility toward both God and His creatures, responsibility that according to him has been put within the very substance of human beings through the act of their creation. Being what they are, human beings are in need of others and therefore bear responsibility toward them. Khayyām also speaks of the necessity of prophecy. The prophets are the most perfect of all and can therefore propagate and promulgate divine laws among people in justice. His assertion about the necessity of prophecy shows how diverse forms of philosophy can flourish in a world dominated by the reality of prophecy and revelation.

As far as differences among people in virtue and evil character are concerned, Khayyām relates them on the one hand to the difference of temperaments, themselves based on bodily fluids and the elements mentioned in traditional Islamic medicine, and on the other to the different makeups of their souls. According to Khayyām, prophets reveal rites of worship so that God will not be forgotten and so that the teachings of God's laws will remain in human society. He then explains more fully the benefits of rites of worship for both the individual human soul and society as a whole. One can hardly imagine a greater difference between the Khayyām who is the author of this treatise and the modern version of him based on free translations of often spurious quatrains interpreted in such a way as to support the skeptical attitudes of certain modern readers of Khayyām in both East and West.

In his Arabic treatise *Ḍarūrat al-taḍādd fi'l-'ālam wa'l-jabr wa'l-baqā'* (The Necessity of Contradiction in the World and Determinism and Subsistence), which Sayyid Sulaymān Nadwī[19] considers as a continuation of *Risālah fi'l-kawn wa'l-taklīf*, Khayyām responds to three further questions; some such as Nadwī consider these to be answers to questions also posed to him by Nasawī. The first question concerns theodicy, that is, how can evil issue from the Necessary Being who being pure goodness cannot be the author of evil and oppression. After analyzing different kinds of attribution, Khayyām states that although it is absolutely true that the Necessary Being alone bestows existence upon things, the very bestowal of existence implies contradiction, which is nonexistence, and it is nonexistence that appears to us as evil and privation. That is why evil cannot be compared either in quantity or quality with the good.

The second question asks which of the two schools, that of determinism or free will, is correct. In a short answer Khayyām leans in favor of determinism, adding that this position is correct provided its followers do not exaggerate and fall into superstition.

The third question involves the quality of subsistence in relation to existence. Khayyām criticizes severely what he considers as a sophism concerning this question. He asserts that *wujūd* and *baqā*ʾ have a single meaning and should not be separated from each other.

In the short Arabic work *Risālat al-ḍiyāʾ al-ʿaqlī fī mawḍūʿ al-ʿilm al-kullī* (Treatise of Intellectual Light concerning Universal Science)[20] Khayyām discusses the relation between existence and quiddity following the views of Ibn Sīnā to whom he refers indirectly. Khayyām makes a clear distinction between quiddity in itself and *wujūd,* which is distinct from *māhiyyah* and is added to it in order to existentiate a quiddity objectively.

One of the important philosophical works of Khayyām is the Persian treatise *Risālah dar ʿilm-i kulliyyāt-i wujūd* (Treatise on the Science of the Universal Principles of Being) also known as *al-Risālah fī ʿilm al-kulliyyāt* (Treatise on Universal Principles) and *al-Risālah mawsūmah bi-silsilat al-tartīb* (Treatise Known as the Hierachic Chain).[21] In this treatise Khayyām discusses the chain of being and the ten intelligences following the views of Ibn Sīnā. It is also in this treatise that Khayyām discusses his classification of those who seek knowledge. Because of the singular significance of this classification for the understanding of Khayyām's philosophical perspective we quote this section in full:

> First, the theologians, who become content with disputation and "satisfying" proofs, and consider this much knowledge of the Creator (excellent is His Name) as sufficient.
>
> Second, the philosophers and sages who use only rational arguments to know the laws of logic, and are never content merely with "satisfying" arguments. But they too cannot remain faithful to the conditions of logic and become helpless with it.
>
> Third, the Ismāʿīlīs who say that the way of knowledge is not verifiable except through receiving instructions from a truthful instructor; for, in bringing proofs about the knowledge of the Creator, His Essence and Attributes, there is much difficulty; the reasoning power of the opponents and the intelligence [of those who struggle against the final authority of the revelation, and of those who fully accept it] is stupefied and helpless before it. Therefore, they say that it is better to seek knowledge from the words of a truthful person.
>
> Fourth, the Sufis, who do not seek knowledge by ratiocination or discursive thinking, but by purgation of their inner

> being and the purifying of their dispositions. They cleanse the rational soul of the impurities of nature and bodily form, until it becomes pure substance. When it then comes face to face with the spiritual world, the forms of that world become truly reflected in it, without any doubt or ambiguity.
>
> This is the best of all ways, because it is known to the servant of God that there is no reflection better than the Divine Presence and in that state there are no obstacles or veils in between. Whatever man lacks is due to the impurity of his nature. If the veil be lifted and the screen and obstacle removed, the truth of things as they are will become manifest and known. And the Master of creatures [the Prophet Muḥammad]—upon whom be peace—indicated this when he said: "Truly, during the days of your existence, inspirations come from God. Do you not want to follow them?"
>
> Tell unto reasoners that, for the lovers of God [gnostics], intuition is guide, not discursive thought.[22]

What is astonishing in this classification is Khayyām's defense of the Sufis and knowledge attained through inner purification, which they call *"kashf,"* as the most perfect and highest form of knowledge. One cannot make any judgment about Khayyām without paying full attention to this classification. Since this work is without doubt authentic, and Khayyām was not the kind of thinker to write a *pièce d'occasion* to satisfy this or that worldly authority, this assertion by him cannot but confirm his devotion to Sufism and makes even more plausible a Sufi interpretation of the authentic verses of Khayyām.

Perhaps the most important single philosophical opus of Khayyām is his Arabic text *al-Risālah fil-wujūd* (Treatise on Being) also known as *al-Risālah fī taḥqīqāt al-ṣifāt* (Treatise concerning Verifications of the Qualities).[23] It begins with two Quranic verses that contain the essence of the content of the treatise: "He gave unto everything its creation, then guided it right" (20: 50), and "He counteth the number of all things" (72: 28). The first asserts that the being of all things issues from God and the second that there is an order to all things. And it is precisely these two issues that comprise the basic elements of this treatise.

Khayyām emphasizes that quiddities receive their existence from another existence *(al-wujūd al-ghayrī)* and calls this process "emanation" *(fayaḍān)*. But at the same time Khayyām asserts that for each existent, it is the quiddity that is principial, and *wujūd* is a conceptual (*i'tibārī*) quality. Although the distinction between the principiality of *wujūd* (*aṣālat al-wujūd*) and the principiality of *māhiyyah* (*aṣālat al-māhiyyah*) goes back only to the School of Isfahan and especially Mullā Ṣadrā,[24] later students of Islamic philosophy have tended to look upon the whole earlier tradition from this point of view and sought to determine who belonged to which school. If we apply this later distinction with its own particular terminology to Khayyām, then we could say that Khayyām, like Suhrawardī, Naṣīr al-Dīn al-Ṭūsī, Ghiyāth al-Dīn Manṣūr Dashtakī, and Mīr Dāmād belongs to the school of principiality of quiddity, although Khayyām does not use the term *aṣālat al-māhiyyah* as was done by Mullā Ṣadrā and many other later philosophers.

In addition to emphasizing emanation and its continuous nature, following the views of both Ibn Sīnā and Suhrawardī, Khayyām also insists that this emanation is based on and contains order and laws. The two verses of the Quran stated at the beginning of the treatise are for Khayyām revealed proofs of this assertion, namely, the continuity of emanation from the Divine Reality, which bestows existences upon all things, and the orderly nature of this emanation. Consequently, the so-called laws of nature and what one observes everywhere in the created realm as order and harmony issue from the very Reality that bestows existence upon things and are inseparable from their ontological reality.

Khayyām is also concerned with the difficult question of God's knowledge of the world, a question that has concerned nearly all Islamic philosophers throughout the ages. He asserts that knowledge or *'ilm* is a quality of *wujūd,* and, therefore, since God bestows *wujūd* upon all creatures, He knows all of His creation simply by virtue of having brought them into being. As for *wujūd,* it is itself an attribute of the Divine Reality (*al-Ḥaqq*) and identical to Its Essence. Divine Knowledge, while ultimately being none other than the Divine Essence, is also none other than emanation. Divine Knowledge is the same as the Presence of God in all beings, even that which possesses only mental existence. Furthermore, since God is the source of reality of all quiddities and essences, all that is thus existentiated is good, and what appears otherwise as nonexistence and hence evil is the result of the necessity of contradiction (*ḍarūrat al-taḍādd*).

Finally among the specifically philosophical treatises of Khayyām there is one that is almost certainly by him, although not noted in the list given by some of the scholars of the subject, and that is a series of responses entitled *Risālah jawāban li-thalāth masā'il* [25] (Treatise of Response to Three Questions). In one manuscript the person posing the questions is Jamāl al-Dīn 'Abd al-Jabbār ibn Muḥammad al-Mishkawī, but in another manuscript he is referred to as "Amīn al-Ḥaḍrah" and at the end of the treatise as "al-Shaykh Jamāl al-Zamān." Although the identity of this person is not clear, it seems that he was a philosopher from Fars. In any case the questions, which are as follows, display the philosophical interests and preoccupations of the questioner:

1. If the rational soul survives after death, it would be necessary for each rational soul to have a specific personal existence.
2. If happenings in the domain of contingent beings have a single cause, this will lead to an infinite regression.
3. It has been proven that time depends on movement and is the quantity of movement of the spheres and that movement is not steadfast by itself (Khayyām does not complete the question).

All of Khayyām's responses are based on Ibn Sīnā's views, to whom he refers as *"al-faylasūf,"* the philosopher. More specifically he refers to the *Fann al-samā' al-ṭabī'ī*, the first book of *Ṭabī'iyyāt* (Natural Philosophy) of the *Shifā'* as well as to the works of Aristotle as sources for response to these questions. Khayyām makes an important philosophical assertion by saying that the *Fann al-samā' al-ṭabī'ī* (which means literally "the art of natural hearing" or that which one should hear first in the study of the natural sciences) contains the principles of all the natural sciences but is itself a branch of universal knowledge. In other words the principles of the sciences are to be sought not in themselves but in metaphysics.

There are a few other short philosophical fragments of Khayyām that deal more or less with the same issues that one finds in the treatises mentioned already. When one examines all of these philosophical treatises together, one sees Khayyām as essentially an Avicennan philosopher with particular acumen in mathematics and interest in mathematical and natural order, on the one hand, and in Sufism, on the other. There are also philosophical insights that are Khayyām's own, and he is far from being simply a repeater of Ibn Sīnā's words. Furthermore, as in the case of the master whom he calls *"the* philosopher," Khayyām's whole philosophical discourse is based on the Necessary Being, the One, who is the Reality who in religious language is called "God." Khayyām goes in fact a step further than many *mashshā'ī* philosophers in using religious references in his philosophical treatises including Quranic verses to which we have already referred.

Let us in conclusion turn to some of the quatrains more strongly attributed to Khayyām and consider their philosophical significance. One of the most famous quatrains states,

Thou hast said that Thou wilt torment me,
But I shall fear not such a warning.
For where Thou art, there can be no torment,
And where Thou art not, how can such a place exist?[26]

This quatrain confirms the utter goodness of God, the fact that the Supreme Reality is Pure Goodness, an idea also confirmed in Khayyām's prose philosophical works. This quatrain reconfirms in novel language an assertion to be found in many Sufi utterances in prose and poetry and also indicates the ultimate victory of good over all that appears as evil. In a sense it is a commentary upon the sacred saying of the Prophet (*ḥadīth qudsī*), "Verily My Mercy precedeth My Wrath."

Another quatrain states,

Thrown in before Fate's Mallet, O man Thou goest,
Struck by blows to left and right, remain silent.
He who hast flung thee with this mad course,
He knoweth, he knoweth, he knoweth and knoweth.[27]

The message in this poem is that *qaḍā*ʾ, translated here as "Fate" but that must be understood as a decree by the Divine Will and not some kind of natural and cosmic fate in the manner of certain Greek philosophers, governs all human existence and that God has knowledge of all things. It is a poetic commentary upon the meaning of the two Divine Names *al-Qādir* (the Omnipotent), and *al-'Alīm* (the All-Knower or Omniscient).

A quatrain, which appears outwardly more problematic, sings of the relativity of human knowledge as follows:

With neither truth nor certitude in scope,
Why waste our lives in doubt or futile hope?
Come, never let the goblet out of hand,
In fog, what if you drunk or sober grope?[28]

This quatrain might seem to be preaching out and out skepticism if taken literally. But would a person who accepted such a philosophy spend so much time and effort writing a work on algebra or reform the calendar? If seen in the context of the Islamic intellectual tradition, the content of these verses reveals their inner meaning to be something else, that is, the relativity of all human or rational knowledge[29] and the certitude derived from gnosis that is symbolized by wine as again found universally in Sufi poetry. In fact, many leading Islamic thinkers, philosophers, and scientists alike, not to speak of Sufis, have composed poems in this vein. In our own times the poems of even such religio-political figures as Mawlānā Mawdūdī and Ayatollah Khumaynī contain many verses in the same vein. The holding of the goblet of wine and drinking it here and now, a theme repeated in several other quatrains of Khayyām, also refers to the preciousness of the present moment, which is our only way of access to the Eternal and the means of gaining of absolute certitude. One must not forget in this context the Sufi adage *al-ṣūfī ibn al-waqt* (the Sufi is the son of the moment).

Many Khayyāmian quatrains also refer to the transience of the world and our rapid journey through it.

> The rotating wheel of heaven within which we wonder,
> Is an imaginal lamp of which we have knowledge by similitude.
> The sun is the candle and the world the lamp,
> We are like forms revolving within it.[30]

Also,

> A drop of water falls in an ocean wide,
> A grain of dust becomes with earth allied;
> What doth thy coming, going here denote?
> A fly appeared a while, then invisible he became.[31]

In the first quatrain the cosmos is likened not only to just any lamp but also to an imaginal lamp indicating the significance of the "world of imagination" (*'ālam al-khayāl*) with all the metaphysical and cosmological significance that it possesses in Islamic thought as we see expounded later in the works of Suhrawardī, Ibn 'Arabī, Mullā Ṣadrā, and others.[32] There is no reason to believe that here Khayyām is using *khayāl* in the modern debased sense of imagination, which implies simply irreality. Rather, by calling the cosmos an imaginal lamp, he not only alludes to the cosmic significance of *'ālam al-khayāl* but also indicates for the philosophically unsophisticated reader the fact that the cosmos is not ultimate reality but that there is a reality beyond it that it reflects as a lamp is the locus wherein light shines upon a scene. Then he points to our transient earthly existence, which is constituted of images and forms caused by the light of a lamp on the shade around it. The second quatrain confirms the same thesis from another point of view starting with the assertion that all things in this world return to their source and principle according to the famous philosophical dictum *kullu shayʾin yarjiʿu ilā aṣlihi,* (all things return to their source or root). In this great coming and going that marks the life of this transient world, our earthly existence is like that of a fly that appears and then disappears in a fleeting moment. It is metaphysically very significant that in this quatrain Khayyām uses the Persian words *padīd* and *nāpaydā* and not *life* and *death.* These two Persian terms mean to become manifest and then nonmanifest, to enter into phenomenal existence and then *dis*appear from that realm or become literally "devoid of appearance" or *nāpaydā,* which also means not to be found. Can one not understand this verse as meaning that we, even if compared to a lowly fly in this vast world of change, come from the unmanifested and the invisible into the world of manifestation and phenomenal existence and then return to that unmanifested and invisible world?

A quatrain of Khayyām with profound eschatological significance asserts,

> If the heart knew the secret of life as it is,
> It would also know the Divine Mysteries at death.
> Today when with thy *self,* thou knowest nothing,
> Tomorrow when stripped of *self,* what wilt thou know?[33]

This quatrain speaks in poetic language of one of the most important doctrines of Islamic eschatology, which has been fully developed by later Islamic metaphysicians and philosophers such as Ibn ʿArabī and Mullā Ṣadrā. According to this doctrine, the soul, while in this world, can both act and know. At the moment of death, it is cut off from both acting on the world and knowing it and will take with it only the fruits of its action and the knowledge that it has gained of spiritual matters while on this earthly journey. These are its "provisions" for the journey of the afterlife that Mullā Ṣadrā discusses in these very terms in one of his works entitled *Zād al-musāfir* (Provisions of the Traveler). This quatrain is nothing but a simple poetic description of a major Islamic eschatological teaching.

Finally, it is necessary to mention at least one quatrain that speaks of man's nothingness in face of the Absolute.

O Thou, unversed in ways of the world, thou art naught;
The bedrock is based on air, hence thou art naught.
Two voids define the limits of thy life,
On thy two sides nothing, in the middle thou art naught.[34]

Many have construed this and similar quatrains in a modern nihilistic manner as if Khayyām were an existential nihilist à la certain schools of twentieth-century Continental philosophy. But this interpretation is totally false if one considers the fact that Khayyām never denied the reality of God, the Absolute. Besides referring to the metaphysical understanding of nothing or void, which is none other than the Quintessential Naught or Beyond-Being to which Khayyām alludes in several verses,[35] this poem can be seen as a clear statement of the relativity of the human state and that from the point of this relativity, if taken only in itself, human beings and indeed the world are literally nothing in the face of the Absolute. In Avicennan language, which Khayyām confirms in his prose philosophical works, man, like all beings in this world, is "contingent" (*mumkin*) and receives his reality from the source of Being through that process of *fayaḍān* discussed above. This and similar quatrains can be read with perfect logic as poetical assertions of the status of contingency, which is complete poverty of existence or nothingness of the world, in contrast to the Necessary Being (*wājib al-wujūd*), which alone possesses and bestows *wujūd* upon all that exists. Moreover, all that exists exists by virtue of existentiation by the Necessary Being. In addition, in these poems there is an allusion to the relativity of even Being vis-à-vis the Beyond-Being, which alone is real in the ultimate sense.[36] The deepest message of such quatrains is that all that is relative is by nature relative and therefore transient, only the Absolute possessing absoluteness as such; or more simply put, only the Absolute is absolute.

These few quatrains, chosen from among those attributed with more certainty to Khayyām, provide a sampling of ideas that, if understood in the context of traditional Islamic philosophy and Sufism, do not only not negate but confirm in poetical language Khayyām's prose philosophical and scientific works in addition to revealing certain Sufi themes of which Khayyām must have had intimate knowledge. His classification of knowers cited above reveals his reverence for and understanding of the Sufi path of knowledge. The major themes of the more authenticated quatrains is the transience of the world, the limited nature of all rational knowledge before that veritable *sophia* that transcends ratiocination, and taking advantage of the present moment and experiencing the effect of that wine that symbolizes realized knowledge or gnosis. None of these themes is contradictory to his prose works. On the contrary, the prose and poetry complement each other and together reveal a fuller picture of Khayyām as metaphysician and philosopher.

It might be said that there are three types of human beings: those who deny all eschatological realities and the Day of Judgment to which Persian Sufis refer as "Tomorrow" *fardā*[37]; those who believe in the traditional eschatological realities and seek to live a virtuous life in this world in fear of hell and hope of paradise; and those who seek God here and now beyond fear of hell and hope of paradise. Since extremes meet, the views of the first and third group might appear to some people who look at the matter superficially to be the same in that both emphasize the here and now at the expense of man's final end in that "Tomorrow" that is beyond time. The first view, however, is the denial of religion from below, and the third view, which is esoteric, is the transcendence of the exoteric view from above. For exoteric pious believers it is sometimes difficult to make a distinction between the two. That is why they have often condemned not only the first view but also the third, their condemnation being in fact justified on its own level, which is not the case of modern agnostics who have deliberately associated the two opposite views together in order to attack those who hold on to the second view.

The limited understanding of ordinary believers is the reason why not only Khayyām but a number of other figures, mostly Sufis, have been condemned by some traditional exoteric authorities over the ages. In the case of other Sufi figures, however, their distinction from hedonists has remained clear enough despite their having received condemnation from some quarters. In the case of Khayyām, a number of factors, among them the intrusion of poems not by him into the corpus of the quatrains attributed to him, caused a number of traditional authorities, including even a few Sufis, to condemn him even before modern times despite the fact that he certainly did not lead a hedonistic life but was deeply revered as an Islamic scholar by his contemporaries. Furthermore, the free translations of Fitzgerald created a Western image of Khayyām, one of whose strong components was pleasure seeking and immediate gratification of the senses. In today's Western world where much more than the Victorian period instant sensual gratification has become practically a pseudo-religion, it is even more difficult than at the time of Fitzgerald to absolve Khayyām of the guilt of being a hedonist. Yet there is no authenticated poem of Khayyām dealing with the afterlife, which cannot be interpreted as belonging to the third rather than the first view stated above. When this celebration of the present moment and taking advantage of life while we have it is taken into consideration, in conjunction with everything he has written and also what his contemporaries wrote about him and even the honorific titles bestowed upon him,[38] it becomes more evident that far from being a hedonist, Khayyām sought to point out the preciousness of human life and the reality of the present moment as the door to the Eternal Realm in a manner consonant with the teachings of the great Sufi masters.

In conclusion, one can assert with assurance that if one studies all of the works of Khayyām, including the more authenticated *rubā'iyyāt*, one is able to discern the philosophical worldview of a major Islamic thinker who in philosophy was mostly a follower of Ibn Sīnā with certain independent interpretations of his own. He was also a major scientist with important views concerning the philosophy of mathematics. In addition he was a poet, who like many other Islamic philosophers and scientists who wrote works with rigorous logical structures, wrote poems on the side with metaphysical and gnostic themes. He was also without doubt personally attracted to Sufism. If we were asked to compare him to another Islamic figure who would most resemble him, we would choose Naṣīr al-Dīn al-Ṭūsī, who was, like Khayyām, an Avicennan (*mashshā'ī*) philosopher and a mathematician, who also wrote some poetry and was interested in Sufism. He also wrote a spiritual autobiography entitled *Sayr wa sulūk* (Spiritual Wayfaring).[39] Of course Ṭusī was also a Twelve-Imam Shi'ite theologian and authority on Ismā'īlī philosophy, in contrast to Khayyām, who was not concerned with these subjects to any appreciable extent.

Khayyām must be resuscitated as an Islamic philosopher and as yet another philosophical flower in the garden watered by the reality of prophecy, even if such an act will take a cultural hero away from modern Arab, Turkish, and especially Persian skeptics and hedonists. His philosophical works which have been translated recently[40] must be studied in their totality along with his poetical and scientific works. The present study should, however, be sufficient to reveal the great significance—philosophical, scientific, and also religious—of a remarkable Islamic philosopher, whose very fame on the mundane plane has caused his philosophical importance to become veiled from the world at large.

CHAPTER 10

Philosophy in Azarbaijan and the School of Shiraz

Centers of Philosophical Activity in the Islamic World

Throughout Islamic intellectual history certain cities and/or areas have become the main focus for philosophical activity during particular periods, while other areas have played little or no role in the cultivation of Islamic philosophy. Such is not the case of Islamic Law or Sufism, whose centers of cultivation have been widespread throughout nearly all of the Islamic world during the whole of Islamic history. When one thinks of philosophy, Baghdad in the third/ninth century, Khurasan from the fourth to the sixth century, Cordova and more generally Andalusia in the fifth and sixth centuries, and Cairo during the Fatimid period come readily to mind, while such major centers of Islamic civilization and culture as Fez, Tlemcen, Damascus, and the holy cities of Mecca and Medina, which have produced a galaxy of Islamic scholars and saints, are not particularly known as loci for the study of Islamic philosophy. The reasons for this historical fact are too complex to analyze here. They include the general religious and educational climate, patronage of the philosophical sciences by rulers and other authorities of influence, social conditions, and so on. But whatever the reasons for such a phenomenon, its reality can hardly be disputed. Even in India where Islamic philosophical texts were taught in *madrasahs* throughout the Islamic regions of the country, only a few places such as Farangi Mahall and Khayabad became major centers of philosophical activity from the late Mogul period onward.[1]

The School of Azarbaijan

In Persia, which became the main arena for the cultivation of Islamic philosophy after Ibn Rushd, one can observe the same phenomenon. The school of Khurasan began to wane after Abū'l-'Abbās al-Lūkarī al-Marwazī, Quṭb al-Zamān Muḥammad al-Ṭabasī, Ḥasan Qaṭṭān al-Marwazī, and 'Umar Khayyām, as already noted the most famous philosophical figure of Khurasan during this period. Gradually Azarbaijan became the center of Islamic philosophy from even before the Mongol invasion and continuing to the first half of the eighth/fourteenth century[2] to the extent that one can speak of the School of Azarbaijan in philosophy as one speaks of the School of Isfahan, which has now become an established term[3] and to which we shall turn in the next chapter.

There is still a great deal of research in manuscripts and monographic studies needed before the full picture of the philosophical life of this school as well as the School of Shiraz, which followed upon its wake, become relatively well known. In fact the period covering these two schools from the seventh/thirteenth to the tenth/sixteenth centuries remains the least known period of the history of Islamic philosophy, and each day new discoveries and studies are made that cast new light upon this very rich period of Islamic intellectual history, not only for Persia but also for the Ottoman world and Muslim India. Just recently a collection was discovered in Persia and named *Majmū'a-yi Marāghah* (The Collection of Maraghah), consisting of nearly twenty works on logic and philosophy copied in the years 596/1200 and 597/1201 less than ten years after the death of Suhrawardī.[4] This collection was copied in the Mujāhidiyyah *madrasah* in which most likely Majd al-Dīn al-Jīlī, the master with whom Suhrawardī studied philosophy in Maraghah, taught. This collection, consisting of writings by al-Fārābī, Abū Sulaymān al-Sijistānī, Ibn Sīnā, Abū Ḥāmid Muḥammad al-Ghazzālī, 'Umar ibn Sahlān al-Sāwajī, and Majd al-Dīn al-Jīlī himself, was copied for the students of the *madrasah* and bears witness to the importance of the teaching of philosophy in Azarbaijan at that time and also makes known the treatises that had been chosen as texts for courses on logic and philosophy.

Philosophical activity in Azarbaijan reached its peak in the seventh/thirteenth century in Maraghah, where the celebrated philosopher and scientist Naṣīr al-Dīn al-Ṭūsī (d. 672/1274) built the Maraghah Observatory, the first major observatory in the history of science built for a group of scientists to work together.[5] The circle around Naṣir al-Dīn is in itself identified by some as the School of Maraghah known especially for its scientific achievements, including the famous Īl-Khānid astronomical tables. But Maraghah was also a major center for the study of Islamic philosophy. In fact it was here that Ṭūsī in revivifying the thought of Ibn Sīnā influenced the whole later course of Islamic philosophy.[6] Until recently Ṭūsī as a philosopher was singularly neglected in Western studies considering his status as one of the colossal figures in Islamic philosophy, as well as the founder of Twelve-Imam systematic theology. A few recent studies have made his philosophical contributions better known,[7] but still much remains to be done to make clear the full significance of Ṭūsī's thought and the role of the circle of Maraghah as a watershed in Islamic intellectual history.

Ṭūsī wrote numerous works on logic, philosophy, and ethics dealing with ontology, the classification of forms of knowledge, the nature of the soul, causality, the relation between the world and the Creator, and numerous other philosophical subjects. He is not only the author of the most extensive work on logic in classical Persian, the *Asās al-iqtibās* (Foundation of Acquiring Knowledge), the most famous Islamic work on philosophical ethics, *Akhlāq-i nāṣirī* (The Naṣīrean Ethics), one of the most beautifully written works on virtue from the perspective of Sufism, *Awṣāf al-ashrāf* (Descriptions of the Noble), but also seminal works on Peripatetic philosophy that established him beyond doubt as the greatest Avicennan philosopher after the master himself. This category of the works of Ṭūsī include his rebuttals to the criticisms of Ibn Sīnā by al-Shahrastānī's *al-Muṣāri'ah* and Rāzī's earlier critical commentary upon Ibn Sīnā's al-*Ishārāt wa'l-tanbīhāt*. Known also as *Sharḥ al-isharāt*, this work, which is a major philosophical masterpiece in both form and content, resuscitated Ibn Sīnā's teachings once and for all in the East. Devoted to expounding the teachings of the master in this work, Ṭūsī refrained from expressing any views of his own except when it came to God's knowledge of the world, where Ṭūsī accepted the views of Suhrawardī, which he also knew well. The work became so famous that it in turn became the subject of many later commentaries, the most famous by Quṭb al-Dīn al-Rāzī.

In the context of the present book, it is not our aim to analyze Ṭūsī's philosophical thought, which is close to that of Ibn Sīnā, but to bring out his significance in the context of the relation between philosophy and prophecy. Here we are faced with a major scientist, one of the greatest in the history of mathematics and astronomy, and also a first-rate philosopher with a powerful analytical mind who is one of the foremost Peripatetic philosophers known in Islamic history. We are also confronted with a figure who wrote many works on logic, yet he was not a rationalist. Ṭūsī not only wrote an important treatise on Ismā'īlī philosophy based on instruction received from the authority of the imam and ultimately revelation but also composed the most important work on Twelve-Imam Shi'ite systematic theology, the *Kitāb al-tajrīd*, which we have already discussed in earlier chapters. He therefore represents a startling example of philosophizing even in a rational vein within a world dominated by the reality of prophecy.

Moreover, it is his path of harmonizing philosophy and revelation that was to have a much greater influence in the Islamic world than the view of independent paths for philosophy and religion proposed by Ibn Rushd.

Ṭūsī was by no means the only philosopher in Maraghah. He was encircled by a number of colleagues and students such as Quṭb al-Dīn Shirāzī, Najm al-Dīn Dabīrān-i Katībī, and Fakhr al-Dīn Marāghī, all of whom were notable philosophers, especially Qutb al-Dīn, who is a major figure in the history of Islamic thought.[8] It is of much interest to note that although Shīrāzī (d. 710/1311) was a prominent scientist, like Ṭūsī he philosophized in a world at whose horizons loomed the reality of revelation and dealt extensively from the point of view of philosophy with religious and spiritual questions derived from revelation.

Although not at Maraghah, Afḍal al-Dīn Kāshānī (d. circa 610/1213–14), is also to be noted in relation to the circle of Maraghah, especially since in later sources he is said to have been related to Ṭūsī, although the latter lived after him, and this relation has not been confirmed by current historical research. Kāshānī is one of the most remarkable of Islamic philosophers, one who combined the rigor of logic and rational philosophy with the vision of Sufism.[9] While he wrote on various aspects of Peripatetic philosophy and even Hermeticism, he emphasized the purification of the soul and self-knowledge as key to metaphysical knowledge. For him autology was the key to metaphysics and ontology. He is revered in Persia to this day as a Sufi saint, and his tomb near Kashan is visited by many pilgrims annually. He represents yet another manner in which philosophy developed in a climate dominated by prophecy in the Islamic world.

Returning to Azarbaijan, it is impossible to discuss this school without mentioning Suhrawardī, whom we have already discussed in this volume and elsewhere. He really marks the beginning of the School of Azarbaijan from which he had hailed, although he was put to death in Aleppo, and his influence continued in the province of his birth long after his death. 'Abd al-Qādir Ḥamzah ibn Yāqūt Aharī, the author of the treatise *al-Bulghah fi᾿l-ḥikmah* (The Sufficient in Philosophy) or *al-Aqṭāb al-quṭbiyyah* (Poles of the State of Being a Pole),[10] written around 628/1230 on the basis of the ideas of Suhrawardī, was perhaps the first *ishrāqī* philosopher after Suhrawardī. He hailed from the town of Ahar in Azarbaijan and was called by the people of that region "philosopher/Sufi." Likewise, the first great commentator of Suhrawardī, Shams al-Dīn Shahrazūrī, who wrote notable commentaries upon the master's *Ḥikmat al-ishrāq* (The Theosophy of the Orient of Light) and the *Talwīḥāt* (Intimations) and who was the author of the major *ishrāqī* text *al-Sharajat al-ilāhiyyah* (The Divine Tree) hailed from Shahrazur, which is located between Hamadan and Irbil and is again within the geographic orbit of the School of Azarbaijan.[11]

Besides Maraghah, other cities in Azarbaijan produced notable philosophers who were near contemporaries of the philosophers of Maraghah. One of the most notable among this group is Athīr al-Dīn Abharī (d. 663/1264), the author of *Kitāb hidāyat al-ḥikmah* (The Book of Guidance for Philosophy), one of the most famous expositions of later Avicennan philosophy upon which many commentaries were written, the most famous being by Maybudī and Mullā Ṣadrā. The commentary of Mullā Ṣadrā known in India as simply *Ṣadrā* was perhaps the most widely studied text of Islamic philosophy in Muslim India. Originally from Abhar, Athīr al-Dīn migrated to Syria and then Anatolia, where he spent the second part of his life. He was one of the most famous students of Fakhr al-Dīn al-Rāzī, the celebrated theologian who also spent some time in Azarbaijan. But in contrast to him and also to Quṭb al-Dīn Shīrāzī, Abharī spent most of his life in Azarbaijan and eastern Anatolia and must be considered as one of the philosophers of the School of Azarbaijan. Abharī was so deeply respected that Ṭūsī wrote a commentary upon his *Tanzīl al-afkār* (Descent of Thoughts), and one of Abharī's treatises on logic dealing with the *Isagogue* was even translated into Latin. It is interesting to note that although known primarily as a Peripatetic philosopher, Abharī was well acquainted with Suhrawardī, a fact to which both Shahrazūrī and Ibn Kammūnah have attested in their writings. Moreover, in two of his other works, *Muntahaʾl-afkār fī ibānat al-asrār* (The Height of Thoughts concerning the Clarification of Mysteries) and *Kashf al-ḥaqāʾiq fī taḥrīr al-daqāʾiq* (The Discovery of Truths concerning the Statement of Subtleties), Abharī himself mentions Suhrawardī.

Another famous contemporary of Abharī who hailed from Azarbaijan was Sirāj al-Dīn Urmawī, who, like Abharī, died in the second half of the seventh/thirteenth century. A commentator of Ibn Sīnā's *Ishārāt*, he also authored a number of independent philosophical works such as *Laṭāʾif al-ḥikmah* (Subtleties of Philosophy) and *Maṭāliʿ al-anwār* (Places of the Rising of Lights). Another contemporary of Abharī, Abū 'Alī Salmāsī, is known as the author of *al-Risālat al-siyāsiyyah* (Treatise on Politics). The appearance of these figures from three different cities of Azarbaijan in addition to Maraghah demonstrates the widespread interest in philosophy during the period in question in the whole province and not primarily in a single city and its environs which is the case of the School of Baghdad or the School of Shiraz.

During the later part of the seventh/thirteenth and beginning of the eighth/fourteenth centuries Tabriz became the most important center of philosophical activity not only in Persia but perhaps throughout the Islamic world. It was here that the great university city Rab'-i rashīdī was built by the Īl-Khānid grand vizier, Rashīd al-Dīn Faḍl Allāh, who was himself not only a great historian but also a physician and philosopher.[12] At that time philosophy was taught extensively in Tabriz, which had become the Īl-Khānid capital and a major cultural center. It was here that Abū 'Abd Allāh Muḥammad Tabrīzī wrote a commentary upon the *Dalāʾil al-ḥāʾirīn* (Guide to the Perplexed) of Maimonides and where his student Abū Isḥāq Tabrīzī , known as Ghaḍanfar, composed a summary of Abū Sulaymān al-Sijistānī's *Ṣiwān al-ḥikmah* (Vessel of Wisdom). Shams al-Dīn Khusrawshāhī, from the nearby town of Khusrawshah, also belongs to the circle of Tabriz. He is known as an expositor of the philosophy of Ibn Sīnā and one who composed a valuable summary of the master's monumental *Kitāb al-shifāʾ*. Likewise, it was near Tabriz in Shabistar that Shaykh Maḥmūd Shabistarī composed one of the greatest masterpieces of Sufi metaphysics and symbolism, *Gulshan-i rāz* (The Secret Garden of Divine Mysteries), at the beginning of the eighth/fourteenth century during the peak of philosophical activity in Tabriz. From around the middle of the eighth/fourteenth century, however, the study of philosophy waned in Azarbaijan and the center shifted to Shiraz.

Before turning to the School of Shiraz, however, it is of value to examine a recently discovered manuscript, *Safīna-yi Tabrīz* (The Vessel of Tabriz), which reveals a great deal about the study in Tabriz of philosophy in relation to the religious sciences derived directly from revelation. This vast compendium bound together in a single work and copied by Abūʾl-Majd Muḥammad Tabrīzī Malakānī Qarashī during the second and third decades of the eighth/fourteenth century was given the name *Safīnah* by the copyist himself.[13] It includes over two hundred works in nearly all the sciences of the day from jurisprudence, theology, and Quranic commentary to philosophy, gnosis, and certain other disciplines such as music. It reflects the syllabi of various centers of learning in Tabriz and the texts that were most widely read. One of the important features of the *Safīnah* is that it contains works of a number of Tabrīzī philosophers not known until now. An important figure who emerges from the study of this precious compendium is Amīn al-Dīn Ḥājjī Bulah, who was apparently a Sufi master as well as philosopher and was the author of a selection from the *Iḥyāʾ 'ulūm al-dīn* (The Revivification of the Sciences of Religion) of al-Ghazzālī, as well as an independent work on knowledge and the intellect.

The philosophical works contained in the *Safīnah* include the famous *al-'Ayniyyah* (Ode to the Soul) poem of Ibn Sīnā and its commentary by Shams al-Dīn Samarqandī; the *Ishārāt* of Ibn Sīnā; *al-Zubdah* (Best Essence) on logic by Bulah; *al-Shamsiyyah fi'l-qawa'id al-manṭiqiyyah* (The Treatise Dedicated to Shams al-Dīn concerning the Rules of Logic), by Najm al-Dīn Dabīrān-i Kātibī, *Ḥikmat al-'ayn* (Philosophy of the Essence) also by Kātibī; a poem on philosophy and logic by Fakhr al-Dīn al-Rāzī, and many works by Suhrawardī and Ṭūsī. It is especially notable that most of Suhrawardī's Persian works, which were not as widely read as his *Ḥikmat al-ishrāq* in later centuries, are contained in this compendium.[14] The very content of this work reveals the extensive interest in Islamic philosophy in the eighth/fourteenth century in Tabriz in conjunction with the transmitted (*manqūl*) sciences.

When one studies the School of Azarbaijan, it is interesting to note that the geographical boundaries of this school were not limited to the present province of Azarbaijan in Iran, although that area constituted the main arena of philosophical activity in the late seventh/thirteenth century and early eighth/fourteenth century. The boundaries stretched into eastern Anatolia all the way to Konya. We know that Quṭb al-Dīn Shīrāzī spent some time in Sivas and that Urmawī also traveled extensively in the eastern cities of Anatolia. The spread of the school of *ishrāq* within the early Ottoman period and the appearance of such figures as Anqarawī[15] have their most likely source in Azarbaijan and not Syria. Just as there was a cultural unity between these Anatolian cities and those of Western Persia as seen by the widespread use of Persian in such cities as Konya where Rūmī composed the greatest works of Persian Sufi literature, so was there a close link in philosophical activity in the region during the period under consideration. When the center of philosophical activity shifted to Shiraz, the development in Anatolia began to part ways from what was taking place in Shiraz although even at this later time such figures as Jalāl al-Dīn Dawānī from Fars were well known and respected even in Istanbul. During the apogee of the School of Azarbaijan, however, the relation was even closer, and eastern Anatolian cities became centers for the study of both Sufism and philosophy closely associated with what was going on in Azarbaijan. One only needs to recall here the name of Dā'ūd al-Qayṣarī, who was both a philosopher and a celebrated commentator of Ibn 'Arabī.

Although the study of philosophical texts of the School of Azarbaijan is far from complete, and still such earth-shaking discoveries as that of the *Safīna-yi Tabrīz* might take place, it is possible to say something about the general characteristics of this school. First of all, it is here that the *mashshāʾī* philosophy of Ibn Sīnā, so acutely criticized in Khurasan by al-Ghazzālī and later al-Shahrastānī and Fakhr al-Dīn al-Rāzī, received a new lease on life and began a second cycle of existence that continues to this day. Not only the epochal commentary of Ṭūsī upon Rāzī's criticism of the *Ishārāt* of Ibn Sīnā and some of his other works revived Avicennan philosophy, but also other important *mashshāʾī* works such as the *Hidāyah* of Athīr al-Dīn Abharī and *Ḥikmat al-ʿayn* of Dabirān-i Kātibī (d. 675/1276), a student of Abharī, were composed by members of this school, works that served as texts for the teaching of *mashshāʾī* philosophy for centuries in Persia, India, and the Ottoman world.

Second, it was in Azarbaijan that the philosophy of *ishrāq* was propagated after its founder Suhrawardī was put to death in Aleppo. Both Quṭb al-Dīn Shīrāzī and Shams al-Dīn Shahrazūrī, the two main commentators upon *Ḥikmat al-ishrāq*, were connected in one way or another with the School of Azarbaijan. Third, perhaps partly due to the influence of *ishrāqī* doctrines but also for independent reasons, many of the philosophers of this school were associated with Sufism, while at the same time much attention was paid in this region to the more metaphysical and philosophical dimensions of Sufism as one sees in the works of Shabistarī, especially his *Gulshan-i rāz*. Finally, it is of interest to note that there was a notable rise of the use of the Persian language for philosophical discourse in the School of Azarbaijan in comparison with the School of Khurasan and also the later School of Isfahan. Suhrawardī, who should be seen as the first major figure of this school, although he lived somewhat earlier than the period of its full flowering, wrote many philosophical treatises that are among the masterpieces of Persian prose. Tūsī is known for a number of Persian philosophical works especially the *Akhlāq-i naṣirī* also a classic of Persian literature. His supposed relative, although from Kashan, Afḍal al-Dīn Kāshānī, wrote almost exclusively in a Persian of exceptional beauty and depth. Ṭūsī's colleague in Maraghah, Quṭb al-Dīn Shīrāzī is the author of a vast Persian encyclopedia of philosophy, the *Durrat al-tāj* (The Jewel in the Crown) and Rashīd al-Dīn Faḍl Allāh, the grand vizier of the Īl-Khānids who was both philosopher and historian wrote his universal history, the first of its kind in human history, in Persian in which he also wrote many of his philosophical and theological discourses. This greater use of Persian, without however neglecting Arabic as the major language of Islamic intellectual discourse, is to be found in Persia and eastern Anatolia in many fields following the Mongol invasion. Persian philosophical treatises of this period, as well as those of the School of Shiraz, became also widely disseminated in India where

Persian was used as an intellectual, as well as mystical, language even more than in Persia itself, although again Arabic was not by any means neglected in India any more than it was in Persia.

In leaving the School of Azarbaijan to travel south to Shiraz, it is important to note that here, as in the schools of Baghdad, Khurasan, and Andalusia, the main concern of philosophers was not only to provide an intellectual vision and a means to understand the nature of things within an intelligible framework but also to respond to the reality of revelation, the knowledge it made possible, including illuminative knowledge, and the challenges it posed to philosophers as an authentic and even the most authentic channel for the attainment of ultimate knowledge by the human mind.

The School of Shiraz

The devastation caused by the Mongol invasion and its aftermath not only obliterated numerous centers of learning in Central Asia, Khurasan, and Iraq but also inaugurated a period of unsettled and chaotic conditions that was to last for a couple of centuries. Thanks to the Atābakān rulers of Fars, Shiraz was spared the fury of the Mongol invasion, and from the seventh/thirteenth to the tenth/sixteenth centuries when the Safavids united Persia, the city and its environs remained a relative oasis of peace. During this period the later dynasties of Āl-i Jalāyir, Āl-i Muẓaffar, and Āq-Quyünlü succeeded in preserving the atmosphere of peace and in encouraging learning. Already during the fourth/tenth century during the Būyid period, Shiraz had become a major center of Islamic learning and was given the title *dār al-'ilm* or "abode of knowledge." It even vied with Baghdad in the domain of scholarship and science. On that historic basis, the Atābakān and the later dynasties mentioned above strengthened the tradition of learning in Shiraz to the extent that after the conquest of Persia by Tamerlane, his governors and later on successors continued to honor the class of learned people in that city. In fact Shiraz continued to be the *dār al-'ilm* of the day into the Safavid period when the center of learning including philosophy was transferred to Isfahan. But one can never forget that the greatest figure of the School of Isfahan, Ṣadr al-Dīn Shirāzī, was not only from Shiraz but also had received his early education in that city. In fact he might be considered the final major product of the School of Shiraz and his journey to Isfahan the point of transfer of the main center of Islamic philosophy to that city, even if in the latter part of his life, Mullā Ṣadrā was to return to Shiraz to teach at the Khan School built for him by the governor of Fars province.[16]

In any case the period from the eighth/fourteenth to the tenth/sixteenth century marks the peak of philosophical activity in Shiraz.[17] The beginning of this school was contemporary with the period of philosophical activity associated with Azarbaijan and the end of the peak of its activity with the founding of the School of Isfahan by Mīr Dāmād and the early decades of the activity of this school. As already mentioned, the period from the seventh/thirteenth to the tenth/sixteenth century is the most unknown and least studied in the history of Islamic philosophy, and consequently many claim that it was in fact a period of languor in Islamic philosophy, a period that did not produce a philosopher of the stature of Fārābī, Ibn Sīnā, Ibn Rushd, Suhrawardī, or Mullā Ṣadrā. Such a judgment can only be made, however, after the works of major philosophers of this school are studied. Certainly Mullā Sadrā himself had as great a respect for some of the philosophers of this period as he did for those of earlier centuries. Without doubt the School of Shiraz was of exceptional influence in the intellectual life of the Ottoman world and Islamic India, as well as of later schools of philosophy in Persia itself, starting with the School of Isfahan, and produced a number of important philosophers.

Culturally and intellectually, although during the period in question Shiraz was not as great a center of Islamic jurisprudence in its Shi'ite form as Najaf, it was a major center of Islamic theology and principles of jurisprudence (*uṣul al-fiqh*), as well as literature and the arts. It was also a major center of Sufism to the extent that it came to be known as *Burj al-awliyā*ʾ (the Tower of Saints) where many major Sufi figures such as Awḥad al-Dīn Kāzirūnī and Shams al-Dīn Muḥammad Lāhījī resided, not to speak of the greatest Sufi poet of the Persian language, Ḥāfiẓ. Moreover, Shiraz soon became a major center of philosophy, heir to the *ishrāqī* school of Suhrawardī as well as the Peripatetic philosophy of the school of Ibn Sīnā.

All of these elements helped create the School of Shiraz, where philosophical discourse became closely wed to theology and Sufism and in certain cases the natural sciences. Many of the philosophers of this school were drawn toward Sufism, others to Ash'arite and later Ithnā 'asharī *kalām*, and yet others to medicine and astronomy, in which they became accomplished masters. The School of Shiraz is in fact almost as important for the history of Islamic theology and science as it is for the history of Islamic philosophy. Furthermore, it was in this school that the rapprochement between *mashshāʾī* and *ishrāqī* philosophy, *kalām* and gnosis (*'irfān*) that characterizes the School of

Isfahan was begun culminating in the rise of the most famous philosopher of Shiraz, Mullā Ṣadrā, who had studied in his early years in his city of birth, Shiraz, probably under figures associated with the circle of Jamāl al-Dīn Maḥmūd Shīrāzī, who was still teaching in 965/1557, and possibly also the circle of Jalāl al-Dīn Dawānī (d. 908/1501). The greatest figures of the School of Shiraz[18] such as 'Aḍud al-Dīn Ījī (d. 756/1355), Mīr Sayyid Sharīf Jurjānī (d. 816/1413), the Dashtakīs, Jalāl al-Dīn Dawānī, and Shams al-Dīn Khafrī (d. 957/1549) were in fact known far beyond the borders of Fars, and many of them exercised the greatest influence on Islamic thinkers of the Ottoman world and Muslim India.

The Major Philosophers of the School of Shiraz

Technically one should start the School of Shiraz with Quṭb al-Dīn Shīrāzī, who, however, left Shiraz as a young man and who belongs more to the School of Maraghah and Azarbaijan as mentioned earlier. As for famous figures such as Ījī and Jurjānī, they produced works of philosophical theology and were essentially experts on *kalām* rather than *falsafah*. We shall therefore confine ourselves to four figures who dominated the philosophical scene in Shiraz from the eighth/fourteenth century to the tenth/sixteenth century before the time of Mullā Ṣadrā and who were full-fledged philosophers. These figures are Ṣadr al-Dīn Dashtakī and his son, Ghiyāth al-Dīn Manṣūr, Jalāl al-Dīn Dawānī, and Shams al-Dīn Khafrī.

Mīr Ṣadr al-Dīn Dashtakī known also as Sayyid-i Sanad

Ṣadr al-Dīn Muḥammad Dashtakī, the real founder of the School of Shiraz was born in 828/1424 in the quarter of Dashtak in Shiraz into a family who descended from the Prophet and who migrated to Shiraz in the fifth/eleventh century.[19] Later in life he was given the honorific title of Ṣadr al-'ulamā᾿ (Foremost among Scholars) and Sayyid al-mudaqqiqīn (Master of Knowledge of the Minutiae of Things), the first title being often the cause of his being confused with Ṣadr al-muta᾿allihīn or Mullā Ṣadrā. Ṣadr al-Dīn Dashtakī studied Arabic and the transmitted sciences with his uncle Sayyid Ḥabīb Allāh Dashtakī and philosophy with Muslim Fārsī, an otherwise unknown figure. Some have also mentioned Mawlā Qawām al-Dīn Muḥammad Kulbārī as his teacher in logic and philosophy. Since the chain of transmission of philosophical knowledge is of great importance, it is worthwhile to mention here Ṣadr al-Dīn's chain (*silsilah*), which connects him to the masters of old, as recounted by his son.

Ibn Sīnā → Bahmanyār → Abū'l-'Abbās al-Lūkarī → Afḍal al-Dīn al-Ghīlānī → Sayyid Ṣadr al-Dīn al-Sarakhsī → Farīd al-Dīn Dāmād al-Nayshābūrī → Naṣīr al-Dīn al-Ṭūsī → Quṭb al-Dīn Shīrāzī → Sayyid Muslim Fārsī (grandfather) → Sayyid Muslim Fārsī (father) → Sayyid Fāḍil Muslim Fārsī → Sayyid Ṣadr al-Dīn Dashtakī.[20]

This chain is of great significance not only for the understanding of the "philosophical lineage" of Ṣadr al-Dīn Dashtakī himself but also for those of his son Ghiyāth al-Dīn, who was his father's student, as well as for the philosophical lineage of later philosophers of Shiraz, Isfahan, and even Muslim India.

Ṣadr al-Dīn became a major scholar and philosopher as well as a powerful public figure. In 883/1478 he established the Manṣūriyyah *madrasah* in Shiraz, named after his son, Ghiyāth al-Dīn Manṣūr, a school where philosophy, logic, and the natural sciences, as well as religious sciences, were taught. It became one of the most influential centers of higher learning in later Islamic history. Ṣadr al-Dīn's life ended tragically when the Turkic ruler of the city, thinking that Ṣadr al-Dīn had been involved in social disturbances, sent a group of ruffians to his house where he was killed in 903/1497. He was buried in the Manṣūriyyah *madrasah,* where his mausoleum survives to this day.

Ṣadr al-Dīn Dashtakī wrote nearly twenty works, many in the form of glosses and commentaries on earlier texts, but these works are not simply repetitions. Rather, they often contain many ideas associated with Ṣadr al-Dīn himself or clarify difficult passages of the earlier classics not elucidated in earlier commentaries.[21] In these texts Ṣadr al-Dīn reveals his mastery of both *falsafah* and *kalām* but writes essentially as a philosopher in the school of Ibn Sīnā. These works, many of which have not been as yet edited and studied carefully,[22] include various subjects on logic, philosophy, and the natural sciences, including a well-known work on agriculture. His most important work perhaps is his commentaries upon the *Tajrīd* of Naṣīr al-Dīn Ṭūsī, which include several sets of glosses, criticisms by Dawānī, and Dashtakī's response to those criticisms. The debate between these two masters was well known in Shiraz and also India, a debate in which Ṣadr al-Dīn usually held the upper hand. The two also debated about the famous "liar's paradox" well known to logicians.[23] These debates led to the discussion of different kinds of attribution (*ḥaml*), which became so important in Mullā Ṣadrā. One can also see questions pertaining to the principiality of existence or quiddity (*aṣālat al-wujūd* or *māhiyyah*), mental existence, unity and gradation of *wujūd*, the immateriality of the imaginative faculty, and many other major philosophical concepts that were to be treated fully by Mullā Ṣadrā. In fact in many places in his writings Mullā Ṣadrā discusses the debates between Ṣadr al-Dīn Dashtakī and Dawānī and usually takes the side of Dashtakī.[24] He even goes so far as to assert that before him Dashtakī believed in the principiality of existence.[25] In any case the revival of Islamic philosophy in Isfahan during the Safavid period and especially the synthesis of Mullā Ṣadrā owes much to Ṣadr al-Dīn Dashtakī, a major philosophical figure who has been greatly neglected in the study of Islamic philosophy until now.

Before leaving this brief discussion of Ṣadr al-Dīn Dashtakī, one must mention the remarkable intellectual role of the Dashtakī family of which he was the patriarch. Besides Ghiyāth al-Dīn, who will be discussed later, he had another son, 'Imād al-Dīn Mas'ūd. Both had many descendents who spread to various parts of Persia, Arabia, and India. Some such as Mīr Niẓām al-Dīn Dashtakī (d. 1015/1607) have left behind a number of notable gnostic works. His son Mīrzā Muḥammad Ma'ṣūm Dashtakī (d. 1032/1622) lived in Mecca where he taught Islamic jurisprudence according to the five schools of Islamic Law. His son Niẓām al-Dīn Aḥmad, born in Ta'if, went to the Daccan in 1055/1645, on the order of the king of Daccan, where he married his daughter and gained political authority. He has left behind a *dīwān* of Arabic poetry. His son Sayyid 'Alī Khān Kabīr was born in Medina in 1066/1655 and studied in Mecca but then left for India to visit his father. There he gained great prominence and became a ruler but at the end of his life returned to Shiraz where he died in 1118/1706. His tomb is in the mausoleum of Shāh Chirāq. It is remarkable how many notable scholars and philosophers appeared in this family and how widespread was their influence in areas as far apart as Mecca and Medina, Herat and Daccan, not to mention Shiraz itself. But wherever they lived, taught, and wrote was still within the confines of "the land of prophecy," and like other Islamic philosophers before and after them, they breathed in a universe where the reality of revelation was ubiquitous.

Jalāl al-Dīn Dawānī

Before turning to Ṣadr al-Dīn's son Ghiyāth al-Dīn Manṣūr, a word must be said about the figure of the School of Shiraz best known in the West, Jalāl al-Dīn Muḥammad ibn Sa'd Kāzirūnī, known as Muḥaqqiq-i Dawānī. Born in Dawan near Kazirun in the vicinity of Shiraz in 830/1427 (hence his name Dawānī, which has by mistake sometimes been referred to as Dawwānī), he studied both *kalām* and *falsafah* in Shiraz. Soon he became a famous scholar occupying the office of *ṣadr* or leader of the *'ulamā'* after which he became teacher of the Begum *madrasah*. Under the Āq Quyūnlū dynasty he became the *qāḍī* of the whole province of Fars. He died at the beginning of the Safavid period in 908/1502–03 and was buried in Dawan.

In his early intellectual life Dawānī was Sunni and an authority on Sunni *kalām* as his commentary upon Taftāzānī's work on Ash'arite *kalām, Tahdhīb al-manṭiq wa'l-kalām* (Refinement of Logic and *Kalām*) makes clear. He also wrote works that attracted the attention of Ottoman scholars, and he was widely popular in that realm. There is little doubt, however, that at the end of his life, as ascertained in traditional sources, on the basis of a dream, he embraced Shi'ism. In any case he remained widely popular in both Sunni and Shi'ite scholarly circles in the Ottoman world, Persia, and Muslim India.[26]

The fame of Dawānī among the general public rests on his very popular work of philosophical ethics entitled *Lawāmi' al-ishrāq fī makārim al-akhlāq* (Flashes of Illumination concerning Ethical Virtues), known more commonly as *Akhlāq-i jalālī* (Jalālean Ethics).[27] This work is the third major opus in this genre of philosophical ethics in Islam. The first well-known work of this kind that sought to deal with ethics as discussed in Greek philosophy from an Islamic point of view and in light of Islamic philosophy, and also Sufism, was Ibn Miskawayh's *Tahdhīb al-akhlāq* (The Refinement of Character)[28] written in Arabic. This famous treatise in turn served as the basis for Naṣīr al-Dīn al-Ṭūsī's *Akhlāq -i nāṣirī*.[29] Written in Persian this very popular work expanded the scope of Ibn Miskawayh's treatise to include "domestic disciplines" and politics.[30] Dawānī in turn based his book on ethics on that of Ṭūsī and like him dealt with law, politics, and certain aspects of economics, as well as moral philosophy, and also dealt with such subjects as the distinction between a legitimate and an illegitimate ruler, good and evil societies, and categories of human beings from the virtuous to the evil.

Dawānī added Quranic references, *ḥadīths*, and sayings of Sufis to his text, and his interpretation of philosophical ethics was more illuminative (*ishrāqī*), whereas Ṭūsī was more Avicennan (*mashshā'ī*). Dawānī also sought to correlate the philosophical teachings of Aristotle concerning the mean with the Quranic doctrine of moderation and emphasized that ultimately the mean in ethical action is attained, as far as the content and not form is concerned, through revelation and Divine Law and not reason. This work of Dawānī along with those of his predecessors and successors on philosophical ethics is very demonstrative of the form that philosophical ethics and practical philosophy take when philosophy is cultivated in the land of prophecy. As far as practical philosophy and ethics are concerned, one can see clear parallels to this Islamic development not only in the Jewish and Christian traditions but also in lands beyond the confines of the Arahamic traditions, such as in the Confucian and Neo-Confucian worlds.

Dawānī was known not only for his works on *kalām* and ethics. He was also fully a philosopher with strong *ishrāqī* tendencies. His most famous work in this domain is *Shawākil al-hūr fī sharḥ hayākil al-nūr* (Forms of Brightness concerning the Temples of Light),[31] a work that clarifies many of the subtleties of Suhrawardī's *Hayākil al-nūr,* (Temples of Light) including clarifying the meaning of the word *haykal* as used by Suhrawardī. Although this work is an important opus in the *ishrāqī* tradition and was popular in both Persia and India, it was strongly criticized in Ghiyāth al-Dīn Manṣūr's own commentary upon the Suhrawardian text.

This *ishrāqī* commentary of Dawānī is not his only *ishrāqī* work. Many of his other writings, such as his metaphysical treatise *al-Zawra',* written in Najaf while he was on pilgrimage and therefore called "Tigris," have a strong *ishrāqī* color. Ideas expressed in these and other works were of keen interest to later philosophers especially those of the School of Isfahan and Mullā Ṣadrā devoted many pages to their discussion, especially in the *Asfār.* Among the most well known views associated with Dawānī is a special interpretation of the unity and principiality of being called *"dhawq al-ta*ʾ*alluh,"* which is discussed extensively but rejected by Mullā Ṣadrā and later Ṣadrian philosophers.

Ghiyāth al-Dīn Manṣūr Dashtakī

Ghiyāth al-Dīn Manṣūr, the oldest son of Ṣadr al-Dīn Dashtakī, is considered by many as the foremost Islamic philosopher of the tenth/sixteenth century, preceding Mīr Dāmād and the greatest *ishrāqī* philosopher between Quṭb al-Dīn Shīrāzī and the foundation of the School of Isfahan,[32] although he was not only an *ishrāqī* philosopher but was also well versed in *mashshā*ʾ*ī* philosophy and *'irfān.* Born in the quarter of Dashtak in Shiraz in 866/1461, he displayed signs of exceptional intelligence from childhood and was for that reason greatly loved by his father, who, as already mentioned, named the famous Manṣūriyyah *madrasah* after him and undertook to educate him himself. Soon Ghiyāth al-Dīn Manṣūr became a major thinker, well versed in the natural and mathematical sciences and philosophy, not to speak of theology and the religious sciences. He was a polymath like Naṣīr al-Dīn al-Ṭūsī and Bahāʾ al-Dīn al-'Āmilī and considered an authority in language and logic, theology and philosophy, jurisprudence and Quranic commentary, astronomy and mathematics, medicine and pharmacology, as well as ethics and *'irfān*.[33] Like Ṭūsī before him, he was given the title of the "eleventh intellect" (in reference to the ten intellects in Ibn Sīnā's philosophy), and like Mīr Dāmād after him, he was called by some the "Third Teacher," following Aristotle, the "First Teacher," and Fārābī, the "Second Teacher."[34] Not only did he teach philosophy and theology in the Manṣūriyyah *madrasah*, but in 927/1521 he was called to Maraghah to repair the observatory constructed by Naṣīr al-Dīn Ṭūsī and to complete the Īl-Khānid Zīj (astronomical tables). As for medicine, his books such as *al-Shāfiyah* (The Healer) and *Ma'ālim al-shifā'* (Milestones of Healing) were taught for a long time to medical students. When the Safavids conquered Persia, Ghiyāth al-Dīn was chosen to the high religious office of *ṣadr* and served in this important function for many years until in 938/1531–32 when he withdrew from politics completely and distanced himself from the Safavid court, retiring to Shiraz, where he died in 948/1542. The political climate which turned against him caused many of his students and learned descendents to leave Shiraz for India or the Hejaz with the result that the School of Shiraz became much weakened after him but also much better known in other regions, especially in the Indian Subcontinent.

Because of political opposition to Ghiyāth al-Dīn Manṣūr and his followers in Shiraz, there are not many extant manuscripts of his writings, and few of his works have appeared in printed form. Works attributed to him include *al-Muḥākamāt* (Trials), in which he compares the glosses of his father and Dawānī upon *Sharḥ al-tajrīd* and criticizes Dawānī severely; his commentary upon the *Hayākil al-nūr* of Suhrawardī, which is much longer than that of Dawānī and again critical of the latter; *Shifā' al-qulūb* (Healing of Hearts) which seeks to clarify the difficulties of Ibn Sīnā's *Kitāb al-shifā'* (The Book of Healing); *al-Ḥikmat al-manṣūriyyah* (Manṣūrean Philosophy), written from an *ishrāqī* point of view and considered by the author as his most important work; *al-Ishārāt wa'l-talwīḥāt* (Directives and Intimations) since it combines the teachings of Ibn Sīnā and Suhrawardī; *Maqāmāt al-'ārifīn* (Stations of the Gnostics), to which we shall turn shortly; a number of treatises on the various sciences such as mathematics and medicine; and *Akhlāq-i manṣūrī* (Manṣūrean Ethics), written within the tradition of philosophical ethics before him but never matching the popularity of either *Akhlāq-i nāṣirī* or *Akhlāq-i jalālī*.

Of special interest among the works of Ghiyāth al-Dīn from the point of view of the relation between philosophy and revelation is his commentary on chapter 76 of the Quran, "*Sūrat al-insān*," entitled *Tuḥfat al-fatā*. Because of the questions that arose about the Makkan or

Medinan origin of the verses of this chapter and the realities to which many of its verses refer, numerous commentaries have been written upon it from the fourth/tenth century commentary of Aḥmad ibn Muḥammad al-'Āṣimī to those of Mawlā Ḥabīb Allāh Kāshānī and Muḥammad 'Alī Hamadānī composed during the last two centuries. In addition this chapter has of course been commented upon by various famous Quranic commentators. Ghiyāth al-Dīn made use of the earlier commentaries, especially those of Fakhr al-Dīn al-Rāzī, al-Zamakhsharī, al-Bayḍāwī, and al-Nayshābūrī. But Ghiyāth al-Dīn's commentary differs in many ways from the views of such commentators, as well as those who wrote commentaries on *Sūrat al-insān* alone in that Ghiyāth al-Dīn's approach is essentially philosophical and gnostic. In fact this work is among the most important in the category of philosophical commentaries on the Quran and is without doubt one of the most outstanding commentaries written by an Islamic philosopher before Mullā Ṣadrā's monumental commentary on the Sacred Text.

Let us now turn to the treatise *Maqāmāt al-'ārifīn,* which contains the summary of the thought of Ghiyāth al-Dīn Manṣūr and is in many ways a synopsis of the teachings of the School of Shiraz.[35] This treatise was written in his later life and has a clear Shi'ite color. It is a commentary upon *"Fī maqāmāt al-'ārifīn"* (On the Stations of the Gnostics), the ninth chapter of Ibn Sīnā's *al-Ishārāt wa'l-tanbīhāt* with material added perhaps inspired by Khwājah 'Abd Allāh Anṣārī's *Manāzil al-sā'irīn* (Resting Places of the Travelers), as well as certain *kalāmī* discussions. Verses of the Quran, *ḥadīths,* and Arabic and Persian poems from classical poets such as Ḥallāj, Rūmī, and Ḥāfiẓ also adorn the text. This work contains discussions of some of the most profound and intricate aspects of *'irfān,* such as the meaning of the sacred saying (*ḥadīth qudsī*) called *"qurb al-nawāfil,"* the transcendent unity of being and the "flow of existence" where the influence of Ibn 'Arabī is evident. He also speaks of the flow of love (*'ishq*) in all things in a manner reminiscent of Mullā Ṣadrā.

One sees in the pages of this work references to Peripatetic philosophy, especially that of Ibn Sīnā, as well as the *kalām* of Fakhr al-Dīn al-Rāzī, which he criticizes several times. He also distances himself from later theologians such as Ījī, Jurjānī, and Taftāzānī. Furthermore, he quotes Suhrawardī, and the work has definitely an *ishrāqī* color. He even refers to his own writings on medicine and psychology in his discussion of love and music. Also in the manner of Mullā Ṣadrā in his *Si aṣl* (Three Principles) and *Kasr al-aṣnām al-jāhililyyah* (Breaking the Idols of the Age of Ignorance), Ghiyāth al-Dīn Manṣūr criticizes the pseudo-Sufis who do not heed the *Sharī'ah,* as well as those who pay attention only to the outward meaning of the religion and not its inward dimension. He seeks to unite *Sharī'ah, Ṭarīqah,* and *Ḥaqīqah* in a context that is both philosophical and gnostic. He himself mentions that this work was written in an *'irfānī* language complementing his *Riyāḍ al-riḍwān* (Garden of Paradise), which was written in a Peripatetic language.[36] He also speaks specifically of Shi'ite gnosis (*'irfān-i shī'ī*). In this context there is also a profound discussion of the *'irfānī* and *ishrāqī* dimensions of prophecy. This section of the work is especially interesting in revealing how in later Islamic philosophy the philosophers dealt with the question of prophecy and how philosophy in the sense conceived by Pythagoras and Parmenides blossomed fully again in a space dominated by prophecy in its Abrahamic form as it had done earlier in ancient Greece where it was wed to prophetic experience as prophecy was understood by the founders of Greek philosophy in the context of the Greek religious universe.

The *Maqāmāt al-'ārifīn* of Ghiyāth al-Dīn Manṣūr is indicative of the rapprochement that was taking place in the School of Shiraz between *mashshā'ī* philosophy, *ishrāqī* philosophy or theosophy, *'irfān,* and *kalām.* It is this rapprochement that prepared the ground for the grand synthesis of Mullā Ṣadrā in the eleventh/seventeenth century. In reading this treatise one becomes aware of how much the School of Isfahan owed to the School of Shiraz and more specifically how indebted Mullā Ṣadrā was to Ghiyāth al-Dīn Manṣūr, whom he cites with such respect in his works, especially the *Asfār.*

Ghiyāth al-Dīn Manṣūr had a number of outstanding students who continued his teachings well into the Safavid period. Among them was his son Amīr Ṣadr al-Dīn Muḥammad Thānī, who taught at the Manṣūriyyah *madrasah* until at least 961/1554 when he composed a work entitled *al-Dhikrā* (Remembrance) dealing with juridical, theological, philosophical, and gnostic themes. Due to politically adverse conditions, he is said to have fled from Shiraz to Gilan, where he spent the rest of his life in an unknown condition and where he died. Ghiyāth al-Dīn's other famous students include Fakhr al-Dīn Sammākī and Jamāl al-Dīn Maḥmūd Shīrāzī,[37] one of whose students may have been the first teacher of Mullā Ṣadrā while he was studying as a young man in Shiraz. In any case, Ghiyāth al-Dīn Manṣūr's influence was to continue for a long time in both Shiraz and Isfahan, as well as in India, and he left a deep imprint on later Islamic philosophy.

Shams al-Dīn Khafrī

After Ghiyāth al-Dīn Manṣūr, the most important student of Ṣadr al-Dīn Dashtakī was Mullā Shams al-Dīn Muḥammad ibn Aḥmad Khafrī, also known as Muḥaqqiq-i Khafrī, who was born in the district of Khafr near Shiraz.[38] The date of his birth is not known, but it is known that he studied philosophy and the sciences in Shiraz mostly with Ṣadr al-Dīn Dashtakī and possibly with Dawānī. Later in life he migrated to Kashan, where he trained his most famous student, Shāh Ṭāhir ibn Raḍī al-Dīn and where he became a major religious and intellectual figure, even attracting the attention of the Safavid court. He died in that city around 957/1552 and was buried near Imāmzādah 'Aṭābakhsh. Already during his lifetime he was celebrated as an outstanding logician, mathematician, and astronomer, as well as philosopher. Although very little research has been done on his scientific works, a recent study of one of his astronomical works has revealed that he was a major astronomer worthy of comparison with Naṣīr al-Dīn Ṭūsī and Quṭb al-Dīn Shīrāzī.[39]

Khafrī's works written mostly in the form of commentaries and glosses deal with philosophy, theology, the mathematical sciences, and even the occult sciences such as geomancy. His philosophical works include glosses on commentaries upon Ṭūsī's *Tajrīd*, a treatise on the *hylé*, commentary upon the *Ḥikmat al-'ayn* by Dabīrān-i Kātibī, a treatise on the transcendent unity of being (*waḥdat al-wujūd*), and a treatise entitled *al-Asfār al-arba'ah* (The Four Journeys), which some believe to have been the source for the title of Mullā Ṣadrā's magnum opus, for it is known that Mullā Ṣadrā was very familiar with Khafrī's works.[40]

Khafrī in fact marks a major further step within the School of Shiraz in the direction of the "transcendent theosophy" (*al-ḥikmat al-muta'āliyah*) of Mullā Ṣadrā. While his teacher Ṣadr al-Dīn Dashtakī wrote on Peripatetic philosophy separately even if he was interested in gnosis and *ishrāq*, Khafrī sought to combine *'irfān* and *ishrāq* with *mashshā'ī* philosophy rather than keeping them apart and even provided demonstration for *waḥdat al-wujūd*, which Ṣadr al-Dīn Dashtakī had considered to be beyond demonstration. Also in the discussion of *waḥdat al-wujūd*, Khafrī dealt with the reality of *wujūd* in a way that is close to Mullā Ṣadrā's view of the principiality of existence (*aṣālat al-wujūd*).[41] Even in writing philosophical commentaries upon the Quran and *Ḥadīth*, in which he sought to bring *al-qur'ān* (the Quran), *burhān* (demonstration), and *'irfān* together in a synthesis, he, like his teacher Ghiyāth al-Dīn Manṣūr, took a major step in the direction of Mullā Ṣadrā whose commentaries on the Quran and *Ḥadīth* are well known. It is no wonder that Mullā Ṣadrā refers in the study of both metaphysics and natural philosophy so often to Khafrī as do later followers of Mullā Ṣadrā such as Sabziwārī.

The School of Shiraz and Islamic Philosophy in India

The rise of interest in Islamic philosophy in India not only coincides with the life of the School of Shiraz but was also directly affected by it. The works of this school as well as a number of scholars trained in it reached India and played a major role in the rise of interest in the Islamic intellectual sciences, especially philosophy, in that land. The reception of the works of the Safavid philosophers such as Mullā Ṣadrā in India was based on the ground prepared by the propagation of the teachings of the School of Shiraz in the Subcontinent not only in philosophy and theology but also in medicine and the natural and mathematical sciences.

The influence of the School of Shiraz in India goes back to the Lodhi period and especially the reign of Sikandar Lodhi, who was much interested in philosophy. It is he who invited Rafī' al-Dīn Shīrāzī, who had been a disciple of Dawānī, to migrate to India to teach both the religious sciences and philosophy.[42] Later, Shāh Ṭāhir ibn Raḍī al-Dīn, the foremost student of Khafrī, became among the most important figures of the School of Shiraz who journeyed to India and played a major role in the history of Indian Islam especially in Daccan.[43] A descendent of the Ismā'īlī imams, he lived in Kashan, where he studied with Khafrī and where he soon became a celebrated philosopher, gnostic, and scientist of his own. Many people would travel to Kashan to meet him. Even the Safavid king, Shāh Ismā'īl, became devoted to him. This interest aroused jealousy at court, however, where his enemies accused him of being an Ismā'īlī and even a heretic. These provocations continued until the shah turned against him and ordered him to be killed, but the prime minister, who was a Sufi and a disciple of Shāh Ṭāhir, informed him beforehand of the danger; so Shāh Ṭāhir set out with his family for Daccan, India, and never returned to Persia. Shāh Ismā'īl later realized his error and invited him to return to his homeland, an invitation that was refused. Shah Ṭāhir settled in Ahmadnagar in Daccan, where soon he became well known to the extent that the king brought him to his court. When the king's son fell ill, Shāh Ṭāhir openly declared his own Shi'ism and asked the king to give alms in the name of the Twelfth Imam. When the son was miraculously cured, the king accepted Twelve-Imam Shi'ism in 928/1513. This event had a major role in the spread of Shi'ism and the Shi'ite sciences in the Daccan. While in such position of eminence, Shāh Ṭāhir continued to write to his teacher, Khafrī, and even sent him his works for criticism and correction.

Shāh Ṭāhir wrote a number of philosophical and literary works in addition to acting as a major public figure. His philosophical works include his glosses upon the metaphysics of the *Shifāʾ* and *Ishārāt* of Ibn Sīnā, glosses upon the *Muḥākamāt* (Trials) of Quṭb al-Dīn Rāzī, and a number of theological and scientific works that have a philosophical component. He died in 952/1545 in Ahmadnagar where he was buried, having transformed in a notable way the history of Islam in the Daccan and having played a major role in the spread of philosophy in India.

The tree planted by Shāh Ṭāhir was further nourished by another figure from the School of Shiraz whose role in the propagation of Islamic philosophy and the sciences in India is also of the greatest importance. He is Mīr Fatḥ Allāh Shīrāzī, who was a student of Jamāl al-Dīn Maḥmūd Shīrāzī and who migrated from Shiraz to India.[44] He was born in Shiraz, where he received his education under the tutelage of such teachers as Jamāl al-Dīn Maḥmūd, himself a student of Ghiyāth al-Dīn and Dawānī, and also directly under Ghiyāth al-Dīn Manṣūr. Soon he became a well-known philosopher and scientist, as well as teacher of the transmitted sciences. The king of Bijapur, 'Alī 'Ādil Shāh, had assembled many men of learning at this court and invited Mīr Fatḥ Allāh Shīrāzī to join them. The latter accepted, leaving Shiraz permanently for India, where he became such an important figure both politically and intellectually that the Indian historian Saiyid Athar Abbas Rizvi writes, "The arrival of Shāh Fatḥ Allāh Shīrāzī [another name by which he was known in India] was the turning point in the history Shi'ism in northern India."[45] Rizvi might have added "and for the intellectual life of the whole of Islam, both Sunni and Shi'ite in India." Akbar wanted Shāh Fatḥ Allāh Shīrāzī at his court, and after the death of 'Ādil Shāh this became possible. In 991/1583 the great Persian savant was received royally at the Mogul court and became one of the most important intellectual, religious, and political figures of the realm. He was instrumental in reforms in taxation, in agriculture, in the invention of many mechanical instruments, in the devising of a new calendar, and most important of all, in educational reform.

Mīr or Shāh Fatḥ Allāh Shīrāzī was a major scientist and engineer. He was the foremost astronomer and mathematician of his day in India and in addition the inventor of many instruments and mechanical gadgets, including a mechanical mill, new means and methods of irrigation, certain forms of military technology, and so on.[46] There are in fact so may inventions associated with him that it is difficult to understand how a man who was also a major philosopher and a political and administrative figure of the highest rank could have had the time to invent them all. Mīr Fatḥ Allāh Shīrāzī was also an accomplished physician. One day when the later history of Islamic science is written in full, he is bound to occupy an important position in it. Moreover, he is yet another example of a philosopher of the School of Shiraz who, like Ghiyāth al-Dīn Manṣūr and Shams al-Dīn Khafrī, was also an accomplished scientist.

Among Mīr Fatḥ Allāh Shīrāzī's most enduring contributions were the educational reforms he carried out on the orders of the Emperor Akbar. Shīrāzī introduced works of philosophical theology by figures such as Jurjānī and Dawānī, as well as works of pure philosophy by Ghiyāth al-Dīn Manṣūr Dashtakī and others into the curriculum of traditional Islamic *madrasahs* both Sunni and Shi'ite. Henceforth the teaching of Islamic philosophy would continue in many centers of learning until our own times in contrast to the Arab world where the intellectual sciences and especially philosophy ceased to be taught in non-Shi'ite *madrasahs* practically after the eighth/fourteenth century.

Mīr Fatḥ Allāh Shīrāzī wrote a number of works, some of which have been lost. These include a Quranic commentary (now lost), a Persian translation of Ibn Sīnā's *al-Qānūn fi'l-ṭibb* (The Canon of Medicine) (attributed to him but possibly by another author with a similar name), and a number of glosses and commentaries upon difficult texts of philosophy and philosophical theology by Ṭūsī, Taftāzānī, and Dawānī. His most important philosophical impact was, however, through his educational reforms and the training of a number of students, many of whom gained great eminence on their own. In Persia the famous philosopher Muḥammad Maḥmūd Dihdār had studied with him and preceded his master to Bijapur, where, after Mīr Fatḥ Allāh's migration, he continued to study philosophy with his old master. Mīr Fatḥ Allāh also had numerous other disciples in India whose names cannot be recounted here. There is, however, one exception who must be mentioned, and that is Mawlānā 'Abd al-Salām of Lahore who studied philosophy under him in the Punjab. He in turn was the master of Mullā 'Abd al-Salām of Dewa, east of Lucknow, who was made mufti of the imperial army by Shāhjahān but who was also a philosopher. His student Daniyāl Chawrasī, also from Lucknow, became in turn the teacher of Mullā Quṭb al-Dīn, one of the most renowned Muslim scholars of the eleventh/seventeenth century in India.

It was upon the violent death of Mullā Quṭb al-Dīn that the emperor Aurangzeb bequeathed to his descendents a mansion in Lucknow that had belonged to the Dutch. This quarter became known as Farangi Mahall and the most important center of Islamic philosophy in India until the partition of 1948.[47] The third son of Mullā Quṭb al-Dīn, Mullā Niẓām al-Dīn, who had studied with several masters of the school of Mīr Fatḥ Allāh Shīrāzī became the principle teacher at Farangi Mahall, and numerous students came from all over India to study with him. He devised the *dars-i niẓāmī* or Niẓāmī curriculum, which included a strong philosophical component along with the religious sciences. These students took the curriculum to the four corners of India, and it became the mainstay of *madrasah* teachings for the next three centuries. The members of the family continued to teach at Farangi Mahall, which remained the main center for the study of Islamic philosophy in India until it closed its doors in the 1960s. It is also interesting to note that the other major center in India for the study of Islamic philosophy, that of Khayrabad, was also based on the teachings of the school of Farangi Mahall because its founder, Mullā 'Abd al-Wāḥid Khayrābādī, had studied at Farangi Mahall.

One therefore sees the immense influence of Mīr Fatḥ Allāh Shīrāzī on the whole later history of Islamic philosophy in India, of which he was himself one of the most outstanding figures.[48] And through Mīr Fatḥ Allāh Shīrāzī one can see the significance of the School of Shiraz itself, of which he was a product, upon the intellectual life of Muslim India from the eighth/fourteenth century onward. Of course there were many other eminent scholars and philosophers of Shiraz who migrated to India, such as Mīrzā Jān Shīrāzī, but never gained the influence nor played as permanent a role in the intellectual and philosophical life of Muslim India as Mīr Fatḥ Allāh Shīrāzī, who remained a major public figure to the end of his life. Mīr Fath Allāh accompanied Akbar to Kashmir, where Mīr Fatḥ Allāh fell seriously ill and died shortly thereafter in 990/1590 and was buried on top of the beautiful Sulaymaniyyah Mountains in that land. The emperor was so bereaved that he said after his death, "Had he fallen into the hands of Franks, and had they demanded all my treasures in exchange for him, I should gladly have entered upon such a profitable traffic, and have bought that precious jewel cheap."[49]

Despite its permanent effect upon the whole development of the Islamic intellectual sciences and particularly philosophy in Muslim India, the most important effect of the School of Shiraz was in making possible the genesis of the Safavid renaissance in the field of philosophy associated with Mīr Dāmād and what has come to be well known as the School of Isfahan, whose most illustrious figure, Mullā Ṣadrā, was also from Shiraz. In his works and that of his followers, many of the most profound dimensions of philosophy, functioning in a land whose intellectual horizons are dominated by prophecy, received their most perfect and complete formulations and many Islamic philosophical issues their most complete and fullest flowering.

CHAPTER 11

The School of Isfahan Revisited

Prelude

Several decades have passed since Henry Corbin and I began to use the term *School of Isfahan,* to which I have already referred in this work. But being a book dedicated to the relations between philosophy and the reality of prophecy, especially in its Islamic form, it is necessary to revisit this school both because of its own significance and because of its role in the training of Mullā Ṣadrā, who is a key figure in the full flowering of prophetic philosophy in Islam. In a sense the School of Isfahan follows upon the wake of the School of Shiraz, and Mullā Ṣadrā is himself the most direct link between the two. But the School of Isfahan also had precedents outside of Shiraz, and there were a number of philosophers not associated directly with the School of Shiraz who had an important role in preparing the intellectual background for the School of Isfahan and who especially sought that unity among different schools of Islamic philosophy, theology, and gnosis for which Mullā Ṣadrā, the supreme figure of the School of Isfahan, is so well known. Here, we shall confine ourselves to three significant and fascinating figures: Ibn Turkah Iṣfahānī, Qāḍī Maybudī (also pronounced Mībudī), and Ibn Abī Jumhūr Aḥsāʾī, all contemporaries of the later luminaries of the School of Shiraz.

Ṣāʾīn al-Dīn Turkah Iṣfahānī (d. 835/1432 or 836/1433) was a member of a famous family of scholars of Isfahan but of Turkeman origin. He began his studies with his older brother, then traveled to the Hejaz, Syria, and Egypt, where he continued to study. He returned to Persia but was exiled for some time by Tamerlane to Samarqand and could return to Isfahan only after the latter's death. He filled important public functions and suffered political persecution, but his life was given mainly to Sufism and philosophy, although he was also an authority on Islamic Law and theology.[1] Ibn Turkah was also a member of the Ḥurūfī school, which considered the highest knowledge to be contained in the symbolism of the letters of the Arabic alphabet, the alphabet of the sacred language of the Islamic revelation.

Established by a mysterious figure named al-Mughīrah in the early Islamic period, the Ḥurūfī school was based on the Islamic science of the esoteric meaning of letters corresponding to the science of the symbolism of letters found in the Jewish Kabbalah. This science in its Islamic form had a deep influence upon certain forms of Sufism, early Ismā'īlism, and Ithnā 'asharī Shi'ism and is said to have been first taught by 'Alī ibn Abī Ṭālib. It is remarkable to note how Ibn Turkah combined theology, philosophy, and Sufism with his Ḥurūfī views.

The writings of Ibn Turkah include several on the esoteric significance of the science of letters known in Arabic as *al-jafr;* commentaries on works of celebrated Sufi figures such as Ibn 'Arabī, Ibn al-Fāriḍ, Fakhr al-Dīn 'Irāqī, and Maḥmūd Shabistarī; works on Islamic theology and philosophy; and Quranic commentaries. His commentary on the verse of the cleaving of the moon reveals his acquaintance with nearly all the different schools of Islamic thought. In this work he discusses the interpretation of this verse by literalists, theologians, Peripatetics, Illuminationists, Sufis of the school of Ibn 'Arabī, the Ḥurūfīs, and Shi'ite esoterists.[2] This discussion and his other works reveal the integrating nature of Ibn Turkah's thought and his attempt to synthesize various intellectual perspectives into a unified vision to accord with the inner meaning of prophecy and revelation.

In discussing Ibn Turkah, a separate word must be said about his most popular work, the *Tamhīd al-qawā'id* (The Disposition of Principles), which is among the most widely studied texts on *'irfān* to this day as seen by the fact that one of the most eminent contemporary philosophers of Persia has recently written an extensive commentary upon it.[3] During the past few centuries those who have been students of the school of Mullā Ṣadrā in Persia have usually been also familiar with the *Tamhīd al-qawā'id,* and many have studied it with a master in order to become fully familiar with the *'irfān* of the school of Ibn 'Arabī, which constitutes such an important component of the "transcendent theosophy" of Mullā Ṣadrā and a major stage for reaching the synthesis that one observes in Mullā Ṣadrā's teachings.

Ibn Turkah was a Shi'ite thinker, but figures preceding the School of Isfahan who sought to synthesize theology, philosophy, and Sufism were not all Shi'ite. A figure of note, who was a Sunni student of Jalāl al-Dīn Dawānī and who was in fact put to death after Shah Ismā'īl conquered Persia, because he was a Sunni and opposed Shi'ism, was Qāḍī Amīr Ḥusayn ibn Mu'īn al-Dīn Maybudī (d. 910/1503–1504), from a town near Yazd. Maybudī was essentially a Peripatetic philosopher but was also deeply immersed in both theology and Sufism. He is best known for his well-known commentaries on the *Ḥidāyat al-*

ḥikmah of Athīr al-Dīn Abharī and *Ḥikmat al-'ayn* of Najm al-Dīn Dabīrān-i Kātibī, which have remained popular to this day. But he also wrote *kalāmī* works and poetry, which reflects more clearly his Sufi leanings, including a commentary on the *dīwān* of poetry attributed to 'Alī ibn Abī Ṭālib. Moreover, he was an accomplished scientist and the author of several mathematical and astronomical works. His attempt to synthesize philosophy, cosmology, and *'irfān* is to be seen most fully in his Persian work *Jām-i gītī-namā* (The Cup Reflecting the Cosmos). Not much research has been carried out concerning Maybudī, but the fact that there was such a figure who wrote such popular works attests to the fact that the continuation of the life of Islamic philosophy in later centuries was not limited to Shi'ite circles but also extended to Sunni ones as seen in the vast influence of the School of Shiraz in Muslim India among both Sunnis and Shi'ites.

The third major figure outside the School of Shiraz worthy of mention here as preparing the ground for the School of Isfahan is Ibn Abī Jumhūr Aḥsā'ī, who died sometime around 906/1501.[4] A Shi'ite Arab who was born in Aḥsā', where he carried out his earliest studied, Ibn Abī Jumhūr also studied in Jabal 'Āmil and then traveled to Persia, where he settled in Khurasan. Known as a jurisprudent, theologian, and a philosopher, he was also an accomplished scholar of *Ḥadīth* cited by Muḥammad Bāqir Majlisī and other later Shi'ite authorities, some of whom, however, criticized his work in this field. In a way he was like 'Allāmah Ḥillī, a major Shi'ite scholar of the transmitted sciences, who was also a philosopher. But Ibn Abī Jumhūr was more immersed in *ishrāqī* philosophy and *'irfān* than his illustrious predecessor. The earlier works of Aḥsā'ī, such as *Kitāb maslak al-afhām fī 'ilm al-kalām* (The Book of the Way of Understandings of the Science of Theology) dealt mostly with *kalām*, but his most important work, for which he remains famous, *Kitāb al-mujlī mir'āt al-munjī* (The Book of the Illuminated, Mirror of the Savior) is primarily an *ishrāqī* work and in fact a major text in that tradition. In the *Kitāb al-mujlī* he deals with themes common to philosophy and theology, such as the nature of God and the question of knowledge; but he foregoes purely theological issues to concentrate on doctrines of the school of Illumination and to some extent *'irfān*. In this essentially *ishrāqī* work there are numerous quotations from Shahrazūrī's major *ishrāqī* text, *al-Shajarat al-ilāhiyyah* (The Divine Tree). Ibn Abī Jumhūr also shows interest in Ibn 'Arabī, and some elements of Ibn 'Arabian gnosis are present in his work.

In any case these three figures, and some others such as Rajab 'Alī Bursī, a Shi'ite philosopher and theologian from Iraq, helped along with the great masters of the School of Shiraz to prepare the ground for the appearance of the School of Isfahan. All of these philosophers were deeply interested in one way or another in the philosophical significance of the reality of prophecy and its consequences, and it was on the basis of their effects that "prophetic philosophy" in its Islamic form reached its peak in the School of Isfahan and especially its most significant representative Mullā Sadrā.

Mīr Dāmād: The Founder of the School of Isfahan

The philosophical school founded in the tenth/sixteenth century in Isfahan by Mīr Dāmād is of exceptional importance in being both a synthesis of nearly a millennium of Islamic thought and the last major school of traditional philosophy in Islamic civilization, one that has cast its influence on Persia, Iraq, and the Muslim parts of the Indian Subcontinent for the past four centuries. This school was established after the Safavids unified Persia under the banner of Shi'ism and made their capital Isfahan, which soon became not only a major center of Islamic art but also of learning. Scholars have differed as to the social and political conditions of the day in relation to philosophical and scientific activity. Some have taken the view that this period marked a major renaissance of all the Islamic sciences, and others consider it to be a period when religious dogmatism suffocated philosophy, which barely survived under heavy persecution.

We believe that extreme views are to be avoided in this matter. It is true that the Safavid period was not witness to a major flowering of the Islamic natural and mathematical sciences as it was in the arts from architecture to miniature painting. At the same time there *was* a major philosophical renaissance that, despite opposition from certain jurists, flowered and flourished not in spite of the social and political conditions of the day but because conditions made such a flowering possible in contrast to, let us say, Mamlūk Egypt at that time. Especially during the early Safavid period, both philosophy and Sufism had supporters among the politically powerful, and a situation was created in which within the world of Shi'ite piety, philosophy and *'irfān* became cultivated despite the opposition of certain powerful jurists.[5]

In any case the School of Isfahan begins with Mīr Muḥammad Bāqir Dāmād.[6] He came from a distinguished religious family, his father, Mīr Shams al-Dīn, having been the son-in-law of one of the most important and influential Shi'ite religious scholars of the day, Muḥaqqiq-i Karakī, hence the title *Dāmād,* which means "son-in-law" in Persian. This relationship provided him not only with the opportunity to have the best religious education, but also to have social and political protection as he turned his attention ever more to philosophical studies. Mīr Dāmād studied in Mashhad and spent some time in Qazwin and Kashan before settling in the capital, Isfahan, during the reign of the greatest Safavid king, Shāh 'Abbās, who held him in great respect. Mīr Dāmād spent most of the latter part of his life in Isfahan, where he wrote extensively and trained many students, but he died in 1041/1631) in Najaf in Iraq, where his tomb is visited by pilgrims to this day.

Mīr Dāmād was a scholar of the religious sciences as well as a major philosopher who was given the title of "Third Teacher" (*al-mu'allim al-thālith*), following Aristotle and al-Fārābī, whom, as alrady mentioned, Muslims considered as the "First and Second Teachers," respectively. This combining of philosophy with jurisprudence and other religious sciences is an interesting phenomenon that is different from what one sees in earlier Islamic history. The famous earlier philosophers such as al-Kindī, al-Fārābī, al-'Āmirī, and Ibn Sīnā all knew something about jurisprudence and other religious sciences, but none except Ibn Rushd was considered an authority on the subject. Rather, they were usually scientists, and many made their living practicing medicine, for example Rāzī and Ibn Sīnā.[7] From Ṭusī onward we begin to see philosophers who were also theologians, jurists, or both as we have seen earlier in this book. But until we come to the School of Isfahan, many of these philosophers continued to be scientists, such as Ṭusī, Ghiyāth al-Dīn Dashtakī, Shams al-Dīn Khafrī, and Fatḥ Allāh Shīrāzī. Mīr Dāmād is the beginning of the new trend in which philosophers are much better versed in the juridical and theological disciplines than in the natural and mathematical sciences. Although what we mention here is not meant to imply that the parting of ways between philosophy and the sciences became absolute, there is definitely a change in the interest of many philosophers in the natural sciences. The later history of Islamic science is yet to be written, and we are the last to believe that activity in the sciences ceased to exist after the eighth/fourteenth century as so many claim. In fact the "discovery" of figures such as Shams al-Dīn Khafrī and Fatḥ Allāh Shīrāzī proves so readily the falsehood of such assertions.[8] There have appeared, moreover, figures like them in Persia, the Ottoman world, and India up to modern times, figures whose scientific works need to be examined. Nevertheless, there is little doubt that there is a shift of interest among many of the leading philosophers of the School of Isfahan and going back to Mīr Dāmād himself from the sciences dealing with mathematical concepts and the natural world toward the religious sciences and the direct fruits of prophecy. This fact has without doubt had an effect on the later history of Islamic science. Also, needless to say, this movement was exactly in the opposite direction of what was taking place in the West at that time. Hence, the radical differences between Cartesianism and the transcendent theosophy or philosophy of Mullā Sadrā, although both were heirs to Greek and medieval philosophy and the Abrahamic world of prophecy.

Some 134 works of Mīr Dāmād have been identified.[9] Some of these deal with Quranic commentary, theology, and Islamic Law, but most are concerned with philosophy and a few with mysticism. Mīr Dāmād also had some knowledge of mathematics and wrote a couple works on the subject, but his knowledge of this field did not at all match that of his friend and contemporary Bahā᾿ al-Dīn al-'Āmilī, who was a major figure in the School of Isfahan but given more to jurisprudence and Sufism, on the one hand, and to mathematics, architecture, and various other pure and applied sciences and the arts, on the other, but who did not write to any appreciable extent on philosophy.[10] The most famous philosophical works of Mīr Dāmād include *Al-Ufuq al-mubīn* (The Manifest Horizon), on aeviternity or metatime (*al-dahr*) corresponding to the Latin *aevum*, time and existence; *Taqwīm al-īmān* (The Straightening of Faith) on the Creator and creation; *Al-Jadhawāt* (Burning Firewood), containing a cycle of his thought and beginning with the symbolism of letters;[11] *al-ṣirāṭ al-mustaqīm* (The Straight Path), dealing with the question of eternity and origination of the world; and his most famous work and masterpiece, *al-Qabasāt* (Firebrands), whose main theme is the relation between time, aeviternity or metatime and eternity. Mīr Dāmād also wrote many commentaries and glosses on works of earlier philosophers such as al-Fārābī, Ibn Sīnā, and Ṭusī. He is also well known for treatises on mystical experience, such as *Khalṣat al-malakūt* (Heavenly Mystical States)[12] and *al-Khal'iyyah* (Disassociation). Finally, it needs to be mentioned that Mīr Dāmād was an accomplished poet who used the pen name *Ishrāq*. His *dīwān* of poetry has in fact been published in Persia.[13]

Mīr Dāmād was essentially an Avicennan philosopher with an *ishrāqī* interpretation of some Peripatetic theses. But he did not remain satisfied with only reinterpreting earlier philosophical ideas. There are several domains in which he formulated distinct ideas, associated with his name. These include new interpretations of the problem of determinism and free will, the structure and meaning of the imaginal world, and the problem of what appears to be change in the Divine Will as reflected in the revealed text (*badā᾿*). Mīr Dāmād is also credited with formulating in a categorial fashion the discussion of the relation of existence and quiddity in terms of the principiality (*aṣālah*) of *wujūd* or *māhiyyah*, a very important formulation that has influenced nearly all later Islamic philosophers, starting with his own foremost student, Mullā Ṣadrā.

The central philosophical concern of Mīr Dāmād was, however, the meaning of time in relation to eternity and the related question of the originated or eternal nature of the world (*ḥudūth wa qidam*). This problem is itself directly related to the reality of prophecy in its Abrahamic form. The Greek philosophers philosophized within a worldview that saw all of existence as a "block without fissure," to quote a formulation of Toshihiko Izutsu. They did not conceive of a temporal origin for the world and a hiatus between God as creator and Pure Being and His creation. Already the Christian philosopher John Philoponus had written again the Greek idea of the eternity of the world in the fourth century.[14] From the beginning of the history of Islamic philosophy, Muslim philosophers, like their Jewish and Christian counterparts, were concerned with the same issue that forms one of the main points of contention among Ibn Sīnā, Ghazzālī, and Ibn Rushd. The debate concerning *ḥudūth* and *qidam* continued long after them and in fact remains to this day.[15]

It is a sign of Mīr Dāmād's full awareness of the philosophical significance of teachings issuing from prophecy that he devoted much of his philosophical writings to the issue of time and its relation to what lies beyond temporality. His main thesis is that we do not only have time and eternity but, eternity (*sarmad*), aeveternity or metatime (*dahr*), and time (*zamān*). They represent both relationality and states of being. *Sarmad* refers to a state of being in which there is relation only between the changeless and the changeless. *Dahr* refers to a state in which there is relation between the changeless and the changing. Finally, *zamān* refers to the relation between the changing and the changing. Everything in the dimension of *zamān* is preceded not by nothingness or *'adam*, but by what exists in *dahr*. The world is therefore not eternal (*sarmadī*) or originated in time (*ḥudūth-i zamānī*). Rather, it is originated in *dahr*, hence the well-known Dāmādean theory of *ḥudūth-i dahrī*, that is, aeveternal or metatemporal origination.[16]

This famous theory was discussed avidly later on and criticized and rejected by a number of major philosophers, including Mullā Ṣadrā, while being defended by others. What is important for us to consider there is the significance of this whole question for the relation between philosophy and prophecy. Neither the ancient Greek philosophers nor modern Western philosophers who deny the reality of prophecy that posits the thesis of *creatio ex-nihilo* have been concerned with this issue. In contrast philosophers in the Abrahamic world, be they Jewish, Christian, or Muslim, have had of necessity to deal with it in one way or another. Moreover, it is interesting to note that in a world with different religious doctrines concerning the nature of the world of time, philosophers have philosophized accordingly. This is true not only of ancient Greece but also of India, where the cyclic nature of cosmic time consisting of *kalpas*, *manvantaras*, and *yugas*, as revealed in the Hindu scriptures, has been the subject of philosophical interpretations and speculation over the ages.

Mīr Findiriskī

One of the most remarkable figures of the School of Isfahan, who along with Mīr Dāmād and Shaykh Bahā᾿ al-Dīn 'Āmilī may be said to be a member of the founding triumvirate of that school is Mīr Abū᾿l-Qāsim Findiriskī. Little is known about the life of this enigmatic figure save that he taught for a long time in Isfahan, mostly the works of Ibn Sīnā, and trained many famous students, such as Rajab 'Alī Tabrīzī; that he also traveled to India where he became acquainted with Hindu philosophy and may have even participated in the movement of translation of Sanskrit texts into Persian; and that he returned to Isfahan, where he died in 1050/1640–41 and where he is buried. Mīr Findiriskī was an exceptional figure in every way. Although known primarily as an Avicennan philosopher, he was also a fine poet and an alchemist, as well as being a pioneer in what today is known as comparative philosophy.[17] Mīr Findiriskī wrote a small number of works of which few have been edited and published until now. His works include a treatise on motion, a response to a question on ontology posed by a philosopher by the name of Āqā Muẓaffar Ḥusayn Kāshānī, the *Risāla-yi ṣinā'iyyah* (Treatise on the Arts), a major work in Persian dealing with the structure and classes of traditional human society; a famous philosophical poem[18] that has been the subject of a number of commentaries; a treatise on alchemy; glosses in Arabic on the *Yoga-Vaisiṣṭha*, translated by Niẓām al-Dīn Panīpātī;[19] and a Persian anthology and commentary on the text by the name of *Muntakhab-i jūk* (Anthology of Yoga).[20] It is unfortunate that the fruits of this pioneering effort in carrying out comparative studies between Islamic and Hindu philosophy have not been properly edited and studied. It is also very significant to note that the writing of commentary on a Hindu philosophical text by an Islamic philosopher preceded by a few centuries Islamic philosophical commentaries on a Western philosophical text, be it medieval, Renaissance, or modern.

The book on alchemy of Mīr Findiriskī also remains in manuscript form. An examination of it reveals the interest of Mīr Findiriskī in spiritual alchemy and the relation of this arcane art to metaphysics. Corbin quite rightly compares it to the *Atalanta fugiens* of Mīr Findiriskī's famous contemporary alchemist in the West, Michael Maier.[21] What is interesting to note from the point of view of the diversity and richness of the philosophical life of the School of Isfahan is that here we have in Mīr Findiriskī a supposed Peripatetic philosopher who is also an alchemist, a fine poet, and a person attracted to the philosophy of Yoga. He complements his contemporary Mīr Dāmād, who was also known as a Peripatetic philosopher but who also wrote on *'irfān* and described his own mystical experiences, which Corbin has called "ecstatic confessions."[22]

Of central importance to our concerns in this book is Mīr Findiriskī's *Risāla-yi ṣinā'iyyah,* where he discusses the relation between philosophy and prophecy.[23] This treatise deals with the hierarchic classification of the arts and the activities of human beings, culminating in a chapter that discusses the relation between philosophers and prophets, which Corbin designates as "prophetic philosophy." The treatise ends with a discussion of the states of being. In the section on philosophers, he asserts their importance and eminence in human society standing below the rank of prophets, and he places philosophical research on a par with *ijtihād* (giving fresh opinion on religious matters on the part of leading religious authorities). For him philosophy in fact replaces theology as the supreme science. Yet he also points out the basic difference between the philosopher and the prophet. The former can err, but the latter does not do so. The former reaches knowledge through the intermediary of thought and the latter through revelation and direct inspiration without need of mental activity. Philosophers know through the light of the intellect, whereas in the case of the prophets intellectual power is boundless, and there is no veil between them and the angelic world.

Having made all these distinctions, Mīr Findiriskī asserts the following statement: "[W]hen philosophers reach the end of their path, this end is the beginning of prophecy. And this station is that of prophets who were not messengers such as Luqmān, the Wise. And it is said of Aristotle that 'Amr ibn 'Āṣṣ insulted Aristotle before the Prophet. The Prophet became angry and said, 'Go easy, O 'Amr. Aristotle was a prophet who was ignored by his people.' "[24] Mīr Findiriskī then adds that the Prophet was using "prophet" metaphorically in the case of Aristotle (meaning most likely Plotinus as is seen often in Islamic texts because of the attribution of the Arabic translation of the *Enneads* to Aristotle), whereas the real differences between the philosopher and the prophet remain.

This important text of Mīr Findiriskī also points to the significance of the Logos or more specifically the Muḥammadan Reality (*al-ḥaqīqat al-muḥammadiyyah*) associated with the Intellect on its highest level for a gnostic and metaphysical understanding of prophecy and the role of the prophetic function vis-à-vis the philosophical one in a human collectivity dominated by the reality of prophecy. The treatise of Mīr Findiriskī is almost unique in the annals of Islamic thought in intertwining the metaphysical and societal aspects of the relationship between prophecy and a philosophy, which in the School of Isfahan is to be identified even more than before as "prophetic philosophy."[25]

The Students of the First Generation

The three earliest masters and founders of the School of Isfahan, Mīr Dāmād, Shaykh-i Bahāʾī, and Mīr Findiriskī trained a galaxy of students, many of whom became celebrated philosophers in their own right. Some studied with one of these masters and some with two but rarely with all three. It has been said by some concerning the most famous of the students of these first generation founders, that is, Mullā Ṣadrā, that he studied with all three, but his rapport with Mīr Findiriskī has not been substantiated, and he does not speak of him in his voluminous works. In any case because he marks the peak of what we can call "prophetic philosophy," we shall deal with Mullā Ṣadrā in the next chapter and turn here to some of the other figures who are of significance from the point of view of this book.

A major figure belonging to the second generation and a contemporary of Mullā Ṣadrā, Mullā Rajab 'Alī Tabrīzī (d. 1080/1669–70) was a student of Mīr Findiriskī and a follower of Ibn Sīnā's metaphysical views. He rejected the idea of the transcendent unity and principiality of being (*waḥdat al-wujūd* and *aṣālat al-wujūd*) and stood totally opposed to Ṣadrian metaphysics.[26] As far as knowledge of God is concerned, he followed the *via negative* and believed that knowledge of the Absolute remains forever beyond the grasp of the human intellect, a view similar to that of the mainstream of Ismā'īlī philosophy. Mullā Rajab 'Alī's works, like those of many later figures, have not been fully studied, and few have even been printed. Besides shorter treatises that reflect his views on particular philosophical issues,[27] there is an important work of his edited by his student Rafīʿ Pīrzādah and entitled *al-Maʿārif al-ilāhiyyah* (The Divine Sciences).

Mullā Rajab ʿAlī was not unique in following a philosophical path totally different from that of Mullā Ṣadrā and his school. A student of Mīr Dāmād, Mullā Shamsā Gīlānī (d. before 1064/1655), who corresponded with Mullā Ṣadrā and even wrote a treatise entitled *al-Ḥikmat al-mutaʿāliyah* (The Transcendent Theosophy) similar in title to Mullā Ṣadrā's major work, was nevertheless primarily an Avicennan with an *ishrāqī* bent, like his teacher Mīr Dāmād, whose doctrine of aeveternal origination he defended despite some criticism of it. But in any case he followed a very different philosophical path from that of Mullā Ṣadrā.[28] Furthermore, Mullā Rajab ʿAlī himself had a number of eminent students, such as Mīr Qawām al-Dīn Rāzī, Mullā ʿAbbās Mawlawī, and Mullā Muḥammad Tunikābunī, who represent a whole strand of Avicennan philosophical thought that develops in the School of Isfahan in a different manner from the philosophy of Mullā Ṣadrā. As mentioned earlier in this book, it is important to remember that although Mullā Ṣadrā's *al-ḥikmat al-mutaʿāliyah* is the most influential and significant result of the flowering of the School of Isfahan, it is not the only result. Another important and long-enduring strand began with Mullā Rajab ʿAlī and has continued to our day. Strangely enough, although those two strands of philosophical thought opposed each other on many issues, there were some who, one might say, had a foot in each camp. The best example is Qāḍī Saʿīd Qummī (d. 1103/1691), one of the major Islamic thinkers of the past few centuries who was a student of Mullā Rajab ʿAlī but also of Mullā Ṣadrā's foremost student, Mullā Muḥsīn Fayḍ.[29]

There are many important members of the School of Isfahan, including Mullā Ṣadrā's own students Mullā Muḥsīn Fayḍ Kāshānī and ʿAbd al-Razzāq Lāhījī, whom we shall not study in this chapter, having dealt with both figures earlier in this book,[30] except to say that each represents a special possibility of the flowering of Islamic philosophy at this juncture in which philosophy becomes wed to the esoteric dimension of prophecy and absorbs and gradually replaces theology. There are two other students of Mīr Dāmād, however, whom we need to mention in light of the relation between philosophy and prophecy before we bring this chapter to a close. They are Quṭb al-Dīn Ashkiwarī and Sayyid Aḥmad ʿAlawī.

Quṭb al-Dīn Ashkiwarī (d. after 1075/1665) is known especially for a voluminous work on a kind of spiritual history of philosophy from Adam to his own teacher, Mīr Dāmād. Entitled *Maḥbūb al-qulūb* (Beloved of Hearts), it is divided into three parts: the ancient philosophers and sages, the Sunni sages and philosophers, and the Shi'ite Imams and philosophers.[31] The whole history reflects the perspective that philosophy is a tree rooted in the ground of revelation and watered over the ages by the messages of various prophets and their spiritual representatives. Concerning this important *historial* treatment of philosophy, Corbin writes: "Special mention must be made of Quṭb al-Dīn Ashkiwarī who composed a sort of immense rhapsody in Arabic and Persian including in three parts the traditions, citations and commentaries concerning the ancient sages, the philosophers and spiritual figures of Sunni Islam and finally the Imams and the great spiritual figures of Shi'ism. It is a sort of *speculum historiale* and 'divine philosophy,' the *Divinalia* beginning with Adam and concluding with Mīr Dāmād, the master of the author."[32]

As for Sayyid Aḥmad 'Alawī (d. between 1054/1644 and 1060/1650), like Ashkiwarī, he was a close disciple of Mīr Dāmād and his son-in-law and nephew. His philosophical perspective was also like that of his teacher Mīr Dāmād, an Avicennism colored by the doctrines of Suhrawardī. Sayyid Aḥmad in fact wrote a commentary upon the *Qubasāt* and remained one of the most faithful followers of his master. Sayyid Aḥmad also wrote one of the most notable commentaries upon the *Shifā*ʾ, which makes him one of the most important of later Avicennian philosophers.[33] He also wrote works on jurisprudence and what would be called today "comparative religious studies." This latter category is of special interest for the relation between philosophy and prophecy. Today in the West it is mostly scholars of religion or theologians who write about different religions in a comparative mode and not ordinary philosophers, except of course those who are followers of the perennial philosophy, there being a few other exceptions. In the School of Isfahan, as philosophy came to absorb theology, this task seems to have been left primarily to the *falāsifah* rather than the *mutakallimūn* when it came to the intellectual and spiritual dimensions of the subject. A major example of this philosophical undertaking is to be found in the works of Sayyid Aḥmad 'Alawī.

The Safavid period was witness to the appearance of a number of attacks against Islam written by Christian missionaries in India and Persia. The works of Sayyid Aḥmad are for the most part responses to this challenge. He wrote three books on Christian doctrines, including *Lawāmi'-i rabbānī* (Lordly Flashes), *Miṣqal-i ṣafā* (Polishing Instrument of Purity), and *Lama'āt-i malakūtiyyah* (Celestial Flashes).[34] The *Lawāmi'* is written in refutation of Pietro della Valle's attack against Islam written in 1621. The second part of the work deals with the question of the possibility of changes in the text of the Gospels and reveals the familiarity of Sayyid Aḥmad with the Gospels.[35] *Miṣqal-i ṣafā* was written in refutation of the famous book *Ā'ina-yi ḥaqq-nāma* (Mirror Reflecting the Truth) written in India by a Catholic missionary. A summary of this work reached Persia, and Sayyid Aḥmad set out to refute its main thesis concerning the truth of Trinitarian doctrine. His response itself elicited further replies by other Christian missionaries.[36]

The *Lama'āt*, which is shorter than the other two works, deals with the inner meaning of the "Word" (*kalimah*) and the three hypostases, that is, Father, Son, and the Holy Ghost, in such a way as to accord with the teachings of the Quran. This work is in reality an *ishrāqī* commentary upon the Gospels and a serious attempt at creating a philosophical and theological harmony between some of the most basic tenets of Islam and Christianity and is of great value for deeper theological discussions between the two religions today.[37] Of special interest in this work is Sayyid Aḥmad's treatment of the theme of the Paraclete in light of Islamic and particularly Shi'ite gnosis.

It is quite remarkable that the author of one of the most extensive commentaries upon the bible of Islamic Peripatetic philosophy, the *Shifā*ʾ of Ibn Sīnā, should write such works on comparative philosophy of religion and theology. Sayyid Aḥmad 'Alawī reveals once again the remarkable diversity of philosophical activity in Safavid Persia and also the different possibilities for philosophical activity in light of the reality of prophecy, including crossing borders from a world dominated by one religion to the verities of prophecy belonging to another religious universe.

Concluding Comments

The works of the few figures of the School of Isfahan mentioned in this chapter reveal the themes and problems with which those philosophizing at this time within the context of prophetic realities in both their outward and inward dimension were concerned. We have also seen philosophers with diverse interests and varying strands of thought, all of which are of philosophical interest. But without doubt the most significant figure of this period, who is not only the most important philosopher of the School of Isfahan but in a sense the representative of the full flowering of "prophetic philosophy" and the synthesis of nearly a millennium of Islamic thought, is Ṣadr al-Dīn Shīrāzī or Mullā Ṣadrā, to whom we now turn.

CHAPTER 12

Mullā Ṣadrā and the Full Flowering of Prophetic Philosophy

Since Henry Corbin and I began to write about Mullā Ṣadrā over forty years ago, a great deal of attention has been paid to this major figure in both the Islamic world and the West and even in lands as far away as Japan. There are now even international and local conferences held on a regular basis on his philosophy. Here our task is not to deal with every aspect of his thought but only certain theses that relate to our concerns in this work. Let it also be repeated, lest one forget, that Mullā Ṣadrā and his followers do not represent the only philosophical current in the School of Isfahan but the major current that was to have the greatest influence in later centuries in Persia and India.[1]

MULLĀ ṢADRĀ

Ṣadr al-Dīn Shīrāzī, known also as Mullā Ṣadrā and Ṣadr al-muta᾿allihīn (foremost among the theosophers or literally those imbued with God-like qualities) is without doubt the greatest of the later Islamic philosophers and perhaps the most outstanding among all Islamic philosophers in the field of metaphysics.[2] Born in Shiraz in 979–80/1571–72, he received his early education in the city of his birth, then set out for Isfahan, where he soon became the most notable student of Mīr Dāmād.[3] After having mastered both the intellectual and the transmitted sciences, his foremost teacher in the latter category having been Bahā᾿ al-Dīn al-ʿĀmilī, Mullā Ṣadrā retired to the village of Kahak near Qom away from the crowd. There he spent years in spiritual training and contemplation. Finally he returned to Shiraz where the Khan School was built for him and where he wrote and taught until his death in 1050/1640 in Basra (or possibly Najaf) upon returning from the pilgrimage to Mecca for the seventh time. He also visited Qom during the last period of his life.

During a remarkably productive life marked by periods of both formal intellectual training and inner purification and spiritual wayfaring and characterized by great faith and piety, Mullā Ṣadrā composed nearly fifty works devoted to both the intellectual and the transmitted sciences ranging from books on logic and Peripatetic philosophy to Quranic commentaries.[4] The most important of these works is *al-Ḥikmat al-muta'āliyah fi'l-asfār al-'aqliyyat al-arba'ah* (Transcendent Theosophy concerning the Four Intellectual Journeys) usually known simply as *Asfar*,[5] which has been commented upon by many later *ḥakīms* as we shall see in the following chapter.[6] In this and many other works, Mullā Ṣadrā presents his vast synthesis of the older schools of Islamic philosophy, theology, and Sufism into the teachings of a new philosophical school, which he calls *"al-ḥikmat al-muta'āliyah,"* a term that can be translated as "transcendent theosophy" if this term is used in its original sense or "transcendent philosophy" if philosophy is also understood to include what Pythagoreans and Parmenides understood by it and not simply as mental machinations and one form or another of rationalism and more recently irrationalism.[7] Mullā Ṣadrā sought to unify the knowledge received through *burhān* or demonstration, *'irfān* or contemplation, intellectual intuition and gnosis and Qu'rān or the Sacred Text made accessible through revelation, thereby giving full expression to philosophy cultivated in the land of prophecy.

We do not wish to dwell extensively here on the principles of Mullā Ṣadrā's philosophy such as the principiality, unity, and gradation of *wujūd*, the union of the intellect and the intelligible, mental existence, the ontological reality of the imaginal world, trans-substantial motion, and many other ideas that together constitute the foundations of his philosophic perspective.[8] What concerns us here is the philosophy of Mullā Ṣadrā in as much as it marks the full flowering of prophetic philosophy in Islam as this term was defined earlier in this book, for as Corbin has written, "Ultimately, Ṣadrā Shīrāzī's philosophy culminates not so much in a philosophy of the creative Spirit, as in a metaphysics of the Holy Spirit."[9]

The Full Flowering of Prophetic Philosophy in the Teachings of Mullā Ṣadrā

There is a famous saying among Islamic philosophers that *al-ḥukamā' warathat al-anbiyā'*, that is, the *ḥakīms* or philosophers are the inheritors of the prophets. Mullā Ṣadrā accepted fully this assertion and lived with awareness of the spiritual universe in which God's beneficent manifestation or *jūd* was evident, in which prophecy had made possible attainment of knowledge not available to unaided human reason, and in which prophecy actualized the inner intellect. In fact he considered inner intellection as distinct from ratiocination to be "partial prophecy" actualized by universal and objective revelation through the prophets. More specifically, as far as the Shi'ite climate in which he philosophized was concerned, he was fully aware of the circle of initiatic and spiritual power (*dāʾirat al-walāyah/wilāyah*) that followed the closing of the prophetic cycle (*dāʾirat al-nubuwwah*) upon the death of the Prophet.[10] Mullā Ṣadrā was keenly aware of the esoteric nature of knowledge associated with *walāyah/wilāyah* and the relation of this knowledge to spiritual hermeneutics (*taʾwīl*) of the Sacred Text. He drank from the fountainhead of this knowledge and gained a vision of the various levels of universal existence and of the Divine Reality Itself.

Mullā Ṣadrā also benefited fully from a thousand years of Islamic intellectual activity, from the writings of nearly all the outstanding philosophers, theologians, and mystics before him, who had contemplated in one way or another a world dominated by the reality of prophecy. In fact, perhaps no major Islamic philosopher was as aware of and as knowledgeable about the history of Islamic philosophy as Mullā Ṣadrā.[11] On the basis of knowledge of this long intellectual heritage, the study afresh of the sources of the Islamic revelation along with the sayings of the Shi'ite Imams and his own experience and intellectual vision of reality made possible by both the outward and inward dimensions of the revelation and the actualization of the intellect within, Mullā Ṣadrā created a major new philosophical school, *al-ḥikmat al-muta'āliyah*. His philosophical synthesis was both rigorously logical and rational and open to the melodies of the rhapsodic intellect and was in fact its fruit. His philosophy combined the logical rigor of the works of Fārābī, Ibn Sīnā, and Ṭūsī; the illuminative knowledge of Suhrawardī's school of *ishrāq*; the mystical theology of Ghazzālī; the concern with spiritual hermeneutics of the Ismā'īlī philosophers such as Nāṣir-i Khusraw and the Sufis; the visionary gnosis of Ibn 'Arabī; and the philosophical efforts by some of the members of the School of Shiraz and other figures mentioned in the last chapters to bring about a rapprochement between these schools. Mullā Ṣadrā's "transcendent theosophy" makes use of extensive logical analysis and demonstration, as well as intellectual vision or what he sometimes calls "what has entered the heart" (*al-wāridāt al-qalbiyyah*) or knowledge received from the Divine Throne (*taḥqīq 'arshī*) and what has been revealed through the Quran and made known to human beings through the sayings of the Prophet and the Imams. But without doubt Mullā Ṣadrā's *ḥikmat* is philosophy in its time-honored sense and not theology or gnosis, which remain distinct from it, although he drew from both of them. Moreover, Mullā Ṣadrā's philosophy represents perhaps the fullest and grandest expression of prophetic philosophy in Islam, one that not only benefits from a millennium of Islamic thought before it but also formulates and crystallizes in an unprecedented manner the various latent modes and dimensions of what can be called "prophetic philosophy" in the Islamic universe.

There are many aspects of Mullā Ṣadrā's philosophy that are especially significant from the point of view of what has been characterized throughout this book as prophetic philosophy. Here we shall mention only seven doctrines of major importance for our present discussion, although there are also others to be considered if one undertakes the task of studying the whole of Mullā Ṣadrā's philosophy from the point of view of prophetic philosophy.

Philosophy of Being

The Quranic revelation speaks not only of God as the Creator and Sustainer of the universe, but also of His Beneficence that concerns all beings and His Mercy that encompasses all things. Understood metaphysically, this means that God is the source and the only source of the being of all things and that like the rays of the sun, which shine upon all things, being flows from its Divine Origin to existentiate all things. This is what Mullā Ṣadrā calls *"sarayān al-wujūd"* (the flow of being). Earlier Islamic philosophers had been deeply concerned with ontology, and as we have seen it was Ibn Sīnā who first formulated the concept of 'Necessary Being,' which he identified with God. But although later philosophers such as Mīr Dāmād and before him Suhrawardī had asserted the absolute reality of the One as the source of all, they had accepted the quiddities (*māhiyyāt*) of things to be what bestowed reality upon them. Mullā Ṣadrā had first accepted this view, but as a result of a vision, he came to realize that it is *wujūd*, a term that, as already mentioned, can be translated into English as "Being," "being," "Existence," and "existence," that is, principial and primary rather than *māhiyyah*. He thereby made the cornerstone of his philosophical edifice the doctrine of the oneness, gradation, and principiality of *wujūd*, which not only accords with the inner meaning of the revealed Text, but is the result of the knowledge that the esoteric meaning of that Text makes possible.

Furthermore, in this universe objects are not simply essences that are existent having been created once by God. Rather, their very essence is inseparable from the act of existence. God's creation did not just take place once upon a time but is taking place anew at every moment. As mentioned earlier in this book, Mullā Ṣadrā was able to make use of both Arabic, where the verb *to be* is not used as a copula, and Persian, which does use 'to be' as copula like other Indo-Iranian-European languages, to create a special vocabulary to speak about *wujūd* not as a thing but as an act, not as *ens* or even *esse* but as *esto*.[12] Being is also presence (*ḥuḍūr*), and ultimately the very being of things marks the presence of the One who ultimately alone *is*. As the Quran says, "Whithersoever ye turn, there is the Face of God." (2: 115)

In this metaphysical perspective being and knowing are not separate from each other. We are what we know, and we know to the degree that we are. In Arabic the Greek term *ousia*, equivalent to the Latin word *essentia*, was not translated as "quiddity" but as "*ḥaqīqah*" or "reality" and "truth." Truth is none other than the real and the real none other than the truth. The Arabic term *al-ḥaqīqah* means both. Moreover, the *ḥaqīqah* of everything is related to its archetypal reality, to God's knowledge of that thing and ultimately to God Himself, one of whose Names is *al-Ḥaqq* or Truth/Reality. And it is this revealed truth that is perceived by the intellect and constitutes the foundation of Mullā Ṣadrā's philosophy.

The Sacred Book

In the Islamic perspective the Sacred Book is inseparable from the reality of prophecy. The Sacred Book, in the case of Islam, the Quran, is not only the source of Divine Law and ethics and the repository of sacred history. It is also the source of knowledge and in fact, in principle, all knowledge. Esoterically it is related to the Muḥammadan Reality (*al-ḥaqīqah al-muḥammadiyyah*) and contains the archetypal reality of the universe. Through it God communicates with man, and knowledge of prophecy, eschatology, and in the case of Shi'ism, knowledge of the Imam, are inseparable from it. The Sacred Text is revealed through a descent (*tanzīl*) and ascends back to its Origin through hermeneutic interpretation (*ta᾿wīl*). It is the Word of God as well as the source of the spiritual energies that carry man back to his celestial home. The Holy Spirit itself is none other than the overflowing of this Word, and it is through union of the intellect within man with the Active Intellect, which is none other than the Holy Spirit, that man gains ultimate wisdom.

It is not accidental that Islamic philosophers from the beginning were concerned with the philosophical meaning of the Quran, and even the master of Islamic Peripatetics, Ibn Sīnā, wrote a number of Quranic commentaries. Classical Ismā'īlī philosophers such as Abū

Ya'qūb Sijistānī, Ḥamīd al-Dīn Kirmānī, and Nāṣir-i Khusraw made *ta'wīl* the basis of their philosophical method and considered their philosophy to be totally embedded in prophecy with the Sacred Text as its central reality.[13] Later Suhrawardī incorporated many verses of the Quran into his philosophical works, and some later philosophers wrote a few commentaries on various Quranic verses or *ḥadīths*. But there is no philosopher in the annals of Islamic philosophy who has written such a vast commentary on the Quran as Mullā Ṣadrā,[14] not to speak of his masterly work, *Mafātīḥ al-ghayb* (Keys to the Invisible), which concerns the relations among metaphysics, cosmology, traditional anthropology, and Quranic exegesis. In this realm as in many others it seems that Mullā Ṣadrā brought the flowering of prophetic philosophy in its Islamic form to its peak.

Prophecy and Illumination

In a spiritual universe in which prophecy is a reality, there is an open passage between Heaven and earth, and the individual intellect has the open possibility to be illuminated by the angelic agency that brought the revelation to the Prophet. Although the term *waḥy* or "revelation" in its technical Islamic sense is reserved for the prophets (*anbiyā'*) in the Quranic sense, the possibility of illumination from above is open to all who fulfill the necessary conditions provided by the revealed religion itself. The Quran itself speaks of *fatḥ*, which means "victory" as well as "illumination" and "opening to the spiritual world," and the bible of Islamic esoteric knowledge by Ibn 'Arabī is entitled *al-Futūḥāt al-makkiyyah* ("Mekkan Illuminations," "Openings," or "Revelations," if this term is not confused with *waḥy*). Prophecy lies at the peak of gnosis and knowledge of the sacred order and at the same time provides the means for illuminative knowledge.

Of course before Mullā Ṣadrā, both Suhrawardī and Ibn 'Arabī, not to speak of their many followers, had spoken of the central role of illumination and unveiling each in his own language and manner of expression. Mullā Ṣadrā was deeply influenced by both these masters. His *Glosses* upon the *Ḥikmat al-ishrāq* of Suhrawardī are among the great masterpieces of the *ishrāqī* school, and his discussions of the science of the soul in his *Asfār*, based largely on Ibn 'Arabī, reveal him as an outstanding commentator of the Murcian master. Mullā Ṣadrā was, therefore, not by any means the first Islamic philosopher to emphasize illumination as the source of knowledge and its relation to prophecy. But here again he integrated the teachings of Suhrawardī and Ibn 'Arabī, along with those of the Shi'ite Imams into his *al-ḥikmat al-muta'āliyah* in such a way that the organic link between objective revelation in the form of prophecy and inner illumination as "partial prophecy" became central to a hierarchical epistemology that characterizes his total synthesis between prophetic and philosophic truth or religion and philosophy.

Angelology

There is ultimately no prophecy without angelology. In the ancient Greek world where Pythagoras and Parmenides philosophized, these angelic realities were identified as gods of the Greek pantheon, and in Hinduism they are identified with various Hindu deities. In the Abrahamic world, however, these intelligible and luminous substances are identified as angels, and the traditional philosophies of all the three monotheistic religions have dealt with them on some level as we see for example in nearly all the writings in the West influenced by the Dionysian corpus.[15] In Islamic philosophy again it was Ibn Sīnā who was the first to seek to create a systematic correlation between the intelligences of the philosophers and the angelic realm as mentioned in religious sources. Suhrawardī expanded greatly the philosophical study of angels, making correlations between the vertical and horizontal orders of light in the *ishrāqī* universe and not only Islamic but also Mazdean orders of angels.[16] In relating angelology to both cosmology and epistemology, Ibn Sīnā and especially Suhrawardī had already paved the way for Mullā Ṣadrā, but again this important dimension of prophetic philosophy finds its full expression in the grand synthesis of the latter.

Eschatology and Sacred Psychology

Left to their own devices, the ordinary human mind and imagination have no means of gaining knowledge of eschatological realities, and ordinary human knowledge of the psyche remains limited to the most outward aspects of the soul. The current philosophical scene exemplifies fully the truth of this assertion. Since the rise of rationalism, mainstream Western philosophers have shown practically no interest in eschatology, and the rare few who have, such as the Swedish visionary Emmanuel Swedenborg, have been philosophically speaking totally marginalized. As for psychology, the modern discipline using that name, does not know what to do with transpersonal psychology, not to speak of traditional psychologies of the Oriental traditions based on intellection and spiritual methods that enable one to penetrate into the depths of the psyche, to transform it and ultimately to transcend it.

In the world of prophecy, the philosopher must deal with the reality of eschatology as asserted by the revelation, as well as with the reality of not only the outer layers of the psyche but also the whole of the immortal soul in itself and in its wedding to the Spirit. Again in this realm earlier Islamic philosophers wrote works of importance such as Ibn Sīnā's *al-Risālat al-aḍḥawiyyah* (Treatise on the Day of Resurrection) on eschatology, and he, Fārābī, and others composed a number of well-known works on psychology. In the latter field, however, most of the earlier works were based on Aristotle's *De Anima* and his Alexandrian commentators. Before Mullā Ṣadrā the more inward studies of psychology were carried out not by philosophers but by Sufis. Mullā Ṣadrā benefited from both types of exposition, and his work marks the peak of the philosophical study of both eschatology and sacred psychology in the framework of prophetic philosophy. In both realms he made contributions that are unsurpassed in their philosophical depth, while at the same time revealing some of the deepest meaning of prophetic teachings on these matters.

The Imaginal World

Revelation not only transforms a human collectivity but in a sense transforms a whole cosmic sector, including the imaginal world, the intermediate world residing ontologically between the physical and the purely intellectual. The forms and images of this world have both a subjective and an objective dimension, both deeply affected by prophecy and the whole universe of symbols and images, which it either reveals or resuscitates with new life. Early Islamic philosophers such as Ibn Sīnā in fact sought to relate the function of the prophet to the imaginal faculty.[17] But it was again Mullā Ṣadrā and before him Suhrawardī and Ibn 'Arabī who brought out for the first time in Islamic metaphysical discourse the central importance of the imaginal world.[18] Mullā Ṣadrā followed those masters in expounding the metaphysics of this world and in bringing out its epistemological, eschatological, and cosmological significance in a masterly way. Moreover, he integrated his exposition of the ontology of the imaginal world into his general ontology based on the unity, principiality, and gradation of *wujūd*. In reading his description of the imaginal world, one senses, on the one hand, the existence and characteristics of this intermediate world and, on the other hand, its familiarity for those living within the context of the Islamic revelation as the locus of events associated with realities revealed by prophecy that concern the life of each believer in both this world and the next.

Trans-substantial Motion

In a cosmos dominated by prophecy and revelation, the human collectivity and the world of nature in a sense participate in the revealed reality. The Ganges is not only a river issuing from the Himalayas, but for those who belong to the Hindu universe, it also has a sacred significance. Likewise, according to Islamic teachings the cosmos is itself the first revelation of God. In such a sacralized cosmos phenomena are at once veils of spiritual realities and symbols that reveal those realities. In the Abrahamic world the world of nature is itself a book to be deciphered but only by virtue of access to prophecy as the Abrahamic religions understand it. More specifically, in Islam the emphasis on the Divine Oneness has as its concomitant consciousness of the interrelatedness of all multiplicity and the harmony that pervades all things, harmony being nothing other than the consequence of the manifestation of the One in the many.

In the universe sacralized by the Quranic revelation through a return to the view of the primordial nature of creation, many philosophies of nature were developed by Peripatetic and Ismā'īlī philosophers, later scholars of *kalām*, *ishrāqīs*, Sufis, and others.[19] All of these philosophies were related directly or indirectly to the reality of prophecy and revelation, and Mullā Ṣadrā was far from being the first Islamic thinker to have developed a natural philosophy relevant to a cosmos dominated by prophetic reality. Nevertheless, Mullā Ṣadrā did develop the doctrine of trans-substantial motion (*al-ḥarakat al-jawhariyyah*), which is both the basis of a profound natural philosophy and also the means to create an ineluctable link between natural philosophy, on the one hand, and metaphysics, cosmology, and eschatology, on the other.

Instead of positing existents with permanent substances in which only accidents could undergo motion in the classical philosophical sense, or asserting the existence of immutable atoms as in classical atomism, Mullā Ṣadrā saw the whole world of nature as partaking in a transformation that affects the very substance of things. He saw the world of corporeal existence—and of course not the immutable intelligible world—as being like a long caravan moving from the lowly state of material existence to the Empyrean without this movement, which Corbin called poetically *"l'inquiétude de l'être,"* implying any form of Darwinian evolution or transformism.[20] In divorcing traditional cosmology from its reliance upon Ptolemaic astronomy, in integrating the dimensions of time and space, in providing a means to understand natural transformations without falling into the error of evolutionary reductionism, and in many other ways, Mullā Ṣadrā created on the basis of the doctrine of trans-substantial motion a natural philosophy that can function and be viable even in a contemporary setting with all the challenges of modern science and yet still remain faithful to the realities of prophecy.

While in the West from the seventh/thirteenth century onward, philosophy and theology began to drift apart, and with Descartes the two became totally separate and in many cases antagonistic, in the prophetic philosophy of Mullā Ṣadrā, in that synthesis that he called "*al-ḥikmat al-muta'āliyah*," all tension and antagonism between philosophy and theology was overcome, and in fact this *ḥikmat* functioned as both, and, as mentioned in chapter 3, it practically devoured Shi'ite *kalām* so that during later centuries in Shi'ism, *kalām* became much less relevant than before. The fully flowered prophetic philosophy of Mullā Ṣadrā not only became the main philosophical current but also played the role that not only philosophy but also theology and especially mystical theology have played in Christianity. In referring to this pact between theology and philosophy in Mullā Ṣadrā, Corbin writes, "From the pact thus concluded, equally from the beginning between prophetic revelation and philosophical meditation, there results a particular situation for philosophy which, promoted to the rank of 'prophetic philosophy,' will henceforth be inseparable from spiritual effort and personal spiritual realization."[21]

The tree of prophetic philosophy can flower many times, and not only once. Mullā Ṣadrā marks the full flowering of prophetic philosophy in the context of Safavid Persia and Ithna 'asharī Shi'ism and is also the fullest flowering of that philosophy, even if one views the whole of Islamic civilization.[22] But even after Mullā Ṣadrā there were other major flowerings of prophetic philosophy in the Islamic world not only in Persia but also in Islamic India, expressions that also represent important expressions of prophetic philosophy, but this time as far as India is concerned, mostly in a predominantly Sunni ambience. One need only recall two of the towering figures of later Islamic thought in India, Shāh Walī Allāh of Delhi and Mawlānā 'Alī Ashraf Thanwī, both of whom were influenced by Mullā Ṣadrā. In their somewhat different syntheses of Islamic philosophy, in which elements of philosophy, theology, principles of jurisprudence, the religious sciences, and Sufism are integrated into an imposing unified structure, the main features of prophetic philosophy to be seen in early Islamic philosophers and in their full flowering in Mullā Ṣadrā are again to be observed. Nor do these flowerings during the past few centuries detract in any way from the possibility of the reflowering of the tree of prophetic philosophy in our own day and age.

The influence of Mullā Ṣadrā in India was substantial,[23] but in contrast the Ottoman world remained indifferent to his teachings, and it is only in the past two decades that the attention of younger Turkish scholars has turned toward him.[24] But it was especially in his home country that after a short period of eclipse, his teachings came to constitute the predominant school of philosophy in Qajar Persia, producing such masters as Ḥajjī Mullā Hādī Sabziwārī[25] and being the main inspiration for the School of Tehran, to which we shall now turn.

CHAPTER 13

From the School of Isfahan to the School of Tehran

The School of Isfahan in Its Later Phase

In its later phase, the School of Isfahan produced a number of significant figures. As mentioned in the last chapter, they include Mullā Ṣadrā's students such as the already cited Mullā Muḥsin Fayḍ Kāshānī[1] and 'Abd al-Razzāq Lāhījī[2] and a number of other important figures such as Mullā Rajab 'Alī Tabrīzī, Mullā Shamsā Gīlānī, Āqā Ḥusayn Khunsārī, Sayyid Aḥmad 'Alawī, and Qāḍī Sa'īd Qummi.[3] Toward the end of the Safavid period, however, the religious atmosphere in Persia turned against philosophy and especially the school of Mullā Ṣadrā. Still, the teaching of philosophy continued in Isfahan under the direction of such masters as 'Ināyat Allāh Gīlānī, Mīr Sayyid Ḥasan Tāliqānī, and Mawlā Muḥammad Ṣādiq Ardistānī.

The tragic life of this last figure exemplifies the plight of philosophy in Isfahan during the reign of Shāh Sulṭān Ḥusayn at the end of the Safavid period in the twelfth/eighteenth century. This outstanding *ḥakīm* and saintly man was a follower of the teachings of Mullā Ṣadrā as one can see in the former's short Persian treatise entitled *Ja'l* (Instauration). He is also known for a treatise entitled *Ḥikmat-i ṣādiqiyyah* (Ṣādiqean Wisdom), which deals with the powers of the soul and is of a mystical character. Despite his great piety and saintly demeanor, however, he was driven away from Isfahan in the winter and lost one of his children to the bitter winter cold. Ardistānī, who is the last major Ṣadrian philosopher of the Safavid period, died in 1113/1701.

Meanwhile, in the latter part of the Safavid period the influence of the School of Isfahan spread to other cities in Persia. Mullā Ṣadrā himself spent the last decades of his life back in Shiraz. Mullā Muḥsin Fayḍ retired to his home town of Kashan, where he continued to teach and where an entourage grew around him. Later in the Qajar period philosophical activity was to continue in Kashan with the appearance of the major intellectual figure Mullā Muḥammad Mahdī Narāqī. Lāhījī settled in Qom, where he and his son Ḥasan Lāhījī and the major expositor of gnosis, Qāḍī Sa'īd, taught. Yet, despite all the opposition to *ḥikmat* in Isfahan during the latter part of Safavid rule, and despite the devastation brought about by the Afghan invasion, *ḥikmat* continued to survive albeit precariously in Isfahan, and once the political situation settled down, it was in this city that philosophical activity and especially the teachings of Mullā Ṣadrā 's *al-ḥikmat al-muta'āliyah* were revived.

A number of philosophers were witness to the storm at the end of the Safavid period, chief among them Mullā Ismā'īl Khājū'ī (d.1173/1760), who survived into the Zand period. In one of his works he describes the devastation caused by the conquest of Isfahan and the suffering he underwent. His own life was endangered, and many of his works were lost, but he survived to continue to teach *ḥikmat* and trained an important student such as Narāqī, among others.[4] The major reviver of Ṣadrean philosophy in Isfahan was, however, Mullā 'Alī Nūrī, who lived about a century and taught *ḥikmat* in Isfahan for some seventy years until his death in 1246/1830–31. No one after Mullā Ṣadrā has done so much to propagate the doctrines of *al-ḥikmat al-muta'āliyah*, through the teaching of numerous important students and writing glosses, commentaries, and annotations upon the works of Mullā Ṣadrā, including the *Asfār*.[5] Nūrī's most important students include his own son Mīrzā Ḥasan Nūrī, as well as Mullā 'Abd Allāh Zunūzī, Mullā Muḥammad Ismā'īl Darbkūshkī Iṣfahānī, Sayyid Raḍī Lārījānī, Āqā Muḥammad Riḍā Qumsha'ī, Mullā Muḥammad Ja'far Langarūdī , Mullā Āqā-i Qazwīnī, and many other well-known figures. The origin of the School of Tehran is to be sought in the Isfahan of the early thirteenth/nineteenth centuries and the circle of Mullā 'Alī Nūrī.

Even after the center of philosophical activity shifted to Tehran, Isfahan remained a vibrant philosophical center, producing such famous philosophers as Jahāngīr Khān Qashqā'ī and in more recent times Āqā Mīrzā Raḥīm Arbāb, who died in the Pahlavi period. Whether one can call the long period of philosophical activity stretching from Mīr Dāmād to someone like Arbāb or Jalāl Humā'ī, who died just two decades ago, the "School of Isfahan" is open to debate,[6] but certainly something of the earlier School of Isfahan survived after the Safavid period into the Qajar period and even into the contemporary era and served as the source for the School of Tehran, which became central in Persia from the thirteenth/nineteenth century onward. The School of Tehran represents both a continuity with the School of Isfahan as far as major philosophical issues and position are concerned, and discontinuity created by the fact that it was in Tehran where the Islamic philosophical tradition in Persia encountered Western thought for the first time and developed in certain directions that make it distinct from the School of Isfahan, from which it originated.

The Beginning of the School of Tehran

Soon after the establishment of the Qajar Dynasty in 1210/1796, Tehran, which was then a small town, was chosen as capital of Persia and grew rapidly into an important city that became not only the political and economic heart of Persia but also its intellectual center. Mosques and *madrasahs* began to be built, and they attracted religious scholars to the city. In 1237/1821–22, Muḥammad Khān Marwī built a major *madrasah* in the heart of what is now the old city, and the king, Fatḥ 'Alī Shāh, invited Mullā 'Alī Nūrī to migrate from Isfahan to Tehran to become the central *mudarris* or teacher of the newly built school. Nūrī was then at an advanced age and had numerous students in Isfahan whom he could not abandon. He therefore declined the king's offer but instead sent one of his foremost students, Mullā 'Abd Allāh Zunūzī, to Tehran. Mullā 'Abd Allāh established himself in the Marwī School during that year and taught Islamic philosophy there for the next two decades until his death in 1257/1841.[7] He marks the first step in the transfer of philosophical activity from the School of Isfahan to what was soon to become the School of Tehran.

Mullā 'Abd Allāh Zunūzī was a follower of the school of Mullā Ṣadrā and of his own teacher Mullā 'Alī Nūrī and by training belonged to the School of Isfahan and more particularly to the circle of Nūrī. Like his teacher, he wrote a number of glosses on the works of Mullā Ṣadrā, including the *Asfār, al-Shawāhid al-rubūbiyyah, al-Mabda᾽ wa᾽l-ma'ād,* and *Asrār al-āyāt,* as well as Ibn Sīnā's *Shifā᾽* and Lāhījī's *Shawāriq al-ilhām.* He also wrote a number of independent works that are perhaps his most significant writings. These treatises, which are in Persian, include *Anwār-i jaliyyah* (Manifest Light), which is a comprehensive commentary upon the tradition transmitted from 'Alī ibn Abī Ṭālib concerning the truth *(al-ḥaqīqah)*,[8] *Lama'āt-i ilāhiyyah* (Divine Splendors) on *tawḥīd* and *ilāhiyyāt bi ma'na᾽l-khāṣṣ* or philosophical theology in the tradition of Mullā Ṣadrā;[9] and *Muntakhab al-khāqānī fi kashf ḥaqā᾽iq 'irfānī* (Royal Selections concerning the Unveiling of Gnostic Truths) on the proof of the Necessary Being and God's Unity and Attributes.[10] What is of great interest in these treaties is not only their philosophical content but also the fact that they were written in lucid Persian and mark the beginning of a movement during the Qajar period to turn once again to fairly extensive use of Persian in addition to Arabic for the expression of philosophical ideas.[11] This movement is clearly evident in the School of Tehran but is also to be seen elsewhere such as in Sabziwar, Qom, Kashan, and Shiraz. It is, however, especially significant for the School of Tehran, for it was in the capital that contemporary philosophical Persian began to develop in the later Qajar period, a development in which traditional philosophical texts written in Persian played an important role.

Before turning to the major figures of the School of Tehran, a few words must be said about two outstanding figures who exercised influence upon the School of Tehran but who did not belong to it. The first is Ḥājjī Mullā Hādī Sabziwārī (1212/1797–98–1289/1872), the most famous philosopher of the Qajar period, who was also the teacher of many of the main early figures of the School of Tehran.[12] Some of Sabziwārī's students came to Tehran, and a number of students from Tehran who were to gain a name for themselves in the field of philosophy journeyed to Sabziwar in Khurasan to study with the venerable philosopher/saint. For several decades the circle of Sabziwar vied with the School of Tehran in importance in the field of philosophy, and Sabziwārī was himself in contact with many figures from Tehran. His *Asrār al-ḥikam* (Secret of Wisdom) was written in Persian at the request of the Persian king, Nāṣir al-Dīn Shāh, and was well known in Tehran, and his *Sharḥ al-manẓūmah* (Commentary upon the *Manẓūmah* [a philosophical poem]) became very popular as a text in the School of Tehran and continues to be so in all centers in Persia where traditional philosophy is being taught. Altogether the figure of Sabziwārī and his works cannot be disassociated from the development of the School of Tehran.

The second seminal figure who must be mentioned is Āqā Sayyid Raḍī Lārījānī, an enigmatic figure about whose life little is known.[13] Apparently after his early life in Larijan near the Caspian Sea, he journeyed to Isfahan, where he soon became one of the foremost students of Mullā 'Alī Nūrī and Mullā Ismā'īl Iṣfahānī and a recognized master in the school of Mullā Ṣadrā. But it is essentially for his knowledge of gnosis, esoterism, and even the occult sciences that he was known to the extent that he was given the title *mālik-i bāṭin* (Master of the Esoteric Realm) or *ṣāḥib-i ḥāl-i mālik-i bāṭin* (Possessor of the Spiritual State of the Esoteric Realm).[14] Those who knew him believed that the truths of gnosis had become fully realized in him. The great master of gnosis of the School of Tehran, Āqā Maḥammad Riḍā Qumsha'ī, to whom we shall turn shortly, writes that when he was in Isfahan he had begun to study the *Fuṣūṣ al-ḥikam* of Ibn 'Arabī with Mullā Muḥammad Ja'far Langarūdī, a major Ṣadrean philosopher of Isfahan, but he was not fully satisfied; so he went to study the text with Lārījānī, who became worried that Āqā Maḥammad Riḍā had changed teachers but added, "The teaching of the *Fuṣūṣ* is the work of a *qalandarī* [an unruly and ecstatic Sufi state] while Ḥājjī Mullā Muḥammad Ja'far is a *hakīm* and not a *qalandar*."[15]

In any case while a formidable authority in *ḥikmat*, Lārījānī was above all a gnostic, an esoterist, and a realized sage. It was these qualities that caused him some problems with anti-Sufi and antiphilosophical religious authorities of Isfahan, and had it not been for one of his physician disciples who bore witness that Lārījānī was "mad," he might have met the same fate as Suhrawardī and 'Ayn al-Quḍāt Hamadānī. In any case, at the end of his life, at the invitation of a Qajar notable, Mīrzā Ismā'īl Gurgānī, Lārījānī came to Tehran, where he settled at the home of his host. He died in 1270/1853–54 in Tehran after only a few years of stay in the capital. Most likely a student of the well-known gnostic Mullā Muḥammad Ja'far Ābādaʾī, Lārījānī became the most important master of the school of Ibn 'Arabī in the early phase of the School of Tehran, his greatest contribution to this school being his training of Āqā Muḥammad Riḍā Qumshaʾī and through him numerous later masters of gnosis such as Āqā Mīrzā Hāshim Rashtī and Mīrzā Muḥammad 'Alī Shāhābādī who was the teacher in *'irfān* of Ayatollah Khomeini.[16]

The Four *Ḥakīms* and the Full Establishment of the School of Tehran

Later Persian scholars have spoken of the four *ḥakīms* (*ḥukamā-yi arba'ah*) who were foundational to the School of Tehran: Āqā 'Alī Ḥakīm Mudarris Ṭihrānī (also known as Zunūzī); Āqā Muḥammad Riḍā Qumshaʾī; Mīrzā Abuʾl-Ḥasan Jilwah, and Mīrzā Ḥusayn Sabziwārī. It is these four masters who established the School of Tehran firmly upon the earlier efforts of Mullā 'Abd Allāh Zunūzī and Lārījānī and who in a sense completed the transfer of the teachings of the School of Isfahan to Tehran.

Āqā 'Alī Ḥakīm Mudarris

Given the title *Ḥakīm-i muʾassis* (The Founding *Ḥakīm*), Āqā 'Alī is the central founding figure of the School of Tehran. The son of Mullā 'Abd Allāh Zunūzī, he was born in 1234/1818 in Isfahan and accompanied his father to Tehran when he was only three years old.[17] He received his early education in literature, logic, and *fiqh* in Tehran and then studied such philosophical and theological texts as the *Shawāriq* of Lāhījī, *Sharḥ al-ishārāt* by Ṭūsī and *al-Mabdaʾ waʾl-maʿād* (The Origin and the Return) by Mullā Ṣadrā with his own father. Upon his father's death, he set out for Iraq to study the transmitted sciences in Najaf and then went to Isfahan to complete his studies in philosophy. In this still vibrant center of Islamic philosophy he studied the *Shifāʾ* of Ibn Sīnā and the *Asfār* and *Mafātīḥ al-ghayb* of Mullā Ṣadrā with the son of Mullā 'Alī Nūrī, Mīrzā Ḥasan Nūrī. He also studied with other major figures of the city such as Sayyid Raḍī and Mullā Muḥammad Ja'far Langarūdī. Then he spent some time in Qazwin studying Mullā Ṣadrā with Mullā Āqā-yi Qazwīnī, whom he considered to be the best teacher of the principles of Ṣadrean philosophy. After that short period, he returned to Isfahan, and about 1270/1853–54 he finished his formal studies in the intellectual sciences.

Finally Āqā 'Alī settled in Tehran, where he continued to study the transmitted sciences with Mīrzā Ḥusayn Āshtiyānī and began to teach philosophy. His career in teaching in Tehran was to last forty years, first in Qāsim Khān *madrasah,* then for a few years in his own home, and then for more than twenty years as official *madarris* in Sipahsālār *madrasah*. The main texts that he taught were the following: *Asfār, al-Mabdaʾ waʾl-maʿād, Sharḥ al-hidāyah* (Commentary upon the Book of Guidance [of Athīr al-Dīn Abharī]) and *al-Shawāhid al-rubūbiyyah* of Mullā Ṣadrā, the *Shifāʾ* of Ibn Sīnā, and *Sharḥ ḥikmat al-ishrāq* (Commentary upon the Theosophy of the Orient of Light [of Suhrawardī and Quṭb al-Dīn Shīrāzī]). His lessons were attended by numerous students and were famous throughout Persia and even in certain other Islamic countries, and he trained a large number of important students belonging to the next generation of philosophers of the School of Tehran. After a long and fruitful life, he died in Tehran in 1307/1889 and was buried in Ḥadrat-i 'Abd al-'Aẓīm in Rayy.

Some twenty-seven works of Āqā 'Alī Mudarris are known to have survived.[18] His works include a number of major annotations (*ta'līqāt)* upon several works of Mullā Ṣadrā, especially his *Asfār* and *Sharḥ ḥikmat al-ishrāq*, glosses upon *Sharḥ al-ishārāt* by Lāhījī and Lāhījī's *Shawāriq*, and his own father's *Lama'āt-i ilāhiyyah;* other works are independent or semi-independent texts on resurrection,[19] attribution (*ḥaml*), the soul, relational existence (*al-wujūd al-rābiṭī*), unity, the transcendent unity of being (*waḥdat al-wujūd)* of the Sufis, a short history of Islamic philosophy, and a short autobiography. In addition to these works and a number of poems Āqā 'Alī wrote *Badāyi' al-ḥikam* (Marvels of Wisdom), which is perhaps his most important text and considered by some to be the most significant work in the school of *al-ḥikmat al-muta'āliyah* after the *Asfār*.[20] Written in Persian, it compares with the works of Afḍal al-Dīn Kāshānī and Suhrawardī in its significance for philosophical prose in that language. It also deals with Ṣadrean metaphysics in a remarkably creative manner. Furthermore, this work is considered by some to be the first in which traditional Islamic philosophy and Western philosophy, mostly Kantian, meet, for Āqā 'Alī sets out in this book to respond to certain philosophical questions brought to him from Europe by the Qajar prince Badī' al-mulk. For this reason some have considered the *Badāyi' al-ḥikam* as being not only the most important text of Ṣadrean philosophy in Persian but also the first text of comparative philosophy (in relation to European philosophy) within the Islamic philosophical tradition,[21] the beginning of a path that was to be followed later in Persia by 'Allāmah Ṭabāṭabā'ī, Mīrzā Mahdī Ḥa'irī Yazdī, and several younger philosophers of this generation.

As for Āqā 'Alī's annotations upon the *Asfār*, they cover nearly the whole text and constitute in themselves a cycle of Ṣadarean philosophy. The glosses of Sabziwārī upon the *Asfār* are among the most detailed and clarifying of the many commentaries written on the text. These glosses have been published in the lithographed edition of the text of Mullā Ṣadrā. The only commentary upon the *Asfār* to compare in significance with that of Sabziwārī is that of Āqā 'Alī, which, however, departs more from the text than does Sabziwārī's. S. J. Āshtiyānī goes as far as to say, "I believe that in philosophical discussions Āqā 'Alī was more meticulous and more confirmed in the truth than Sabziwārī."[22] Some in fact consider Āqā 'Alī Mudarris to be the greatest figure of the school of *al-ḥikmat al- muta'āliyah* after Mullā Ṣadrā himself,[23] but others bestow this honor upon Mullā 'Alī Nūrī. Although it is true that Āqā 'Alī must be considered along with Mullā Ṣadrā himself, Mullā 'Alī Nūrī, Ḥājjī Mullā Hādī Sabziwārī, Āqā Muḥammad Riḍā Qumsha'ī, and one or two others as the greatest master of the school of *al-ḥikmat-al-muta'āliyah*, he was not simply an imitator and commentator of Mullā Ṣadrā. Rather, he expressed certain views not found in Ṣadr al-Dīn's works and may be said to have begun a new chapter in the history of the Ṣadrean school rather that being simply a continuation of the same chapter. Not only did he criticize certain Ṣadrean tenets, but he also formulated several new theses of his own concerning such questions as corporeal resurrection, attribution, knowledge, second philosophical intelligibles, trans-substantial motion, the principiality of being, gradation, the unity of the arc of descent and the arc of ascent, and many other major issues. A thorough study of

Āqā 'Alī will reveal him to be not only a major commentator of Mullā Ṣadrā but also the founder of a new phase in the development of the school founded by the great *ḥakīm* of Shiraz.

Āqā 'Alī had extensive contact with the notable figures of his day both among the class of religious scholars and those at court, such as I'timād al-Salṭanah, who was one of Nāṣir al-Dīn Shāh's closest confidants and at the same time very respectful of Āqā 'Alī. He was in fact Āqā 'Alī's disciple. I'timād al-Salṭanah was a channel whereby Āqā 'Alī gained some knowledge of what was transpiring philosophically in Europe. I'timād al-Salṭanah was also instrumental in spreading the fame of Āqā 'Alī in courtly circles and also among these also were becoming interested in Western education and thought.

As far as the contact of Āqā 'Alī with the West is concerned, it is especially important to mention Comte de Gobineau, the French philosopher who came to Tehran for two years as a minister in the French embassy. In his well known work *Les Religions et les philosophies dans l'Asie central*,[24] he mentions Āqā 'Alī, and the information that Gobineau transmits concerning later Persian philosophers is from Āqā 'Alī, whom he had met in Tehran. Some traditional Persian religious scholars have transmitted the account of an invitation given by Gobineau to Āqā 'Alī to go to France and teach Islamic philosophy at the Sorbonne. The account also mentions that at first he accepted the invitation but that he was later dissuaded from going by his many students.[25] One wonders what would have happened in the West as far as Islamic philosophy was concerned and in the Islamic world itself, especially Persia, if a colossal figure of Islamic metaphysics and philosophy and a figure of great spiritual stature such as Āqā 'Alī Mudarris had gone to France in the nineteenth century. In any case, even though the journey did not take place, Āqā 'Alī was able to establish the School of Tehran on a firm Ṣadrean foundation while at the same time being ready to encounter the challenges of Western philosophies and schools of thought that were soon to penetrate into the capital of Qajar Persia.

Āqā Muḥammad Riḍā Qumshaʾī

Although a definite master of the school of Mullā Ṣadrā, Āqā Muḥammad Riḍā was above all a master of gnosis of the school of Ibn 'Arabī and in fact the greatest representative of this school in Persia during the past few centuries. Ayatollah Khomeini referred to him as "the master of our masters." This remarkable figure, who was called "the second Ibn 'Arabī" and who used the pen name Ṣahbā, was born in Qumshah near Isfahan in 1241/1825 and carried out his early studies in the city of his birth before coming to Isfahan to study *ḥikmat* with Mullā Muḥammad Ja'far Lāhījī and Mīrzā Ḥasan Nūrī, the already mentioned son of Mullā 'Alī Nūrī. His most important teacher was, however, Sayyid Raḍī Lārījānī, and it was in his hands that Āqā Muḥammad Riḍā reached the station of realization in gnostic knowledge. It is important to note in this context that Āqā Muḥammad Riḍā had a spiritual teacher and confirmed the necessity of having a spiritual master in order to realize the truths of gnosis.[26] In this context he is said to have cited the verse,

> Do not traverse this stage without the companionship of Khiḍr.[27]
> For there is darkness, have fear of being lost.

In any case what is known of the life of Āqā Muḥammad Riḍā reveals that he taught both *'irfān* and *ḥikmat* in Isfahan and then, after giving all his worldly possessions to the poor, set out to settle in Tehran some time around 1294/1877. The cause for his migration from Isfahan to Tehran is not certain, but later scholars have mentioned his dissatisfaction with some of the authorities in Isfahan and also the migration of a number of major scholars such as Mullā 'Abd Allāh Zunūzī and Mīrzā Abūʾl-Ḥasan Jilwah to Tehran.[28] Āqā Muḥammad Riḍā was to teach hundreds of students in Tehran until he died in that city in 1306/1888 and was buried, according to most authorities, in Ibn Babūyah near Rayy. In describing the breadth of his knowledge Āshtiyānī writes, "Āqā Muḥammad Riḍā was one of those people who could teach the *Shifāʾ*, and other *mashshāʾī* texts with perfect ease and domination and was a sagacious master in the teaching of the books of Shaykh al-ishrāq and Ṣadr al-mutaʾallihīn. As for gnosis and the teaching of the *Fuṣūṣ, Tamhīd al-qawā'id, Miṣbāḥ al-uns* ("Lamp of Spiritual Familiarity"), and *Futūḥāt-i-makkiyyah* ("Meccan Illuminations") he was peerless."[29] One cannot describe more clearly and justly the intellectual activities of this supreme master of gnosis of his day.

Āqā Muḥammad Riḍā lived simply as a darvish and often met his students in the ruins outside of Tehran. There is an account by the great Iṣfahānī *ḥakīm* Jahāngīr Khān Qashqāʾī, who had come to Tehran to meet Āqā Muḥammad Riḍā, which casts much light on the master's countenance and presence. Jahāngīr Khān has provided the following account:

> I had the impulsion to study with Ḥadrat-i Qumshaʾī in Tehran and therefore in the very night of my arrival I went to his

> presence. He did not have any characteristics of a religious scholar and was like muslin sellers of Sidah [a town near Isfahan]. I was in a state of spiritual attraction (*jadhbah*). When I made the request [to see him], he said that I should come the next day to the ruins (*kharābāt*). The ruins were a place outside the ditch [surrounding Tehran] and a darvish had a coffee-house there where people of spiritual taste would meet. The next day I went to that location and found him sitting in a place of spiritual solitude (*khalwatgāh*) on a mat. I opened the *Asfār* and he read it from memory and made such a verification of it that I almost fell into a state of madness. He discovered my spiritual state and said, "Power does break the jar."[30]

It is perhaps this manner of living that caused many of Āqā Muḥammad Riḍā's works to be lost, including most of his poems. The few poems that have survived being in ghazal form in the 'Irāqī style reveal his great poetic power and the immensity of the loss of the majority of his poems for Persian Sufi poetry of the Qajar period. The prose works of Āqā Muḥammad Riḍā that are known include a treatise on *walāyat/wilāyat, Risālah fī waḥdat al-wujūd bal al-mawjūd* ("Treatise on the Unity of Existence or Rather of the Existent), *al- Khilāfat al-kubrā* (The Greatest Vicegerency), treatise on the difference between the Essence and the Qualities of God, treatise on *'ilm* or knowledge, a treatise about the *Asfār*, and a number of glosses and annotations upon the *Asfār* and the *Shawāhid,* as well as major gnostic texts such as the *Fūṣūs, Miftāḥ al-ghayb* (Key to the Invisible World) of Qunyawī, and *Tamhīd al-qawā'id* of Ibn Turkah Iṣfahānī.[31]

One can hardly overestimate the significance of Āqā Muḥammad Riḍā in both *ḥikmat* and *'irfān* for the School of Tehran and his influence over succeeding generations to our own day. A sage and saint who lived simply and always with humility, he left a deep spiritual expression upon those who met him while imparting the profoundest teachings of *'irfān* and *ḥikmat* to those capable and worthy of receiving the pearls of wisdom that he disseminated. He established the school of *'irfān* in Tehran on a solid foundation, and it was from there that his students were to spread his teachings to many other cities such as Qom itself. If one only goes over the long list of his students,[32] which includes such names as Āqā Mīrzā Hāshim Ashkiwarī, Mīrzā Shihāb al-Dīn Nayrīzī, Mīrzā Ḥasan Kirmānshāhī, and Mīrzā Mahdī Āshtiyānī, one will realize the remarkably extensive influence of Āqā Muḥammad Riḍā over the later intellectual life of Persia. In any case he is the second major figure of the School of Tehran after Āqā 'Alī Mudarris, and the two complement each other in many ways.

Mīrzā Abū᾿l-Ḥasan Jilwah

The third of the four major founders of the School of Tehran, Mīrzā Abū᾿l-Ḥasan Jilwah, was born in 1238/1822 in Ahmadabad in Gujarat. His father had migrated from Persia to Hydarabad in Sindh, and had married the daughter of the prime minister and was even chosen as ambassador. But he fell out with those at court and went to Ahmadabad and then Bombay, returning finally to Isfahan when Jilwah was seven years old.[33] It was in this city that after the death of his father and the period of youth spent under financial duress, Jilwah turned to the field of religious studies and especially philosophy. He studied both Ṣadrean and Avicennan philosophy, as well as some medicine with famous masters such as Mīrzā Ḥasan Nūrī, Mullā 'Abd al-Jawād Tūnī (who was known especially as a master of traditional medicine), Mīrzā Ḥasan Chīnī, and Mullā Muḥammad Ja'far Langarūdī and soon became himself a well-known philosopher. In 1273/1856, dissatisfied with his situation in Isfahan, he set out for Tehran and settled there to teach philosophy and write until the end of his life in 1314/1896. He was buried in Ibn Babūyah near Rayy.

Jilwah taught mostly in the Dār al-Shifā᾿ *madrasah* and became so famous and respected that Nāṣir al-Dīn Shāh would visit him from time to time at his school. Like Āqā 'Alī and Āqā Muḥammad Riḍā, Jilwah taught the works of Mullā Ṣadrā, but his main interest was Ibn Sīnā and the *mashshā᾿ī* school. As already mentioned in chapter 11, in the School of Isfahan one can detect two main philosophical trends: The *ḥikmat al-muta'āliyah* associated with Mullā Ṣadrā and the continuation of Avicennan philosophy in its later interpretations as one sees in Mullā Rajab 'Alī Tabrīzī and in a somewhat different manner in Mullā Shamsā Gīlānī. Jilwah represents more this second trend than the first, and he was essentially a *mashshā᾿ī ḥakīm* even if he also taught Mullā Ṣadrā and commented upon his works. Jilwah was even critical of Mullā Ṣadrā, accusing him of having taken various ideas from earlier philosophers without acknowledging his sources. Although he was a gifted poet whose *dīwān* has in fact been published, Jilwah was more of a philosopher with strong rational tendencies than an illuminationist or intuitive thinker and possessed a very rigorous and rational mind although also having a mystical side. One of his main contributions was in fact in correcting and editing with great exactitude all the texts that he taught, paying attention to every word and phrase. The corrected texts include *Tamhīd al-qawā'id* of Ibn Turkah, the *Shifā᾿* of Ibn Sīnā, and *Miṣbāh al-uns* of Shams al-Dīn Fanārī.

The works of Jilwah include his glosses upon the *Mashā'ir* (The Book of Metaphysical Penetrations), *Sharḥ al-hidāyah, al-Mabda᾿ wa᾿l-*

ma'ād, and *Asfār* of Mullā Ṣadrā, annotations upon the introduction of Qayṣarī to his commentary upon the *Fuṣūs*, and a number of independent treatises including those on the relation between the created and the eternal, trans-substantial motion, universals, and existence. He also wrote a series of glosses upon the *Shifā*ʾ along with the correction of the text, which was one of the main works that he taught. Jilwah was also so much interested in Sufi poetry that he corrected the text of the *Mathnawī* of Jalāl al-Dīn Rūmī. Unfortunately, most of his works, like those of Āqā Muḥammad Riḍā, remain unedited. Also like his illustrious contemporaries, Jilwah trained numerous students among whom one can mention especially Āqā Sayyid Ḥusayn Bādkūbaʾī, who established a circle for the study of Islamic philosophy in Najaf in Iraq; Mīr Sayyid Shihāb al-Dīn Nayrīzī, the well-known authority on *'irfān* and philosophy; Mīrzā Ṭāhir Tunikābunī, one of the foremost later masters of philosophy in the School of Tehran; and Ākhūnd Mullā Muḥammad Hīdajī Zanjānī, known especially for his famous commentary upon the *Sharḥ al-manẓūmah* of Sabziwārī.

Mīrzā Ḥasan Sabziwārī

We know much less about the last of the four founders of the School of Tehran, Mīrzā Ḥasan Sabziwārī, except that he was a student of Ḥājjī Mullā Hādī Sabziwārī and migrated later from Sabziwar to Tehran, where he taught in the 'Abd Allāh Khān *madrasah* in the bazaar. Although he taught philosophy, his main concern was with mathematics, for which he became justly famous. He also had a number of famous students including Hīdajī and Mīrzā Ibrāhīm Riyāḍī Zanjānī. What is significant about him is not only his fame among his contemporaries but that in the thirteenth/nineteenth century in the School of Tehran the study of mathematics had not become as yet completely separated from that of philosophy and that the traditional link between philosophy and mathematics that one observes in Ṭūsī, Quṭb al-Dīn Shīrāzī, the Dashtakīs, Shams al-Dīn Khafrī, and Faṭh Allāh Shīrāzī was still alive, although it was soon to become greatly weakened. The presence of Mīrzā Ḥasan assured that something of this important link would survive into this later period. My own teachers, Sayyid Muḥammad Kāẓim 'Aṣṣār and Sayyid Abuʾl-Ḥasan Rāfi'ī Qazwīnī and a major later representative of the School of Tehran, Abūʾl-Ḥasan Sha'rānī, had extensive knowledge of the traditional Islamic mathematical sciences, in addition to their great mastery of philosophy.

After the Four Founding Ḥakīms

Among the most important students of those four masters, besides those already mentioned, were Mīrzā Ḥasan Kirmānshāhī, who was a specialist in the teachings of *mashshāʾī* philosophy, mathematics, and medicine, and Mīrzā Hāshim Rashtī, who was a notable exponent of *'irfān* and *ishrāqī* doctrines. Their students and the generation that followed are too numerous to name here.[34] We must confine ourselves to only a few of the most famous who later became masters of the School of Tehran during the late Qajar and the Pahlavi periods. One can mention, in addition to those already cited, Mīrzā Maḥmūd and Mīrzā Aḥmad Āshtiyānī, who resided in Tehran and who were known as great authorities in the teaching of spiritual ethics and *'irfān*; Mīrzā Muḥammad 'Alī Shāhābādī, who moved to Tehran where in addition to philosophy he taught the main texts of *'irfān*; Muḥammad Taqī Āmulī, one of the leading philosophers of the School of Tehran during the Pahlavi period; and three figures about whom we need to say a few more words: Mīrzā Mahdī Āshtiyānī, Sayyid Abūʾl-Ḥasan Rafī'ī Qazwīnī, and Sayyid Muḥammad Kāẓim 'Aṣṣār, all of whom lived well into the Pahlavi era but were trained in the late Qajar period in the School of Tehran.

Mīrzā Mahdī Āshtiyānī, at once an outstanding philosopher and *faqīh*, was born in 1306/1888 in Tehran. His first teacher was his father, with whom he studied *fiqh* and *uṣūl*. He also studied these subjects with Shaykh Masīḥ Ṭāliqānī and Shaykh Faḍl Allāh Nūrī and philosophy with Āqā Mīr Shīrāzī and Mīrzā Ḥasan Kirmānshāhī. Āshtiyānī was also very knowledgeable in traditional mathematics and medicine. He even studied Western medicine, which was then spreading in Persia, with such famous Qajar physicians as Nāẓim al-aṭibbāʾ and Raʾīs al- aṭibbāʾ. He then set out for Iraq, where he studied rational *fiqh* and *uṣūl* with such famous *faqīhs* as Sayyid Muḥammad Kāẓim Yazdī. After becoming established as an authority in *fiqh* as well as *ḥikmat* and *'irfān*, he returned to Persia, teaching for a while in Qom, Isfahan, and Mashhad and finally settled in Tehran. He spent the rest of his life in the capital teaching and writing a number of important works, becoming recognized as the leading *ḥakīm* and a notable *'ārif* of his day in Tehran. During this period he also traveled to India, Central Asia, Europe, and Egypt, where he explained Islamic philosophy to many audiences. He died in Tehran in 1372/1952.[35]

The philosophical works of Āshtiyānī include his commentary in Arabic and the Persian paraphrase of the *Asfār* of Mullā Ṣadrā and an *'irfānī* commentary upon his *Mafātīḥ al-ghayb*, as well as commentaries upon various parts of Sabziwārī's *Sharḥ al-manẓūmah.*[36] Āshtiyānī was also the author of an independent work on *ḥikmat*, *Asās al-tawḥīd* (Foundations of Unity), which reveals his remarkable philosophical profundity.[37] Furthermore, he authored a number of shorter treaties on various philosophical subjects.

One should not think for one moment that Āshtiyānī was simply a commentator who only clarified the meaning of earlier texts. Like many members of the School of Tehran and those before them, his commentaries are original philosophical treatises written in commentary form much like the commentaries of Mullā Ṣadrā upon *Ḥikmat al-ishrāq* and *Shifā*ʾ. For example, Āshtiyānī's commentary upon Sabziwārī is much more *'irfānī* in character than Sabzwārī's own commentary and reveals the text as almost an *'irfānī* work rather than a systematic and rational presentation of Mullā Ṣadrā's ideas. As T. Izustu writes:

> Sabziwārī, despite the fact that his entire philosophizing is at bottom based on a personal mystical existence, does not disclose this concept of philosophy on the surface. Āshtiyānī on the contrary is openly *'irfānī* throughout the whole commentary. This fact comes out more clearly in the introductory part of the work. But in the main part of the book, too, he never fails to seize the opportunity of leaving Sabziwārī behind at any moment and going into long fully developed *'irfānī* discussions of the philosophical concept in question. . . . [T]he same feature of Āshtiyānī's general attitude in writing his commentary is remarkable in that it turns the book into an original work of his own.[38]

In any case Mīrzā Mahdī Āshtiyānī was a towering intellectual figure of his day who wielded much influence in traditional circles of learning. He was also the teacher of a number of well-known philosophers of our own day such as Abūʾl-Ḥasan Sha'rānī, Muḥammad Taqī Ja'farī, Murtaḍā Muṭahharī, Mahdī Ḥāʾirī Yazdī, Jawād Falāṭūrī, and Sayyid Jalāl al-Dīn Āshtiyānī, all of whom are well-known Islamic thinkers of the fourteenth/twentieth century.[39]

Sayyid Abūʾl-Ḥasan Rafī'ī Qazwīnī, with whom I had the honor of studying the *Asfār* for some five years, was born in Qazwin in 1315/1897, where he carried out his early studies. Then he came to Tehran and Qom studying in both cities with such masters as Mīrzā Ḥasan Kirmānshāhī, Mīrzā Hāshim Āshkiwarī, Sayyid Muḥammad Tunikābunī, Shaykh 'Alī Rashtī, Shaykh 'Abd al-Karīm Ḥāʾirī, and others. He soon became famous as an authority in both philosophy and *fiqh,* becoming in fact one of Persia's leading ayatollahs and, after the death Ayatollah Burūjirdī, a source of emulation (*marja'-i taqlīd*) for many Shi'ites. He taught in Qom, Qazwin, and Tehran, where he died in 1396/1975, his body being buried in Qom.[40]

Qazwīnī was a masterful teacher especially of the work of Mullā Ṣadrā and in the explanation (*taqrīr*) of the *Asfār* in which he was unequalled among his contemporaries. He had a majestic countenance and exuded great authority. Although he taught mostly Ṣadrean philosophy, he did not agree on every point with Mullā Ṣadrā and Sabziwārī, in questions such as the exact meaning of the unity of the knower and the known (*ittiḥād al-'āqil wa'l-ma'qūl*). He also would often say that he was not totally satisfied with the explanation of the earlier Islamic philosophers of the relation between the created order and eternity (*ḥudūth* and *qidam*). He loved Sufi poetry but never spoke about it in public. This intimacy with the greatest works of Persian literature enabled him to possess a very lucid and flowing Persian prose, but he hated to write, and the few philosophical treatises that have survived from his pen and now edited and published by the outstanding contemporary *ḥakīm* from Qom, Ayatollah Ḥasanzādah Āmulī, were produced as the result of my insistence.[41] These treatises are masterpieces both in their success in clarifying in readily understandable terms some of most difficult issues of Islamic philosophy and also in their literary quality. They are among the best examples of philosophical Persian written in recent decades. Qazwīnī was also the author of a commentary upon the *Sharḥ al-manẓūmah.*

The influence of Ayatollah Qazwīnī in the domain of philosophy was primarily through the training of students in Qazwin, Qom, and Tehran, such figures as Mīrzā Mahdī Ḥā'irī and Sayyid Jalāl al-Dīn Āshtiyānī. The latter told me often over the years that Qazwīnī was the most acute commentator and lucid expositor of Ṣadrean philosophy whom he had known among the all the teachers of his day.

As for Sayyid Muḥammad Kāẓim 'Aṣṣār, he has been considered by some the last outstanding representative of the School of Tehran.[42] He was born in a family of religious scholars in Tehran in 1302/1884, where he carried out his early studies in *fiqh, uṣūl, kalām,* and logic with his father, who was a well-known teacher at that time.[43] In order to learn the modern sciences, he went to Dār al-funūn (the first institution of higher learning based on Western models in Iran), which he completed. He was then asked to teach the modern sciences, especially mathematics, along with French in Tabriz. It was there that he developed a close friendship with the famous religious scholar, Thaqat al-Islām Tabrīzī who apparently benefited from 'Aṣṣār's knowledge of the *Asfār*. After the violent death of Thaqat al-Islām, 'Aṣṣār left Tabriz for Europe through Caucasia and spent some time studying in the West. He was in fact the first member of the traditional class of *'ulamā'* in Persia to have done so. He then returned to the East, studying for some fourteen years in Najaf to complete his mastery of the transmitted sciences before coming to Tehran, where he settled and where he devoted himself completely to teaching both *fiqh* and philosophy. He taught at the Sipahsālār School, where he gave a regular course on *fiqh* followed by one in philosophy in which usually the *Sharḥ al-manẓūmah* of Sabziwārī was used as text. But he was also professor of Islamic philosophy in both the Faculty of Divinity and the Faculty of Letters of Tehran University. The latter position was particularly important because the philosophy department of the Faculty of Letters was then the most important philosophy department in Persia and one in which the teaching of Western philosophy was predominant. The doctoral students of the department, who became teachers in philosophy throughout the country, were therefore instructed in Islamic philosophy by 'Aṣṣār.[44] This great master died in Tehran in 1396/1975.

Sayyid Muḥammad Kāẓim 'Aṣṣār was a recognized authority in both the religious and philosophical sciences. He was at once a great *mujtahid, ḥakīm,* and *'ārif* who had an incredible intelligence and a wonderful sense of humor which caused him to laugh at the follies of the world. He refused to receive religious tax or to enter into the political and economic aspects of the life of many *mujtahids.* He devoted his life entirely to teaching and writing and gave of his time freely to those who sought his advice or yearned to learn from him. Although he had spent some time in Europe, he avoided all modernistic mannerisms and even in his teaching rarely referred to Western thought. He had penetrated the mask of the modern world, and knew fully well what stood behind it and was therefore not fooled by modernist tenets. Often he would make fun of not only modernized Persians, but also those among the *'ulamā'* who would make reference to some modern idea in a shallow way in order to appear up to date.

As a philosopher he was both a master of traditional texts and a creative interpreter of them. He had studied *ḥikmat* and *'irfān* with such luminaries as Āqā Mīrzā Ḥasan Rashtī, who was himself a student of Āqā 'Alī Mudarris; Āqā Muḥammad Riḍā Qumsha'ī; Āqā Mīrzā Ḥasan Kirmānshāhī, that celebrated philosopher and physician of the Qajar period; and Āqā Mīrzā Shihāb al-Dīn Nayrīzī, who was also a foremost disciple of Āqā Muḥammad Riḍā; and Āqā 'Alī Mudarris. Having studied with such masters was fully reflected in

'Aṣṣār's approach to texts of *ḥikmat* and *'irfān*. He knew every nuance of the texts and ideas involved. While teaching at the Sipahsālār School and Tehran University he would follow the assigned text carefully, but in private classes the text would serve as the point of departure into the vast empyrean of sacred knowledge within which 'Aṣṣār could journey with remarkable ease.[45]

Besides his commentaries and annotations to works concerning *fiqh* and *uṣūl*, 'Aṣṣār has left behind a small but very significant number of writings devoted to some of the most different questions of *ḥikmat* and *'irfān*. These include the treaties on *waḥdat al-wujūd* and *badā'* (apparent change in the Divine Will) and two works that appear to deal with the religious sciences but that like the *naqlī* works of Mullā Ṣadrā are also treatises of *ḥikmat* and *'irfān*, these being *'Ilm al-ḥadīth* (Science of *Ḥadīth*) and commentary upon the opening chapter of the Quran, *al-Fātiḥah*.[46] The study of these treatises reveals 'Aṣṣār to be a major philosopher casting the light of his own Godgiven intelligence upon the works of the earlier masters and displaying much intellectual creativity. His works are far from being simply an elucidation of what had gone before. Although primarily a Ṣadrean philosopher, 'Aṣṣār was also *ishrāqī* in a sense independent of Mullā Ṣadrā. He was also given the exceptional gift of bringing out both the intellectual and spiritual dimension of terms, ideas, and formulations associated with the religious sciences and in creating a synthesis between the transmitted (*naqlī*) and intellectual (*'aqlī*) sciences crowned and also held together by the purest doctrines of *'irfān*.[47]

The Significance of the School of Tehran

The School of Tehran is important not only in making possible the continuation of the tradition of Islamic philosophy from the end of the Zand period and beginning of the Qajar period to the Pahlavi era. It is also very significant because more than any other philosophical center in Persia, Tehran became the locus where Western ideas began to penetrate into Persia and the main battleground for the struggle between tradition and modernism in later years. It was in Tehran that the *Discourse on Method* of Descartes was first translated into Persian and where Western philosophical ideas began to hold sway over the modernized classes. Because of the political weakness of Qajar Persia and dominance of colonial powers, many Persians, like other Asian and Africans of that time, Muslims and non-Muslims alike, developed a cultural inferiority complex vis-à-vis the West that still continues in many non-Western circles. This attitude caused most of the modern educated classes to turn away from traditional philosophy and to become infatuated with modern Western philosophers, especially French ones. So, while the School of Tehran continued during the Qajar period, modern Western philosophy came to be also studied, often totally separate from the existing philosophical tradition that still breathed in the land of prophecy. Consequently, this tradition came to be belittled and more or less ignored among the modern educated classes of society.[48]

The current of Western philosophy cultivated in Tehran is not of course a part of the School of Tehran as we define it. Often the two existed in parallel fashion to each other, but sooner or later there was bound to be interaction. This interaction occurred in a wider context than before in the second half of the fourteenth/twentieth century.[49] The two most important figures of this later encounter were not trained in the School of Tehran but became nevertheless associated with it. The first was the remarkable master of Islamic thought, 'Allāmah Sayyid Muḥammad Ḥusayn Ṭabāṭabāʾī, who hailed from Tabriz, studied in Najaf, and revived Islamic philosophy in Qom, where he resided. He also taught in Tehran until his death in1404/1983.[50] This monumental figure of Islamic thought during the past century belonged to and in fact founded the new School of Qom in Islamic philosophy, but his meetings with Marxist thinkers, which led to his ground-breaking work *Uṣūl-i falsafa-yi riʾālism* (Principles of the Philosophy of Realism) took place in Tehran. This work, which marks the first extensive encounter between traditional Islamic philosophy and a Western philosophical school, in this case Marxism, is therefore related to the School of Tehran, although 'Allāmah Ṭabāṭabāʾī did not belong to that school, strictly speaking. It must also be mentioned that the discourses and debates between him and Corbin were carried out almost completely in Tehran and not in Qom.

The second major figure who encountered Western thought from the background of Islamic philosophy was Mīrzā Mahdī Ḥāʾirī Yazdī, who was trained in Qom but spent much of his life in Tehran, where he died in 1419/1999. Ḥāʾirī was the first *'ālim* in Persia who went to Europe and America and spent years studying Western philosophy, primarily the analytical school, until he attained his doctorate in Western philosophy and even taught for some time in Britain, Canada, and the United States. He authored a number of important works, such as *Hiram-i hastī* (The Pyramid of Being) and *'Ilm-i ḥuḍūrī* (Knowledge by Presence), in which philosophizing is carried out in dialogue between Islamic and Western philosophy and more specifically Anglo-

Saxon analytical philosophy. His *Knowledge by Presence,* which is now available in English,[51] reveals his philosophical acumen and is the first work of its kind in English by a traditional Islamic philosopher. Technically speaking Ḥāʾirī belonged to the School of Qom rather than Tehran but like Ṭabāṭabāʾī was related to the School of Tehran, where he also taught for many years.[52]

When one meditates upon the works of Ṭabāṭabāʾī and Ḥāʾirī, one wonders why a member of the School of Tehran did not write a response based on the principles of Islamic philosophy to Descartes' *Discourse on Method* when this work first appeared in Tehran in the Qajar period. Had such a criticism come forth, it would have been more like the response of a Hamann or a von Baader to Descartes rather than the simple emulation of Cartesianism that we see among the modernized students of philosophy in Tehran. In any case the response did not come, and one had to wait a century before serious Islamic philosophical responses began to appear to various currents of Western thought. As a result, the School of Tehran became ever more separated from the concern of modernized circles who turned to Western thought wholeheartedly becoming Cartesian, as well as Kantian, Hegelian, Comptian, Marxist, and in more recent decades, Heideggerian, Popperian, and the like. Even after the Revolution of 1979 intense interest in the Islamic response to Western thought has not succeeded in weaning all the Persians given to philosophical discourse away from blind emulation of various currents of Western philosophy, although interest in Islamic philosophy has certainly grown even among many followers of Western thought.

Despite this parting of ways in Tehran between traditional and modern philosophy, the School of Tehran exercised a definite influence upon Persian philosophical prose in general. Muḥammad ʿAlī Furūghī, who translated works of European philosophy including Descartes into Persian and whose *Sayr-i ḥikmat dar Urūpā* (The Development of Philosophy in Europe) was the single most influential text in introducing European philosophy to Persians, was in touch with a number of living members of the School of Tehran, such as Faḍīl-i Tūnī, Mīrzā Ṭāhir Tunikābunī, Mīrzā Mahdī Āshtiyānī, and Sayyid Muḥammad Kāẓim ʿAṣṣār; and he developed his philosophical style and vocabulary with their help. Others, who wrote Persian philosophical prose well, such as Yaḥyā Mahdawī, were also very well acquainted with the Persian philosophical texts of the Qajar period, as well as those of earlier ages. Although of course there was much development of new vocabulary for the expression of new Western ideas during the Pahlavi period, there is no doubt that there is a great deal of continuity in the style and vocabulary of Persian philosophical prose between the School of Tehran, and through it with earlier schools of Islamic philosophy, and the modern currents of philosophy in the Pahlavi and also post-Pahlavi period. The revival of Persian prose, philosophical prose included, during the Pahlavi period is in many ways the continuation of what began in the Qajar period, even if, as far as philosophy is concerned, the content of many philosophical works changed drastically from the Islamic to the Western.

Another feature of the School of Tehran, resulting from the centrality of the capital and modern means of transportation and communication, is that it was more in contact with other centers of learning than were the Schools of Isfahan and Shiraz. Many of the philosophers of the School of Tehran journeyed to other Persian and Iraqi cities to become well-known scholars. Conversely many figures from other centers would travel to Tehran and spend some time there. During the last few decades some of the most famous Persian philosophers can be said to belong to this category. As examples one can cite 'Allāmah Ṭabāṭabāʾī, trained in Tabriz and resident in Qom, who journeyed to Tehran every other week for some thirty years; Murtaḍā Muṭahharī, trained in Qom but who resided in Tehran; Ḥāʾirī Yazdī, likewise trained in Qom but like Muṭahharī a resident of Tehran and professor of Tehran University; Sayyid Jalāl al-Dīn Āshtiyānī, trained in Qom and professor of Mashhad University, who traveled and stayed in Tehran often and even studied there for a while; and Jawād Muṣliḥ, trained in Shiraz, but a resident of Tehran for the second part of his life, where he taught at Tehran University. From the later Qajar period until the weakening of the School of Tehran, members of this school were therefore in constant contact with other centers in Persia where Islamic philosophy was taught, such as Shiraz, Isfahan, Qom, and Mashhad, and the reverse was also true.

After the Iranian Revolution, Qom soon became the most important center for the teaching of Islamic philosophy thanks to the foundation laid by 'Allāmah Ṭabāṭabāʾī and his training of such illustrious students as Ḥasan Ḥasanzādah Āmulī, 'Abd Allāh Jawādī Āmulī, and Miṣbāḥ Yazdī, all of whom teach *ḥikmat* to a large number of students in Qom today. Perhaps at no time in Islamic history has as large a percentage of religious students turned to *al-'ulūm al-'aqliyyah* and particularly philosophy as today in Qom. But this remarkable growth did not rise from a vacuum. Rather, it is based on the revival of interest in Islamic philosophy in the 1950s, 60s, and 70s resulting from the activities of 'Allāmah Ṭabāṭabāʾī and his students in Qom and Corbin and myself in university circles in Tehran, along with the important activity of a number of prominent figures among the *'ulamā'*, such as Muṭahharī, Maḥmūd Shihābī, Ḥā'irī, and Āshtiyānī in Tehran and Mashhad.

One of the living symbols and results of this growth of interest was the establishment of the Iranian Academy of Philosophy, which we founded by me in 1973 and in which Ḥā'irī, Muṭahharī, and Āshtiyānī, not to speak of Corbin and Izutsu, were active. All of those activities may be said to have been based on the heritage of the School of Tehran, while in the field of traditional Islamic philosophy in the *madrasah* style, the center of activity was shifting to Qom. Even after this shift, however, Tehran remained important, and although there is no longer a figure of the stature of Sayyid Muḥammad Kāẓim 'Aṣṣār to represent the School of Tehran, something of the School of Tehran survives even now. In any case Tehran remains still the most important locus for the encounter between Islamic and Western philosophy and along with Qom the main arena for an intense philosophical activity in Persia not to be found to the same extent in other Islamic countries.

While the School of Tehran was flourishing in the thirteenth/nineteenth century, other Islamic countries were also facing the onslaught of Western thought. In Egypt and North Africa the Islamic response came primarily from the *fuqahā'* and Sufis as it did in the Ottoman Empire. In India however, from Shāh Walī Allāh of Dehli to Mawlānā 'Alī Ashraf Thanwī, there was also a strong response that contained philosophical as well as *fiqhī* and *'irfānī* elements. In fact, in comparison with other Islamic lands, the situation in India most resembles that of Persia. Nevertheless, it was primarily in the School of Tehran, and to some extent its extension in Iraq in Najaf,[53] that the integral Islamic intellectual tradition has been preserved and that the first philosophical contact was made with Western philosophy. The historical significance of the School of Tehran lies in that it both preserved the Islamic philosophical tradition into modern times and produced the first Islamic philosophical responses to the challenges of Western philosophical thought. The process of providing Islamic answers to questions and to problems posed by Western thought and in opening a new chapter in the history of Islamic philosophy that is both authentically Islamic and therefore still "prophetic philosophy" and responsive to problems presented by various currents of modern thought is still going on. This chapter in the history of Islamic thought has not as yet been fully written. But there is no doubt that the School of Tehran is of great importance in this process and knowledge of it necessary not only for a better understanding of the later history of Islamic philosophy or the intellectual history of Persia during the past two centuries but also in order to be able to continue the process of writing this latest chapter of Islamic philosophy with greater firmness and surer footing. The heritage of the School of Tehran is of much importance not only for Persians but also for all Islamic thinkers and philosophers concerned with the task of preserving authentic and traditional Islamic thought. It is, furthermore, important in providing responses based on Islamic philosophy to the many challenges of the modern world that are primarily intellectual and philosophical and that even on the level of popular culture, so appealing to the young, present a particular philosophy of life and of existence that poses the greatest challenge to the Islamic understanding of the nature of God, of man, and of the rest of His creation.

PART 4

The Current Situation

CHAPTER 14

Reflections on Islam and Modern Thought

Despite the survival of the School of Tehran and other centers of traditional Islamic philosophy, without doubt a good deal of Islamic thought has been concerned with modernism since the late nineteenth century, and this concern continues in new forms to this day. Let us now consider this challenge from the point of view of traditional Islamic philosophy not only rooted in the Intellect but also living and functioning in the land of prophecy. The discussion of this chapter is therefore a response to modern thought from the perspective of the philosophical and metaphysical tradition discussed so far in this book. Needless to say, few issues arouse more passion and debate among Muslims today than the encounter between Islam and modern thought, which is divorced from both the light of the Intellect and the verities of revelation. The subject is of course vast and embraces fields ranging from politics to sacred art, subjects whose debate often causes volcanic eruptions of emotions and passions and vituperations that hardly lead to an intellectual and objective analysis of causes and a clear vision of the problems involved. Nor is this debate, which consumes so much of the energies of Islamic thinkers, helped by the lack of clear definition of the terms of the debate and an insight into the actual nature of forces and ideas involved and by separation from over a millennium of Islamic philosophy nurtured in the land of prophecy. The whole discussion is also paralyzed by a psychological sense of inferiority by many Muslims no longer rooted in their own tradition, Muslims who have a sense of enfeeblement before the challenges of various modern philosophies. This state of affairs in turn prevents most modernized Muslims from making a critical appraisal of the situation from the authentic Islamic intellectual point of view and of stating the truth irrespective of whether it is fashionable and acceptable to current opinion or not. Let us then begin by defining what we mean by modern thought, which for us includes also postmodernism to which older forms of modernism have given rise.

It is amazing how many hues and shades of meaning have been given to the term *modern*, ranging from contemporary to simply "innovative," "creative," or in tune with the march of time. The question of principles and in fact the truth itself is hardly ever taken into consideration when modernism is discussed. One hardly ever asks whether this or that idea or form or institution conforms to some aspect of the truth. The only question is whether it is modern (and now for some, postmodern) or not. The lack of clarity, precision, and sharpness of both mental and artistic contours, which characterizes the modern world itself, seems to plague the contemporary Muslim's understanding of modernism whether he or she wishes to adopt its tenets or even to react against it. The influence of modernism seems to have dimmed that lucidity and blurred that crystalline transparency that distinguish traditional Islam in both its intellectual and artistic manifestations.[1]

When we use 'modern' we mean neither contemporary nor up-to-date nor successful in the conquest and domination of the natural world nor given to a way particularly favored in the West for fashioning society. Rather, for us "modern" means that which is cut off from the transcendent, from the immutable principles that in reality govern all things and that are made known to man through revelation in its most universal sense and also through the Intellect as already defined in earlier chapters. Modernism is thus contrasted with tradition (*al-dīn*): the latter implies all that is of Divine Origin along with its manifestations and deployments on the human plane, and the former by contrast implies all that is merely human and now ever more increasingly subhuman, and all that is divorced and cut off from the Divine Source.[2] Obviously, tradition has accompanied and in fact characterized human existence over the ages, whereas modernism is a very recent phenomenon. As long as human beings have lived on earth they have buried their dead and believed in the afterlife and the world of the Spirit. During the "hundreds of thousands" of years of human life on earth, people have been traditional in outlook and have not "evolved" as far as their belief in Divine Reality and relation with nature seen as the creation and theophany of that Divine Reality are concerned.[3] Compared to this long history during which man has continuously celebrated the Divine and performed his function as God's viceregent (*khalīfah*) on earth, the period of the domination of modernism stretching from the Renaissance in Western Europe in the fifteenth century to the present day appears as no more than the blinking of an eye.[4] Yet, it is during this fleeting moment that we live: hence the apparent dominance of the power of modernism before which so many

Muslims retreat in helplessness or that they join with a superficial sense of happiness that accompanies the seduction of the world.

A word must also be said about the term *thought* as it appears in the expression *modern thought* since this term has been used to an even greater extent by Muslim thinkers during the last century. 'Thought' as used in this context is itself modern rather than traditional. The Arabic term *fikr* and the Persian *andīshah,* which are used as its equivalents, hardly appear with the same meaning in traditional texts. In fact what would correspond to the traditional understanding of the term would be more the French word *pensée* as used by Pascal, a term that can be better rendered as "meditation" in addition to "thought." Both *fikr* and *andīshah* are in fact related to meditation and contemplation rather than only to a purely human and therefore nondivine mental activity that the modern term "thought" usually evokes.[5] If then we nevertheless use 'thought' it is because we are addressing an audience nurtured on all that this term implies and are using a medium and language in which it is not possible without being somewhat contrite to employ another term with the same range of meaning embracing many forms of mental activity but devoid of the limitation in the vertical sense that 'thought' possesses in contemporary parlance. Also it is because the classical term '*fikr*' itself has undergone a transformation in the writings of modern Muslim authors to reflect more the current meaning of thought in English.

All forms of mental activity that together comprise modern thought and that range from science to philosophy, psychology, and even certain aspects of religion itself, possess certain common characteristics and traits that must be recognized and studied before the answer of traditional Islamic philosophy to modern thought can be provided on a serious intellectual plane. Perhaps the first basic trait of modern thought to be noted is its anthropomorphic nature. How can a form of thought that negates any principle higher than man be anything but anthropomorphic? It might of course be objected that modern science is certainly not anthropomorphic, but that rather it is the premodern sciences that must be considered man-centered. Despite appearances, however, this assertion is mere illusion if one examines closely the epistemological factor involved. It is true that modern science (excluding the recent theory of the anthropic principle) depicts a universe in which man as spirit, mind, and even psyche is but an accident and an irrelevant minor phenomenon, and the universe thus appears as "inhuman" and not related in a meaningful manner to the human state. But it must not be forgotten that although modern man has created a science that excludes the reality of man and consciousness from the general picture of the universe,[6] the criteria and instruments of knowledge that determine this science are merely and purely human. It is the human reason and the human senses that determine modern science. The knowledge of even the farthest galaxies is held in the human mind.[7] This scientific world from which man has been abstracted is, therefore, nevertheless based on an anthropomorphic foundation as far as the subjective pole of knowledge, the subject who knows and determines what science is, is concerned.

In contrast, the traditional sciences were profoundly nonanthropomorphic in the sense that for them the locus and container of knowledge was not the human mind but ultimately the Divine Intellect made accessible to human beings through objective revelation and inner intellection. True science was not based on purely human reason but on the Intellect, which belongs to the supra-human level of reality yet illuminates the human mind. If medieval cosmologies placed man in the center of things, it is not because they were humanistic in the Renaissance sense of the term, according to which terrestrial and fallen humanity was the measure of all things, but it was to demonstrate that human beings stood on the lowest level of reality with a vast hierarchy of levels of existence before and above them and to enable them to gain a vision of the cosmos as a crypt through which they must travel and that they must transcend. And certainly one cannot begin a journey from anywhere except where one is.[8]

If the characteristic of anthropomorphism is thus to be found even in modern science, it is to be seen in an even more obvious fashion in other forms and aspects of modern thought whether it be psychology, anthropology, or philosophy. Modern thought of which philosophy is in a sense the father and progenitor became profoundly anthropomorphic the moment man was made the criterion of the knowledge of reality. When Descartes uttered, "I think, therefore I am" (*cogito ergo sum*), he placed his individual awareness of his own limited self as the criterion of existence for certainly the "I" in Descartes' assertion was not meant to be the Divine "I" who through Ḥallāj exclaimed, "I am the Truth" (*anaʾl-Ḥaqq*), the Divine "I" that, according to traditional doctrines, alone has the ultimate right to say "I."[9] Until Descartes, it was Pure Being, the Being of God that determined human existence and the various levels of reality. But with Cartesian rationalism individual human existence, consciousness, and reason became the criterion of reality and also the truth. In the mainstream of Western thought, and excluding certain peripheral developments, ontology gave way to epistemology, epistemology to logic, and finally by way of reaction logic became confronted with those antirational "philosophies" so prevalent today.[10]

What happened in the postmedieval period in the West was that higher levels of reality became eliminated on both the subjective and the objective domains. There was subjectively nothing higher accessible to man than his reason and nothing higher in the objective world than what that reason could comprehend with the help of ordinary human senses. The reality of prophecy therefore became illusory or irrelevant, as far as knowledge was concerned, and intellect was reduced to reason. This was of course bound to happen if one remembers the well-known principle of adequation (the *adaequatio* of St. Thomas Aquinas), according to which to know anything there must be an instrument of knowledge adequate and conforming to the nature of that which is to be known. And since modern man refused to accept a principle higher than himself, obviously all that issued from his mind and thought could not but be anthropomorphic, and the reality known had to be reduced to what human reason and human senses could comprehend and detect.

A second trait of modernism closely related to anthropomorphism is the lack of principles in the metaphysical sense. Human nature is too unstable and turbulent to be able to serve as metaphysical principle for anything. That is why a mode of thinking that is not able to transcend the human level and that remains anthropomorphic cannot but be devoid of principles understood metaphysically. In the realm of the life of action—namely, the domain of morality (although morality cannot be reduced simply to external action) and, from another point of view, politics and economics—everyone senses this lack of principles. But one might object as far as the sciences are concerned. But here again it must be asserted that neither empiricism nor the validation through induction nor reliance upon the data of the senses as confirmed by reason can serve as a principle in the metaphysical sense. They are all valid in their own level as is the science created by them. But they are divorced from immutable principles as is modern science, which has discovered many things on a certain level of reality but because of its divorce from higher principles has brought about disequilibrium through its very discoveries and inventions. Only mathematics among the modern sciences may be said to possess certain principles in the metaphysical sense: the reason is that mathematics remains, despite everything, a Platonic science, and its laws discovered by the human mind continue to reflect metaphysical principles, as reason itself cannot but display the fact that it is a reflection, even if a dim one, when it seeks to turn upon itself, of the Intellect. The discoveries of the other sciences to the extent that they conform to some aspect of the nature of reality of course possess a symbolic and metaphysical significance, but that does not mean that these sciences are attached to metaphysical principles and are integrated into a higher form of knowledge. Such an integration could take place, but as a matter of fact it has not. Modern science, therefore, and its generalizations, like other fruits of that way of thinking and acting that we have associated with modernism, suffer from the lack of principles, a trait that characterizes the modern world. This lack is in fact felt to an even greater degree as the history of the modern world unfolds.

It might be asked what other means of knowledge were available to other civilizations before the modern period. The preceding chapters should have already provided a response to this question as far as the Islamic tradition is concerned. The answer should in fact be quite clear at least for those Muslims who know the intellectual life of Islam: prophecy and revelation, on the one hand, and intellectual intuition or vision (*dhawq*, *kashf* or *shuhūd*), on the other.[11] The traditional Muslim intellectual saw prophecy and revelation as the primary source of knowledge not only as the means to learn the laws of morality concerned with the active life as we have already discussed in this book. He was also aware of the possibility for human beings to purify themselves until the "eye of the heart" (*'ayn al-qalb*) residing at the center of their being would open and enable them to gain the direct vision of the supernal realities through the functioning of the heart/intellect. Finally, he accepted the power of reason to know, but this reason was always attached to and derived sustenance from revelation, on the one hand, and intellectual intuition, on the other. The few in the Islamic world who would cut this cord of reliance and declare the independence of reason from both revelation and intuition were never accepted into the mainstream of Islamic thought. They remained marginal figures, while in a reverse fashion in the postmedieval West those who sought to sustain and uphold the reliance of reason upon revelation and the Intellect and who still wanted to philosophize in the land of prophecy became marginalized, since the mainstream of modern Western thought rejected both revelation and intellectual intuition as means of knowledge. In modern times in the West even philosophers of religion and theologians rarely defend the Bible as a source of a sapiental knowledge that could determine and integrate *scientia* into *sapientia* in the manner of a St. Bonaventure. The few who look upon the Bible for intellectual guidance are for the most part limited by such shallow literal interpretations of the Holy Book (usually identified with fundamentalism) that in their feuds with modern sciences the rationalistic camp comes out almost inevitably as the victor.

When one ponders over these and other salient features of modernism, one comes to the conclusion that in order to understand modernism and its manifestations, it is essential to comprehend the conception of man that underlies it. One must seek to discover how modern man conceives of himself and his destiny, how he view the *anthropos* vis-à-vis God and the world. Moreover, it is essential to understand what constitutes the soul and mind of men and women whose thoughts and ideas have molded and continue to mold the modern world. For surely if such men as Ghazzālī and Rūmī, or for that matter Erigena or Eckhart, were the occupants of the chairs of philosophy in leading universities in the West today, another kind of philosophy would issue forth from such universities. A person thinks according to what he or she is, or as Aristotle said, knowledge depends upon the mode of the knower. A study of the modern concept of man as being "free" of Heaven, complete master of his own destiny, earth-bound but also master of the earth, oblivious to all eschatological realities which he has replaced with some future state of perfection in profane historical time, indifferent if not totally opposed to the world of the Spirit and its demands and lacking a sense of the sacred will reveal how futile have been and are the efforts of those modernistic Muslim "reformers" who have sought to harmonize Islam and modernism in the sense that we have defined it. If we turn even a cursory glance at the Islamic conception of man, as the *homo islamicus*, we shall discover the impossibility of harmonizing this conception with that of modern or postmodern man.[12]

The *homo islamicus* is at once the servant of God (*al-'abd*) and His vicegerent on earth (*khalīfat Allāh fiʾl-arḍ*),[13] not an animal that happens to speak and think but a being who possesses a soul and spirit/intellect created by God. The *homo islamicus* contains within himself or herself the plant and animal natures as he or she is the crown of creation (*ashraf al-makhlūqāt*) but has not evolved from the lower forms of life. Man has always been man. The Islamic conception of human beings envisages that they are beings who live on earth and have earthly needs but are not only earthly, and their needs are not limited to the terrestrial. They rule over the earth, not in their own right, but rather as God's vicegerents before all creatures. They therefore also bear responsibility for the created order before God and are the channels of grace for God's creatures. *Homo islamicus* possesses the power of reason, of *ratio* that divides and analyzes, but his or her mental faculties are not limited to reason. He or she possesses the possibility of knowing intuitively through the use of the intellect as well as analytically through the employment of reason and also has the capability to gain inward knowledge, the knowledge of his or her own inner being, which is in fact the key to the knowledge of God according to the famous prophetic *ḥadīth* "He who knoweth himself knoweth His Lord" (*man 'arafa nafsahu faqad 'arafa rabbahu*). The *homo islamicus* is innately aware of the fact that his or her consciousness does not have an external, material cause but that it comes from God and is too profound to be affected by the accident of death.[14]

The *homo islamicus* thus remains aware of the eschatological realities, of the fact that although he or she lives on this earth, he or she is here as a traveler far away from his or her original abode. He or she is aware that his or her guide for this journey is the message that issues from his or her home of origin, from *the* Origin, and this message is none other than revelation to which such as person remains bound not only in its aspect of law as embodied in the *Sharī'ah* but also in its inner aspect as truth and knowledge (*Ḥaqīqah*). Such a being is also aware that human faculties are not bound and limited to the senses and reason but that to the extent that human beings are able to regain the fullness of their being and bring to actualize all the possibilities that God has placed within them, through faith and spiritual practice, their minds and reason can become illuminated by the light of the spiritual world, and they are able to gain direct knowledge of the spiritual and intelligible world to which the Noble Quran refers as the invisible or absent world (*'ālam al-ghayb*).[15]

Obviously such a conception of humanity differs profoundly from that envisaged in most schools of contemporary philosophy and in modern thought, which sees human beings as beings who are purely earthly creatures, masters of nature, but responsible to no one but themselves. No amount of wishy-washy apologetics can harmonize the two different conceptions of the meaning of being human. The Islamic conception of man removes the possibility of a Promethean revolt against Heaven and brings God into the minutest aspect of human life.[16] Its effect is therefore the creation of a civilization, an art, a philosophy, and a whole manner of thinking and seeing things that is completely nonanthropocentric but theocentric and that stands opposed to anthropomorphism, which is such a salient feature of modernism as well as postmodernism. That is why nothing can be more shocking to authentic Muslim sensibilities than the Titanic and Promethean "religious" art of the late Renaissance and the Baroque, which stand directly opposed to the completely nonanthropomorphic art of Islam. Man in Islam thinks and makes in his function of *homo sapien* and *homo faber* as the *'abd* of God and not as a creature who has rebelled against Heaven. His function remains not the glorification of himself but of his Lord, and his greatest aim is to become "nothing" before God, to undergo the experience of *fanā'* that would enable him to become as the perfect *'abd* the mirror in which God contemplates the reflections of His own Names and Qualities and the channel through which His grace and the theophanies of His Names and Qualities are reflected in the world in a central manner.

Of course what characterizes the Islamic conception of human beings has profound similarities with the conception of human beings in other traditions, including Christianity, and we would be the last to deny this point. But modernism is not Christianity or any other tradition and it is the confrontation of Islam with modern thought that we have in mind here and not Islam's encounter with Christianity. Otherwise what could be closer to the Islamic teaching that man is created to seek perfection and final spiritual beatitude through intellectual and spiritual growth, that man is man only when he seeks perfection (*ṭālib al-kamāl*) and attempts to go beyond himself than the scholastic saying *Homo non proprie humanus sed superhumanus est* (to be properly human one must be more than human).

The characteristics of modern thought discussed earlier, namely, its anthropomorphic and by extension secular nature, the lack of metaphysical principles in various branches of modern thought, and the reductionism that is related to it and that is most evident in the realm of the sciences, are obviously in total opposition to the tenets of Islamic thought, as the modern conception of man from whom issue these thought patterns is opposed to the Islamic conception. This opposition is clear enough not to need further elucidation here.[17] There are a few elements of modern thought, however, that need to be discussed in greater detail as a result of their pervasive nature in the modern world and their lethal effect upon the religious thought and life of those Muslims who have been affected by them, chief among them, the theory of evolution.[18]

In the West no modern theory or idea has been as detrimental to religion as the theory of evolution, which instead of being taken as a hypothesis in biology, zoology, or paleontology, parades around as if it were a proven scientific fact and functions as an unquestionable ideological basis for a whole worldview. It has become a fashion of thinking embracing fields as far apart as astrophysics and the history of art. The effect of this manner of thinking has had negative effects on Muslims affected by it, but this effect has not as yet been as extensive as what we observe among Christians in the West. In any case, usually modernized Muslims have tried to come to terms with evolution through all kinds of unbelievable interpretations of the Quran, forgetting that there is no way possible to harmonize the conception of man (Adam) to whom God taught all the "names" and whom He placed on earth as His *khalīfah* and the evolutionist conception that sees mankind as "ascended" from the ape. It is strange that except for a few fundamentalist Muslim thinkers who reject the theory of evolution on purely religious grounds, as have their Christian counterparts, few modern educated Muslims have bothered to study Western works written on its logical absurdity and all the scientific evidence brought against it by such men as Louis Bounoure, Douglas Dewar, Michael Behe, and others,[19] despite the ecstatic claims of its general acceptance by most standard works in the West such as dictionaries and encyclopaedias. In fact as it has been stated so justly by E. F. Schumacher, "evolutionism is not science; it is science fiction, even a kind of hoax."[20] Some Western critics of evolution have gone so far as to claim that its proponents suffer from psychological disequilibrium,[21] and recently a whole array of arguments drawn from information theory and design have been brought against it.[22]

It is not my aim here to analyze and refute in detail the theory of evolution, although such a refutation by Muslim thinkers is essential from a scientific as well as metaphysical, philosophical, logical, and religious points of view, as it has been already carried out in the Occident.[23] What is important to note here is that the evolutionary point of view, which refuses to see permanence anywhere, for which the greater somehow "evolves" from the "lesser," and which is totally blind to the higher states of being and the archetypal realities that determine the forms of this world, is but a result of that loss of principles alluded to above. Evolutionism is but a desperate attempt to fill the vacuum created by man's attempt to cut the Hands of God from His creation and to negate any principle above the merely material and in a sense the human, who then falls of necessity to the level of the subhuman. Once the Transcendent Principle is forgotten, the world becomes a circle without a center, and this experience of the loss of the center remains an existential reality for anyone who accepts the theses of modernism, whether he or she is a Jew, a Christian, or a Muslim.

Closely allied to the idea of evolution is that of progress and utopianism, which both philosophically and politically have shaken the Western world to its roots during the past two centuries and have also affected the Islamic world profoundly. The idea of unilateral progress has fortunately ceased to be taken seriously by many noted thinkers in the West today and is gradually being rejected by many in the Islamic world as an "idol of the mind" before which the earlier generation of modernized Muslims prostrated without any hesitation.[24] But the utopianism that is closely related to the idea of progress bears further scrutiny and study as a result of the devastating effect it has had and continues to have on a large segment of the modernized Muslim "intelligentsia."

Utopianism is defined by the *Oxford English Dictionary* as follows: "impossible ideal schemes for the amelioration or perfection of social conditions." Although the origin of this term goes back to the well-known treatise of Sir Thomas More entitled *Utopia* and written in 1516 in Latin, the term *utopianism* as employed today has certain implications antedating the sixteenth century, although the term itself derives from More's famous work. The Christian doctrine of the incarnation and a sense of idealism that characterizes Christianity were of course present before modern times. Utopianism grafted itself upon the caricature of these characteristics and whether in the form of the humanitarian socialism of such figures as St. Simon, Charles Fourier, or Robert Owen or the political socialism of Marx and Engels, led to a conception of history that is a real parody of the Augustinian *City of God*. The utopianism of the last centuries, which is one of the important features of modernism, combined with various forms of Messianism led and still lead to deep social and political upheavals whose goals and methods cannot but remain completely alien to the ethos and aims of Islam.[25] Utopianism seeks to establish a perfect social order through purely human means. It disregards the presence of evil in the world in the theological sense and aims at doing good without God, as if it were possible to create an order based on goodness but removed from the Source of all goodness.

Islam has also had its descriptions of the perfect state or society in works such as those of al-Fārābī describing the "Virtuous City" (*madīnat al-fāḍilah*) or the texts of Shaykh Shihāb al-Dīn Suhrawardī referring to the land of perfection, which is called in Persian *"nā kujā-ābād,"* literally the "land of nowhere *u-topia*." But then it was always remembered that this land of perfection is "no where," that is, beyond the earthly abode and therefore identified with the eighth clime above the seven geographic ones. The realism present in the Islamic perspective combined with the strong emphasis of the Quran and *Ḥadīth* upon the gradual loss of perfection of the Islamic community as it moves away from the origin of revelation prevented the kind of utopianism present in certain strands of modern European philosophy from growing in the soil of Islamic thought. Moreover, the traditional Muslim remained always aware that if there were to be a perfect state, it could only come into being through Divine help. Hence, although the idea of the cyclic renewal of Islam through a "renewer" (*mujaddid*) has been always alive, as has the wave of Mahdiism that sees in the Mahdī the force sent by God to return Islam to its perfection, Islam has never faced within itself that type of secular utopianism that underlies so much of the poltico-social aspects of modern thought. It is therefore essential to be aware of the profound distinction between modern utopianism and Islamic teachings concerning the *mujaddid* or renewer of Islamic society or the Mahdī himself. It is also basic to distinguish between the traditional figure of the *mujaddid* and the modern reformers, who usually, as a result of their feeble reaction to modern thought, have hardly brought about the renewal of Islam. Nor have the so-called Islamic fundamentalists, who are in general opposed to the Islamic intellectual tradition, succeeded where the modernists have failed. In fact, "Islamic fundamentalism" is itself a form of reform opposed to traditional Islam. Moreover, certain forms of so-called fundamentalism have combined with Mahdiist trends in some parts of the Islamic world to create a dangerous new form of utopianism. It is true that this form of utopianism is different from what one sees in the West, but it is nevertheless something alien to the integral Islamic tradition. Moreover, it is highly anti-intellectual and while claiming to strengthen Islam often leads to the further secularization of Islamic society. It is remarkable how such movements, while opposed to the modernists on a certain level, join the supporters of modernism in opposing the millennial intellectual traditions of Islam and especially that philosophy that flourished in the land of prophecy in its Islamic form.

There is finally one more characteristic of modern thought that is essential to mention and that is related to all that has been stated above. This characteristic is the loss of the sense of the sacred.[26] Modern man can practically be defined as that type of man who has lost the sense of the sacred, and modern thought is conspicuous in its lack of awareness of the sacred. Nor could it be otherwise seeing that modern humanism is inseparable from secularism. But nothing could be further from the Islamic perspective, in which there does not even exist such a concept as the 'profane' or 'secular,'[27] for in Islam, as already mentioned, the One penetrates into the very depths of the world of multiplicity and leaves no domain outside the domain of tradition. This is to be seen not only in the intellectual, philosophical, and scientific aspects of Islam that breathed in the land of prophecy[28] but also in a blinding fashion in Islamic art. The Islamic tradition can never accept a thought pattern that is devoid of the perfume of the sacred and that replaces the Divine Order by one of a purely human origin and inspiration. The fruitful response of Islamic thought to modernism cannot be given on a serious level if the primacy of the sacred in the perspective of Islam and its lack in modern thought is not taken into consideration. Islam cannot even carry out a dialogue with the secular on an equal footing by placing it in a position of legitimacy equal to that of religion, although Muslims have been encouraged by the traditional sources to have a dialogue and carry out discourse even with those who do not accept the reality of God. But Islam must face the secular with full awareness of what it is, namely, the negation and denial of the sacred that ultimately alone *is* while the desacralized, profane, or secular only *appears* to be.

In conclusion, it is necessary to mention that the reductionism that is one of the characteristics of modern thought has itself affected Islam in its confrontation with modernism. One of the effects of modernism upon Islam has been to reduce Islam in the minds of many to only one of its dimensions, namely, the *Sharī'ah*, and to divest it of those intellectual means that alone can withstand the assault of modern thought upon the citadel of Islam. The *Sharī'ah* is of course basic to the Islamic tradition: it is the ground upon which the religion is based. But the intellectual challenges posed by modernism in the form of secularism, evolutionism, rationalism, existentialism, agnosticism, relativism, nihilism, humanism, and the like can only be answered intellectually and on the basis of authentic Islamic philosophical thought and not only juridically or by ignoring or disregarding the tenets of modern thought and expecting some kind of magical wedding between the *Sharī'ah* and modern science and technology. The successful encounter of Islam with modern thought can only come about when modern thought is fully understood in both its roots and ramifications by means of the principles of Islamic thought, and the whole of the Islamic intellectual tradition, much of which has been discussed in this work, brought to bear upon the solution of the enormous problems that modernism and postmodernism pose for Islam. At the center of this undertaking stands the revival of that wisdom, that *ḥikmah* or *ḥaqīqah*, that lies at the heart of the Islamic revelation and that has been elaborated in the Islamic intellectual tradition in general and Islamic gnosis and philosophy in particular, over the ages, a wisdom that will remain valid as long as human beings remain human beings and bear witness to Him according to their theomorphic nature and their state of servitude before the Lord (*'ubūdiyyah*), the state that for Islam is the *raison d'être* of human existence.

CHAPTER 15

Philosophy in the Land of Prophecy Yesterday and Today

There is much that goes on by the name of philosophy today, but the question is whether there are still living schools of philosophy in the world that function in an authentic manner in light of the realities of prophecy and the perennial wisdom that resides at the heart of the messages of Heaven. In the West for several centuries philosophy has become ever more separated from prophecy, and this secularized philosophy in its various modes and currents, which claims that it alone is legitimate philosophy as distinct from theology, not only dominates over the Western world but also holds sway in academic philosophical circles from Tokyo to Rabat. Even in the non-Western world where the intellectual dimension of what has been revealed through prophecy is still alive and more accessible than in the West, it is postmedieval Western philosophy in its mainstream forms that dominates the academic philosophical discourse as one can see, for example, in the 2003 World Congress of Philosophy, which was held for the first time in the Islamic world (in Istanbul), but as far as Islamic philosophy is concerned, it might as well have been held in Boston, as was the 1998 Congress.

The domination of the type of philosophical activity that is divorced from prophecy in most philosophy departments in universities all over the globe does not, however, tell the whole story. In the West, as already mentioned at the beginning of this book, the number of those who call themselves Christian philosophers is on the rise as is interest in Jewish philosophy as philosophy and not only as intellectual history. More specifically, Thomistic philosophy, which witnessed a revival in the twentieth century in the hands of such figures as Maurice De Wulf, Etienne Gilson, and Jacques Maritain continues its life in North America and various Catholic countries of Europe and South and Central America. Even the philosophical schools of Buddhism and Hinduism, both based on the possibility of illumination and intellection that we have identified with the more universal meaning of prophecy and revelation, are gaining some adherents among Western philosophers.

As for the rest of the world, Buddhist philosophies, especially in the schools of Mahāyāna and Vajrāyāna, continue to thrive in Japan, among the Tibetans of the diaspora, especially in India, and elsewhere even if mostly outside academic circles and universities. There are in fact today even some well-known Buddhist philosophers associated with a number of universities. Likewise, in India various schools of what is called "Hindu philosophy" are still alive, although nearly all university departments are dominated by Western philosophy as they are also for the most part in Japan, where again Buddhist philosophies nevertheless survive both outside and inside academic circles. In China, after a long period of subservience to the rationalism of modern philosophy followed by the official Marxist philosophy of the Communist era, there has been of late a notable rise of interest in Neo-Confucian and Taoist philosophies. Likewise, in Russia after the long period of Marxist domination and its extreme reaction against all forms of prophecy and religion, there has been recently a notable rise of attention paid to Russian Orthodox philosophers of the nineteenth and early twentieth centuries. As for the Islamic world, to which we wish to turn in greater detail, a similar situation is to be found, that is, the domination of modernist educational institutions by secularized Western philosophies and at the same time the continuation and in fact revival of Islamic philosophy.

Before turning to the Islamic world, however, it is necessary to mention the central role played by the formulation of traditional metaphysics and the perennial philosophy in the twentieth century by René Guénon, Ananda K. Coomaraswamy, Frithjof Schuon, Titus Burckhardt, and others in the revival of various forms of traditional philosophy in both East and West and in providing the necessary critique of modern philosophy that opens an intellectual space in the contemporary scene for traditional philosophies that always function in a world dominated by prophecy, as we have already defined this term. The perennial philosophy in fact is inseparable from prophecy in its most universal sense, and to speak of philosophy in the land of prophecy is also to speak of various schools of perennial philosophy expressing in different dialects the same universal truths.

Let us then in conclusion turn in greater detail to the Islamic world. In the late nineteenth and early twentieth centuries as modern-style universities began to be established in various Islamic countries, in such places as Istanbul, Cairo, Tehran, and Lahore, Western philosophy began to become disseminated and soon dominated the study of philosophy in such universities and similar institutions that came to be established later. In many places Islamic philosophy was reduced to a shell and taught as the *history* of Islamic philosophy, and even that was seen from the point of view of Western scholarship. Where Islamic philosophy was taught, if it was taught at all, was in faculties of theology (*ilāhiyyāt*) rather than in the faculties of arts and letters where the central role of philosophy was by and large fulfilled by modern Western philosophy.

This situation continues to some extent to this day in universities from Bangladesh and Pakistan to Morocco, but during the past few decades matters *have* begun to change. First, the history of Islamic philosophy has gradually come to be seen from the point of view of the integral Islamic intellectual tradition itself and not in its truncated version. One needs only look at the *History of Philosophy* of De Boer being taught at the beginning of the twentieth century in Muslim India and the *History of Islamic Philosophy* edited by S. H. Nasr and O. Leaman, which is now being taught all over the Islamic world, to see the differences in how Islamic philosophy, in both its depth and breadth, has been taught to Muslim students during most of the last century. Second, the living Islamic philosophical tradition has been revived to a large extent and is now entering academic circles, where Western philosophy divorced from prophecy has held sway for so many decades.

As has become clear from previous chapters, it was most of all in Persia and to some extent in Muslim India that Islamic philosophy as a living tradition survived into the modern period. As mentioned earlier, the School of Tehran was witness to major philosophical activity in the traditional Islamic mode. In India, British rule, the loss of endowment (*waqf*) for religious schools, and many other factors led to an eclipse of the Islamic philosophical traditions of Farangi Mahall and other centers, despite the appearance of such a major figure as Mawlānā ʿAlī Ashraf Thanwī in the late nineteenth and early twentieth centuries. Nor did the partition of India help in the revival of Islamic philosophy in Pakistan or among Indian Muslims. In fact, the figure who is most associated with the idea of Pakistan and whose influence has remained great in that country—namely Muḥammad Iqbāl—although very philosophically minded and interested in Islamic philosophy, did not philosophize for the most part within that tradition. His poetry in fact was associated more with the reality of prophecy than was his philosophy, which was also influenced by nineteenth-century Western philosophy, although he was a Muslim thinker with firm belief in the reality of prophecy. It is interesting to note that one of his best known interpreters in the West, the German scholar Annemarie

Schimmel, wrote a book on him in German with the title *Prophetische Poet und Philosoph* and not *Prophetische Philosoph.*

The situation in Persia was quite different. With the advent of the Pahlavi Dynasty in 1921, modern education became fully implemented, and Tehran University was soon established in its present form to be followed by many others based more or less on its model. And as far as the philosophy department in the Faculty of Arts (Letters) was concerned, it came to be dominated completely by French and to some extent German philosophy, but Islamic philosophy was taught mostly at the Faculty of Theology. This way of teaching philosophy continued in most other universities that came to be established one after another. As already mentioned, it was only in the 1960s that more emphasis began to be placed on Islamic philosophy in the philosophy department of the Faculty of Arts (Letters) at Tehran University itself.

Outside of the university system within the traditional *madrasahs,* however, Islamic philosophy not only survived but was definitely revived in the latter half of the twentieth century. A number of major figures cited already such as Sayyid Abūʾl-Ḥasan Rafīʿī Qazwīnī, Sayyid Muḥammad Kāẓim ʿAṣṣar, Abūʾl-Ḥasan Shaʿrānī, ʿAllāmah Ṭabāṭabāʾī, and several other figures kept the older tradition of Islamic philosophy alive through both teaching and writing. Ṭabāṭabāʾī was in fact responsible for introducing the teaching of philosophy formally within the curriculum of the *madrasahs* in Qom rather than confining it to private and more exclusive circles of students. Before his death in 1983, some four to five hundred students would attend his courses in Qom on Ibn Sīnā and Mullā Ṣadrā. A later generation, some of whom have died and others are still alive, such as Mīrzā Mahdī Ḥāʾirī, Murtaḍā Muṭahharī, Sayyid Jalāl al-Dīn Āshtiyānī, Miṣbāḥ Yazdī, ʿAbd Allāh Jawādī Āmulī, Ḥasan Ḥasanzādah Āmulī, and Muḥaqqiq-i Dāmād have continued the tradition, and in fact there is today an unprecedented interest in Persia among general religious students and the larger public in a philosophy that breathes in a world dominated by prophecy, and also in the interaction of this philosophy with various schools of Western philosophy.

Nor is this revival of Islamic philosophy confined today to clerical circles. There are a number of Iranian philosophers who are not clerics but who are well-known authorities in Islamic philosophy such as Ibrāhīm Dīnānī, Ghulām Riḍā Aʿwānī, and Riḍā Dāwarī. Moreover, university departments of philosophy are becoming ever more interested in Islamic philosophy and are no longer simply second-rate copies of Western philosophy departments, while a strong interest in

Western philosophy continues to be present. In this task of bringing about a more creative interaction between the living Islamic philosophical tradition and Western schools of philosophy, the dialogues between 'Allāmah Ṭabāṭabā'ī and Henry Corbin, in which I acted for the most part as translator and interpreter, the writings of Corbin addressed to modern educated circles, the founding of the Iranian Academy of Philosophy by myself and its later activities to this day, and other factors have played decisive roles. In any case today there is no land in the Islamic world in which Islamic philosophy as well as its interaction with Western philosophy is as avidly pursued as in Persia.

As for other Islamic countries, the second half of the twentieth century was also witness to a rise of interest in the Islamic philosophical tradition. In Iraq this tradition continued to be studied and produced a major figure in Muḥammad Bāqir al-Ṣadr, who was put to death at the prime of his intellectual life. Perhaps when the dust settles in that land, this tradition will continue more openly. In Turkey, whose universities are still heavily dominated by Western philosophy, a number of younger philosophers have turned their gaze upon the Islamic philosophical tradition seen in light of what we have characterized as "prophetic philosophy" in this book. They include Ilhan Kutluer, Mahmut Erol Kiliç, Mustafa Armagan, Beşir Ayvazoglu, Mustafa Tahrali, and Ibrahim Kalin. Nearly all of these scholars and thinkers are interested deeply in the perennial philosophy and traditional metaphysics as well as in the Islamic intellectual tradition.

In Pakistan and Muslim India, the influence of both Western philosophy and Iqbāl still looms large, but Iqbāl himself was interested in Suhrawardī and other Islamic philosophers so that his influence is not an impediment to the serious espousal of the Islamic philosophical tradition. On the contrary, many have used his own references to earlier Islamic thought to seek to revive that tradition as one sees in the activities of the director of the Iqbal Academy in Lahore, Suheyl Umar, who has played a major role in the spread of the perennial philosophy and the revival of the Islamic philosophical tradition in that land following upon the wake of the earlier efforts of Mian Muhammad Sharif, M. M. Ahmad, Saeed Shaikh, and others. As for the Malay world, although Sufism was of course prevalent in that area from the beginning of the spread of Islam there, and was in fact very instrumental in that spread, the integral tradition of Islamic philosophy did not begin to attract any serious attention in Indonesia, Malaysia, and Singapore until a few decades ago. Since then, centers for the study of this tradition from within have been set up in these lands, and a number of well-known scholars from these areas, such as Naquib al-Attas, Osman Bakar, and Muḥammad Bāqir, have made important contributions to the restatement and spread of Islamic philosophy in its authentic sense.

The case of the Arab world outside of Iraq is somewhat different. On the one hand, many works of and about Islamic philosophy continue to appear in Arabic, and there seems to be much interest in Islamic philosophy in such countries as Syria, Jordan, and Egypt and to some extent the Maghrib. On the other hand, the philosophical scene is dominated mostly by one form or another of rationalism, and even the Islamic philosophical tradition is often interpreted rationalistically with open opposition to what some call in a pejorative sense "merely" mystical philosophy. This tendency is to be seen in the case of the Moroccan thinker Muḥammad al-Jābirī, while some forms of philosophical thought that remain popular such as those of 'Abd Allāh Laroui and Ḥasan Ḥanafī have a leftist tinge, and, while often possessing penetrating insights, especially in the case of Ḥanafī, they cannot be said to be an organic continuation of the Islamic philosophical tradition as defined above.

Interestingly enough, this tradition has also found a home for itself outside the Islamic world. The seminal writings of Corbin, Izutsu, and some of my own humble works have introduced this "prophetic philosophy" to the world at large, and there are those in the West, such as Christian Jambet and Gilbert Durand in France, who have been deeply influenced by it as philosophers and not just as scholars. In Germany the Persian philosopher Jawād Falāṭūrī, who was a student of the great master Mīrzā Mahdī Āshtiyānī, taught Islamic philosophy for many years as I have done for over a quarter century in America. Recently, a whole journal entitled *Transcendent Philosophy* has begun to appear in London devoted to the presentation of this philosophical tradition (especially its later currents) in the contemporary world and its interaction with various schools of Western philosophy. Many younger philosophers, Muslim and non-Muslim, who are attracted to this "prophetic philosophy" contribute to this journal and the philosophical activities associated with it.

The vast majority of Muslims still live in a world that can be characterized as the land of prophecy, and they have faith in the reality of revelation. Yet many think and philosophize as if prophecy were a reality associated only with faith and action and unrelated to the activities of the mind. This attitude has given rise to a crisis that has paralyzed to a large extent intellectual creativity among the Muslim intelligentsia and brought about a chasm between faith and reasoning in the souls and minds of many, a chasm that classical Islamic thought was able to bridge in different fashions. Yet because faith in prophecy remains strong, and individuals seriously engaged in philosophical thought do not cease to appear, Islamic philosophy continues as a living intellectual tradition and in fact, after relative eclipse during the colonial period in many lands, is now reasserting itself with ever greater vigor.

As for the world at large, although both secular philosophy and a formalistic interpretation of religion opposed to in-depth philosophical introspection continue to dominate the public scene, interest in philosophy functioning in the land of prophecy, which means in a world dominated by the sense of the sacred and ultimate meaning, also continues to grow. The ever-greater interest in perennial philosophy is also related to this deep need to discover a mode of knowing related to the inner and sacred dimensions of existence. So, as already mentioned, we can detect in the West itself ever greater interest in different expressions of the perennial philosophy in general and in Christian and Jewish philosophical thought in particular. As for other civilizations, we see the revival of interest in Hindu, Buddhist, Taoist and Neo-Confucian philosophies in various Asian countries even amidst ever greater entanglement with secularist philosophies issuing from the West.

As for the Islamic world, which stands between the West and the Oriental worlds of India and the Far East, it is one in which the reality of prophecy remains as strong as ever, while the long philosophical tradition that was created in light of this reality and in response to it while making use of the intellectual and rational faculties that make philosophizing possible, although partly weakened, has survived and is now being revived and renewed in a contemporary context. This philosophical tradition needs to respond not only to secular philosophies but also to other schools of philosophy outside the abode of Islam that have come into being over the ages in the various lands of prophecy defined in its most universal sense. The Islamic philosophical tradition is in fact itself one of the most powerful and multi-faceted of all traditional philosophies; it is one of the main expressions of what earlier Islamic philosophers Muskūyah (Miskawayh) and Suhrawardī referred to as "*Jāwīdān-khirad/al-ḥikmat al-khālidah*" and that came to be known later in Latin as *philosophia perennis*.

The reality of prophecy is like that of the Sun; it can be eclipsed, but it always returns as an abiding reality. As for philosophy understood in its time-honored sense, it is the quest for the truth, for wisdom, for a vision of the whole, for insight into the nature and causes of things. As long as there are human beings, there will be men and women drawn to this quest, and there will be philosophy in the sense defined here. Therefore, philosophy in the land of prophecy is a reality that is of central concern now as it was yesterday, and it will remain of central concern tomorrow as it is today. The deepest philosophies whose truths are perennial and that speak to us today, as they did to our forefathers before us, are those that, while using the inner intellectual and rational faculties with which human beings are endowed, are fruits of philosophizing in a world whose landscape has been illuminated by the light of prophecy and permeated by the perfume of the Sacred. Such was the situation yesterday, such it is today, and such it will be tomorrow.

Notes

Introduction

1. One should remember that Pythagoras established a religious society in Croton centered around Apollo, and he provided it with a rule of life much like the prophet founders of other religions. See Kenneth S. Guthrie, compiler and trans., *The Pythagorean Sourcebook and Library* (Grand Rapids, MI: Phanes, 1987); see especially "The Life of Pythagoras" by Iamblichus, pp. 57ff. where there is even allusion to Pythagoras being divine and identified with Apollo himself (p. 80). See also the seminal work of Peter Kingsley, *Ancient Philosophy, Mystery and Magic* (Oxford: Clarendon, 1995), which deals with both Pythagoras and Empedocles.

2. See Peter Kingsley, *In the Dark Places of Wisdom* (Inverness, CA: The Golden Sufi Center, 1999); and *Reality* (Inverness, CA: The Golden Sufi Center, 2004).

3. In what follows concerning Parmenides I have relied on the work of Kingsley, *Reality*, pp. 31ff.

4. See my "Spiritual Chivalry," in ed. S. H. Nasr, *Islamic Spirituality*, vol. 2 (New York: Crossroad, 1991), pp. 304–15.

5. See 'Allāmah Sayyid Muḥammad Ḥusayn Ṭabāṭabā'ī, *'Alī wa'l-ḥikmat al-ilāhiyyah*, in his *Majmū'a-yi rasā'il*, Sayyid Hādī Khusrawshāhī (ed.) (Tehran: Daftar-i Nashr-i Farhang-i Islāmī, 1370 A. H. [solar]), pp. 191ff.

6. Kingsley, op. cit., p. 33.

7. Ibid., p. 40.

8. Martin Lings, *The Secret of Shakespeare* (New York: Inner Traditions International, 1984), p. 18.

9. In classical Islamic texts the prophet Idrīs or Ukhnūkh (Enoch), who was identified with Hermes, was given the title Abū'l-Ḥukamā' or Father of Philosophers. See "Hermes and Hermetic Writings in the Islamic World" in Nasr, *Islamic Life and Thought* (Chicago: ABC International Group, 2001), pp. 102–19.

10. Kingsley, op.cit., p. 46.

11. Ibid., p. 87.

12. Ibid., p. 62.

13. Ibid., p. 320. See also Kingsley, *Ancient Philosophy, Mysticism, and Magic,* in passim.

14. Kingsley, *Reality,* p. 323.

15. See S. H. Nasr, *An Introduction to Islamic Cosmological Doctrines* (Albany: State University of New York Press, 1993), chapter 15, "Nature and the Visionary Recitals," pp. 263–74.

16. Throughout this book whenever two dates are given in this manner, the one on the left refers to the Islamic lunar calendar and the one on the right to the Christian calendar or what is now called "Common Era."

17. See Huston Smith, *Forgotten Truth* (San Francisco: Harper, 1992), especially chapter 3, "Levels of Reality," pp. 34–59; and chapter 4, "Levels of Selfhood," pp. 60–95; also René Guénon, *The Multiple States of Being,* trans. Joscelyn Godwin (Burdett, NY: Larson, 1984).

18. One need only read about the teachings of the great Sioux sage Black Elk to realize what a profound philosophy existed albeit orally among a people for whom prophecy was the central reality of their spiritual lives. See Joseph E. Brown, *The Sacred Pipe* (New York: Penguin Metaphysical Library, 1986).

19. Henry Corbin has dealt with this issue in many of his works to which we shall turn later in this volume.

20. See the seminal works of Frithjof Schuon on this subject, especially his *Transcendental Unity of Religions* (Wheaton, IL: Theosophical Publishing House, 1993); and *Form and Substance in the Religions* (Bloomington: World Wisdom Books, 2002).

Chapter 1. The Study of Islamic Philosophy in the West in Recent Times

1. We shall deal more fully with the meaning of *al-falsafah* and *al-ḥikmat al-ilāhiyyah* in the next two chapters.

2. See Harry A. Wolfson, *The Philosophy of Kalam* (Cambridge: Harvard University Press, 1976).

3. For complete bibliographical information about the writings of these and later figures mentioned in this chapter see the magisterial work of Hans Daiber, *Bibliography of Islamic Philosophy,* 2 vols. (Leiden: Brill, 1999); for a guide to references and sources for the study of Islamic philosophy see Oliver Leaman, "A Guide to Bibliographical Sources," in Nasr and Leaman (eds.), *History of Islamic Philosophy* (New York: Routledge, 2001), pp. 1173–76.

4. In order for comparative philosophy to be fruitful and meaningful when it involves a traditional form of philosophy on the one hand and postmedieval Western philosophy on the other, there are important pitfalls that must be avoided and principles that must be kept in mind. See S. H. Nasr, *Islam and the Plight of Modern Man* (Chicago: ABC International Group, 2001), part 2, "The Comparative Method and the Study of the Islamic Intellectual Heritage in the West," pp. 39–68. Concerning the confusion in comparative philosophy as it is often carried out, Harry Oldmeadow writes, "One of the principal sources of this confusion is a failure to understand the crucial distinction between metaphysics as a *scientia sacra* on the one hand, wedded to direct spiritual experience and complementing revealed religious doctrines, and what is usually meant in the modern West by 'philosophy': an autonomous and essentially rational and analytical inquiry into a range of issues and problematics." *Journeys East: Twentieth Century Western Encounters with Eastern Religious Traditions* (Bloomington: World Wisdom Books, 2003), p. 338. Although the "East" with which Oldmeadow is concerned in this book excludes the Islamic world, his comments are very relevant and applicable *mutatis mutandis* to comparative philosophy when it involves the Islamic intellectual tradition.

5. On their works and the philosophical scene in Persia in general in the decades of the 50s and 60s, see S. H. Nasr, *The Islamic Intellectual Tradition in Persia* (London: Curzon, 1996), part 4, "Islamic Thought in Modern Iran," pp. 323ff.

6. In this section of this chapter fewer names are provided, and when they are mentioned they are meant as examples and not to deliberately exclude or slight anyone. This is an especially sensitive issue because most of the scholars active during this period are still alive, and we do not want to commit the sin of omission in not mentioning every significant scholar in each group.

7. The origin of this encounter in a serious manner must be sought most of all in the seminal writings of Mahdī Ḥāʾirī Yazdī, some of which have been rendered into English. See his *Principles of Epistemology in Islamic Philosophy: Knowledge by Presence* (Albany: State University of New York Press, 1992).

8. The *philosophia perennis* refers to a wisdom or *sophia* that its followers believe has existed from time immemorial at the heart of different religions and traditional philosophies, the wisdom being one but expressed in different formal languages. On the usage of the history of this term in Western thought see Charles Schmitt, "Perennial Philosophy: Steuco to Leibnitz," *Journal of the History of Ideas*, vol. 27, 1966, pp. 505–32 (printed also in his *Studies in Renaissance Philosophy and Science* (London: Variorum Reprints, 1981); and his introduction to "*De perenni philosophia*" by Augustinus Steuchus (New York: Johnson Reprint Corp., 1972). Frithjof Schuon writes, "The inward and timeless Revelation is present still, but it is hidden away beneath a sheet of ice which necessitates the intervention of outward Revelations; but these cannot have the perfection of what might be termed 'innate religion' or the immanent

philosophia perennis." Islam and the Perennial Philosophy, trans. J. Peter Hobson (London: World of Islam Festival Publishing Group, 1976), p. 195.

9. Among the writings of these authors on the subject of philosophy see especially René Guénon, "Metaphysical Thought and Philosophical Thought Compared," in his *Introduction to the Study of Hindu Doctrines*, trans. Marco Pallis (Ghent, NY: Sophia Perennis et Universalis, 2001), chapter 8, pp. 92ff. (by "philosophy" here Guénon means modern Western philosophy); Ananda K. Coomaraswamy, "The Pertinence of Philosophy" in his *What is Civilization? and Other Essays* (Ipswich: Golgonooza, 1989), pp. 13–32; and Frithjof Schuon, "Tracing the Notion of Philosophy," in his *Sufism: Veil and Quintessence*, trans. William Stoddart (Bloomington: World Wisdom Books, 1981), pp. 115–28. This last essay is very nuanced in its explanation and critique of the very concept of 'philosophy.'

10. On these figures whose role in the spread of traditional doctrines is central and who have also played an important role sometimes directly and sometimes indirectly in bringing about better understanding of Islamic philosophy and especially metaphysics in the West, see S. H. Nasr, *Knowledge and the Sacred* (Albany: State University of New York Press, 1989), pp. 100ff.

11. The al-Furqan Foundation established by Shaykh Aḥmad Zakī Yamānī in Wimbledon, Great Britain, is the leading institution in the West dedicated to the task of preserving, cataloging, and making available Islamic manuscripts. It has already achieved much since it began its activities in earnest in the late 1980s, and although it is not particularly interested in Islamic philosophy, its support for the cataloging of many different libraries has already helped to make known a number of philosophical manuscripts.

12. This series made available a number of important philosophical texts by Ibn Sīnā, Nāṣir-i Khusraw, Suhrawardī, Mullā Ṣadrā, and others in critical editions that were edited mostly by Corbin himself and often in collaboration with Persian and Arab scholars such as Osman Yahya, Mohammad Mo'in, S. H. Nasr, and Sayyid Jalāl al-Dīn Āshtiyānī.

13. For more thorough information about texts translated into European languages see Daiber, op.cit., in passim.

14. For certain fields of Islamic philosophy French is even richer than English, especially as far as translations are concerned. This includes figures as important as Ibn Sīnā and Suhrawardī.

15. See Daiber, op. cit., under their names for bibliographical information on their translations.

16. There is not in fact even one satisfactory philosophical dictionary of Arabic and Persian terms with English equivalents. The only work of this kind available is that of Suhail Afnan, *A Philosophical Lexicon in Persian and Arabic* (Beirut: Dar el-Mashreq, 1969). This work is, however, far from being ad-

equate, especially as far as technical vocabulary of later schools of Islamic philosophy is concerned.

17. The titles that have appeared so far include among others: al-Ghazzālī, *The Incoherence of the Philosophers,* trans. Michael Marmura (Provo: Brigham Young University Press, 1997); al-Ghazzālī, *The Niche of Light,* trans. David Buckman (1998); and Suhrawardī, *The Philosophy of Illumination,* trans. Hossein Ziai (1999).

18. See, for example, Hossein Ziai's translation of Suhrawardī's *Partaw-nāmah* as *The Book of Radiance* (Costa Mesa, CA: Mazda, 1998). There are also a number of such bilingual texts available in French and German as well as a small number of texts translated into English and published with the Arabic text many years ago. Among these perhaps the most notable is Richard Walzer's translation of al-Fārābī's *al-Madīnat al-fāḍilah* as *Al-Farabi on the Perfect State* (Oxford: Clarendon, 1985). Criticisms have been made by M. Mahdi and others of both the reading of some of the original Arabic text and certain translations of it by Walzer. Nevertheless, it remains an important bilingual edition. The Ismaili Institute in London has also embarked upon a publication series that includes both original texts and translations of texts concerned primarily with Ismā'īlī philosophy.

19. See Shams al-Dīn Muḥammad Shahrazūrī, *Nuzhat al-arwāḥ wa rawḍat al-afrāḥ,* trans. Maqṣūd 'Alī Tabrīzī, ed. Muḥammad Tāqī Dānishpazhūh and Muḥammad Sarwar Mawlā'ī (Tehran: Shirkat-i Intishārāt-i 'Ilmī wa Farjangī, 1365 [A.H. solar]). The lengthy introduction by Dānishpazhūh deals in a masterly way with the long tradition of the writing of the history of Islamic philosophy in classical Islamic civilization.

20. See "Hermes and Hermetic Writings in the Islamic World," in Nasr, *Islamic Life and Thought* (Chicago: ABC International, 2001), chapter 9, pp. 102–19. We shall turn to this subject again later in this book.

21. This usage was later adopted by Arab scholars of the history of philosophy because of nonscholarly reasons associated with the ideology of Arab nationalism. It has taken a great deal of effort during the past few decades by both Muslim and some Western scholars to make the use of *Islamic philosophy* the correct manner of referring to the prevalent subject, while, for the most part because of political reasons, the term *Arabic philosophy* still survives in certain circles.

22. For particulars on these works see Hans Daiber, op. cit.

23. This was translated by Edward R. Jones from German into English as *The History of Philosophy in Islam* with numerous editions (first printed in London in 1903).

24. Originally published by Gallimard in Paris in 1964.

25. Translated by Philip Sherrard (London: Kegan Paul International, 1993).

26. Published originally by the Harvard University Press in Cambridge in 1964 but now available through Caravan Books in Delmar, NY.

27. It was first published in two volumes in Wiesbaden by Otto Harrassowitz, 1963–1966.

28. In 2 vols. (Madrid: Alianza Universidad Textos, 1981).

29. London and New York: Routledge, 1989.

30. New York: Columbia University Press, 1983.

Chapter 2. The Meaning and Role of Philosophy in Islam

1. See S. H. Nasr, *An Introduction to Islamic Cosmological Doctrines*, pp. 18ff.; and Frithjof Schuon, *L'Oeil du Coeur* (Paris: Dervy-Livres, 1974), pp. 91–94.

2. See Frithjof Schuon, *Understanding Islam* (Bloomington: World Wisdom Books, 1994), pp. 127ff. See also Sachiko Murata and William Chittick, *The Vision of Islam* (New York: Paragon House, 1994).

3. On the rapport between *al-Ḥaqīqah* and traditional philosophy, see Henry Corbin (with the collaboration of S. H. Nasr and O. Yahya), *History of Islamic Philosophy*, pp. 1–14.

4. See S. H. Nasr, *Islamic Life and Thought*, chapters 8 and 9; also Nasr, *Three Muslim Sages* (Delmar, NY: Caravan Books, 1986), introduction and chapter 1. We shall turn to this issue in later chapters of this book.

5. "Nous n'avons aucun droit d'en refuser la qualification à ceux qui veulent être des *ḥokamā*, des *falāsifa*, de la leur refuser sous prétexte qu'ils sont en même temps des *'orafā*, des théosophes mystiques, et que leur idée que certains d'entre nous, en Occident, se font de la 'philosophie'. La cassure, hélas! est vieille de plusieurs siècles; elle remonte jusqu'à la scholastique médiévale. Cette cassure ne s'est pas produite en Islam, chez nos penseurs iraniens, parce que l'on peut dire symboliquement que pour eux l'Ange de la revelation divine est le même que l'Ange de la connaissance. Le sommet de l'intellect (*'aql, Nous*) est l'*intellectus sanctus*, l'intellect prophétique; il y a quelque chose de commun entre la vocation du philosophe et la vocation du prophet." Introduction of Henry Corbin to Sayyid Jalāl al-Dīn Āshtiyānī and Corbin, (ed.), *Anthologie des philosophes iraniens*, vol. 1, (Téhéran-Paris: Andrien Maisonneuve and Institut Franco-Iranien, 1972), p. 3.

6. For example, Louis Gardet writes, "La question centrale est celle posée naguère par M. Gilson: peut-on parler d'une 'philosophie musulmane' au—sens analogique—où nous parlons d'une 'philosophie chrétienne'?" He answers this negatively adding, "De ce point de vue historique, on peut donc

appeler Fārābī, Avicenne, Ibn Tufayl et Averroès des 'philosophes musulmans'. Mais si l'on entend parler *mutatis mutandis* d'une 'philosophie musulmane' au sens ou l'on parlera d'une 'philosophie chrétienne' des grands médiévaux, il faut renoncer à leur donner ce titre. On ne peut guère les designer que comme philosophes d'inspiration hellénistique, d'expression arabe ou persane, et d'influences musulmanes." In "Le problème de la philosophie musulmane," *Mélanges offerts à Étienne Gilson* (Paris: Vrin, 1959), p. 282.

It is difficult to sustain the view of Gardet if we take into consideration such figures as Suhrawardī and Mullā Ṣadrā or the Islamic philosophers of Farangi Mahall and Khayrabad in India. Even the earlier Peripatetic (*mashshāʾī*) Islamic philosophy is much more Islamic than an appraisal such as that of Gardet would indicate. Ibrāhīm Madkour answers the claim of Gardet and others holding a similar view in these words: "Nous avons démontré il y a longemps, qu'il existe une philosophie arabe, comme il existe une philosophie grecque et une philosophe latine. Nous pouvons dire aujourd'hui qu'il existe une métaphysique arabe ou musulmane. Elle est musulmane par ses problèmes et par sa façon de les résoudre." "La Métaphysique en terre d'Islam," *Mélanges Inst. Dominicain d'Études Orientales du Caire*, 7, 1962-63, p. 30. See also the introduction to his *Fiʾl-falsafat al-islāmiyyah* (Cairo: Dār al-Maʿārif, 1968).

7. See Fernand van Steenberghen, *La Philosophie au XIIIe siècle* (Louvain: Publications Universitaires, 1966), pp. 533–40.

8. We have dealt with the Islamicity of Islamic philosophy in many of our writings. See for example, "The Qur'ān and *Ḥadīth* as Source and Inspiration of Islamic Philosophy," in Nasr and Leaman (eds.), *History of Islamic Philosophy*, pp. 27ff. Max Horten came close to expressing this close link between Islamic philosophy and religion when he wrote, "Für den Philosophen ist die Philosophie seine Religion; denn sein philosophisches System ist die Forum, in der er sich Gott und des Weltall denkt und zugleich die Grundsätze, nach denen er sein sittliches Leben einrichtet. Die Religion des Islam will aber nichtes anderes sein als seine lehre über Gott und die Welt und eine Direktion des sittlichen Handelns—*Philosophia theoretica et practica*," "Religion und Philosophie in Islam," *Der Islam*, 1913, p. 1.

9. On the significance of Hermes for Islamic philosophy see Nasr, *Islamic Life and Thought*, chapter 6. Mīr Findiriskī, the eleventh/seventeenth century Persian philosopher, calls Aristotle (or in reality Plotinus, for he was thinking of the author of the *Theology of Aristotle*) "a prophet who was not a messenger [of Divine Law] (*ghayr mursal*)." See Āshtiyānī, *Anthologie des philosophes iraniens*, p. 73.

10. Already Ibn Khaldūn in his *Muqaddimah*, trans. Franz Rosenthal, vol. 3 (London: Routledge and Kegan Paul, 1958), pp. 52ff., considered the later school of *kalām* as philosophy, and many recent Muslim authors have emphasized the importance of *kalām* and also Sufism as forms of "Islamic philosophy." See for example Muṣṭafā ʿAbd al-Rāziq, *Tamhīd li-taʾrīkh al-falsafat*

al-islāmiyyah (Cairo: Lajnat al-Ta᾿līf wa᾿l-Tarjumah wa᾿l-Nashr, 1959); and the works of 'Abd al-Ḥalīm Maḥmūd.

11. The works of Corbin, Izutsu, Nasr, and to a certain extent M. Horten before them have dealt with Islamic philosophy in an integral manner and in all its richness and diversity, preparing the ground for greater awareness in the West during the past three decades of the totality of the Islamic philosophical tradition. Before those writings appeared Islamic philosophy had become identified in the West with early Peripatetic philosophy, to which an appendix concerning Ibn Khaldūn and one or two other later Islamic philosophers were added. The writings of Corbin are particularly important in dispelling this illusion. See also S. H. Nasr, *The Islamic Intellectual Tradition in Persia.*

12. On the meaning of *falsafah,* the problems of its study, and its definitions with citations of the views of many scholars, see Georges C. Anawati, "Philosophie médiévale en terre d'Islam," in his *Etudes de philosophie musulmane* (Paris: Vrin, 1974), pp. 1–67; and Christel Hein, *Definition und Einteilung der Philosophie von der spätantiken Einleitungs-Literature zur arabischen Enzyklopädie* (Bern and New York: Lang, 1985).

13. This verse has of course been interpreted in other ways by other schools of thought in Islam.

14. Al-Dārimī, in the *Muqaddimah,* p. 34.

15. Ibid.

16. Muṣṭafā 'Abd al-Rāziq, *Tamhīd li-ta᾿rīkh al-falsafat al-islāmiyyah,* p. 45, where reference is also made to various other Islamic sources using the term *ḥikmah.*

17. See *The Fihrist of al-Nadīm,* trans. B. Dodge (New York: Columbia University Press, 1970), vol. 2, p. 581.

18. From his *On First Philosophy* quoted by Ahmed Fouad El-Ehwany, "Al-Kindi," in *A History of Muslim Philosophy,* M. M. Sharif (ed.), vol. 1, p. 424.

19. The meaning of *demonstration* as used in Islamic thought is not exactly the same as one finds in modern Western logic and has an element of certitude in it that is derived from the illumination of the mind by the light of the Intellect.

20. See al-Fārābī, *Kitāb al-ḥurūf* (Book of Letters), Muhsin Mahdi (ed.) (Beirut: Dār al-Mashriq, 1968), pp. 153–57.

21. See *al-Jam' bayn ra᾿yay al-ḥakīmayn Aflāṭūn al-ilāhī wa Arisṭū* (Hyderabad, Daccan: Dāiratu᾿l-Ma'ārifi᾿l-Osmānia, 1968), pp. 36–37.

22. Ibn Sīnā, *'Uyūn al-ḥikmah* (Cairo: Hindiyyah, 1326), p. 30.

23. *Rasāʾil* (Cairo: al-Maṭbaʿat al-ʿarabiyyah, vol. 1, 1928), p. 23. The Ikhwān have a conception of philosophy very close to that of the *ishrāqīs* and the whole later tradition of Islamic philosophy, in which philosophy is considered as veritable philosophy only if it is able to transform the being of man and enable him to have a new vision of things made possible by this very transformation. As such it is nothing other than a particular expression of the esoteric dimension of (*al-bāṭin*) of religion, accessible only through spiritual exegesis or hermeneutic interpretation (*taʾwīl*) of the revealed truths contained in religious sources. See Nasr, *An Introduction to Islamic Cosmological Doctrines*, pp. 33ff.

24. This aspect of Suhrawardī's teachings has been dealt with amply in our *Three Muslim Sages*, chapter 2, and "Suhrawardī," in our *Islamic Intellectual Tradition in Persia*, pp. 125–53. See also the numerous studies of H. Corbin on this theme including his *En Islam iranien*, vol. 2 (Paris: Gallimard, 1971), and his two prolegomenas to Suhrawardī, *Ouevres philosophiques et mystiques*, vols. 1 and 2 (Tehran: Institut d'Etudes et des Recherches Culturelles, 2001).

25. Suhrawardī, *Ouevres philosophiques et mystiques*, vol. 3, ed. S. H. Nasr, p. 69. See also M. Ziai's translation of the *Partaw-nāmah, The Book of Radiance*, p. 72. In another work he states after quoting Plato that "philosophy (*ḥikmah*) is to leave one's body and to ascend to the world of light. *Talwīḥāt* in *Oeuvres philosophiques et mystiques*, H. Corbin (ed.) (Tehran: Institut d'Etudes et des Recherches Culturelles, 2001), p. 113.

26. This saying, which appears in many Islamic sources of *Ḥadīth* such as Bukhārī, reveals clearly the function of philosophy in the land of prophecy.

27. From *Risāla-yi ṣināʿiyyah* in *Antholgie des philosophes iraniens*, vol. I, p. 73 (of the Arabic and Persian text).

28. *Al-Ḥikmat al-mutaʿāliyah fiʾl-asfār al-arbaʿah*, vol. 1, part 1 (Tehran: Dār al-Maʿārif al-Islāmiyyah, 1387 [A.H. lunar]), p. 20.

29. Introduction of S. J. Āshtīyānī to Ṣadr al-Dīn Shīrāzī, *al-Shawāhid al-rubūbiyyah* (Mashhad: Mashhad University Press, 1967), p. seven.

30. *Al-Ḥikmat al-mutaʿāliyah* . . . known usually simply as the *Asfār*, p. 21.

31. Ibid. The views of Mullā Ṣadrā were to be reflected in many later philosophers, such as the fourteenth/twentieth-century master ʿAllāmah Ṭabāṭabāʾī, who called "philosophy the science which can prove the real existence of things." See his *Uṣūl-i falsafa-yi riʾālism*, vol. 1 (Qom: Dār al-ʿIlm, 1332 [A.H. solar]), pp. 2–4.

32. I have had occasion to refer to this matter in several of my works, including *An Introduction to Islamic Cosmological Doctrines*, introduction, and *Science and Civilization in Islam*, introduction (Chicago: ABC International, 2000).

33. See chapter 3 of this work.

34. For a discussion of this matter from somewhat a different view, see Max Massimo Campanini, "al-Ghazālī," in Nasr and Leaman, *History of Philosophy*, pp. 258–74.

35. See Max Horten, *Die philosophischen Ansichten von Rāzī und Tūsī* (Bonn: P. Hanstein, 1910); S. H. Nasr, "Fakhr al-Dīn Rāzī," in *The Islamic Intellectual Tradition in Persia*, pp. 107–1221; also Louis Gardet and M. M. Anawati, *Introduction à la théologie musulmane*, vol. 1 (Paris: Vrin, 1948). One must mention also the criticism by the Ash'arite theologian al-Shahrastānī of Ibn Sīnā in his *Kitāb al-muṣāra'ah* (The Book of Struggle). His criticism is, however, also on the basis of certain Ismā'īlī doctrines and not Ash'arite *kalām*. See Muhammad 'Abd al-Karīm al- Shahrastānī, *Struggling with the Philosopher: A Refutation of Avicenna's Metaphysics*, ed. and trans. Wilfred Madelung and Toby Mayer (London: I.B. Tauris, 2001).

36. This did not mean that members of this group did not in turn criticize rationalistic philosophy.

37. See my "The Relation between Sufism and Philosophy in Persian Culture," *Hamdard Islamicus*, vol. 6, no. 4 (winter 1983), pp. 33–47.

38. One day a full study must be made of the relation between Sufism and *falsafah* throughout the whole of the Islamic intellectual tradition. For a summary treatment of this subject see S. H. Nasr, "Introduction to the Mystical Tradition," in Nasr and Leaman (eds.), *History of Philosophy*, pp. 367–73.

39. On the positive role accorded by Rūmī to the Intellect and correct thought in contrast to rationalism and thought veiled by the passions and the type of philosophy that he criticizes see Jalāl Humāʾī, *Mawlawī cha mīgūyad*, vol. 2 (Tehran: Shawrā-yi 'Ālī-yi Farhang wa Hunar, 1956), pp. 686ff., 946ff.

40. *The Mathnawi*, trans. R. A. Nicholson (London: Luzac), vol. 2, p. 115 (with some modification).

41. Quoted by Jawād Muṣliḥ in his *Falsafa-yi 'ālī yā Ḥikmat-i Ṣadr al-mutaʾallihīn* (Tehran: Tehran University Press, 1377 [A.H. lunar]), pp. yz–yḥ.

42. Referring to the Quranic story of Joseph.

43. Muṣliḥ, op. cit., p. yḥ. The same type of debate can also be found in the annals of Arabic literature.

44. See S. H. Nasr, *Three Muslim Sages*, chapter 1.

45. See S. Pines, "Quelques tendances antipéripatéticiennes de la pensée scientifique islamique," *Thalès*, vol. 4, 1940, pp. 210–20.

46. We have dealt more fully with this subject in the introduction to *Science and Civilization in Islam.*

47. See S. H. Nasr, *Sufi Essays* (Chicago: ABC International, 1999), pp. 123ff.

48. Unfortunately, little attention has been paid until now to the philosophical and scientific works of Rashīd al-Dīn, save his interest in medicine. But this philosophical aspect of his personality and thought deserves a much more extensive treatment. For a preliminary study see "The Status of Rashīd al-Dīn Faḍl Allāh in the History of Islamic Philosophy and Science," in my *The Islamic Intellectual Tradition* in Persia, pp. 228–36.

49. On this matter see *Introduction to Islamic Cosmological Doctrines*, pp. 11ff.

50. For a reference to this tradition see Zia Ülken, *La Pensée de l'Islam*, trans. G. Dubois, M. Bilen, and the author (Istanbul: Fakülteler Matbaasi, 1953), chapter 15; also Mubahat Türker, *Üç Tehāfut Bakimindan Felsefe ve Din Münasebeti* (Ankara: Türk Tarih Kumuru Basimevi, 1956). See also Bilal Kuşpinar, *Ismā'īl Ankavarī on the Illuminative Philosophy* (Kuala Lumpur: International Institute of Islamic Thought and Civilization, 1996).

51. Henry Corbin, *En Islam iranien*, vol. 4, pp. 10–122; and his *La Philosophie iranienne islamique aux xviie et xviii*[e] *siècles* (Paris: Buchet/Chastel, 1981). See chapter 12 of this book for Mullā Ṣadrā. As far as India is concerned, there is unfortunately no systematic study of the Islamic philosophical tradition in that land in Western languages. For the philosophers of Farangi Mahall see Francis Robinson, *Islam and Muslim History in South Asia* (New Delhi: Oxford University Press, 2001); idem, *The 'Ulama of Farangi Mahall and Islamic Culture in South Asia* (London: Hurst, 2001); and Jamal Malik, *Islamische Gellehrtenkultur in Nordindien: Entwicklungsgeschichte und Tendenzen am Beispiel von Lucknow* (Leiden: Brill, 1997).

52. See "The Pertinence of Islamic Philosophy Today," in my *Islamic Life and Thought*, pp. 153–57.

CHAPTER 3. *AL-ḤIKMAT AL-ILĀHIYYAH* AND *KALĀM*

1. See H. Corbin, "La place de Mollâ Sadrâ Shîrâzî (ob. 1050/1640) dans la philosophie iranienne," *Studia Islamica*, vol. 18, 1963, pp. 81–113. We shall trace the development of this synthesis in chapters 12 and 13 of this book.

2. See especially his *Philosophy of the Kalam*.

3. See for example George Makdisi, "Ash'arī and the Ash'arites in Islamic Religious History," *Studia Islamica*, vol. 17, 1962, pp. 37–80, and vol. 18, 1963, pp. 19–39.

4. See Frithjof Schuon, "Dilemmas of Moslem Scholasticism," in his *Christianity/Islam: Essays on Esoteric Ecumenism*, trans. Gustavo Polit (Bloomington: World Wisdom Books, 1985), pp. 203ff.

5. See Ibrāhīm Dīnānī, *Shu'ā'-i andīshah dar falsafa-yi Suhrawardī* (Tehran: Ḥikmat, 1364 [A.H. solar]).

6. The systematic study of the numerous commentaries and glosses written upon this major work during the past seven centuries by both the *mutakallimūn* and *falāsifah* would be a major contribution to the history of both Shi'ite *kalām* and *ḥikmat-i ilāhī*.

7. Concerning Mullā Ṣadrā 's teachings as the synthesis of the different schools preceding him, see H. Corbin, prolegomena to Mullā Ṣadrā 's *Le Livre des pénétrations métaphysiques* (Tehran-Paris: Department d'lranologie—Andrien-Maisonneuve, 1964); and his *En Islam iranien*, vol. 4, pp. 54ff. I have also dealt fully with this subject in Nasr, *Ṣadr al-Dīn Shīrāzī and His Transcendent Theosophy* (Tehran: Institute for Humanities and Cultural Studies, 1997). We shall turn to this subject in chapter 12.

8. For example in the *Asfār* (Tehran: lithographed edition, 1222 [A.H. lunar]), p. 147, he confirms the arguments of the *mutakallimūn* against the possibility of a movement or a chain of causes and events continuing ad infinitum, and in the section on proofs for the existence of God, p. 548, he confirms their arguments for God's existence based on motion.

9. An example is on p. 345, where their views about time are rejected, and the whole last section of the fourth *safar*, vol. 4 of the *Asfār*, where their views on eschatology are completely refuted.

10. *Si aṣl*, S. H. Nasr (ed.), (Tehran: Tehran University Press, 1340 [A.H. solar]), pp. 5–6.

11. Ibid., p. 7.

12. *Kasr al-aṣnām al-jāhiliyyah*, M. T. Danechepazhuh (ed.) (Tehran: Tehran University Press: 1340 [A.H. solar]), pp. 91–92.

13. Concerning Lāhījī see H. Corbin, *La Philosophie iranienne islamique aux xviie et xviiie siècles*, pp. 96ff. See also *Yādnāma-yi Ḥakīm Lāhījī* (Tehran: Wizārat-i Farhang wa Irshād-i Millī, 1374 [A.H. solar]).

14. See Ya'qūb Ja'farī, "Ta'rīf-i 'ilm-i kalām az dīdgāh-i Mullā 'Abd al-Razzāq Lāhījī," in *Yādnāma-yi Lāhījī*, p. 667.

15. On the philosophical views of Lāhījī, see S. J. Āshtiyānī, in *Yādnāma-yi Lāhījī*, pp. 91–156. In vol. 1 of *Anthologie des philosophes iraniens*, ed. H. Corbin, J. Āshtiyānī has selected a number of the more philosophical passages of Lāhījī's writings. See pp. 272–361 of the Arabic-Persian section.

16. What Lāhījī refers to is the Islamic injunction that it is the duty of the believer to penetrate intellectually to the extent possible for that person into the articles and principles of faith. But if he or she does not have the intellectual acumen necessary for this task, it is sufficient to imitate (*taqlīd*) the

founder of the religion and in the case of Shi'ism also the Imams in order to gain salvation. But for the person who does possess the capability, it is essential to seek to understand the intellectual basis of religious injunctions and doctrines.

17. Lāhījī, *Gawhar-i murād* (Tehran: Islāmiyyah, 1377 [A. H. lunar]), pp. 15–21.

18. On Ḥasan Lāhījī see the introduction of 'Alī Ṣadrāʾī Khuʾī to his edition of *Rasāʾil-i fārsī taʾlīf-i Ḥasan ibn 'Abd al-Razzāq Lāhījī* (Tehran: Markaz-i Farhangī-yi Nashr-i Qiblah, 1375 [A.H. solar]). See also Corbin, *La Philosophie iranienne islamique . . .*, pp. 291–300.

19. Translated by Marcie Hermansen (Leiden: Brill, 1995); Shāh Walī Allāh, *The Sacred Knowledge*, trans. G. N. Jalbani, ed. David Pendleburg (London: Octagon, 1982). See also Hafiz Ghaffar Khan, "Shah Walīullāh," in Nasr and Leaman (eds.), *History of Islamic Philosophy*, pp. 663–70.

Chapter 4. The Question of Existence and Quiddity and Ontology in Islamic Philosophy

1. "The distinction between 'quiddity' and 'existence' is undoubtedly one of the most basic philosophical theses in Islamic thought. Without exaggeration the distinction may be said to constitute the first step in ontologico-metaphysical thinking among Muslims; it provides the very foundation on which is built up the whole structure of Muslim metaphysics." Toshihiko Izutsu, "The Fundamental Structure of Sabzavārī's Metaphysics," introduction to the Arabic text of Sabzavari's *Sharḥ-i manẓūmah*, Mehdi Mohaghegh and T. Izutsu (eds.) (Tehran: McGill University Institute of Islamic Studies, Tehran Branch, 1969), p. 49.

2. For the metaphysical distinction between Being and Non-Being, see F. Schuon, *From the Divine to the Human*, trans. Gustavo Polit and Deborah Lambert (Bloomington: World Wisdom Books, 1982), part 1; and his *Survey of Metaphysics and Esoterism*, trans. G. Polit (Bloomington: World Wisdom Books, 1986), part 1. Schuon writes, "Beyond-Being or Non-Being is Reality absolutely unconditioned, while Being is Reality insofar as It determines Itself in the direction of Its manifestation and in so doing becomes personal God." *Stations of Wisdom*, trans. G. E. H. Palmer (Bloomington: World Wisdom Books, 1995), p. 213, note 1.

3. See A. M. Goichon, "L'Unité de la pensée avicennienne," *Archives Internationales d'Histoire des Sciences* 20–21 (1952), 29ff.

4. E. Gilson, *L'Être et l'essence* (Paris: Vrin, 1948), p. 90; also quoted in Izutsu, "The Fundamental Structure," pp. 54–55.

5. Although some scholars have doubted the attribution of this work to al-Fārābī and consider it to be by Ibn Sīnā (see S. Pines, "Ibn Sīnā et l'auteur de la *Risālat al-fuṣūṣ fi'l-ḥikma*," *Revue des Etudes Islamiques* [1951], 122–24), we see no convincing reason to doubt the view of Islamic philosophers held during the past millenium that the work is by al-Farābī. S. H. Nasr, *Three Muslim Sages*, p. 136.

6. On Ibn Sīnā 's views concerning *wujūd* and *māhiyyah*, see A. M. Goichon, *La Distinction de l'essence et de l'existence d'après Ibn Sīnā (Avicenna)* (Paris: Desclée, 1937); and Fazlur Rahman, "Essence and Existence in Avicenna," in *Mediaeval and Renaissance Studies*, vol. 4 (London: Warburg Institute, 1958), pp. 1–16. For Ibn Sīnā 's discussion of *wujūd* in general, see S. H. Nasr, *An Introduction to Islamic Cosmological Doctrines*, pp. 197ff.

7. On Suhrawardī's metaphysics, see S. H. Nasr, *Three Muslim Sages*, chapter 2; H. Corbin, *En Islam iranien*, vol. 2.

8. See *Kashf al-murād—Sharh tajrīd al-i'tiqād*, of which the text is by Ṭūsī and the commentary by Ḥillī, ed. with trans. and commentary by Abū'l-Ḥasan Sha'rānī (Tehran: Islāmiyyah Bookshop, 1351 [A. H. solar]/1972), chapter 1.

9. On this most obscure period in the history of Islamic philosophy, see chapter 11 of this work; also H. Corbin (in collaboration with S. H. Nasr and O. Yahya), *Histoire de la philosophie islamique* (Paris: Gallimard, 1986), especially part 2, which was written entirely by Corbin; and M. Cruz Hernández, *Historia de pensamiento en el mundo islámico* 2 (Madrid: Alianza University, 1981). Needless to say, the Peripatetic school of the Maghrib, which survived from the time of al-Ghazzālī to the beginning of this period, also addressed extensively the question of *wujūd* and *māhiyyah*, as can be seen in the commentary of Ibn Rushd on the *Metaphysics* of Aristotle as well as in many of Ibn Rushd's other works.

10. We shall turn in later chapters to the significance of this school. See also Corbin, *En Islam iranien*, vol. 4, pp. 9–201.

11. Mullā Ṣadrā devoted the whole of the first book of his *Asfār* to the discussion of *wujūd*, to which he returned in several of his other works, especially the *Kitāb al-mashā'ir* and *al-Shawāhid al-rubūbiyyah*. See H. Corbin's introduction to his edition of the *Kitāb al-mashā'ir* (*Le Livre des pénétrations métaphysiques*); the introduction of S. J. Āshtiyānī in Persian and of S. H. Nasr in English to Āshtiyānī's edition of *al-Shawāhid al-rubūbiyyah* (Mashhad: Mashhad University Press, 1967); S. H. Nasr, *Ṣadr al-Dīn Shīrāzī and His Transcendent Theosophy*; and F. Rahman, *The Philosophy of Mullā Ṣadrā* (Albany: State University of New York Press, 1976). We shall deal more fully with Mullā Ṣadrā in chapter 12 of this work.

12. See S. H. Nasr, "Sabziwārī," in *The Islamic Intellectual Tradition in Persia*, pp. 304–319; Nasr, "The Metaphysics of Ṣadr al-Dīn Shirāzī and Islamic Philosophy in Qajar Persia," in *Ṣadr al-Dīn Shirāzī*, chapter 6, pp. 99ff. See also Manuchihr Ṣaddūqī Suha, *Tārīkh-i ḥukamā wa 'urafā-yi muta'akhkhir* (Tehran: Ḥikmat, 1423 A.H.). S. J. Āshtiyānī has also dealt with the figures of this

period in several introductions to their works, especially those of Sabziwārī and the two Zunūzīs. See, for example, Mullā 'Abd Allāh Zunūzī, *Lama'āt-i ilāhiyyah* (Divine Splendors) (Tehran: Imperial Iranian Academy of Philosophy, 1976), Persian prolegomena of Āshtiyānī and English and Persian introductions of S. H. Nasr. See also the long Persian introduction of Āshtiyānī to his edition of Mullā Ṣadrā's *Shawāhid.*

13. See, for example, his *Fayṣalat waḥdat al-wujūd wa waḥdat al-shuhūd* (Delhi, n.d.); and his *Lamaḥāt*, in *Sufism and the Islamic Tradition*, trans. G. N. Jalbani and ed. D. B. Fry (London: Octagon, 1980). We shall discuss more fully some of these figures in chapter 13 of this work.

14. Such works as 'Allāmah Sayyid Muḥammad Ḥusayn Ṭabāṭabā'ī's *Uṣūl-i falsafah wa rawish-i ri'ālism*, with commentary by Murtaḍā Muṭahharī, 5 vols. (Qum: Dār al-'Ilm, 1332 [A. H. solar]/1953); Sayyid Muhammad Kāẓim 'Aṣṣār, *Waḥdat-i wujūd wa badā'* in Sayyid Jalāl al-Dīn Āshtiyānī (ed.), *Mujmū'a-yi āthār-i Aṣṣār* (Tehran: Amīr Kabīr, 1376 [A.H. solar]), pp. 5–30; Sayyid Jalāl al-Dīn Āshtiyānī, *Hastī az naẓar-i falsafah wa 'irfān* (Mashhad: Khurasan, 1379 [A. H. lunar]/1960); Mahdī Ḥā'irī Yazdī, *Hiram-i hastī* (Tehran: Cultural Studies and Research Institue, 1363 [A. H. solar]/1984); and M. R. Ṣāliḥī Kirmānī, *Wujūd az naẓar-i falsafa-yi islām* (Qum, n.d.), bear witness to the living character of traditional Islamic metaphysics in general and the study of *wujūd* or *hastī* (in Persian) in particular.

15. Metaphysics or the science of Ultimate Reality is called *"ma'rifah"* or *"'irfān"* in the Islamic esoteric tradition or Sufism. In the philosophical tradition, it is called *"al-ḥikmat al-ilāhiyyah"* in Arabic or *"ḥikmat-i ilāhī"* in Persian. See the previous chapter.

16. See S. H. Nasr, *Islamic Life and Thought*, chapter 17, "The Polarization of Being," pp. 182–87.

17. T. Izutsu quite justifiably translated *'māhiyyah'* in the first sense as "quiddity" and in the second as "essence." See his "Fundamental Structure," p. 73.

18. It is remarkable how the three terms *wujūd, wijdān*, and *wajd* resemble so closely the famous *sat, chit*, and *ānanda* in Hinduism, where their combination *satchitananda* is considered a Name of God and the metaphysical characterization of Reality. See S. H. Nasr, *Knowledge and the Sacred*, p. 1.

19. In his introduction to Mullā Ṣadrā's *Kitāb al-mashā'ir*, H. Corbin, who was the first person to translate Martin Heidegger into French, has made a profound comparison between the Islamic philosophy of being and Heidegger's thought on the subject of existence.

20. These three ways of envisaging quiddity, namely, in itself, in the mind, and in its actualization in the external world, are called *"al-i'tibārāt al-thalathah."* See Izutsu, "The Fundamental Structure," p. 65.

21. For a summary and clear Avicennan expression of the distinction between *wujūd* and *māhiyyah*, see his *al-Ishārāt wa᾿l-tanbīhāt* (Cairo: Dār al-Ma'ārif, 1960), vol. 1, pp. 202–03.

22. Classical works on Islamic philosophy usually have in fact separate sections or chapters devoted to the principles pertaining to *wujūd* (*aḥkām al-wujūd*) and those pertaining to *māhiyyah*. The *aḥkām al-wujūd*, moreover, are divided into the affirmative (*al-ījābiyyah*) and negative (*al-salbiyyah*), the first dealing with unity and multiplicity, causality, potentiality, actuality, and the like, and the negative with such themes as the fact that *wujūd* has no definition, that it has no parts, and so on. As for *aḥkām al-māhiyyah*, they are concerned with such issues as whether a *māhiyyah* is simple (*basīṭ*) or compound (*murakkab*), the question of species, genus, or specific difference, and so on. See S. H. Nasr, *Islamic Life and Thought* chapter 17, pp. 182ff.

23. It is the famous sentence from the *Shifā᾿*, "These quiddities (*māhiyyāt*) are by themselves 'possible existents' and existence (*wujūd*) occurs (*ya'riḍ*) to them from the outside" that has been the main source of this misunderstanding. See Izutsu, "The Fundamental Structure, pp. 109–10, where he quotes from Āshtiyānī's discussion of this passage. In section 6 of this work entitled "Is Existence an Accident?" Izutsu has given an excellent summary of this question and the reason for the misunderstanding that followed Ibn Sīnā's assertion of the "accidentality" of *wujūd*.

24. Izutsu, "The Fundamental Structure," pp. 110–11. It is interesting, as far as the later history of Islamic philosophy is concerned, to note that this very passage was quoted by Mullā Ṣadrā in his *Kitāb al-mashā'ir*.

25. From Ṭūsī's *Sharḥ al-ishārāt*, trans. Izutsu, p. 105. We have made a slight change by translating *wujūd dhihnī* as "mental existence" rather than "rational existence," which Professor Izutsu prefers in the text, although he refers to "mental existence" as an alternative translation in one of his footnotes.

26. See, for example, the *Ilāhiyyāt* of the *Shifā᾿* (Tehran: Lithograph edition, 1305/1887), pp. 597ff; and the *Najāh* (Cairo: Muḥyī al-Dīn Ṣabrī al-Kurdī, 1938), pp. 224ff.

27. Contingency or possibility also has another meaning, which is related to potentiality that can become actualized and that refers to the potentialilties latent in an existent. It is interesting to note that both potentiality and possibility are derived from the same Latin root *posse*, which, furthermore, bears the meaning of power. In this sense possibility is related to the latent creative power of the Divinity. For an in-depth discussion of this basic metaphysical issue, which cannot, however, be expanded here, see Frithjof Schuon, *From the Divine to the Human*, "The Problem of Possibility," pp. 43–55.

28. What Ṭūsī means in this poem must not be confused with the question of predestination and determinism, although they are philosophically and theologically related.

29. In one of the best known verses of the *Sharḥ-i manẓūmah,* Sabziwārī says,

> *mafhūmuhu min aʿrafiʾl-ashyāʾ-i*
> *wa kunhuhu fī ghāyatiʾl-khifāʾ-i*
>
> Its notion is one of the things best known.
> But its deepest reality [*kunh*] is hidden in the extreme.

Sharḥ-i ghurar al-farāʾid or *Sharḥ-i manẓūmah,* part 1 "Metaphysics," M. Mohaghegh and T. Izutsu (eds.) (Tehran: McGill University Institute of Islamic Studies-Tehran Branch, 1969), p. 4. The term *kunh* is used by Sabziwārī as being synonymous with *ḥaqīqah.*

30. In his introduction to Mullā Ṣadrā 's *Kitāb al-mashā'ir,* besides dealing with the thought of Heidegger, Corbin provides an excellent comparison between the course of ontology in the history of Islamic thought and that of the West. See also Alparsalan Açikgenç, *Being and Existence in Ṣadrā and Heidegger: A Comparative Ontology* (Kuala Lumpur: International Institute of Islamic Thought and Civilization, 1993).

31. Since the 1980s with the rise of interest in Shi'ism, a politicized usage of the term "School of Isfahan" has come into vogue employing the term originally coined by Corbin and myself, but in a very different context.

32. See chapter 12 of this work.

33. On the doctrine of *waḥdat al-wujūd,* see Martin Lings, *A Sufi Saint of the Twentieth Century* (Los Angeles: University of California Press, 1971), chapter 5; Titus Burckhardt, *An Introduction to Sufi Doctrine,* trans. D. M. Matheson (Wellingborough: Crucible, 1990), chapter 7; and T. Izutsu, "The Basic Structure of Metaphysical Thinking in Islam," in M. Mohaghegh and H. Landolt (eds.), *Collected Papers on Islamic Philosophy and Mysticism* (Tehran: McGill University Institute of Islamic Studies, Tehran Branch, 1971), pp. 39–72.

34. There have been of course those who have grasped the knowledge of *waḥdat al-wujūd* intuitively without the corresponding spiritual discipline, but they are the few exceptions bound to be present, for the "spirit bloweth where it listeth."

35. See Carl Ernst, *Words of Ecstasy in Sufism* (Albany: State University of New York Press, 1985).

36. On these two doctrines and an attempt at their synthesis, see Mir Valiuddin, "Reconciliation between Ibn Arabī's *Waḥdat al-Wujud* and the Mujaddid's *Waḥdat al-Shuhūd,*" *Islamic Culture* 25 (1951), 43–51. This attempt at reconciliation goes back to Shāh Walī Allāh himself.

37. See al-Jandī, *Sharḥ fuṣūṣ al-ḥikam,* ed. S. J. Āshtiyānī (Mashhad: Mashhad University Press, 1361[A. H. solar]/1983). Āshtiyānī's own work *Hastī az naẓar-i falsafah wa 'irfān* contains a fine summary of various views on

waḥdat al-wujūd and demonstrates how much the issue has remained alive to this day.

38. William Chittick has devoted numerous studies to this school, including his introduction to Jāmī's *Naqd al-nuṣūṣ fī sharḥ naqsh al-fuṣūṣ* (Tehran: Imperial Iranian Academy of Philosophy, 1977). See also his "Mysticism versus Philosophy in Earlier Islamic History: The al-Ṭūsī, al-Qūnawī Correspondence," *Religious Studies* 17 (1979), pp. 87–104; also his "Ibn 'Arabī and His School," in S. H. Nasr (ed.), *Islamic Spirituality: Manifestations*, vol. 20 of *World Spirituality: An Encyclopedic History of the Religious Quest* (New York: Crossroad, 1991), pp. 49–79; and his "Ṣadr al-Dīn Qūnawī on the Oneness of Being," *International Philosophical Quarterly*, vol. 21, 1981, pp. 171–84. See also Chittick, "The School of Ibn 'Arabī," in Nasr and Leaman, *History of Islamic Philosophy*, pp. 510–23.

39. He was a major commentator of Ibn 'Arabī and his doctrine of *waḥdat al-wujūd*. See H. Corbin, *En Islam iranien*, vol. 3, pp. 149–213; and Corbin and O. Yahya (eds.), *La Philosophie shi'ite* (Tehran/Paris: A. Maisonneuve, 1969), which contains the text of Āmulī's *Jāmi' al-asrār* as well as his *Fī ma'rifat al-wujūd* (On the Knowledge of Being).

40. His *Tamhīd al-qawā'id*, ed. S. J. Āshtiyānī, with Persian and English introductions by S. H. Nasr (Tehran: Imperial Iranian Academy of Philosophy, 1976), shows clearly the philosophical concern for this gnostic doctrine. See also his commentary upon the *Fuṣūṣ* of Ibn 'Arabī, ed. Muḥsin Bīdārfar, 2 vols. (Qom: Bīdār, 1420 A.H.).

41. By gnosis is meant *'irfān* or *ma'rifah*, that is, that knowledge which transforms and illuminates, and not the sectarianism of the early history of Christianity.

42. The history of this idea was treated in the famous work of Arthur Lovejoy, *The Great Chain of Being* (Cambridge: Harvard University Press, 1936).

43. On Ibn Sīnā 's teachings concerning the chain of being, see Nasr, *An Introduction to Islamic Cosmological Doctrines*, pp. 203ff.; see also pp. 51ff. for the significance of this idea in the *Rasā'il* of the Ikhwān al- Ṣafā'. Ibn Sīnā devoted numerous pages to this doctrine in many of his works and in addition wrote a treatise entitled *Risālah dar ḥaqīqat wa kayfiyyat-i silsila-yi mawjūdāt wa tasalsul-i asbāb wa musabbabāt* (Treatise on the Reality and Mode of the Chain of Beings and the Sequence of Causes and Effects) (Tehran: Tehran University Press, 1952).

44. The Ṣadrean exposition of this doctrine is very similar to what Suhrawardī states concerning the nature of light. The light of the sun and a candle are distinguished from each other by nothing other than light. What unites them is the same as what distinguishes them from each other.

45. "In the earlier days I used to be a passionate defender of the thesis that the 'quiddities' are *aṣīl* and 'existence is *i'tibārī*, until my Lord gave me guidance and let me see His demonstration. All of a sudden my spiritual eyes

were opened and I saw with utmost clarity that the truth was just the contrary of what the philosophers in general had held. Praise be to God who, by the light of intuition, led me out of the darkness of the groundless idea and firmly established me upon the thesis which would never change in the present world and the Hereafter. . . . As a result (I now hold that) the 'existences' (*wujūdāt*) are primary 'realities', while the 'quiddities' are the 'permanent archetypes' (*a'yān thābitah*) that have never smelt the fragrance of 'existence'. The 'existences' are nothing but beams of light radiated by the true Light which is the absolutely self-subsistent Existence, except that each of them is charactacterized by a number of essential properties and intelligible qualities. These latter are the things that are known as 'quiddities,'" (Izutsu, "The Fundamental Structure," pp. 77–78).

46. There have been a few men such as Shaykh Aḥmad Aḥsāʾī who have sought to accept the views of both schools as being valid, but their claims have not been intellectually satisfactory and have not been favorably received by the most eminent representative of the various schools of *ḥikmat-i ilāhī*.

47. See Sabziwārī, *The Metaphysics of Sabzavari*, M. Mohaghegh and T. Izutsu (eds.), pp. 32ff. Two of these arguments have been summarized by Izutsu in his "Fundamental Structure," pp. 80ff.

48. It must not be forgotten that one of the titles of Mullā Ṣadrā was Ṣadr al-mutaʾallihīn, literally, "foremost among the theosophers."

49. See the masterly analysis of Izutsu in his "Fundamental Structure," section 7.

50. See the next chapter of this book; see also Richard M. Frank, "Attribute, Attribution, and Being: Three Islamic Views," pp. 258–78; and P. Morewedge, "Greek Sources of Some Near Eastern Philosophies of Being and Existence," in Parviz Morewedge (ed.), *Philosophies of Existence* (New York: Fordham University Press, 1982), pp. 285–336, in the same volume.

51. See Izutsu, "The Fundamental Structure," pp. 143–44.

Chapter 5. Post-Avicennan Islamic Philosophy and the Study of Being

1. As already mentioned, Ibn Sīnā or Avicenna has in fact been called first and foremost a "philosopher of being." See A. A. Goichon, "L'Unité de la pensée avicennienne," 290ff. Many Western scholars of medieval Western philosophy such as Etienne Gilson have also recognized him as the father of ontology or the philosophy of being as this discipline came to be cultivated in the medieval West.

2. This major work, edited for the first time by Muhsin Mahdi (Beirut: Dār al-Mashriq, 1969), caused contemporary scholars to revise completely

their views concerning the study of ontology among the earlier Islamic philosophers.

3. See Parviz Morewedge, *The Metaphysics of Avicenna (Ibn Sīnā)* (New York: Columbia University Press, 1973); for the ontology of Avicenna, see also A. M. Goichon, *La Distinction de l'essence et de l'existence d'après Ibn Sīnā (Avicenne)*; and S. H. Nasr, *An Introduction to Islamic Cosmological Doctrines*, chapter 12.

4. See F. Schuon's *Logic and Transcendence*, trans. P. Townsend (New York: Harper and Row, 1975), chapters 7 and 13; as well as his *Islam and the Perennial Philosophy*.

5. On Suhrawardī's view of existence see his *Ḥikmat al-ishrāq*, H. Corbin (ed.), in *Oeuvres philosophiques et mystiques* 2 (Tehran: Institut d'Etudes et des Recherches Culturelles, 2001), pp. 186ff. and in passim; vol. 1 of the same work containing the *Talwīḥāt*, pp. 26ff.; and Ibrāhīmī Dīnānī, *Shu'āʾi andīshah wa shuhūd*, pp. 309ff.

See also Hossein Ziai, "Shihāb al-Dīn Suhrawardī: Founder of the Illuminationist School," in Nasr and Leaman, *History of Islamic Philosophy*, pp. 434ff; and Chittick, *The Sufi Path of Knowledge* (Albany: State University of New York, 1989) and *The Self-Disclosure of God* (Albany: State University of New York Press, 1998).

6. While asserting that Ibn 'Arabī provided "an inexhaustible ocean of meditation upon the Unity of God and its relationship with the manyness of things," William Chittick writes, "Ibn 'Arabī took over most of the vocabulary connected to the discussion of *wujūd* from the Muslim philosophers." *The Sufi Path of Knowledge*, pp. 79, see also 80. See also pp. 77–144 of this work for a profound exposition of Ibn 'Arabī's ontology.

7. On Ibn 'Arabī in general, see Nasr, *Three Muslim Sages*, chapter 3. As for his doctrine of Divine Mercy, see Chittick, *The Sufi Path of Knowledge*, pp. 127ff.; and Izutsu, *Sufism and Taoism: A Comparative Study of the Key Philosophical Concepts* (Berkeley: University of California Press, 1983), pp. 7ff. In a section entitled "Ontological Mercy," Izutsu quotes the famous commentator of Ibn 'Arabī, 'Abd al-Razzāq Kāshānī, as saying, "Existence [*wujūd*] is the first overflowing of the Mercy which is said to extend to everything" (p. 116).

8. On this basic doctrine, which has often been mistaken for philosophical pantheism, existential monism, and the like, see Burckhardt, *An Introduction to Sufi Doctrine*, trans. chapter 3; Lings, *A Sufi Saint of the Twentieth Century*, chapter 5; and Chittick, *The Sufi Path of Knowledge*, pp. 79–80.

9. *La Philosophie shi'ite*, H. Corbin and O. Yahya (eds.) (Tehran and Paris: Andrien-Maisonneuve, 1969), pp. 620ff. of the Arabic text.

10. On the meaning of these terms, see Toshihiko Izutsu, *The Concept and Reality of Existence*, pp. 99ff. The School of Isfahan will be treated later in

this book—especially as far as the flowering of philosophy in a land dominated by prophecy is concerned.

11. All these three schools are represented in the second volume of the anthology of the philosophers of Persia since Mīr Dāmād. See their *Anthologie des philosophes iraniens*, vol. 2. The discussion of the three schools, as described by Corbin on p. 5, occupies nearly the entire volume. See also Corbin's "Présence de quelques philosophes iraniens," in his *Philosophie iranienne et philosophie comparée* (Paris and Tehran: Imperial Iranian Academy of Philosophy, 1977), part 2, pp. 55–81.

12. The *Mashā'ir* is in fact devoted to ontology and is one of the master's last works on the subject. See the analysis of its content by H. Corbin in his edition and translation of the work, *Le Livre des pénétrations métaphysiques*.

13. On Mullā Ṣadrā's doctrine of the unity of being, see "Mullā Ṣadrā and the Doctrine of the Unity of Being," in my *Islamic Life and Thought*, chapter 16, pp. 171ff. See also Zailan Moris, *Revelation, Intellectual Intuition and Reason in the Philosophy of Mullā Ṣadrā* (New York: Routledge Curzon, 2003).

14. See Corbin's introduction to the introduction of Mullā Ṣadrā's *Mashā'ir*, in *Le Livre des pénétrations métaphysiques*, pp.62ff.

15. See my *Islamic Intellectual Tradition in Persia*, pp. 278ff; see also Izutsu, *Concept and Reality of Existence*, part 4.

16. See F. Schuon, *Dimensions of Islam*, trans. P. Townsend (London: Allen and Unwin, 1970), chapter 2.

17. The following famous verses of Rūmī attest this truth:

> I died as mineral and became a plant,
> I died as plant and rose to animal,
> I died as animal and I was Man.
> Why should I fear? When was I less by dying?
> Yet once more I shall die as Man, to soar
> With angels blest; but even from angelhood
> I must pass on; all except God doth perish.
> When I have sacrificed my angel-soul,
> I shall become what no mind e'er conceived.
> O, let me not exist! for Non-existence
> Proclaims in organ tones: "To Him we shall return."

Reynold A. Nicholson, *Rumi: Poet and Mystic*
(London: Allen and Unwin, 1950), p. 103

18. *Logic and Transcendence*, p. 44. Schuon also quotes (ibid.) Franz von Baader's formulation to the same effect, the German theosopher having said, in answer to Descartes, *cogitor, ergo cogito et sum* ("I am thought [by God], therefore I think and I am").

Chapter 6. Epistemological Questions

1. There is still no thorough work in a European language dealing with the relation of faith and reason or reason and revelation in Islamic thought as one finds in the famous study of Etienne Gilson for Christian thought. Arthur J. Arberry wrote a short treatise entitled *Reason and Revelation in Islam* (London: Allen and Unwin, 1957), but it is far from being adequate.

2. On the distinction between intellect and reason see our *Knowledge and the Sacred*, especially chapters 1 and 4. For a penetrating critique of rationalism based on reason alone and traditional doctrines based on intellection see Schuon, *Logic and Transcendence*, especially the first three chapters.

3. See for example, "They also say: If we had only heard, and had understood (*na'qilu*) we would not have been of the inhabitants of the Blaze." Quran (53:10) (Arberry translation). In this verse the refusal to understand, or literally "intellect," is equated with the loss of paradise. In many other verses various forms of the verb *faqaha* are used with the same meaning as *'aqala*, for example: "We have distinguished the signs for a people who understand (*yafqahūn*). Quran (6: 98).

4. Concerning this distinction, which became central with Suhrawardī, see Corbin, *En Islam iranien*, vol. 4, pp. 65ff., 137; Ziai, "Suhrawardī," in Nasr and Leaman, *History of Islamic Philosophy*, pp. 451ff.; and Ibrāhimī Dīnānī, *Shu'ā'-i andīshah*, pp. 310ff. The most complete work on *'ilm al-ḥuḍūrī* in light of contemporary Anglo-Saxon analytical philosophy is Mahdī Hā'irī Yazdī, *The Principles of Epistemology in Islamic Philosophy* (Albany, State University of New York, 1992).

5. On the relation between faith and intellect or revelation and reason, see Schuon, *Stations of Wisdom*, "If 'no man cometh unto the Father but by me,' this truth or this principle is equally applicable to the pure Intellect in ourselves: in the sapiential order—it is only in this order that we may speak of Intellect or intellectuality without making implacable reservation—it is essential to submit all the powers of the soul to the pure Spirit, which is identified, but in a supra-formal and ontological manner, with the fundamental dogma of the Revelation and thereby with the *Sophia Perennis*." Schuon, *Dimensions of Islam*, p. 76.

6. On Ash'arite voluntarism see F. Schuon, *Islam and the Perennial Philosophy*, chapter 7, pp. 118–51. For a more general discussion of Ash'arite "voluntarist thought," see Daniel Gimaret, *La Doctrine d'al-Ash'ari* (Paris: Les Edition du Cerf, 1990).

7. On Ash'arism and its views concerning the intellect, see L. Gardet, *Introduction à la théologie musulmane* (Paris: Vrin, 1948).

8. On these schools see the histories of Islamic philosophy of Fakhry, Corbin, and Nasr and Leaman (eds.) already cited. For the third school see especially Nasr, *The Transcendent Theosophy of Ṣadr al-Dīn Shīrāzī.*

9. Classical Greek philosophy, before its decadence, cannot itself be reduced to rationalistic philosophy and is not merely of human inspiration. Rather, as already pointed out in the case of Pythagoras, Parmenides, and Empedocles, it is based on a wisdom of Divine Origin. It is only the rationalism of modern thought that has reduced the whole of ancient philosophy to a "harmless" antecedent of modern philosophy and refuses to see in a Pythagoras or a Plato, who made such a clear distinction between intellect or *nous* and reason, anything more than somewhat more intelligent professors of philosophy as one would find in any contemporary Western university. It must be remembered that the Muslims called Plato the "Divine Plato" (*Aflāṭūn al-ilāhī*). Concerning intellectual intuition as it functions in the context of traditional wisdom or the *philosophia perennis* and ratiocination in modern philosophy, F. Schuon writes, "Intellectual intuition communicates a priori the reality of the Absolute. Reasoning thought infers the Absolute by starting from the relative; thus it does not proceed by intellectual intuition, though it does not inevitably exclude it. For philosophy arguments have an absolute value; for intellectual intuition their value is symbolical and provisional. *Spiritual Perspectives and Human Facts*, p. 112.

10. These treatises had a profound influence upon Western Scholasticism and were well known to medieval masters such as St. Thomas and Duns Scotus. See Herbert Davidson, "Alfarabi and Avicenna on the Active Intellect," *Viator*, 1972, pp. 109–78.

11. See Ibn Sīnā, *Le Livres des directives et remarques*, pp. 324–26; Ibn Sīnā, *La Métaphysique; du shifāʾ*, trans. Georges C. Anawati, *see* (Paris: Vrin, 1985) vol. 2, pp. 111ff. and Nasr, *An Introduction to Islamic Cosmological Doctrines*, pp. 257ff.; also Fazlur Rahman, *Prophecy in Islam: Philosophy and Orthodoxy* (London: Allen and Unwin, 1958), pp. 11–29, which contains the translation of the relevant sections from the *Shifāʾ*.

12. See E. Gilson, "Les sources gréco-arabes de l'augustinisme avicennisant," *Archives d'Histoire Doctrinale et Littéraire du Moyen-Age*, vol. 4 (Paris, 1929), pp. 5–149.

13. Suhrawardī 's purely *ishrāqī* epistemology is expounded especially in the second book of his *Ḥikmat al-ishrāq* but can hardly be fully understood without the commentaries of Quṭb al-Dīn al-Shīrāzī and Shams al-Dīn al-Shahrazūrī. See the prolegomena of H. Corbin to vol. 2 of Suhrawardī, *Oeuvres philosophiques et mystiques.*

14. Concerning Mullā Ṣadrā, in addition to my *Ṣadr al-Dīn Shīrāzī and His Transcendent Theosophy* and the introduction of H. Corbin to Mullā Ṣadrā, *Le Livre des pénétrations métaphysiques*, see F. Rahman, *The Philosophy of Mullā*

Ṣadrā, which, however, gives a somewhat excessively rationalistic interpretation of the master of "the transcendent theosophy." On the epistemological teachings of Mullā Ṣadrā, see Seyed Gh. Safavi (ed.), *Perception according to Mulla Sadra* (London: Institute of Islamic Studies, 2002) where various aspects of his epistemology and doctrine of perception are discussed in matters ranging from the relevance of the philosophy of physics to prophecy to Mullā Sadrā's views on other issues of philosophy.

15. The impoverished modern vision of reality did not only banish the angels from the cosmos after Leibnitz, but also reduced the *mundus imaginalis* to pure whim and fancy with which the word *imagination* is identified today. With H. Corbin, we use the term *imaginal* to distinguish the traditional meaning of "*imaginalis*" from all that the word *imaginary* brings to mind. Concerning this imaginal world, see H. Corbin, *Alone with the Above: Creative Imagination in the Sufism of Ibn 'Arabī*, trans. R. Mannheim (Princeton: Princeton University Press, 1997); and Corbin, *Spiritual Body and Celestial Earth: from Mazdean Iran to Shi'ite Iran*, trans. N. Pearson (Princeton: Princeton University Press, 1977). In Ibn 'Arabī the faculty of imagination plays a major epistemological as well as cosmological and eschatological role. See Chittick, *The Sufi Path of Knowledge*, p. 112ff. See also Chittick, *Imaginal Worlds—Ibn al-'Arabī and the Problem of Religions Diversity*, (Albany: State University of New York, 1994).

16. See S. H. Nasr, "The Heart of the Faithful Is the Throne of the All-Merciful," in James Cutsinger (ed.), *Paths to the Heart: Sufism and the Christian East* (Bloomington: World Wisdom Books and Fons Vitae, 2002), pp. 32–45.

17. Quoted in *Sayings of Muhammad*, ed. and trans. Mirza Abu'l-Fadl (Allahabad, 1924), p. 51.

18. Ibid., p. 229.

19. On the symbolism of the "eye of the heart," see Frithjof Schuon, *The Eye of the Heart: Metaphysics, Cosmology, Spiritual Life* (Bloomington: World Wisdom Books), pp. 3–12.

Chapter 7. A Framework for the Study of the History of Islamic Philosophy

1. Among the issues in which I differed from Corbin was that he had little interest in the later development of philosophy outside of Persia and Shi'ite circles, while I have always thought that there are two important branches of Islamic philosophy in the later Sunni world: one in the Ottoman world and the second in Muslim India. Also, Corbin showed little interest in the revival of Islamic philosophy in the Arab world with Jamāl al-Dīn Asadābādī (Afghānī) in Egypt, while I believe that any thorough history of Islamic philosophy must include the development in the Arab world in modern times, despite the shallowness of some of the ideas of many of the figures

involved, and that this discussion should include philosophical Sufism in the Sunni world as it does Shi'ite gnosis, which was so important for Corbin. I also emphasize the relation of the sciences to philosophy more than he does. In any case my views on this matter are not the same as Corbin's, although we shared much and developed a framework for the general study of the history of Islamic philosophy together.

See the outline of the contents and the introduction of Corbin et al. to *History of Islamic Philosophy*.

2. See Nasr, "The Qur᾿ān and *Ḥadīth* as Source and Inspiration of Islamic Philosophy," in Nasr and Leaman, *History of Islamic Philosophy*, chapter 2, pp. 27–39.

3. See chapter 4 of this book.

4. Joel Kraemer has made an important study of this circle, but the more philosophical aspects have not as yet been integrated into general histories of Islamic philosophy. See Kraemer's *Humanism in the Renaissance of Islam* (Leiden: Brill, 1999).

5. Although earlier histories of Islamic philosophy neglected Ismā'īlī philosophy completely, Corbin was deeply interested in this school and wrote much about it. Also, the second volume of *The Anthology of Philosophy in Persia*, ed. S. H. Nasr with Mehdi Aminrazavi (New York: Oxford University Press, 2001) (a new edition is to appear in London: I.B. Tauris soon) is devoted completely to Ismā'īlī philosophy. Still, Ismā'īlī philosophy has not as yet made its way into general histories of Islamic philosophy, even those in Islamic languages, most of which are based on European models.

6. The pioneering studies of Paul Kraus on him such as his edition of his extant philosophical works as *Rasā᾿il falsafiyyah* (Beirut: Dār al-Āfāq al-Jadīdah, 1977); and his "Râzîna" *Orientalia*, vol. 4, 1935, pp. 200–04, and vol. 5, 1936, were not followed to any appreciable extent in the West. In Persia some interest has been shown in not only his medical but also his philosophical teachings. Rāzī is one of those figures whose philosophy of science must be considered in any serious history of the Islamic philosophy of science. For the most recent extensive study on Rāzī's works and philosophy see Parwīz Adhkā᾿ī, *Ḥakīm Rāzī* (Tehran: Tarḥ-i Naw, 1382 [A. H. solar]).

7. I have edited this work with Mehdi Mohaghegh as *al-As᾿ilah wa᾿l-ajwibah* (Kuala Lumpur: International Institute of Islamic Thought and Civilization, 1995). I have also dealt with al-Bīrūnī's philosophy of nature extensively in my *Introduction to Islamic Cosmological Doctrines*, pp. 116ff. Yet his philosophy of nature is hardly considered in various histories of Islamic philosophy.

8. It is noteworthy to mention here that although known as an Ash'arite theologian, al-Shahrastānī must have also had certain Ismā'īlī tendencies, for in his *Struggle with the Philosopher* (*al-Muṣāri'ah*) he criticizes Ibn Sīnā's philosophy more from the point of view of Ismā'īlī philosophy than that of Ash'arite *kalām*.

9. See Max Horten, *Die philosophischen Ansichten von Rāzī und Ṭūsī* (1209 and 1273) (Bonn: Haustein, 1910).

10. See chapter 10.

11. This period will be discussed extensively later in this book.

12. This period will be discussed more fully in chapter 13.

13. On the contemporary period of Islamic philosophy, see Nasr and Leaman, *History of Islamic Philosophy*, section 9, pp. 1037–1140.

14. In our *History of Islamic Philosophy*, Leaman and I tried to pay some attention to this matter by devoting a whole section (section 7, "Philosophy and Its Parts," pp. 783–998) to the philosophical aspects of various domains from science to law. But in the present state of scholarship such studies could not be completely integrated into the main body of the work, and most of the essays also reflect the incomplete state of the study of the subject.

15. This last suggestion about the philosophy of various disciplines to be integrated into the general history of Islamic philosophy as well as being treated independently in separate histories is my own and was not included in the original structure and framework devised by Corbin and myself for the periodization of the history of Islamic philosophy.

Chapter 8. Dimensions of the Islamic Intellectual Tradition

1. This is the definition given by 'Aḍud al-Dīn al-Ījī, one of the later masters of the science of *kalām*, in his *Mawāqif* (Stations) (translated in the article of G. C. Anawati entitled "Kalām" in the new *Encyclopedia of Religion* [New York: Macmillan, 1987] vol. 8, p. 231).

2. On the Mu'tazilites, see J. van Ess, "Mu'tazilah," in the *Encyclopedia of Religion*, 10:220–29; Josef van Ess, *Theologie und Geselschaft im 2. und 3. Jahrhundert Hidschra* (New York: de Gruyter, 1991–1997); W. Montgomery Watt, *The Formative Period of Islamic Thought* (Oxford: One World, 1998); Albert Nader, *Le Système philosophique des mu'tazila* (Beirut: Editions Des Lettres Orientales, 1956); Richard Frank, *The Metaphysics of Created Being according to Abū'l-Hudhayl al-'Allaf* (Istanbul: Nederlands Historisch-Archaeologisch Institut in Het Nabije Oosten, 1966); idem., *Beings and their Attributes* (Albany: State University of New York Press, 1978); and Richard Martin et al. (eds.), *Defenders of Reason in Islam* (Oxford: One World, 1997). On Islamic *kalām* as a whole, see Max Horten, *Die philosophischen Systeme der spekulativen Theologen in Islam* (Bonn: Cohen, 1912); Harry A. Wolfson, *The Philosophy of the Kalam* (Cambridge, MA: Harvard University Press, 1976); Louis Gardet and G. C. Anawati, *Introduction à la théologie musulmane*, vol. 1 (Paris: J. Vrin, 1970); and J. Windrow Sweetman, *Islam and Christian Theology*, (2 vols. (London: Lutterworth, 1945).

3. See George Hourani, *Islamic Rationalism: The Ethics of 'Abd al-Jabbār* (London: Oxford University Press, 1971).

4. Trans. M. Abdul Hye in his "Ash'arism," in *A History of Muslim Philosophy*, vol. 1, p. 223.

5. This work is one of the most exhaustive among a whole class of writings in Islam, usually called *"firaq"* or "sects," literature associated with the names of al-Nawbakhtī, al-Baghdādī, Ibn Ḥazm, al-Shahrastānī, and others. Al-Ash'arī's work is also among the most thorough and detailed work in this category of religious writings usually composed by scholars of *kalām*.

6. On the metaphysical critique of Ash'arite voluntarism, see Frithjof Schuon, *Christianity/Islam: Essays on Esoteric Ecumenism*, trans. G. Polit (Bloomington: World Wisdom Books, 1981), 203ff. Many studies and translations have been made of al-Ash'arī. See, e.g., Walter C. Klein, *The Elucidation of Islam's Foundation* (New Haven: American Oriental Society, 1940), which contains a translation of *al-Ibānah*; Richard J. McCarthy, *The Theology of al-Ash'arī* (Beirut: Imprimerie Catholique, 1953), which contains a study of al-Ash'arī and the translation of two of his creeds; Daniel Gimaret, *La Doctrine d'al-Ash'ari* (Paris: Les Editions du Cerf, 1992); and Duncan B. Macdonald, *Development of Muslim Theology: Jurisprudence of Constitutional Theory* (New York: Scribner's Sons, 1926).

7. On Ash'arite atomism and occasionalism, see the still valuable work of S. Pines, *Beiträge zur islamischen Atomenlehre* (Berlin: Heine, 1936) trans. by Michael Schwarz as *Studies in Islamic Atomism* (Jerusalem: Magnus Press, 1997); and Majid Fakhry, *Islamic Occasionalism* (London: Allen and Unwin, 1958). Ash'arite atomism was not new in Islam in the sense that certain Mu'tazilites had already developed such a theory, but it became much more elaborated than before by the Ash'arites and was made a cornerstone of their theological system.

8. The Islamic philosophers refuted this view strongly, as seen in the arguments offered by Averroes in his *Incoherence of the Incoherence* against al-Ghazzālī on this issue. See S. H. Nasr, *Science and Civilization in Islam*, pp. 318ff. It is of interest to note that David Hume used the same argument as the Ash'arites to refute causality and even mentioned the example of fire and cotton given by al-Ghazzālī and referred to by Averroes. Needless to say, Hume did not reach the same conclusion as the Ash'arites, because he did not see the Divine Will as the cause of all things.

9. This is the translation of *kalām al-muta'akhkhirīn* given by G. C. Anawati in his article on *kalām* in the new *Encyclopedia of Religion*, vol. 8, p. 238.

10. He was well versed in Islamic philosophy as well as in medicine, astronomy, and even the "hidden sciences" (*al-'ulūm al-gharībah* or *khafiyyah*).

See S. H. Nasr, "Fakhr al-Dīn al-Rāzī ," in *The Islamic Intellectual Tradition in Persia*, pp. 107–21. On later Islamic theology, see also Horten, *Die philosophischen Systeme*; van Ess, *Die Erkenntniss Lehre des 'Aduḍaddīn al-Īčī* (Wiesbaden: Harrassowitz, 1966); and Gardet and Anawati, *Introduction à la théologie musulmane*, vol. 1, pp. 76ff.

11. F. Schuon, *Christianity/Islam*, p. 221.

12. Ibid., pp. 220–21.

13. Some of these ideas have been treated already by Azim Nanji in his article "Ismā'īlism," in *Islam, Islamic Spirituality: Foundations*, S. H. Nasr (ed.), *World Spirituality* 19 (New York: Crossroad, 1987), pp. 179–98. See also Corbin et al., *History of Islamic Philosophy*, pp. 79ff.

14. See *Kashf al-murād fi sharḥ tajrīd al-i'tiqād*, trans. and commented upon by Abū'l-Ḥasan Sha'rānī (Tehran: Kitābfurūshī-yi islāmiyyah, 1351 A.H. solar). On Shi'ite theology, especially of the earlier period before it became systematized by Ṭūsī, see Wilfred Madelung, *Religious Schools and Sects in Medieval Islam* (London: Variorum Reprints, 1985) vii–xv.

15. A contemporary example of this division is to be found in the popular two-volume work of Muḥyī al-Dīn Mahdī Ilāhī Qumsha'ī, *Ḥikmat-i ilāhī 'āmm wa khāṣṣ* (Tehran: Islāmī, 1363 [A.H. solar]) p. 204.

16. For an extensive bibliography concerning all the figures mentioned in this chapter see Hans Daiber. With this important reference available, we have not found it necessary to provide bibliographical notes for every philosopher or theologian cited in this survey.

17. See Nasr, *Three Muslim Sages*, chapter 1.

18. Translated by R. Walzer in his "Islamic Philosophy," in *The History of Philosophy, Eastern and Western*, S. Radhakrishnan (ed.) (London: Allen and Unwin, 1953) 2:131.

19. That is why a person such as Mullā Ṣadrā refers to inner intellection as being like "partial prophecy."

20. See *Three Muslim Sages*, p. 12.

21. This becomes evident when one studies the technical philosophical terminology used by al-Fārābī and Ibn Sīnā.

22. The question of the classification of the sciences is of great importance in Islamic thought and is very relevant to the relation between philosophy and prophecy. See Osman Bakar, *Classification of Knowledge in Islam* (Cambridge: The Islamic Texts Society, 1998).

23. The title "teacher" (*mu'allim*), which was also to be used later by Thomas Aquinas and other Scholastics, is not of Greek origin. It is Islamic and refers in this context to the function of defining and classifying the sciences. See Nasr "Why Was al-Fārābī Called the Second Teacher?" in *The Islamic Intellectual Tradition in Persia*, pp. 59–65.

24. Al-Fārābī was particularly interested in the question of the relation of words to their meaning, as seen in his important opus *Kitāb al-ḥurūf.* Arabic philosophical vocabulary owes its final crystallization to him more than to anyone else.

25. One of great masters of traditional Islamic philosophy in Persia during the twentieth century, Muḥyī al-Dīn Mahdī Ilāhī Qumsha'ī, taught this text with two levels of meaning, one philosophical (*falsafī*) and one gnostic (*'irfānī*). See his *Ḥikmat-i ilāhī 'āmm wa khāṣṣ* vol. 2, pp. 1–232.

26. It is important to note here that many Islamic philosophers had Jewish and Christian students and in the early period some also had Jewish and Christian teachers.

27. For a description of the climate of Baghdad, in which interest in philosophy was combined with literary discussions, and the teachings of al-Sijistānī , see J. L. Kramer, *Philosophy in the Renaissance of Islam: Abū Sulaymān al-Sijistānī and His Circle.*

28. Technically speaking, Miskawayh is more of an independent philosopher than a Peripatetic one. He is mentioned here because of his having studied with a well-known Peripatetic philosopher, that is, al-'Āmirī.

29. The term was actually used before Leibnitz by Agostino Steuco, who lived in the sixteenth century. It is interesting to note that Steuco used the term *antiqua* as well as *perennis,* the former corresponding to Suhrawardī's *al-ḥikmat al-'atīqah* or *philosophia antiqua* (also *philosophia priscorium*). See Charles Schmitt, "Perennial Philsoophy: Steuco to Leibnitz." See also chapter 1, ft. nt. 8.

30. There is a vast literature on Ibn Sīnā in Islamic as well as European languages. As far as the spiritual significance of his philosophy is concerned, see H. Corbin, *Avicenna and the Visionary Recital,* trans. Willard Trask (Princeton, NJ: Princeton University Press, 1960); S. H. Nasr, *Three Muslim Sages,* I; idem, *An Introduction to Islamic Cosmological Doctrines,* pp. 177ff., which also contains an extensive bibliography of primary and secondary sources concerning him.

31. For the significance of the "Oriental Philosophy" of Ibn Sīnā, see Corbin, *Avicenna,* pp. 271ff.; and Nasr, "Ibn Sīnā's 'Oriental Philosophy,' " in Nasr and Leaman, *History of Islamic Philosophy,* chapter 17, pp. 247–51. This is an issue that is a major point of contention between the later followers of Ibn Sīnā with an *ishrāqī* bent in the Islamic world and most modern Western scholars. For an example of strong opposition to the interpretation of Corbin and I concerning the "Oriental Philosophy" see Dimitri Gutas, *Avicenna and the Aristotelian Tradition* (Leiden: Brill, 1981).

32. We shall duscuss this figure extensively in chapter 10.

33. A. M. Goichon, "L'Unité de la pensée avicenienne," *Archives Internationales d'Histoire des Sciences* 20–21 (1952) pp. 290ff.

34. See also Nasr, *Islamic Cosmological Doctrines*, pp. 198ff; and Lenn Goodman, *Avicenna* (London: Routledge, 1992) pp. 49ff.

35. This scheme is described in the *Shifāʾ* of Ibn Sīnā. See *Avicenne, La Métaphysique du Shifāʾ*, vol. 2, trans. G. C. Anawati pp. 137ff. It is summarized in Nasr, *Islamic Cosmological Doctrines*, pp. 202ff.; see also A. Davidson, "Alfarabi and Avicenna on the Active Intellect," *Viator: Medieval and Renaissance Studies* 3 (1972) pp. 134–54.

36. See Fazlur Rahman, *Prophecy in Islam* (London: Allen and Unwin, 1958).

37. Abūʾl Barakāt's physical theories are especially important. See Shlomo Pines, *Studies in Abūʾl-Barakāt al-Baghdādī* (Leiden: Brill, 1979).

38. See al-Bīrūnī, *Epître de Beruni contenant le repértoire des ouvrages de Muḥammad Zakariya al-Razi*, trans. and ed. Paul Kraus (Paris: Maisonneuve, 1936).

39. For a list of Rāzī's works see Mehdi Mohaghegh, *Fīlsūf-i Rayy* (Tehran: Society for Protection of National Monuments, 1970), pp. 53ff. The most extensive study of the scientific thought and philosophy of Rāzī interpreted mostly from a "positivistic" point of view is Parwiz Adhkā'ī, *Ḥakīm Rāzī*.

40. See Shlomo Pines, "al-Rāzī," in the *Dictionary of Scientific Biography*, vol. 11, pp. 34ff; and Syed Nomanul Haq, "The Indian and Persian Background," in Nasr and Leaman, *History of Islamic Philosophy*, p. 58.

41. See Lenn Goodman, "al-Rāzī," in Nasr and Leaman, op. cit., p. 203. This essay is one of the more recent in English to contain a fine summary of Rāzī's philosophical views.

42. See Nasr, *Islamic Life and Thought*, "From the Alchemy of Jābir to the Chemistry of Rāzī," pp. 120–23.

43. See *al-Asʾilah waʾl-ajwibah* already mentioned. See also "Ibn Sīnā: Al-Bīrūnī Correspondence," trans. Rafik Berjak and Muzaffar Iqbal, *Islamic Science*, vol. 1, no. 1, June 2003, pp. 91–98; vol. 1, no. 2, December 2003, pp. 253–60.

44. See our *Introduction to Islamic Cosmological Doctrines*, pp. 107ff. where his philosophical views as far as they concern the nature of the cosmos is concerned is studied on the basis of not only the two works cited here but also passages in his other books.

45. Persian was an important language for this whole philosophical tradition. Even the *Umm al-kitāb* has reached us in an archaic Persian transla-

tion rather than Arabic; see *Ummu'l-Kitāb*, ed. and trans. P. Filippani Ronconi (Naples: Istituto Universitario Orientale, 1966).

46. On the history and major ideas of this tradition see Corbin et al., *History of Islamic Philosophy*, pp. 74ff.; and his *Cyclical Time and Ismā'īlī Gnosis*, trans. Ralph Mannheim and James Morris (London: KPI, 1983). See also Azim Nanji, "Ismā'īlī Philosophy" in Nasr and Leaman, *History of Islamic Philosophy*, pp. 144-54, where the main tenets of Ismā'īlī philosophy are summarized.

47. See S. H. Nasr, *Islamic Life and Thought*, "Hermes and Hermetic Writings in the Islamic World," pp. 102ff.

48. On Islamic alchemy and its philosophy, see H. Corbin, *L'Alchimie comme art hiératique*, P. Lory (ed.) (Paris: Edition L'Herne, 1986); Corbin, *Le Livre des sept statues*, ed. Pierre Lory (Paris: L'Herne, 2003); P. Lory, *Alchimie et mystique en terre d'Islam* (Paris: Verdier, 1989); P. Kraus, *Jābir ibn Ḥayyān* (Paris: Les Belles Lettres, 1986); and Nasr, *Science and Civilization in Islam*, pp. 242–82.

49. See Nasr, *Islamic Cosmological Doctrines*, part 1, pp. 25–104; see also Ian R. Netton, *Muslim Neoplatonists: An Introduction to the Thought of the Brethren of Purity* (London: Allen and Unwin, 1982).

50. Corbin et al., *History of Islamic Philosophy*, pp. 79–80; see also Wilfred Madelung, "Aspects of Ismā'īlī Theology: The Prophetic Chain and the God beyond Being," in *Ismā'īlī Contributions to Islamic Culture*, S. H. Nasr (ed.) (Tehran: Imperial Iranian Academy of Philosophy, 1977) pp. 51–65.

51. It is important to remember that many important Ismā'īlī philosophical and theosophical treatises were kept hidden from the public at large and did not become publicly available until recently.

52. See Miguel Asín Palacios, *Ibn Masarra y su escuela: Origenes de la filosofía hispano-musulmana* (Madrid: Imprenta Iberica, 1914); translated somewhat imperfectly by Elmer Douglas and Howard Yoder as *The Mystical Philosophy of Ibn Masarra and His Followers* (Leiden: Brill, 1978). On Islamic philosophy in Spain, see Miguel Cruz Hernández, *Historia del pensamiento en el mundo islámico*, vol. 2, pp. 9–270; see also Titus Burckhardt, *Moorish Culture in Spain*, trans. Alisa Jaffe (London: Allen and Unwin, 1972) chap. 9, pp. 129–37, which treats the spiritual significance of Islamic philosophy in Spain. See also Lenn Goodman, "Ibn Masarrah," in Nasr and Leaman, *History*, pp. 277–93. A number of scholars such as Samuel M. Stern have criticized and refuted Asín's views concerning "Empedoclean cosmology," which they relate more to al-'Āmirī's description of Empedocles without their views altering appreciably the description of the thought of Ibn Masarrah as reconstructed by Asín and others who have followed him.

53. The significance of these ideas in relation to prophecy becomes clear in light of Peter Kingsley's study of Empedocles mentioned at the beginning of this book.

54. There are numerous works devoted to Ibn Ḥazm, especially in Spanish. See M. Asín Palacios, *El cordobes Abenhazam: Primer historiador de las ideas religiosas* (Madrid: Imprentas de Estanislao Maestre, 1924); idem, *Abenhazam de Cordoba y su historia critica de las ideas religiosas,* 6 vols. (Madrid: Ediciones Turner, 1984). As for his *Ṭawq al-ḥimāmah* on Platonic love, it is the most translated work of Ibn Ḥazm. See *The Ring of the Dove: A Treatise on the Art of Arab Love,* trans. Arthur J. Arberry (London: Luzac, 1953).

55. See Miguel Asín Palacios, *El regimen del solitario* (Madrid and Granada: Imprentas de la Escuela de Estudios Arabes de Granada y Fransisco Roman Camacho, 1946). See also Daniel M. Dunlop, "Ibn Bājjah's *Tadbiru'l Mutawaḥḥid* (*Rule of the Solitary*)," *Journal of the Royal Asiatic Society* 4C (1945) 61–81. See also Leann Goodman, "Ibn Bājjah," in Nasr and Leaman, *History,* pp. 294–312.

56. This is an interpretation given to the text by many scholars in the West over the centuries. For the latest example of this interpretation, see Sami S. Hawi, *Islamic Naturalism and Mysticism: A Philosophic Study of Ibn Ṭufayl's Ḥayy bin Yaqẓān* (Leiden: Brill, 1974). See also *Ibn Ṭufayl, Ḥayy ibn Yaqẓān,* trans. Lenn E. Goodman (Los Angeles: University of California Press, 1983).

57. In his *Averroes et l'averroisme* (Paris: Levy Frères, 1861), Renan makes of Averroes a "freethinker" opposed to the submission of reason to faith and the ancestor of modern rationalism and skepticism. There is an extensive European literature on Averroes; see, e.g., O. Leaman, *Averroes and His Philosophy* (London: Oxford University Press, 1988).

58. The Latin translations followed Hebrew ones and go back to the seventh/thirteenth century and the efforts of Michael Scot. The Latin texts of Averroes's commentaries on Aristotle are being published by the Mediaeval Academy of America in the series *Corpus phiiosophorum medii aevi corpus commentariorum Averrois in Aristotelem.*

59. See George Hourani, *Averroes: On the Harmony Religion and Philosophy* (London: Luzac, 1961). This contains the translation of the *Faṣl al-maqāl,* Ibn Rushd's most important treatise on the relation between philosophy and religion. For a later translation and commentary see Charles Butterworth, *The Book of the Decisive Treatise Determining the Connection between the Law and Wisdom* (Provo, Utah: Brigham Young University Press, 2001).

60. See Simon van den Bergh, *Averroes' Tahāfut al-tahāfut* (*The Incoherence of the Incoherence*) 2 vols. (Oxford: Oxford University Press, 1954).

61. This seems unlikely, because Ibn Sab'īn was a pious Muslim who followed the *Sharī'ah,* which forbids suicide. All of these views are discussed by Abū'l-Wafā' al-Taftāzānī in his *Ibn Sab'īn wa falsafatuhu'ṣ-ṣūfiyyah* (Beirut: Dār al-Kutub al-Lubnānī, 1973). This is by far the most thorough and detailed study of Ibn Sab'īn, who has not been studied extensively in the West. For references in Western languages, see Corbin et al., *History of Islamic Philosophy,*

2:366–68; Cruz Hernández, *Historia*, 2:249–57; and Taftāzānī and Leaman, "Ibn Sab'īn," in Nasr and Leaman, *History*, pp. 346–49.

62. See "The Hidden Sciences in Islam," by Jean Canteins in *Islamic Spirituality*, S. H. Nasr (ed.), chapter 23, pp. 447–68.

63. This is one of the few works of Ibn Sab'īn to have been studied and translated into a Western language. See E. Lator, "Ibn Sab'īn de Murcia y su 'Budd al-'Ārif'," *Revista al-Andalus* 9/2 (1944) pp. 371–417.

64. Cruz Hernández refers to the school represented by Ibn Sab'īn as "*gnosofia*" (*Historia*, 2:249). This school, sometimes referred to as the Sab'iyyah, was represented after Ibn Sab'īn by the great Sufi poet al-Shustarī, who was one of his students.

65. On Ibn Khaldūn's philosophy of history see Muhsin Mahdi, *Ibn Khaldūn's Philosophy of History* (Chicago: Chicago University Press, 1974).

66. See Abderramane Lakhsassi, "Ibn Khaldūn," in Nasr and Leaman, *History*, pp. 356–61.

67. See S. H. Nasr, *Science and Civilization in Islam*, pp. 62–64; S. Johnson, "The 'Umranic Nature of Ibn Khaldūn's Classification of the Sciences," *Muslim World*, vol. 81, 1991, pp. 254-61.

68. This village in the Zagros Mountains south of Zanjan is also the original home of the Suhrawardī family of Sufis, to whom Shaykh al-ishrāq was not, however, related. On Suhrawardī, his life, and works, see Corbin, *En Islam iranien*, vol. 2; Nasr, *Three Muslim Sages*, chapter 2; idem, "Suhrawardī," in *The Islamic Intellectual Tradition in Persia*, pp. 125–83; Corbin et al., *History of Islamic Philosophy*, pp. 205–20; Mehdi Aminrazavi, *Suhrawardī and the School of Illumination* (London: Curzon, 1997); Hossein Ziai, "Shihāb al-Dīn Suhrawardī: Founder of the Illuminationist School," in Nasr and Leaman, *History* . . ., pp. 434-64; and Ibrāhīm Dīnānī, *Shu'ā'-i andīshah wa shuhūd-i falsafa-yi Suhrawardī*.

69. See the translations of this major opus as *Le Livre de la sagesse orientale*, trans. H. Corbin; C. Jambet (ed.); and *The Philosophy of Illumination*, trans. J. Walbridge and H. Ziai.

70. The recitals of Suhrawardī have been translated into elegant French by H. Corbin as *L'Archange empourprée* (Paris: Fayard, 1976); they have also been translated but less successfully into English by W. Thackston as *The Mystical and Visionary Treatises of Suhrawardī* (London: Octagon Press, 1982).

71. See Suhrawardī, *Opera Metaphysica et Mystica*, vol. 1, ed. H. Corbin (Tehran and Paris: A. Maisonneuve, 1976) p. 503; see also John Walbridge, *The Leaven of the Ancients* (Albany, NY: The State University of New York Press, 2000) whose understanding of this subject is quite different from ours.

72. For the later tradition of the school of Illumination see Hossein Ziai, "The Illuminationist Tradition," in Nasr and Leaman, *History . . .*, pp. 465-96.

73. For an explanation of the complex angelology of Suhrawardī, which is discussed in many of his works, especially the *Ḥikmat al-ishrāq*, see Corbin, *Les Motifs zoroastriens dans la philosophie de Sohrawardī* (Tehran: Société d'Iranologie, 1946); see also Nasr, "Suhrawardī," in *The Islamic Intellectual Tradition in Persia*, pp. 138-140.

74. We shall turn more fully to this subject in chapter 10.

75. See chapters 11 and 12.

Chapter 9. The Post-Scientist 'Umar Khayyām as Philosopher

1. Thanks of course to the free translation of a number of quatrains by Edward Fitzgerald that created something of a cult in Victorian England, the like of which has not been seen in modern times. There is a whole library of works on Khayyām's quatrains written in various European languages.

2. On Khayyām as mathematician see Dirk Struik, "Omar Khayyām, Mathematician," *The Mathematics Teacher*, vol. 51, April 1958, pp. 280–85; Adolf P. Youschkevitch, *Les Mathématiques arabes* (8–15 siécles), trans. M. Cazevane and K. Jaouiche (Paris: Vrin, 1976); and especially the recent comprehensive work of Roshdi Rashed and Bijan Vahabzadeh, *Al-Khayyām mathématicien* (Paris: Librairie Scientifique et Technique Albert Blanchard, 1999).

3. On Khayyām's treatment of the fifth postulate of Euclid, see Ali Amir-Moez's partial translation of Khayyām's treatise, "Discussion of Difficulties in Euclid," *Scripta Mathematica*, vol. 24, 1959, pp. 275–303; and Ja'far A. Chavooshi, *Ḥakīm 'Umar Khayyām, Nayshābūrī* (Tehran: Iranian Academy of Philosophy, 1979).

4. We have devoted a short study to his philosophical ideas in our *Islamic Intellectual Tradition in Persia*, "'Umār Khayyām: Philosopher-Poet-Scientist," pp. 175–77. On Khayyām's philosophical ideas and influence in the West see the extensive work of Mehdi Aminrazavi, *The Wine of Wisdom* (Oxford: One world, 2005) which came out after our book had gone to press.

5. In his *al-Zājir liʾl-ṣighār 'an mu'āra al-kibār*, quoted in Badī' al-Zamān Forouzanfar, "Qadīmītarīn iṭṭilā' az rindagī-yi Khayyām," *Nashriyya-yi Dānishkada-yi adabiyyāt-i Tabrīz* (1327 [A.H. solar]), pp. 1ff.; quoted by Sayyid Muḥammad Riḍā Jalālī Nāʾīnī, "Ḥakīm 'Umar ibn Ibrāhīm Khayyām-i Nayshābūrī," in *Farhang* (Tehran), vol. 12, no. 29–32, Spring 2000, p. 4.

6. In his *Kharīdat al-qasr*, 'Imād al-Dīn Kātib Iṣfahānī says about Khayyām, "There was no one like him in his own time and he had no peer in the science of astronomy and philosophy." Quoted by Raḥīm Riḍā-zādah Malik, *Dānish-nāma-yi Khayyāmī* (Tehran: Maḥārat, 1327 [A.H. solar]), p. 19.

7. See for example, Nā'īnī, op. cit., pp. 2–3.

8. See Hedayat, *Tarānihā-yi Khayyām* (Tehran: Rawshanāʾī, 1313 [A.H. solar]).

9. See Muhammad Mahdī Fūlādwand, *Khayyām-shināsī* (Tehran: Bīnā, 1347 [A.H. solar]). See also his "Sahm-i Hedayat dar shināsānīdan-i Khayyām," *Farhang,* op. cit., pp. 33ff. We agree fully with Fūlādwand's assessment of how Hedayat, like so many modernized Iranians after him, was reading his own inner thoughts and states into the Khayyām he had created in his mind.

10. In the 1960s I had the honor of studying the *Asfār* of Mullā Ṣadrā for several years with the late Sayyid Abūʾl Ḥasan Raf ī'ī Qazwīnī in both Tehran and Qazwin. This venerable master was a grand ayatollah, a *marja'-i taqlīd* (a source of emulation in matters of the *Sharī'ah),* one of the greatest masters of the school of Mullā Ṣadrā in his day, and an authority in traditional mathematics. His countenance was always serious, and of course he exuded religious authority by his very presence. One day while a group of us consisting of Badī' al-Zamān Forouzanfar, Sayyid Jalāl al-Dīn Āshtiyānī, and others were waiting in his study in Qazwin for the master to come and begin the lesson, I stood up and walked to a shelf of books along the wall of the room to browse. I found one of the works of Mullā Sadrā inside which there were small pieces of paper with quatrains written by Ayatollah Qazwīnī very much in the spirit of some of Khayyām's quatrains. A few minutes later the master came in and became angry that I had found the poems. He said these are just doodlings not meant to be read by us. Suddenly I thought of how the Khayyāmian quatrains that are authentic must be related to the thought of Khayyām and also to the rest of his works.

11. On Khayyām's commentary on the *Difficulties in the Postulates of Euclid's Elements,* see in addition to works cited in note 3, Nasser Kanānī, "Omar Khayyām and the Parallel Postulate," in *Farhang,* op. cit., pp. 107ff; and Jalāl Humāʾī, *Khayyāmī-nāmah* (Tehran: Anjuman-i Millī, 1346 [A.H. solar]), pp. 9ff., which contains a detailed discussion of Khayyām's views in relation to those who came before him and also in light of the principles of Islamic philosophy and logic. See also Osman Bakar, "'Umar Khayyām's Criticism of Euclid's Theory of Parallels," in his *The History and Philosophy of Islamic Science* (Cambridge: Islamic Texts Society, 1999), pp. 157–72.

12. "We find here [in reference to Khayyām's proof of the parallel postulate], apparently for the first time in history, the three situations later known as the hypothesis of the acute angle (case a), that of the obtuse angle (case b) and that of the right angle (case c). These three situations are now known to lead respectively to the non-Euclidean geometry of Bolai-Lobacevskii, and to that of Rieman." Dirk J. Struik, "Omar Khayyām, Mathematician."

13. See Wolfgang Smith, *The Quantum Enigma,* Peru (Ill.), Sherwood Snyder, 2000; see also S. H. Nasr, "Perennial Ontology and Quantum Mechanics," *Sophia,* vol. 3, no. 1, Summer 1997, pp. 135–59.

14. The complete text of Khayyām's philosophical works, as far as they are known today, is to be found in R. Raḥīmzādah Malik, *Dānish-nāma-yi Khayyāmī*. See also Swami Govinda Tirtha, *The Nectar of Grace* (Allahabad: Ketabistan, 1941); Muḥammad 'Abbāsī, *Kulliyyāt-i āthār-i pārsī-yi 'Umar Khayyām* (Tehran: Kitāb-furāshī-yi Bārānī, 1338 [A.H. solar]); Sayyid Sulaymān Nadwī (ed.), *Khayyām-Awr us ke savānih va taṣānīf* (A'zamgarh: Dār al-Muṣannifīn, 1979); and Boris A. Rosenfeld and Adolf P. Youschkevitch, *Omar Khaiiam* (Moscow: Nauka, 1965).

15. For the English translation of this text see K.A.M. Akhtar, "A Tract of Avicenna," *Islamic Culture*, vol. 9, 1935, pp. 221–22. For the original text see Raḥīmzādah Malik, op. cit., pp. 305ff. Throughout this chapter, I will mention only the source of the original text as contained in this work and that of Swami Govinda Tirtha. Raḥīmzādah Malik has cited other printings of treatises of Khayyām in his introduction to each work in question.

16. See Raḥīmzādah Malik, op. cit., pp. 321ff. See Swami Govinda Tirtha, op. cit., pp. 46 and 83–99 which contain both the Arabic text of this treatise and an English translation by Abdul-Quddūs.

17. The fact that an eminent religious authority far away from Khurasan should write to Khayyām on such matters is itself proof of Khayyām's status as an Islamic thinker in the eyes of his contemporaries. Such a request would be unconceivable if Khayyām had been seen at that time as the skeptical and hedonistic figure that many modern people envisage him to be.

18. For the summary of Ibn Sīnā's views on these matters, see S. H. Nasr, *An Introduction to Islamic Cosmological Doctrines*, pp. 197ff.

19. See Sayyid Sulaymān Nadwī, *Aw rus ke savāniḥ va taṣānīf*. For the text of the treatise see Raḥīmzādah Malik, op. cit., pp. 343ff. See also Swami Govinda Tirtha, op. cit., pp. 99–110 for both the Arabic text and an English translation by M.W. Rahman.

20. See Raḥīmzādah Malik, op. cit., pp. 369 ff.

21. See Raḥīmzādah Malik, op. cit., pp. 377ff. See also Arthur Christensen, "Un traité de métaphysique de 'Omar Khayyām," *Le Monde Oriental*, vol. 1, no. 1, 1906, pp. 1–16. The Persian text and an English translation of it is to be found in Swami Govinda Tirtha, op. cit., pp. 47–48 and 117–29.

22. Op. cit., pp 389–90. See Nasr, *Science and Civilization in Islam*, pp. 33–34. See also pp. 52–53 of the same work; also F. Schuon, *Spiritual Perspectives and Human Facts*, pp. 76–77.

23. See Raḥīmzādah Malik, op. cit., pp. 395 ff. See also Swami Govinda Tirtha, *The Nectar of Grace*, pp. 110–116.

24. See S. H. Nasr, *Ṣadr al-Dīn Shīrāzī and His Transcendent Theosophy*, pp. 109ff.

25. See Raḥīmzādah Malik, op. cit., pp. 411ff.

26. The translation is ours.

27. Modified translation of the *Rubā'iyāt of Omar Khayyām*, trans. and annotated by Ahmad Saidi (Berkeley: Asian Humanities Press, 1991), no. 59, p. 116.

28. Saidi, op. cit., no. 60, p. 117. Such verses must be read in conjunction with those that affirm in no uncertain terms Khayyām's certitude concerning the knowledge of God and that He is ultimately the only Reality. For example,

> His is, and not but Him exists, I know,
> This truth is what creation's book will show,
> When heart acquired perception with His Light,
> Atheistic darkness changed to faithly glow.

Swami Govinda Tirtha, *The Nectar of Grace*, p. 1

Khayyām also speaks of the divine grace that makes such a knowledge possible. In one of his rare Arabic poems, quoted by Shams al-Dīn Shahrazūrī in his *Nuzhat al-arwāḥ*, Khayyām sings,

> I soar above both Worlds to Highest Realm
> With lofty courage and with sober thoughts.
> The Guiding Light of Wisdom dawns in me
> In the Darkness, and Delusion is dispelled.
> The foe may try to extinguish the Light,
> But God maintains it by his Grace Divine.

Swami Govinda Tirtha, op. cit., p. 131,
with some modification

29. This theme of the relativity of all human knowledge when measured with the yardstick of Divine Knowledge is a recurrent theme in many of these quatrains, for example,

> Of science naught remained I did not know,
> Of secrets, scarcely any, high or low,
> All day and night for three scores and twelve years,
> I pondered just to learn that naught I know.

Saidi, op. cit., no. 68, p. 125

30. The translation is our own highly modified version of Saidi, op. cit., no. 63, p. 120.

31. Modified translation of Saidi, op. cit., no. 64, p. 121.

32. See Henry Corbin, *Alone with the Alone—Creative Imagination in the Sufism of Ibn 'Arabī*; and E. Zolla, *The Uses of Imagination and the Decline of the West* (Ipswich: Golgonooza, 1978).

33. Highly modified translation of Saidi, op. cit., no. 65, p. 122.

34. Modified translation of Saidi, op. cit., no. 70, p. 127.

35. "Being Itself, which is none other than the Personal God, is in its turn surpassed by the Impersonal or Supra-Personal Divinity, Non-Being, of which the Personal God or Being is simply the first determination from which flow all the secondary determinations that make up cosmic Existence. Exoterism cannot, however, admit either this unreality of the world or the exclusive reality of the Divine Principle, or above all, the transcendence of Non-Being relative to Being." Frithjof Schuon, *The Transcendent Unity of Religions*, trans. Peter Townsend (London: Theosophical Publishing House, 1993), p. 38.

36. On this issue see S. H. Nasr, *Knowledge and the Sacred*, chapter 4, pp. 130ff.

37. The thirteenth/nineteenth-century Persian philosopher and saint Ḥājjī Mullā Hādī Sabziwārī in fact refers to eschatology as "the science of Tomorrow" (*fardā-shināsī*).

38. Some of these titles include *al-imām* (the leader), *ḥakīm al-dunyā* (the philosopher of the world), *ḥujjat al-ḥaqq* (proof of the Truth), *al-shaykh al-ajall* (the exalted master), and *faylasūf al-waqt* (the philosopher of the time). See Raḥīmzādah Malik, op. cit., pp. 32–33.

39. This work has been translated as *Contemplation and Action*, by Sayyed Jalal Badakhchani (London: Tauris, 1999).

40. See Aminrazavi, op. cit., pp. 283ff.

Chapter 10. Philosophy in Azarbaijan and the School of Shiraz

1. See Francis Robinson, *The 'Ulama of Farangi Mahall and Islamic Culture in South Asia* (Delhi: Permanent Black, 2001).

2. On the School of Azarbaijan, see Nasrollah Pourjavady, "Jāygāh-i Ādharbāyjān dar tārīkh-i falsafah," *Nashr-i Dānish*, vol. 19, no. 2, 1381 (A.H. solar), pp. 10–14.

3. As we discussed earlier in this book, scholars now speak readily of the School of Isfahan because of the usage of this term and research carried out under the name of the school by Henry Corbin and myself from over forty years ago.

4. See Nasrollah Pourjavady (ed.), *Majmū'a-yi Marāghah* (Tehran: Markaz-i Nashr-i Dānishgāhī, [1380 A.H. solar]).

5. See Aydin Sayili, *The Observatory in Islam* (Ankara: Türk Tarih Kumuru Basimevi, 1960), chapter 6, pp. 187–223; and S. H. Nasr, *Islamic Science: An Illustrated Study* (Chicago: Kazi [distributor], 2000), chapter 6, pp. 91ff.

6. See S. H. Nasr, *The Islamic Intellectual Tradition in Persia*, chapter 18, pp. 207–15; see also John Cooper, "From al-Ṭūsī to the School of Isfahan," in Nasr and Leaman (eds.), *History of Islamic Philosophy*, pp. 585ff.

7. See for example, Ṭūsī, *La Convocation d'Alamut: Rawdat al-taslīm*, trans. Christian Jambet (Paris: Verdier/UNESCO, 1996); Ṭūsī , *Contemplation and Action*, ed. and trans. Sayyed Jalal Badakhshani (London: Taurus, 1999); Nasrollah Pourjavady and Živa Vesel (eds.), *Naṣīr al-Dīn Ṭūsī: Philosophe et savant du XIIIe siècle* (Tehran: Institut Français de Recherche en Iran, 2000). For the climate of thought and intellectual background of Ṭūsī see Hamid Dabashi, "Khwājah Naṣīr al-Dīn al-Ṭūsī: The Philosopher/Vizier and the Intellectual Climate of his Times," in Nasr and Leaman (eds.), *History of Islamic Philosophy*, chapter 32, pp. 527–85; and Bakhtyar Husain Siddiqi, "Naṣīr al-Dīn Ṭūsī," in M. M. Sharif (ed.), *A History of Muslim Philosophy*, vol. 1, chapter 29, pp. 564ff.

Several philosophical treatises of Ṭūsī have been collected and translated by Parviz Morewedge as *The Metaphysics of Ṭūsī* (New York: Society for the Study of Islamic Philosophy and Science, 1991).

8. See Nasr, *The Islamic Intellectual Tradition in Persia*, chapter 19, pp. 216–27; also John Walbridge, *The Science of Mystic Lights: Quṭb al-Dīn Shīrāzī and the Illuminationist Tradition in Islamic Philosophy* (Cambridge: Harvard University Press, 1992). See also Sabine Schmidtke, "The Doctrine of the Transmigration of Souls according to Shihāb al-Dīn Suhrawardī and His Followers," *Studia Iranica*, vol. 28, 1999, pp. 237–54. It is important to note that although Ṭūsī also knew of Suhrawardī, it was Quṭb al-Dīn who for the first time sought to synthesize different elements of Ibn Sīnā and Suhrawardī in his own philosophical works, especially in his vast philosophical encyclopedia *Durrat al-tāj* (The Jewel of the Crown). One also needs to mention another of the students of Ṭūsī, 'Allāhmah al-Ḥillī, who was a major Shi'ite theologian and jurist but was also a philosopher who wrote a commentary on Suhrawardī's *Talwīḥāt* and was also familiar with the teachings of Ibn 'Arabī.

9. On Kāshānī, see William Chittick, *An Introduction to Islamic Philosophy* (New York: Oxford University Press, 2001), which is completely devoted to him with numerous translations of his works. See also Nasr, *The Islamic Tradition in Persia*, chapter 17, pp. 189–206.

10. Edited by Mohammad Taghi Daneshpazhuh (Tehran: Anjuman-i Falsafa-yi Īrān, 1358 [A.H. solar]).

11. See Hossein Ziai's introduction to his edition of Shahrazūrī, *Commentary on the Philosophy of Illumination* (Tehran: Institute for Humanities and Cultural Studies, 2001), pp. xivff. In his Persian introduction, pp. 55ff., Ziai analyzes the contents of Shahrazūrī's major philosophical encyclopedia, *al-Shajarat al-ilāhiyyah*, which influenced many later Islamic philosophers, such as Mīr Dāmād and Mullā Ṣadrā. This text was published in its entirety for the first time, in Tehran, edited by Ḥ. Najafī, only recently. See also Muḥammad Najīb Kūrkūn's edition of the work (Istanbul: Elif Yayinlari, 2004).

12. See Nasr, *The Islamic Intellectual Tradition in Persia*, chapter 20, pp. 228–36.

13. This work has been published in facsimile form under the direction of Nasrollah Pourjavadi (Tehran: Iran University Press, 2003) with the title *Safīna-yi Tabrīz*. On the content of this very important discovery, see 'Abd al-Ḥusayn Ḥāʾirī, "Safīna-yi Tabrīz, kitābkhāna-yi bayn al-daftayn," *Nāma-yi bahāristān*, vol. 2, no. 4, Autumn-Winter 1380/1422, pp. 41–64.

14. When during the 1960s I edited the complete Persian philosophical works of Suhrawardī, which appeared as the third volume of his *Opera Metaphysica et Mystica*, the first two volumes having been devoted to various Arabic works of Suhrawardī edited by Henry Corbin, this important manuscript was not known to me or in fact to the scholarly circles in Persia in general. One hopes that in a future edition of the Persian works, the *Safīnah* will be taken into full consideration.

15. See Bilal Kuşpinar, *Ismā'īl Anḳaravī on the Illuminative Philosophy* (Kuala Lumpur: International Institute of Islamic Thought and Civilization, 1996).

16. See S. H. Nasr, *The Transcendent Theosophy of Ṣadr al-Dīn Shirāzī*, pp. 37–38.

17. The use of this term and the study of some of the figures of this school can be found in the writings of Qāsim Kākāʾī, a contemporary Shīrāzī philosopher, especially in a series of articles written by him in *Kheradnameh-e Sadra*, from 1995 to 1997. Already in *The History of Islamic Philosophy* by Corbin (with the collaboration of S. H. Nasr and O. Yahya), pp. 335–37, Corbin refers to the Dashtakī family as constituting the "School of Shiraz," but he devotes little attention to the writings of this school. As for his *En Islam iranien*, Corbin limits his discussion of the School of Shiraz in this major work to a single footnote in vol. 2, pp. 352–53. I have used this term before in the introduction to Leonard Lewisohn and David Morgan (eds.), *The Heritage of Sufism*, vol. 3 (Oxford: One World, 1999), pp. 5–6.

18. The figures of the School of Shiraz either hailed from the city of Shiraz itself and towns nearby, such as Bayḍaʾ, Ij, Kazirun, Lar, Fasa, Dawan, and Khafr, or they had come from other regions to study in Shiraz and its adjacent areas. See Kākāʾī, "Shiraz—mahd-i 'irfān—zādgāh-i Mullā Ṣadrā," *Kheradnameh-e Sadra*, vol. 1, no. 2, serial 2, August 1995, p. 63.

19. On his life and works see Q. Kākāʾī, "Āshnāʾī bā maktab-i Shīrāz, 1—Mīr Ṣadr al-Dīn Dashtakī (Sayyid-i Sanad)," *Kheradnameh-e Sadra*, vol. 1, no. 3, serial 3, March 1996, pp. 82–89. See also the introduction of Parwīn Bahārzādah to her edition of Ghiyāth al-Dīn Manṣūr Dashtakī, *Tuḥfat al-fatā fī tafsīr sūrah hal atā* (Tehran: Markaz-i Nashr-i Mīrāth-i Maktūb, 1381 [A.H. solar]), pp. 30ff.

20. This chain is mentioned by Ghiyāth al-Dīn Manṣūr Dashtakī in his *Kashf al-ḥaqā'iq al-muḥammadiyyah,* quoted by Q. Kākā'ī in his "Shiraz—mahd-i 'irfān," op. cit., p. 65.

21. Earlier Western scholars of Islamic thought, and even some Western-educated Muslim scholars, have often written that such later figures in the history of Islamic philosophy and theology were mere imitators because they simply wrote glosses upon earlier works. Of course these scholars have not usually bothered to read such glosses; otherwise they would not have made such a statement. One needs only to point to the glosses of Mullā Ṣadrā upon the *Ḥikmat al-ishrāq* of Suhrawardī, which is one of the most important works of Mullā Ṣadrā, to realize how creative and "original" in fact many glosses are in the later Islamic intellectual tradition. On this point see T. Izutsu's English introduction to Mīrzā Mahdī Āshtiyānī, *Commentary on Sabzawārī's Sharḥ-i Manẓūmah,* 'Abd al-Jawâd Falâṭûrî, and Mehdi Mohaghegh (eds.) (Tehran: Tehran University Press, 1973), pp. 1–5.

22. Concerning the list of books of Ṣadr al-Dīn Dashtakī, including fourteen mentioned by his son Ghiyāth al-Dīn and also including others not found on his list, see Kākā'ī, "Āshnā'ī bā maktab-i Shīrāz," pp. 85–86; also Bahārzādah, op. cit., pp. 47–50.

23. This paradox is known in Arabic as *shubhah jadhr al-aṣamm.* For the text of Dashtakī on this subject see Aḥmad Farāmarz Qarāmalikī (ed.), "Mīr Ṣadr al-Dīn Dashtakī, *Risālah fī shubhah jadhr al-aṣamm," Kheradnameh-e Sadra,* vol. 92, no. 5–6, Autumn–Winter 1997, pp. 74–82. Dashtakī refers in this work to earlier Islamic thinkers such as Ṭūsī and Ibn Kammūnah and especially Dawānī, who had dealt with this logical paradox.

24. This is to be seen for example in the first part of the *Asfār* on mental existence. *Al-Asfār al-arba'ah, al-juz' al-awwal,* ed. Sayyid Muḥammad Ḥusayn Ṭabāṭabā'ī (Qum: Dār al-Ma'ārif al-Islāmiyyah, 1378 [A. H. solar]), pp. 314ff.

25. Ibid., pp. 321–22.

26. On the influence of Dawānī in the Ottoman world, see Sherif Mardin, "The Mind of the Turkish Reformer 1700–1900," in *The Western Humanities Review,* vol. 14, 1960, pp. 418ff.

27. This work, written in Persian, was so popular among Indian Muslims that it became one of the first books to be translated into English by the British, who were then ruling India. See W. F. Thompson (trans.), *Practical Philosophy of the Muhammadan People* (London: Oriental Translation Fund, 1839). Dawānī also wrote a number of other works on *falsafah* and *kalām* in Persian, most of which were published in the journal *Taḥqīq dar mabda'-i āfarīnish* in the 1970s by I. Wā'iẓ Jawādī. For a summary of Dawānī's life and thought, see Mahdī Dihbāshī, "Taḥlīlī az āndishahā-yi falsafī wa kalāmī-yi Jalāl al-Dīn Muḥaqqiq-i Dawānī," *Kheradnameh-e Sadra,* vol. 1, no. 3, March 1996,

pp. 41–51; and Bakhtiyar Ḥusain Siddiqi, "Jalāl al-Dīn Dawwāni," M. M. Sharif (ed.), *A History of Muslim Philosophy*, vol. 2, pp. 883-88.

28. Translated by Constantine Zurayk (Beirut: American University of Beirut Press, 1966). For Ibn Miskawayh see S. H. Nasr and M. Aminrazavi (eds.), *An Anthology of Philosophy in Persia* (New York: Oxford University Press, 1999), pp. 275ff.; Oliver Leaman, "Ibn Miskawayh" in Nasr and Leaman (eds.), pp. 252–57; Mohammad Arkoun, *Contribution à l'étude de l'humanisme arabe au IVe/Xe siècle: Miskawayh (320/325–421)=(932/936–1030)* (Paris: Vrin, 1970); and Majid Fakhry, *Ethical Theories in Islam* (Leiden: Brill, 1991).

29. Translated by G. M. Wickens as *The Nasirean Ethics* (London: Allen and Unwin, 1964).

30. On his political views see Erwin I. J. Rosenthal, *Political Thought in Medieval Islam* (Cambridge: Cambridge University Press, 1958), pp. 210–23.

31. See Muḥammad 'Abdul Ḥaq (ed.), *Shawākil al-hūr fī sharḥ hayākil al-nūr* (Madras: Government Oriental Manuscripts Library, 1953). On the life and works of Dawānī, see also 'Alī Dawānī, *Sharḥ-i zindigī-yi Jalāl al-Dīn Dawānī* (Qom: Ḥikmat, 1375 [A.H.]). Dawānī also composed poetry from time to time. His Persian poems have been assembled by Ḥusayn 'Alī Maḥfūẓ in *Shi'r-i fārsī-yi Jalāl al-Dīn Dawānī* (Baghdad: Dār al-Ma'ārif, 1973).

32. See Qāsim Kākāʾī, "Shaykh-i ishrāq wa maktab-i Shīrāz," in *Majmū'a-yi maqālāt: International Congress on Suhrawardī*, Zanjan, 2001 (Zanjan: International Congress on Suhrawardī, vol. 3, 2001), pp. 190ff.

33. On his life see Q. Kākāʾī, "Āshnāʾī bā maktab-i Shīrāz—3. Mīr Ghiyāth al-Dīn Dashtakī Shīrāzī," *Kheradnameh-e Sadra*, vol. 2, no. 5–6, Autumn–Winter 1997, pp. 83ff. See also 'Alī Aṣghar Ḥalabī, *Tārīkh-i falāsafa-yi īrānī* (Tehran: Zawwar, 1361 [A.H. solar]), pp. 498–99, where he gives the title of eighteen works attributed to him, although this list is incomplete. Two treatises of Mīr Ghiyāth al-Dīn have been edited critically by 'Alī Awjabī (ed.) in *Ganjīna-yi bahāristān: Ḥikmat I* (Tehran, Kitābkhāna-yi Mūzih, 2000). See also the Quranic commentary of Ghiyāth al-Dīn, *Tuḥfat al-fatā fī tafsīr sūrat 'hal atā'*, ed. Parwīn Bahārzādah. In the important introduction dealing with the life and works of Mīr Ghiyāth al-Dīn as well as of his father along with a history of this illustrious family, the editor cites some fifty-five works of this remarkable figure in philosophy, medicine, the natural and mathematical sciences, the religious sciences and *'irfān*, the majority of which have never been edited or studied carefully.

34. As already mentioned the term "teacher" (*al-mu'allim*) in this context has a special meaning. See "Why was al-Fārābī Called the Second Teacher?" in Nasr, *The Islamic Intellectual Tradition in Persia*, chapter 5, pp. 59–65.

35. The Arabic text of this work has been critically edited with introduction and commentary by Q. Kākāʾī in the *Journal of Religious Thought* (Shiraz), vol. 1, no. 2, pp. 83–144.

36. This work seems to have been lost.

37. On the students of Ghiyāth al-Dīn Manṣūr, see Q. Kākāʾī, "Shāgirdān-i Ghiyāth al-Dīn Manṣūr Dashtakī Shīrāzī," in *Kheradnameh-e Sadra*, vol. 11, Spring 1998, pp. 23ff.; also P. Bahārzādah's introduction to *Tuḥfat al-fatā*, pp. 62–67.

38. See Q. Kākāʾī, "Āshnāʾī bā maktab-i Shīrāz —2. Muḥaqqiq-i Khafrī," *Kheradnameh-e Sadra*, vol. 1, no. 4, June 1996, pp. 71–79.

39. See the study of his commentary on Ṭūsī's *Tadhkirah* by George Saliba, "An Arabic Critique of Ptolemaic Astronomy," *Journal of the History of Astronomy*, vol. 25, 1994, pp. 15–38. Saliba writes about Khafrī, "We are dealing with a planetary theorist of the highest rank. . . . Khafrī not only continues this long established tradition of criticism of Ptolemaic astronomy, but brings to it a fresh vision and a rare creativity not known before." Op. cit., pp. 32–33.

40. It is of much interest for the history of Islamic science to ask why Mullā Sadrā, who was so close in many ways to Khafrī, although much interested in natural philosophy, did not share the interest of the latter and also of other masters of the School of Shiraz in the natural and mathematical sciences themselves. This is a question that has not as yet been investigated.

41. See Q. Kākāʾī, op. cit., pp. 73–74.

42. See Hafiz A. Ghaffar Khan, "India," in Nasr and Leaman (eds.), *History of Islamic Philosophy*, chapter 62, p. 1060.

43. See Kākāʾī, op. cit., pp. 77–79.

44. On his life in both Persia and India, see Saiyid Athar Abbas Rizvi, *A Socio-Intellectual History of the Isna 'Ashari Shi'is in India*, vol. 1 (Canberra, Australia: Ma'rifat), pp. 222ff; and Hafiz A. Ghaffar Khan, op. cit., pp. 1062–63.

45. Rizvi, op. cit., p. 222.

46. On his scientific and engineering achievements see M. A. Alvi and Abdur Rahman, *Fath*[u]*'llāh Shīrāzī* (Delhi, 1968) (publisher unknown); and Rizvi, *A Socio-Intellectual History*, vol. 2, pp. 196ff.

47. See Francis Robinson, *The 'Ulama of Farangi Mahall*.

48. It is remarkable that there is still not a single work in any European language that deals in a satisfying manner with the development and history of Islamic philosophy in India.

49. Rizvi, *A Socio-Intellectual History*, vol. 1, p. 226, quoted from the *Akbar-nāmah* of Abūʾl-Faḍl.

Chapter 11. The School of Isfahan Revisited

1. On Ibn Turkah, see Corbin, *En Islam iranien*, vol. 3, pp. 233–74. This essay, which analyzes a treatise of Ibn Turkah on the meaning of the Quranic verse on the cleaving of the moon (*shaqq al-qamar*), remains after several decades still the most notable work on Ibn Turkah in European languages. For the text of the works of Ibn Turkah, see Sayyid 'Alī Mūsawī Bihbahānī and Sayyid Ibrāhīm Dībājī (eds.), *Collected Works of Ṣā᾿in al-Dīn ibn Turkah Iṣfahānī*, part 1, (Tehran: Taqī Riḍā᾿ī, 1351 [A.H. solar]), in which fourteen of the fifty-seven known treatises of Ibn Turkah are published. See also his *Tamhīd al-qawā'id*, Sayyid Jalāl al-Dīn Āshtiyānī (ed.) (Tehran: The Imperial Iranian Academy of Philosophy, 1976); refer to my English and Persian introductions for the content and significance of this work. For the life and list of works of Ibn Turkah, see S. A. M. Bihbahānī, "Aḥwāl wa athār-i Ṣā᾿in al-Dīn Turka-yi Iṣfahānī," in Mehdi Mohaghegh and Herman Landolt (eds.), *Collected Papers on Islamic Philosophy and Mysticism* (Tehran: Tehran University Press, 1971), pp. 97–145.

2. See Corbin, op. cit., pp. 237ff.

3. See 'Abd Allāh Jawādī Āmulī, *Taḥrīr tamhīd al-qawā'id* (Qom: Intishārāt al-Zahrā᾿, 1372 [A.H. solar]). This famous book is actually a commentary by Ṣā᾿in al-Dīn on a treatise on *tawḥīd* by his ancestor Ṣadr al-Dīn Abū Ḥāmid Muḥammad Turkah. The complete title of the text of Ṣā᾿in al-Dīn, which has become known as *Tamhīd al-qawā'id* is in fact *al-Tamḥīd fi sharḥ qawā'id al-tawḥid* (The Disposition in the Commentary of the Principles of Unity). Ibn Turkah is one of the most neglected in the West among the major figures of Islamic thought and deserves to be studied much more thoroughly as a "philosopher of being," a Shi'ite interpreter of Ibn 'Arabī, and a synthesizer of the various intellectual perspectives in Islam.

4. Fortunately in contrast to Qāḍī Maybudī, Ibn Turkah and many other major intellectual figures of this period, there is a fine scholarly monograph in a European language on Ibn Abī Jumhūr, including a list of his works, nearly all of which remain in manuscript form. See Sabine Schmidtke, *Theologie, Philosophie und Mystik im zwölferschiitischen Islam des 9./15. Jahrhunderts* (Leiden: Brill, 2000). See also her "Recent Studies on the Philosophy of Illumination and Perspectives for Further Research," *Dâneshnâmeh: The Bilingual Quarterly of the Shahîd Beheshtî University*, vol. 1, no. 2, Spring and Summer 2003, pp. 101–19. Corbin also refers to him often in his *En Islam iranien*, especially vols. 1 and 4. Corbin has written some important passages on Ibn Abī Jumhūr's study of the Shi'ite Imams and his identification of the Paraclete with the Twelfth Imam.

5. See Hamid Dabashi, "Mīr Dāmād," in Nasr and Leaman (eds.), *History of Islamic Philosophy*, pp. 598ff., where, under the title "Philosophy under the Safavids," this issue is discussed. See p. 601, where Dabashi quotes a poem by Mullā Muḥammad Ṭāhir Qummī, one of the most severe opponents of the Sufis and philosophers, against philosophy.

6. On the School of Isfahan, see Corbin, *En Islam iranien*, vol. 4, livre 5, pp. 7ff.; and Nasr, "The School of Isfahan," in *The Islamic Intellectual Tradition in Persia*, pp. 239–70. On Mīr Dāmād, in addition to the above chapters, see Dabashi, op. cit.; Izutsu, "Introduction: Mīr Dāmād and His Metaphysics," in Mīr Dāmād, *al-Qabasāt*, ed. Mehdi Mohaghegh et al. (Tehran: Tehran University Press, 1977), pp. 1–15. See also Sayyid 'Alī Mūsawī Mudarris Bihbahānī, *Ḥakīm-i Astarābād Mīr Dāmād* (Tehran: Tehran University Press, 1377 [A.H. solar]); and Corbin, *La Philosophe iranienne islamique*, pp. 26–31.

7. That is why in my *Three Muslim Sages* I refer to Ibn Sīnā and figures like him as philosopher-scientists.

8. As far as the Safavid period is concerned, there was important scientific activity in medicine, mathematics, and as recent discoveries have shown cartography. See David King, *The World about the Ka'ba: The Sacred Geography of Islam* (Leiden: Brill, forthcoming). See also his earlier work, *World Maps for Finding the Direction and Distance to Mecca: Innovation and Tradition in Islamic Science* (Leiden: Brill; London: al-Furqan Islamic Heritage Foundation, 1999), pp. 128ff. There is still so much as yet unstudied scientific material in various Islamic libraries that every few years we are presented with major new discoveries that force scholars to revise their whole view of the history of science of a particular period as the work of David King, Rushdi Rashid, and George Saliba over the past three decades has amply demonstrated.

9. For a listing of his works see Mūsawī Mudarris Bihbahānī, op. cit., pp. 107ff.

10. That is why we are not dealing with this fascinating religious scholar, poet, mystic, and scientist in this book. We have discussed briefly his life and works in "School of Isfahan," op. cit., pp. 243ff.

11. For a brief analysis of this major work, see Nasr, *The Islamic Intellectual Tradition in Persia*, pp. 250ff.

12. Corbin has given a very poetic analysis of the "ecstatic confessions" of Mīr Dāmād in his *En Islam iranien*, vol. 3, pp. 30ff.

13. Many of Mīr Dāmād's works remain, however, in manuscript form. During the last few years more attention is being paid to his writings, and a number of them are beginning to see the light of day. See for example, *Jazāvat va Mavāqīt*, 'Alī Owvjabī (Awjabī) (ed.) (Tehran: Daftar-i Nashr-i Mīrāth-i Maktūb, 2001); *al-Ṣirāṭ al-mustaqīm*, 'Alī Owvjabī (ed.) (Tehran: Daftar-i Nashr-i Mīrāth-i Maktūb, 2002); Sayyid Aḥmad al-'Alawī al-'Āmilī, *Sharḥ al-qabasāt*, Ḥāmid Nājī Iṣfahānī (ed.) (Tehran, Mu'assasa-yi Muṭāli'āt-i Islāmī, 1376 [A.H. solar]); and *Taqwīm al-īmān* 'Alī Owvjabī (ed.) (Tehran: Daftar-i Nashr-i Mīrāth-i Maktūb, 2003). This work contains also the text of Sayyid Aḥmad 'Alawī's *Kashf al-ḥaqā'iq*, which is a commentary upon *Taqwīm al-īmān*, along with an extensive discussion of the works and philosophy of Mīr Dāmād (pp. 22–131 of the introduction) and an account of the life, works, and thought of his student Sayyid Aḥmad 'Alawī (pp. 138–53 of the introduction).

14. See John Philoponus, *On the Eternity of the Cosmos against Proclus* (Leibzig: Teubner's, 1899); and his *On the Creation of the World* (Leibzig: Teubner's, 1897).

15. One of our great teachers of Islamic philosophy, Sayyid Abū᾿l-Ḥasan Rafī'ī Qazwīnī, used to say that this is the one problem that has never been satisfactorily solved philosophically in the annals of Islamic philosophy, not even by Mīr Dāmād or Mullā Ṣadrā, who provided a solution very different from that of his master.

16. See Izutsu, op. cit., pp. 8–10. See also Dabashi, op. cit., pp. 609ff.

17. On Mīr Findiriskī, see Corbin, *La Philosophie iranienne islamique*, pp. 37ff; and Nasr, *The Islamic Intellectual Tradition in Persia*, pp. 254–58.

18. For the translation of this Persian *qaṣīdah*, see our *Islamic Intellectual Tradition*, pp. 255–56.

19. See Fathullah Mojtabai, *Hindu Muslim Cultural Relations* (Delhi: National Book Bureau, 1978), pp. 41ff. He also mentions that Mīr Findiriskī assembled a glossary of Sanskrit technical philosophical terms in Arabic and Persian (p. 102).

20. See Corbin, op. cit., p. 37.

21. Ibid., p. 48.

22. Corbin, *En Islam iranien*, vol. 4, pp. 9ff.

23. For the original text of this work, see Sayyid Jalāl al-Dīn Āshtiyānī and Corbin (eds.), *Anthologie des philosophes iraniens depuis le XVIIe siècle jusqu'à nos jours*, vol. 1 (Tehran and Paris: Department d'Iranologie de l'Institut Franco-iranien de Recherche and Andrien-Maisonneuve, 1972), pp. 63ff. The *Risāla-yi ṣīnā'iyyah* was also edited and published by 'Alī Akbar Shihābī (Tehran: Sa'ādat, 1317 [A.H. solar]). For an analysis of this text see Corbin, *La Philosophie iranienne islamique*, pp. 37ff.

24. *Anthologie*, p. 73 of the Arabic and Persian texts.

25. Mīr Findiriskī concludes this section of his book with a most interesting passage about the relation between true philosophy and prophecy. He first asserts that some have accepted only the inward (*bāṭin*) of religion and rejected the outward (*ẓāhir*), and some the other way around. Both have deviated from the straight path. Then he adds concerning the true philosophers: "And a group have preserved the just mean and marched between the *ẓāhir* and the *bāṭin*, this being the straight path (*ṣirāṭ-i mustaqīm*). They made the word of the prophets concerning intellectual matters to conform to the intellect and brought out the truth of what the prophets had intended. And in transmitted and practical matters they made their intellects to obey the intellect of the prophets. God—praised and exalted is He—was referring to this

group in the *Fātiḥah* of His Book [the Quran] in His Word, 'Lead us unto the straight path." *Anthologie*, p. 77. One hardly need comment upon the significance of this text for how this late tradition of Islamic philosophy viewed the relation between philosophy and prophecy and of course also reason and revelation.

26. On Mullā Rajab 'Alī, see Corbin, *La Philosophie iranienne*, pp. 83ff.

27. Selections of his writings and those of some of his contemporaries and the philosophers of the next generation are to be found in Āshtiyānī and Corbin (eds.), *Anthologie des philosophes iraniens*.

28. On Mullā Shamsā, see Ibrāhīm Dībājī, "Aḥwal wa āthār-i Mullā Shamsā Gīlānī," in *Collected Papers on Islamic Philosophy and Mysticism*, pp. 52–85. The author lists forty known works of Mullā Shamsā. See also Corbin, *La Philosophie iranienne*, pp. 120ff.

29. Corbin has made a profound study of Qāḍī Sa'īd's work on the symbolism of the Ka'bah. See his *Temple and Contemplation*, trans. Philip and Laidain Sherrard (London: KPI, 1986), pp. 183–262. Qāḍī Sa'īd's most important work is perhaps his commentary on the *Kitāb al-tawḥīd* (The Book of Unity) of Ibn Babūyah. Another of his major works is his commentary upon the *Enneads* of Plotinus known to Muslims as *The Theology of Aristotle*. Qāḍī Sa'īd represents another remarkable type of flowering of Islamic philosophy in the full light of the verities of revelation and prophecy. He deserves to be much more studied as a philosopher who was also a theologian and mystic. On Qāḍī Sa'īd in addition to the above cited work, see Corbin, *La Philosophie iranienne*, pp. 245ff.; and Corbin, *En Islam iranien*, vol. 4, pp. 123–201. This latter chapter is among the most significant written by Corbin on a member of the School of Isfahan.

30. The most important contribution of Fayḍ to philosophy was in the domain of philosophical ethics, while he also wrote some works on Mullā Ṣadrā's philosophy. His great fame, however, is primarily in the field of the religious sciences and gnosis. As for Lāhījī, as we saw earlier, he was a great authority in Shi'ite *kalām* and also well versed in *falsafah*.

31. See Ashkiwarī, *Maḥbūb al-qulūb*, 2 vols., Ibrāhīm Dībājī and Ḥamīd Ṣidqī (eds.) (Tehran: Daftar-i Nashr-i Mīrāth-i Maktūb, 1998–2003).

32. Corbin, *En Islam iranien*, vol. 4, pp. 27–28. See also Corbin, "L'idée du Paraclet en philosophie iranienne," in his *Face de Dieu, face de l'homme* (Paris: Flammarion, 1983), especially pp. 341–45.

33. On Sayyid Aḥmad 'Alawī, see Corbin, *La Philosophie iranienne islamique*, pp. 168ff; see Corbin, *Philosophie iranienne et philosophie comparée* (Tehran: Iranian Institute of Philosophy, 2004), pp. 63–66; and Sayyid Aḥmad ᶜAlawī, *Sharḥ al-qabasāt*, the introduction of Ḥ. Nājī Iṣfahānī. In his edition of *Taqwīm al-īmān*, 'Alī Awjabī has provided a scholarly biography and bibliography of 'Alawī, pp. 138–53.

34. See the introduction of Rasūl Ja'fariyān to Mīr Muḥammad Bāqir ibn Ismā'īl Khātūnābādī's translation of the Four Gospels, *Turjuma-yi anājīl-i arba'ah* (Tehran: Daftar-i Nashr-i Mirāth-i Maktūb, 1375 [A.H. solar]), pp. 20ff.

35. See ibid., p. 22. The second part of this book has been translated into English. See Henry Martyn, *Controversial Tracts on Christianity and Mohammedanism* (Cambridge: Smith, 1824) with additions by Samuel Lee.

36. Rasūl Ja'fariyān in the above cited work refers to two Latin works, one by Bonaventura Malvasia, *Dilucidatio Speculi verum monstrantis . . .* , and the second by Filippo Guandagudi, *Apologia pro Christianan religione . . .* , both published in Rome, the first in 1628, and the second in 1631.

37. The text of this work has been published in *Sālnāma-yi mīrāth-i islāmī-i Īrān* (Tehran, 1374 [A.H. solar]).

Chapter 12. Mullā Ṣadrā and the Full Flowering of Prophetic Philosophy

1. See Ibrāhīm Dīnānī, "Daw jaryān-i mutafāwit-i fikrī dar ḥawza-yi falsafī-yi Iṣfahān," in his *Niyāyish-i fīlsūf* (Mashhad: Dānishgāh-i 'Ulūm Islāmī-yi Raḍawī, 1377 [A.H. solar]), chapter 18, pp. 335–50.

2. See S. H. Nasr, *Ṣadr al-Dīn Shīrāzī and His Transcendent Theosophy*; H. Corbin ed. and trans., *Le Livre de pénétrations métaphysiques* of Mullā Ṣadrā (Paris: Verdier, 1993); Fazlur Rahman, *The Philosophy of Mullā Ṣadrā* (Albany: State University of New York Press, 1976); chapters by Hossein Ziai and Nasr on him in Nasr and Leaman (eds.), *History of Islamic Philosophy*, pp. 635–62; and "Sadr al-Dīn Shīrāzī," in Nasr, *The Islamic Intellectual Tradition in Persia*, chapter 22, pp. 271–303. There is a whole foundation in Persia devoted to the propagation of his teachings. It organized a major international conference on him in Tehran in 1999 and another one in 2004. It has also planned several conferences on him in London in collaboration with the Islamic Institute of England. The foundation in Iran publishes the journal *Kheradnameh-e Sadra* primarily in Persian, and the Islamic Institute of England publishes the journal *Transcendent Philosophy* in English devoted mostly to the thought of Mullā Ṣadrā and his school.

3. Although Mullā Ṣadrā differed from his teacher on many points, he also followed him closely in many matters as for example in accepting the famous principle "There is no efficient cause in existence except God" (*lā muʾaththir fiʾl-wujūd illaʾLlāh*). See 'Alī Awjabī, "Dūrnamāʾī az andīshahā wa naẓariyyāt-i Mīr Dāmād," *Kheradnameh-e Sadra*, vol. 4, no. 14, March 1999, pp. 64–70.

4. Corbin, Sayyid Jalāl al-Dīn Āshtiyānī, and myself have provided a bibliography of his writings, the latest in this series being in Nasr, *Sadr al-Dīn Shīrāzī*, pp. 39–50. Since the compilation of these lists, however, much research

on manuscripts of his writings has been carried out in Persia. A work that is comprehensive and incorporates not only our earlier efforts but also those of later scholars is Ibrahim Kalin, "An Annotated Bibliography of the Works of Mullā Ṣadrā with a Brief Account of His Life," *Islamic Studies* (Islamabad), vol. 42, no. 1, Spring 2003, pp. 21–62. The most complete bibliographical study of the Ṣadrean corpus is Khurramdashtī, Nāhid Bāqirī, and Aṣgharī, Fāṭimah (eds.), *Kitābshināsī-yi jāmi'-i Mullā Ṣadrā* (Tehran: Bunyād-i Ḥikmat-i Islāmī-yi Ṣadrā, 1999).

5. See Nasr, *Ṣadr al-Dīn Shīrāzī*, chapter 3, pp. 55–68.

6. As yet no translation of this work exists in a European language, but one is planned in English. So far the following works of Mullā Ṣadrā have been translated into European languages: *al-Ḥikmat al-'arshiyyah* translated by James Morris as *The Wisdom of the Throne* (Princeton: Princeton University Press, 1981); the *Kitāb al-mashā'ir*, trans. Corbin as *Le Livre des pénétrations métaphysiques*, and by Parviz Morewedge (in an unsuccessful translation as far as many passages are concerned) as *The Metaphysics of Mullā Ṣadrā* (New York: Society for the Study of Islamic Philosophy and Science, 1992), and by S. H. Nasr with his own commentary, Ibrahim Kalin (ed.) (forthcoming); *Risālat al-ḥashr*, trans. Christian Jambet as *Se rendre immortel: Traité de la résurrection* (Paris: Fata Morgana, 2000); *Risālah fī ḥudūth al-'ālam*, trans. Sayed Bagher Talgharizadeh as *Die Abhandlung über die Entstehung* (Berlin: Schwarz, 2000); and *Iksīr al-'ārifin*, trans. William Chittick as *The Elixir of the Gnostics* (Provo, UT: Brigham Young University Press, 2003).

7. On the meaning of *al-ḥikmat al-muta'āliyah*, see Nasr, *Ṣadr al-Dīn Shīrāzī*, chapter 5, pp. 85–97.

8. Several of the works cited above deal in depth with these philosophical ideas. In addition to them, see Corbin, *En Islam iranien*, vol. 4, pp. 54–122; and Zailan Moris, *Revelation, Intellectual Intuition and Reason in the Philosophy of Mullā Ṣadrā*.

9. Corbin, *The Voyage and the Messenger*, trans. Joseph Rowe (Berkeley: North Atlantic Books, 1998), pp. 206–07. For the relation between prophetic philosophy and Mullā Ṣadrā's metaphysics, see the chapter of this book entitled "Prophetic Philosophy and the Metaphysics of Being," pp. 205–15. On Corbin's views on prophetic philosophy, see also his *En Islam iranien*, vol. 1, pp. 43–53; and his *A History of Islamic Philosophy*, pp. 23–104.

10. Although this doctrine is usually associated with Shi'ism as studied extensively by Corbin, especially in the first two volumes of his *En Islam iranien*, it has its correspondence in Sufism within the Sunni world. On this notion in Ibn 'Arabī, see Michel Chodkiewicz, *Seal of the Saints*, trans. Liadain Sherrard (Cambridge: Islamic Texts Society, 1993).

11. See S. H. Nasr, *Islamic Life and Thought* chapter 15, "Mullā Ṣadrā as a Source for the History of Islamic Philosophy," pp. 169–73.

12. "The secret of the act of being, of existing, must not be sought in the substantive form of the verb (Latin *ens*), but in its imperative form (Arabic *K-N*, Latin *esto*, not *fiat*)." Corbin, *The Voyage and the Messenger*, p. 206.

13. On selections of the writings of Ismāʿīlī philosophers, see S. H. Nasr and Mehdi Aminrazavi (eds.), *An Anthology of Philosophy in Persia*, vol. 2. Corbin has also dealt in many of his studies with this issue. See for example his *Trilogie ismaélienne* (Tehran-Paris: Andrien Maisonneuve, 1961). That is why in this book we have not devoted a separate chapter to Ismāʿīlī philosophy in relation to prophetic philosophy. In speaking of prophetic philosophy in Islam one must, however, always remember the importance of Ismāʿīlī philosophy.

14. The complete Quranic commentaries of Mullā Ṣadrā have been assembled and published in one series by Muḥammad Khwājawī as *Tafsīr al-qurʾān al-karīm*, 7 vols. (Qom: Intishārāt-i Bīdār, 1363–67 [A.H. solar]). On Mullā Ṣadrā's Quranic commentaries, see also chapter 7, "The Quranic Commentaries of Mullā Ṣadrā," in my *Ṣadr al-Dīn Shīrāzī . . .*, pp. 123–35.

15. On angels in Christian thought, see Steven Chase (trans.), *Angelic Spirituality* (New York: Paulist, 2002).

16. See H. Corbin, *Les Motifs zoroastriens dans la philosophie de Sohrawardī*, 1946; and *En Islam iranien*, vol. 2, pp. 81ff.

17. See Fazlur Rahman, *Prophecy in Islam*; and his "Ibn Sīnā," in Sharif, *A History of Muslim Philosophy*, vol. 1, pp. 498–501.

18. It was Henry Corbin who singlehandedly revived the significance of the imaginal world in the modern West where the term *imagination* is almost always associated with unreality. From the Center for the Study of the Imaginary founded by Gilbert Durand in France to the Temenos Academy founded by Kathleen Raine in Britain, the central influence of Corbin's teachings about the imaginal world or *mundus imaginalis*, based on the teachings of Islamic metaphysicians, is evident. See Corbin's classical study *Alone with the Alone: Creative Imagination in the Sufism of Ibn ʿArabī*. On Ibn ʿArabī's doctrine of the imaginal world, see also W. Chittick, *Imaginal Worlds: Ibn al-ʿArabī and the Problem of Religious Diversity*; and his *Self-Disclosure of God* (Albany: State University of New York Press, 1998), chapter 10, pp. 331ff. As mentioned earlier, in order not to cause confusion between the Islamic metaphysicians' view of *khayāl* (imagination), and the modern understanding of this term, many years ago Corbin and I decided to use the adjective *imaginal* rather than imaginary for the Islamic concept of imagination, and the term has now come to be accepted in many European languages.

19. See Nasr, *Islamic Life and Thought*, chapter 8, pp. 96ff.

20. On the meaning of trans-substantial motion in relation to natural philosophy and physics, see Ibrahim Kalin, "Between Physics and Metaphys-

ics: Mullā Ṣadrā on Nature and Motion," *Islam and Science*, vol. 1., no. 1, June 2003, pp. 59–90.

21. *En Islam iranien*, vol. 1, pp. 43–53.

22. For a study of Mullā Ṣadrā's philosophy in light of revelation and prophecy, see Zailan Moris, op. cit.; and Christian Jambet, *L'Acte d'être: La philosophie de la révélation chez Molla Ṣadrā* (Paris: Fayard, 2002). See also Joseph Lumbard, "The Place of Prophecy in Mullā Ṣadrā's Philosophy of Perception," in Seyed G. Safavi (ed.), *Perception according to Mullā Ṣadrā* (London: Institute of Islamic Studies—Salmān-Āzādeh Publication, 2002) pp. 129–50.

23. The full extent of the influence of Mullā Ṣadrā in India has not as yet been studied. Over four decades ago when I visited some of the major libraries of India specifically in order to study manuscripts of Mullā Ṣadrā, I was amazed at the number of manuscripts of his works in such places as the Rampur and Khudābakhsh Libraries. Among them the number of manuscripts of the *Kitāb al-hidāyah* and the very large number of commentaries and glosses written upon it (much more than in Persia itself) was truly amazing. See Akbar Thubūt, "Sharḥ-i hidāya-yi Mullā Ṣadrā dar Hind," in *Kheradnameh-yi Sadra*, vol. 1, no. 3, March 1996, pp. 100–07; and "Mullā Ṣadrā dar Hindūstān," in S. H. Nasr, *Ma'ārif-i islāmī dar jahān-i mu'āṣir* (Tehran, Shirkat-i Kitābhā-yi Jībī, 1348 [A.H. solar]), pp. 123–1323.

24. See Mahmut Kiliç, "Mullā Ṣadrā dar dāʾira-yi andīshmandān-i turk," *Kheradnameh-e Sadra*, vol. 2, no. 8–9, 1997, pp. 102–104.

25. At once logician, epistemologist, metaphysician, poet, and saint, Sabziwārī represents the concrete example of the teaching and the living of prophetic philosophy in a period not far from our own, he having died in 1289/1878. See our *Islamic Intellectual Tradition in Persia*, chapter 23, pp. 304–19; and T. Izutsu, "The Fundamental Structure of Sabziwārī's Metaphysics," which is the introduction to *Sharḥ-i ghurar al-farāʾid* or *Sharḥ-i manẓūmah* of Sabziwārī, part 1, "Metaphysics" (Tehran/McGill University, Montreal: Institute of Islamic Studies, Tehran Branch, 1969), pp. 1–152. This is the most extensive and masterly treatment of Sabziwārī's metaphysics in a European language. See also Ghulām Ḥusayn Riḍā Nizhād, *Ḥakīm Sabziwārī* (Tehran: Sanāʾī, 1371 [A.H. solar]).

There is definitely a need for an extensive monographic study in the English language on this remarkable figure.

Chapter 13. From the School of Isfahan to the School of Tehran

1. On this important figure who was at once philosopher, theologian, gnostic, and poet, see S. H. Nasr, "The School of Isfahan," in *The Islamic Intellectual Tradition in Persia*, pp. 258–62; and Fayḍ Kāshānī, *Uṣūl al-ma'ārif*,

ed. S. J. Āshtiyānī (Mashhad: Faculty of Theology, 1354 [Q.H. solar]), including an English introduction by S. H. Nasr; and Corbin, *La Philosophie islamique iranienne*, pp. 179–87.

2. Like Fayḍ Kāshānī, Lāhījī was also an accomplished poet and a major Shi'ite theologian whom we discussed in chapter 3. See *Yād-nāma-yi Ḥakīm Lāhījī;* and Corbin, op. cit., pp. 96–115.

3. On these figures, some of whom were discussed in chapter 11, see the introduction of S. J. Āshtiyānī to his edition of Ṣadr al-Dīn Shīrāzī, *al-Shawāhid al-rubūbiyyah* with the commentary of Sabziwārī (Mashhad: Mashhad University Press, 1967), pp. 85ff.; also Manūchihr Ṣadūqī Suhā, *Tārīkh-i ḥukamā᾽ wa 'urafā-yi muta᾽ākhhir* (Tehran: Intishārāt-i Ḥikmat, 1381 [A.H. solar]); and H. Corbin, *La Philosophie iranien islamique aux xviie et xviiie siècles.*

4. See 'Alī Aṣghar Ḥalabī, *Tārīkh-i-falāsafa-yi Īrān* (Tehran: Zawwār, 1361 [A.H. Solar]), pp. 558–59. See also S. H. Nasr with M. Aminrazavi, *Anthology of Philosophy in Persia,* vol. 3 (London: Taurus, [in press]).

5. See Āshtiyānī's introduction to *al-Shawāhid al-rubūbiyyah,* pp. 106 ff.; and Āshtiyānī (ed.), *Muntakhābātī az āthār-i ḥukamā-yi ilāhī-yi Īrān,* vol. 4 (Mashhad: Mashhad University Press, 1357 [A. H. Solar]), pp. 537ff. See also M. Ṣaduqī Suhā, op. cit. pp. 33ff.

6. The history of the development of *ḥikmat* in Isfahan after Mullā 'Alī has not been well studied, although Jalāl Humā᾽ī has provided much useful information on this subject in his general study of the history of Isfahan (*Tārīkh-i Iṣfahān*), which, as far as we are aware, has never been published in full.

7. There is a short biography of Mullā 'Abd Allāh by his son, the celebrated philosopher Mullā 'Alī Mudarris, to whom we shall turn shortly. This biography was discovered by Āshtiyānī and has been translated in our English introduction to Āshtiyānī's edition of Zunūzī, *Lama'āt-i ilāhiyyah—Divine Splendor* (Tehran: Cultural Studies and Research Institute, 1982), pp. 6–8.

8. Edited by S. J. Āshtiyānī, op. cit.

9. Edited by S. J. Āshtiyānī (Tehran: Imperial Iranian Academy of Philosophy, 1976), with English and Persian introductions by S. H. Nasr.

10. Edited by Mayel Herawi, *Montaxab-Al-Xaqani . . .* (Tehran: Mawlā, 1361 [A.H. Solar]).

11. We have said "once again" because from the time of Nāṣir-i Khusraw until Afḍal al-Dīn Kāshānī, Naṣīr al-Dīn al-Ṭūsī, and Quṭb al-Dīn Shīrāzī, the use of philosophical Persian was on the rise, and this tendency continued to a large extent in the School of Shiraz as we see in the writings of Jalāl al-Dīn Dawānī, and Maḥmud Dihdād. With the coming of the Safavid period Persian became to some extent eclipsed, and Arabic became once again more dominant in the field of philosophy. It is enough to compare the ratio between

Persian and Arabic writings of a Mullā Ṣadrā with that of a Suhrawardī or a Ṭūsī to realize the truth of this assertion. The reason for this phenomenon is probably the migration to Persia of a number of Arab Shi'ite scholars who did not know Persian at the beginning of the Safavid period. With the Qajar period the tendency to use Persian to a greater extent, but of course not exclusively, became strengthened in comparison to the Safavid period.

12. See chapter 12, note 25 for references on him.

13. See Ṣaduqī Suhā, op. cit., pp. 46–47; and Āshtiyānī, introduction to *Shawāhid*, pp. 108–09, 122.

14. Ṣaduqī Suhā, op. cit. p., 46.

15. Ibid., p. 47.

16. There is an initiatic line of transmission of esoteric teachings, not to be confused with the theoretical understanding of gnosis and Sufi metaphysics, that existed among Shi'ite scholars stretching from Mullā Ṣadrā, and even before him, to 'Allāmah Ṭabāṭabā᾿ī and before him certain other fourteenth/twentieth century figures, including such famous Shi'ite scholars as Baḥr al-'ulūm. Both Lārījānī and Qumsha᾿ī, as well as a number of his students in the School of Tehran, belonged to this initiatic line about which little has been written until now, although some points of intersection between the chain of Shi'ite *'urafā᾿* and the Sufi orders in Persia, especially the Dhahabī and the Ni'matullāhī, is known. See our preface to Sayyid Muḥammad Ḥusayn Ṭabāṭabā᾿ī, *Kernel of the Kernel*, trans. Mohammad H. Faghfoory (Albany: State University of New York Press, 2003) pp. xiii–xix. See also Christian Bonnard, *L'Imam Khomeyni, un gnostique méconnu du XXe siècle* (Beirut: Al-Bouraq, 1997).

17. Fortunately we now have the monumental study of Āqā 'Alī and the critical edition of his writings by Muḥsin Kadīwar (ed.), *Majmu'a-yi muṣannafāt-i Ḥakīm-i Mu᾿assis Āqā 'Alī Mudarris Ṭihrānī*, 3 vols. (Tehran: Intishārāt-i Iṭṭilā'āt, 1378 [A.H. solar]). A fourth volume containing the text of the *Badāyi' al-ḥikam* is planned to complete the project. This work contains all the available and authenticated texts of Āqā 'Alī in addition to an extensive introduction by Kadīwar on his life and thought. These volumes are unique in their thoroughness and scholarly quality as far as a figure of the School of Tehran is concerned. An edition of the *Badāyi' al-ḥikam* has already appeared under the care of Aḥmad Wā'iẓī (Tehran: Mu᾿assisa-yi Chāp wa Nashr-i 'Allāmah Ṭabāṭabā᾿ī, 1376 [A.H. solar]).

18. For a complete list, see Kadīwar, op. cit., pp. 61–64.

19. His treatise on resurrection, *Sabīl al-rishād* (Path of Guidance) was among his most popular works.

20. Ibid. p. 59.

21. See K. Mujtahidī, "Dhikr-i falāsafa-yi gharb dar *Badāyi' al-ḥikam*," *Rāhnāma-yi kitāb*, vol. 18, no. 10–12 (1354 [A. H. Solar]); and Mujtahidī, "Mīrzā

'Imād al-Dawlah wa Evellene fīlsūf-i Farānsawī," *Rāhnāma-yi kitāb*, vol. 19, no. 11–12 (1355).

22. See the introduction of Āshtiyānī to his edition of the *Rasā'il* of Sabziwārī (Mashhad: Mashhad University Press, 1970), p. 52.

23. "In his comprehension of the words of Mullā Ṣadrā and understanding of the mysteries and difficulties of his philosophy, Āqā 'Alī was more perfect than all those who have written either glosses or independent works concerning the foundation of Mullā Ṣadrā's [thought]." S. J. Āshtiyānī, introduction to *Sharḥ risālat al-mashā'ir* of Mullā Ṣadrā by Mullā Muḥammad Ja'far Lāhījānī (Mashhad: Mashhad University Press, 1964), p. 48.

24. Published in Paris, Dedier et cie, 1865.

25. Kadīwar, op. cit. p. 49.

26. Ṣaduqī Suhā, op. cit., pp. 51–52. Ṣaduqī Suhā also writes that the teacher of Āqā Muḥammad Riḍā's teacher, Āqā Sayyid Raḍī Lārījānī, a mysterious figure whose name was Ākhūnd Mullā Ismā'īl Waḥid al-'Ayn, was one of the spiritual masters of the Dhahabī Order. (Ibid., p. 52).

27. Khiḍr or al-Khaḍir refers of course to the mysterious prophet mentioned in the Noble Quran who symbolizes the guide upon the spiritual path in Islamic esoterism.

28. Ṣaduqī Suhā, op. cit., p. 49.

29. Āshtiyānī's, introduction to the *Shawāhid*, p. 124.

30. Ṣaduqī Suhā, op. cit., p. 58.

31. Unfortunately most of those works have yet to be critically edited and published. One hopes that someone will do for the works of Āqā Muḥammad Riḍā what Muḥsin Kadīwar has done for the writings of Āqā 'Alī Mudarris.

32. For a long list of Āqā Muḥammad Riḍā's students, see Ṣaduqī Suhā, op. cit., pp. 59–105.

33. Like Āqā 'Alī Mudarris, Jilwah has written a short account of his own life, which has been published in Ṣaduqī Suhā, op. cit. pp. 159–61. On Jilwah, see Ghulām Riḍā Gulī Zawwārah, *Mīrzā Abū'l-Ḥasan Jilwah: Ḥakīm-i Furūtan* (Tehran: Sāzimān-i Tablīghāt-i Islāmī, 1372 [A.H. solar]). This work deals with the family background, biography, and certain features of his thought, as well as reflections upon him by his contemporaries and students.

34. Ṣaduqī Suhā has given the name of dozens upon dozen of the students of the founders of the School of Tehran and their immediate successors to the present day. See his op. cit., pp. 59ff. There are many figures mentioned briefly by Ṣaduqī Suhā and Āshtiyānī who deserve to be more fully studied. We do not wish to give simply a catalog of their names here but must emphasize that many of them are worthy of separate monographic studies.

35. For an account of his life, see the Persian introduction of M. Mohaghegh to A. Falâṭûrî and M. Mohaghegh (eds.), Āshtiyānī, *Commentary* on *Sabzawārī's Sharḥ-i manẓūmah* (Tehran: McGill University, Institute of Islamic Studies, Tehran Branch, 1973). See also the English introduction written by T. Izutsu to this volume.

36. See ibid. where the complete Arabic commentary has been printed in a critical edition.

37. Published in Tehran by the Tehran University Press, 1330 (A.H. Solar).

38. Āshtiyānī, *Commentary*, English introduction, pp. 5–6. This description also holds true for a number of other commentaries written by members of the School of Tehran on the earlier texts of Islamic philosophy not to speak of *'irfān*.

39. All of these figures either belong to or have been closely associated with the School of Tehran, and one day when the full history of this school and Islamic philosophy in general during the fourteenth/twentieth century is written, their ideas must be analyzed and discussed fully. I have had the honor and pleasure of knowing all of them well and having collaborated for years with some of them, especially Murtaḍā Muṭahharī and Sayyid Jalāl al-Dīn Āshtiyānī, on various projects dealing with Islamic philosophy and Islamic thought in general.

40. See the brief introduction of Sayyid Ḥasan Ḥasanzādah Āmulī to Qazwīnī, *Ittiḥād-i 'āqil wa ma'qūl* (Tehran: Markaz-i Intishārāt-i 'Ilmī wa Farhangī, 1401 [A.H. Solar]).

41. When I planned to publish a commemoration volume on the occasion of the four hundredth anniversary of the birth of Mullā Ṣadrā, which came out as S. H. Nasr (ed.), *Mullā Ṣadrā Commemoration Volume* (Tehran: Tehran University Press, 1961), I asked him to contribute an article. He kindly accepted and wrote a masterly essay in Persian on trans-substantial motion, which was also translated into English by me for that volume (pp. 7–21). This is the only work of his available in English until now. Then in the late 1960s and early 1970s, when I visited Qazwin regularly, often with Sayyid Jalāl al-Dīn Āshtiyānī and Badī' al-Zamān Furouzānfar to benefit from Qazwīnī's presence, I gave him a notebook in which he wrote short treatises to answer questions that I posed to him. These questions included such thorny issues as *ittiḥād al-'āqil wa'l-ma'qūl, ḥudūth-i dahrī, 'ālam al-mithāl*, and eschatology. In the mid-1970s, after his death, M. T. Danechpazhuh asked me if he could make a copy of this notebook for the Central Library of Tehran University, to which I fortunately acquiesed because, with the plunder of my library in 1979, the original notebook was lost to me. Later Ḥasanzādah Āmulī published these treatises together, but I do not know whether they were from the Tehran University Library microfilms or from the original, which had fallen into his

hands. In any case fortunately these masterly treatises are now available in published form.

42. I have had an intense personal relationship with this master since my childhood days. He was an intimate friend of my father and like a second father to me. Upon returning to Persia in 1958, I studied both *ḥikmat* and *'irfān* with him regularly until shortly before his death.

43. On the life of Sayyid Muḥammad Kāẓim 'Aṣṣār, see the introduction of S. J. Āshtiyānī to his edition of *Majmū'a-yi āthār-i 'Aṣṣār* (Tehran: Intishārāt-i Amīr Kabīr, 1376 [A.H. solar]), pp. 1ff. See also the moving poetic account of this master by his daughter, Shusha Guppy, in her autobiography, *The Blind Horse: Memories of a Persian Childhood* (London: Heinemann, 1988). Written in elegant English, this work reveals much about the personal traits of this remarkable sage.

44. Upon his retirement he was succeed by Abū ʾl-Ḥasan Sha'rānī. When I became professor in this same department in 1958, the only course on Islamic philosophy was taught by 'Aṣṣār, but I was able to expand the curriculum to some extent. For some years Corbin and I taught a graduate seminar on the subject, and I also devised and taught a new course that was an introduction to Islamic philosophy and a requirement for all philosophy majors and many other students.

45. For over fifteen years I studied various traditional texts with the master at the house of Dhu ʾl-Majd Ṭabāṭabāʾī, a lawyer dedicated to the study of *ḥikmat* and *'irfān*. We met with 'Aṣṣār three afternoons a week for study. About five years of this period was spent in studying the *Ashi'at al-lama'āt* of Jāmī, which is a commentary upon ʿIraqī's *Lama'āt* (Divine Flashes) and a gnostic text of great literary beauty, 'Aṣṣār having been very well versed in classical Sufi literature, especially poetry, which he quoted often in his classes. He would read one or two lines of Jāmī and then carry out a discourse of his own for an hour or two. After five years when we had finished the introduction, the master said, "We do not need to continue. You should be able to read the rest of the text on your own." It was also at the house of Dhu ʾl-Majd that the weekend sessions with 'Allāmah Ṭabaṭabāʾī were held, sessions that were joined by Corbin during the fall season, which he spent in Tehran.

46. All of those works have been edited with commentary by Āshtiyānī in *Majmū'a-yi āthār-i 'Aṣṣār.*

47. It is an enigma that 'Aṣṣār did not write a work confronting Western thought as did 'Allāmah Ṭabāṭabāʾī and Mīrzā Mahdī Ḥāʾirī Yazdī. I asked him several times about this matter, but he always shrugged off the proposal to write such a work in a manner suggesting that such an enterprise was not worthwhile because of the lack of depth of modern philosophical ideas.

48. Muḥsin Furūghī, the oldest son of Muḥammad 'Alī Furūghī, who wrote the major text on Western philosophy in modern Persia (*Sayr-i ḥikmat*

dar Urūpā), told us that when he was a child, there was keen interest in their household in European philosophy, which was highly revered, while when one spoke of Mullā Ṣadrā, it was considered something very ordinary, and uninteresting, like meat bought at a butcher's shop. If this was the case in a household whose master was interested in Islamic philosophy and who translated a part of the *Shifāʾ* of Ibn Sīnā into Persian, one can imagine what it must have been like in other modernized households.

49. See our analysis especially in reference to Islamic thought of the philosophical scene in Persia at that time in *Islamic Intellectual Tradition in Persia*, chapter 24, "Islamic Philosophy in Modern Persia," pp. 323–40.

50. On his life and works, see our introduction to his *Shi'ite Islam*, ed. S. H. Nasr, (Albany: State University of New York Press, 1975); and 'Allāmah Sayyid Muḥammad Ḥusayn Ḥusaynī Ṭihrānī, *Mihr-i tābān* (Mashhad: Mashhad University Press, 1417 [A.H. solar]). I had the honor and privilege of studying both philosophy and *'irfān* with 'Allāmah Ṭabāṭabāʾī for some nineteen years between 1958 to 1978. Ṭihrānī, who was himself among the best students of 'Allāmah, was a major scholar and philosopher in his own right and the author of over a hundred works, many dealing with *ḥikmat*. He studied and taught in Qom and belongs properly speaking more to the School of Qom than the School of Tehran.

51. See his *Principles of Epistemology in Islamic Philosophic-Knowledge by Presence*, (Albany: State University on New York Press, 1992), and my forward to the work about the author.

52. There were of course other traditional philosophers, such as Ḥusayn 'Alī Rāshid and Muḥammad Taqī Ja'farī, who dealt with Western thought, but we consider Ṭabāṭabāʾī and Ḥāʾirī to be the most important in this group and therefore have not dealt with the others here.

53. In this context it is important especially to refer to the works of Muḥammad Bāqir al-Ṣadr, who was a prominent member of the philosophical School of Najaf.

Chapter 14. Reflections on Islam and Modern Thought

1. Islam is based on intelligence, and intelligence is light as expressed in the *ḥadīth "innaʾl-'aqla nūr^{un}"* ("Verily intelligence is light"). The characteristic expression of Islam is the courtyard of an Alhambra whose forms are so many crystallizations of light and whose spaces are defined by the rays of that light that symbolizes in this world the Divine Intellect.

2. On tradition and modernism as used here and in fact in all of our writings see Frithjof Schuon, *Light on the Ancient Worlds*, trans. Lord Northbourne (Bloomington: World Wisdom Books, 1984); and René Guénon,

The Crisis of the Modern World, trans. Marco Pallis and Richard Nicholson (Ghent, NY: Sophia Perennis et Universalis, 1996).

If we are forced to redefine these terms here, it is because despite the considerable amount of writing devoted to the subject by outstanding traditional writers such as Guénon, Schuon, Ananda K. Coomaraswamy, Titus Burckhardt, Martin Lings, and others, there are still many readers, especially Muslim ones, for whom the distinction between tradition and modernism is not clear. They still identify tradition with customs and modernism with all that is contemporary.

Many Western students of Islam also identify 'modern' with "advanced," "developed," and the like as if the march of time itself guarantees betterment. For example, Carl Leiden, a political scientist and student of contemporary Islam, writes, "Equally important is how the term modernization can itself provide insight into these questions. This is not the first time in history that societies have undergone confrontation with other 'advanced' societies and have learned to accommodate to them. Every such confrontation, was, in a sense, a clash or contact with modernization." James A. Brill and Carl Leiden, *Politics in the Middle East* (Boston: Little, Brown, 1979), p. 63. The author goes on to cite as example the confrontation of the Romans with the Greeks and the Arabs with the Byzantine and Persians. However, despite the decadent nature of late Greek culture, neither the Greeks nor certainly the theocratic Byzantines and Persians were modern in our definition of the word. If modernism is understood in our sense, then this is the first time that traditional societies are confronting modernism.

3. Despite the totally antitraditional character of the perspective that dominates modern anthropology, even certain anthropologists have come to the conclusion that from a metaphysical and spiritual point of view, man has not "evolved" one iota since the Stone Age. If in the early decades of the twentieth century this view was championed by a few scholars such as Alfred Jeremias and Wilhelm Schmidt, in recent years it has received a more powerful support based on extensive evidence reflected in the studies of such men as Jean Servier and, from the point of view of religious anthropology, Mircea Eliade.

4. It must be remembered that even during this relatively short period of five centuries, the Muslim world has remained for the most part traditional and did not feel the full impact of modernism until a century or two ago. See S. H. Nasr, *Islam and the Plight of Modern Man;* and *Traditional Islam in the Modern World.*

5. In the famous Persian poem

Invoke until thy invocation gives rise to meditation (*fikr*)
And gives birth to a hundred thousand virgin "thoughts" (*andīshah*)

the relation between mental activity in a traditional context and spiritual practice and contemplation is clearly stated.

6. There have been recent attempts by some Western thinkers to escape from the reductionism of classical physics and to introduce both life and even the psyche as independent elements in the universe. But the general view of modern science retains the reductionist one that would reduce spirit to mind, mind to the external aspects of the psyche, the external aspects of the psyche to organic behavior, organisms to molecular structures, and so on. The man who knows and who has the certitude of his own consciousness is thus reduced to chemical and physical elements that in reality are concepts of his own mind imposed upon the natural domain. See Arthur Koestler and J. R. Smythies (eds.), *Beyond Reductionism* (Boston: Beacon, 1971). See also the article of Victor E. Frankl, "Reductionism and Nihilism," where he writes that "the present danger does not really lie in the loss of universality on the part of the scientist, but rather in his pretence and claim of totality. . . . The true nihilism of today is reductionism. . . . Contemporary nihilism no longer brandishes the word nothingness; today nihilism is camouflaged as *nothing-butness*. Human phenomena are thus turned into mere epiphenomena." See also the remarkable work of Ernst Friedrich Schumacher, *A Guide for the Perplexed* (New York: Harper and Row, 1977), especially chapter 1, where this question is discussed.

7. See Fernand Brunner, *Science et réalité* (Paris: Aubier, 1956), where the author displays clearly the nonanthropomorphic nature of the traditional sciences based or their reliance upon the Divine Intellect rather than mere human reason. See also the important works of Wolfgang Smith such as *The Wisdom of Ancient Cosmology: Contemporary Science in Light of Tradition* (Oakton, VA: Foundation for Traditional Studies, 2004).

8. Concerning the study of the cosmos as a crypt as far as Islam is concerned, see S. H. Nasr, *An Introduction to Islamic Cosmological Doctrines*, chapter 15.

9. See S. H. Nasr. "Self-awareness and Ultimate Selfhood," in *The Need for a Sacred Science* (London: Curzon, 1993), pp. 15–23.

10. The classical study of Etienne Gilson, *The Unity of Philosophical Experience* (Westminster, MD: Christian Classics, 1982), is still valuable in tracing this development in Western thought, although it does not of course cover the history of postmodernism and the relativism and nihilism that are the expected results of the trend in question.

11. As stated earlier in this book, in the context of Islamic philosophy, it was especially Ṣadr ad-Dīn Shīrāzī who elucidated, perhaps more than any other Islamic philosopher, the relations among the three paths of reason, intuition, and revelation open to human beings in their quest for the attainment of knowledge.

12. There are of course many men and women living in the present day world who would not accept this description of modern people, as far as it

concerns themselves. But such people, whose number in fact grows every day in the West, are really contemporary rather than modern. The characteristics that we have mentioned here pertain to modernism as such and not to a particular contemporary individual who may in fact stand opposed to them.

13. On the Islamic conception of man, see S. H. Nasr, "Who Is Man? The Perennial Answer of Islam," in Jacob Needleman (ed.), *The Sword of Gnosis* (London: Arkana, 1986), pp. 203–17.

14. Consciousness has no origin in time. No matter how we try to go back in the examination of our consciousness, we cannot obviously reach a temporal beginning. At the heart of this consciousness in fact resides the Infinite Consciousness of God who is at once the Absolute and Transcendent Reality and the Infinite Self residing at the center of our being. In general, Sufism has emphasized more the objective and Hinduism the subjective pole of the One Reality that is at once pure Object and pure Subject, but the conception of the Divinity as pure Subject has also been always present in Islam as the reference in the Noble Quran to God as the Inward (*al-Bāṭin*), the prophetic *ḥadīth* already cited and such classical Sufi treatises as the *Conference of the Birds* (*Manṭiq al-ṭayr*) of 'Aṭṭār reveal. See F. Schuon, *Spiritual Perspectives and Human Facts*, pp. 102ff. See also S. H. Nasr, "In the Beginning of Creation Was Consciousness," *Harvard Divinity Bulletin*, fall/winter 2002, pp. 13–16, 43.

15. It is of interest to note that one of the outstanding treatises of Islamic philosophy dealing with metaphysics and eschatology is a work by Ṣadr al-Dīn Shīrāzī entitled *Mafātīḥ al-ghayb*, literally "Keys to the Invisible World."

16. "In Islam, as we have seen, the Divine ray pierces directly through all degrees of existence, like an axis or central pivot, which links them harmoniously and bestows upon each degree what is suited to it; and we have also seen how the straight ray curves on its return and becomes a circle that brings everything back to its point of departure." Leo Schaya, "Contemplation and Action in Judaism and Islam," in Yusuf Ibish and Ileana Marculescu (eds.), *Contemplation and Action in World Religions* (Seattle: University of Washington Press, 1978), p. 173.

17. Of course the ramification of this opposition and the details as they pertain to each field are such that they could be discussed indefinitely. But here we have the principles rather than their applications in mind. We have discussed some of these issues in detail in *Islam and the Plight of Modern Man*.

18. "[I]n the modern world more cases of loss of religious faith are to be traced to the theory of evolution as their immediate cause than to anything else . . . for the more logically minded, there is no option but to choose between the two, that is, between the doctrine of the fall of man and the 'doctrine' of the rise of man, and to reject altogether the one not chosen." Martin Lings, review of Douglas Dewar, *The Transformist Illusion*, in *Studies in Comparative Religion*, vol. 4, no. 1, 1970, p. 59.

One might also explain the rapid spread of the theory of evolution as a pseudo-religion in the West by saying that to a large extent at least, it came to fill the vacuum already created by the weakening of faith. But as far as Islam is concerned, its effect has been to corrode and weaken an already existing faith that has remained strong as it was the case for those Christians who still possessed strong religious faith when the theory of evolution spread in the late nineteenth century and is in fact still the case up to this day.

19. See Louis Bounoure, *Determinisme et finalité, double loi de la vie* (Paris: Flammarion, 1957); ibid., *Recherche d'une doctrine de la vie: Vrai savants et faux prophètes* (Paris: Laffont, 1964); Douglas Dewar, *The Transformist Illusion* (Murfreesboro: Dehoff, 1957); Evan Shute, *Flaws in the Theory of Evolution* (Nutley, NJ: Craig, 1961); M. Bowden, *The Rise of the Evolution Fraud* (Bromley, Kent: Sovereign, 1982): Giuseppe Sermonti and Roberto Fondi, *Dopo Darwin: Critica all' evoluzionismo* (Milan: Rusconi, 1980): Roberto Fondi, *La Révolution organiciste* (Paris: Le Labyrinthe, 1986); and Michael Denton, *Evolution: A Theory in Crisis* (Bethesda, MD: Adler and Adler, 1986). We have also dealt with this question in our *Man and Nature* (Chicago: ABC International, 1997); and our *Knowledge and the Sacred*, chapter 7, pp. 221ff.

20. Schumacher, *Guide for the Perplexed*, p. 114. "It is far better to believe that the earth is a disc supported by a tortoise and flanked by four elephants than to believe, in the name of 'evolutionism,' in the coming of some 'superhuman' monster. . . . "A literal interpretation of cosmological symbols is, if not positively useful, at any rate harmless, whereas the scientific error—such as evolutionism—is neither literally nor symbolically true; the repercussions of its falsity are beyond calculation." F. Schuon, *Spiritual Perspectives and Human Facts*, p. 118.

21. "If we present, for the sake of argument, the theory of evolution in a most scientific formulation, we have to say something like this: 'At a certain moment of time the temperature of the Earth was such that it became most favorable for the aggregation of carbon atoms and oxygen with the nitrogen-hydrogen combination, and that from random occurrences of large clusters molecules occurred which were most favorably structured for the coming about of life, and from that point it went on through vast stretches of time, until through processes of natural selection a being finally occurred which is capable of choosing love over hate and justice over injustice, of writing poetry like that of Dante, composing music like that of Mozart, and making drawings like those of Leonardo. Of course, such a view of cosmogenesis is crazy. And I do not at all mean crazy in the sense of slangy invective but rather in the technical meaning of psychotic. Indeed such a view has much in common with certain aspects of schizophrenic thinking." Karl Stern, *The Flight from Woman* (New York: Farrar, Straus and Giroux, 1965), p. 290. The author, a well-known psychiatrist, reached this conclusion not from traditional foundations but from the premises of various contemporary schools of thought.

22. See especially the works of Wilbur Smith. More recently works on intelligent design have posed a major scientific challenge to evolutionism. See especially William Dembski, *Intelligent Design: The Bridge between Science and Theology* (Downers Grove, IL: Intervarsity, 1999); and Michael Behe, *Darwin's Black Box* (New York: Free Press, 1996).

23. On a more popular level, the Turkish thinker Harun Yahya has written a number of works on this subject. See his *Evolution Deceit* (London: Ta-Ha, 2001).

24. We have discussed the idea of progress and its refutation in our *Islam and the Plight of Modern Man*. See also Maryam Jameelah, *Islam and Modernism* (Lahore: Muhammad Yusuf Khan, 1968). For an eloquent refutation of the notion of progress see Martin Lings, *Ancient Beliefs and Modern Superstitions* (Cambridge, UK: Quinta Essentia, 1991); also Lord Northbourne, *Looking Back on Progress* (London: Perennial Books, 1970). On the criticism of Teilhardism, which seeks to synthesize evolutionism and the idea of progress with Christian theology, see Wolfgang Smith, *Teilhardism and the New Religion* (Rockford, IL: Tan Books, 1988); and our *Knowledge and the Sacred*, pp. 240–44.

25. On the deeper roots of utopianism in the West, see Jean Servier, *Histoire de l'utopie* (Paris: Presse Universitaire de France, 1992).

26. See our *Knowledge and the Sacred*, chapter 1, pp. 1ff.

27. This is proven by the lack in classical Arabic or Persian of terms for secularism.

28. We have dealt with the sacred quality of all aspects of Islamic learning, even the sciences of nature, in our *Science and Civilization in Islam*; also *Islamic Science: An Illustrated Study*.

Index

'Abbās, Shah, 213
Abbasids: destruction of caliphate of, 45; rise of Ash'arite power among, 44
'Abd al-Ḥalīm Maḥmūd. *See* Maḥmūd, 'Abd al-Ḥalīm
'Abd al-Ḥaqq ibn Sab'īn. *See* Ibn Sab'īn, 'Abd al-Ḥaqq
'Abd al-Ghanyī al-Nābulusī, 45
'Abd al-Jabbār. See Qāḍī 'Abd al-Jabbār
'Abd al-Qādir Ḥamzah ibn Yāqūt Aharī. *See* Aharī, 'Abd al-Qādir Ḥamzah ibn Yāqūt
'Abd al-Raḥmān Badawī. *See* Badawī, 'Abd al- Raḥmān
'Abd al- Raḥmān ibn Khaldūn. *See* Ibn Khaldūn, 'Abd al- Raḥmān
'Abd al- Raḥmān Jāmī. *See* Jāmī, 'Abd al- Raḥmān
'Abd al-Razzāq Kāshānī. *See* Kāshānī, 'Abd al-Razzāq
'Abd al-Razzāq Lāhījī. *See* Lāhījī, 'Abd al-Razzāq
'Abd al-Wahhāb al-Sha'rānī. *See* Sha'rānī, 'Abd al-Wahhāb
'Abduh, Muḥammad, 128
Abharī, Athīr al-Dīn, 162, 189, 192, 211
Aborigines, Australian, 7
Abrahamic: monotheism, 1, 6; philosophies, 7; Pythagoreanism, 148; terms, 3
Absāl, 153
the Absolute, 180
Absolute Being, 66
abstractions, 102
Abū 'Abd Allāh al-Shawdhī. *See* Shawdhī, Abū 'Abd Allāh
Abū 'Abd Allāh Muḥammad Tabrīzī. *See* Tabrīzī, Abū 'Abd Allāh Muḥammad
Abū 'Alī al-Jubbā'ī. *See* Jubbā'ī, Abū 'Alī
Abū Ḥanīfah, Imam, 121, 127
Abū Ḥatīm al-Rāzī. *See* Rāzī, Abū Ḥatīm
Abū Ḥayyān al-Tawḥīdī. *See* Tawḥīdī, Abū Ḥayyān
Abubacer. *See* Ibn Ṭufayl, Abū Bakr Muḥammad
Abū Bakr al-Bāqillānī. *See* Bāqillānī, Abū Bakr
Abū Bakr ibn Bājjah. *See* Ibn Bājjah, Abū Bakr
Abū Bakr Muḥammad ibn 'Alī Khusrawī. *See* Khusrawī, Abū Bakr Muḥammad ibn 'Alī
Abū Bakr Muḥammad ibn Ṭufayl. *See* Ibn Ṭufayl, Abū Bakr Muḥammad
Abū Isḥāq al-Naẓẓām. *See* Naẓẓām, Abū Isḥāq Ibrāhīm
Abū Isḥāq al-Warrāq. *See* Warrāq, Abū Isḥāq
Abū Isḥāq Tabrīzī. *See* Tabrīzī, Abū Isḥāq
Abū'l-'Abbās al-Lūkarī al-Marwazī. *See* Lūkarī al-Marwazī, Abū'l-'Abbās
Abū'l-'Abbās Īrānshahrī. *See* Īrānshahrī, Abū'l-'Abbās
Abū'l-Ḥasan al-Shādhilī, Shaykh. *See* Shādhilī, Shaykh Abū'l-Ḥasan

Abū'l-Barakāt al-Baghdādī, 141
Abū'l-Fatḥ al-Shahrastānī. *See* Shahrastānī, Abū'l-Fatḥ
Abū'l-Ḥasan al-'Āmirī. *See* 'Āmirī, Abū'l-Ḥasan
Abū'l-Ḥasan al-Sha'rānī. *See* Sha'rānī, Abū'l-Ḥasan
Abū'l-Hudhayl al-'Allāf. *See* 'Allāf, Abū'l-Hudhayl
Abū'l-Ḥukamā', 34, 281*n*9
Abū'l-Qāsim al-'Irāqī. *See* 'Irāqī, Abū'l-Qāsim
Abū Manṣūr al-Māturīdī. *See* Māturīdī, Abū Manṣūr
Abū Muḥammand 'Alī ibn Ḥazm. *See* Ibn Ḥazm, Abū Muḥammand 'Alī
Abū Naṣr al-Fārābī. *See* Fārābī, Abū Naṣr
Abū Rayḥān al-Bīrūnī. *See* Bīrūnī, Abū Rayḥān
Abū Sulaymān al-Sijistānī, 25. *See* Sijistānī, Abū Sulaymān
Abū'l-Majd Muḥammad Tabrīzī Malakānī Qarashī. *See* Qarashī, Abū'l-Majd Muḥammad Tabrīzī Malakānī
Abū Ya'qūb al-Sijistānī. *See* Sijistānī, Abū Ya'qūb
Active Intellect, 98, 99, 142, 152
actus essendi, 67, 73, 89
adaequatio rei et intellectus, 99
Adam, 78, 133, 219, 220, 268; Celestial, 149
Adhkā'ī, Parwīz, 305*n6*, *310n39*
'Aḍūd al-Dīn al-Ījī. *See* Ījī, 'Aḍūd al-Dīn
Afandī, Bālī. *See* Bālī Afandī
Afḍāl al-Dīn Kāshānī. *See* Kāshānī, Afḍāl al-Dīn
Affifi, 'Alā' al-Dīn, 18
Afghānī, al-. *See* Asadābādī, Jamāl al-Dīn
Afnan, Suhail, 284*n16*
Aga-Khanid, 147
agkhinoia, 98
agnosticism, 172, 271
Aḥṣā'ī, Ibn Abī Jumhūr, 53
Aharī, 'Abd al-Qādir Ḥamzah ibn Yāqūt, 188
Aḥmad, M. M., 277
Aḥmad ibn Ḥanbal, Imam. *See* Ibn Ḥanbal, Imam Aḥmad
Aḥmad ibn Muḥammad al-'Āṣīmī. *See* 'Āṣimī, Aḥmad ibn Muḥammad
Aḥmad ibn Muskūyah. *See* Ibn Muskūyah, Aḥmad
Aḥmad ibn Ṭayyib al-Sarakhsī. *See* Sarakhsī, Aḥmad ibn Ṭayyib
Ahmadnagar, 204, 205
Aḥmad Sirhindī, Shaykh. *See* Sirhindī, Shaykh Aḥmad
Ā'īna-yi ḥaqq-namā (Mirror Reflecting the Truth), 221
Ā'īna-yi ḥikmat (The Mirror of Philosophy), 59
Ajwibah yamāniyyah 'an as'ilat al-ṣiqilliyyah (Yemeni Answers to Sicilian Questions), 156
Akbar, 43
Akhlāq-i jalālī (Jalālean Ethics), *198*
Akhlāq-i nāṣirī, (Naṣīrean Ethics) *116, 187, 192*
'Alā' al-Dawlah Simnānī. *See* Simnānī, 'Alā' al-Dawlah
The 'Alā'ī Book of Science (Ibn Sīnā), 64, 86, 111, 112
'ālam al-amr, 148
'ālam al-ibdā', 148
'ālam al-khalq, 148
'ālam al-khayāl, 100, 179
Alamut fortress, 146
'Alawī, Sayyid Aḥmad, 219, 220, 235
Albert the Great, 152
alchemy, 144, 145, 147, 216, 217
Aleppo, 158, 188, 192
Alexandrian: commentators, 77, 98
Algebra (Khayyām), 170

Algeria: Islamic philosophy in, 157
'Alī Aṣghar Ḥalabī. *See* Ḥalabī, 'Alī Aṣghar
'Ali ibn Abī Ṭālib, 2, 120, 211
Āl-i Jalāyir, 193
'Alīm, al-, 178
'Alī Mudarris Ṭihrānī, Mullā Āqā. *See* Mudarris Ṭihrānī, Āqā 'Alī
'Alī Nurī, Mullā. *See* Nurī, Mullā 'Alī
'Alī Sāmī al-Najjār. *See* Najjār, 'Alī Sāmī
'Allāf, Abūʾl-Hudhayl, 121, 123
Allah: divinity of, 74; Quranic teachings about, 64
Allah Transcendent (Netton), 28
'Allāmah al-Ḥillī, 51. *See* Ḥillī, 'Allāmah
'Allāmah Ṭabāṭabāʾī. *See* Ṭabāṭabāʾī, 'Allāmah Sayyid Muḥammad Ḥusayn
Ameer Ali, Syed 128–129
Almeria school, 150
Almohads, 127
Ālūsī, Ḥusām al-, 26
Amad 'alaʾl-abad, al- (On the Soul and its Fate), 23
'Āmilī, Bahāʾ al-Dīn al-, 199, 214, 223
Amīn, 'Uthmān, 26
Amīn al-Dīn Ḥājjī Bulah. *See* Bulah, Amīn al-Dīn Ḥājjī
Amīn al-Ḥaḍrah, 177
Aminrazavi, Mehdi, 19, 305*n5*, 330*n13*
'Āmirī, Abūʾl-Ḥasan al-: philosophical defense of Islam by, 139; works of, 23, 110, 139
amr biʾl-ma'rūf waʾl-nahy 'an al-munkar, al-, 122, 123
'Amr ibn Baḥr al-Jāḥiẓ. *See* Jāḥiẓ, 'Amr ibn Baḥr
Āmulī, Muḥammad Taqī, 247
Āmulī, Sayyid Ḥaydar, 53, 76, 87, 134
Anatolia, 158; Islamic philosophy in, 189, 191, 192; Seljuq rule in, 168; Sufi music in, 138
Anawati, Georges C., 18, 26, 50, 288*n12*, 290*n*35, 303*n*11, 306*n2*, 310*n35*
Anawati, M.M., *See* Anawati, Georges C.
Andalusia: Islamic philosophy in, 150, 193; philosophical activities in, 148
angelology, 229; Mazdaean, 115, 159
angels: banished from cosmos, 155; Mazdaean, 160
Anglo-Saxon: philosophy, 7, 19
animae caelestes, 155
annihilation, 90
anthropomorphism, 262, 266
Anwār, Qāsim-i, 146
Anwār-i jaliyyah (Manifest Light), 237
Aphrodisias, Alexander, 98
Apollo, 3, 281*n1*
Āqā 'Alī Mudarris Ṭihrānī, Mullā. *See* Mudarris Ṭihrāni, Mullā Āqā 'Alī
Āqā -i Qazwīnī, Mullā. *See* Qazwīnī, Mullā Āqā-i
Āqā Mīrzā Raḥīm Arbāb. *See* Arbāb, Āqā Mīrzā Raḥīm
Āqā Muḥammad Riḍā Qumshāʾī. *See* Qumshaʾī, Āqā Muḥammad Riḍā
Āqā Muḥammad Riḍā Rashtī. *See* Rashtī, Āqā Muḥammad Riḍā
'aql, al-, 67, 70, 94, 95, 134
'aql al-fa''āl, al-, 98, 142
'aql al-juzʾī al-, 94
Aqṭāb al-quṭbiyyah, al- (Poles of the State of Being a Pole), 188
Aquinas, St. Thomas. *See* St. Thomas Aquinas
Arabic, 158; Hermetic works in, 147; need for knowledge of, 24; Peripatetic thought in, 109; philosophical texts translated, 13, 22; philosophic vocabulary, 3, 110, 137; philosophy, 25; Sufism, 132

'arad̤, 69
Arbāb, Āqā Mīrzā Raḥīm, 236
Arberry, Arthur, 23, 302*n1*, 312*n54*
architecture, 33, 212, 214; Christian, 33; Islamic, 33
Ardistānī, Mawlā Muḥammad Ṣādiq, 235
Aristotelianism, 39, 41, 109, 136, 138, 140, 151
Aristotle, 14, 23, 63, 64, 67, 77, 98, 110, 138, 141, 150, 153, 154, 155, 159, 177, 213, 217, 218, 230, 265, 287*n9*, 312*n58*; teachings of, 42
Arkoun, Mohammad, 18, 322*n28*
Armagan, Mustafa, 277
'arsh, 78
art: Christian, 33; history of, 267; Islamic, 270; philosophy of, 118
Asadābādī, Jamāl al-Dīn al-, 45, 60, 117, 304*n1*
aṣālah, 74, 77
aṣālat al-wujūd, 71, 87
Asās al-iqtibās (Foundation of Acquiring Knowledge), 187
Asfār al-arba'ah, al- (The Four Journeys of Mullā Ṣadrā), 22, 53, 55, 65, 79, 88, 117, 203, 224, 228
Asfār al-arba'ah, al- (The Four Journeys of Mullā Shamsā Gīlānī), 219
Asfār al-arba'ah, al (The Four Journeys of Shams al-Dīn Khafrī), 203
Asfār. See Asfār al-arba'ah, al-
Ash'arī, Abū'l-Ḥasan al-, 43, 97, 124–126, 125, 126
Ash'arism, 97, 112, 126, 130, 168; anti-intellectualism of, 131; attacks against philosophy by, 140; early, 124–126; later, 127, 128; message of, 129–132; opposition to, 51; spiritual significance of, 129
Ash'arite: domination, 169; *kalām*, 46, 60, 86, 168; *mutakallim*, 168; omnipotentialism, 129, 130; rise of theology, 50; school, 81, 97; theology, 53, 123; theories of atomism, 131, 144, 307*n7*; voluntarism, 302*n6*, 307*n6*
Ash'arite school, 38, 39, 112
Ashkiwarī, Āqā Mīrzā Hāshim, 244
Ashkiwarī, Quṭb al-Dīn, 139, 219, 220
Āshtiyānī, Sayyid Jalāl al-Dīn, 18, 241, 254, 284*n12*, 328*n4*
Āshtiyānī, Mīrzā Aḥmad, 247
Āshtiyānī, Mīrzā Mahdī, 72, 88, 117, 244, 247, 248, 321*n21*, 328*n4*
Asian: traditions, 15, 17
'Āṣimī, Aḥmad ibn Muḥammad al-, 201
Asín Palacios, Miguel, 15, 150, 311*n52*
Asrār al-ḥikam (Secrets of Wisdom), 238
'Aṣṣār, Sayyid Muḥammad Kāẓim, 88, 117, 246, 249–251, 276, 295*n14*
astronomy, 187, 200, 308*n10*; anti-Ptolemaic, 152; Ptolemaic, 231
'Aṭābakhsh, Imām-zādah, 203
Athar Abbas Rizvi, Saiyid. *See* Rizvi, Sayyid Athar Abbas
atheism, 143
Athīr al-Dīn Abharī. *See* Abharī, Athīr al-Dīn
atomism, 123, 130, 131, 134, 144, 307*n7*
Attas, Naquib al-, 17, 19, 277
Autology, 188
avatārs, 7
Avempace. *See* Ibn Bājjah, Abū Bakr
Averroes. *See* Ibn Rushd
Averroes' Commentary on Plato's "Republic" , 23
Averroism, 154
Avicenna. *See* Ibn Sīnā
Awṣāf al-ashrāf (Descriptions of the Noble), 187
A'wānī, Ghulām Riḍā, 276
Āwāz-i par-i Jibra'īl (The Chant of the Wing of Gabriel), 158
Awḥad al-Dīn Kāzirūnī. *See* Kāzirūnī, Awḥad al-Dīn
'ayn al-qalb, 102

'Ayn al-Quḍāt Hamadānī. *See* Hamadānī, 'Ayn al-Quḍāt
'Ayniyyah, al- (Ode to the Soul), 191
Ayvazoglu, Beşir, 277
Azarbaijan: school of philosophy in, 185–193
Azhar, al (University), 128
Azhar, Shaykh al-, 117

Baader, Franz von, 301*n18*
Bābā Afḍal. *See* Kāshānī, Afḍal al-Dīn
Badajoz, 148
Badakhshānī, Sayyid Jalāl, 318*n38*, 319*n7*
Badāyi' al-ḥikam (Marvels of Wisdom), 240
Badawī, 'Abd al-Raḥmān, 18
Badī' al-Mulk, 241
Baghdad: Islamic philosophy in, 156, 183, 193
Baghdādī, Abū'l-Barakāt al-, 141, 143
Baghdādī, Muḥammad al-, 165
Bahā' al-Dīn al-'Āmilī. *See* 'Āmilī, Bahā' al-Dīn
Bahmanyār ibn Marzbān, 140, 169
baḥth, 77
baṣīrah, 95
Bājūrī, al-, 128
Bakar, Osman, 277, 308*n22*
Bālī Afandī, 45
Bangladesh, 275
baqā': meaning of, 174
Bāqillānī, Abū Bakr al-, 43, 126
Bāqir, Imam Muḥammad al-, 111, 146, 277
Baṣrī, Ḥasan al-, 121
Baroque period, 266
Basra, 223
Basṭāmī, Bāyazīd al-, 156, 159
Bayān wa'l-tabyīn (Declaration and Explanation), 35
Bāyazīd al-Basṭāmī. *See* Basṭāmī, Bāyazīd
Bayhaqī, Ẓahīr al-Dīn, 168
Behe, Michael, 268
being, 63; absolute, 66, 78; annihilation and, 90; chain of, 64, 77; contingent, 141; of God, 2, 232, 251, 253, 262; necessary, 66, 71, 72, 141, 142, 181, 237; negation of, 148; philosophy of, 88, 226, 227; pure, 90, 215; study of, 85–91; transcendent unity of, 74–78, 83, 87
Beloved of Hearts (Ashkiwarī), 219
Berjak, Rafik, 310*n43*
Best Essence (Bulah), 191
Ben Gabirol, Solomon, 150
Bezels of Wisdom (al-Fārābī), 64, 138
Bibliothèque Iranienne, 22
Bihbahānī, Sayyid 'Alī Mūsawī, 324*n1*
Bijapur, 206
Bilen, M., 291*n50*
Bill, James, 337*n2*
bi'l-malakah, 98
bi'l-ma'na'l-a'amm, 66
bi'l-quwwah, 98
Bīrūnī, Abū Rayḥān al-, 42, 112, 143, 144, 145, 151
Black Elk (Sioux), 282*n18*
Blumberg, Harry, 23
Boehme, Jakob, 158
The Book about Events which Constitute a Lesson (Ibn Khaldūn), 157
The Book of Guidance for Philosophy (Abharī), 189
The Book of Accord between the Ideas of the Divine Plato and Aristotle (al-Fārābī), 138
The Book of Attainment (Bahmanyār ibn Marzbān), 140
The Book of Circles (Ibn al-Sīd), 148
The Book of Critical Detailed Examination of Religions, Sects, and Philosophical Schools (Ibn Ḥazm), 151
The Book of Directives and Remarks (Ibn Sīnā), 22, 64, 86, 98, 111–113, 162, 172
The Book of Guidance (al-Juwaynī), 127

The Book of Healing (Ibn Sīnā), 22, 64, 86, 98, 110, 140
The Book of Letters (Ibn Masarrah), 150
The Book of Light (al-Ash'arī), 125
The Book of Metaphyiscal Penetractions (Mullā Ṣadrā), 88, 310*n12*
The Book of Opinions of the Citizens of the Virtuous City (al-Fārābī), 110, 138
The Book of Penetrating Explanations (Ibn Masarrah), 150
The Book of Salvation (Ibn Sīnā), 64, 86, 98, 111
The Book of Science Dedicated to 'Alā' al-Dawlah (Ibn Sīnā), 64, 86, 111, 112
The Book of the Attainment of Happiness (al-Fārābī), 138
The Book of the Emerald (al-Rāwandī), 143
The Book of the Illuminated, Mirror of the Savior (Aḥṣā'ī), 211
The Book of the Way of Understandings of the Science of Theology (Aḥṣā'ī), 211
The Book of What is Established by Personal Reflection (Baghdādī), 141
Bounoure, Louis, 268
Breaking the Idols of the Age of Ignorance (Mullā Ṣadrā)54
Breath of the Compassionate, 82, 90
Brethren of Purity (Ikhwān al-Ṣafā'), 36, 148, 298*n43*
Brigham Young University, 24
Brown, Joseph E., 282*n18*
Buckman, David, 285n*17*
Budd al-'ārif (The Object of Worship of the Gnostic), 156
Buddha, 7
Buddhism, 6, 273, 274; Mahāyāna, 7; Tibetan, 7; Vajrāyāna, 274; Zen, 1
Bukhārī, 101
Bulah, Amīn al-Dīn Ḥājjī, 190
Bulghah fi'l-ḥikmah, al- (The Sufficient in Philosophy), 188
Burckhardt, Titus, 274, 297*n33*, 300*n8*, 311*n52*, 337*n2*
burhān, 36
Burning Firewood (Mīr Dāmād), 214
Burrell, David, 19, 50
Bursī, Rajab 'Alī, 211
Butterworth, Charles, 23, 312*n59*

calendar, Christian, 282*n16*
Canada: analytical philosophy in, 19; study of Islamic philosophy in, 20
The Canon of Medicine (Ibn Sīnā), 140, 206
Canteins, Jean, 313*n62*
Carra de Vaux, Bernard, 17, 25
Cartesianism, 214
Catharsis of Doctrines (al-Ṭūsī), 133
Catholicism: Scholastic tradition, 15, 19; "Spanish identity" and, 15
Celestial Adam, 149
Celestial Flashes ('Alawī), 220
Celestial Intellects, 149
Chahār-maqālah (Four Articles), 166
The Chant of the Wing of Gabriel (Suhrawardī), 158
Chartres cathedral, 33
Chavooshi, Ja'far, 314*n3*
Chawrasī, Daniyāl, 206
Children of Israel, 37
China, 274; sages of, 1
Chīnī, Mīrzā Ḥasan, 245
Chittick, William, 19, 23, 286*n2*, 298*n38*, 300*n5*, 329*n6*, 330*n18*
Christ, 7; on Kingdom of God, 101
Christian: architecture, 33; art, 33; philosophy, 1, 7, 8, 9, 33, 63, 85, 94, 110, 137, 141; scholastic tradition,16, 15; theology, 5, 52; writers on Islamic philosophy, 26
Christianity, 120, 268, 269, 302*n1*; Catholicism, 221; Divinity of the Founder in, 7–8; knowledge of by Islamic philosophers, 156; philosophy as rival to religion in, 9; prophetic philosophy and, 109; traditional, 129
City of God (St. Augustine), 269

cogito ergo sum, 91
Commentary upon the Book of Directives and Remarks (al-Rāzī), 113, 169
Commentary upon the Ishārāt (al-Rāzī). *See Commentary upon the Book of Directives and Remarks*
Commentary upon the Ishārāt. *See* al-Ṭūsī
Commentary upon the Manẓūmah (Sabziwārī), 238
Commentary upon the Stations (al-Rāzī), 128
communism, 274
Companions, 57
The Conclusive Argument from God (Shāh Walī Allāh of Delhi), 23
Confucianism, 6; Chinese philosophical tradition in, 7; prophecies of, 7
consciousness: unity of, 76
contingency, 141; distinction from impossibility and necessity, 71–73, 110
Coomaraswamy, Ananda K., 20, 274, 284*n9*, 337*n2*
Cooper, John, 19, 319*n6*
Corbin, Henry, 16, 17, 19, 20, 22, 27, 79, 107, 108, 209, 217, 220, 224, 231, 232, 252, 254, 255, 277, 278, 282*n19*, 284*n12*, 286*n3*, 288*n11*, 291*n51*, 292*n7*, 293*n17*, 294*n9*, 298*n24*, 298*n39*, 302*n4*, 304*n1*, 304*n15*, 305*n5*, 306*n15*, 311*n46*, 313*n68*, 317*n32*, 318*n3*, 320*n14*, 325*n6*, 326*n17*, 327*n29*, 330*n18*
Cordovan Sierra (Andalusia), 150
cosmology, 118, 152, 211, 231; angelology and, 229; Aristotelian, 161; Avicennan, 141, 142; Manichaean, 146; of the natural sciences, 147; pseudo-Empedoclean, 150; Quranic, 149; traditional, 21
Cruz Hernández, Miguel, 15, 25, 28, 311*n52*, 313*n61*, 313*n64*
The Cup Reflecting the Cosmos (Maybudī), 211
cycle of initiation, 37, 225
cycle of prophecy, 37, 225

Dabashi, Hamid, 319*n7*
Dabīrān-i Kātibī Qazwīnī. *See* Qazwīnī, Dabīrān-i Kātibī
Daccan, 204, 205
Daiber, Hans, 20, 282*n3*
dāʾirat al-nubuwwah. *See* cycle of prophecy
dāʾirat al-walāyah/wilāyah. *See* cycle of initiation
Dalāʾil al-ḥāʾirīn (Guide to the Perplexed), 190
Dāmād, Mīr Muḥammad Bāqir, 5, 40, 41, 46, 74, 78, 116, 143, 163, 167, 199, 200, 220, 301*n11*, 325*n6*; founding of School of Isfahan by, 87, 212–216; in Safavid period, 88, 116; school of principiality of quiddity and, 176
Dāneshpazhūh, Mohammad Taghi. See Dānishpazhūh, Muḥammad Taqī
Daniel, 5
Dānish-nāma-yi ʿalāʾī (The Book of Science Dedicated to ʿAlāʾ al-Dawlah), 64, 86, 111, 112
Dānishpazhūh, Muḥammad Taqī, 21, 285n*19*, 319n10
Dante Alighieri, 154
Dārā Shukūh, 43
ḍarūrat al-taḍādd, 176
ḍarūrat al-taḍādd fiʾl-ʿālam waʾl-baqāʾ (The Necessity of Contradiction in the World and Determinism and Subsistence), 173
Dasein, 67
Dashtakī, Ghiyāth al-Dīn Manṣūr, 53, 65, 197, 198, 199–202, 206, 213, 323n37, 213; school of principiality of quiddity and, 176
Dashtakī, ʿImād al-Dīn Masʿūd, 197
Dashtakī, Mīr Niẓām al-Dīn, 197
Dashtakī, Mīr Ṣadr al-Dīn Muḥammad, 195–197

Dashtakī, Mīrzā Muḥammad Ma'ṣūm, 197
Dashtakī, Niẓām al-Dīn Aḥmad, 197
Dashtakī, Ṣadr al-Dīn, 53, 203, 321*n22*
Dashtakī, Sayyid Ḥabīb Allāh, 195
Dashtakī, Sayyid 'Alī Khān Kabīr, 197
Dā᾽ūd al-Qayṣarī, 51. *See* Qayṣarī, Dā᾽ūd
Davidson, Herbert, 23, 303*n10*
Dawānī, Jalāl al-Dīn, 39, 51, 53, 134, 191, 195, 197–199, 203, 204, 206, 210; on structure of reality, 80
Dawānī, Riḍā, 276
De Anima (Aristotle), 230
De Boer, Tjitze, 25
The Decisive Treatise (Ibn Rushd), 115
Declaration of the Virtues of Islam (al-'Āmirī), 139
deconstructionism, 19
De intellectu (al-Kindī), 109, 137
The Deliverance from Error (al-Ghazzālī), 113
De Mineralibus (Ibn Sīnā), 77
Demiurge, 112
Democritus, 144
Descartes, René, 2, 91, 232, 251, 253, 262
Descent of Thoughts (Abharī), 189
De Scientiis (al-Fārābī), 138
Descriptions of the Noble (al-Ṭūsī), 187
Deus absconditus, 133
The Development of Metaphysics in Persia (Iqbāl), 26
The Development of Philosophy in Europe (Furūghī), 253
Dewar, Douglas, 268
De Wulf, Maurice, 15, 273
Dhāt, al-, 86
Dhāt al-ilāhiyyah, al-, 63
dhawq, 77, 95
dhawq al-ta᾽alluh, 80
Dhū᾽l-Nūn al-Miṣrī, 147,159
Dībājī, Sayyid Ibrāhīm, 324*n1*
Dihdār, Muḥammad Maḥmūd, 206
Diogenes Laertius, 25
Dionysius the Areopagite, 120
Discourse on Method (Descartes), 251, 253
The Discovery of Truths concerning the Statement of Subtleties (Abharī), 189
The Disposition of Principles (Ibn Turkah), 210
Dissassociation (Mīr Dāmād), 214
Divinalia, 220
Divine Attributes, 50, 125; and, 52
Divine Comedy (Dante), 154
Divine Essence, 86; Beyond-Being of, 63
Divine Intellect, 32, 39
Divine Knowledge, 132, 176
Divine Law, 121, 122, 127, 198, 227
Divine Mercy, 87
Divine Names, 178
Divine Nature, 126
Divine Origin, 170
Divine Principle, 151; relation of world of multiplicity to, 81
Divine Reality, 53, 176
The Divine Sciences (Tabrīzī), 219
Divine Splendor (Zunūzī), 237
Divine Throne, 78, 225
The Divine Tree (Shahrazūrī), 189, 211
Divine Unity, 59
Divine Will, 50, 126
Divine Witnesses, 55
Divine Word: meaning of, 50
Doctrines of the Muslims (al-Ash'arī), 125
Douglas, Elmer, 311*n52*
dualism, 143
Dubois, G., 291*n50*
Dugat, Gustave, 25
Dunlop, Daniel, 312*n55*
Duns Scotus, 303*n10*
Durand, Gilbert, 17, 278, 330*n18*
Durrī, Ḍiā᾽ al-Dīn: works of, 107

Egypt, 155, 209, 278; ancient prophecies and, 1; Islamic

philosophy in, 117, 155, 156, 157, 183, 255, 304*n*; Mamluk, 212; revival of Islamic philosophy in, 108; works of Islamic philosophy from, 107
Eighth/Fourteenth Century: School of Shiraz in, 194
El-Ahwany, Fuʾād, 18
Eleventh Intellect, 200
Eliade, Mircea, 338*n3*
Elucidation concerning the Principles of Religion (al-Ash'arī), 125
emotion: reason and, 102
Empedocles, 4, 150, 281*n1*, 303*n9*, 311*n52*
empiricism, 263
Enneads (Plotinus), 137, 218
Enoch, 281*n9*
Epimenides, 2
epistemology, 2, 141, 159, 161, 232, 251, 253, 262, 303*n13*; angelology and, 229
Erigena, 265
eschatology, 6, 231, 318*n37*; sacred psychology and, 229, 230
esoterism: Islamic, 40
Eternal Wisdom (Ibn Muskūyah), 139
Ethics, 116, 144, 198, 199, 200; philosophical, 139, 187, 198; rational, 123
Euclid, 165, 170, 314*n3*
Europe: histories of Islamic philosophy in, 165
evolution, 267, 268; Darwinian, 231
evolutionism, 271
existence, 67, 293*n1*; of all accidents, 69, 70; death and, 90; distinct from quiddity, 141; external, 70; giver of, 90; of individual man, 90; inner discipline and, 90; levels of, 64; meaning of, 90; mental, 68, 70, 321*n*; nuances of meaning in, 67; principiality of, 87; quiddity and, 70, 175; spiritual experience of, 91; universal, 90
existentialism, 19, 90, 271
existentiation: expansive mode of *wujūd* and, 82

faith: harmonization with reason, 115; meaning of, 122, 123; practice and, 123; reason and, 93; test of, 124
Fakhr al-Dīn al-Rāzī. *See* Rāzī, Fakhr al-Dīn
Fakhr al-Dīn As'ad Gurgānī. *See* Gurgānī, Fakhr al-Dīn As'ad
Fakhr al-Dīn Marāghī. *See* Marāghī, Fakhr al-Dīn
Fakhry, Majid, 18, 23, 28, 307*n7*, 322*n28*
Fākhūrī, Ḥannā al-, 26
Faṣl al-maqāl (The Decisive Treatise), 23, 115
falāsifah, 38, 292*n6*; truth for, 43. *See also* *faylasūf*
Falāṭūrī, Jawād, 19, 278
falsafah, 13, 14, 26, 31, 32, 33, 35, 108, 119, 169, 282*n1*; banning of teaching of, 44; ceases to exist in western lands of Islam, 45; concern with science, 42; criticism of, 40, 41; in development of intellectual sciences, 42; opposition to, 38; opposition to *kalām*, 50; in post-Ibn Rushdian phase of philosophy, 44, 45; reciprocal influence with *kalām*, 49; role in eastern lands of Islam, 45, 46; role in tools of analysis, logic, and rational inquiry, 42; struggle with *kalām*, 43; study in Cairo, 60; truth as one for, 43; in the universities, 44; waning of, 44
falsafah maẓnūnah, 36
falsafah yaqīniyyah, 36
falsafat al-islāmiyyah, al-, 33
Fanārī, Shams al-Dīn al-, 45
Fann al-samā' al-ṭabī'ī, 177
Fārābī, Abū Naṣr al-, 36, 42, 63, 64, 74, 86, 138, 139, 152, 156, 157, 159, 186, 194, 213, 225, 288*n20*, 308*n21*,

Fārābī, Abū Naṣr al- *(continued)* 309*n24*; commentaries on Aristotle, 138; discusses *wujūd* and *māhiyyah;* as father of formal logic in Islamic world, 110; as founder of Peripatetic school, 110; founding of Islamic political philosophy by, 138; interest in music, 138; scientific teaching of, 138; as "Second Teacher," 138; as successor to al-Kindī, 110, 137; systematization of emanation scheme of ten intellects from the One by, 110; works on Plato and Aristotle, 110; treatise on the intellect, 98
Farangi Mahall, 44; Islamic philosophy in, 183
Far East: metaphysics, 17
Fars: Atābakān rulers of, 193
Fārsī, Sayyid Muslim, 196
fāsiqūn, 122
fatā/jawān, 2
Fatḥ 'Alī Shah, 237
Fāṭimid period: Islamic philosophy in Egypt, 183
Fāṭimids, 44, 112, 147
Fawzī al-Najjār. *See* Najjār, Fawzī
Fayḍ Kāshānī, Mullā Muḥsīn. *See* Kāshānī, Mullā Muḥsin Fayḍ
fayḍ al-muqaddas, al-, 90
faylasūf, 50, 177. *See* also *falsāsifah*
Fazlur Rahman. *See* Rahman, Fazlur
fedeli d'amore, 151
Fifth/Eleventh Century: continuation of school of Ibn Sīnā during, 169
Fifth/Sixth Century: Islamic philosophy in Andalusia, 183
Fī ḥaqīqat al-'ishq (On the Reality of Love), 158
Fi'l-'aql (On the Intellect), 109
Fi'l-falsafat al-ūlā (On Metaphysics), 109, 137
Fī māqāmāt al-'ārifīn (On the Stations of the Gnostics), 201
Findiriskī, Mīr Abū'l-Qāsim, 37, 216–218, 287*n9*
fiqh: rivalries of, 55
Fiqh al-akbar (The Great Knowledge), 121
First Intellect, 141, 148, 149
"First Originated," 148
Fitzgerald, Edward, 166, 167, 182, 314*n1*
Five Divine Presences, 90
Flashes of Illumination concerning Ethical Virtues (Dawānī), 198
Forms of Brightness concerning the Temples of Light (Dawānī), 199
Forouzanfar, Badī' al-Zamān, 314*n5*
Foundations of Acquiring Knowledge (al-Ṭūsī), 187
Four Articles (Samarqandī), 166
Fourier, Charles, 269
The Four Journeys (Mullā Ṣadrā), 22, 53, 55, 65, 79, 88, 117, 203, 224, 228
The Four Journeys (Mullā Shamsā Gīlānī), *219*
The Four Journeys (Shams al-Dīn Khafrī), 203
Fourth/Sixth Century: Islamic philosophy in Khurasan, 183
France, 242; philosophical traditions, 20
Frank, Richard, 306*n2*
Frederick II (Emperor), 156
Fu'ad Sezgin. *See* Sezgin, Fu'ad
Fūlādwand, Muḥammad Mahdī, 315*n9*
fundamentalism, 270
Furūghī, Muḥammad 'Alī, 253
Futuḥāt al-makkiyyah, al- (Mekkan Illuminations), 228
futuwwah, 2
Fuṣūṣ al-ḥikmah (Bezels of Wisdom), 64, 138

Gabriel (Archangel), 7, 96, 137
Galen, 25
Gardet, Louis, 15, 17, 50, 286*n6*, 290*n35*, 302*n7*

Gauthier, Léon, 16, 25
Gawhar-i murād (The Sought Jewel), 55, 56
Genequand, Charles, 23
geomancy, 203
geometry, 171
German: philosophical developments, 24; philosophy, 6; Romantic movement in, 6
Geschichte der Philosophie im Islam (De Boer), 25
Ghaḍanfar. *See* Tabrīzī, Abū Isḥāq
ghayb al-ghuyūb, 148
Ghazzālī, Abū Ḥāmid Muḥammad al-, 38, 39, 45, 50, 53, 56, 75, 97, 112, 113, 114, 127, 131, 148, 155, 156, 168, 169, 186, 192, 265, 285n*17*, 294*n9*
Ghīlanī, Afḍal al-Dīn al-, 196
Ghiyāth al-Dīn Manṣūr Dashtakī. *See* Dashtakī, Ghiyāth al-Dīn Manṣūr
Gholam Safavi. *See* Safavi, Gholam
Ghulām Ḥusayn Ibrāhīmī Dīnānī. *See* Ibrāhīmī Dīnānī, Ghulām Ḥusayn
Gīlānī, ʻInāyat Allāh, 235
Gīlānī, Mullā Shamsā, 219, 235
Gilson, Etienne, 15, 16, 273, 286nb, 293*n4*, 302*n1*, 303*n12*, 339*n10*
Gimaret, Daniel, 302*n6*, 307*n6*
gnosis, 32, 35, 36, 37, 40, 41, 46, 49, 74, 87, 119, 131, 139, 190, 194, 203, 209, 211, 236, 239, 243; faculty of the heart and, 94; illumination and, 76; Islamic, 159; knowledge and, 99; meaning, 298*n41*; meaning of intellect and, 100; of the purified heart, 102; Shi'ite, 36, 111, 146, 304*n1*; shortcomings of Ash'arite approach and, 52; theoretical, 108
Gobineau, Comte de, 242
God, 3, 55; Being of, 2, 232, 251, 253, 262; bestowing of *wujūd* by, 176; communication from, 227; creations of, 123; on Day of Judgment, 125; Essence and Qualities of, 244; as eternal, 142; existence of, 67, 292*n8*; goodness of, 178; guidance from, 144; knowledge of, 93, 102, 218; knowledge of particulars by, 113; knowledge of the world by, 52, 100, 187; light of, 135; manʾs position in reference to, 34; nature of, 134; as Necessary Being, 71; omnipotence of, 125, 126; Oneness of, 72; path to, 101; possession of *wujūd* by, 76; power of creation in, 72; praise of, 171; presence of, 130; as Pure Being, 215; in Quranic revelation, 226; reaching, 39; as reality, 67, 80, 129, 172, 181; remembering, 173; returns Islam to perfection, 270; science of, 132; servants of, 175; soul recreated by, 134; source of single reality, 78; speaking to Moses, 7; transcendence of, 81; unity of, 120, 121, 137, 237, 300*n6*; "unknowable," 133; will of, 86, 97, 126; Word of, 96, 148; *wujūd* given by, 67
Godʾs Names and Qualities, 132
Godwin, Joscelyn, 282*n17*
Gohlmann, William E., 23
Goichon, A.M., 15, 293*n3*, 294*n6*, 300*n3*, 310*n33*
Goldziher, Ignaz, 15
Goodman, Lenn, 19, 23, 310*n41*, 311*n52*, 312*n55*
gradation: of being, 89; of *wujūd*, 77–78
"Grand Resurrection," 146
Great Britain: analytical philosophy in, 19, 20
Greece: ancient prophecies and, 1; early philosophers of, 43; intellectual activity in, 1; philosophical tradition in, 2, 8, 18, 25

Greek: philosophers, 150, 159; philosophy, 6, 63, 108, 109, 146, 156, 198, 214, 215, 303*n9*; religion, 4; sages, 139; thinking on "chain of being," 77; thought translated into Arabic, 123
Guarded Tablet, 149
Guénon, René, 20, 274, 284*n9*
Guide for the Perplexed (Maimorides), 190
Gujarat: Ismā'īlism in, 147
Gulshan-i rāz (Secret Rose Garden of Divine Mysteries), 146, 190, 192
Gurgānī, Fakhr al-Dīn As'ad, 172
Gurgānī, Mīrzā Ismā'īl, 239
Gutas, Dimitri, 309*n31*
Guthrie, Kenneth S., 281*n1*

ḥaḍarāt al-ilāhiyyat al-khams, al-, 90
Ḥadīth, 74, 101, 102, 120, 121, 124, 127, 133
Ḥāfiẓ, 194
Ḥā'irī, 'Abd al-Ḥusayn, 320*n13*
Ḥā'irī Yazdī, Mīrzā Mahdī, 18, 19, 241, 252, 254, 276, 283n7, 295n*11*, 302n4
Ḥājjī Mullā Ḥādī Sabziwārī. *See* Sabziwārī, Ḥājjī Mullā Ḥādī
Ḥājjī Khalīfah, 24
ḥakīm: defining, 42
Ḥalabī, 'Alī Aṣghar, 27
Ḥallāj, Manṣūr al-, 156, 159
Hamadānī, 'Ayn al-Quḍāt, 239
Ḥamīd al-Dīn al-Kirmānī. *See* Kirmānī, Ḥamīd al-Dīn
Ḥanafī, Ḥasan, 278
Ḥannā al-Fākhūrī. *See* Fākhūrī, Ḥannā
ḥaqīqah, 31
ḥaqīqat al-muḥammadiyyah, al-, 227
Ḥaqq, al- 33, 176
Harvard University, 27
Ḥasan al-Baṣrī. *See* Baṣrī, Ḥasan
Ḥasan Qaṭṭān al-Marwazī. *See* Marwazī, Ḥasan Qaṭṭān
Ḥasan-zādah Āmulī, Ḥasan, 254
Hātif, 102
Ḥayākil al-nūr (Temples of Light), 199, 200
Ḥayy ibn Yaqẓān (Living Son of the Awake), 114, 153,154
The Healer (Dashtakī), 200
heart: eye of, 102; knowledge and, 100, 101, 102; mind as projection of, 102
Heavenly Mystical States (Mīr Dāmād), 214
Hedayat, Sadegh, *166*
hedonism, 183
Hegel, Georg W. F., 158
Heidegger, Martin, 6, 295*n19*
The Height of Thought concerning the Clarification of Mysteries (Abharī), 189
Hein, Christel, 288*n12*
Hejaz, 200, 209
Hellenic: thought, 123
Hermansen, Marcia, 23, 293*n19*
hermeneutics: esoteric, 133; spiritual, 111
Hermes, 25, 34, 43, 109, 159, 281*n9*
Hermeticism, 39, 111, 147–150, 156
Hesychia, 3
Hesychasm, 3
Hidāyat al-ḥikmah (Guide of Philosophy), 162
ḥikmah, 25, 30, 31, 34, 35, 36, 40, 97, 135; relation to Sufism, 59; revival of, 59
ḥikmah baḥthiyyah, 85, 99
ḥikmah dhawqiyyah, 85, 99
Ḥikmat al-'arshiyyah, al- (Wisdom of the Throne), 23
ḥikmat al-'atīqah, al-, 158
Ḥikmat al-'ayn (Wisdom from the Source), 162
ḥikmat al-'ilāhiyyah, al-, 13, 14, 36, 119, 135; as bridge between formal religious science and gnosis, 36; followers refusal to

accept methods of *kalām*, 52; relation to *kalām*, 49–60; in Shi'ite circles in Iraq, 60
Ḥikmat al-ishrāq (the Theosophy of the Orient of Light) 115, 158, 160, 188, 192
ḥikmat al-mashriqiyyah, al-, 11, 140
ḥikmat al-muta'āliyah, al-, (the transcendent theosophy).*See* transcendent theosophy
Ḥikmat al-muta'āliyah fi'l-asfār al-'aqliyyat al-arba'ah, al- (Transcendent Theosophy). *See Asfār al-arba'ah*
ḥikmat-i ilāhī, 53
Ḥillī, 'Allāmah Jamāl al-Dīn al-, 51, 52, 59, 65, 133, 211
Hindu: *avatārs*, 7; philosophical traditions, 8; prophecies, 1; sages, 4
Hinduism, 145, 156, 229, 273, 295*n18*; *rishis* of, 7
Hiram-i hastī (The Pyramid of Being), 252
Histoire de la philosophie islamique (Corbin, Nasr, Yahya), 27, 107, 108
Historia del pensamiento en el mundo islámico (Cruz Hernández), 28
history: philosophy of, 157, 313*n65*
History of Islamic Philosophy (Fakhry), 28
The History of Islamic Philosophy (Nasr and Leaman [eds.]), 27, 108
Hobson, J. Peter, 283*n8*
Holy Spirit, 152
homo islamicus, 265, 266
Horovitz, Saul, 15, 50
Horten, Max, 17, 50, 113, 287*n8*, 288*n11*, 290*n35*, 306*n2*, 306*n9*
Hossein Ziai. *See* Ziai, Hossein
Hourani, George, 23, 307*n3*, 312*n59*
ḥuḍūr, 89
ḥukamā', 32, 33
Humā'ī, Jalāl, 236, 290*n39*
humanism, 270
Ḥusām al-Ālūsī. *See* Ālūsī, Ḥusām

īlahiyyāt bi ma'na'l-'āmm, al-, 134
Iatromantis, 1, 2, 3
Ibānah 'an uṣūl al-diyānah, al- (Elucidation concerning the Principles of Religion), 125
Ibn Abī Jumhūr Aḥsā'ī, 209, 211, 212
Ibn Abī Uṣaybi'ah, 24
Ibn 'Adī, Yaḥyā, 139
Ibn al-'Arīf, 150
Ibn al-Fātik, 139
Ibn al-Haytham, 170, 171
Ibn al-Nadīm, 24
Ibn al-Nā'imah al-Ḥimsī, 137
Ibn al-Qifṭī, 24
Ibn al-Rāwandī, 143
Ibn al-Sīd, 148
Ibn Ḥanbal, Imam Aḥmad, 124
Ibn 'Arabī, 27, 38, 40, 46, 74, 75, 76, 115, 116, 131, 132, 135, 150, 151, 156, 162, 163, 179, 180, 191, 228, 242, 300*n6*; effect on Sufism, 87; Islamic philosophy and, 87; metaphysical doctrines of, 45; transcendent unity of being and, 87
Ibn Ḥayyān, Jābir. See Jābir ibn Ḥayyān
Ibn Baḥr al-Jāḥiẓ, 'Amr. *See* Jāḥiẓ, 'Amr ibn Baḥr
Ibn Bājjah, Abū Bakr, 114, 152, 156
Ibn Barrajān, 150
Ibn Fātik, 25
Ibn Ḥazm, 24, 114, 115, 151
Ibn Kammūnah, 189
Ibn Khaldūn, 23, 26, 39, 45, 50, 51, 115, 127, 155, 157, 287*n10*, 288*n11*, 313*n65*
Ibn Khallakān, 24
Ibn Marzbān, Bahmanyār. *See* Bahmanyār ibn Marzbān
Ibn Masarrah, 114, 150, 151, 156, 157

Ibn Miskawayh. *See* Ibn Muskūyah
Ibn Muskūyah, Aḥmad, 112, 139
Ibn Nadīm, 35
Ibn Ṭufayl, 152, 156
Ibn Qasyī, 156
Ibn Rushd, 16, 23, 26, 27, 29, 41, 45, 108, 114, 150, 152, 154, 155, 156, 169, 188, 194, 213, 215, 294*n9*, 312*n59*; on accidentality of *wujūd*, 69; commentaries on Aristotle by, 114, 115; harmonization of faith and reason by, 115; understanding of Ibn Sīnā, 70; works of, 96
Ibn Sab'īn, 45, 75, 115, 156, 157; knowledge of Judaism and Christianity, 156; pro-Shi'ite tendencies of, 155
Ibn Hārūn, Sahl, 35
Ibn Sīnā, 4, 5, 22, 27, 29, 36, 39, 41, 42, 46, 49, 50, 67, 68, 69, 74, 114, 115, 118, 133, 134, 138, 140, 141, 143, 145,152, 155, 159, 165, 167, 169, 171, 172, 174, 177, 192, 194, 196, 200, 205, 215, 218, 225, 226, 240, 276, 284*n12*, 288*n22*, 290*n35*, 294*n6*, 296*n23*, 298*n43*, 305*n8*, 308*n21*, 309*n31*, 310*n35*, 312*n61*, 313*n63*, 319*n8*; on accidentality of *wujūd*, 79; chain of being and, 77; formulation of distinctions of necessity, contingency, and impossibility by, 71; Hermetic prototypes in, 147; on intellectual intuition, 99; as philosopher of being, 64, 141; structure of reality and, 81; study of in Turkey, 60; synthesis of Peripatetic thought by, 110; treatment of the intellect by, 98; use of Persian by, 112; visionary recitals of, 111, 147; works of, 69, 86, 111
Ibn Taymiyyah, Taqī al-Dīn, 38, 76
Ibn Ṭufayl, 23, 114, 152, 156
Ibn Tumart, 127
Ibn Turkah Iṣfahānī, 65, 76, 116, 163
Ibrāhīm Madkour. *See* Madkour, Ibrāhīm
Ibrāhīmī Dīnānī, Ghulām Ḥusayn, 27,276,292n5, 313n68
identity: Spanish, 15
Idrīs, 25, 43, 109, 159
Idrīs 'Imād al-Dīn, Sayyidunā, 174
'ifrān-i naẓarī, 108
Iḥyā' 'ulūm al-dīn (The Revivification of the Sciences of Religion), 190
Ījī, 'Aḍud al-Dīn al-, 39, 43, 128, 195, 201, 306*n1*
Ikhwān al-Ṣafā'. *See* Brethren of Purity
Iksīr al-'ārifīn (The Elixir of the Gnostics), 23
Ilāhī Qumsha'ī, Muḥyī al-Dīn Mahdī, *308n15*
ilāhiyyāt, 132
ilāhiyyāt bi ma'na'l-khāṣṣ, al-, 134
I'lām bi-manāqib al-islām, al- (Declaration of the Virtues of Islam), 139
Īl-Khānid, 43, 190
illumination, 32, 40, 41, 42, 46, 49, 76, 118, 210, 211; defining, 161; inner, 153; of the intellect, 96; knowledge as result of, 99; locus in the heart, 84; possibility of from above, 228; prophecy and, 228, 229; prophetic function and, 94, 228, 229; reception of, 77; school of, 51, 64, 80, 86, 99, 115, 116, 140, 157, 158–160. See also *ishrāqī*
Illuminationist, 13
'ilm al-hūḍūrī, al-, 76, 95
'ilm al-uṣūl, 135
'Ilm-i ḥuḍūrī (Knowledge by Presence), *252, 253*
'Imād al-Dīn Mas'ūd Dashtakī. *See* Dashtakī, 'Imād al-Dīn Mas'ūd
imagination: knowledge and, 100; power of, 100; world of, 179
Imām al-Ḥaramayn al-Juwaynī. *See* Juwaynī, Imām al-Ḥaramayn

Imamology, 134, 147
īmān, 31
imkān, 71, 86, 141
impossibility, 141; distinction from contingency and necessity, 71–73
imtinā', 71, 86, 141
Inati, Shams, 23
inbi'āth, 149
Incoherence of the Incoherence (Ibn Rushd), 114, 115
Incoherence of the Philosophers (al-Ghazzālī), 113
India, 189, 200; Alamut tradition in, 147; *al-ḥikmat al-ilāhiyyah* in, 60; Christian missionaries in, 220; intellectual life in, 46; Islamic philosophy in, 28, 88, 160, 163, 183, 192, 194, 204–207; Ismā'īlism in, 112, 147; libraries in, 21; metaphysics in, 17; Moghul period in, 43; philosophical traditions of, 7; philosophy of Mullā Ṣadrā in, 117; religions of, 6; Sufi music in, 138; Sufism in, 128; unity of consciousness school in (*See* Simnānī, 'Alā᾽ al-Dawlah)
Indian: sages, 139; Sufism, 132
Indonesia, 277; students studying in the West from, 19
Indo-Pakistani: Islamic texts, 26; teaching of *falsafah* in schools of, 44
initiation: cycle of, 37
insān al-kāmil, al-, 100
Institut Franco-Iranien, 22
intellect: ability to distinguish between *wujūd* and *māhiyyah* by, 67; Active, 98, 99, 142, 152; degrees of, 99; Eleventh, 200; First, 141, 148, 149; growth of, 99; intuition and, 99; Islamic perspectives on, 93–103; meaning of, 93, 95, 100; revelation and, 96; Second, 141, 149; Tenth, 141, 149; Third, 149; universal, 98; universal function of, 100
The Intellect (al-Kindī), 109
intellectus in actu, 142
intelligence: material, 98; potential, 98
Intimations (Suhrawardī), 188
intuition, 95; gaining knowledge and, 94; inner, 94; intellect and, 99; Islamic perspectives on, 93–103; meaning of, 93
Investigations concerning India (al-Bīrūnī), 145
Iqbāl, Muḥammad, 26, 117, 129, 275
Iqbāl, Muẓaffar, 310*n43*
Iqtiṣād fi᾽l-i'tiqād, al- (The Just Mean in Belief), 127
Iran: Council of the Islamic Revolution in, 117; Islamic philosophy in, 191; new manuscripts in, 21; religions in, 1, 6; students studying in the West from, 19; works of Islamic philosophy from, 107. *See* also Persia
Irānī, Taqī, 166
Iranian Academy of Philosophy, 255
Iranian Revolution, 117, 254
Īranshahrī, Abū᾽l-'Abbās, 49, 109, 144
Iraq, 211; *al-ḥikmat al-ilāhiyyah* in, 60; Mongol invasion of, 193; Mu'tazilites in, 121; philosophical activity in, 45, 116; philosophical traditions in, 110; religious debates in, 120; Seljuq rule in, 168
'Irāqī, Abū᾽l-Qāsim al-, 147
'irfān, 32, 35, 119,200; *ḥikmah* and, 46
irrationalism, 224
Isagogue, 189
Isfahan: Islamic philosophy in, 158; revival of Islamic philosophy in, 197; school of, 162, 163
Isfahan School. *See* School of Isfahan
Iṣfahānī, Muḥammad ibn Dā᾽ūd al-, 151
Iṣfahānī, Mullā Muḥammad Ismā'īl Darbkūshkī, 236

Işfahānī, Ṣāʾin al-Dīn Turkah, 209, 210
Ishārāt waʾl-tanbīhāt, al-. *See Kitāb al-ishārāt waʾl-tanbīhāt*
ishrāq, 4, 13, 32, 36, 51, 64, 95, 97, 116, 117, 159, 161, 192; philosophy of, 160–162; theosophy of, 53. *See* also illumination
Islam, 2; esoterism in, 37; fate of *falsafah* in, 45–47; Indian, 88; *mashshāʾī* school in, 97; meaning and role of philosophy in, 31–47; meaning of divinity in, 74; modern thought and, 259–271; philosophical traditions differing from Western, 85; Shiʿite, 39, 74, 132–135, 163, 204; Sunni, 39, 51, 97, 128, 163; Twelve-Imam, 38, 51, 97, 116, 128, 132, 133, 183, 187, 204
Islamic: architecture, 33; esoterism, 40; law, 214; metaphysics, 65; ontology, 67; philosophy, 33, 49, 275; revelation, 100; sciences, 42, 43, 213, 214, 323*n39*; spirituality, 148; theology, 49; universities, 44, 274, 275, 276
Ismāʿīlī, 38; doctrine, 290*n35*; philosophy, 23, 81, 108, 111, 112, 145–150, 305*n5*, 311*n46*, 330*n13*; thinking, 133
Ismāʿīlism, 112, 146, 210, 227
istidlāl, 95; criticism of, 40
Iʿtimād al-Ṣaltanah, 242
Ivanow, Vladimir, 23
Ivry, Alfred, 23
Izutsu, Toshihiko, 17, 19, 215, 255, 278, 293*n1*, 301*n15*
ʿIzz al-Dīn al-Jaldakī. *See* Jaldakī, ʿIzz al-Dīn

Jābirī, Muḥammad al-, 278
Jadhawāt, al- (Burning Firewood), 214
Jābir ibn Ḥayyān, 147
Jaʿfar al-Ṣādiq, Imam, 149
Jaʿfarī, Yaʿqūb, 292*n14*
Jaffe, Alisa, 311*n52*
Jahāngīr Khān Qashqāʾī. *See* Qashqāʾī, Jahāngīr Khān
Jāḥiẓ, ʿAmr ibn Baḥr, 35, 121
Jalāl al-Dīn Dawānī. *See* Dawānī, Jalāl al-Dīn
Jalālean Ethics (Dawānī), 198
Jalāl Humāʾī. *See* Humāʾī, Jalāl
Jalālī Nāʾīnī, Muḥammad Riḍā, 314n5
Jalāyir, Āl-i. *See* Āl-i Jalāyir
Jalbani, G.N., 293*n19*
Jaldakī, ʿIzz al-Dīn al-, 147
Jamāl al-Dīn al-Asadābādī. *See* Asadābādī, Jamāl al-Dīn
Jamāl al-Zamān, al-Shaykh, 177
Jambet, Christian, 20, 278, 319*n7*
Jāmī, ʿAbd al-Raḥmān, 76
Jāmiʿ al-ḥikmatayn (The Sum of Two Wisdoms), 112, 146
Jām-i gītī-namā (The Cup Reflecting the Cosmos), 211
Jandī, Muʾayyīd al-Dīn al-, 45, 76, 116
Japan, 274
Jār Allāh Zamakhsharī. *See* Zamakhsharī, Jār Allāh
Jawād Falāṭūrī. *See* Falāṭūrī, Jawād
Jawādī Āmulī, ʿAbd Allāh, 254
jawānmardī, 2
jawhar, 98
Jawharat al-tawḥīd (The Substance of Unity), 128
Jāwīdān-khirad (Eternal Wisdom [philosophia perennis]), 112, 139
Jeremias, Alfred, 338*n3*
Jewish: Kabbalah, 210; philosophy, 1, 7, 8, 9, 28, 33, 63, 110, 137, 141, 152; Scholasticism, 15, 16, 19
Jīlī, Majd al-Dīn al-, 186
Jilwah, Mīrzā Abūʾl-Ḥasan, 243, 245, 246
jism al-ṭabīʿī, al-, 171
jism al-taʿlīmī, al-, 171
Jonah, 5
Jones, Edward R., 28522
Jordan, 278

Jubbāʾī, Abū ʿAlī al-, 121, 124
Judaism, 5, 156; knowledge of by Islamic philosophers, 156; prophetic philosophy and, 109; traditional, 129
Junayd, Abūʾl Qāsim al-, 156
jurisprudence, 54, 124, 135, 190, 194, 197, 200, 220; Catholic, 96; principles of, 232; Quranic principles of, 13, 133
Jurjānī Sayyid Sharīf al-, 43, 51, 53, 116, 128, 195
Jurr, Khalīl al-, 26
The Just Mean in Belief (al-Ghazzālī), 127
Juwaynī, Imām al-Ḥaramayn al-, 39, 50, 168
juzʾ lā yatajazzā, 126

kalām, 14, 26, 34, 35, 108, 119; Ashʿarite, 46, 60, 86, 125, 128; basis in voluntarism, 86; differing views on, 49; Divine Attributes and, 52; early, 120, 121; eclipse of, 59; extension of borders of, 57, 58; in modern world, 128, 129; in Muslim intellectual life in western regions, 45; Muʿtazilite, 133; new, 57, 58; opposition from *falsafah,* 50; philosophical, 128; relation to *al-ḥikmat al-ilāhiyyah,* 49–60; relation to Sufism, 56, 57, 58; religious truth and, 54; replacement of role and function of, 52; resuscitation of, 128; school, 117; Shiʿite, 59, 132–135; Sunni, 60; teaching of in *madrasahs,* 113; Twelve-Imam Shiʿite, 38, 51, 128, 132, 133
kalām-i jadīd, 59
Kalin, Ibrahim, 277, 330*n20*
Kamal, Selim, 23
Kant, Immanuel, 2, 7
Karakī, Muḥaqqiq-i, 212
Kashan, 203, 204, 213, 238
Kāshānī, ʿAbd al-Razzāq, 87, 116, 300*n7*
Kāshānī, Afḍal al-Dīn, 5, 23, 162, 167, 188, 192, 241
Kāshānī, Āqā Muẓaffar Ḥusayn, 216
Kāshānī, Mawlā Ḥabīb Allāh, 201
Kāshānī, Mullā Muḥsin Fayḍ, 65, 88, 134, 219, 235
Kashf al-ḥāqāʾiq fī taḥrīr al-daqāʾiq (The Discovery of Truths concerning the Statement of Subtleties), 189
Kashf al-maḥjūb (Unveiling of the Veiled), 146
Kashf al-murād (The Unveiling of the Desired), 133
Kasr al-aṣnām al-jāhiliyyah (Breaking the Idols of the Age of Ignorance), 54
Kātibī Qazwīnī, Najm al-Dīn Dabīrān-i, 162, 188, 191, 192, 203, 211
Kay Khusraw, 159
Kāzirūnī, Awḥād al-Dīn, 194
Keys to the Invisible (Mullā Ṣadrā), 228
Khafrī, Shams al-Dīn Muḥammad ibn Aḥmad, 195, 202, 203, 206, 213
Khājūʾī, Mullā Ismāʿīl, 236
Khalṣat al-malakūt (Heavenly Mystical States), 214
Khālid ibn Yazīd, 35
Khalīl al-Jurr. *See* Jurr, Khalīl
Khalʿiyyah, al- (Disassociation), 214
khamīrat al-azaliyyah, al-, 159
Khān, Ḥāfiẓ Ghaffār, 293*n19*
Khan, M.S., 23
Khān, Sayyid Aḥmad, 128
Khān School, 194, 223
khāriq al-ʿādah, 126
Kharyrābādī, Mullā ʿAbd al-Wāḥid, 207
Khayabad: Islamic philosophy in, 183
khayāl, 179

Khayyām, 'Umar, 5, 113, 118, 141, 163, 165–183, 186, 314*n14*, 315*n10*, 315*n11*, 315*n12*, 317*n28*; cult of, 167; defense of Sufism by, 175; knowledge of, 166; works of, 167, 168, 178–183
Khumaynī, Ayatollah Rūḥ Allāh, 117, 179
Khunsārī, Āqā Ḥusayn, 235
Khurasan: as center of philosophic activity, 110, 139; Islamic philosophy in, 193
Khusraw, Nāṣir-i. *See* Nāṣir-i Khusraw
Khusrawī, Abū Bakr Muḥammad ibn 'Alī. 171
Khusrawshāhī, Shams al-Dīn, 190
Khuṭbat al-gharrā', al- (The Splendid Sermon), 171
Khwājah Naṣīr al-Dīn al-Ṭūsī. *See* Ṭūsī, Khwājah Naṣīr al-Dīn
Khwājah Niẓām al-Mulk. *See* Niẓām al-Mulk
Kiliç, Mahmut Erol, 277
Kindī, Abū Ya'qūb al-, 49, 98, 110, 136, 145; founding of Peripatetic school and, 109, 136; as "Philosopher of the Arabs," 109; treatises on intellect by, 98; works of, 109
King, David, 325*n8*
Kingsley, Peter, 2, 4, 281*n1*, 282*n13*, 311*n53*
Kirmānī, Ḥamīd al-Dīn al-, 111, 133, 146, 147, 148, 227
Kirmānshāhī, Mīrzā Ḥasan, 244, 247
Kitāb al-ḥurūf (The Book of Letters), 86, 150
Kitāb al-ishārāt wa'l-tanbīhat (The Book of Directives and Remarks), 22, 64, 86, 98, 111–113, 162, 172
Kitāb al-mawāqif (The Book of Stations), 39
Kitāb al-fiṣal fi'l-milal wa'l-ahwā' wa'l-niḥal (The Book of Critical Detailed Examination of Religions), 151
Kitāb al-ḥadā'iq (The Book of Circles), 148
Kitāb al-'ibar (The Book about Events which Constitute a Lesson), 157
Kitāb al-irshād (The Book of Guidance), 127
Kitāb al-jam' bayn ra'yay al-ḥakīmayn Aflāṭūn al-ilāhī wa Arisṭū (The Book of Accord between the Ideas of the Divine Plato and Aristotle), *138*
Kitāb al-luma' (The Book of Light), 125
Kitāb al-maslak al-afhām fī 'ilm al-kalām (The Book of the Way of Understandings of the Science of Theology), 211
Kitāb al-mujlī mir'āt al-munjī (The Book of the Illuminated, Mirror of the Savior), *211*
Kitāb al-mu'tabar (The Book of What Is Established by Personal Reflection), 141
Kitāb al-najāh (The Book of Salvation), 64, 86, 98, 111
Kitāb al-shifā' (The Book of Healing), 22, 64, 86, 98, 110, 140
Kitāb al-tabṣirah (The Book of Penetrating Explanations), 150
Kitāb al-taḥṣīl (The Book of Attainment), 140
Kitāb al-zumurrud (The Book of the Emerald), 143
Kitāb ārā' ahl al-madīnāt al-fāḍilah (The Book of Opinions of the Citizens of the Virtuous City), 110, 138
Kitāb hidāyat al-ḥikmah (The Book of Guidance for Philosophy), 189
Kitāb taḥsīl al-sa'ādah (The Book of the Attainment of Happiness), 138
Klein, Walter, 307*n6*
knowledge: accessibility of, 93; acquisition of, 57, 58, 99; attained, 102; by demonstration, 58; direct, 102; Divine, 132, 176; esoteric,

228; gained by the heart, 101, 102; of God, 102, 218; hierarchy of, 102; imaginary, 102; intellectual, 102; intuitive, 95; as light, 161; metaphysical, 99; of particulars of the world of multiplicity, 93; path of, 101; power of imagination and, 100; presential, 95, 102; principal, 102, 135; as quality of *wujūd*, 176; rational, 102; representative, 95; as result of illumination, 99; revealed, 93; sharing attribute of, 94; of state of creatures according to the *Sharī'ah*, 58; supreme form of, 102; theory of, 98; through inner purification, 175; unitive, 102

Knowledge by Presence (Yazdī), 252, 253

Kouros, 2

Kraemer, Joel, 305*n4*

Kraus, Paul, 15, 305*n6*

kuffār, 122

Kulbārī, Mawlā Qawām al-Dīn Muḥammad, 195

kullī al-ṭabī'ī, al-, 121, 123

kullu shay'in yarji'u ilā aṣlihi, 180

kumūn wa burūz, 123

kun, 148

Kurland, Samuel, 23

Kuşpinar, Bilal, 291*n50*

Kutluer, Ilhan, 277

Lāhījī, 'Abd al-Razzāq, 65, 134, 167, 219, 235; works of, 55, 56

Lāhījī, Mīrzā Ḥasan: works of, 59

Lāhījī, Mīrzā Ibrāhīm, 59

Lāhījī, Mullā Muḥammad Ja'far, 243

Lāhījī, Shams al-Dīn Muḥammad, 194

Lahore, 206

la ilāha illa'Llāh, 74

Lama'āt-i ilāhiyyah (Divine Splendors), 237

Lama'āt-i malakūtiyyah (Celestial Flashes), 220

Landolt, Herman, 19, 324*n1*

Langarūdī, Mullā Muḥammad Ja'far, 240, 245

language(s): Arabic, 131, 158, 192, 193, 227, 284*n16*, 321*n23*; Arabic philosophical, 110; Avicennan, 181; distinction between intellect and reason in, 94; English, 28, 261, 310*n41*, 313*n70*; European, 8, 13, 20, 23, 27, 309*n30*, 329*n6*, 330*n18*; French, 285n*18*, 313*n70*; German, 285n*18*; Greek, 227; Indo-European, 131; Indo-Iranian-European, 227; Latin, 156, 189, 227, 269; Persian, 192, 193, 198, 227, 310*n45*; philosophical, 112; Urdu, 117; Western, 94

Lārījānī, Āqā Sayyid Raḍī, 238, 239, 243

Laraoui, 'Abd Allāh, 278

Laṭā'if al-ḥikmah (Subtleties of Philosophy), 189

law, 14; Divine, 121, 122, 127, 198, 227; Islamic, 183, 197, 214; philosophy of, 118; Sunni schools of, 121

Lawāmi' al-ishrāq fī makārim al-akhlāq (Flashes of Illumination concerning Ethical Virtues), 198

Lawāmi'-i rabbānī (Lordly Flashes), *220*

Lawḥ al-maḥfūẓ, al-, 149

Leaman, Oliver, 19, 20, 28, 108, 282*n3*, 287*n8*, 290*n34*, 298*n38*, 302*n4*, 306*n13*, 309*n31*, 311*n46*, 313*n61*, 319*n7*, 322*n28*, 328*n2*

Leiden, Carl, 337*n2*

Les Religions et les philosophies dans l'Asie central (Gobineau), 242

Lewisohn, Leonard, 320*n17*

liar's paradox, 196

The Life of Ibn Sīnā (Gohlmann*)*, *23*

light: knowledge as, 161; of lights, 160; metaphysics of, 160; symbolism of, 161

Lings, Martin, 281*n8*, 297*n32*, 337*n2*

literature, 194, 240; Arabic, 290*n43*

Living Son of the Awake (Ibn Ṭufayl), 114, 153, 154

Lodi, Skandar, 43, 204
Loeb Library, 24
logic, 2, 42, 156, 187, 189, 191, 196, 200, 224, 232, 240, 251, 253, 262; Aristotelian, 78; formal, 110, 113; Greek, 3; spiritual union and, 46, 47; teaching of, 44; Western, 2
Logos, 43
loquentes, 119
Lordly Flashes ('Alawī), 220
love: Platonic, 114, 115, 312*n54*
Lovejoy, Arthur, 298*n42*
Lūkarī al-Marwazī, Abū ʾl-'Abbās, 169, 172, 196
Luther, Martin, 120

ma'ād, al-, 134
Ma'ālim al-shifāʾ (Milestones of Healing), 200
ma'ārif, 59
Ma'ārif al-ilāhiyyah, al- (The Divine Sciences), 219
ma'ārif-i ilahī, 56
mabdaʾ, al-, 90
Mabdaʾ waʾl-ma'ād, al- (The Origin and the End), 55
Macdonald, Duncan, 307*n6*
Madelung, Wilfred, 50, 290*n35*, 308*n14*, 311*n50*
Madkour, Ibrāhīm, 18, 26
madrasahs, 113, 276, 277; banning of *falsafah* in, 44
Mafātīḥ al-ghayb (Keys to the Invisible), 228
Maghrib, 15; Ash'arite teachings in, 127; Islamic philosophy in, 114, 115, 152, 154, 155, 157, 158
Maḥbūb al-qulūb (Beloved of Hearts), 219
Mahdawī, Yaḥyā, 253
Mahdi, Muhsin, 18, 19, 23
Mahdī Āshtiyānī, Mīrzā. *See* Āshtiyānī, Mīrzā Mahdī
Mahdiism, 270
maḥdūd, 148, 149
māhiyyah , 86, 172, 174, 215; appearance in the mind, 68; as container of the mind, 71; contingency and, 71–73; distinction from *wujūd*, 67–68; experience of *wujūd* and, 82–84; historical survey of study of, 64–65; impossibility and, 71–73; meaning of, 65–67; necessity and, 71–73; principiality of, 176; relation to *wujūd*, 63
Maḥmūd, 'Abd al-Ḥalīm, 26, 117
Maḥmūd Shabistarī, Shaykh. *See* Shabistārī, Shaykh Maḥmūd
Maier, Michael, 217
Maimonides, 190
Majd al-Dīn al-Jīlī. *See* al-Jīlī, Majd al-Dīn
Majid Fakhry. *See* Fakhry, Majid
Majlisī, Muḥammad Bāqir, 38, 211
Majmū'a-yi Marāghah (The Collection of Maraghah), 186
Majrīṭī, Abū Maslamah al-, 147
Makdisi, George, 291*n3*
Malaysia, 277; students studying in the West from, 19
Mali: libraries in, 21
Malik, Jamāl, 291*n51*
Maʾmūn, al-, 121
Manichaeans, 120, 143
The Manifest Horizon (Mīr Dāmād), 214
Manifest Light (Zunūzī), 237
Mannheim, Ralph, 311*n46*
Manṭiqī, al-. *See* Sijstānī, Abū Sulaymān al- Manṭiqī
Manṣūr al-Ḥallāj. *See* Ḥallāj, Manṣūr
manzilah bayn al-manzilatayn, al-, 122, 123
Maqāṣid al-falāsifah (The Purposes of the Philosophers), 113
Maqālāt al-islāmiyyīn (Doctrines of the Muslims), 125
Maqāmāt al-'ārifīn (Stations of the Gnostics), 201
Maraghah, 162; Islamic philosophy in, 188, 189

Marāghī, Fakhr al-Dīn, 188
marātib al-wujūd, 64
ma'rifah, 35, 57, 58, 100, 108, 119, 132, 135
ma'rifat. *See ma'rifah*
Maritain, Jacques, 273
Marmura, Michael, 23
Martin, Richard, 306*n2*
Marvels of Wisdom (Āqā 'Alī Mudarris), 240
Marwazī, Ḥasan Qaṭṭān al-, 185–186
Marwī, Muḥammad Khān, 237
Marwī School, 237
Marxism, 252, 253, 269, 274; Islamic philosophy and, 16
Mashā'ir, (The Book of Metaphysical Penetrations), 88, 329*n6*, 382*n2*
Mashhad, 213
mashiyyat Allāh, 157
mashshā'ī, 13, 116, 139, 145; doctrine; 99; school 99, 108, 109, 117; relation to *kalām*, 49. *See* also Peripatetic
Massignon, Louis, 15
materia prima, 112, 151
materia secunda, 151
mathematics, 170, 177, 187, 199, 200, 203, 212, 213, 214, 247, 263; geometry, 171; philosophy of, 170, 183
Matheson, D.M., 297*n33*
Mathnawī (Rūmī), *40, 41*
matter: intelligible, 151; spiritual, 151
Māturīdī, Abū Manṣūr al-, 127
Māturīdism, 97, 126, 127
Mawdūdī, Mawlānā, 117, 179
mawjūd, 67
Mawlā Ḥabīb Allāh Kāshānī. *See* Kāshānī, Mawlā Ḥabīb Allāh
Mawlā'ī, Muḥammad Sarwar, 285n*19*
Mawlānā 'Alī Ashraf Thanwī. *See* Thanwī, Mawlānā 'Alī Ashraf
Mawlānā Mawdūdī. *See* Mawdūdī, Mawlānā
Mawlawī, Mullā 'Abbās, 219
Maybudī, Qāḍī Amīr Ḥusayn ibn Mu'īn al-Dīn, 209, 210, 211
Mayer, Toby, 290*n35*
Mazdaeans, 120
McCarthy, Richard J., 307*n6*
McGill University (Canada), 20
meaning: of intellect, 100
Mecca, 156, 157, 197, 223; Islamic philosophy in, 183
Medina, 197; Islamic philosophy in, 183
Mehdi Aminrazavi. *See* Aminrazavi, Mehdi
Mehdi Mohaghegh. *See* Mohaghegh, Mehdi
messianism, 269
metaphysics, 2, 35, 131, 134, 156, 159, 165, 177, 203, 205, 217, 231, 294*n7*, 295*n15*, 329*n9*; Aristotelian, 67; with Being as first principle, 87; essentialistic, 86, 88; existentialistic, 88; Far Eastern, 17; of the Holy Spirit, 224; Indian, 17; Islamic, 65, 90; knowledge and, 99; of light, 160; of the *Najāh*, 64; reality and, 295*n18*; Ṣadrian, 218, 241; of the *Shifā'*, *64;* shortcomings of Ash'arite approach and, 52; Sufi, 39, 46, 81, 82, 115, 132, 147, 190; the three directions and, 71; traditional, 21, 274, 277; transcending ontology, 87
Metaphysics (al-Kindī), 23
Metaphysics (Ibn Rushd), 23
Mian Muhammad Sharif. *See* Sharif, Mian Muhammad
Middle Ages, 5; Christian art in, 33
Milal wa'l-niḥal literature, 24
Milestones of Healing (Dashtakī), 200
Millás-Vallicrosa, Jose, 15
*Miṣqal-i ṣafā (*Polishing Instrument of Purity), *220*
Mīr Abū'l-Qāsim Findiriskī. *See* Findiriskī, Mīr Abū'l-Qāsim
Mīr Dāmād. *See* Dāmād, Mīr
Mīr Firdiriskī. *See* Firdiriskī, Mīr

Mīr Niẓām al-Dīn Dashtakī. *See* Dashtakī, Mīr Niẓām al-Dīn
Mīrzā Ḥasan Kirmānshāhī. *See* Kirmānshāhī. Mīrzā Ḥasan
Mīrzā Ḥasan Lāhījī. *See* Lāhījī, Mīrzā Ḥasan
Mīrzā Ibrāhīm Lāhījī. *See* Lāhījī, Mīrzā Ibrāhīm
Mirzā Ismā'īl Gurgānī. *See* Gurgānī, Mīrzā Ismā'īl
Mīrzā Mahdī Āshtiyānī. *See* Āshtiyānī, Mīrzā Mahdī
Mīrzā Mahdī Ḥā'irī. *See* Ḥā'irī, Mīrzā Mahdī
Mīrzā Muḥammad 'Alī Shāhābādī. *See* Shāhābādī, Mīrzā Muḥammad 'Alī
Mīrzā Muḥammad Ma'ṣūm Dashtākī. *See* Dashtakī, Mīrzā Muḥammad Ma'ṣūm
Miṣbāḥ Yazdī, Muḥammad Taqī, 254
Miskawayh. *See* Ibn Muskūyah
Mishkawī, Jamāl al-Dīn 'Abd al-Jabbār ibn Muḥammad, 177
modernism, 1, 259, 260, 266, 269, 271
Moghul period, 43
Mogul court, 205
Mohaghegh, Mehdi, 17, 18, 293*n1*, 297*n29*, 305*n7*, 310*n39*, 324*n1*, 325*n6*
monadology, 148
Mongols: destruction by, 112; destruction of Abbasid caliphate by, 45; invasion of Anatolia, 192; invasion of Azarbaijan by, 186
monotheism, 2, 141; Abrahamic, 1, 6, 109
More, Sir Thomas, 269
Morewedge, Parviz, 23, 300*n3*, 329*n6*
Morgan, David, 320*n17*
Moris, Zailan, 301*n13*, 329*n8*
Morocco, 275, 278; Islamic philosophy in, 152; Sufi orders in, 76
Morris, James, 19, 23, 311*n46*, 329*n6*
Moses, 5, 34; spoken to by God, 7
motion, trans-substantial, 231, 232
Mt. Sinai, 7
Mu'allim al-thānī, al-, 138
Mu'ayyid al-Dīn al-Jandī. *See* Jandī, Mu'ayyid al-Dīn
Mubda' al-awwal, al-, 90, 148
Mudarris Ṭihrānī, Āqā 'Alī Ḥakīm, 65, 88, 117, 239–242
Mufīd, Shaykh al-, 133
Mughīrāh, al-, 210
Muḥākamāt, al- (Trials), 113, 200
Muḥammad 'Abduh. *See* 'Abduh, Muḥammad
Muḥammad Shams al-Dīn al-Dīn Shahrazūrī. *See* Shahrazūrī, Muḥammad Shams al-Dīn
Muḥammad al-Sanūsī. *See* Sanūsī, Muḥammad
Muhammad Arkoun. *See* Arkoun, Muhammad
Muḥammad Bāqir al-Ṣadr. *See* Ṣadr, Muḥammad Bāqir
Muḥammad ibn Dā'ūd al-Iṣfahānī. *See* Iṣfahānī, Muḥammad ibn Dā'ūd
Muḥammad ibn Zakariyyā' al-Rāzī. *See* Rāzī, Muḥammad ibn Zakariyyā'
Muḥammad Iqbāl. *See* Iqbāl, Muḥammad
Muḥammad Khān Marwī. *See* Marwī, Muḥammad Khān
Muḥammad Maḥmūd Dihdār. *See* Dihdār, Muḥammad Maḥmūd
Muḥammad (Prophet). *See* the Prophet
Muḥammad Taqī Dānishpazhūh. *See* Dānishpazhūh, Muḥammad Taqī
Muḥammad Tunakābunī, Mullā. *See* Tunakābunī, Mullā Muḥammad
Muḥammad Ismā'īl Darbkūshkī Iṣfahānī, Mullā. *See* Iṣfahanī, Mullā Muḥammad Ismā'īl Darbkūshkī

Muḥsin Fayḍ Kāshānī, Mullā. *See* Kāshānī, Mullā Muḥsin Fayḍ
Muhsin Mahdi. *See* Mahdi, Muhsin
Muḥyī al-Dīn ibn 'Arabī. *See* Ibn 'Arabī, Muḥyī al-Dīn
mukāshafah, 95
Muṣlih, Jawād, *254,* 290*n41*
Mullā Ṣadrā. *See* Ṣadrā, Mullā
Mullā Bāqir Majilsī. *See* Majlisī, Mullā Bāqir
Mullā Mahdī Narāqī. *See* Narāqī, Mullā Mahdī
mu'min, 59
mumkin, 71
mumkin al-wujūd, 141
mumtani', 71
mundus imaginalis, 100
Munk, Salomo, 15, 25, 50
Munqidh min al-ḍalal, al- (The Deliverance from Error), 113
Muntaha'l-afkār fī ibānat al-asrār (The Height of Thoughts concerning the Clarification of Mysteries), 189
Muntakhab al-khāqānī fi kashf ḥaqā'iq 'irfānī (Royal Selections concerning the Unveiling of Gnostic Truths), 237
Muqaddimah, al- (Prolegomena), 115
Murata, Sachiko, 286*n2*
Murcia: Islamic philosophy in, 155
Muṣāri'ah, al- (Wrestling with the Philosopher), 169
Murtaḍā Muṭahharī. *See* Muṭahharī, Murtaḍā
music, 138, 190
muta'allih, 36
Muṣṭafā 'Abd al-Rāziq, Shaykh. *See* 'Abd Rāziq, Shaykh Muṣṭafā
Muṭahharī, Murtaḍā, 18, 117, 254
mutakallim, 38, 50, 51, 119, 129, 133, 135, 292*n6*
Mu'tazilism, 97, 121–124, 306*n2,* 307*n7*; compulsory practice of, 124; five principles of, 122, 123; theology, 53; theories of atomism, 144
Mu'tazilite school, 38; dominance in *kalām,* 49
Mystery of mysteries, 148
The Mystical Treatises (Suhrawardī), 23
mysticism, 214

Naẓẓām, Abū Isḥāq al-, 121, 123
nabī, al-, 149
Nābulusī, 'Abd al-Ghanyī al-, 45
Nader, Albert, 306*n2*
Nadwī, Sayyid Sulaymān, 173
nafas al-Raḥmān. See Breath of the Compassionate
nafs, 134
Nahj al-balāghah (Path of Eloquence), 120
Najaf, 240, 255
Najjār, 'Alī Sāmī al-, 26
Najjār, Fawzī al-, 23
Najm al-Dīn Dabīrān-i Kātibī Qazwīnī. *See* Qazwīnī, Najm al-Dīn Dabīrān-I Kātibī
Names and Qualities (Ibn 'Arabī), 87
Nanji, Azim, 308*n13*
Naqd al-nuqūd fī ma'rifat al-wujūd (Criticism of Criticisms concerning Knowledge of Beings) (Āmulī), 87
Naquib al-Attas. *See* Attas, Naquib al-
Narāqī, Mullā Muḥammad Mahdī, 59, 235
Nasawī, Abū Naṣr, 172, 173
Nāṣir al-Dīn al-Ṭūsī. *See* Ṭūsī, Naṣīr al-Dīn
Naṣīr al-Dīn Shah, 242
Nāṣir-i Khusraw, 5, 111, 133, 146, 148, 167, 227, 284n12
Naṣīrean Ethics (al-Ṭūsī), 116, 187
Nasr, S.H., 17, 18, 19, 107, 281*n9,* 282*n15,* 283*n4,* 284*n10,* 284*n12,* 286*n1,* 286*n3,* 287*n8,* 288*n11,* 290*n34,* 290*n46,* 292*n7,* 294*n5,* 294*n9,* 294*n12,* 298*n23,* 298*n38,*

Nasr, S.H. *(continued)* 300*n3*, 301*n15*, 302*n4*, 304*n1*, 305*n2*, 305*n5*, 306*n13*, 307*n8*, 308*n10*, 309*n31*, 310*n34*, 311*n46*, 313*n61*, 313*n62*, 318*n5*, 318*n36*, 319*n6*, 319*n7*, 320*n12*, 320*n16*, 322*n28*, 325*n6*, 328*n2*, 330*n13*, 331*n1*, 338*n4*, 339*n8*
nationalism, Arab, 285n*21*
Native Americans, 7
Natural Philosophy (Ibn Sīnā), 177
Nature: Divine, 126; God's, 130; philosophy of, 126
Nayrīzī, Mīrzā Shihāb al-Dīn, 244
Nayshābūrī, Farīd al-Dīn Dāmād al-, 196, 201
Necessary Being, 66, 71, 72, 141, 142, 181, 237
necessity, 141; of contradiction, 176; distinction from contingency and impossibility, 71–73, 110
The Necessity of Contradiction in the World and Determinism and Subsistence (Khayyām), 173
Neo-Confucian: philosophical traditions, 8
Neoplatonism, 40, 109, 115, 136, 138, 140, 151
Neopythagoreanism, 39, 111, 112
Neo-Thomism, 15
Netton, Ian, 20, 28
Nicholson, Reynold A., 290*n4*, 301*n17*
Nicholson, Richard, 337*n2*
Nihāyat al-iqdām (The Extremity of Action or *Summa Philosophiae*), 127
nihilism, 271, 339*n6*
Nineteenth Century: French rationalism, 154; introduction of Islamic philosophical texts to the West, 22, 25; philosophical developments in, 24; philosophical traditions, 15
Niẓām al-Mulk, Khwājah, 44, 164
Niẓām al-Dīn Aḥmad Dashtakī. *See* Dashtakī, Niẓām al-Dīn Aḥmad
Niẓāmī curriculum, 207
Niẓāmiyyah *madrasah*, 169
Niẓamiyyah school system, 44
Niẓāmī 'Arūḍī Samarqandī. *See* Samarqandī, Niẓāmī 'Arūḍī
Noble Quran. See Quran
nonexistence, 65
North Africa: Islamic philosophy in, 156
Notions (al-Ṭūsī), 147
Nūr al-anwār, 160
Nūrī, Mīrzā Ḥasan, 236, 240, 243, 245
Nūrī, Mullā 'Alī, 65, 88, 117, 236, 243

The Object of Worship of the Gnostic (Ibn Sab'īn), 156
occasionalism, 126, 130, 307*n7*
Occidental Exile (Suhrawardī), 152
Ode to the Soul (Ibn Sīnā), 191
Oldmeadow, Harry, 283*n4*
Omar Khayyam. *See* Khayyām, 'Umar
omnipotentialism, 129, 130
the One, 148
On Metaphysics (al-Kindī), 109, 137
On the Enumeration of the Sciences (al-Fārābī), 138
On the Reality of Love (Suhrawardī), 158
ontology, 2, 86, 172, 216, 226, 232, 251, 253, 262, 300*n6*; Avicennan, 141, 142
Organon (Aristotle), 110
"Oriental Philosophy," 153, 309*n31*
"Orient of Light," 155
Orients of Divine Inspiration ('Abd al-Razzāq Lāhījī), 55
The Origin and the End (Mullā Ṣadrā), 5555
the Originator, 149, 151
the Orthodox Church, 3
Ottoman: *madrasahs*, 44
Owen, Robert, 269

Pahlavi period, 117
Pahlawī (sages), 79–82

Pakistan, 275; creation of center for Islamic philosophy, 27–28; Islamic texts from, 26; Jamā'at Islamī in, 117; libraries in, 21; students studying in the West from, 19
Pallis, Marco, 337*n2*
Palmer, G.E.H., 293*n2*
Panīpātī, Niẓām al-Dīn, 216
Paraclete, 221
Parmenides, 2, 3, 4, 224, 229, 303*n9*
Partaw-nāmah (The Book of Radiance), 36
Pascal, Blaise, 261
Path of Eloquence ('Ali ibn Abī Ṭālib), 120
Pendleburg, David, 293*n19*
perfection: imitation of philosophers and, 59
Peripatetic philosophy, 25, 35, 36, 38, 39, 42, 45, 46, 49, 50, 52, 53, 55, 80, 86, 87, 97, 100, 109–111; founding of, 110; synthesis of Islamic tenets in, 109
Persia, 204, 209, 283*n5*, 320*n14*; *al-ḥikmat al-ilāhiyyah* in, 60; Ash'arite teachings in, 127; Christian missionaries in, 220; conditions in, 140; conquered by Safavids, 200; effect of Āmulī on philosophy in, 87; integration of *ḥikmah* and *kalām* in, 51; intellectual sciences in, 44; Islamic philosophy in, 26, 28, 155, 158, 160, 162, 163, 190, 192, 194; Ismā'īlī philosophy in, 146; Ismā'īlī power in, 112; Marwī School in, 237; Mongol invasion of, 8; Pahlavi period in, 247, 251, 254, 276; philosophical activities in, 116, 169; philosophical traditions in, 236, 255; Qajar period in, 237, 238, 247, 251, 252; rapport beween *falsafah* and religion in, 43; religious atmosphere in, 235; revival of Islamic philosophy in, 108; role of *falsafah* in, 45, 46; Safavid dynasty in, 116; School of Illumination in, 116; School of Isfahan in, 87; Seljuq rule in, 168; teaching of *falsafah* in, 44; Zand period, 251
Persian: philosophical texts translated, 22; poets, 39; rise of as a major philosophical language of Islam (*See* Nāṣir-i Khusraw); sages, 79; Sufism, 182
pharmacology, 200
phenomenology, 19
Philoponus, John, 215, 326*n14*
philosophia perennis, 20, 21, 40, 112, 139, 279, 283*n8*, 303*n9*
philosophia priscorium, 158
The Philosophical Way of Life (al-Rāzī), 33, 144
Philosophos Autodidactus (Ibn Ṭufayl), 114, 153
philosophy: Almeria school, 150; American, 9; analytical, 19, 253; Andalusian, 150; Anglo-Saxon, 7, 19, 253; anti-Peripatetic, 145; Arabic, 25, 285n*21*; argumentative, 99; Aristotelian, 64, 98, 140; of art, 118; authentic, 273–280; Avicennan, 112, 113, 115, 158, 163, 169, 177, 183, 187, 192, 214, 216, 219, 220, 245; in Azarbaijan, 185–193; of being, 88, 226, 227; Cartesian, 253; Christian, 33, 63, 85, 94, 110, 141, 215, 273, 279; contemporary, 266; Continental, 181; discursive, 85; early Peripatetic, 136–141; eastern *mashshā'ī*, 152; European, 241, 269; of existence, 89; Greco-Alexandrian, 108, 120, 137; Greek, 6, 108, 146, 214, 215, 303*n9*; harmonization with spirituality, 158; Hegelian, 253; Hermetico-Pythagorean, 145–150; Hindu, 112, 144, 216, 274; of history, 157, 313*n65*; illuminationist, 97, 100, 142; intuitive, 85, 99; *ishrāqī*, 159, 160–162, 211; Isma'īlī, 81, 108, 111,

philosophy *(continued)*
112, 142, 145–150, 183, 187, 218, 305*n5,* 311*n46,* 330*n13*; Jewish, 28, 33, 63, 110, 141, 150, 152; Kantian, 241, 253; of law, 118; Marxist, 274; *mashshā'ī,* 136–141, 199, 203, 247; of mathematics, 170, 183; medieval, 214; modern, 274, 303*n9*; mystical, 278; natural, 112, 123, 145, 171, 203, 231; of nature, 126, 305*n7*; Neoplatonic, 98, 140; oral form, 7; Oriental, 111, 140, 153, 161, 309*n31*; perennial, 8, 158, 220, 274, 277, 279; Peripatetic, 25, 35, 36, 38, 39, 42, 45, 46, 49, 50, 52, 53, 55, 80, 86, 88, 97, 100, 109–111, 140, 142, 146, 155, 156, 158, 162, 187, 201, 203, 210, 214, 217, 221, 224, 288*n11,* 294*n9*; Persian, 88; Platonic, 115; political, 110; post-Ibn Rushdian phase of, 44, 45; practical, 199; preparation of the mind for intellection and, 77; prophetic, 9, 109, 209, 212, 217, 218, 221, 223–233, 255, 277, 278, 329*n9,* 330*n13*; purpose of, 77; of quantum mechanics, 171; rapport with religion, 36; rational, 99; relation to prophecy, 146; relation to religion, 312*n59*; relation to theology, 60; religion and, 145, 154; rooted in certainty, 36; Russian Orthodox, 274; Ṣadrian, 236, 240, 245, 298*n44*; of science, 118, 305*n6*; secular, 273, 279; speculative, 138; study of history of, 107–118; Taoist, 274; "tasted," 85, 99; against theology, 113, 114; Thomistic, 273; traditional, 35, 87, 274; transcendent, 224; of various disciplines, 118; Western, 85, 94, 98, 150, 241, 252, 253, 255, 274, 275; of Yoga, 217
philosophy, Islamic, 33, 49, 135; after Suhrawardī, 163; Andalusian school, 155, 156, 157; in contemporary Islamic world, 117, 118; effect of Ibn 'Arabī on, 87; epistemological questions in, 93–103; existence and, 63–84; influence of other intellectual perspectives on, 108; *māhiyyah* in, 83, 84; as major intellectual tradition in Islamic world, 108; meaning of the intellect and intuition in, 97; methodology of knowledge in, 97; ontology in, 63–84; origin of, 108, 109; Persia as main home of, 108; post-Avicennan, 85–91; rapprochement between schools of, 162, 163; rationalism in, 113; relations between intellect, reason, and intuition, 93–103; Safavid renaissance of, 65; School of Isfahan and, 116, 117; in Spain, 114, 115; on structure of reality, 80–84; study of being in, 85–91; Sufism, 100; traditional, 107; in the West, 13–30; in western lslamic lands, 150–158; *wujūd* and, 63–84
physics, 141, 171, 339*n6*; Aristotelian, 114
Picatrix, 147
Pines, Shlomo, 15, 307*n7,* 310*n37*
Pīrzādah, Rafī', 219
Plato, 3, 7, 37, 64, 138, 144, 150, 159, 303*n9*; political philosophy of, 110
Platonism, 159; Muslim, 151
Pléiades, 27, 107
Plotinus, 137, 218, 287*n9*
pneumatology, 6
poetry, 211
poets: Persian, 39; Sufi, 39
Poles of the State of Being a Pole (Aharī), 188
Polishing Instrument of Purity ('Alawī), 220
Polit, Gustavo, 291*n4*
postmodernism, 1, 259, 266, 271
post-Renaissance period: philosophical traditions of, 38

Pourjavady, Nasrollah, 318*n2*, 319*n7*, 320*n13*
presence, 89
Pre-Socratic, 4
principiality, 215; of being, 89; of existence, 87; of *māhiyyah* , 176; of *wujūd*, 77–80, 176
Proclus, 88
Prolegomena (Ibn Khaldūn), 115, 157
prophecy: Abrahamic, 93, 215; accessibility of knowledge through, 93; angelology and, 229; cycle of, 37; function of, 133; illumination and, 228, 229; reality of, 94, 129, 135, 227, 273; relation to philosophy, 146
the Prophet, 57, 101, 120, 125, 132, 161, 175, 178, 217, 225, 228
Prophet of Islam. See the Prophet
Provisions of the Traveler (Mullā Ṣadrā), 180
psychology: traditional, 6
Pure Being, 90, 215
Purification of Morals (Ibn Muskūyah), 112, 139
The Purposes of the Philosophers (al-Ghazzālī), 113
The Pyramid of Being (Yazdī), 252
Pythagoras, 2, 4, 7, 150, 229, 281*n1*, 303*n9*
Pythagoreans, 159, 224

Qāḍī 'Abd al-Jabbār. *122*
Qāḍī Sa'īd Qummī. *See* Qummī, Qāḍī Sa'īd
Qādir, al-, 178
qahr, 151
Qajar period, 135
Qānūn fi'l-ṭibb, al- (The Canon of Medicine), 140, 206
Qarāmalikī, Aḥmad Farāmarz, 321*n23*
Qarashī, Abū'l-Majd Muḥammad Tabrīzī Malakānī, 190
Qashqā'ī, Jahāngīr Khān, 236, 243
Qayṣarī, Dā'ūd al-, 39, 45, 51, 76, 116, 191
Qazwin, 240
Qazwīnī, Dabīrān-i Kātibī. *See* Kātibī Qazwīnī, Dabīrān-i
Qazwīnī, Mullā Āqā-yi, 236, 240
Qazwīnī, Sayyid Abū'l-Ḥasan Rafī'ī, 117, 246, 249, 276, 326*n15*
Qom, 59, 235, 238, 252, 254, 255
Quadri, Goffredo, 25
Quantum Enigma (Wolfgang Smith), 171
quiddity, 141, 172, 215, 293*n1*; distinct from existence, 141; existence and, 70, 175; intellect and, 70
Qummī, Qāḍī Sa'īd, 219, 235
Qumsha'ī, Āqā Muḥammad Riḍā, 236, 238, 239, 241– 244
Qunyawī, Ṣadr al-Dīn al-, 45, 74
Quran, 7, 35, 37, 64, 102; commands from God in, 148; cosmology of, 149; on God as First and Last, 75; hierarchy of beings and, 77; interpretations of, 268; nature of revelation in, 96; shortcomings of Ash'arite approach and, 52; as source of philosophical speculation, 109; teaching on transcendent unity of being, 74; teachings of, 108; traditional scholars of, 121; verses of, 175, 176, 177
Quranic: commentary, 14, 133, 190, 200, 201, 206, 224, 227, 330*n14*; doctrine of revelation, 98; jurisprudence, 133; revelations, 6, 25, 26, 226, 231; verses, 228, 324*n1*
Quṭb al-Dīn al-Shīrāzī. *See* Shīrāzī, Quṭb al-Dīn
Quṭb al-Dīn Ashkiwarī. *See* Ashkiwarī, Quṭb al-Dīn
Quṭb al-Zamān Muḥammad al-Ṭabasī. *See* Ṭabasī, Quṭb al-Zamān Muḥammad

Rab'-i Rashīdī (Tabriz), 44, 190
Riḍā-zādah Malik, Raḥīm, 314*n6*, 318*n38*

Rafī' al-Dīn Shīrāzī. *See* Shīrāzī, Rafī' al-Dīn
Rāḥat al-'aql (Repose of the Intellect), 111, 146
Rahman, Fazlur, 18, 19, 294*n6*, 303*n11*, 310*n36*, 328*n2*
Raine, Kathleen, 330*n18*
Rajab 'Alī Tabrīzī, Mullā. *See* Tabrīzī, Mullā Rajab 'Alī
Rashid, Roshdi, 325*n8*
Rashīd al-Dīn Faḍl Allāh, 43, 44, 190, 192, 291n48
Rashtī, Āqā Muḥammad Riḍā, 239
Rashtī, Mīrzā Hāshim, 247
ratiocination, 77, 95, 99; criticism of, 40
rationalism, 113, 224, 229, 271; Aristotelian, 157; French, 154
Rāzī, Abū Ḥatīm al-, 133, 144
Rāzī, Fakhr al-Dīn al-, 39, 43, 49, 50, 53, 64, 69, 70, 74, 97, 113, 128, 162, 168, 189, 192, 201
Rāzī, Mīr Qawām al-Dīn, 219
Rāzī, Muḥammad ibn Zakariyyā᾽ al-, 42, 112, 143; atomism and, 144; celebrated as physician, musician, alchemist, 144, 145; denial of necessity of prophecy by, 144; ethics and, 144; independence of, 145; philosophical views of, 144, 145
Rāzī, Quṭb al-Dīn al-, 113, 205
reality: absolute, 81; cosmic, 131; diversity of thoughts on structure of, 80–84; Divine, 176; of God, 67, 80, 129, 172, 181; metaphysics and, 295*n18*; Muḥammadan, 218, 227; in relation to *wujūd*, 71; as the Principle, 90; of prophecy, 94, 135, 227; of revelation, 135; structure of, 80–84; supernal, 102; Ultimate, 295*n15*; understanding nature of, 65; of *wujūd*, 73–74, 80–84
reason: emotion and, 102; faith and, 93; harmonization with faith, 115; Islamic perspectives on, 93–103; possession of faculty of, 102; as reflection of intellect, 94–95
Reconstruction of Religious Thought in Islam (Iqbāl), 129
reductionism, 267, 271, 339*n6*
Regimen of the Solitary (Ibn Bājjah), 114, 152
relativism, 271
religion(s): comparative, 220, 221; documentation of foundations of, 57; Indian, 6; Iranian, 6; philosophy of, 145, 154; rapport with *falsafah*, 43; relation to philosophy, 36, 312*n59*
Renaissance, 13, 131, 158, 217, 260, 262, 266
Renan, Ernst, 16, 29, 154, 312*n57*
Repose of the Intellect (al-Kirmānī), 111, 146
revelation: alpha and omega of, 102; complementary nature with intellection, 96; defense of, 135; illumination of intellect and, 96; Islamic, 100; as means for attainment of truth, 96; messages of the heart and, 100, 101; partial, 96; Quranic, 98, 231; reality of, 135; universal, 96; verities of, 95
The Revivification of the Sciences of Religion (al-Ghazzālī), 190
Rhazes. *See* Rāzī, Muḥammad ibn Zakariyyā᾽
The Ring of the Dove (Ibn Ḥazm), 114
Risālah dar 'ilm-i kulliyyāt-i wujūd (Treatise on the Science of the Universal Principles of Being), 174
Risālah fi᾽l-'aql (Treatise on the Intellect), al-, 98
Risālah fi᾽l-kawn wa᾽l-taklīf, al- (Treatise on the Realm of Existence and Human Responsibility), 172
Risālah fi᾽l-wujūd, al- (Treatise on Being), 175
Risālah fī taḥqīqāt al-ṣifāt, al- (Treatise concerning Verifictions of the Qualities), 175
Risālah fī waḥdat al-wujūd bal al-mawjūd (Treatise on the Unity

Existence or Rather of the Existent), 244
Risālah jawāban li-thalāth masā'il (Treatise of Response to Three Questions), 176
Risālah mawsūmah bi-silsilat al-tartīb, al- (Treatise Known as the Hierarchic Chain), 174
Risālat al-aḍḥawiyyah, al- (Treatise on the Day of Resurrection), 230
Risālat al-ḍiyā' al-'aqlī fi mawḍū' al-'ilm al-kullī (Treatise of Intellectual Light concerning Universal Science), 174
Risālat al-siyāsiyyah, al- (Treatise on Politics), 189
Risālat al-tawḥīd (The Treatise of Unity), 128
Risāla-yi ṣinā'iyyah (Treatise on the Arts), 216, 217
rishis, 7
Rizvi, Saiyid Athar Abbas, 205
Robinson, Francis, 291*n51*, 318*n1*
The Romance of Wīs and Ramīn (Gurgānī), 172
Rose Garden of Divine Mysteries (Shabistarī). *See The Secret Rose Garden of Divine Mysteries*
Rosenthal, Erwin, 15, 23, 322*n30*
Rosenthal, Franz, 23, 287n10
Rowe, Joseph, 329*n9*
Rowson, Everett K, 23
Royal Selections concerning the Unveiling of Gnostic Truths (Zunūzī), 237
Rubā'iyyāt (Khayyām), 167, 183
Rūḥ Allāh Khumaynī, Ayatollah. *See* Khumaynī, Ayatollah Rūḥ Allāh
Rūmī, Jalāl al-Dīn, 141, 191, 265, 290*n39*
Russia, 274

Sabaeans, 43
Ṣabbāḥ, Ḥasan al-, 146
sābiq, 149
Sabziwārī, Ḥājjī Mullā Hādī, 65, 79, 88, 117, 167, 203, 238, 318*n37*
Sabziwārī, Mīrzā Ḥasan, 246
The Sacred Book, 227, 228, *See* also the Quran
Sacred Effusion, 66
Sa'd al-Dīn al-Taftāzānī. *See* Taftāzānī, Sa'd al-Dīn
Ṣādiq, Imam Ja'far al-. *See* Ja'far al-Ṣādiq
Ṣadr, Muḥammad Bāqir al-, 117, 277
Ṣard al-Dīn al-Qunyawī. See Qunyawī, Ṣadr al-Dīn
Ṣadr al-Dīn Shīrāzī. See Ṣadrā, Mullā
Ṣadrā, Mullā, 5, 22, 23, 34, 37, 40, 46, 49, 52, 68, 73, 78, 97, 116, 131, 150, 162, 163, 167, 176, 179, 180, 189, 193–194, 197, 199, 221, 204, 207, 209, 212, 214, 215, 223–233, 236, 237, 240, 242, 276, 284*n12*, 291*n51*, 292*n7*, 294*n11*, 298*n29*, 298*n31*, 301*n13*, 303*n14*, 315*n10*, 321*n21*, 326*n15*, 327*n30*, 328*n2*; acceptance of unity, gradation, and principiality of *wujūd* by, 80; acquaintance with important theologians, 53; attack on basis of *kalām* by, 55; development of *al-ḥikmat al-ilāhiyyah* and, 51; familiarity with Khafrī, 203; identification of *wujūd* with light, 80; on importance of power of imagination in knowledge, 100; integration of heritage of *kalām* in works of, 55; *Kasr al-aṣnām al-jāhiliyyah* of, 54; in Safavid period, 87–88, 88; sayings of Shi'ite Imams in works of, 109; on structure of reality, 80; School of Isfahan and, 74, synthesis of, 94; traditional Islamic conception of history of philosophy by, 107; transcendent theosophy of, 53, 77; on truth of the position of *aṣālat al-wujūd*, 79; understanding of *waḥdat al-wujūd*, 76–77

Saeed Shaikh. *See* Shaikh, Saeed
Safavi, Gholam, 20
Safavid period, 59, 134, 143, 163, 193, 197, 200, 203, 204, 207, 213, 220, 235, 236, 325*n8*; *ḥakīms* and, 36; intellectual life in, 46; synthesis associated with, 116
Safīna-yi Tabrīz (The Vessel of Tabriz), 190, 191
sages: Greek, 139; Indian, 139; Islamic, 83; Khusrawānī, 79; Native American, 282*n18*; Pahlawī, 79–80, 81, 82; Persian, 15, 79; Sunni, 220
ṣaḥābah, 57
Ṣahbā. *See* Qumshāʾī, Āqā Muḥammad Riḍā.
Sahl al-Tustarī. *See* Tustarī, Sahl al-
Sahl ibn Hārūn. *See* Ibn Hārūn, Sahl
Saidi, Ahmad, 317*n27*
St. Augustine, 98, 99, 269
St. Bonaventure, 264
St. Simon, 269
St. Thomas, 33, 69, 99, 119, 126, 263, 303*n10*, 309*n23*
Saliba, George, 323*n39*, 325*n8*
Salmāsī, Abū ʿAlī, 189
salvation, 94; knowledge of the heart and, 101
Salvation (Ibn Sīnā), 64, 86, 98, 111
Samarqand, 209
Samarqandī, Niẓāmī ʿArūḍī, 166, 168
Samarqandī, Shams al-Dīn, 191
Sanāʾī, 39, 146
Sanskrit, 216; translations into Persian, 43
Sanūsī, Muḥammad al-, 128
Sarakhsī, Aḥmad ibn Ṭayyib al-, 110, 137
Sarakhsī, Sayyid Ṣadr al-Dīn al-, 196
sarayān al-wujūd, 226
Sāwajī, ʿUmar ibn Sahlān al-, 186
Sayili, Aydin, 318*n5*
Sayr-i ḥikmat dar Urūpā (The Development of Philosophy in Europe), 253
Sayyid Abūʾl-Ḥasan Rafīʿī Qazwīnī. *See* Qazwīnī, Sayyid Abūʾl-Ḥasan Rafīʿī
Sayyid Aḥmad Khān. *See* Khān, Sir Sayyid Aḥmad
Sayyid ʿAlī Khān Kabīr Dashtakī. *See* Dashtakī, Sayyid ʿAlī Khān Kabīr
Sayyid Haydar Āmulī. *See* Āmulī, Sayyid Ḥaydar
Sayyid Jalāl al-Dīn Āshtiyānī. *See* Āshtiyānī, Sayyid Jalāl al-Dīn
Sayyid Muḥammad Ḥusayn Ṭabāṭabāʾī. *See* Ṭabāṭabāʾī, Sayyid Muḥammad Ḥusayn
Sayyid Muḥammad Kāẓim ʿAṣṣār. *See* ʿAṣṣār, Sayyid Muḥammad Kāẓim
Sayyid Sharīf al-Jurjānī. *See* Jurjānī, Sayyid Sharīf al-
Schimmel, Annemarie, 275, 276
Schmidt, Wilhelm, 338*n3*
Schmidtke, Sabine, 319*n8*, 324*n4*
Schmitt, Charles, 283*n8*
Schmölders, Augustus, 25
Scholasticism, 69, 89, 108, 153, 156; Catholic, 19; Christian, 16; Jewish, 15, 16, 19; Latin, 15, 137; Western, 303*n10*
Scholastics. *See* Scholasticism
School of Azarbaijan, 195, 318*n2*
School of Baghdad, 189
School of Ibn ʿArabī, 162, 163
School of Illumination, 34, 64, 80, 86, 99, 115–117, 140, 157, 158–160, 163, 314*n72*
School of Isfahan, 51, 53, 65, 74, 87, 116, 117, 134, 162, 163, 176, 192–195, 207, 209–221, 219, 220, 254, 297*n31*, 300*n10*, 325*n6*, 327*n29*; development of *al-ḥikmat al-ilāhiyyah* in, 51; late phase, 235–237
School of *ʿirfān*, 117
School of Khurasan, 192
School of Mahāyāna, 274
School of Maraghah, 195

School of kalām
School of *mashshā*ʾ, 117
School of Qom, 252
School of Shiraz, 189, 190, 192, 193–195, 200, 203, 209, 212, 225, 254, 320*n17*; rise of Islamic philosophy in India and, 204–207
School of Tehran, 235–256, 259, 275; beginnings, 237–239; four *ḥakīms* and, 239–247; full establishment of, 239–247; Jilwah and, 245, 246; later period, 247–251; Mudarris in, 239–242; Qumshaʾī and, 242–244; Sabziwārī and, 246; significance of, 251–256
School of Vajrāyāna, 274
Schumacher, Ernst, 268, 339*n6*
Schuon, Frithjof, 20, 91, 274, 282*n20*, 283*n8*, 284*n9*, 286*n1*, 291*n4*, 293*n2*, 296*n27*, 300*n4*, 302*n5*, 303*n9*, 307*n6*, 318*n35*, 337*n2*
Schwarz, Michael, 307*n7*
science, 140, 193, 194, 261; applied, 214; Chinese, 43; classification of, 42, 308*n22*; divine, 56, 59; esoteric, 44; of God, 132; "hidden," 308*n10*; intellectual, 35, 41, 46, 206, 207, 223, 224, 240; interaction with Islamic culture, 42; Islamic, 35, 42, 43, 213, 214, 323*n39*; of logic, 42; mathematical, 14, 199, 203, 212, 213; modern, 7, 130, 261, 262, 264, 265, 271, 339*n6*; natural, 13, 14, 196, 199; occult, 203; philosophical dimensions of, 108; philosophy of, 118, 305*n6*; physics, 171; Platonic, 263; pre-Islamic, 35, 42, 43; premodern, 261; principles sought in metaphysics, 177; proof in, 170; of Quranic commentary, 96; religious, 2–4, 38, 95, 96, 134, 135, 199, 207, 214, 232; supreme, 217; traditional, 262; transmitted, 42, 195, 205, 211, 223, 224, 240; Western, 47
scientia sacra, 35
Second Intellect, 141, 149
The Secret Garden of Divine Mysteries (Shabistarī), 146, 190, 192
Secrets of Wisdom (Sabziwārī), 238
secularism, 270, 271
Sédillot, Amélie, 165
Seiende, das, 89
Sein, das, 67, 89
Seljuq rule, 113, 168; rise of Ash'arite power among, 44
semiotics, 20
Servier, Jean, 338*n3*
"Seven Cherubim," 149
Seventh/Thirteenth Century: reappearance of School of Illumination, 160
Sezgin, Fūʾad, 21
Shabistar, 190
Shabistarī, Shaykh Maḥmūd, 190, 192
Shādhilī, Shaykh Abūʾl Ḥasan al-, 76
Shāfiyah, al- (The Healer), 200
Shah Ṭāhir ibn Raḍī al-Dīn, 203, 204
Shah Walī Allāh, 293n19, 297n36
Shāhābādī, Mīrzā Muḥammad 'Alī, 239, 247
Shahrastānī, Abūʾl-Fatḥ al-, 50, 113, 127, 146, 192
Shahrazur: Islamic philosophy in, 189
Shahrazūrī, Shams al-Dīn Muḥammad, 24, 115–116, 139, 160, 188, 189,192, 211, 285n*19*
Shaikh, Saeed, 26
Shajarat al-ilāhiyyah, al- (The Divine Tree), 211
Shamanic religions, 1
Shamsā Gīlānī, Mullā. *See* Gīlānī, Mullā Shamsā
Shams al-Dīn al-Fanārī. *See* Fanārī, Shams al-Dīn
Shams al-Dīn Khusrawshāhī. *See* Khusrawshāhī, Shams al-Dīn
Shams al-Dīn Muḥamad ibn Aḥmad Khafrī. *See* Khafrī, Shams al-Dīn Muḥammad ibn Aḥmad
Shams al-Dīn Muḥammad Shahrazūrī. *See* Shahrazūrī, Shams al-Dīn Muḥammad

Shamsiyyah fi'l-qawā'id al-manṭiqiyyah, al- (The Treatise Dedicated to Shams al-Dīn concerning the Rules of Logic), 191
Sharajat al-ilāhiyyah, al- (The Divine Tree), 189, 211
Sha'rānī, 'Abd al-Wahhāb al-, 45
Sha'rānī, Abū'l-Ḥasan, 276, 308*n14*
Sharḥ al-hidāyah (Commentary upon the Guidance), 22
Sharḥ al-ishārāt (Commentary upon the Book of Directives and Remarks by Fakhy al-Dīn al-Rāzī), 169
Sharḥ al-ishārāt (Naṣīr al-Dīn al-Ṭūsī). *See* al-Ṭūsī
Sharḥ al-manẓūmah (Commentary upon the *Manẓūmah* of Sabziwārī), 79, 238
Sharḥ al-mawāqif (Commentary upon the Stations), 128
Sharī'ah, al-, 31, 56, 57, 58, 122, 123, 135, 154, 271; begging assistance from, 59; injunctions of, 58
Sharif, Mian Muḥammad, 18, 27–28, 277, 288*n18*
Shawāḥid al-rubūbiyyah, al- (Divine Witnesses), 55, 88
Shawākil al-hūr fī sharḥ hayākil al-nūr (Forms of Brightness concerning the Temples of Light), 199
Shawāriq al-ilhām (Orients of Divine Inspiration), 55, 59
Shawdhī, Abū 'Abd Allāh al-, 155
Sherrard, Philip, 285*n25*
Shifā', al-, (Healing). *See Kitāb al-shifā'*
Shihāb al-Dīn Suhrwardī. *See* Suhrwardī, Shihāb al-Dīn
Shihābī, Maḥmūd, 255
Shi'ism (Ithnā-'asharī or Twelve-Imam), 37, 38, 40, 51, 97, 116, 128, 132, 133, 183, 187, 204, 210, 220, 292*n16*, 297*n31*, 308n14, 329*n10*; commentaries on *Tajrīd*, 39; gnosis, 36, 146; (Ismā'īlī branch), 111; (Zaydī), 122, 132, 133. See also Ismā'īlism
Shiraz, 223
Shīrāzī, Jamāl al-Dīn Maḥmūd, 195, 205
Shīrāzī, Mawlānā Sayyid Quṭb al-Dīn Muḥammad, 40
Shīrāzī, Mīr Fatḥ Allāh, 206, 207
Shīrāzī, Quṭb al-Dīn al-, 52, 65, 116, 160, 162, 188, 189, 191, 192, 195, 196, 199, 203, 240, 319*n8*
Shīrāzī, Rafī' al-Dīn, 204
Shīrāzī, Ṣadr al-Dīn. *See* Ṣadrā, Mullā
shuhūd, 89
Si aṣl (Three Principles), 53
Siddiqi, Bakhtyar Husain, 319*n7*
Siger of Brabant, 69
Sijistānī, Abū Sulaymān al-, 25, 110, 111, 139, 186, 190
Sijistānī, Abū Ya'qūb al-, 111, 146, 148, 227
Simnānī, 'Alā' al-Dawlah, 76
sin, 122
Singapore, 277
Sipahsālār School, 251
Sīrat al-falsafiyyah, al- (The Philosophical Way of Life), 144
Ṣirāṭ al-mustaqīm, al- (The Straight Path), 214
Sirhindī, Shaykh Aḥmad, 76
Ṣiwān al-ḥikmah (Vessel of Wisdom), 190
Sixth/Twelfth century: anti-Ptolemaic astronomy in, 152; cosmology in, 152
skepticism, 165, 172, 183
Smith, Huston, 282*n17*
Smith, Wolfgang, 171, 339*n7*
socialism, 269
Socrates, 144, 150
Solomon, 34, 43
sophia, 7, 283*n8*
sophia perennis, 161
Sorbonne (France), 242
soteriology, 161

The Sought Jewel (Lāhījī), 55
soul, 134
Soul of the First Sphere, 141
Soviet Union: Marxism in, 16
space, 112
Spain: Islamic philosophy in, 114, 115, 152, 154, 156, 311*n52*
Spanish: "identity," 15
speculum historiale, 220
spirituality: harmonization with philosophy, 158
The Spiritual Physick (al-Rāzī), 23, 144
The Splendid Sermon (Ibn Sīnā), 171
Springs of Wisdom (Ibn Sīnā), 98
Stagirite, 64. *See* also Aristotle
Steengerghen, Fernand, 287*n7*
Steinschneider, Moritz, 15, 50
Stern, Samuel, 311*n52*
Stoddart, William, 284*n9*
The Story of the Occidental Exile (Suhrawardī), 161
The Straight Path (Mīr Dāmād), *214*
The Straighting of Faith (Mīr Dāmād), 214
Struik, Dirk, 314*n2*
Suarez, Francisco, 86
The Substance of Unity (al-Bājūrī), 128
Subtleties of Philosophy (Urmawī), 189
The Sufficient in Philosophy (Aharī), 188
Sufi: *ḥukamāʾ*, 37; metaphysics, 46, 81, 82; poets, 39
ṣufī ibn al-waqt, al-, 179
Sufism, 13, 14, 27, 34, 35, 116, 128, 131, 146, 147, 150, 155–157, 175, 179, 188, 192, 194, 204, 209, 210, 212, 224, 277, 295*n15*. *See* Iṣfahānī, Muḥammad ibn Dāʾūd al-; Kāshānī, Afḍal al-Dīn; ascetic practices of, 36; combined with philosophy, 155; criticism of, 40; doctrinal, 23, 108, 136; effect of Ibn 'Arabī on, 87; identified with esoteric dimension of Islam, 100; exeriential knowledge of, 74; *falsafah* and, 45; on illumination, 76; Indian, 132; integration of *ḥikmah* and *kalām* and, 51; meaning of divinity in, 74; metaphysics and, 46; North African, 132; Persian, 182; philosophical dimensions of, 108; prophets of, 37; Qādirī, 76; relation to *ḥikmah*, 59; relation to *kalām*, 56, 57, 58; Shādhiliyyah Order, 76; in Spain, 114, 115; on structure of reality, 80; Turkish, 132
Suhrawardī, Shihāb al-Dīn, 4, 5, 23, 27, 29, 36, 38, 39, 45, 49, 64, 79, 140, 152, 153, 156, 157, 167, 179, 188, 189, 192, 194, 225, 228, 239, 241, 269, 284*n12*, 294*n7*, 298*n24*, 300*n5*, 303*n13*, 313*n68*, 321*n21*; defense of correspondence of *māhiyyah* to the reality of an object, 79; essentialistic metaphysics and, 79; execution of, 115; founding of School of Illumination by, 86; identified with school of *aṣālat al-māhiyyah* , 80; *ishrāqī* doctrines of, 52; school of illumination and, 99, 115, 116, 158–160; school of principiality of quiddity and, 176; study of angels by, 229; study of in Turkey, 60; traditional Islamic conception of history of philosophy by, 107
Sulaymān Nadwī, Sayyid. *See* Nadwī, Sayyid Sulaymān
The Sum of Two Wisdoms (Nāṣir-i Khusraw), 112, 146
sunnah: shortcomings of Ash'arite approach and, 52
Sunni: philosophical activity in Syria, 45
Sunnism, 38, 44
Supreme Principle, 102, 131, 148

Supreme Reality, 63
sūrah, 101
Swedenborg, Emmanuel, 229
Sweetman, J. Windrow, 306*n2*
Syed Ameer Alī. *See* Ameer 'Alī, Syed
symbolism: of light, 161; mathematical, 148; Sufi, 190
sympatheia, 153
Syria, 209, 278; Islamic philosophy in, 189; libraries in, 21; philosophical activity of Sunni Arabs in, 45; religious debates in, 120; Seljuq rule in, 168

ta'aqqul, 99
taṣawwuf al-'ilmī, al-, 108
Taṣawwurāt (Notions), 147
Ṭabasī, Quṭb al-Zamān Muḥammad al-, 185
Ṭabāṭabāʾī, 'Allāmah, Sayyid Muḥammad Ḥusayn 18, 60, 117, 241, 252, 254, 276, 277, 295*n14,* 298*n31*
Ṭabīʾiyyāt (Natural Philosophy), 177
Tabrīzī, Abū 'Abd Allāh Muḥammad, 190
Tabrīzī, Abū Isḥāq, 190
Tabrīzī, Maqṣūd 'Alī, 285n*19*
Tabrīzī, Mullā Rajab 'Alī, 88, 216, 218, 235
Tadbīr al-mutawaḥḥid (Regimen of the Solitary), 114, 152
ṭafrah, 123
tafsīr, 13
Taftāzānī, Sa'd al-Dīn al-, 128, 201, 206
Tahāfut al-falāsifah (Incoherence of the Philosophers), 113, 155, 169
Tahāfut al-tahāfut (Incoherence of the Incoherence), 23, 114, 115, 162, 169
Taḥāwism, 126, 127
Tahdhīb al-akhlāq (Purification of Morals), 112, 139
Ṭāhir Tunikābūnī, Mīrzā Ṭāhir. *See* Tunakābūnī, Mīrzā Ṭāhir
Taḥqīq mā liʾl-hind (Investigations concerning India), 145
Tahrali, Mustafa, 277
Tajrīd al-i'tiqād (Catharsis of Doctrine), 38, 39, 52, 55, 133, 134
talī, 149
Ṭaliqānī, Mīr Sayyid Ḥasan, 235
Tā'līqāt (Glosses), 69
Talwīḥāt (Intimations), 188
Tamerlane, 193, 209
Tamhīd al-qawā'id (The Disposition of Principles), 210
Tanzīl al-afkār (Descent of Thought), 189
Taoism, 1, 6; prophecy and, 7
Taqī al-Dīn ibn Taymiyyah. *See* Ibn Taymiyyah, Taqī al-Dīn
Taqī Irānī. *See* Iranī, Taqī
taqlīd, 58
Taqwīm al-īmān (The Straightening of Faith), 214
Ṭarīqah, al-, 31
tashkīk, 74, 77, 78
tawḥīd, al-, 102, 146, 148
Tawḥīdī, Abū Ḥayyān al-, 111, 139
taʾwīl, 111, 133, 145, 154.
Ṭawq al-ḥamāmah (The Ring of the Dove), 114
Temples of Light (Suhrawardī), 199
Tenth Intellect, 141, 149
Tenth/Sixteenth Century: rapprochement between schools of Islamic philosophy, 162, 163; School of Shiraz in, 194
Thackston, Wheeler, 23
Thanwī, Mawlānā 'Alī Ashraf, 51, 60, 232, 255
Themistius, 98
theodicy, 173
Theologica Germanica, 120
theology, 14, 141, 190, 194, 200, 203, 209, 210, 219, 232, 321*n21.* *See* also Islam; acceptable, 126; Ash'arite,

50, 52, 53, 123; Catholic, 15; Christian, 5, 52, 120; dogmatic, 127; Islamic, 49, 194; Mu'tazilite, 53, 143; mystical, 225; nature of God and, 134; new, 128; philosophical, 7, 23, 108, 206, 237; against philosophy, 113, 114; relation to philosophy, 60; Scholastic, 108; Shi'ite, 97, 308*n14*; speculative, 127; Sufi, 113; Sunni, 97; as supreme science, 217; Twelve-Imam, 38, 51, 97, 128, 132, 133, 183, 187, 204
Theology of Aristotle (Plotinus), 137
theophany, 87
Theophrastus, 25, 64, 77
theorems: non-Euclidean, 170
theory: Empedoclean, 151; of evolution, 267, 268; of projectile motion, 152
theo-sophia, 65, 119
theosophy, 14, 135, 158; defining, 117; *ishrāqī,* 53; Ismā'īlī, 147; tasting of, 80; transcendent, 34, 53, 65, 68, 77, 81, 117, 203, 210, 214, 224, 225
The Theosophy of the Orient of Light (Suhrawardī), 115, 158, 188
Third Intellect, 149
Third/Ninth Century: Islamic philosophy in Baghdad in, 183
Thirteenth Century: Islamic philosophy from, 25
Thomism, 15, 18
Three Muslim Sages (Nasr), 27, 107
Three Principles (Mullā Ṣadrā), 53
Ṭibb al-rūḥānī, al- (Spiritual Physick), 144
Tibet, 274
"The Tigris" (Dawānī), 199
Timaeus (Plato), 144
time, 112
Toynbee, Arnold, 158
tradition: Christian Scholastic, 15; Oriental, 15, 17
Transcendent Philosophy (Journal), 20, 65
transcendent theosophy, 53, 68, 77, 81, 117, 219
Transcendent Theosophy concerning the Four Intellectual Journeys (Mullā Ṣadrā). *See Asfār, al*
The Transcendent Theosophy (Gīlanī). *See Asfār, al*
The Transcendent Theosophy (Khafrī). *See Asfār al-*
transformism, 231
Treatise concerning Verifications of the Qualities (Khayyām), 175
The Treatise Dedicated to Shams al-Dīn concerning the Rules of Logic (Kātibī), 191
Treatise Known as the Hierarchic Chain (Khayyām), 174
Treatise of Intellectual Light concerning Universal Science (Khayyām), 174
Treatise of Response to Three Questions (Khayyām), 176
The Treatise of Unity ('Abduh), 128
Treatise on Being (Khayyām), 175
Treatise on Politics (Urmawī), 189
Treatise on the Arts (Mīr Findiriskī), 216
Treatise on the Day of Resurrection (Ibn Sīnā), 230
Treatise on the Realm of Existence and Human Responsibility (Khayyām), 172
Treatise on the Science of the Universal Principles of Being (Khayyām), 174
Treatise on the Unity of Existence (Qumshā'ī), 244
Trials (Dashtakī), 200
truth: binding to, 94; direct knowledge of, 95; tasting of, 77; transcending time, 107
Tunakābunī, Mīrzā Ṭāhir, 253
Tunakābunī, Mullā Muḥammad, 25, 219
Tūnī, Mullā 'Abd al-Jawād, 245

Tunisia: Islamic philosophy in, 155, 157
Turba Philosophorum, 147
Turkey: Islamic philosophy in, 163, 192; Islamic texts from, 26; new manuscripts in, 21; Ottoman, 163; philosophical activity in, 45; school of illumination in, 116; students studying in the West from, 19; study of Islamic philosophy in, 60; Sufism in, 132
Ṭūsī, Naṣīr al-Dīn al-, 22, 34,38, 39, 44, 46, 53, 55, 64, 65, 133, 134, 162, 163, 167, 169, 171, 187, 188, 192, 196, 199, 200, 203, 206, 213, 225, 240, 294*n8*, 296*n24*, 296*n28*, 308*n14*, 319*n7*, 321*n23*, 323*n39*; founding of Shi'ite systematic theology by, 52; founds Twelve-Imam Shi'ite *kalām*, 51, 183; poetry of, 72, 183; resuscitation of Avicennian philosophy by, 113, 116; school of principiality of quiddity and, 176; understanding of Ibn Sīnā, 70
Tustarī, Sahl al-, 159
Twentieth Century: deconstructionism in, 19; interaction of Western and Islamic philosophical traditions, 20; nihilism in, 181; philosophical traditions, 14, 17, 18; study of being in, 88; Western approaches to philosophy, 26

Ufuq al-mubīn, al- (The Manifest Horizon), 214
Ukhnūkh, 281*n9*
'ulamā': opposition to teachings of Mullā Ṣadrā by, 53
Ülken, Zia, 26, 291*n50*
Ultimate Reality, 295*n15*
'ulūm al-'aqliyyah, al-, 35
'Umar ibn Sahlān al-Sāwajī. *See* Sāwajī, 'Umar ibn Sahlān
Umm al-kitāb (The Archetypal Book), 111, 146
United States: analytical philosophy in, 19; publishing of Islamic texts in, 24; study of Islamic philosophy in, 20
unity, 146; of being, 74–78, 89; doctrine of, 89; of God, 120, 121, 137, 300*n6*; Islamic doctrine of, 102; multiplicity in the light of, 94; realization of, 102; transcendent, 74–78, 77, 218
unity of consciousness doctrine, 76
universal: natural, 68
Universal Existence, 90
Universal Intellect, 43
Universal Man, 100
Universal Soul, 112
universe: Avicennan, 142
universities: *falsafah* in, 44; Islamic, 44
The Unveiling of the Desired (al-Ḥillī), 133
Unveiling of the Veiled (al-Sijistānī), 146
'urafā', 32
Urmawī, Sirāj al-Dīn, 189, 191
Ushida, Noriko, 17
'Uthmān Amīn. *See* Amīn, 'Uthmān
Utopia (More), 269
utopianism, 268, 269, 270
uṣul al-dīn, 13
uṣūl al-khamsah, al-, 122

Vajda, Georges, 15
Valiuddin, Mir, 297*n36*
van der Bergh, Simon, 15, 22
Vatican II, 15.
Vatican Library: cataloging, 21
Vernet, Juan, 15
Vesel, Ziva, 319*n7*
Vessel of Wisdom (al-Sijistānī), 190
Vico, Giambattista, 158
Visionary Recitals (Ibn Sīnā), 4
voluntarism, 86; Ash'arite, 130
von Ess, Joseph, 50

wa'd, al-, 122
waḥdah, 74, 77

waḥdat al-shuhūd, 76
waḥdat al-wujūd, 74, 76, 115, 156, 203
Wāhib al-ṣuwar, 142
Wāḥid, al-, 148
waḥy al-juzʾī, al-, 96
waḥy al-kullī al-, 96
Waṣī, al-, 149
Waṣiyyah, al- (Testament), 121
Wājib, al-, 71
Wājib al-wujūd, 141, 181
wājib biʾl-ghayr, 72
walāyah/wilāyah, 133
Walbridge, John, 23, 319*n8*
Walker, Paul, 23
Walzer, Richard, 15, 23
Warrāq, Abū Isḥāq al-, 143, 144
Wāṣil ibn 'Aṭāʾ, 121
Watt, W. Montgomery, 306*n2*
Wensinck, A.J., 15
wijdān, 66
Wisdom from the Source (Qazwīnī), 162
Wīs wa Rāmīn (The Romance of Wīs and Rāmīn), 172
witness, 89
Woepke, Franz, 165
Wolff, Christian, 86
Wolfson, Harry, 14, 15, 50, 282*n2,* 306*n2*
World Congress of Philosophy (2003), 273
"World of Divine Command," 148
"World of Origination," 148
World War II, 16
Wrestling with the Philosopher (al-Shahrastānī), 169
wujūb, 71
wujūd, 86, 141, 172, 203, 215, 226, 227, 230, 295*n18,* 296*n21*; absoluteness of, 80, 83; accidentality of, 69–71; belonging to God, 75; concept of, 73–74; as conceptual quality, 175–176; contingency and, 71–73; difficulty in defining, 65; distinction from *imkān,* 110; distinction from *māhiyyah* , 67–68; emanation of Divine Origin from, 170; expansive mode of, 81, 82; experience of, 82–84; four meanings of, 80; gradation of, 77–78; historical survey of study of, 64–65; impossibility and, 71–73; intensification of, 83; in Islamic philosophy, 63–84; knowledge as quality of, 176; light and, 80; meaning of, 65–67, 174; mentally posited, 80; necessity and, 71–73; negatively and non-conditioned stages of, 81, 82; pertaining to God, 67; portion of, 80; possession of reality by, 71; principiality of, 77, 78–80, 175–176; reality of, 73–74, 80–84; relation to *māhiyyah,* 63; significance of, 63–64; single reality of, 78; unity of, 74–77; universal knowledge of, 66
wujūd al-munbasiṭ, al-, 82, 90
wujūd dhihnī, 70
wujūd khārijī, 70

Yahya, Osman, 27, 284*n12*
Yamānī, Shaykh Aḥmad Zakī, 284*n11*
Yazd, 210
Yemen, 122; Ismā'īlī philosophy in, 146; Ismā'īlī power in, 112; Ismā'īlism in, 147; *kalām* in, 133; libraries in, 21; Sufi orders in, 76
Yemeni Answers to Sicilian Questions (Ibn Sab'īn), 156
Yoder, Howard, 311*n52*
Yoga, 217
Youshkevitch, Adolf, 314*n2*

Zād al-musāfir (Provisions of the Traveler), 180
Ẓahīr al-Dīn Bayhaqī. *See* Bayhaqī, Ẓahīr al-Dīn
Zamakhsharī, Jār Allāh, 165, 168, 201
Zanjānī, Mīrzā Ibrāhīm Riyāḍī, 246
Zawāhir al-ḥikam (The Flowers of Philosophical Sciences), 59

zawj tarkībī, 68
Zawra', *al-*, 199
Ziai, Hossein, 19, 23, 285n17, 300n5, 313n68, 314n72, 319n11
Zia Ülken. *See* Ülken, Zia
Zimmerman, Fritz W., 23

Zoroaster, 1
Zoroastrianism, 156
Zubdah, *al-* (Best Essence), 191
Zunūzī, Mullā 'Abd Allāh, 236, 237, 243, 294n12
Zurayk, Constantine, 322n28

www.ingramcontent.com/pod-product-compliance
Lightning Source LLC
Chambersburg PA
CBHW030125240426
43672CB00005B/31
* 9 7 8 0 7 9 1 4 6 8 0 0 5 *